T0366470

THE WANDERING ARMY

The Wandering Army

THE CAMPAIGNS THAT TRANSFORMED
THE BRITISH WAY OF WAR, 1750–1850

HUW J. DAVIES

YALE UNIVERSITY PRESS
NEW HAVEN AND LONDON

Published with assistance from the Annie Burr Lewis Fund.

For information about this and other Yale University Press publications, please contact:
U.S. Office: sales.press@yale.edu   yalebooks.com
Europe Office: sales@yaleup.co.uk   yalebooks.co.uk

Set in Adobe Caslon by IDSUK (DataConnection) Ltd
Printed in Great Britain by TJ Books, Padstow, Cornwall

Library of Congress Control Number: 2022941287

ISBN 978-0-300-21716-2

A catalogue record for this book is available from the British Library.

10 9 8 7 6 5 4 3 2 1

This book is dedicated to the memory of my grandparents

Doris McCarthy
(1921–2014)

Howard McCarthy
(1921–2012)

Contents

9   The 'Wandering Army': The Rebirth of the British Army,   257
    1799–1801

10 The 'Universal Soldier': Shorncliffe and the Light Division,   287
    1803–1812

11 'The Scientifics': High Wycombe and the British Way of   316
    Warfare, 1803–1815

12 'The Dread of Innovation': From Enlightenment to   342
    Ignorance, 1815–1856

    Conclusion: 'Every Fertile Genius': Britain's Accidental   369
    Military Enlightenment Explained

    Notes   *389*
    Bibliography   *445*
    Index   *473*

Illustrations and Maps

Plates

1. *William Augustus, Duke of Cumberland (1721–1765)* by David Morier, 1750. © Courtesy of the Council of the National Army Museum, London (NAM 1978-03-40-1).
2. *The Battle of Fontenoy* by Pierre L'Enfant. © Heritage Image Partnership Ltd / Alamy Stock Photo.
3. *The Shooting of General Braddock at Fort Duquesne, Pittsburgh, 1755* by Edwin Willard Deming, 1903. © Bridgeman Images.
4. *John Campbell, 4th Earl of Loudoun, 1705–1782* by Allan Ramsay, c. 1747. © National Galleries of Scotland.
5. Engraving of Major Robert Rogers, 1780. © Courtesy of the Council of the National Army Museum, London (NAM 2006-12-85-1).
6. Fort Ticonderoga, Ticonderoga, New York. © Roy Johnson / Alamy Stock Photo.
7. *Sir Jeffrey Amherst* by James Watson, mezzotint after Joshua Reynolds, 1766. © National Portrait Gallery, London (NPG D7002).
8. *View of the Taking of Quebec, 13 September 1759*, artist unknown, 1797. © Courtesy of the Council of the National Army Museum, London NAM (1971-02-33-314-1).
9. *The Death of General Wolfe* by Benjamin West, 1776. © William L. Clements Library, University of Michigan.
10. *General Lloyd* by Nathaniel Hone, 1773. © Fitzwilliam Museum / Bridgeman Images.
11. Engraving of British officers of the American Revolutionary War by J. Rogers, date unknown. © William L. Clements Library, University of Michigan.

Maps

Abbreviations

AB	Abercromby Papers
Add MS	Additional Manuscript
AHM	Arquivo Histórico Militar, Lisbon
AN	Archives Nationale, Paris
AP	Amherst Papers
APAC	Asia, Pacific & Africa Collection
ATL	Alexander Turnbull Library, Wellington
BL	British Library
BRBML	Beinecke Rare Book and Manuscript Library, Yale University
CC	Ross, Charles (ed.), *Correspondence of Charles, First Marquis Cornwallis*, 3 vols (London: J. Murray, 1859)
CHLWG	Lloyd, Henry, *Continuation of the History of the Late War in Germany Between the King of Prussia and the Empress of Germany and Her Allies* (London: Hooper, 1781)
CO	Colonial Office
CP	Clinton Papers
CPW	Aspinall, A. (ed.), *The Correspondence of George, Prince of Wales 1770–1812*, 8 vols (London: Cassell, 1964)
CUL	Cambridge University Library
DCP	Papers of the Duke of Cumberland
DUN	Dundas Papers
FMC	Fitzwilliam Museum, Cambridge
FTA	Fort Ticonderoga Archive

GSGP	Germain Papers
HEH	Henry E. Huntington Library, San Marino, California
HL	Henry Lloyd Papers
HLWG	Lloyd, Henry, *The History of the Late War in Germany, Between the King of Prussia, and the Empress of Germany and her Allies* (London: Privately Published, 1766)
HM	Huntington Manuscripts
HMC	Historical Manuscripts Commission
HO	Home Office
IHR	*International History Review*
IOR	India Office Records
JMH	*Journal of Military History*
JRL	John Rylands Library, University of Manchester
JSAHR	*Journal of the Society for Army Historical Research*
KHLC	Kent History and Library Centre, Maidstone
LAC	Library and Archives of Canada, Ottawa
LCG	Aspinall, A. (ed.), *The Later Correspondence of George III*, 5 vols (Cambridge: Cambridge University Press, 1966)
LCP	Loftus Cliffe Papers
LO	Loudoun Papers
LOC	Library of Congress, Washington, DC
LSC	Library of the Society of the Cincinnati, Washington, DC
LWL	Lewis Walpole Library, Yale University
MSA	Maharashtra State Archives, Mumbai, India
NAI	National Archives of India, New Delhi
NAM	National Army Museum
NLA	National Library of Australia, Canberra
NLS	National Library of Scotland, Edinburgh
NMM	National Maritime Musuem, Greenwich
NRS	National Records of Scotland, Edinburgh
NYCD	O'Callaghan, E. B. and B. Fernow (eds), *Documents Relative to the Colonial History of the State of New York*, 15 vols (Albany: Argus & Co., 1853–87)
NYHS	New York Historical Society
NYPL	New York Public Library
PAL	Punjab Archives, Lahore
PHB	Stevens, S. K., Donald H. Kent and Autumn L. Leonard (eds), *The Papers of Henry Bouquet*, 6 vols (Harrisburg: Pennsylvania Historical and Museum Commission, 1951)

PRC   Sarkar, Jadunath and G. S. Sardesai (eds), *English Records of Maratha History: The Poona Residency Correspondence* (Bombay: Modern India Press, 1936–51)

RD   Martin, Montgomery (ed.), *The Dispatches, Minutes, and Correspondence of the Marquess Wellesley, K.G., During His Administration in India* (London: John Murray, 1836–7)

RA   Royal Archvies, Windsor Castle

SD   Wellington, 2nd Duke of (ed.), *Supplementary Dispatches and Memoranda of Field Marshall Arthur Duke of Wellington, 1797–1818*, 14 vols (London: John Murray, 1858)

SLNSW   State Library of New South Wales, Sydney

SRO   Suffolk Record Office

SSCL   Albert & Shirley Small Special Collections Library, University of Virginia, Charlottesville

TCD   Trinity College Dublin Library, Dublin

TNA   The National Archives

TNSA   Tamil Nadu State Archives, Chennai

TP   Townshend Papers

UDL   University of Durham Library

USL   University of Southampton, Hartley Library

WCL   William L. Clements Library, University of Michigan, Ann Arbor

WD   Gurwood, John (ed.), *The Dispatches of Field Marshal the Duke of Wellington During His Various Campaigns in India, Denmark, Portugal, Spain, The Low Countries and France*, 13 vols (London: John Murray, 1852)

WO   War Office

WP   Wellington Papers, University of Southampton Library

Acknowledgements

This book sprang unexpectedly to life in 2012 during a research trip to the William L. Clements Library, at the University of Michigan in Ann Arbor. My first book, *Wellington's Wars*, had just been published, and I had decided to focus my research on how lessons had been learned by the British Army during the American Revolutionary War and applied during the French Revolutionary and Napoleonic Wars. At most, I expected to produce an article. Whilst in Ann Arbor, Dr Brian Dunnigan, then curator of the extensive map collection at the Clements, pointed me to the recently acquired papers of Sir Eyre Coote. Amongst the many orderly books, journals and memoranda, I found the quote that brilliantly encapsulated for me the character of the British Army in the eighteenth and nineteenth centuries and furnished me with the title for this book.

I am particularly indebted to Brian for his advice, not least because it opened a fresh seam of research and set me on a path that would allow me to travel the world, following the trail of Britain's wandering soldiers. In the process, I have incurred many other debts. Besides Brian, who continues to proffer advice during his retirement, this book would not have been possible without the sage advice of his colleague, Clayton Lewis, curator of graphics materials. I have him to thank for highlighting some of the wonderful images which have been reproduced in this book. Thanks also to Cheney J. Schopieray and Jayne Ptolemy, curator and assistant curator of manuscripts, as well as the rest of the brilliant staff at the Clements. The happy months I spent there bookended my research, having won a Jacob M. Price Fellowship in 2012 and a Howard H. Peckham Fellowship in 2019.

My research into Britain's North American military history continued in 2014 with a short-term research fellowship at the Huntington Library in San Marino, California, and a visiting fellowship at the Lewis Walpole Library, Yale University. The then research director at the Huntington, Dr Steve Hindle, and the whole library staff were so welcoming and helpful, and really facilitated my access to the enormous collection of papers and correspondence of John Campbell, Fourth Earl of Loudoun. At the Lewis Walpole, Susan Walker, Kristen McDonald and the library staff were generous with their time and knowledge. My thanks as well for the permission to reproduce an image from the library's collections.

In 2019, I received a Georgian Papers Fellowship to research the Cumberland and York correspondence at the Royal Archives at Windsor Castle. My gratitude to Professor Arthur Burns of the King's College London History Department for his advice and guidance on this collection, as well as for all the work he has done to make the Georgian Papers Programme such a success. I am also indebted to Dr Oliver Walton for his support when he was a curator at the Royal Archives. Material from that collection, as well as from the Wellington Papers held at the University of Southampton Hartley Library, is quoted with the generous permission of Her Majesty Queen Elizabeth II.

The same year, I received a Society of Colonial Wars in the State of Maryland Fellowship at the American Revolution Institute of the Society of the Cincinatti in Washington, DC. I was delighted to be able to access under one roof such a vast collection of early modern literature on the art of war, but little did I realise that I would stumble upon that thing every historian dreams of: a genuinely previously undiscovered primary source. The library catalogue contained a reference to an anonymous notebook 'describing mistakes of tactics employed in various battles in Europe between 1645 and 1755'. My interest piqued, I asked for it to be retrieved and slowly began to realise that the author was Henry Clinton, commander in chief of the British Army in North America. The notebook had been bought from a private collection in 1997 and never accessed. The contents form a major element of several of the early chapters of this book. The only person more excited than me, I think, was Ellen Clark, the director of the library, particularly when we received confirmation that my suspicions were correct and the handwriting matched other examples from Clinton's papers. Ellen was so generous with her time, and I remain in her debt, not least for permission to reproduce a photograph of 'West's Military Figures', a wonderful set of items which arrived mere hours before I was due to leave Washington, DC.

None of the work historians undertake would be possible without the support and expertise of the archivists, librarians and curators who care for and maintain the primary sources on which we rely. I am grateful to the staffs of the many archives and libraries I have visited in the course of this research project. I would like to extend my gratitude to the present Duke of Wellington, who gave me access to his library at Stratfield Saye, and enabled me to inspect the volumes Colonel Arthur Wesley carried with him to India in 1797. In 2013, I travelled to Pakistan to conduct research at the Punjab Archives in Lahore, a trip that would not have been possible without the help and support of then Captain, now Lieutenant Colonel, Mark Luson. Though the research was for a different project, the material I found revealed the degree to which the British were dismantling their own imperial knowledge networks in the nineteenth century.

Academic conferences are the lifeblood of the profession, offering opportunities to test theories and arguments. In the decade I have been researching this book, I have had the pleasure of giving papers at many conferences across the world. Friends and colleagues who regularly attend the Consortium on the Revolutionary Era and the annual meeting of the Society for Military History will recognise many of the arguments in this book. The opportunity offered at those conferences to test my ideas in safety was, and is, invaluable, and I am particularly indebted to Professors Rick Herrera, Wayne Lee and Christy Pichichero for their expert advice and guidance.

In 2013 and 2016, I attended military history conferences in Canberra, the first at the invitation of the late Professor Jeffrey Grey. Alongside meeting scholars with similar interests, these afforded me the opportunity to visit the National Library of Australia and the State Library of New South Wales in Sydney. In 2015, Professors David Lambert and Peter Merriman accepted my proposal to present my arguments on a panel they organised at the International Congress of Historical Geographers. Their interrogation of the resultant paper introduced me to new literature on the history of colonial knowledge creation, and helped me refine my arguments. To them, my thanks. As a result of connections made at that conference, I began corresponding with Professor Charlotte Macdonald, who in 2017 invited me to present at the 'Garrison Towns in the 19th Century Empire' symposium in Wellington, New Zealand. Again, the opportunity to test my evolving arguments proved invaluable, so to Charlotte and her colleagues, my thanks.

For the time and financial assistance for all those trips which were not covered by fellowships, I am grateful for the support of my employer, King's College London, and particularly the research fund of the Defence Studies Department based at the Joint Services Command and Staff College, Shrivenham. This has been my professional home for nearly two decades; I consider it to be the finest department at which to study military history, and I have benefited on a daily basis from the advice, guidance and suggestions of my colleagues. In particular, I am indebted to Professor Niall Barr, and Drs Anna Brinkman-Schwartz, Jonathan Fennell, Aimée Fox, Robert Foley and David Morgan-Owen, as well as my former colleague Dr Huw Bennett. I would also like to thank my former PhD student, and now, I am proud to say, current colleague, Dr William Fletcher. In 2019, he completed a brilliant thesis on the staff system during the Peninsular War which redefines our understanding of the subject. As I wrote up the final chapters of the book, he patiently answered questions about Robert Craufurd and George Murray. It is a privilege as well to be able to teach members of the armed forces. Though separated by centuries, there is much to be learned about the eighteenth-century army from its twenty-first-century incarnation, and vice-versa. To the students of my special subject, 'Britain as a Military Power', which I taught in 2012, 2019 and 2020, particular thanks. Invariably, my research was turbo-charged as a result of these sessions.

I began writing this book during my Peckham Fellowship at the Clements Library in the autumn of 2019, and finished the first draft in the summer of 2021. That draft was a good deal longer than the final product, and I am grateful for the advice and guidance of my editors at Yale, Heather McCallum, Katie Urquhart and Meg Pettit, and my copy-editor, Jenny Roberts. Heather, in particular, has supported me since 2008, and this book would certainly not have seen the light of day were it not for her encouragement and patience. Thanks also to the anonymous reviewers for their useful comments and criticisms, and to Martin Brown for the superb job he has done on the maps. Any errors that remain are, of course, mine alone.

The majority of the book was written during the pandemic. I am grateful to my colleagues, friends and family for their (remote) support during what was a challenging time for everyone, and particularly to my parents, Janet and John, for their continuous encouragement and enthusiasm for my work. Words cannot express my gratitude to my partner, Liz, for her love and support, as well as her tolerance of the 'zombie' writing phases, when the officers and soldiers of the eighteenth century British Army became unexpected members of our isolated household.

This book is dedicated to the memory of my grandparents, Doris and Howard McCarthy. They lived to see work commence on this project, but sadly not to see it completed. Every historian can pinpoint the things that got them interested in the subject. One of those for me was the stories my grandparents would tell of their wartime experiences. My grandmother was a nurse in London during the Blitz, whilst my grandfather served in the Merchant Navy, wandering the world twice over. Both escaped untimely deaths by little more than a whisker, and this instilled in them an earnest desire to create better lives for their children and grandchildren – something for which I will be eternally grateful. Granno & Gramps – this one's for you!

Huw J. Davies
Oxfordshire
August 2022

Introduction

'A Science Covered with Darkness': British Military Knowledge in the Eighteenth Century

O<small>N</small> 11 May 1745, on a long plain, gently inclined towards the tiny village of Fontenoy, 15,000 redcoats advanced methodically into action. They had been formed by the British infantry commander, General John Ligonier, into two lines and, by all accounts, were in perfect order.[1] The Battle of Fontenoy was only the second major battle the British Army had fought on European soil since the end of Marlborough's campaigns in 1714. Nevertheless, the small force retained a fierce reputation on the continent; a reputation based largely on the British soldier's skill with a musket. Moreover, this was an army in which its soldiery felt pride, and in which, in the words of one of its junior officers, 'every private man seemed worthy to command in chief . . .'.[2] At its head was the Duke of Cumberland. Inexperienced but passionate for the profession of arms, Cumberland was flanked by the much more seasoned veteran, Ligonier, and his aide-de-camp, Captain Joseph Yorke. 'I reckon it might be about a mile from the entrance into the Plain to the [entrenchment] just behind the Brow of which the enemy had formed their troops', Yorke recalled two weeks after the battle. 'His Royal Highness', he continued, '(whose youth full Heroism is unparalleled) got on Horseback & joined the Troops at the head' of the advance.[3] But the French commander, Maurice, Comte de Saxe, had constructed a series of entrenchments and fortifications designed specifically to obviate the superiority of British fire-power. The redcoats were marching into a trap, the effects of which, once sprung, would help catalyse Britain's military enlightenment.

The outbreak of the War of Austrian Succession in 1742 ended three decades of peace. Much of the training and drill used by the British Army was based on ideas and concepts that had barely evolved since the end of the previous war. Moreover, there was a deficit of operational experience in the officer cadre. 'A cessation of Arms for twenty-eight years', wrote one officer, 'must unavoidably have been attended with the loss of most of our old Generals and Officers, and their Posts fill'd with many who have never served abroad.'[4]

This deficit of experience was rendered abundantly apparent during the so-called War of Jenkins's Ear between Britain and Spain. During a combined operation against the Spanish Port of Cartagena in April 1741, the British general officer commanding, Thomas Wentworth, proved incapable of adapting his tactics to meet the challenges posed by the Spanish defenders. After he repeatedly hesitated to launch assaults on poorly defended positions, an attempt to take the main fort guarding the entrance of Cartagena resulted in heavy casualties. The operation, which was also marked by poor interservice relations with the Royal Navy, was a total failure, and the British were forced to withdraw, humiliated.[5]

Inexperience and ill-discipline nearly resulted in disaster at a battle against the French at Dettingen on 27 June 1743. There, the British infantry discharged their muskets at much too great a range to have a meaningful effect on their adversaries; once 'the first flurry was over,' noted one participant, Captain Jeffrey Amherst, 'they fired much better & the French soon gave way but rallied to make a second stand'.[6] The speed and accuracy of the second and third rounds made all the difference. The British attacked the French 'with great fury, which gained us a complete victory', noted another participant, Lieutenant James Wolfe, 'and forced the enemy to retire in great haste'.[7]

Victory had been snatched from the jaws of defeat, thanks largely to the speed with which the British had been able to reload and fire, outclassing their opponents. With more training and better discipline, British infantry firepower would pose a formidable challenge to any enemy it engaged on the field of battle. Training and exercises were ordered on a daily basis following Dettingen, with 'the awkward men to be out every day'.[8] In the 22 months between Dettingen and the next major engagement in Europe at Fontenoy in Flanders, British infantry discipline improved markedly.[9] It was on this superior firepower capability that the British were again to rely at Fontenoy.

Cumberland, aged just 24, was in overall command. He relied on the considerable experience of the Austrian commander, Dominik von Königsegg-Rothenfels, whose five-decade career included exposure to traditional European fighting methods, as well as the irregular and unpredictable tactics of the Ottomans.[10] But the British and Austrians were not alone in learning the lessons of recent campaigns: Maurice de Saxe had witnessed the superiority of British firepower and had fortified the battlefield to mitigate this strength. Without properly taking account of Saxe's adjustments, Cumberland elected to launch a huge infantry assault against the main French line, banking on the superior capabilities of his soldiers. Attempts to destroy the French defences prior to the main infantry attack proved abortive, however, and French artillery was able to fire with impunity into the exposed British flank.

Nevertheless, the British continued to advance and, unlike at Dettingen, the British infantry held their nerve and did not fire until they were well within range of the muskets they carried. When the British opened fire at 30 yards, their adversaries 'ran away in a most shameful manner', recalled Amherst, who again found himself in the thick of the action. 'More battalions & more squadrons moved up but we likewise obliged them to retire.'[11] The British infantry continued to advance and broke into the French encampment 300 yards behind Fontenoy. Despite this breakthrough, the failure to suppress the heavy weaponry in the flanking fortresses rendered the British position untenable. 'The Enemy had a fort which fired grap-shot in our rear which I imagined we had been in possession of many hours before and by what fatality it was not taken I cannot tell,' wrote Lord Charles Hay, commanding the First Foot Guards.[12] In reality, the officer sent to capture the fortifications had been harassed by French irregulars – *grassin* – which had disrupted his ability to launch an assault.[13]

Cumberland was forced to withdraw. British casualties at Fontenoy were severe: of the 15,000 who had gone into action, nearly six thousand lay dead or wounded on the battlefield; French losses were as great.[14] Cumberland's aide-de-camp, Captain Joseph Yorke, thought 'it providential it was no worse, considering all our slips. This will make us better soldiers, braver it cannot . . . [T]hat day convinced me in open ground the French will never stand us.'[15] In looking for a positive outcome from the defeat at Fontenoy, Yorke had perhaps unwittingly exposed the reasons for that failure.

Saxe had recognised that his infantry would be no match for the British, and this had influenced his choice of dispositions at Fontenoy. He used the natural features of the terrain, embellished them with redoubts and other hastily constructed fortifications, and then allowed the British to march into a trap. From now on, British troops would have to learn how to counteract the use of natural and artificial obstacles, as well as the effect of irregular troops. Late in life, as he tried to offer insights into war-fighting, 'a science', he said, 'covered with darkness', Saxe himself would record that 'nature is infinitely stronger than the works of man'.[16]

Moreover, the use of irregular troops, which disrupted Cumberland's plans, and denuded him of tactical intelligence, while furnishing plenty for Saxe, illustrated significant shifts in European fighting methods for which the British were ill-prepared. Saxe's systematic use of terrain, fortifications and well-posted infantry, cavalry and artillery helped spark a century-long debate about universal systems of warfare, proponents of which argued that war could be reduced to scientific principles and laws that, if followed precisely, could guarantee success.[17] This argument proved extremely attractive to some in the British Army who began searching for solutions to the problems presented by the surprise defeat.

The defeat prompted a fundamental re-evaluation of the fighting practices of the British Army. This book is about the creation of new military knowledge during the years after this defeat, how officers and soldiers responded to new and unexpected challenges, developed new approaches to fighting war and implemented those ideas in the face of organisational tradition, institutional resistance and personal suspicion of change. The process would take decades, and would be facilitated by, and help perpetuate, an accidental military enlightenment in Britain.[18] This period of military change, innovation and adaptation reflected a much larger, European-wide movement which Madeleine Dobie termed 'the first true meta-discourse on the aims and effects of war'.[19]

As ideals such as compassion, restraint and humanity in war began to emerge in both the theory and practice of warfare, so the armies of Europe began to undergo a military enlightenment. The British Army, largely separated, as it was, from European military developments, remained insulated from the European military enlightenment. However, the impact of the defeat at Fontenoy helped perpetuate the phenomenon, perhaps most immediately through a marked shift in reading preferences, as traditional classical texts, military histories and personal memoirs were superseded by new military treatises packed with new concepts and thinking of war, produced largely on the continent.

If the growth in popularity of new military thought originating on the continent provided the intellectual underpinning of Britain's military transformation in the eighteenth century, then it was driven by the wealth of experience which personnel were to gain in the practice of warfare as the British Army was deployed to North America, South

Asia, Europe and Africa, with smaller deployments to South America and Australasia. According to Enlightenment philosophers, experience was seen to be at the heart of knowledge creation, while the breadth of Britain's strategic ambition in the late eighteenth century also meant that this knowledge was circulated. This book is about the interconnected relationship of these three areas: military thought, experience and knowledge exchange, which together drove Britain's accidental military enlightenment.

The mid-century paucity of original thought on the art of war and the profession of arms illustrated that British officers were, prior to the calamities of the War of Austrian Succession, broadly satisfied with the organisation, command and tactical arrangements of the British Army. Prior to 1754, officers preferred to read the classics – Vegetius, Polybius and Thucydides – and campaign histories rather than continental treatises on the art of war.[20] Adding to this the fact that many officers selected recent successful campaign histories of the British Army, which easily recalled the glories of the most recent war, then it is evident that British officers saw themselves on a par with their classical heroes.

Senior officers of the British Army, an intensely conservative institution, in particular those with experience of warfare, frowned upon anything which challenged this dynamic. In 1736, for example, Brigadier Richard Kane wrote his *Campaigns of King William and Queen Anne*, which appended a *New System of Military Discipline*, though it was not published until 1745.[21] Kane had 'with great Contempt, read some Books, which pretended to Teach the whole Military Art'.[22]

The near-catastrophic defeats of the 1740s, however, produced a discernible and almost unstoppable shift in the selection of professional reading by British officers, as illustrated by the recommendations of James Wolfe to a friend and colleague, Thomas Townshend, who had requested suggestions for his brother, recently commissioned as an army officer. 'As to the books that are fittest for his purpose,' Wolfe had written, 'Comte de Turpin's book . . . is certainly worth looking into as it contains a good deal of plain practice.' Beyond that:

> he may begin with the 'King of Prussia's Regulations for his Horse and Foot', where the economy and good order of an army in the lower branches are extremely well established. Then there are the 'Memoirs' of the Marquis de Santa Crus, Feuquières, and Montecuculli; Folard's 'Commentaries upon Polybius'; the 'Projet de Tactique'; 'L'Attaque et la

Défense des Places', par le Maréchal de Vauban; 'Les Mémoires de Goulon', 'L'Ingénieur de Campagne'. La St Remi for all that concerns artillery ... There is an abundance of military knowledge to be picked out of the lives of Gustavus Adolphus and Charles XII, King of Sweden, and of Zisca the Bohemian; and if a tolerable account could be got of the exploits of Scanderbeg, it would be inestimable; for he excels all the officers, ancient and modern, in the conduct of a small defensive army ... There is a book lately published that I have heard commended, 'L'Art de la Guerre Pratique' – I suppose it is collected from all the best authors that treat of war; and there is a little volume, entitled 'Traité de la Petite Guerre', that your brother should take in his pocket when he goes upon out-duty and detachments.[23]

But the new interest in continental military thought was only one way in which Britain's accidental military enlightenment manifested. In the period between 1745 and 1815, which has been labelled the Seventy Years' War, British troops bore arms on all continents of the globe.[24] They fought in the wilderness of North America during the so-called French and Indian War (1754–1760), as well as the American Revolutionary War (1775–1783); on the plains of Europe during the Seven Years' War (1756–1763), the French Revolutionary War (1793–1802) and the Napoleonic War (1803–1815); and in a mixture of terrains – from jungles to deserts – in South Asia during three wars in the Carnatic (1746–1748, 1749–1754 and 1756–1763), four wars with Mysore (1767–1769, 1780–1784, 1790–1792 and 1798–1799) and two wars with the Maratha Confederacy (1775–1782 and 1803–1805).[25] Each campaign brought with it different challenges borne of terrain, environment and adversary.

These challenges required innovative responses driven by the necessity of the soldiers, and the ambitions of their officers, and prompted by the different experiences of warfare in different parts of the world. In America, the British redcoats gradually adapted to the conditions they faced by incorporating irregular tactics into their approach to warfighting and modifying their uniforms and weaponry accordingly. Officers sought to offset the difficulties of campaigning in distant lands by adapting the way they used their resources. In South Asia, local ideas and methods were incorporated into the ways in which the British Army used force. In Europe, traditional Continental tactics and methods were formally adopted, but the combination of local circumstance and personal experience saw adaptations to these centrally proscribed doctrines. The collective experience of these wars on a global scale offered the British Army, or more precisely its officers and soldiers, a qualitative advantage in the creation, adaptation and application of the resultant 'military knowledge': a combination of formal training, institutional memory, professional education and personal experience of war.

Any focus on the formal organisation of the British Army alone, controlled, as it was, from headquarters in Horse Guards in London, and maintained through the regimental system, discounts the informal influence and agency of individuals within the organisation. These individuals could and did bring to bear their personal experience when in command of their own units, and while serving on expeditions and operations. The combination of formal training and personal experience produced 'military knowledge', unique to individuals, but available to the wider army. This military knowledge was bound together across the army by an informal network which facilitated the exchange of that knowledge in a variety of fashions. This interaction of different personnel, with different experiences in different cultures and geographies, ensured that military knowledge was 'made and remade, rather than simply transferred or imposed'.[26]

This knowledge was communicated through correspondence and reading, conversation and discussion, and reflected interconnected sensationalist moral philosophies advocated by, among others, John Locke (1632–1704), David Hume (1711–1776) and Étienne Bonnot de Condillac (1714–1780). These philosophies helped drive the emergence of the military enlightenment in Europe. Alongside the development of new knowledge, the emergence of the military enlightenment in Europe was marked by increasingly important notions of humanity, compassion and restraint in war. In Britain, as elsewhere, these notions were viewed and applied unevenly, but the emerging humanity exhibited between European adversaries was itself the product of the culture of *sensibilité*, which had come to be seen in the eighteenth century as the quintessential human trait. A key component of military as well as elite culture of the period, *sensibilité* was the foundation for human knowledge and identity and was responsible for creating the idea of fellow feeling between human beings. As a result, the chivalric code, which had helped govern the practice of war since medieval times, was replaced by the notions of respect, benevolence and compassion while waging war.[27]

Indeed, the experience of war offered raw insight into what sensationalist philosophies saw as the intimate linkage between physical experience, emotion and the self. Philosopher and historian David Hume argued that thinking was itself an involuntary association of ideas, connected only by past physical experience. It was, sensationalists reasoned, meaningless to speak about things with which one had no personal experience. Ideas that were not rooted in these experiences, in the senses, were mere delusions.[28] All humans had the ability to experience and to sense, so common soldiers with direct experience of war were better equipped to understand it than the socially superior armchair theorist. The natural extension of these arguments saw the experience of different emotions manifest in a physical reaction.

Soldiers reported the extraordinary sensations they experienced as a result of defeats as well as victories. The prospect of action alone was invigorating for some. 'Instead of creating gloomy sensations,' wrote one British participant in the Napoleonic Wars, the onset of a new campaign, in fact, 'was viewed with sincere delight.'[29] Taken to extremes, sensationalists, such as Claude Adrien Helvétius, argued that 'physical pain and pleasure are the unknown principles of all human actions'.[30] In other words, all human emotions, and by extension actions, could be reduced to the pursuit of sensory pleasure or avoidance of sensory pain.[31]

Personal – both physical and emotional – experience, or sensation, was, therefore, seen to be at the root of knowledge. Without such experiences, it was impossible to acquire new knowledge, or remake existing knowledge, while the way in which knowledge was exchanged could be controlled through the threat or application of pain or pleasure. Military personnel embraced these principles wholeheartedly, where the acquisition of experience, of experiential learning and with it of personal valour was privileged above any other form of knowledge creation. Conversely, the same principles also helped officers and soldiers to justify as punitive measures acts of brutality and atrocities against civilians, largely though not solely focused on indigenous populations.

Education – such as that gained by reading and travelling – was sufficient for preparation, but it would never supplant the experience of war itself. Experience, then, was seen to be central to knowledge creation during the military enlightenment, and British soldiers had a unique set of experiences on which to draw. Britain's uniquely global experience of warfare in the 70 years between Fontenoy and Waterloo, generated military knowledge, on which no other army had access to. This helped also to promote experimentation with new ideas and facilitate the communication and exchange of those ideas.

Other forms of military knowledge could be obtained through reading, accessed in libraries or archives or imparted at training and educational institutions. This knowledge was exchanged horizontally, that is to say, across ranks rather than up and down the chain of command. These individuals were often senior officers with widespread experience, or well-connected junior officers with the necessary political relations or patronage networks that ensured influence, and therefore had the means to communicate widely. Occasionally, brilliant innovations were introduced by private soldiers, such as adjustments to uniforms or adaptations to weaponry to better suit the physical environment in which they were being used. While these might have discernible impacts within a unit, battalion or even brigade, the onward communication of that idea depended very much on the interest and connections of their officers.

Well-connected officers formed what historian Tony Ballantyne describes as a 'web of empire'. Within this web, information passed from one colony to the next, from one war zone to the next and from there back to Britain. In so doing, the web drew 'material together, cataloguing and organizing knowledge, and disseminating it throughout the system'. These officers 'played a key role in the circulation of knowledge that was the very lifeblood', in this case, of a military knowledge structure.[32]

Most commonly, the personal experience of senior officers was implemented in action during a deployment to a war zone. In so doing, a new generation of personnel, junior officers at the beginning of their careers, would learn from the experience of their superiors. They would then mobilise that knowledge and remake and refashion it for use later in their careers.[33] Possibly just as commonly, but less easy to demonstrate, personal experience was exchanged in less active settings: in conversations in the mess, where heated debates about the conduct of the campaign were punctuated and illustrated by the evidence of past experience; during periodic visits to historical battlefields, offering a direct connection with recent military history, and the opportunity, again, for discussion and debate; in correspondence and personal diaries, shared with colleagues and comrades in arms; and in the collective reading of published memoirs, military histories and treatises on the art and science of war, and through the review of maps of increasing sophistication and complexity.[34]

Loose and informal knowledge networks were evident across the generations of officers and across the continents on which they served. Evidence exists of the acquisition, making, remaking and exchange of military knowledge through various means in Britain, Europe, North America and India. It remains challenging to trace the exchange of ideas borne of experience between theatres and wars. On the one hand, similar tactical or operational responses could be formulated as a reaction to similar challenges posed by the terrain or an enemy. On the other, they could be the result of an idea passed through a network of knowledge exchange that existed within the British Army. Take, for example, the simple idea of ordering troops to lie down, or use dead ground, to shield themselves from enemy artillery fire. At the battle on the Plains of Abraham outside Quebec on 13 September 1759, as the French 'came within reconnoitring view they halted ... at the same time playing with three field pieces on our line', General James Wolfe 'ordered the line to lay down till the enemy came close, when they were to rise up and give their fire'. The tactic proved devastatingly successful. 'The enemy, thinking by our disappearing, that their cannon disconcerted us, they thought proper to embrace the opportunity ... but received and sustained such a check that the smell of gun-powder became nautious.'[35]

The tactic was reused a number of times over the succeeding decades. In 1778, during the British attack on the West Indies, Colonel George Harris ordered his troops to 'lie down, and cover themselves in the brush-wood as much as possible, to prevent their being seen as marks' by the French defenders.[36] Two years later, Colonel William Baillie used the same tactic at the Battle of Pollilur in South India. There, on 10 September 1780, Baillie's detachment was encircled as it tried to rejoin the main company force. 'Surrounded on all sides ... it appeared that the enemy had placed batteries to command every part of the road through which our troops must necessarily pass,' recorded one survivor. 'In this situation exposed to a heavy cannonade of 30 pieces of cannon the troops were ordered to sit down.'[37] On this occasion, the tactic proved rather less effective, as the British rear guard was simultaneously attacked, and the line collapsed, forcing Baillie to surrender.[38]

During the Second Anglo-Maratha War (1803–1805), Major General Arthur Wellesley ordered his men to lie down in order to shield them from the well-aimed artillery fire of Rajhoji Bhonsle's 40,000-strong Maratha army at the commencement of the Battle of Arguam on 29 November 1803. On this occasion, Wellesley's sepoys had panicked after an intense bombardment commenced as they marched into battle. Three battalions had fled to the rear, and Wellesley had intervened personally to restore order, before marching them back into the field. 'Did you ever see a battle restored like this?' Wellesley had asked his subordinates.[39] This was purportedly the first time Wellesley had employed a tactic for which he would become famous during his command of the Anglo-Portuguese Army during the Peninsular War (1808–1814).[40]

What do these four seemingly unconnected instances of the use of the same tactic illustrate? The tactical decisions were unusual, taken by unorthodox commanders, which, as a violation of the traditional approach to line discipline of the era, was generally frowned upon. Were they a response to the specific tactical situation faced by each commander at the time? Or was each commander drawing on a loose network of knowledge exchange that helped ideas, innovations and experience communicate across both decades and continents? A loose connection exists between these disparate events. Wellesley, an avid reader of history prior to and during his deployment to India, read the memoir of the Third Anglo-Mysore War (1790–1792) by Captain Alexander Dirom, who had himself served alongside Major General Archibald Campbell in Madras between 1782 and 1786. Both had served under the command of the Earl of Cornwallis, who, as well as Governor-General of India, was also colonel of Wellesley's regiment, the 33rd Foot. Campbell had himself studied the events of the Second Anglo-Mysore War (1780–1784), and a diary documenting Baillie's use of the tactic at Pollilur can be found among Campbell's personal papers.[41]

Having served in North America during the War for Independence, Campbell sought to import to India ideas and innovations he had seen successfully applied in America, including weapons designs and infantry training and drill. Indeed, in his 'Regulations and Discipline', written specifically for service in India, Campbell aimed to allow the whole army to 'observe one uniform principle in their movements'.[42] In some respects, Campbell's regulations bore a striking resemblance to a light infantry drill manual written by Major General William Howe in 1774, following his experiences under the command of, among others, James Wolfe at Quebec.[43] Campbell's aide-de-camp, Alexander Dirom, critiqued the regulations and suggested adaptations based on his own local experience.[44]

There is limited evidence of a direct connection between Campbell and Howe, who had in 1775 also commanded Harris at Bunker Hill. Indeed, Campbell had been captured during the siege of Boston in 1775, and only exchanged in 1778 after Howe had left the North American command. But the two served in the same war and had relationships with the same groups of officers. It is therefore not unreasonable to conclude that Howe's ideas might have influenced Campbell, who had employed the light infantry during the capture of Savannah in December 1778 in much the same manner as Howe at Quebec.[45] Many of these ideas were later reflected in the works of military theorists, notably Henry Lloyd, who gained fame after the publication of an essay on the philosophy of war in the 1780s. Widely read, Lloyd's book had been part of Arthur Wellesley's library for his voyage to India in 1797.[46] There is insufficient evidence to confirm a connection which may have resulted in the communication of this simple idea from the Heights of Abraham outside Quebec to southern and central India, and on to Spain and Portugal, but there is enough circumstantial evidence to suggest a connection between these officers.

The knowledge networks themselves were a symptom of the so-called European military enlightenment, in which ideas of compassion and restraint in war began to influence decision making, and in which different philosophical concepts helped influence the way in which officers and, to some extent, soldiers thought about war. The gunpowder revolution had placed projectile weaponry firmly at the centre of European military thought, but Enlightenment thinkers looked to the classics for inspiration for modern military institutions, while thinking of war as governed by rational and universal principles; war was, in the words of Jean-Charles, chevalier de Folard (1669–1752), 'a science, more speculative than experimental'.[47] Underpinning these assumptions was the concept of military spirit, which many argued, Folard among them, was more influential than gunpowder in the outcome of a battle. The military enlightenment therefore encouraged military thinkers to look for advantages and innovations outside the technological progress that had dominated European military development up to 1745.[48] Britain's military enlightenment was a more accidental and selective endeavour, but new ideas of knowledge, learning and experience began to permeate the officer corps. Indeed, the way knowledge itself was thought of began to change, with an emerging focus on the importance of experience as a critical factor in the formation of new knowledge. In so doing, the understanding of the art and science of war began to evolve. New ideas gained from the experience of war, and interaction with enemies and allies, in continental Europe, North America and India were adopted. Combined, this new knowledge offered the army specific advantages and opportunities for success.[49]

In this book, I explore the informal knowledge networks that developed within and across the British Army, the impact of the wider military enlightenment on British thinking about war, and the effect that the resulting knowledge creation and exchange had on the capabilities and conduct of the army in action. I expose the basis of these networks by examining the experiences of a collection of individuals who were able to influence decision making or were themselves decision makers, and thereby able to apply military knowledge they had acquired elsewhere or from others. I expose connections between these individuals and attempt to chart the transmission of different ideas. In so doing, I argue that new military knowledge was created as a result of the experience of war, which in turn fostered a process of gradual improvement through speculative activity and experimentation with ideas learned in one theatre and applied in a new one. This was an uneven process. Experimentation carried with it risk of failure, and in war there is limited opportunity for refinement of intellectually risky actions. This partly explains the emergence of different 'schools' of thought within the army, as the overwhelmingly conservative organisation favoured the tried-and-tested methods of the continental school, while the more innovative individuals of the American school sought to experiment with new ideas. In some ways, this is a story of two armies: the change-resistant organisation versus the body of innovative individuals who sought to improve that organisation.

In seeking to illustrate this argument, I have returned to the archive, to re-engage with the diaries, papers and correspondence of officers and, in some cases, soldiers who embodied these networks of military knowledge. Even so, the scope for understanding how those individuals learned and thought is limited to that which they chose to record. Some are more forthcoming than others. In addition to his extensive correspondence, for example, John Campbell, Fourth Earl of Loudoun, commander of British forces in North America in 1756–1758, kept a series of equally extensive memoranda books which documented in considerable detail his conversations and decision-making processes. Henry Clinton, commander-in-chief of the British Army during the American Revolutionary War, likewise minuted conversations, made copious notes and kept numerous pocket-books filled with observations of historical and contemporary campaigns. Christopher Hely-Hutchinson, a major during the French Revolutionary War, maintained a strikingly detailed diary of his military experiences, choosing to record everyday events, such as conversations at dinner, which most correspondents glossed over in favour of details of the military actions they were involved with. Thomas Mitchell, an ensign in the 95th Rifles, kept detailed fieldnotes of his reading and activities during the Peninsular War. The papers and correspondence of Eyre Coote, whose career encompassed the American and French Revolutionary wars, are punctuated by a series of orderly books which document his everyday regimental activities in North America. Indeed, orderly books provide useful records of regimental adaptation and innovation in the field.

These archival sources open a window on an otherwise somewhat poorly illuminated corner of British military history: the everyday mundanity of life in the army, which created the space for learning, adaptation and innovation. What they reveal is a portion of the officer corps with an interest in the profession of arms. This interest extended to conversations, historical battlefield visits and common reading selections. Rather than isolated instances of intellectual discussion, professional interest in learning was reasonably widespread, occurring in messes and barrack rooms in North America, India and Europe. This allowed officers and soldiers to learn from their own experience, from that of others and from the lessons of history and geography.

If the calamity of defeat at the Battle of Fontenoy in May 1745 prompted the professional re-evaluation of the literature of war available to British military personnel, it was the commencement of the Seven Years' War which transformed the military knowledge available to the British Army. Labelled the first truly global war, because of the interconnected campaigns fought by Britain in North America, India and Europe, the conflict transformed Britain from a medium-sized European power into a global imperial superpower. Known in North America as the French and Indian War, hostilities between Britain and France commenced there two years before the European conflict which gave the war its name. Back country skirmishes escalated until the very future of Britain's North American colonies was threatened by seemingly interconnected series of French incursions. In July 1755, a British army was virtually wiped out in an ambush on the river Monongahela in the Ohio Valley. Its commander, General Sir Edward Braddock, was killed in action, and Horse Guards scrambled to find a replacement able to restore order in a rapidly deteriorating situation. Cumberland appointed one of his favourites, and General John Campbell, Fourth Earl of Loudoun, embarked for North America, carrying with him a wealth of military knowledge from his experiences during the last war.

CHAPTER I

'Grasping in the Dark'

Defeat and Humiliation, Adaptation and Innovation, 1745–1758

A T 3 o'clock in the morning on 23 July 1756, John Campbell, Fourth Earl of Loudoun, the newly appointed commander-in-chief of the British Army in North America, set foot unceremoniously on American soil at the quayside in New York. So early was it, that, according to the *New York Mercury*, the 'City Regiment could not be drawn out to receive him, as was intended'.[1] Thus, with literally no fanfare, did Lord Loudoun formally assume his new position. He was taking command of a defeated and discontented regular force, which was – with some justification – regarded with suspicion by the local colonial forces. Although war with France had not yet been declared, an effective state of hostility existed in North America. Loudoun's mission was therefore both immense and ill-defined.

Not only was he tasked with meeting the challenge posed by a French strategy of encirclement of the Thirteen British North American colonies and simultaneous violent incursions by hostile Native Americans, but he also had to establish close cooperation between the Thirteen Colonies, man, train and equip colonial defence forces and rebuild the tattered reputation of the regular British Army after a series of defeats and humiliations in both Europe and America. It was a challenge which neither he nor any of his successors would fully meet. 'In an American campaign everything is terrible,' wrote one veteran, 'the face of the country, the climate, the enemy. There is no refreshment for the healthy, nor relief for the sick. A vast unhospitable desart, unsafe and treacherous, surrounds them, where victories are not decisive, but defeats are ruinous; and simple death is the least misfortune which can happen to them.'[2]

The new commander-in-chief owed his appointment to the Duke of Cumberland, the now 35-year-old favourite son of King George II and Captain-General of the British Army. Loudoun had been in Cumberland's close circle of trusted officers during the War of Austrian Succession and had played a pivotal role in the suppression of the Jacobite Rebellion in 1745–1746. It was during these conflicts that the British Army suffered a series of humiliating defeats, which ruined its reputation, but created the conditions for a mid-century transformation based largely on the accumulation of global experiences of warfare, and set in train Britain's accidental military enlightenment.

*　*　*

A decade earlier, Loudoun had been posted to Scotland, tasked with raising new regiments of Highland soldiers. News reached him that Charles Edward Stuart, the Young Pretender to the throne, had landed in Scotland, assembled a strong army of rebellious Jacobite Highlanders and was heading to Edinburgh.[3] Loudoun joined the main British force under the command of General Sir John Cope, and together offered battle at Prestonpans on 21 September 1745.

On the field, the British under Cope outnumbered the Jacobites by two to one and had occupied a strong position. Significantly better trained, the British expected to win the day. But the Jacobites offered a very different threat to that posed by conventional European forces. 'They come on slowly 'til they be within distance of firing, which, because they keep no rank or file, doth ordinarily little harm,' recalled Lieutenant General Hugh Mackay, who had commanded against them during an earlier rising in 1715. 'When their fire is over, they throw away their firelocks, and everyone drawing a long broad sword, with his targe (such as have them) on his left hand, they fall a running toward the enemy.'[4]

On the morning of the battle, the Jacobite commander, Lord George Murray, surprised his opponent by quickly changing his disposition and attacking Cope's flank. The Jacobites did not level their muskets 'until they were very near, being always sure that their one fire should do execution'.[5] Thereafter, the Jacobites charged into the redcoats, and heavy hand-to-hand fighting developed, in which the British purportedly put up a good, though brief, fight. The second line of Jacobites now entered the fray. 'We left our guns, drew our swords and targes like lions,' recorded one participant, Captain James Mor, 'yet we were obliged to draw our pistols to break the first rank; then they broke, and we hashed them and slaughtered at them like fury.'[6]

The battle was over in minutes as the British infantry collapsed and fled for cover in the buildings of the nearby town. For Loudoun, who had been in Scotland since the spring, the shock of the defeat was palpable. 'We had lain on our arms all night and were perfectly formed to receive them but they came on in five collumbs or rather squares with such astonishing rapidity that not one of our people could stand their shock,' he wrote to a confidante a couple of days after the battle. 'The Dragoons shrunk as soon as they were carryed up to them and the Foot popped off a few fires and fled and all the power of man could not make them make a face again.'[7] Edinburgh fell shortly after, and with the Jacobites in command of the Scottish capital, the way was now open for an invasion south into England.

Prestonpans had been a catastrophic defeat for the British Army. In the wake of Fontenoy four months earlier, the previously ferocious reputation of the British Army had completely disintegrated, suffering defeat at the hands of an opponent who capitalised on British weaknesses in an unconventional manner. Cumberland was recalled from Flanders to head up the response, and began implementing hastily devised reforms to try to counteract the perceived strengths of his new adversaries. In the wake of the defeat at Prestonpans, a flurry of short treatises on how to resist such tactics began to appear in periodical magazines. It is 'the constant aim of a tumultuous and cunning enemy', wrote one commentator, 'to render discipline useless by introducing confusion; if by a sudden shock, or desperate push they acquire this, certain victory is generally the consequence'.

Such comments accurately foreshadowed the military challenges the British would face over the next decade. 'To prevent all future attempts of so dangerous a consequence,' continued the armchair theorist, 'two or three regiments of loyal Highlanders might be rais'd, for the government's use, that may continue their own method of fighting, without going thro' the discipline of ours.'[8] It was on precisely such a mission that Loudoun was dispatched to Inverness to oversee the raising of further Highland companies and counter the Jacobite force at the source of its strength.

The British government had been proactively recruiting Highland soldiers for service in the British Army since the previous Jacobite rising of 1715, mainly as a local police force, containing criminality rather than suppressing political dissent. Upon the outbreak of war with Spain in 1739, however, these units were reformed into a Highland Regiment, the 42nd. Loudoun had been sent to Scotland to raise a second Highland Regiment, the 64th, for service abroad.[9] Originally trained to respond to the particular problems presented by service in Scotland, from 1739 onwards, the Highlanders were now also subject to the same training and discipline as the rest of the army. With two distinctive roles, the Highland regiments therefore gained an unusual duality: they were to be capable of responding to the largely irregular challenges present in the Highlands, as well as the general circumstances with which the British Army at large was expected to deal.[10]

Essentially, Loudoun was deployed behind enemy lines to try to persuade the local population to resist the rebellion. 'I begun with 150 men in town ready to cut my throat and my neighbours ... threatening to attack me every night,' Loudoun wrote during his mission. 'I augmented by very slow degrees and with numberless difficulties to about 2000.' The Scottish irregulars

> were more suitably attired and of greater utility than those of the line, who were unused to a mountainous and difficult country where even the language was not understood ... They could traverse peat bog and mountain with ease, where the cumbersomely clad and accoutred soldiers of the line, whether horse or foot, would flounder helplessly or be unable to proceed or only with difficulty.[11]

Slowly but surely, Loudoun began to exert pressure on Jacobite support, and arguably was engaged in what today might be termed a counterinsurgency. His main objective was the recruitment of a highland fighting force capable of countering the irregular strengths of the main Jacobite army. Trained to fight in both a regular and irregular order of battle, the Highlanders hampered the movements of the rebels for some time. Facing regular rebel ambushes, Crown 'irregulars were to be detach'd in small patroles, supported by parties of the regulars, with orders to attack any patroles of the rebels'.[12] The Jacobites were surprised by the effectiveness of the Crown Forces. 'Lord Loudoun with his corps frequently harassed and annoyed us,' remarked one rebel leader, 'keeping us constantly on the alert.'[13]

Nevertheless, Loudoun encountered significant problems: 'want of arms, want of money were after my base ... my daily bread', he later wrote.[14] Only to a very limited extent was he able to gather intelligence, or counter the intelligence activities of the Jacobites. For the most part, he found himself manoeuvring his sizeable force to avoid battle with significantly larger opponents, and eventually had to give up Inverness in the face of a superior rebel force. He found the entire campaign exhausting and might have begun to wonder if success in 'this curs't rebellious country' was possible. 'I am really worn out. . . .'[15]

The onus therefore rested with the main army to work out how to resist the effectiveness of the Highland charge on the battlefield. In October, Cumberland arrived from the continent, and immediately began implementing changes designed to counter this threat that had proved so effective at Prestonpans. He accurately identified that the British infantry were firing their muskets prematurely, provoked by the Jacobites who fired their muskets 'at a distance & then immediately Lay themselves flat to the ground, in order to avoid & draw off our fire'. The rebels would then 'rush in with their Broadswords' against unloaded muskets. This, Cumberland argued, 'they will never dare to do, if the [British] fire is kept up'. In November 1745, Cumberland ordered the adoption of a new firing system, designed to increase British firepower, so long as it remained disciplined. 'If the Rebels should advance in a hasty disorderly manner,' Cumberland explained, 'the commanding officer must keep up the fire of his Battalion til the Enemy is within 10 to 12 yards of them, not answering their fire.'[16] To instil this level of discipline, Cumberland established a training camp at Aberdeen in March 1746.

If this approach was successfully deployed on the battlefield against the Jacobite army, the weight of firepower would be enough to disrupt the oncoming charge. But firepower was only half the battle. Cumberland also noted that the bayonet was being used ineffectually. British infantrymen were being trained to use the bayonet in the same way they would have been trained to use a pike: the Jacobites therefore found it easy to tarry a bayonet thrust with their targe (a small shield) and thus render the infantryman defenceless. A simple modification to the way the musket and bayonet was held and used would neutralise the Jacobite method. Instead of attacking the Jacobite directly in front of him, a redcoat would instead attack the exposed flank of the man to the right.[17] This would not only prove decidedly more effective, but also bred an extreme degree of trust among the men: for this system to work, one man had to depend on the discipline of his neighbour. Cumberland 'took the pains to confer with every Battalion of Foot, on the proper method of using the Musket and Bayonet to advantages against the Sword and Targe'.[18]

Cumberland also reorganised the army. An advanced guard would operate at a distance from the main army in order to collect intelligence, while the main body of the army marched in four columns (three of infantry and one cavalry). The infantry was deployed in columns of battalions, with each battalion marching on a frontage of three. This mirrored the Jacobite style of marching and foreshadowed later European tactical and operational manoeuvre. The formation bestowed greater mobility and ensured that the army could form very swiftly into line of battle facing any direction. It was thus able to anticipate an unexpected assault, though success depended on meticulous training and adherence to drill regulations.

In deploying his army in such a flexible fashion, Cumberland was probably drawing on what he had learned the previous year from his Austrian allies. Their experience of the mobile and unpredictable warfare practised by the Turks now seemed particularly relevant against the mobile and unpredictable Jacobites.[19] 'It is what Königsegg taught me,' he was reported to have said when asked about the formations he had adopted. 'It is what he used against the Turks.'[20] Such a plan of action effectively prepared the army for battle as it was manoeuvring. Cumberland's reforms were not, therefore, restricted to tactical-level thinking, but they ensured that his army was operationally capable as well. Now he needed to track down the Jacobite army and force it to battle.

The Jacobites made it as far south as Derby before Charles and his advisers grew concerned they had overstretched themselves, and retreated north. A final confrontation occurred when the two armies met again at Culloden on 16 April, on a barrel-shaped ridge that formed a stretch of Drumossie Moor. The geology here produced a ridged bog, with channels that ran roughly east to west, which had the effect of canalising the Highland charge when it came and compartmentalising the different aspects of the battle.

As news arrived that the Jacobite army was within striking distance, Cumberland wheeled his army into two lines of battle, with the cavalry covering the exposed left flank. Cumberland had also positioned his strongest infantry regiments here. As at Prestonpans, the Jacobite army sought to force the British troops to fire too early. They clearly expected the royal cavalry to launch the attack in the same disorderly fashion that had occurred at earlier battles. When none came, the Jacobites became impatient, and the order for the attack was eventually given.[21]

At this point, Cumberland was seen 'speaking to every platoon ... and undoubtedly had a wonderful effect. "Depend," he said to the men as he rode by ... "depend on your bayonets, let them mingle with you, let them know the men they have to deal with." '[22] Soon after, the Jacobites 'after firing irregularly at a considerable distance ... rush'd furiously in upon' the royal troops, 'thinking to carry down all before 'em, as they had unfortunately done on former occasions. However, they soon found themselves grossly mistaken ...'.[23]

This fighting, on Cumberland's left, was the most intense of the battle. The redcoats 'first gave one fire, the fore rank kept them off with their bayonets till the second rank charged [loaded] again and gave them so close a fire that our fore rank was bespattered with their blood and brains'.[24] Nevertheless, the Jacobite 'mass, which seemed undiminished, still pressed forwards, and by its weight ... bore its opponents from their ranks, and intermixing with them everywhere ... both sides at last formed a sort of mass themselves'.[25]

The close-quarter, hand-to-hand action favoured the bayonet over the broadsword, which the Jacobites needed space to wield effectively.[26] As Cumberland hoped, the British infantry had developed a close bond and each man trusted his neighbour implicitly. The result was a cohesive unit that proved greater than the sum of its parts. From his position on Cumberland's staff, Captain James Wolfe observed that the Jacobites were 'repulsed, and ran off with the greatest precipitation, and the Dragoons falling in amongst them completed the victory with much slaughter'.[27]

Cumberland's adaptations had proved highly effective. The infantry was prepared for the Highland charge and withstood its psychological effect. Musket fire was held until the Jacobites were within a few yards of the front line. The bayonet played an important role in defeating the charge, and Cumberland noted that the royal troops 'fairly beat them with their Baionets'.[28] In the space of a year, then, the British Army had demonstrated itself capable of learning and adapting in the face of new threats and challenges. Fontenoy and the Jacobite uprising had illustrated that the reliance on firepower alone was outdated and needed reform.

Over the next few months, Cumberland orchestrated a brutal and punitive suppression of support for the rebellion, earning himself the sobriquet 'Butcher Cumberland', an image he would never fully shake. He returned to the continent the following year to continue operations against the French. On 2 July 1747, he commanded at the Battle of Lauffeldt, outside Maastricht.

Cumberland, however, made serious errors of judgement during the opening stages of the battle, by abandoning key positions and then ordering their recapture. 'It seems we know not, whether a Village, in Front of the Line, ought to be occupied or no', remarked Colonel George Townshend, 'for, a little before the Battle, it was once ordered to be *burnt*, and twice to be *evacuated* and *repossessed*'.[29] This gave his opponent, once again Maurice de Saxe, the opportunity to pin down the British infantry at Lauffeldt and outflank and cut their communications with Maastricht. Saxe ordered several attacks on the village, where the fighting was intense: the village changed hands four or five times in as many hours. Cumberland, fearful that the French were breaking through, ordered a withdrawal, unaware it seems that his left was being flanked by Saxe's cavalry. General Sir John Ligonier, commanding Cumberland's cavalry, ordered a general advance, which prevented the British infantry from being cut off.[30] Cumberland's poor handling of the battle did not go unobserved. 'The honour of saving the army was envied Ligonier', remarked Townshend, 'by those who had reaped none themselves.'[31] Colonel Jeffrey Amherst, who served on Ligonier's staff, noted the importance of meticulous reconnaissance and planning, while James Wolfe, who had commanded his unit in the thick of the fighting at Lauffeldt, was frustrated by the indecision at the outset of the battle.[32]

The Battle of Lauffeldt had been bloody indeed, with as many as 14,000 casualties between the two armies. It had also effectively exhausted Britain and France, but the subsequent peace treaty signed the following year at Aix-la-Chappelle was little more than a fragile truce. Prussia and Austria remained at loggerheads, and Anglo-French relations remained precarious over the situation in North America, where the British colonies still felt threatened by French encirclement. Unsurprisingly tensions flared when in 1754 French colonial forces established a presence at the confluence of the Monongahela and Allegheny rivers in the Ohio Valley.

The new fortification, named DuQuesne, along with a series of other strategically positioned forts along the Great Lakes shores, controlled river access from the St Lawrence in the north to the Mississippi in the south. This effectively encircled the Thirteen British Colonies, and increasing incursions from Native Americans allied with the French, particularly in the back country of Pennsylvania and Virginia, further destabilised the British position.[33] Consequently, the British government decided to send a force of regular troops to unpick the French strategy of encirclement, focused principally on capturing Fort DuQuesne.

To that end, then, in the summer of 1755, General Sir Edward Braddock took command of two battalions of understrength British regulars – the 44th and 48th Regiments of Foot, supplemented by colonial militia, principally from Virginia. Braddock was ordered to march his troops 120 miles through some of the most densely wooded terrain in North America, carving a new military road as they did so.[34] Braddock has been criticised for the inflexibility of his approach in planning and executing the expedition to DuQuesne, but recent research has illustrated that, once the target was decided, the operation was effectively and systematically planned and

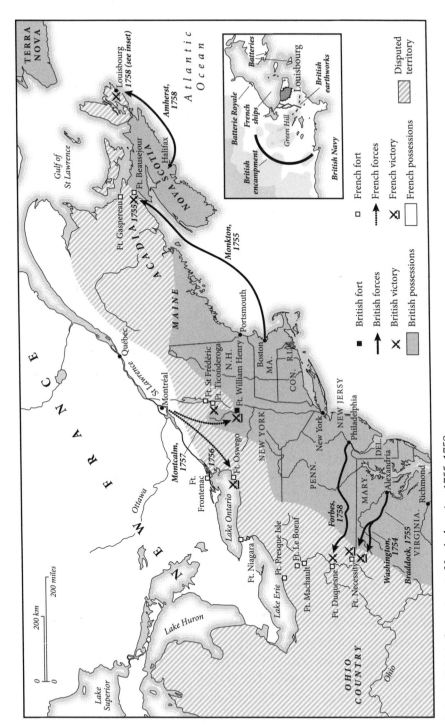

Map 1. British Campaigns in North America, 1755–1758.

executed, albeit with difficulties, which no British general in 1755 would likely have anticipated or overcome.[35]

Many of the adaptations that would eventually help achieve success in North America from 1758 onwards were foreshadowed by Braddock in preparation for the march to DuQuesne. For example, in anticipation of the harsh conditions the troops would encounter, linen waistcoats and breeches were issued instead of the conventional wool garments, while brown gaiters were worn to protect the men's legs while cutting the road. On top of this, Braddock ensured that the load his soldiers each carried was considerably reduced. The men were permitted to leave behind their heavy leather shoulder belts and waist belts and carry only a linen haversack for rations, a tin canteen, a knapsack for personal kit and a blanket. Fusils – light and shorter muskets – became the weapon of choice as being 'more use . . . in the Woody Country'.[36]

Moreover, during the march itself, Braddock took measures to increase the confidence and capability of his troops. In contrast to criticism that he neglected his flank security, Braddock repeatedly deployed flanking parties consisting of light horsemen and friendly Native American guides. The regulars were deployed in what two years later would have been recognised as light infantry formations, small parties of men spread out into a skirmish line half a mile wide, with orders to sweep the flanks of the column, flushing out enemy fighters who concealed themselves the night before.[37] As the army continued its slow march, the confidence of the regulars and colonial soldiers alike gradually increased.

Braddock, though, remained concerned that the march was not proceeding at a fast enough pace, and on 17 June split his force into two, with the regular battalions, the Virginian militia, and the artillery moving swiftly ahead, while the remainder brought up the rear escorting the main supply train. Braddock's 'flying' detachment, numbering in total 2,000 men, unencumbered by the supply train, would be able to move more rapidly and descend on DuQuesne, creating surprise and confusion. Braddock's quartermaster, Lieutenant Colonel Sir John St Clair viewed this arrangement as suitable for marching but did not think it a sensible formation for the successful investment of the fort. 'No General had hitherto march'd up at midday to the Gates of the Town he was to besiege, lacking his Convoy,' he remarked on 7 July, 'and if General Braddock attempted it he must look to the consequences.'[38]

On the morning of 9 July, the advanced party was within a few miles of DuQuesne. At 8 a.m., Braddock ordered his men, with Lieutenant

Colonel Thomas Gage in command of the vanguard, and St Clair in command of the road clearers, to ford the river Monongahela. It took nearly six hours to get the whole party across.[39] Once across, Braddock's flying column arrived at a wide clearing about a quarter of a mile from the river. Here, a small party of French and Native American warriors ambushed the British and American soldiers.

Robert Orme, one of Braddock's aides-de-camp, 'heard an excessive quick and heavy firing in the Front. The General imagining the advanced Parties were very warmly attacked' immediately sent reinforcements forward.[40] Gage ordered his troops to 'halt with a design of forming into a line of battle, but when that was attempted it proved ineffectual the whole falling into confusion'. Gage could not persuade his men to 'get . . . into any regular form, & being by this time within reach of the Enemy's fire, they appeared struck with a panic'.[41] With the attackers seemingly hidden behind the trees at the edge of the clearing, but the British and colonial soldiers badly exposed in the middle of it, confusion and panic quickly spread. St Clair was shot trying to stabilise the situation, but remained able to deliver a few remaining orders to try to re-establish order, and beseeched Braddock to take the rising ground which might have given the British some advantage.

As the ambush unfolded, Braddock rushed to support his advanced guard, but faced with firing from unknown locations from the thick wood, accompanied by the fear-inducing yell of Native American warriors, the advanced guard panicked and collapsed. A British officer observed that 'the Indians whether ordered or not I cannot say kept an incessant fire on the Guns & killed the Men very fast. These Indians', he continued, 'from their irregular method of fighting by running from one place to another obliged us to wheel from right to left, to desert the Guns . . . .'[42] As the redcoats fled back in the direction from which they had marched, they collided with troops coming to their aid. Formed up in a regular line, but with nothing to aim at, these troops also began to panic. Some fired at their own comrades, others into the air.[43] 'The men were so extremely deaf to the exhortations of the general officers', recalled Orme, 'that they fired away in the most irregular manner all their ammunition, and then ran off leaving the enemy the artillery, ammunition, provisions and baggage.'[44]

All the while, the fire of the French and Native Americans began to take a devastating toll on the officers, including Braddock. 'The general had five horses shot under him', recalled Orme, who was himself severely wounded, and 'at last received a wound through his lungs of which he died' four nights later in agonising pain.[45] With over 900 soldiers killed or wounded, including 60 of 86 officers, the entire advanced column began to flee the clearing and attempt to get back across the Monongahela.

The failure of an expedition that was supposed to be the centrepiece of the British effort to evict the French from the Ohio Valley would elicit recriminations which produced far-reaching consequences. Unsurprisingly, given the confusion of the combat itself, recollections were also varied and contradictory. Orme emphasised the calm and professional conduct of the officers in a very difficult and challenging situation, which was undone, he argued, by the indiscipline specifically of the colonial soldiers.[46]

In contrast, George Washington, who commanded three Virginian Provincial Companies, firmly blamed the British regulars for the failure: 'The dastardly behaviour of the English Soldiers, exposed all those who were inclined to do their duty to almost certain death, and at length in despite of every effort to the contrary, broke and ran like sheep before the hounds.' Any attempts to restore order were met 'with as much success as if we had attempted to stop the wild bears of the mountains'. The Virginians, meanwhile, 'behaved like men and died like soldiers'.[47]

Gage firmly disagreed with this version of events. He specifically recalled 'frequent conversations of the Provincial troops & country people ... that if they engaged any Indian in the European manner of fighting, they would be beat'. The implication was that such talk, combined with harassing attacks by enemy Native American warriors, undermined the morale and discipline of the redcoats, inexperienced as they were in American wilderness warfare.

Horatio Gates, a British officer who had served in North America since the War of Austrian Succession, was more inclined to blame the officers for making poor decisions. He reported that:

> the main body of the army instead of being form'd in a line of battle, on the Vanguards being attacked, moved up in a line of march, therefore were flank'd on both sides by the enemy which caused an immediate confusion and so great was the disorder that there was no setting it to right and from that instant all was lost.[48]

For both Gage and Gates, it was the fact that the redcoats held a poor position, and continued to do so – Gage estimated for about three hours, exhausting their supply of ammunition in the process – that resulted in the disaster. Asked to summarise why the fiasco had occurred, he concluded that it was because of 'the novelty of an invisible enemy & the nature of the country, which was entirely a forest'.[49] The Native Americans were firing from behind trees, and with nothing to aim at, the soldiers discharged their weapons at anything that moved: more often than not, other British soldiers. When asked for reasons for the fiasco, Gage suggested 'the want of Indians or other irregulars to give timely notice of the enemy's approach'.[50]

Whatever the actual causes of the catastrophe – recent research has suggested that the redcoats behaved as well as might be expected in such circumstances, and the best chance they had was to maintain discipline – the perception that emerged in the wake of the battle indicated that regular European continental drill methods were inadequate to the challenge posed in America.[51] This perception, so much more important than reality, drove a debate which also dovetailed with new and innovative thinking emerging from Europe. There, continental armies had long accepted the value and utility of irregular units. During the War of Austrian Succession, Frederick the Great had formed the *Feld Jäger Corps*, levied from Central European hunters, skilled in the use of rifles, while the French formed *chasseurs à pied*. Saxe would go on to write eloquently of the utility of such units as a supplement and compliment to the regular order of battle. In the absence of formal doctrine, such treatises offered soldiers the only real access to distilled experience of practical value.[52]

By contrast, as historian John Grenier argues, the British never really embraced irregular forces in the same way. Rather, they were seen as interim solutions to be deployed in the suppression of rebellion. This viewpoint had been illustrated in an 'Essay on Regular and Irregular Forces', published in *Gentleman's Quarterly* in January 1746. The author argued that regular formations of disciplined infantry would overcome irregular adversaries so long as they were not facing overwhelming numbers, were competently led and properly trained.[53] The essay effectively captures the prevailing opinion within a British Army heavily focused on the European experience of war, where regular training was considered essential, and any modifications were temporary solutions to specific problems. The emergence of adaptations and innovations, such as irregular tactics, light infantry and *petite guerre*, and their successful incorporation into British fighting practices, was therefore an organic process separate from the experience of war in Europe. Key to this process of development was the experience of key personnel, their personal networks and the global scope of their professional knowledge.

When news of the calamity at the Monongahela reached London, Cumberland set about revising his plans for the 1756 campaign. Insanely ambitious, they included 'the Reduction of *Montreal* and *Quebec* with the Forts which lie between those Places'. For this to succeed, 'we must be masters of Lake *Champlain* by having a proper Number of armed Vessels upon it'. To facilitate this, 'an *experienced & active* General Officer' was needed.[54] Into this difficult situation, Cumberland appointed an officer he trusted implicitly, John Campbell, the Earl of Loudoun.

*   *   *

Setting aside the ridiculously ambitious plan Cumberland had devised, Braddock's defeat at the Monongahela had laid bare the severe shortcomings of the British Army in North America. Not only did it seem that British troops were tactically incapable of dealing with the threats they faced, but severe logistical and command shortcomings had only accentuated internal fissures between British and colonial forces, and between the British command and colonial assemblies. On top of this, the British had alienated almost all of their Native American support.

Previously friendly Native American tribes turned bloodthirsty enemies, as the latter sought to bolster their position alongside their new allies, the French. Raids and massacres took place across the Thirteen Colonies. Newspapers carried stories of atrocities, of villages 'laid in ashes, men, women, and children cruelly mangled and massacred'.[55] The bloody raids continued throughout 1756. Even 'those we call friends', Loudoun dryly observed, 'are no more than Neutrals'.[56] This was, of course, part of a French strategy designed to spread terror throughout the Thirteen Colonies and thus undermine the British will to continue the war.

The French were also bolstering their regular army. Loudoun learned 'by the best intelligence we had, the Enemy had sent in single vessels, from France to North America, 4000 Troops, 3500 of which had escaped our Fleets in the Channel'.[57] Unknown to the British at the time, this reinforcement carried with it the new commander of French forces in Canada, Louis-Joseph, Marquis de Montcalm-Gozon de Saint-Véran.[58] Montcalm would prove a tenacious enemy for Loudoun and the British; a superb strategist, he understood how to obtain results with limited means. His actions would bring the British to the verge of defeat by 1758. Loudoun, meanwhile, lacked the tactical brilliance to take on the French, but at least understood that long-term success was predicated on a well-trained and resourced army.

Loudoun's immediate attention was focused on laying the structural foundations for the British Defence of North America. This, he believed, rested on Canada and the Great Lakes. The day after his arrival, Loudoun wrote to Admiral Charles Lawrence, commanding at Halifax, demanding 'with impatience' a 'particular account of all Military Affairs in Your Province'.[59] Loudoun's haughty tone belied both his attitude and the gravity of the situation. He was fearful that the French at Louisbourg could launch a strike against Halifax and cut off access to the St Lawrence for the British.

Loudoun was likewise concerned that the network of fortifications that commanded the waterways into British North America were also vulnerable to a French attack. In early August, he sent Major General Daniel Webb and the 44th Regiment to the fort at Oswego, where the commanding officer had been ordered to begin building a naval task force which would secure command of Lake Ontario.[60] On his march to Oswego, Webb was to 'review all the troops in their different posts . . . examine the state of all the Forts twixt Skenectady and Oswego & give directions to put them in the best posture of defence . . .'.[61] Similar instructions were sent to Lieutenant Colonels Bunton and Montressor, who were deployed respectively to Fort William Henry, which commanded the southern shore of Lake George, and Fort Edward on the Hudson River.[62]

But success depended on more than strategically important fortresses. The British Army in North America was poorly trained, inadequately led and riven with internal feuds which paralysed decision making. Added to this was the complexity of the environment. British training had proved inadequate to the challenges presented in North America: European tactics of fighting in columns and lines, concentrating firepower to mitigate the effects of inaccurate musketry, had seemingly been shown wanting in the wilderness back country of Virginia and Pennsylvania. Nor would the shortcoming be met simply by recruiting 'irregular' soldiers for service in the British Army.

Just two months after their surprise success at the Monongahela, the French had suffered an equally surprising defeat. In September 1755, French, Canadian and Native American forces had attacked a British post on Lake George commanded by William Johnson, who was soon to be appointed as superintendent of Northern Indian Affairs. Despite employing similar tactics to those deployed at the Monongahela, the French and Native American attack was disrupted by well-aimed artillery. 'The French regulars kept their ground and order for some time with great resolution and good conduct, but the warm and constant fire from our artillery and troops put them into disorder.' Five hours after the engagement began, 'our men and the Indians jumped over the breastwork, pursued the enemy, slaughtered numbers and took several prisoners'.[63]

In such close terrain, then, and in a situation where the main strategic objective was a fortification, simply assembling trained irregulars alongside regular forces was unsatisfactory. Something more sophisticated was required, something that combined the discipline and technical training of regular soldiers with the dynamism and innovation exhibited by irregular soldiers. In this regard, Loudoun considered his experience in Scotland as essential preparation for his command in America.

Given the evident parallels – untamed terrain, local irregular forces and challenging geography – Loudoun was always going to draw on his experiences in Scotland for inspiration. The hybrid regular–irregular pattern he employed in the Highlands, where locally recruited soldiers combined their regular training with irregular techniques learned while fighting in the Highlands, offered lessons of evident value in America.

Loudoun still needed to learn how to integrate his personal experience and understanding with the wealth of local knowledge available in the Thirteen Colonies. This would prove no easy task. Loudoun encountered significant resistance to adaptation both from within the British Army and from those with whom he sought to work, who viewed service alongside the British Army redcoats with deep suspicion. As Benjamin Franklin succinctly observed, the Colonial troops feared that 'Regulars join'd with them, would claim all the Honour of any Success, and charge them with the Blame of any Miscarriage'.[64]

Loudoun ordered his regular officers to employ friendly Native Americans to support their operations. When he ordered General Webb to march to Oswego, Loudoun advised him to recruit 'a body of Indians to march along with you . . . to Protect and cover the workmen at [Oswego], by scouting in conjunction with the Troops'.[65] Loudoun had integrated regular and irregular practices while serving in Scotland, and he was seeking to repeat the process in North America. He was nevertheless far too late to save Oswego, which the Governor-General of New France, Pierre de Rigaud Vaudreuil de Cavagnial, had recognised could be used as a staging post by the British to raid French fortresses of Niagara and Frontenac along the Great Lakes. Left in British hands, Oswego could be the launch-pad for a strategy that would gradually unpick the French position on Lake Ontario, and with it North America.

Vaudreuil therefore determined to besiege, capture and destroy Oswego, thus preventing the possibility of any meaningful military assault on

Niagara.[66] This he achieved quickly and decisively, forcing the British garrison to surrender on 14 August 1756. A riot broke out as the prisoners of war left the fort and according to one 'the Enemy Indians, who, not satisfied with taking away our Baggage, murther'd several of our soldiers'.[67] Webb learned of the fall of Oswego on 25 August. Believing an invasion of New York was imminent, he raised the wooden fortresses at the Great Carrying Place, erected a wooden dam across the portage at the Mohawk River and beat a hasty retreat.[68] The French, satisfied that they had prevented any British threat to their position on Lake Ontario, turned their attention to Lake George and the Hudson Valley in New York.

With the latest version of his strategy in tatters, Loudoun had to reassess, but he was engaging in a campaign in an area of the world about which he knew little. 'We are at present grasping in the dark,' he wrote to Cumberland with an air of melodrama. 'No Intelligence; no part of the country reconnoitred; few men to act with; no one thing provided for moving them; but Provisions which I have the greatest difficulties to transport to the places where wanted.'[69] He wanted to learn more about the geography of North America, but his forces were ill-equipped to collect this information.

Loudoun realised he could not successfully prosecute a campaign until his army was sufficiently manned, trained and equipped. He therefore turned his attention to remedying the shortage of manpower in the provincial armies. He remained convinced that the root of the colonies' security problems lay in their inherent fragmentation, and therefore the solution to that problem could be found in a loose colonial military union. Loudoun sought to build relationships with the colonial governors and, in anticipation of the 1757 campaign, he met with commissioners from the four New England colonies, held a council of war at Philadelphia with the southern governors and dealt directly with the governors of New York and New Jersey. In return for their agreeing to raise a certain number of provincial troops for service alongside regulars, Loudoun agreed to local provincial courts martial.

With the Crown funding victualling, transportation, ammunition and medical care, Loudoun envisaged a considerable financial saving for the colonial assemblies, whose responsibility would be limited to raising, paying, arming and clothing their recruits. In so doing, Loudoun sought to corral the military resources of the colonies under his command, an unprecedented concentration of effort. As ever, the plan did not survive contact with the colonial assemblies, who refused to vote through their share of provincial recruits, instead agreeing in some cases to the 1754 requirement. Despite this setback, and though they were not ready for deployment by the commencement of the 1757 campaign, Loudoun still had managed to convince the various colonial governors to suborn their provincial recruits to royal – and therefore his – command. Though it fell short of bestowing the level of authority Loudoun desired, this was the most unified the military power of the colonies had ever been, and Loudoun was at least able to direct the military resources of the colonies to the defence of any part of the 1,500-mile frontier.[70]

Loudoun's European experiences, meanwhile, provided solutions to colonial transport and logistics problems: British contractors were employed to secure the supply of adequate rations at a reasonable price to the British soldiery.[71] Centrally located Crown storehouses enabled the more efficient storage and distribution of victuals, which from 1757 were transported using a Crown-procured wagon train, saving £3,400 on the colonial contracted costs.[72] Loudoun had begun implementing such solutions almost as soon as he arrived in America. When he despatched Daniel Webb to Oswego in May 1756, Loudoun had instructed Webb to 'order Store Houses and Barracks to be erected in the different Forts. For that end, you will have it under Consideration what number of men will be sufficient to Garrison those Forts during the Winter'.[73] Such a move was designed to facilitate military operations across strategically significant and extended areas of North America. Historians have noted that this solution illustrates the application of European military knowledge in America,[74] but in the field of tactical innovation and reform, it is quite clear that European tactics, techniques and procedures were adapted and integrated with American military knowledge to produce a solution that combined the strengths of both.

Loudoun employed several approaches before he finally succeeded in effectively combining different schools of tactical thought. Initially, he favoured recruiting provincial soldiers to serve as irregular troops, but it swiftly became apparent that the lack of formal training of any capacity meant that they proved significantly less adaptive to the varied challenges evident in wilderness warfare. If not the provincials, then Loudoun contemplated recruiting regiments of Native Americans. In the wake of Braddock's defeat, and the continued Native American attacks in the back country and frontier settlements,[75] Loudoun surmised that the best troops to counter these activities were friendly Native American warriors. Such a force would counter the irregular activities of his adversaries, collect intelligence and scout the terrain. The scheme was costly – a full regiment of 500 men was predicted to cost over £30,000 a year – but the idea failed because it proved impossible to recruit sufficient numbers of Native Americans.[76]

Instead, Loudoun turned to rangers, another solution organic to the Thirteen Colonies. Ranging emerged as a colonial response to Native American raids against frontier farmsteads and settlements during King Philip's War (1675–1678). Benjamin Church of Plymouth Colony had argued then that colonists 'must make a business of the war as the enemy did'. Enlisting the support of friendly Native Americans, Church recruited like-minded colonists capable of withstanding gruelling campaigning conditions, and launched an expedition against the Narragansetts.

Rather than 'lie in any town or garrison,' he and his men would 'lie in the woods as the enemy did'.[77] This might not have been the first such attempt,[78] but the success of the expedition – Church reported the 'killing of many of the enemy' – illustrated the value to colonial defence of a military unit that incorporated Native American wilderness warfare tactics. Consequently, Governor Edward Winslow agreed to commission Church in July 1676; the first American ranging unit was born.[79] Church returned to lead his unit during subsequent colonial wars, while other ranging companies sprang up elsewhere in the colonies, illustrating the value of organic military adaptation to the irregular tactics favoured by Native American adversaries.

During King George's War, as Acadian and Mi'kmaq raiding parties struck terror into the colonists and settlers of Nova Scotia, John Gorham, the third generation of a family of experienced 'ranger' officers, organised a small unit of about 50 rangers in New England. Governor Shirley promptly recognised the value of Gorham's Rangers and sent them to help defend Annapolis Royal in Nova Scotia. Gorham's Rangers, as Church had in earlier wars, utilised Native American tactics as a form of 'applied terror', gaining a reputation by 1747 as being 'far more terrible than European Soldiers'.[80] The tactics employed by Gorham bore immediate results by collecting intelligence and intercepting Native American raiding parties. On 4 October 1746, for example, Gorham related how he used a Native American 'stratigem' and 'trappned a Couple of the [French] Inhabitants' in order to 'gain any Inteligenc [sic]' of enemy plans.[81]

Over the course of the next few years, Gorham's Rangers became the premier military unit in Nova Scotia. As conflict with the Mi'kmaq and the Acadians escalated, so the British became ever more reliant on the irregular skills of the rangers. In 1750, the new governor of Nova Scotia, Edward Cornwallis, ordered more ranger units to be raised, including one commanded by Captain Francis Bartelo, recently arrived from Europe, where he had served under the Duke of Cumberland in Flanders. There, he had waged *petite guerre* against French *grassin*.[82]

European practices were influencing the organic development of an American response to the challenges posed by complex terrain and adversaries. Although Gorham and Bartelo made some significant gains against the Mi'kmaq and Acadians, their opponents proved as flexible, adopting a Fabian strategy and seeking to draw the rangers into compromising situations.[83] Bartelo himself was killed after finding 'himself intirely surrounded' on 16 September, while reconnoitring an enemy position on the banks of the river Maragash.[84] The ambush eerily foreshadowed the much larger ambush on the Monongahela five years later and perhaps illustrates the limitations of European irregular practices.

When war broke out again in 1754, the rangers continued to use exemplary violence to spread terror in what was a deliberate targeting of noncombatant populations in North America. By 1755, the rangers had been instrumental in subduing the Mi'kmaq and the forcible exclusion of over 4,000 Acadians from Nova Scotia. No wonder, then, that Loudoun, with his own personal experience of *petite guerre* and irregular tactics from Scotland, saw the rangers as a possible solution to the growing challenge posed by the French and Native Americans across New England, Virginia and Pennsylvania in 1756.

With provincial irregular soldiers and Native American warriors proving unreliable, Loudoun ordered the incorporation of American rangers into the British order of battle. 'It is impossible for an army to act in this country, without Rangers,' Loudoun wrote to Cumberland in November, 'there ought to be a considerable body of them.'[85] During the 19 months Loudoun commanded in North America, the rangers were expanded to nine companies. Their role was multifaceted: regular and timely intelligence collection, guiding and route finding, and the more traditional irregular activities of detecting and countering enemy ambushes and skirmishers. At the end of 1756, Loudoun asked the famed ranger Robert Rogers to provide a set of written instructions for regular soldiers who had volunteered to serve as skirmishers.

Rogers had made a reputation for himself in the early 1750s, with regular newspaper reports in the *Boston Gazette* highlighting his zeal and seemingly boundless energy in prosecuting irregular warfare.[86] On 24

March 1756, William Shirley commissioned Rogers as a captain of an independent company of rangers, consisting of 60 privates, three sergeants, an ensign and a lieutenant.[87] Shirley had insisted that, when recruiting men to the rangers, 'none may be employed, but good officers, fit for the Wood Service, and to be depended upon ...'. They were to wear 'A good Hunting Coat, Vest & Breeches, a pair of Indian Stockings, shoes', while they were to be armed with 'a Hatchet' and 'Firelocks to be delivered to them at Boston, which they are to return at the end of the Service'.[88] Rogers, meanwhile, trained his recruits 'with the manner of and practices in scouting & fighting in the woods ...', which he distilled into a series of instructions so 'that their errors may be avoided & want of greater regularity if found necessary pointed out to them for their observation and improvement'.[89]

Rogers derived these instructions from his own experience of scouting, collecting intelligence and fighting French and Native American warriors in the wilderness of North America. In January 1757, for example, he led 70 officers and men on a scout north from Fort William Henry with a view to obtaining intelligence on enemy intentions for the forthcoming campaign. After a chance encounter on the frozen Lake Champlain with 10 sleighs travelling between Forts Carillon and Crown Point, Rogers and his men captured seven prisoners whom they immediately interrogated.

Learning that the French were reinforcing Fort Carillon, Rogers quickly and correctly assumed that a French and Native American raiding party would be sent out to hunt down the Rangers. Early the following morning, the Rangers set out for Fort William Henry. As they marched through a valley, 'a volley of two hundred shot or there about was fired upon us from the Enemy who formed themselves into a half moon to intercept & surround us which killed [three] and wounded several of our party & myself slightly in the head'. In the ensuing battle, Rogers and his Rangers employed a range of tactics and techniques designed to take advantage of close terrain and mitigate French and Native American abilities to do the same.

After giving orders to kill the prisoners captured the day before, a move which demonstrated that both sides practised brutality in this conflict, Rogers ordered his men to form a double line in order to return fire. 'The Enemy pursued us so close thro' the valley that they took some prisoners and killed ... several of our men; but were beaten back again from the Bush fire of' a flanking party that Rogers had deployed to cover a retreat.

'The enemy soon after made an attempt to push up to us', Rogers noted in a record of the encounter sent to Lord Loudoun once he returned to

Fort William Henry, 'but having the advantage of the Ground & good shelter from Trees we obliged them ... to retreat as they could not stand our continual fire upon them'. Rogers selected strong ground to try to hold out until dusk, at which point he elected to fall back under cover of darkness and before his adversary received any reinforcement. The scout returned to Fort William Henry the following evening, having suffered 25 casualties. Rogers estimated enemy strength to be in the region of 250 French and Native American warriors.[90]

Rogers employed and also learned a range of tactics and techniques in this battle, which would later appear in his instructions, including the use of terrain for cover, and how to maintain a continuous fire. The reality was that Rogers expected his men to learn tactics, techniques and procedures that a regular redcoat would never dream of performing on a battlefield, for to do so would be a violation of the close-knit discipline required to achieve superior firepower, and with it psychological dominance over an adversary.

By contrast, tight tactical formations were, for Rogers, a liability in certain circumstances. 'If your number be small,' he instructed, 'march in a single file, keeping at such a distance from each other as to prevent one shot from killing two men.' If the opportunity arose to attack an irregular adversary, 'push upon them with the greatest resolution with equal force in each flank and in the centre, observing to keep at a due distance from each other, and advance from tree to tree, with one half of the party before the other ten or twelve yards'. He had observed his adversary using a similar approach in January 1757.

If the rangers found themselves under attack, and 'obliged to receive the enemy's fire, fall, or squat down, til it is over, then rise and discharge at them'. In the event that the 'enemy push upon you, let your front fire and fall down, and then let your rear advance thro' them and do the like', Rogers wrote. At this point, 'those who before were in front will be ready to discharge again, and repeat the same alternately as occasion shall require ...'.[91] The specifics of these instructions varied significantly to the parade-ground training of regular soldiers. In 'Exercises for the American Forces', which Cumberland had issued in April 1756, the Captain-General of the British Army offered strict guidelines not only on how and when to fire, but also on a number of options for deployment of the platoon.[92] But built into these instructions was an inherent expectation: organic adaptation. Cumberland, and by extension Loudoun, clearly believed redcoats serving in America would naturally adapt to the conditions, challenges and combat that they found.

True, Rogers's instructions broke the mould – with loose-order tactics, using natural cover for protection, and in many cases the complete abandonment of traditional discipline – but these movements required skill and dexterity, and the confident use of the available weaponry: skills that were at the heart of the traditional drill employed by European armies. Indeed, Rogers expected the same cast-iron discipline from his men as Cumberland had expected at Culloden. If awaiting an enemy attack, 'reserve your fire 'til they approach very near,' Rogers wrote, 'which will put them into the greater surprise and consternation, and give you an opportunity of rushing upon them with your hatchets and cutlasses to the better advantage'.[93] When Rogers selected his men, then, he was looking not just for the experienced woodsmen and back country huntsmen, which was the archetypal early American ranger, he was looking for skilled marksmen and disciplined infantrymen.

While Rogers' rules and instructions were designed principally to train newly raised ranging units, there is also some evidence of the exchange of these ideas directly into British Army units. In 1757, George Augustus, Lord Howe, arrived in North America with his regiment, the 55th.[94] Keen to understand the methods of warfare employed in the wilderness, Howe accompanied Rogers on one of his scouting expeditions. He was interested to learn the Rangers' 'method of marching, ambushing, retreating &c.',[95] and during the scout Howe abandoned traditional European discipline in favour of the tactics and techniques, as well as the dress, employed by the Rangers.[96] He then adapted these methods and began instructing his own men accordingly.

'Lord Howe always lay ... with the regiment which he commanded which he modelled in such a manner that they were ever after considered an example to the whole American Army,' wrote one observer. 'Lord Howe laid aside all pride and prejudice, and gratefully accepted counsel from those whom he knew to be best qualified to direct them.'[97] He ordered changes to the men's uniforms and armaments, such as cutting the skirts from their coats, browning their muskets and providing leggings to protect the lower limbs.

'We are now literally an army of roundheads,' exclaimed one soldier. 'Our hair is about an inch long; the Flaps of our Hats, which are slouched, about two inches and a half broad. Our coats are docked rather shorter than the Highlanders ... Swords and sashes are degraded, and many have taken up the Hatchet and wear Tomahawks.'[98] Finally, more subsistence was provided for each man to carry personally, creating a more independent and mobile fighting force.[99] Howe was not alone in arguing for the adoption of local practices. 'Our cloaths, our arms, our accoutrements, nay even our shoes and stocking are all improper for this country,' wrote Brigadier James Wolfe shortly after his arrival in Halifax. 'Lord Howe is so well convinc'd of it that he has taken away all the men's breeches.'[100]

The reality was, however, that many in the army remained resistant to change. At the end of 1756, Loudoun wrote, in considerable frustration, of his experience at all levels of military recruitment. The regular regiments were seriously undermanned, and Loudoun was forced to collapse several into single battalions for the winter. The ranger units were 'a considerable expence' and the colonial establishment, moreover, was wildly overesti-mated.[101] While Rogers was able to pick his men, and fashion highly effec-tive units, the talent pool from which he drew was very shallow.

Though the instructions and training helped transform these 'selected' men into highly effective warriors, there still remained the question about what role Lord Loudoun envisaged for the rangers. Rogers had his own ideas, and in late 1756, he proposed to Loudoun 'that a Party of Rangers consisting of two hundred with such Officers as Scouts' should serve 'our interest by distressing the Enemy at their Settlements in Canada'.[102] Rogers' preference was terrorism against the noncombatant population of New France, a strategy of violence that historian John Grenier has termed the 'First Way of War', and the natural successor to the developments in raiding which was the colonial response to Native American attacks.[103]

Such an approach proved too much for Loudoun to stomach. Though similar violence had been meted out by the British to the Highland popu-lation of Scotland during the Jacobite Rebellion a decade earlier, Loudoun did not, at this stage at least, wish to spread terror among the civilian population of North America – he was hardly likely to reform colonial civilisation if he advocated practices which directly contradicted such principles when working out how to fight the adversaries he found in the colonies. He ordered Rogers instead to concentrate on intelligence collection, which had been his original concern in August 1756.

Unhappy though Rogers might have been with a seemingly limited and constrained portfolio of missions, for Loudoun, timely and accurate intelli-gence was the key to transitioning to a more offensive strategy from the defensive posture he had been forced to adopt since arriving in America. 'I expect ... those Ranging Companies ... to prevent the Enemy from making incursions into the settled country', he had written to Fox, 'and hope, totaly to prevent scalping parties. If we have early enough Intelligence by our Rangers, we shall be strong enough everywhere to meet them, and drive them back, and if they should escape us ... we must be able to cut off their retreat.'[104]

Though the Rangers proved an effective intelligence-collection unit, Loudoun found them unreliable in other roles. Frequently insubordinate and tardy, the rangers clearly saw themselves primarily as scouts. Moreover, the nine companies – numbering no more than 500 men – were £15,000 a year more expensive than a regiment of regular redcoats, who usually cost approximately £20,000 to maintain.[105] Cumberland had advised Loudoun to 'teach your Troops to go out upon Scouting Parties: for, 'till Regular Officers with men they can trust, learn to beat the woods, and to act as Irregulars, you never will gain any certain Intelligence of the Enemy'.[106] Sceptical as he was that the rangers could fulfil this duty, Loudoun had every intention of training British redcoats to do the same job.

Indeed, he found that British regulars had been adapting of their own accord to the conditions they faced. 'When I arrived, I found there was a disposition in the Soldiers, to go out with Indians and Rangers,' he wrote to Cumberland in August 1756. 'I shall encourage it all I can, and if the parties that are now out, have success and escape, we shall soon get a knowledge of this unknown country, and be able to march with much more safety than at present.'[107] Those soldiers and officers who did go on scouts were similarly sceptical of the reliability and effectiveness of the rangers. 'I assure you it is necessary to encourage young fellows to go out', wrote General Abercromby to Colonel John Forbes, Loudoun's Adjutant-General, after the return of one volunteer from a scout, 'for the officers of the Rangers are a set of thugs and Rascals & not any of them except Rogers knows any thing of the country.'[108] If not the Native Americans or the Rangers, then who would provide the much-needed irregular support to the British Army? A solution readily presented itself in the form of the Royal American Regiment.

In late 1755, Swiss émigré officer Lieutenant Colonel James Prevost had tabled a proposal to the British government, to raise two battalions of continental troops drawn from the Low Countries, Switzerland and the smaller German states.[109] The government was initially wholly supportive, and Prevost was dispatched to Europe in October 1755 to recruit officers for his battalions, enrolling 43 officers by 1 January 1756, including his older brother Augustine, and Lieutenant Colonels Henry Bouquet and Frederick Haldimand, who had served in the army of the Dutch Republic. Haldimand had also served a stint under Frederick the Great's command,

and Bouquet in the *petit guerre* in Corsica in the 1740s. Perhaps inevitably, however, the plan met opposition in parliament, suspicious as it was of foreign battalions. It was eventually agreed that, while the number of battalions would be increased from two to four, fewer than half of the officers would be foreign, the majority of the recruits would be raised in America. The regiment itself was now dubbed the Royal American. Rather than being its chief, Prevost would become colonel of the most junior battalion. By contrast, Haldimand and Bouquet were appointed to command its most senior battalions.[110] By the end of 1756, Loudoun saw the new unit not just as a solution to the recruitment difficulties faced by the British in North America, but also as a potential solution to the tactical challenges. Recognising a sensible suggestion when he saw it, Loudoun copied the instructions laid down by Frederick Haldimand and ordered the whole regiment to train 'to fire at Marks, and in order to qualify them for the Service of the Woods, they are to be taught to load and fire, lyeing on the Ground and kneeling'. Also channelling the words of Robert Rogers, Loudoun similarly expected the men to be 'taught to march in Order, slow and fast in all sortes of Ground'.[111]

At the same time, regular British units were also beginning to experiment with innovative irregular tactics. When acting as a covering party, British soldiers learned to march in single file, making it easier, if they fell into an ambush, to obey the command 'Tree all', and find themselves a tree for cover.[112] Loudoun championed rather than proscribed such ground-up innovation, while his second-in-command and adjutant-general advocated for the incorporation of ranger tactics into the regular infantry battalions. This, Abercromby argued, 'requires coming speedily to a resolution to form a respectable body of men under proper discipline which I am in good hopes may be accomplished, and by training one company of each Regt into Rangers you have the very thing they have done at home'.[113] This thinking chimed with Loudoun's own experiences in Scotland a decade earlier. There, he had been responsible for organising parties of irregular troops whose mission it was to harass enemy supplies and communications and inhibit the ability of the rebels to recruit to their cause. At the same time, he recognised the need for a hybrid approach: the rebellion would not be defeated by irregular means alone, and the British army would have to fight major battles in which close discipline, concentration of firepower and the measured use of the bayonet were essential elements of success.[114] Though Loudoun did not seek to impose this experience as a blueprint on North America, he used it as a guide for creating the conditions for adaptation.

Unfortunately, these adaptations and innovations would come too late to save Loudoun's command. For the winter of 1756, Loudoun had to rely on the rangers alone, and he positioned a company of 50 rangers, with each regular battalion defending Britain's various lake forts, 'to get them intelligence in order to prevent sudden surprises'. Rogers interpreted his instructions more liberally, using intelligence collection as a cover for deeper incursions into enemy territory. In October 1756, for example, Rogers captured a French sentry from outside the gates of the French-held Fort Carillon. On their return to Fort William Henry on 31 October, the prisoner was promptly interrogated and revealed information about the defensive capacity and military complement of Forts Carillon and Crown Point, and French plans for the capture of Fort William Henry in the forthcoming spring.[115]

* * *

Following the loss of Oswego, fears began to grow of the imminent collapse of the colonial economy.[116] The reality was that the North American economy could sustain significantly more damage from the war, but Loudoun was looking for ways to strike a blow against New France, while preserving the integrity of the Thirteen Colonies. He was aware from the activities of Robert Rogers that the French intended to strike a blow in the direction of the Hudson Valley in 1757, but he was also cognisant that Cumberland expected him to attack the heart of New France. He therefore planned a direct assault on the seat of French power in Canada, 'by striking at the root'.[117]

Initially he proposed to attack Quebec. 'They would keep their whole Force, to defend their Capital, as their whole depends upon it,' he wrote to a subordinate officer. 'When once that is taken, there is an end of all their Forts ... and of Course, of their Influence and Command over the Indians.'[118] Attacking New France directly would forestall any French invasion of New York. According to the *New York Gazette*, 'a bold push' to the St Lawrence that would make the British 'masters of Quebec and, in consequence, of all Canada; whereas the present manner of carrying on the war among thick woods, where a single Indian can fire his piece without discovery, may linger on without effect for many years'.[119] Not for the last time would there be a disagreement over which military strategy to pursue: whether to seek a direct, war-winning decisive battle, or by orchestrating a campaign of indirect activities, manoeuvring the enemy into a position in which the chances of defeating them were high.

A change of government in London, which sidelined Cumberland, resulted in the rise of William Pitt, who now insisted that Louisbourg become the principal objective, on the basis that the fortified port commanded the entrance to the St Lawrence.[120] Loudoun appeared mildly frustrated by the orders, noting upon their arrival that he barely had time to distribute a call to arms to the provincial governments if he was to get his operation underway before the summer months.[121] Further weather-related delays meant Loudoun did not get to Halifax until mid-June, where an immediate assault was rendered impossible by thick fog and then adverse winds.

Loudoun made the most of the situation, taking the opportunity to train his forces, landing them at Halifax to learn the basics of siege warfare, and fight mock battles,[122] 'in order to make the troops acquainted with the nature of their service they are going upon; also to render the smell of powder more familiar to the young soldiers'.[123] Loudoun's use of war games and mock sieges provoked derision in some segments of the army. Major General Lord Charles Hay in particular saw the practice as a waste of time. 'I shall find a method of letting the Mother Country know what is doing here,' he publicly exclaimed in frustration, 'that we have taken up building show forts and making Approaches to them, when we should be Employ'd in Real attacks'.[124]

Despite the evident disdain of some, field training was commonplace throughout the British Army and had been a feature of deployed units from at least as early as Marlborough's campaigns at the beginning of the century.[125] In the absence of formalised training practices during peacetime, and the infrequency of wartime training encampments, field training was the last – and, in many cases, only – opportunity for soldiers and officers within units to harmonise their drill practice, as well as to learn how to fight alongside other units. Field training was also adapted to meet the particular and unique challenges presented by different environments. Loudoun's army was preparing for siege warfare at Halifax, but field training was the principal means by which innovations and adaptations would be communicated to newly arrived units. However, those units training in Halifax would find little use for their new skills until 1758.

Continued poor weather prevented any assault on Louisbourg, and then intelligence was received which indicated that the French had managed to sneak in three fleets, carrying a reinforcement of four battalions of infantry. Under such circumstances, a successful attack was deemed impossible, as 'the Force the Enemy now have in Louisbourg' was too strong.[126] Thus ended hopes of 'striking at the root'. A direct assault on the seat of French power in North America would have to wait, not least because while Loudoun and half the regular units of the British Army were floating in a small fleet of transports anchored off Halifax, Montcalm struck deep into British territory, just as Robert Rogers' intelligence had suggested.

Loudoun urged General Daniel Webb to take the initiative against the French in New York, by laying siege to either Fort Carillon, on the small land bridge between Lakes Champlain and George, or Crown Point, positioned halfway along the western shore of Lake Champlain. The threatened French attack on Fort William Henry, at the foot of Lake George, would 'be entirely prevented, if you are able to take both or either of those Forts'.[127] Unfortunately, Webb, a man whose health was poor and confidence badly shaken by the previous year's fiasco, failed completely to take Loudoun's advice. Despite mounting intelligence of an imminent French attack, Webb not only failed to go on the offensive early, he sent only 2,500 of his 7,500 men to reinforce the British garrison of William Henry.[128]

On the morning of 3 August, William Henry's sentries 'discovered a large number of boats on the lake close under a point of Land on the west shore' about five miles north of the fort, which proceeded to disembark their combined 1,500 strong force of regulars, Canadians and Native American warriors. By noon, 'we could plainly see from the Fort that the Enemy were throwing up an entrenchment and erecting a Battery at the distance of about 7 or 800 yards on a Clear Ground'. The first battery opened on the 5th, with a second completed two days later, precipitating 'the hottest days action from all quarters'.[129] Garrison morale remained high until a letter from Webb was brought in under a flag of truce, informing the fortress commander that he could expect no relief. With the fortress defences weakened and under strain, and with no prospect of relief, William Henry surrendered. In the wake of the siege, French-allied Native Americans, who hailed from as many as 33 nations, ranging from Michigan to the Ohio Valley, descended on a column of prisoners of war as they were led from the fortress. As many as 185 were killed before the French could regain control.[130]

Vaudreuil now urged a move against Fort Edward, but Montcalm, who had commanded the siege of Fort William Henry, declined, fearing the British were concentrating their forces there and that a move into the Hudson Valley might overextend his position. He destroyed Fort William Henry and withdrew with 2,300 prisoners back to Fort Carillon.[131] Montcalm was right: the northern colonies had rallied to the cause and dispatched militia units to defend Fort Edward,[132] proving perhaps that Loudoun had indeed achieved a moderate level of success in creating a colonial military union.

If this was a modest administrative achievement, it was overshadowed by the humiliating failure to capture Louisbourg, and yet another devastating defeat at Fort William Henry. Loudoun cannot bear sole responsibility for the failures of 1757: his plans in Canada were undermined by the weather, and he was lacking capable generals to leave in command in New York. Yet he had not insisted that Fort William Henry be strengthened, despite warnings that it awaited the same fate as Oswego, nor had he ensured naval superiority on Lake George – crucial for preventing any siege of Fort William Henry.[133]

Nevertheless, Loudoun continued to press for adaptations to the tactical and operational organisation of the British Army in North America. As more regular soldiers were trained in irregular fighting methods, Loudoun and his adjutant-general, Colonel John Forbes, ensured that for the 1758 campaign every regular battalion in North America had a company of light infantry trained in such tactics.[134] When in December 1757 Lieutenant Colonel Thomas Gage proposed to 'raise, cloath & accoutre a Reg^t of light armed men', Loudoun quickly approved.[135] 'All the men furnished' for the new regiment, were, according to Forbes, 'to be active, young, strong and healthy'.[136] Gage's sceptical colleagues, among them Forbes, saw this move as little more than a blatant attempt to obtain a colonelcy. Forbes described the plan as 'a Most flagrant jobb' in an unsigned memorandum, in which he proposed, instead, training the entire British regular contingent in light infantry tactics and techniques.[137]

Loudoun, however, suspected that Gage's detractors were simply jealous because they too had mooted the idea of forming a regiment of light infantry, demonstrating that the plan had currency.[138] For Loudoun, Gage's plan was 'the only one that has been offered or occurred to me for ... making the Rangers a real fighting corps'.[139] These units were to be attired for the conditions they would face. Their long coatskirts were cut away, small caps replaced tall, cumbersome shakers, while hatchets and powder horns prepared them for action in difficult terrain.[140] Historian Stanley Pargellis sees the proposal to form the regiment as historically significant. Not only did it represent the creation of the first lightly armed fighting unit, it also marked the point at which Loudoun stopped experimenting with local solutions and accepted the incorporation of fighting methods thought relevant only in America into the regular order of battle of the British Army.[141]

Undoubtedly the genesis of the plan was the fruit of the synthesis of military knowledge taught in Europe with the experience of warfare in

America. As well as responding to the challenges posed by Native American tactics and the North American terrain, Gage's plan also sought to remedy some of the logistical difficulties wilderness warfare posed. For instance, '500 fierlocks' were ordered 'for the Light Armed Regt intended ... to be cut shorter and the stocks dressed to make them lighter'.[142] Loudoun gave Gage discretion over who he selected to officer his new regiment, but it quickly became apparent that Gage's choices did not match those that Loudoun expected, so he intervened with more focused suggestions. 'As he did not seem to intend to take Quenton Kennedy,' Loudoun recorded in his memorandum book, 'I [said] I thought it would be a discouragement to officers going a-Ranging if he were left out who had done more than all the rest in that way.' Moreover, he also encouraged Gage to select officers from the 42nd Highland Regiment, especially those who had acquitted themselves well, but who lacked the means to obtain promotion.[143]

While he was making these decisions, Loudoun must have been aware that his position was in jeopardy. The failure to even attempt a siege of Louisbourg and the loss of Fort William Henry could not be compensated by the so far untried reforms he had made to the army. In Europe his patron, the Duke of Cumberland, suffered a calamitous defeat at Hastenbeck in Germany in August 1757, and soon after he fell from grace. Pitt, having successfully deposed his political rivals, was now free to direct policy and strategy, and wanted rid of those he perceived to be under Cumberland's influence. Under the shadow of humiliations and military setbacks, Loudoun was recalled, departing North America as unceremoniously as he had first set foot on it.

Though he received word of his recall in March 1758, the impact of Loudoun's reforms were evident for the remainder of the war in North America, most immediately in the campaign to capture Fort DuQuesne. Loudoun and Forbes had in fact already devised the plan prior to Loudoun's recall. Forbes was to command and do 'whatever can be done in those parts to cutt off ... the Communication between Canada & Louisiana, by which one or the Country must fall'.[144] Faced with an 'immense uninhabited Wilderness overgrown everywhere with trees and underbrush, so that no where can anyone see twenty yards ...', Forbes implemented Loudoun's ideas.[145] He had 'long been in ... Opinion of equiping Numbers of our Men like the Savages', he wrote to his newly appointed second-in-command, Henry Bouquet, and was consequently 'resolved upon getting some of the best people in every Corps to go out a

Scouting in that stile'.[146] It was essential that 'in this Country, wee must comply and learn the Art of Warr', Forbes argued, 'from Ennemy Indians or any thing else who have seen the Country and Warr carried on inn itt.'[147] In so doing, an 'Experienced officer or soldier secure's himself directly behind some tree Stumpp or Stone, where he becomes his own Commanding Officer, Acting to the best of his judgement for his own defence and General Good of the whole'.[148]

Planning an autumn campaign to avoid the excessive temperatures of June and July, Forbes and Bouquet spent the summer months assembling an army composed of regular British soldiers, provincial units from Virginia and Pennsylvania and friendly Native American warriors.[149] Progress was frustratingly slow, but by September the army was ready to move. While the tactical training of the army had been informed by the experience of war in North America, Forbes was inspired by the arguments of European military thinkers in developing his campaign plan. 'As my offensive operations are clogged with many Difficultys, owing to the great distance & badness of the roads, through an almost impenetrable wood,' he explained, 'I am therefore lay'd under the Necessity of having a stockade Camp, with a Blockhouse & cover for our Provisions, at every forty Miles distance.'[150]

Based on a 'project that I took from *Turpin's Essay Sur la Guerre*', Forbes planned to 'advance but gradually,' and 'go more Surely by Lessening the Number, and immoderate long train of provisions Waggons &c,'.[151] This would offer his army 'constant Supply security', while also ensuring a 'sure retreat, leaving a road always practicable to penetrate into those back Countrys'.[152] The methodical nature of the plan, the intricate details and the focus on an advance with a broad frontage bore all the hallmarks of Turpin de Crissé's ideas.[153]

The operation proceeded slowly and methodically. An ill-advised reconnaissance-in-force sanctioned by Bouquet went badly awry when it found itself dangerously outnumbered,[154] but by the time Forbes got to Fort DuQuesne, a combination of factors had persuaded the French to withdraw. Concurrent operations against Forts Carillon – which the British called Ticonderoga – and Frontenac had achieved mixed success. Though Abercromby's frontal assault on strong defences at Ticonderoga had been a disaster,[155] a subsequent smaller operation against Frontenac, commanded by the experienced and competent colonial officer John Bradstreet, had been startlingly successful. 'The Garrison made no scruple of saying that their Troops to the Southward and Western Garrisons will suffer greatly if not intirely starve for want of the provisions and vessels we have destroy'd,' Bradstreet explained to Abercromby.[156] Facing a winter without either reinforcement or replenishment, and now also facing a well-supplied British army, the French commandant of Fort DuQuesne saw little point in trying to fight, and so destroyed the encampment and withdrew south to Louisiana.

Any thoughts the French had of recapturing Fort DuQuesne were permanently derailed when Fort Niagara was captured by a British expedition under Brigadier John Prideaux in July 1759. Niagara was, in the words of Charles Lee, one of the participants in the expedition, the 'absolute Empress of the Inland parts of North America', and its capture effectively forced the French frontier back to Oswegatchie, just 115 miles from Montreal.[157] The forts at Presque Isle, LeBoeuf and Machault were all abandoned, and trading posts as significant as Detroit and Michilimackinac were cut off from New France. The series of defeats undermined Indian confidence in the French, who would now have to fight the British unsupported.[158]

Loudoun was, within two years of his departure from America, proved right, both strategically and operationally. The successful defence of the Thirteen Colonies lay in controlling the waterways that connected the St Lawrence and Mississippi Rivers. Once the British had captured fortresses that controlled key positions on the Great Lakes and the Ohio rivers, the French were unable to go on the offensive against British North America. British strategy switched now to the offensive, aiming once and for all to dismantle the French North American empire. Tactically as well, the 1758 and 1759 expeditions all bore the hallmarks of the synthesis of regular and irregular warfare, of European and American fighting methods.

Forbes had established elite light infantry units, but employed them within a campaign plan derived from European experience. During the advance to Ticonderoga, Abercromby's second-in-command, George Howe, had sought to implement the lessons he had learned while observing Rogers, including marksmanship training for all troops. At the subsequent abortive assault on the defences of Ticonderoga, Abercromby had tried to use marksmen to pick off the French defenders, though if he had used his irregular forces to outflank his adversary, the result might have been less costly and more successful.[159] This had been evident when light infantry units had been used to enhance the firepower of the British defenders during an attempted French counterattack at Niagara. In combination with more traditional European techniques – according to Lee, when the regular infantry 'rush'd in with their Bayonets, the victory was quick & decisive' – the British infantry proved irresistible.[160]

Though he had been killed during the Ticonderoga operation, many of Howe's ideas and much of his thinking were carried forward at the battalion level and recorded by his aide-de-camp, Captain Alexander Monypenny. During the subsequent and ultimately successful advance on Ticonderoga in 1759, this time commanded by General Jeffrey Amherst, Monypenny noted that all troops 'were to fire two rounds at marks',[161] thus regularly improving their marksmanship skills. Moreover, Amherst had directed that light infantry companies be formed into larger battalions, providing a more flexible tactical fighting force.[162] Irregular troops had proved essential in all three operations, but so too had European discipline. This would be illustrated starkly in the campaigns that would capture Louisbourg, Quebec and Montreal.

In the wake of his recall to London, Loudoun was publicly derided, and his reputation remains in tatters: his 'management in the conduct of affairs is by no means admired', wrote James Wolfe with an air of understatement.[163] But the reality was much more complex. Loudoun had set the conditions for success in his reforms to the administration and composition of the British Army in North America.[164] Over the course of 20 months, he had laid the foundations for a military union of the colonies. Whether his successor chose to build on this or not, it was nevertheless an administrative achievement.[165] Loudoun's reforms had created a more stable basis for logistical support for military operations across the breadth of the frontier, and while certainly not perfect, his system ameliorated many of the issues the British had faced in 1755 and 1756. Perhaps most significantly, Loudoun created the conditions for the adaptation of the redcoats to the environment they found in North America, most evident in his advocacy for the incorporation of ranger units into the British Army, and then later his support for the recruitment and training of regular troops capable of performing those functions. In neither pursuit was he totally successful, but he was successful enough. Adaptation was crucial to the British Army's survival, not just in North America, but anywhere.

Loudoun was also an important part of a much wider military knowledge network, that spanned the continent of Europe and extended into North America. Historians have long debated how specific knowledge was transferred from one place to another, and there is evidence of a widespread network of diplomatic, scientific, mercantile, cultural and political knowledge that facilitated the exchange of ideas across vast distances and preserved that knowledge through time. The British military was no different, and, if anything, more diverse in the different experiences upon which its personnel could draw. The arms of the network included the expansion of the printing press and with it the democratisation of military literature, and the widespread correspondence networks that existed within and beyond the armed forces. But the role of individuals in the transmission of knowledge was key. Loudoun is the first of many individuals who helped facilitate the exchange of experience and knowledge, in his case from Scotland and Flanders to North America. But he did not merely imprint that knowledge on his new command. His interaction with individuals with experience of wilderness warfare meant that his military knowledge was remade, and likewise the existing military knowledge in North America – by a process of gradual adaptation and innovation – was also remade. This flexibility of thought, borne of the informal exchange of military experience and knowledge, was key to British success in North America after 1757.

CHAPTER 2

'I Was Come to Take Canada'

LOUISBOURG, QUEBEC AND MONTREAL, 1758–1760

'HITHERTO there has been the most profound ignorance of the nature of the war upon this continent,' James Wolfe declared upon his arrival in North America. 'I believe no nation ever paid so many bad soldiers at so high a rate.'[1] He had been promoted to brigadier and deployed to America on the advice of General Sir John Ligonier, whom Pitt, as the new prime minister, had asked to replace Cumberland as captain-general of the British Army. Pitt wanted competent officers to take charge of what he deemed to be the most important operations in North America: the capture of Louisbourg, Quebec and Montreal, and with it, the elimination of a French presence in Canada. Wolfe was too junior for overall command, so Ligonier recommended Jeffrey Amherst be promoted to major general and appointed to command the expedition. Despite sharing many of the same experiences, including the battles of Dettingen, Culloden and Lauffeldt during the War of Austrian Succession, Amherst and Wolfe had very different views on the planning and prosecution of war. Where Amherst saw the need for caution, good intelligence and detailed planning of operations to bring about battle in optimal circumstances, Wolfe's self-education and military experiences had inculcated the requirement for decision and action. This subtle but crucial difference in approach would define the campaign to conquer New France.

Both had recent experience of operations in Europe. In July 1757, Amherst was serving as Cumberland's aide-de-camp and was responsible for describing unfolding events at the Battle of Hastenbeck (26 July 1757) to the short-sighted duke. Cumberland's left, which had previously been thought secure, had been outflanked by a brigade of French infantry. Amherst relayed these events to Cumberland who duly sent reinforcements, but in so doing weakened his centre, which was then unable to withstand the main French assault.[2] Cumberland's army was forced to withdraw in humiliation, and the battle effectively marked the end of his field career. Reviewing the battle, Amherst concluded that Cumberland, who had reasonably sound intelligence, should have attacked the French earlier in the month, before they had received reinforcements. 'All defence, without offensive when the occasion offers', Amherst wrote in his notebook, 'must end in ruin to the defensive!'[3] For Amherst, Hastenbeck should not have been fought, and he believed a more effective outcome would have been achieved with better operational planning.

By contrast, Wolfe had spent much of his time in the early stages of the Seven Years' War focused on tactical development. After news broke of Braddock's catastrophic defeat on the Monongahela, and as diplomatic relations with the French began to crumble, Wolfe and the 20th Regiment were deployed to the south coast of England, with orders to prepare to resist any French invasion. Wolfe was justifiably worried that the British infantry were improperly trained for combat in both Europe and America. 'You know how readily the infantry under the present method of training are put into disorder even on the battlefield of Europe,' he wrote to his uncle, Walter Wolfe, soon after learning of Braddock's defeat. 'How much more then when they are led on to encounter a horde of savages ambush'd behind timber in an unknown trackless country! Some day we will learn the lesson: meanwhile we can only look on and marvel at the insensate stupidity which tollerates this laxity in our affairs.'[4] Wolfe therefore issued a series of training instructions for the units now under his command. The influence of Frederick the Great, who advocated strict discipline and an emphasis on firepower, can be detected in the essence of these orders,[5] because, as he wrote to the Duke of Richmond, 'natural courage seldome prevails against experience & military knowledge'.[6]

At the heart of Wolfe's tactical planning was the deadly combination of disciplined musketry and the shock action of the bayonet. He ordered that his unit adopt the 'alternate fire' system which would avoid much of the confusion he had witnessed earlier in his career.[7] Musket fire was 'to begin by platoons', Wolfe ordered, 'either from the wings or from the center, it is to proceed in a regular manner, till the enemy is defeated, or till the signal is given for attacking them with bayonets'. In the event that his regiment was attacked by an enemy column, his soldiers were to load 'two or three bullets in their pieces' if there was time, and only 'when the [enemy] column is within about twenty yards they must fire with a good aim, which will necessarily stop them a little'. Wolfe continued, 'it is highly probable, that, after firing a few rounds, they will be commanded to charge them with their bayonets, for which the officers and men should be prepared'. Wolfe also advocated a method of combining infantry and cavalry action, in which the infantry would 'march forward and pierce the enemy's battalion in four places', so that the 'cavalry behind us may get in amongst them and destroy them'. In this scenario, the infantry were to fire one musket volley and then 'immediately present their bayonets, and charge'.[8] A distillation of Wolfe's military experience to date, this would become a central aspect of his approach during his service in North America.

In 1757, Wolfe was appointed to be quartermaster general on a raiding expedition against the French Atlantic port of Rochefort, which vague intelligence reports suggested was poorly defended. Wolfe's friend, the Duke of Richmond, was hopeful of success,[9] but Wolfe was more sceptical, branding the expedition 'no Scene of Instruction'.[10] He was proved right when the expedition arrived at its target, the Isle d'Aix, only to find it much better defended then intelligence had suggested. The expedition commander, General Sir John Mordaunt, faced with contradictory reports, dithered over what action to take, only to have his impatient naval counterpart, Admiral Edward Hawke, call off the expedition.

Wolfe considered the expedition to have 'been conducted so ill that I am ashamed to have been of the party', though he appreciated the opportunity to 'pick up something useful from amongst the most fatal errors'. It was quite apparent to him that 'the season of the year and the nature of the enterprise called for the quickest and most vigorous execution,' as he wrote to his uncle, 'whereas our proceedings were quite otherwise'.[11] Wolfe's experience suggested the importance of taking the initiative, making swift decisions and acting with vigour and speed. Indeed, he had come to believe 'that in war something must be allowed to chance and fortune ... and that, in particular circumstances and times, the loss of a thousand men is rather an advantage to a nation than otherwise, seeing that gallant attempts raise its reputation and make it respectable ...'.[12] In short, Wolfe was willing to take extreme risks in moments of uncertainty.

It was with this attitude that Wolfe learned of his promotion and deployment to North America. He arrived in Halifax well ahead of Amherst. He was unimpressed by the army that he found, believing

Loudoun's training policies would inevitably lead it to defeat, 'unless they fall into some method more suited to the country and to the kind of enemy they have to deal with'.[13] Such a view, in part at least designed to allow Wolfe to claim maximum credit for any successes that might follow his arrival, deliberately overlooked the considerable efforts already under way to reform the British Army in North America. Far from adhering 'so literally and strictly to the one, two and three firings', as Wolfe claimed, Loudoun had laid the foundations for a more adaptive fighting force, reforms which Wolfe himself would seek to implement.[14]

Training was already under way, however, closely supervised by Brigadier Charles Lawrence, commanding at Halifax until Amherst's arrival. He sought to combine the best elements of European drill and discipline with the successful tactics developed as a result of the experience of warfare in North America. 'A Body of Light Troops are now training to oppose the Indians, Canadians & other painted Savages', Lawrence wrote in his general order of May 1758. These troops would 'entertain' the enemy 'in their own way & preserve the Women & Children of the Army, from their unnatural barbarity'. In so doing, Lawrence sanctioned different rules of engagement depending on the adversary. It was an approach that Amherst would later support, and Wolfe wholeheartedly endorsed.

Wolfe considered the Rangers in 'appearance ... little better than *canaille*'.[15] He was therefore happy to discover that Lawrence had incorporated them into a single light infantry corps under the command of Major George Scott, who, Lawrence wrote, 'must teach his Corps to attack, & to defend themselves judiciously, always endeavouring to get upon the enemy's flank'. 'They must be instructed to chuse good Posts & to lay themselves in Ambuscade to advantage to be alert, silent, vigilant and obedient'. At the same time, the light infantry must be prepared 'for their ready forming in a variety of Situations'. In particular, 'when any of our Troops are to attack the French Regular Forces, they are to march close up to them discharge their pieces, loaded with two Bullets, & then rush upon them, with their Bayonets fixed'.[16] As Loudoun had envisaged, light infantry units were expected to master the art of irregular warfare, but be capable of acting as regular infantry when the need arose.

Halifax afforded the British the opportunity to train their troops in all kinds of conditions, such as 'bush fighting after the Indian manner, making fascines [bundles of brushwood], raising redoubts, attacking, defending them, etc.'.[17] As a result, the troops became proficient in dealing with unexpected obstacles 'and delays occurring in a line of march from some trifling circumstances as fallen trees, muddy creeks, close thickets'.[18] As the first objective would entail an opposed amphibious assault, the troops 'frequently landed in the boats of the transports, and practised in the woods the different manuvres they were likely to act'.[19] Once ashore, troops were to fix bayonets and clear the beach immediately, ready for the following landing.[20] The landing techniques that evolved during this period of interservice training became standard practice in amphibious operations in succeeding years. By the time Wolfe and Amherst arrived in Halifax, then, the troops with which they were to attack Louisbourg had received a comparatively large amount of relevant and effective training. This was evident when the joint naval and military force made its assault on Louisbourg.

By the 1750s, Louisbourg, with its large natural harbour, was the centre of French North American trade and fishing. It was therefore suitably well-defended, with the town itself encompassed by 30-foot-high walls following a Vauban design. The garrison consisted of 3,000 regular soldiers and 236 heavy guns emplaced in the walls. It was possible for the British to circumvent the fortified port, but any military operation aimed at Quebec and Montreal would always remain vulnerable if the French remained in command of the entrance to the St Lawrence River.[21]

On 28 May, the British fleet, commanded by Admiral Edward Boscawen, and consisting of 23 ships of the line and 16 frigates, sloops and gunboats, sailed from Halifax. It escorted 127 transports carrying 13,142 men, including 15 battalions of infantry, gunners and carpenters necessary for the construction of the siege works. Amherst arrived, after a laborious 11-week crossing, just in time to take command. Scrapping an overcomplicated plan that had been devised by Lawrence, Amherst selected Gabarus Bay, to the west of Louisbourg and the site of the successful 1745 landings, as the single point of attack. Though better defended than other possible landing locations, Amherst judged that the shelter offered by the bay and proximity to the objective were worth the additional risk.[22]

Several days of inclement weather repeatedly delayed the landings, but before dawn on 8 June, Amherst was advised that it was safe enough for the troops to attempt to land. Amherst planned to surprise his adversary by launching a night attack. Dividing his force into three waves, Wolfe was given command of the initial attack, while Lawrence and Brigadier Edward Whitmore commanded the other waves, with orders to divert the enemy and exploit any landing made by Wolfe.[23] 'By dividing their force we may be sure to succeed somewhere', Amherst argued.[24] The intricacy

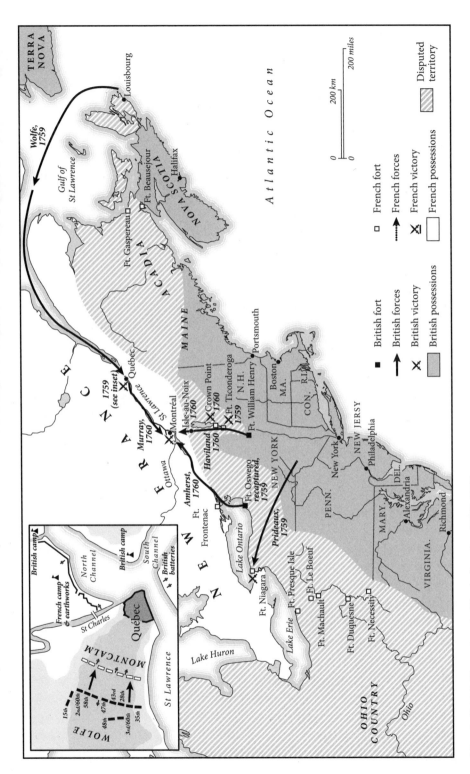

Map 2. British Campaigns in North America, 1758–1760.

of the plan speaks to the impressive levels of cooperation that Amherst and Boscawen had been able to achieve, but the key to success was undoubtedly the weeks of training specifically focused on an amphibious assault landing. Officers, soldiers and sailors alike all understood what was needed to achieve success.

Intricate though the plan was, it nearly came unstuck, thanks to unexpectedly rough seas, and the effective defence which the French had been able to construct. The French did not return fire until the boats were in the bay, and then 'threw in a cross fire of one 24-Pounder, four 6-Pounders, and the fire of the Infantry that had lined the whole bay'.[25] The impact was devastating. One shot hit a lieutenant of the Highland regiment 'and tore his body into shivers' before 'cutting off both the legs of the poor fellow that held the tiller of the boat'.[26] The fire was so severe that 'it was hardly possible for the Men to Continue in their Boats. Many of them were shot to pieces & several killed by their small Arms'.[27]

Wolfe had already given the order to retire, when a boat managed to get ashore on his right. Three more boats followed and this was the breakthrough Wolfe needed.[28] The intensive training the soldiers had received immediately paid off, as a scratch force was assembled consisting of 'Light Infantry, Highlanders and Grenadiers intermixed'. After scrambling up the rock face, the troops found themselves on the flank of the French defensive position.[29] With their powder wet, the men charged with their bayonets and cleared out the French trenches. 'The Enemy by this motion being taken in Flank soon began to retreat', and Wolfe 'pursued as fast as he could get the Troops landed'. Amherst ordered in Lawrence and Whitmore's waves, which began to arrive about half an hour later. By then, the French had abandoned their position, and were withdrawing to Louisbourg. 'Their retreat was through the Roughest and worst ground I ever saw,' Amherst noted in his journal, 'and the Pursuit ended with a Cannonading from the Town'.[30] Amherst came ashore at 6 a.m., and within two hours, the army as a whole was headed toward the fortress. The British suffered 46 dead and 61 wounded, with a further seven sailors killed and 33 wounded.

Once ashore, it took over a month to land all the required stores, tools, tents and artillery pieces in order to prosecute a siege. Poor weather contributed to the delays, more than a hundred boats were destroyed, and soldiers and sailors were crushed to death or drowned in the pounding surf.[31] In order to transport the heavy artillery and stores, a road had to be constructed across the marshy terrain between Gabarus Bay and the walls of Louisbourg. Throughout the operation, Amherst tightened his grip on Louisbourg slowly and methodically. On 12 June, Wolfe seized Lighthouse Point on the opposite side of the harbour, and installed a battery which on 25 June destroyed a French emplacement on an island in the entrance to the harbour. Thereafter, Amherst was free to concentrate solely on establishing batteries on high ground outside the walls of Louisbourg. The rocky terrain precluded the usual siege works, and batteries were constructed using fascines. In late June, the first battery opened fire on the walls and Wolfe seized Gallows Hill, only 300 yards from one of the seven bastions. There work commenced on building another battery, which was ready by the fifth week of the siege. Wolfe despaired at the 'exceedingly slow and injudicious' pace of the operation.[32] 'The many difficulties of landing every thing in allmost a continual Surf', Amherst explained to Pitt on 6 July, 'the making of Roads, draining and passing of Bogs, and putting ourselves under Cover, renders our Approach to the Place much longer than I could wish'.[33]

Further delays were imposed by the activities of the French defenders and their Native American allies, who launched a number of sorties designed to disrupt the British siege works. These efforts were largely mitigated by the increasingly superior quality and training of the British Light Infantry, who were, in the words of Amherst's younger brother and aide-de-camp, William, 'certainly of great use, & should always accompany an Army in this country . . . These troops drive them out of their shelter, harass them continually & treat them in their own way'.[34] The enemy irregulars, who numbered as many as 300, endeavoured to harass the construction of the batteries, but their efforts were neutralised by the erection of prefabricated blockhouses. These had been designed by George Scott – who now commanded the light infantry – in 1757 for Loudoun's original abortive operation against Louisbourg. Each blockhouse was two stories and could hold 100 men, four light guns and mortars, and could be assembled by 12 men in less than eight hours.[35] Sorties from the fort proved more problematic. A particularly large attack took place on 9 July, when 724 French troops surprised the British right flank, killing several men.[36]

Wolfe often withdrew his own light infantry forces behind sand dunes, encouraging the attackers to overextend their assault, and render themselves vulnerable. This, Wolfe claimed, he learned from his reading of classical military history. During a conversation at mess one evening, one of the junior captains remarked that Wolfe's tactics reminded him of irregular warfare described in Xenophon's *Anabasis Kyrou* (*The Expedition of Cyrus*). Following Cyrus's defeat at the Battle of Cunaxa, Xenophon helped orchestrate a retreat, but was harassed by the Kardouchoi. By appearing to withdraw precipitately, Xenophon drew the adversary into a trap and successfully turned the tables. Wolfe, it seems, was pleased his subordinates were so well read. 'I had it from Xenophon', he remarked, 'but our friends here are astonished at what I have done because they have read nothing'.[37] The anecdote reveals Wolfe's practical application of his deep study of history, but also illustrates that such reading was more wide-spread. More importantly, the conversation reveals that informal discussions among military personnel of varying ranks, which explicitly linked military history and theory and past experiences to contemporary circumstances, were commonplace in the eighteenth-century British Army.

By 26 July, with the town and fortress completely invested, all French naval support destroyed or evacuated, and external support neutralised, the bombardment was beginning to take its toll. 'Each cannon shot from English batteries shook and brought down immense sections of the ruinous walls', wrote one French officer.[38] Wolfe estimated that 'two days more' and the British 'should certainly have carried it'.[39] The French commandant, Augustin de Boschenry, chevalier de Drucour, asked for terms, but Amherst and Boscawen demanded unconditional surrender. Drucour had little option but to accept, and on the morning of 27 July, the Louisbourg garrison, numbering 5,637, surrendered their arms. 'Thus with much perseverance, loss and fatigue,' recalled one participant, 'we had taken the strongest garrison in North America, and opened the road to Canada'.[40] The French had suffered 400 dead and 1,300 wounded. In comparison, British losses were modest – 222 killed and 354 wounded. The French civilian population, almost 4,000 in total, would be deported to France.[41] All of this would take time, as would securing and rebuilding the fortress defences, refitting Boscawen's fleet and dismantling the siege works. Wolfe appeared oblivious to the obvious delays such arrangements imposed. 'I do not penetrate our General's intentions', he wrote in frustration on the day of the French capitulation. 'If he means to attack Quebec, he must not lose a moment'.[42]

* * *

Wolfe's frustration would continue. In early August, Boscawen concluded that it was impossible to launch an expedition to Quebec, not least because his fleet was badly in need of repair, and the chances of completing such a complex siege before the St Lawrence River froze was limited. Wolfe was ordered to sail to the Bay of Gaspé in the Gulf of St Lawrence and 'rob the fisherman of their nets, and to burn their huts'.[43] Dissatisfied with what he considered to be a trivial operation, upon its completion Wolfe returned to England.

The siege of Louisbourg revealed in Amherst and Wolfe two contrasting approaches to warfighting. Amherst planned methodically, ensuring that all factors and variables that might influence the course of a campaign were accounted for. The price he paid for this approach was the speed with which he conducted his campaigns.

This was a source of significant frustration to Wolfe, whose eagerness for action and decision often translated into taking unwarranted risks. More often than not, this produced a positive outcome, and Wolfe was keen to seize the resulting plaudits. He, rather than Amherst, acquired what his biographer, Stephen Brumwell, has described as the status of the 'first truly *transatlantic* hero',[44] but was this accolade entirely justified? His aide-de-camp, Lieutenant Thomas Bell, was particularly enamoured. During the siege, Wolfe's 'small corps came and took post within 200 yards of the town, while the engineers were still bouggering' about, Bell wrote zealously. 'He open'd the trenches, called in the army, and pushed them within forty yards of the glacis and in short took the place without the assistance of any one regular bred fumbler. He has been general, soldier, and engineer.'[45] This is obviously something of an exaggeration, but similar accounts were published and republished in the British press, and thereby clouded the reality of the situation.

Wolfe, of course, had considerable credit to bear for the success of both the landing and the siege. He also inspired the soldiers under his immediate command and, as his fame spread, the rest of the army, not least for the care and consideration he showed them. Though he was a proponent of training programmes tailored to the circumstances in which the army was to fight, it is absurd to argue that in the three weeks between his arrival in Halifax and the deployment of the expedition, he alone shaped the capabilities of the army that was to land and besiege Louisbourg. Such an assertion does a disservice to the considerable efforts already under way to reform the Army, both in the short and long term. Loudoun had done much to reorient the culture of the Army, introducing practices that drew on European and American experiences. Though he left the role of commander-in-chief before he completed this task, he nevertheless instituted reforms that would set the conditions for success, including creating a professional environment where learning and particularly training were an acceptable and necessary aspect of army life. Much of the training conducted in Halifax in 1758 had been instituted there by Loudoun during the abortive 1757 operation.

Moreover, British officers with experience of warfighting in America were willing to integrate the techniques of 'wilderness warfare' into their practices. In some cases, this was done by regimental staff and distributed through general and daily orders to the individual companies.[46] In other cases, innovations were developed at the unit level and sometimes gradually fed up the chain of command. Frequently, such 'ground-up' innovations were not adopted, but the better and more practical ones were. George Howe, for example, had made alterations to the uniforms of his regiment after training with Rogers' Rangers.[47] George Scott, meanwhile, had successfully pitched his invention of prefabricated blockhouses to Loudoun, and had seen them used with some measure of success by Amherst during the siege of Louisbourg.[48] While Wolfe himself was an advocate of simpler drill and firing methods, such as the alternate-fire system, this had been adopted by Charles Lawrence, along with the more central use of the bayonet, before either Wolfe or Amherst arrived in the theatre.[49] Indeed, Amherst would adopt some aspects of Lawrence's general order word for word in his own orders issued at Louisbourg.[50]

The arrival of Amherst and Wolfe in America, then, brought to the fore two very different approaches to warfighting, which characterised tensions that existed within the British Army of the eighteenth century over the strategic, rather than tactical, use of military power. Amherst's methodical style contrasted sharply with the decisive, high-risk approach taken by Wolfe. Reflecting the loneliness of command, Amherst had to consider the wider picture of logistics, sustainment and resilience. There would have been no point in taking Louisbourg if he had lost the best part of his army in doing so. He would have witnessed such considerations when acting as Cumberland's assistant and aide during the years of peace, as well as in the Hastenbeck campaign. Wolfe, on the other hand, was a highly experienced regimental commander, where he trained his men for action and witnessed in them the strong desire for battle. His one campaign as a staff officer — the abortive expedition to Belle Isle — had failed because of indecision. This line of thought clearly influenced his assessment of the campaign as a whole in 1758. 'We had Canada in our hands last year', he wrote to his uncle. 'If the siege of Louisbourg had been pushed with vigour, Quebec would have fallen'.[51]

In December, having been in England for just over a month, Wolfe was summoned to Downing Street to learn of his next deployment. He had been hoping for a role in Germany, but 'it is my fortune to be cursed with American service,' he wrote to his friend Captain Henry Parr, 'yours to serve in an army commanded by a great and able Prince, where I would have been if my choice and inclination had been consulted'.[52] Long an admirer of Frederick the Great, Wolfe would have relished the opportunity to serve under the Duke of Brunswick, one of the Prussian King's closest confidantes and Cumberland's successor as commander of the British contingent in Europe. Here were generals who acted in the same way Wolfe wanted to, striking decisive blows and achieving brilliant victories. Ligonier, however, had told him there was no vacancy for an officer of his rank, and so Wolfe was expecting to be sent back to America, again to serve under Amherst in an operation against Quebec. Instead, he learned, to his palpable shock, that he was to command the Quebec expedition, with the temporary rank of major general. 'I am to act a greater part in this business that I wished or desired', Wolfe wrote with a degree of melancholy to his uncle.[53] A great commander of men in battle, Wolfe was now to be tested in the organisation of a campaign.

In North America, meanwhile, Amherst had received news in late October 1758 that Pitt had appointed him commander-in-chief, replacing the tired and ineffective Abercromby. The army Amherst inherited consisted of 22 battalions of infantry, seven independent companies, 13 companies of rangers, 25 of artillerymen and fewer than 20 engineers; totalling 21,000 officers and men. This was over 4,000 troops short of its full complement.[54] Amherst received Pitt's instructions for the 1759 campaign in March: while Wolfe was to command the expedition to Quebec, Amherst was to attack Canada by way of Lakes George and Champlain, capturing the key French fortresses of Ticonderoga and Crown Point as he did so. 'By baffling the Enemy in different quarters,' he wrote to Whitmore, 'I hope to reap the benefit of their surprise and confusion'.[55] It was clear that Wolfe's expedition had priority, and Amherst conceived a strategy which would coordinate his operations on Lakes George and Champlain with an operation against Niagara led by Brigadier John Prideaux. In so doing, Amherst hoped that French strength would be divided, and as a result 'they shall weaken themselves every where, which I hope will ensure Success to Us'.[56]

Amherst was confident of victory, despite the challenges he faced in preparing for the campaign. Of his 21,000-strong army, a total of 9,000 – among them the best troops in the army – would head to Louisbourg to link up with Wolfe. Amherst therefore had to bolster his substantially reduced force with provincial soldiers. Like Loudoun and Forbes before him, he faced the tedious problem of negotiating with colonial governors and assemblies over adequate recruitment quotas. Eventually, in addition to his 3,000 regulars, Amherst cobbled together nearly 14,000 troops, of varying quality and experience, from the north and mid-Atlantic colonies.

5,000 were immediately detached with Prideaux to Niagara and another 3,000 were needed for garrison duty, leaving just 8,000 men for the Ticonderoga operation.[57]

Having witnessed their value during the Louisbourg campaign, and confirmed the widespread view held across the army that the Rangers and Light Infantry were indispensable for operations in North America, Amherst authorised Robert Rogers to recruit his units to full strength, which was managed by the beginning of May. As in previous years, these units excelled at targeted intelligence collection. On 3 March, Rogers led 356 men, including 169 light infantry from the Royal Americans to scout Fort Carillon at Ticonderoga.[58] An engineer attached to the party sketched the fort and reconnoitred the new defences built to replace the ones Abercromby had unsuccessfully attacked the previous July.[59] This proved useful for Amherst as he planned his expedition.

During the operation itself, however, Amherst was disappointed by the performance of his Rangers. 'They are unknowing for every part of the Service that is to be Conceived', he wrote in frustration to Gage. 'At their rate of going on they must always be beat; I have tryed to rub them up, and Shew them the way to March in the Woods, for those I have had with me know nothing of the matter'.[60] Later still, he described them as 'the most Careless, Negligent, Ignorant Corps I ever Saw . . .'.[61] Like his predecessors, then, Amherst found the Rangers unreliable and useful only in specific circumstances. This confirmed his view that a light infantry arm composed of regular British soldiers was essential for operational and strategic success in North America.

To achieve this, Amherst sought to incorporate light infantry more fully into the regular order of battle of the British Army. During the winter, he ordered the army to begin training using drill methods imported from Frederick the Great's army, which had enabled the Prussians to fight successful battles when themselves outnumbered, and which incorporated light infantry units into every battalion of the army.[62] In February 1759, 10 per cent of each regular battalion were to be formed into a corps of light infantry.[63] They were to be 'clothed and accoutred as light as possible', were to be armed with carbines rather than muskets, and were provided with 'what ammunition they want, so that I don't doubt but they will be excellent marksmen'.[64] Trained to move swiftly through the wilderness, using the terrain to their advantage, these light infantry units were also primed with the drill and tactics of the regular infantry, while regular soldiers received rudimentary instruction in light infantry drill.[65] The process started by Loudoun, and championed by Forbes, now reached fruition under Amherst.

Having planned to be under way by the beginning of June, it was not until the 21st that Amherst got to Lake George, and by then he had fewer than 6,500 troops. The balance of his army was guarding the supply route through to Albany. It took another month to get the force prepared for its expedition down the Lake to Ticonderoga, and early in the morning of 21 July, the army embarked in hundreds of the flat-bottomed, double-ended boats known as batteaux. The following day, the force arrived at a sawmill, three miles from Ticonderoga, and Amherst established a magazine there prior to commencing an attack on the fortress itself. As he planned his siege, he observed the French giving up their defences and hurriedly with-drawing inside the fortress. Over the next four days, Amherst prepared a systematic siege, and by the evening of the 26th a battery of six 24-pounders was 'preparing to open . . . at daybreak'.

At this point, 'a Deserter came in & said the Garrison was to get off and to blow up the Fort'. Amherst wrote to 'Major Rogers immediately to attack them, and soon we saw the Fort on fire and an Explosion but as the Deserter said a Match was laid to blow the whole up I would not order any men into it'. By midnight, some volunteers had concluded there was no more danger, so Amherst 'sent hands and Camp kettles to try all we could to extinguish the fire', though it took them another five days to quench the flames.[66] Having received intelligence that Crown Point had also been abandoned, Amherst advanced on 4 August to find the place 'in part blown up'.[67] He was aston-ished by the rapidity of his advance and by the willingness of the French to withdraw after posing virtually no resistance. This, however, was soon to end.

The local French commander, Brigadier General François-Charles de Bourlamaque, had retreated north to the Isle-au-Noix, at the foot of Lake Champlain. The island had been turned into a formidable fortress, surrounded by flooded and swampy terrain. Bourlamaque had 3,500 men with him, a mixture of regulars, colonial marines, Canadian militia and Native Americans. Moreover, four French warships carried a total of 32 cannon. Amherst could not get close to the fortress without his own warship, and the one which he had ordered be built following the capture of Ticonderoga would be insufficient for the job. A radeau (flat-bottomed rigged vessels designed for carrying guns), mounting six 24-pounders, would be needed to outrange the French warships.[68]

Amherst, however, remained concerned that the precipitate French withdrawal to Isle-au-Noix was actually nothing more than bait to make him overextend his position. He was aware of the capture of Niagara, and had detached Gage to take command following Prideaux's death during the siege. But he had yet to hear anything definitive from Quebec, and was only willing to move when he was certain all the pieces were in place. 'If we all do our Parts,' he wrote to Gage, 'the French must fall.'[69] In dispatching Gage to Niagara, Amherst informed him that 'no time must be lost . . . in proceeding to La Galette with all Expedition possible . . .'.[70] La Galette was a fortress at the confluence of the Oswegatchie and St Lawrence Rivers, and Amherst believed that a strong movement against it would force the French, who were now perilously weak on the upper St Lawrence, to withdraw. With Amherst pressuring from the south, Gage from the west, and Wolfe from the east, the pieces would soon be in place to encircle the French in Canada.

Unfortunately, the pieces did not start falling into place as Amherst had expected them to. When he arrived at Niagara, Gage found the supply situation was perilously close to collapse, while he also needed to divert men to complete building works on the new fort at Oswego. As a result, he believed he would be unable to move against La Galette. 'I can't but say that it is with some concern', Amherst wrote in a rare expression of frustration, 'that . . . I find you have determined not to take post at La Galette . . . .'[71] Amherst was convinced the French would be unable to send reinforcements if Gage attacked. For his part, Gage claimed not to have understood Amherst's strategy. 'If your plan of operations was not to concern yourself with Forts, but push on all sides for the Whole Country, I was certainly in a condition to make a Vigorous Effort on this Side toward it,' he wrote defensively to Amherst; but 'if your plan is to secure what you have gained by building a respectable Fort here, without posts of communication with the Inhabited Country, this I hope to be able to Effect'. Gage argued, though, that he could 'execute either but if I attempt both, I shall do Neither'.[72] Amherst now realised that he would be unable to surround Canada on all sides in 1759.

Nor did events progress well for Amherst. It took six weeks to build the gunboats he needed, while an attempt to burn the French sloop at Isle-au-Noix in mid-September failed.[73] On 9 October, the silence from Quebec was finally broken, but the news appeared dire. At the time the messengers left Quebec, 7 September, Wolfe appeared convinced that he would be unable to take the place. If this was true, Wolfe must now have either been defeated or abandoned the siege.[74] Worried, then, that he would soon face a huge French reinforcement from Quebec, Amherst made arrangements to strike against the French gunboats, while he would, 'with what Troops can be Spared, accompany them to See what may be further attempted'.[75]

In the event, Amherst had to settle for naval control of the lake and leaving Isle-au-Noix in French hands until another attack could be made the following year. Though the British moved quickly, bad weather set in and Amherst's 4,300-strong army was forced to seek shelter ashore. After pinning the two French gunboats in a bay overnight on 12 October, in the morning the British discovered that their crews had scuttled them.[76] The storm continued for several more days, rendering further operations impossible. Then, on 18 October, Amherst received news from Gage and then Lieutenant Governor de Lancey that Quebec had in fact fallen on 13 September.[77]

While British naval control had been confirmed on Lake Champlain, news that Quebec was in British hands, but that the French army had managed to escape, albeit with heavy losses, convinced Amherst to give up any pretensions of continuing onward to Isle-au-Noix. Concerned that the French were now free to attack him, Amherst was ultimately 'very glad to give it over' after news arrived of Wolfe's decisive victory, 'which is an infinitely more important Event'.[78] Amherst was disappointed with the outcome of his arm of the operation, though his contemporaries saw the wider strategic significance of his decisions. 'It is extremely probable', wrote Thomas Hutchinson of Massachusetts, 'that, if a great part of the French forces had not been withdrawn from Quebec to attend the motions of General Amherst, the attempt made by General Wolfe must have failed.'[79]

* * *

Wolfe's expedition to Quebec had begun successfully enough. The fleet, commanded by Vice-Admiral Charles Saunders and composed of 22 ships of the line and frigates and 119 transport and supply vessels had departed Louisbourg on 6 June. The transports carried 8,535 troops, including 'six new-raised companies of North American Rangers—not complete, and', Wolfe commented, 'the worst soldiers in the universe'.[80] This was fewer than Wolfe expected, even by his pessimistic estimation. Insufficient in quantity though they were, Wolfe was confident that his troops would not fail for want of ability, despite his low opinion of the rangers. Declaring them to be his 'American Army', Wolfe believed, like Amherst, these troops to be capable of close combat and manoeuvring in challenging terrain, as well as the tactics of conventional European warfare should the opportunity present itself. Indeed, his principal aim in the operation was to draw the French defenders into an open battle. 'I could not flatter myself that I should be able to reduce the place', he subsequently wrote, but 'sought . . . an occasion to attack their army, knowing well, that with these troops I was able to fight, and hoping that a victory might disperse them'.[81]

An advance squadron had mapped much of the treacherous river, and after three weeks of event-free sailing, the first part of the fleet arrived on the southern edge of Île d'Orléans, just to the east of Quebec. There, the advanced troops of Wolfe's army made an unopposed landing. Wolfe was now able to get his first view of his objective. It presented a formidable challenge. Quebec, though in Wolfe's view 'poorly fortified', was perched on a high clifftop, with dwellings running down to the shoreline beneath the fortress walls.[82] The garrison had swollen to just under 14,000 men, some of relatively little experience, others having served throughout the war. To the west, the cliffs, topped with rolling terrain known as the Plains of Abraham, continued to be apparently insurmountable for several miles toward the village of St Michel. Quebec was bounded on its north-eastern edge by the St Charles River, which flowed into the St Lawrence, but the terrain east of here permitted an amphibious landing. Understandably, then, the French had spent a great deal of time entrenching this shoreline, running past the small dwelling of Beauport toward the Montmorency River. On the southern shore of the St Lawrence, relatively little had been done to secure or defend the Lévis heights, which would, if seized by the British, allow them to bombard Quebec with impunity.[83]

Wolfe faced several difficulties which governed all his decisions. The first was the problem posed by 'the nature of the river', with its fierce ebb-tide and prevailing winds conspiring to render it impossible for the British to get past the gun emplacements of Quebec.[84] This prevented Saunders getting enough warships and, crucially, flat-bottomed landing craft west of the city. Until this challenge was overcome, Wolfe would be limited to operating east of the city. The next difficulty, once a suitable landing zone was identified and sufficient naval support amassed to enable a landing, was to determine how to get his men ashore in sufficient numbers swiftly enough to concentrate a fighting force capable of defeating the French, and before his adversary could react and push the British back into the river. These difficulties help explain the delays and seeming indecision that blighted Wolfe as he attempted to capture Quebec.

Expecting Amherst to threaten Montreal, Wolfe predicted that Montcalm would divide his force, 'but, as the loss of the capital implies the loss of the colony, their chief attention will naturally be there'. Wolfe therefore proposed to cut the line of communications and supply between Quebec and Montreal, by occupying the high ground to the west of the city, 'with our right to the River St. Lawrence, and our left to the river St. Charles'. To do this, Wolfe would occupy the Lévis heights on the south shore of the St. Lawrence to threaten the city, and land his force on the Beauport shore, cross the St. Charles and thus surround the city. 'I reckon we shall have a smart action at the passage of the river St. Charles,' Wolfe predicted, 'unless we can steal a detachment up the river St. Lawrence, and land them three, four, five miles, or more, up the river . . . and get time to entrench so strongly that they won't care to attack.'[85] This plan was confirmed after Wolfe 'reconnoitred the enemy's situation' on 27 June and 'determined to land at Levy and below the Falls of Montmorency'.[86]

Wolfe had organised his army into three brigades, under the command of Brigadiers Robert Monckton, George Townshend and James Murray.[87] He sent Monckton to occupy Point Lévis during the night of 29 June. The position was captured with little resistance, but Wolfe was unimpressed by Monckton's handling of the operation, after some of his troops got pinned down on the beach.[88] Now in possession of Lévis, and with the construction of artillery batteries under way, Wolfe turned his attention to the north shore, and early on 9 July landed 10 battalions east of Montmorency Falls, completely surprising the French. Still, the river itself – in particular its steep embankments – offered a considerable obstacle. Wolfe had to be content for the time being with limited night-time raids across the river, and over the next few weeks, a vicious *petite guerre* broke out in the woods on either side of the river. On 12 July, the batteries at Point Lévis commenced their bombardment of Quebec, delivering a devastating fire that set the town aflame in several locations. A fortnight later, Wolfe ordered his ranger units 'to burn and lay waste the country for the future'.[89] In what amounted to an increasingly brutal campaign of terror, Wolfe sought to drive a wedge between the French military garrison and the civilian population of both the town and surrounding countryside, justifying his actions as 'deterring and dreadful vengeance'.[90]

Exploring all possible options, Wolfe reconnoitred the shoreline west of Quebec, accompanied by the ranger Major Joseph Goreham and the naval cartographer Captain-Lieutenant Samuel Holland. As the party marched along the southern shoreline, Wolfe observed a small group of Native Americans 'playing in their canoes and then bathing in the river'. This, Holland noted, was 'nearly opposite to the Cove of Foulon'. Wolfe then ordered Goreham to 'be particularly attentive to the movements on the opposite side and discover the number of people that came to the water edge, the time of their coming down, the length of their stay etc.'. The following day, Goreham informed Holland that the inhabitants 'came down to the beach merely for the purpose of washing, beating their clothes, linen etc. Their stay was but short as they soon disappeared in the bush and were afterwards seen at the top of the hill spreading and drying their clothes'.

According to Holland, 'after much serious deliberation in his own mind', Wolfe 'exclaimed' in French: 'There, my dear Holland, will be my Last Resort, but only after my other projects are tried, and have failed.' As a result of these observations, Wolfe divined that there must be a pathway through what otherwise looked like a steep cliff and impenetrable wood-land. It was also apparent that the French were either unaware of the pathway or did not consider it a risk, for they were 'not in any number or in any shape on their guard'.[91] Any landing here was still imbued with considerable risk, however, based as it was on intuition and incomplete intelligence. Wolfe would also need the navy to force its way past Quebec for a landing at the 'cove of Foulon' to be an option. Hence, he would try more obvious options first.

At the end of July, plans were finalised for an attack on the Beauport shore. According to one eyewitness, 'the Beach was commanded by a very high Steep Bank, on the Top of which was a Strong Intrenchment, with Traverses & Redouts.'[92] Aiming to establish a foothold on the west bank of the Montmorency, Wolfe proposed to focus an attack on the redoubt closest to the river, which he believed was positioned just outside the range of the other beach defences. The grenadiers would lead the attack, supported by 200 Royal Americans. Townshend would follow up the initial assault from the east bank of the Montmorency, fording the river at low tide. Diversionary assaults would be led by Rear Admiral Holmes against St Michel, and Colonel William Howe against a ford further up the Montmorency River. Naval support would come in the form of gunships providing fire support as close in shore as possible, which, it was estimated, would suppress the French batteries on the shoreline. The evening before the attack, however, a deserter leaked details of the attack to the French. Wolfe nevertheless decided to proceed.[93]

Between 4 p.m. and 6 p.m. on 31 July, 'the first line of boats was landed, and the grenadiers . . . rushed on with the greatest impetuosity for the bank,' recorded one eyewitness, 'where they received from the enemy such an incessant fire of musquetry, as must be far easier to conceive than to describe.'[94] Unfortunately for Wolfe, the river was far shallower along this shoreline than his naval colleagues had estimated, and the gunships were kept out of range of the French batteries. Worse, Wolfe himself had misread the terrain, and although the defenders withdrew from the redoubt on the shoreline, it remained within range of the other defences. 'They kept up such a constant fire from the Breast work above', recorded Townshend in his journal, 'that it was impossible for men to stand under it.'[95]

Wolfe had no option but to call off the attack, having sustained 440 casualties, including 47 dead, compared to about 60 killed and wounded among the defenders.[96] In the wake of the failure at Beauport, Wolfe sent Murray 20 miles west of Quebec in an effort to divert French strength and interrupt their supply line to Quebec. Murray got bogged down with several attempted landings, and it was only on 25 August that he and his sizeable detachment of nearly one thousand troops returned to Île d'Orléans. Almost the whole month of August had been lost to an operation designed merely to divert French attention. 'Murray, by his long stay above and by detaining all our boats', Wolfe wrote in frustration to Monckton, 'is actually master of the operations, or rather puts an entire stop to them.'[97]

The defeat and delays further compromised what was already a deteriorating relationship between Wolfe and his brigadiers. Wolfe was already irritated with Monckton's lackadaisical performance during the operation to capture Point Lévis and clearly perceived Murray to be sluggish and indecisive, while Townshend publicly doubted Wolfe's competence. Though 'the advantage of the ground, not their number, fought against us' at Beauport, Wolfe's confidence was shaken.[98] The setback also bolstered faltering French morale. News began to leak, both into Quebec and New York, that Wolfe 'was not sanguine about taking Quebec'.[99] French confidence was given a further boost at the end of August when intercepted dispatches from Amherst indicated the latter would be unable to support Wolfe.[100] Nevertheless in preparation for a decisive engagement, Wolfe continued to implement a programme of rigorous training among the troops that remained at Quebec. On 7 August, for instance, 'large detachments' were 'sent to scour the woods' in order 'to use the troops to the country, to oblige the enemy to keep at a fit distance and to prepare the troops for a decisive action'.[101]

As the campaigning season advanced, and winter loomed, Wolfe was willing to resort to almost any measure to bring about a general action. Throughout the month of August Wolfe intensified his campaign of terror against the civilian population. He issued proclamations in the villages surrounding Quebec, inviting the local inhabitants to acquiesce to British control, refrain from encouraging the *petite guerre* and abandon support for the French, or face retribution. It was clear from the outset that this proclamation would achieve little, and even before its expiry on 10 August, Wolfe ordered detached units to begin burning settlements, storehouses and crops.[102] Though these operations were ostensibly punitive, Wolfe clearly hoped to force Montcalm to seek 'to try the event of a battle to prevent the ravage' from continuing.[103] In this ambition, Wolfe was again to be disappointed.

Having apparently exhausted all options, and with naval strength on the St. Lawrence west of Quebec still precarious, on 27 August Wolfe wrote a memorandum to his brigadiers, outlining three possible options, all focused on the Montmorency River, the Beauport Shore and the St. Charles river,[104] and for which Wolfe had been rigorously training his forces.[105] That very night, however, as the wind shifted to an easterly, Saunders managed to squeeze five of his vessels past Quebec's defences, this being 'their fourth attempt they had made to gain their passage'.[106] Four nights later, another three ships got past. The strategic situation shifted, for there was now a 'tolerable fleet above' Quebec.[107] Monckton, Townshend and Murray, in consultation with Saunders, rejected Wolfe's suggested plan of operations and instead advocated a move upriver, where the army might land unopposed and thus threaten Montcalm's supply lines.[108] Weakened by a severe and debilitating fever, Wolfe conceded, and a plan was duly formed to convey '4 or 5000 men (which is nearly the whole strength of the army) . . . to draw the enemy from their present situation, and bring them to an action'.[109] In reality, Wolfe was far from confident of success. 'My antagonist has wisely shut himself up in inaccessible entrenchments, so that I can't get at him without spilling a torrent of blood', he wrote despondently in what would be his final letter to his mother, 'and that perhaps to little purpose.'[110]

Recovering from his illness, Wolfe conducted a personal reconnaissance of the north shore of the St. Lawrence west of Quebec. He initially planned on sailing as far upstream as Pointe-aux-Trembles, 18 miles from Quebec, but cancelled that plan when he rediscovered the narrow lane at the Anse au Foulon, which ran from the shore up the cliff to the Plains of Abraham, and which he had observed months earlier with Goreham and Holland. On closer inspection, the lane was too difficult an obstacle, 'but about 200 yards to the right', according to engineer Patrick Mackellar, 'there appeared to be a slope in the bank which was thought might answer the purpose'.[111]

It was here that Wolfe proposed to make his initial assault. He 'thought that a Sudden brisk Attack, a little before daybreak, would bring his Army on the plain, within two miles of the Town'. In contrast to his earlier indecision, Wolfe sought no advice or guidance from his brigadiers, and set the ambitious plan in motion. The troops would embark by 10 p.m. on 12 September, and sail beyond the proposed landing area 'a convenient distance for the boats and armed vessels to fall down to the *Foulon*', Wolfe explained. They would aim to land at 4 a.m., but 'the impetuosity of the Tide; the darkness of the Night; and the great chance of exactly hitting the very Spot intended, without discovery or alarm; made the whole extremely difficult'.[112] Howe was given command of the initial landing, numbering 400 light infantry, and a further 1,300 regulars.

They sailed at 10 p.m., the tide turned at midnight, and the transports floated back down the river. The initial landing commenced at 4.07 a.m.[113] The operation was a complete surprise. Within minutes, Howe had scrambled up the cliff, which Knox described 'as one of the steepest precipices that can be conceived, being almost a perpendicular'. Outflanking the French defenders, the Anse au Foulon was soon open for Wolfe's regulars to come ashore and ascend to the Plains of Abraham. Wolfe, Monckton and Murray came ashore in the first wave, and witnessed the redcoats 'formed with much regularity'.[114] Within four hours, the troops of the second wave had been landed, and Wolfe had marched east toward Quebec. Observing his adversary decamp from Quebec, he ordered his army of 4,500 troops to form a line of battle, two rather than three ranks deep, in contravention of Cumberland's doctrinal guidance. Monckton commanded the right of the line, with Murray in the centre and Townshend on the left. The light infantry and Royal Americans covered the flanks. The total frontage was extensive.

For John Johnson, Quartermaster Sergeant of the 58th Regiment of Foot, Wolfe's deployment was in response to the terrain. 'Our line of Battle would admit of us to be drawn two deep only, from the smallness of our number,' he wrote in his journal of the campaign, 'as well as the quantity of ground we had to cover to secure our flanks'. Whether a response to the challenges posed by terrain or an innovative idea forged by Wolfe to capitalise on the superior marksmanship and musketry skills of the British infantry, the deployment would prove overwhelmingly successful. 'Although our fire was very light,' Johnson continued, 'yet being well directed, and as well sustained on their heavy lines, it had the greater effect upon them, and consequently the greater Loss.'[115] This was the so-called and quintessential 'thin red line'.[116]

Deceived by a well-executed operation on the Beauport shore, in which Saunders had sent all available boats close to the beaches, Montcalm did not learn about Wolfe's landing until 6 a.m.; it was another three hours before the French commander at Trois Rivières was informed. Realising that Quebec would not be able to survive a sustained siege, Montcalm elected to strike back sooner rather than later, and he marched his force as quickly as possible to meet Wolfe on the Plains of Abraham outside Quebec. Gradually, the French forces began to filter onto the battlefield.

By 10 a.m., Montcalm had assembled his army, also numbering about 4,500, and was ready to launch a counterattack. They 'began to advance briskly in three columns with loud shouts and recovered arms, two of them inclining to the left of our army, and the third towards our right, firing obliquely at the two extremities of our line, from the distance of one hundred and thirty yards', recalled Knox.[117] On the British side, 'Wolfe had given positive Orders, not to fire a Shot until the Enemy should be within Forty Yards of the point of our Bayonets,' noted one eyewitness.[118] The impact of the French fire was limited, but that of the British was devastating. When Montcalm's men came 'within 20 or 30 yards of closing', the British 'gave a general' discharge, and 'the enemy's whole line turned their back from right to left in the same instant'.[119]

A general advance was ordered, with bayonets fixed, while the Highlanders drew their broadswords. This, it turned out, was the most dangerous moment of the battle, as Canadian militia were now able to use the cover on the right and left of the field to take aim at the advancing British soldiers. The Highlanders, in particular, suffered heavy casualties during this part of the battle, and Wolfe himself received several wounds, before being shot twice in the chest. Carried to the rear of the battle-lines, he lived long enough to hear one of his attendants exclaim 'They run, see how they run ... The enemy ... they give way everywhere'.[120]

Supposedly with his dying breath, Wolfe gave the order to close off any avenue of retreat along the St Charles River, but in the chaos of the battle, this was never carried out. Command had devolved on Townshend, after Monckton too was severely wounded. He scrabbled to reconstitute the British line, so that when French reinforcements from Trois Rivières arrived in the early afternoon, they elected not to attack the British. Montcalm was himself mortally wounded in the French retreat, but the remnants of his army were able to escape. Quebec itself surrendered on 18 September, after the British had quickly erected siege lines on the Plains, and Saunders had brought up seven line-of-battle ships to threaten to bombard the lower town.

As with many great military victories, the perception of the event endures longer than the reality. Quebec is seen as the classic decisive victory, but though an undoubted tactical success, it did not achieve the same strategic impact. By escaping, the French army in Canada was able to survive to fight another day. More generally, the overwhelming nature of the tactical victory imprinted on the minds of the surviving participants the importance of pursuing a decisive battlefield engagement. Wolfe was undoubtedly a proponent of such an approach, rigorously training his men so that when they encountered the French in a traditional battlefield setting, their superior discipline would guarantee success. But it is also worth noting that Quebec offered limited options. Wolfe's critics have suggested that he should have acted earlier to interrupt the supply lines between Montreal and Quebec, and, in such circumstances, Montcalm would have been forced, eventually to surrender. In reality, Quebec was too well supplied and Wolfe was well aware that Montcalm would be able to withstand an investment at least until the onset of winter compelled Wolfe to withdraw.

This argument also overlooks the fact that not until late August was Saunders able to pass sufficient naval forces past Quebec. Until he was able to do this, Wolfe was effectively unable to operate in any strength west of the city. Circumstances therefore forced him to pursue options along the heavily defended Beauport shore. When Saunders was able to push sufficient numbers of ships and transports past Quebec – thanks in part to a fortuitous change in the wind direction – Wolfe was able to pursue options west of the city. By then, however, the season was so advanced that an investment of Quebec – cutting the city off from Montreal – was not an option. As a result, Wolfe was forced to pursue a decisive engagement – admittedly his objective all along, but one that was necessary to achieve any success against Montcalm's dispositions at Quebec, and the particular circumstances in which both forces found themselves.

Wolfe clearly preferred such an approach. The books he chose to privilege in his self-education, and his professional military experiences so far, all pointed to the centrality and importance of the decisive battlefield engagement. The way in which he conducted his command also pointed in this direction. 'Mr Wolfe had a very peculiar turn for war,' wrote one of his staff officers. 'Personal bravery to excess ... firmly attach'd to officers who distinguish'd themselves in military exploit ... Thus a friend of the brave, an enemy to the base, he work'd up courage to such a pitch in his little army that it became necessary often to desire the soldiers not to expose themselves without a necessity for it.'[121] A decisive showdown was the only option likely to result in success for Wolfe at Quebec, but on the back of this victory it became easy to conclude that the main purpose of the British Army in the eighteenth century was the pursuit of the decisive tactical battlefield victory, not least because of the plaudits and laurels that such victories brought, as opposed to the tactically less decisive, but strategically more important, campaigns of manoeuvre favoured by other generals. This issue would dominate British military thinking and decision making for the remainder of the century, and failure to understand the importance and place of both tactical battles and strategic campaigns would result in significant difficulties.

*   *   *

If the capture of Quebec was an illustration of the importance of a decisive field engagement to military success, then the capture of Montreal would illustrate the importance of operational manoeuvre and coordination. Following news of the fall of Quebec, Amherst returned to New York, leaving Colonel William Haviland in command of the garrison at Crown Point, and began preparations for a coordinated advance on Montreal. Pitt gave him permission to plan the invasion 'either in one body, or by different operations, at one and the same time ... according as you shall, from your knowledge of the Countries, thro' which the War is to be carried, and from emergent circumstances not to be known here...'.[122] Amherst planned a simultaneous advance on three fronts. Murray, who had remained in command at Quebec, would advance up the St. Lawrence, Haviland would advance up Lake Champlain from Crown Point, taking the Isle-au-Noix, while Amherst would move down the St. Lawrence from Oswego.[123] Preparations went well, but the recruitment and retention of sufficient numbers of colonial troops once more caused delays for both Amherst and Haviland. Murray, meanwhile, had his own set of problems to contend with.

The new garrison of Quebec had been left ill-prepared and poorly supplied for winter, such that by early April Murray's men were suffering from scurvy, food supplies were running perilously short and soldiers were forced to demolish old houses for firewood. Word then reached Quebec that General François Gaston de Lévis was marching from Montreal, as expected, with the intention of besieging Quebec before a British relief force could get up the St. Lawrence from Louisbourg. On 28 April, the French arrived on the Plains of Abraham, and Murray deployed his army on high ground overlooking the field, with the intention of building redoubts and entrenchments.

However, as Lévis deployed his force into line, Murray thought he saw an opportunity to attack and destroy his adversary in detail.[124]

This was a staggeringly ill-judged decision and surrendered a perfectly defendable position in exchange for a difficult manoeuvre through boggy terrain. The result, predictably enough, was essentially a re-enactment of the battle of 13 September on almost the same ground, this time with the British in an attacking role. Vicious hand-to-hand fighting broke out on the flanks, and Murray's exhausted army was unable to match the French, who outnumbered them by nearly two to one. In the end, Murray was forced to withdraw to Quebec, having lost a third of his fighting force, and his artillery, spiked and stuck in the mud of the battlefield. His soldiers were unforgiving in their criticism. 'His conduct on this occasion', wrote Malcolm Fraser, 'is universally condemned by all.'[125] French losses were also high, but Lévis was left in possession of the field, and free to commence a siege of Quebec.

It took some time for the French to construct the siege works, hampered as they were by British sorties mounted with a spirit at odds with their recent battlefield calamity. Just as the French were ready to open their batteries, however, a British frigate anchored at Quebec on 9 May, disembarking reinforcements and supplies. Aware now that his position was hopeless, Lévis gave up the siege and withdrew. As 'Quebec is not now in danger', Murray wrote to Amherst, and with the French in retreat, 'the moment I can, which will be soon, I will move up the River'.[126]

As ever, it took several months for Amherst and his staff to coordinate the build-up of supplies, recruit and move sufficient numbers of Provincial soldiers, and establish reliable communications across vast expanses of wilderness terrain. In addition, Captain Joshua Loring, who had overseen the naval operations on Lake Champlain the previous year, was once more required to secure naval command of Lake Ontario. On 6 July, three French sloops had threatened Oswego, so Loring was dispatched to hunt them down and ensure Amherst was able to transport his army to the St. Lawrence unmolested. Though there were several close encounters, by 23 July, the French ships had escaped into the St. Lawrence. 'No person can be more uneasy that I am at this Disappointment,' wrote Loring, 'especially after having been so near them.' At one point, the British had been gaining steadily on the French craft, only for the wind to ease. Under the power of their oars, the French were able to make their escape.[127] Still, the main objective, command of Lake Ontario, had been achieved, and by 10 August, Amherst was ready to commence his advance with a force totalling 10,961 troops. At Crown Point, Haviland began his march with 3,600 men on 11 August, while Murray had departed Quebec with 4,000 men on 14 July.[128]

Murray had managed to cobble his column together from the remnants of his garrison, which had more than 2,400 reported sick and wounded on 15 June. No single unit was able to report its complement, so Murray created composite battalions for the purpose of the campaign, divided into two brigades commanded by Colonels Ralph Burton and William Howe. Major George Scott commanded a separate Light Infantry battalion. They were to be conveyed up the St. Lawrence in a flotilla of transports escorted by two sloops, two frigates and nine floating batteries which Amherst had proclaimed were 'excellent things against the few Ships' the French 'have remaining'.[129] A force under the command of Captain Jean-Daniel Dumas, numbering approximately 1,200 troops, 300 of them Canadian militia, garrisoned three defensive locations between Quebec and Montreal – the first at Jacques-Cartier River, the second at Trois Rivières and the third on the south shore at Sorel, where the Richelieu River joined the St. Lawrence.

The fleet reached Jacques-Cartier on 16 July, and despite a fortification 'situated on a bold commanding eminence, its works consisting of fascines, earth and stockades', the French defences posed no obstacle as the British were able to sail past, out of reach of the French guns.[130] Murray was more interested in sending landing parties ashore to secure the neutrality of the civilian population, who were surprised at the generous terms the British offered. Having been told by Governor Vaudreuil of the barbarism and brutality of the British Army, when they were allowed instead to continue to enjoy their property and religion so long as they stopped supporting the French, most accepted the terms with little hesitation.[131] Murray's force reached Trois Rivières on 26 July, and was again able to bypass the strong French defences. Moreover, word had spread of British policy to the Canadian population, and the French could muster no resistance among the civilian communities. As the force advanced, Murray sent landing parties ashore at every settlement, taking oaths of loyalty, in exchange for militia arms and intelligence, all of which pointed to a general collapse in French morale.[132]

At Sorel on 12 August, however, Murray found the French willing to make a stand, and the militia also remained active. Though he was delayed by contrary winds, on 21 August Murray landed two battalions under Scott's command. Finding 'the inhabitants . . . had deserted' the town and were 'in arms', Scott's orders put him 'under the cruel Necessity of burning the greatest part of these poor unhappy peoples houses'.[133] The tactic proved effective, and the combination of the virtual certain defeat of the

French with exemplary punitive measures persuaded more and more the Canadian militia to abandon support for the French government. For their part, the French acknowledged that Murray 'did us during his march more harm by his policy than by his army'.[134]

In many ways, Murray's five-week campaign along the St. Lawrence was more akin to a counterinsurgency operation designed to win hearts and minds than a military operation contributing to the conquest of an adversary colony. Like several of his professional colleagues, Murray was evidently influenced by the writings of European military thinkers like Frederick the Great and Turpin de Crissé, not least in the combination of intelligence collection and rapport building with the local population, designed in part to ensure ready access to supplies. His application of those ideas was also clearly informed by the principles of the emerging military enlightenment, and his actions were designed to be exemplary rather than vengeful. 'I pray God this Example May suffice,' he wrote to Pitt, 'for my nature revolts, when this becomes a necessary part of my duty.'[135] Contrary winds once more enforced a delay of more than a week on Murray's advance, during which time he sought to establish communications with Amherst and Haviland.

Commanding the column heading from the south through Lake Champlain and the Richelieu River, William Haviland had departed Crown Point on 11 August, with a force including two battalions of regular soldiers, five of colonial troops, and five companies of Rangers commanded by Robert Rogers himself. They were transported on a small flotilla of batteaux and radeaux, and escorted by the vessels Amherst had commissioned during the 1759 campaign. In June, in a raid into French territory, Rogers had acquired plans of the defences of Isle-au-Noix, which suggested it was better to isolate the fortress, rather than attack it directly.[136]

Haviland reached the Isle-au-Noix on 16 August, and work on three siege batteries commenced. Once completed, fire from these covered the construction of a fourth much closer to the fortress. While this was under way, Rogers was sent with two companies of light infantrymen and grenadiers to attempt to seize the small flotilla of French craft moored north of the island. Under cover of darkness, Rogers was able to get level with one of the vessels, and 'by firing from shore, gave an opportunity to some of my party to swim on board with their tomahawks', successfully capturing it.[137] Meanwhile, the light infantry seized one of the French armed radeaux and turned it on the remainder of flotilla, one of which was driven ashore by the wind. The 'rangers kept up such a fire on them after shooting the Captain's head off, the others were glad to surrender on any terms'.[138]

Now the British were in command of naval vessels on both sides of the island, the French position on Isle-au-Noix was rendered untenable. This complete, the batteries opened and had an immediate impact. 'They had a sight of us everywhere,' recalled one French eyewitness, 'back, face and side-ways, and so near us that at the south staccado they killed several of our soldiers by their musket shots.'[139] After a two-day bombardment, the French evacuated the fortification under cover of darkness on 27 August, with-drawing cross-country toward Montreal. In the wake of his success at Isle-au-Noix, Haviland issued similar orders to those given by Murray along the St. Lawrence, ensuring the Canadians had no reason to resist the British advance. On 2 September, he commenced the march to Chambly, the final leg of his invasion of Canada, in anticipation of linking up with Amherst, who had made good progress since his departure from Oswego on 10 August.

Amherst's was the strongest of the three columns, as he intended his advance to both surprise the French and cut off the main avenue of retreat from Montreal. His force was composed of 5,258 British infantrymen, including several veteran battalions and Gage's 80th Light Infantry. This substantial body of regularly trained soldiers was augmented by 4,479 colonial soldiers and 706 Native American warriors. Supplied with a strong artillery train, the army was transported aboard a fleet of 800 batteaux and whaleboats, escorted by two well-armed sailing vessels – named the *Onondaga* and the *Mohawk* – and five row-galleys crewed by American colonial troops. These ships, according to Amherst, appeared 'to be much larger & finer Vessels than the Enemys'.[140]

The fleet reached the Thousand Islands at the head of the St. Lawrence on 15 August, and began the perilous navigation of the poorly mapped area, reaching within a few days the open river and the abandoned forts at La Présentation and Oswegatchie. The next obstacle was Fort Lévis, about five miles downriver of Oswegatchie; though small, it was in a defensible state and commanded the river with a single 12-pounder gun. Amherst would have to take the small fort before he could proceed, and ordered an investment on 18 August. Light infantry units, under William Amherst's command, would take the lead, 'two boats abreast' and hugging the north shore of the river as far as possible from the French gun emplacements in Lévis. They took with them some light artillery. As they advanced, the British sustained some loss in the brisk fire from the fort, though this did not slow their progress.[141] Once past Fort Lévis, Amherst's units were to land on two islands north of Fort Lévis, where batteries were built no further than 650 yards from their target, well within the range of the 24-pounders in the British siege train. To the south-east, Lieutenant Colonel Frederick Haldimand of the 4th Battalion Royal Americans established a further battery on the south shore of the river within 1,000 yards of the Lévis. Amherst assigned working parties numbering 500 men to build the batteries in three eight-hour shifts a day, and by 23 August, one of the batteries was ready to open fire.

The same day, Amherst attempted an amphibious assault, covered by the sailing vessels under Loring's command. Poor seamanship and an unexpectedly spirited defence from the French turned the attempted assault into a fiasco, with two of Amherst's vessels sustaining severe damage and running aground. After Loring was shot in the leg, the crew of the *Onondaga* actually struck its colours, only for a company of Grenadiers to row over to the stricken vessel and attempt to restore order.

Despite this setback, work continued apace to bring the other two artillery batteries into service, which commenced their bombardment on the 24th. As well as focusing on the fortress walls, mortars fired combustible bombs and red-hot shot into the fort itself, setting the wooden blockhouses on fire. Captain Pierre Pouchot, commandant of Fort Lévis, complained to Amherst of 'this method of making war, which was only used against rebels and not against a brave garrison that did not deserve such treatment'.[142] The following day, a breach was opened in the north bastion of Fort Lévis, and Amherst summoned the garrison. Pouchot agreed to terms and surrendered Fort Lévis at 8 p.m. Casualties were modest, 21 killed and 23 wounded, almost all in the abortive amphibious assault. Pouchot had lost only 12 men in the bombardment. Amherst ordered work to begin immediately on reconstructing the fort, which he renamed William Augustus, in honour of the Duke of Cumberland, his former mentor.

The advance to Montreal recommenced on 31 August, and had immediately to contend with four sets of rapids, the first of which were overcome with relative ease. On 4 September, however, the British entered the set of rapids known as the Cedars, the Buisson and the Cascades. Amherst sent most of the men ashore to march along the riverbank, but 55 boats were destroyed, drowning 84 men.[143] Amherst's judicious deployment of light infantry units to protect his flanks forestalled any intention the French had of attacking him.

With the rapids successfully negotiated, Amherst commenced the final advance on Montreal, and landed there on 6 September, immediately deploying his army into line of battle. He was aware that Murray's army was landing on the eastern end of the island, and news had arrived that

Haviland was closing in from the south. 'I believe never have three Armys, setting out from different & very distant Parts from each other joined in the Centre as was intended, better than we did,' Amherst wrote in a some-what out-of-character self-congratulatory tone. 'It could not fail of having the effect of which I ... now see the consequence.'[144] In total, Amherst could now rely on 17,000 men; his adversary merely 2,500, currently encamped within the crumbling ruins of the town wall.

Amherst has in many ways been unfairly judged in comparison to Wolfe, whose reputation benefitted immensely from his glorious death on the field of battle. Wolfe was evidently the more tactically innovative general, willing to take risks that promised great rewards if they came off. Amherst was perhaps a more tactically conservative general officer, but his strategic planning was considerably more ambitious and imaginative. Wolfe could win the battle, but Amherst understood how to win the war. Self-congratulatory he might have been, but he was also right: the coor-dination of three army columns from Oswego in the west, Quebec in the east and Albany in the south, and the execution of a plan to converge on Montreal within 48 hours of each other was no mean feat, but it was one that was as much to do with the quality of the army as it was to do with Amherst's imagination. This army was the product of its experiences in North America, in Europe and Britain; of its informal interactions with the Native Americans, the French and Britain's colonial allies; and of the resultant military knowledge that was made and remade in the course of the war, and which allowed it to develop innovative tactics, and the ability to execute complex orders and decisions.

On 7 September 1760, Vaudreuil and Lévis elected, sensibly, to surrender Montreal. During the subsequent negotiations, when the French sought a truce to verify rumours that a general peace had been signed,[145] Amherst informed them curtly that 'I was come to take Canada and I did not intend to take anything less'.[146] At noon on 7 September, Vaudreuil's proposals were presented to Amherst, most of which he accepted, though he refused to grant the garrison of Montreal the honours of war, owing to 'the infamous part the troops of France had acted in exciting the savages to perpetuate the most horrid and unheard of barbar-ities in the whole progress of the war'.[147]

The American war had indeed been extremely brutal, and this memory more than any other would persuade British officers to consider the expe-rience of war in the wilderness to be unique to the continent of North America. It was impossible for them to separate the innovations and lessons of warfare in the wilderness from the brutality of the adversary they faced. Similarly, by compartmentalising the war as a uniquely American experience, British officers could justify their own brutality in the course of the war there. Such atrocities would, and could, never be perpetrated in Europe, they argued. After all, the finest authorities on the rules of war in Europe agreed that the normal standards of conduct would not apply when 'the war is with a savage nation, which observes no rules'.[148] For this reason, then, the lessons of America were considered irrelevant to the European theatre. The lessons, of course, were not irrelevant, and it would take another war to relearn them for application elsewhere.

The tactical response to the conditions of North America were not the only innovations to be tried and tested during this six-year colonial campaign. Wolfe and Amherst had very different strategic and operational approaches to warfighting, with Wolfe seeking the decisive battle that would bring the war to a swift conclusion. Amherst recognised this approach as a gamble, with the effects of losing potentially devastating. In contrast, he preferred a methodical approach, positioning his forces in strategically important locations, like the pieces on a chessboard. Such an approach could reap enormous benefits, but it took time, patience and skill to execute successfully. While the practical challenges of the two approaches had been visibly demonstrated during the campaign to seize Canada from the French, the merits of both approaches also occupied the pens of theorists in Europe.

CHAPTER 3

The 'Great Book of War'

FORMS OF BRITISH MILITARY KNOWLEDGE IN THE EIGHTEENTH CENTURY

VISITING the Westphalian town of Bergen in May 1774, the future commander of British forces in North America, Henry Clinton, remarked that the town was 'beautifully situated on the Maine [sic], look[ing] over the Rhine at a great distance, & bounded on that side by ... mountains'.[1] But Clinton was not sightseeing. Rather, the purpose of his visit was to study the battle that had taken place there on 13 April 1759 between an Anglo-Hanoverian army under the command of Duke Ferdinand of Brunswick and a French army commanded by Victor-François, duc de Broglie. Brunswick had succeeded Cumberland following the humiliation of Hastenbeck, and gone on the offensive successfully in 1758, defeating a 70,000 strong French army at Krefeld on 23 June. His aim in 1759 was to clear the French from Westphalia before they received reinforcements sent by Paris. At Bergen, then, Brunswick took the opportunity to attack Broglie who had adopted a defensive position outside the fortified town.

As he approached Bergen, Brunswick believed that Broglie was still forming up, so decided on an immediate attack before all his forces had arrived on the field of battle. Outlying villages and surrounding hills were captured by Brunswick's *Jäger* light troops, commanded by Heinrich Wilhelm von Freytag. Brunswick, perceiving that Bergen was the key to the battle, decided on a frontal assault, any flanking attack being denied by Bergen's position on the Main River. Though Brunswick's initial assault carried some success, Broglie had kept a substantial reserve of infantry in column, which he now fed with some rapidity into the battle. Brunswick's men were beaten back, but then regained momentum as his trailing forces started to arrive. Broglie, though, was able to counterattack once more, causing some disharmony in the allied army. Having reached a stalemate, Brunswick withdrew in the evening after a substantial artillery duel, heading toward Minden.[2]

Fifteen years later, Clinton was travelling through Europe and took the opportunity to visit several battlefields from the War of Austrian Succession and the Seven Years' War. A lover of history, Clinton often referred to past campaigns to help him form views on leadership and command in war.[3] After touring the field, Clinton analysed the battle and concluded that the 'village of Bergen might have been turned by the left'. In this scenario, he suggested that 'a column of infantry might have penetrated close under the wall of that village, unexposed to a single shot in flank as there are no towns to flank it, & no firing from the walls'. It was, however, extremely risky. 'It would have been difficult to have turned the whole position of the left', he continued, 'owing to a marshy rivulet which still kept you from the town.'[4] Clinton evidently believed that Brunswick was overconfident and underestimated the strength and capability of his enemy. Despite his observations on the possibility of flanking the town, Clinton clearly would not have fought a battle at Bergen if he had been in command.

Nine years after Clinton's visit, Prince Frederick, favourite son of George III and future Duke of York and commander-in-chief of the British Army, also visited the battlefield, commenting to his father that the 'field of Battle . . . is very curious'.[5] For Frederick, the visit was part of a curriculum designed to prepare him for a life in the military, which incorporated visits to many of the major battles fought on European soil, as well as regular attendance at military reviews held by the Great Powers of Europe. When not on the road, Frederick underwent tuition in the science of war, including the geometry of fortification design, arcs of fire and weapon design. Such a curriculum was not merely the preserve of royal students but provided the European social elite with the means of communicating 'notions of admirable male conduct' to young men embarking on careers not only in the military, but also in politics and other areas of society where men needed to demonstrate their 'elite masculinity'. Besides the 'drama, spectacle and entertainment', such activities afforded opportunities to socialise in fashionable company and build and enhance personal networks that might accelerate both political and military careers.[6]

Throughout the eighteenth century, then, military officers visited former battlefields and siegeworks, accompanied either by experienced veterans or with recorded histories in hand, to learn the art of war, in the words of historian Sarah Goldsmith, 'by drawing the military past into the present'. Frequent destinations included the coastal defences of northern France, the fortifications of the Low Countries, the historical and recent battlefields of Switzerland, Germany and Austria, as well as strategically important locations on the frontiers of France, Germany and Switzerland.[7] Terrain, geography and military structures can be seen in this way to be the means of the transmission of knowledge and learning, as the visible and undying reminder of past military experience.

Conducting his own battlefield tour when still a junior officer based in Scotland, James Wolfe had observed that 'the more a soldier thinks of the false steps of those that have gone before him, the more likely is he to avoid them; on the other hand The Examples worthiest of imitation should never be lost sight of, as they will be the best & truest guides in every undertaking'.[8] Grand tourists would need to familiarise themselves with the wars fought on the terrain they were visiting or learn directly from those who fought those wars. Maps and books relating to the campaigns being studied were therefore an essential prerequisite for a successful martial grand tour and would allow tourists to understand not just the battlefield they were visiting but the broader political and strategic aspects of the wider war.[9] The strength of memory associated with physical place was profound. Individuals 'sought to inscribe experience and memory' upon landscapes and places in the wake of traumatic encounters.[10] As geographer Karen Till has noted: 'places are never merely backdrops for action or containers for the past. They are fluid mosaics and moments of memory . . . Through place making, people mark social spaces as haunted sites where they can return,' and, for soldiers and officers, make and remake military knowledge.[11]

* * *

Frederick was accompanied on his tours by Heinrich Wilhelm von Freytag, veteran of the Seven Years' War, and comrade in arms both of the Duke of Brunswick and Frederick's great-uncle, the Duke of Cumberland. Freytag proved an invaluable guide, recounting events with the precision only an eyewitness could offer. Indeed, in 1781 the two visited the field of the Battle of Hastenbeck, on the anniversary of Cumberland's infamous final defeat. 'Four and twenty years before on that very same day,' Frederick wrote to his father, Freytag 'was posted in the same place ... and looked with as much unconcern upon ... the place, as he did now ...'.[12] Like Bergen, Hastenbeck offered opportunities to learn from defeat.

Later the same year, Frederick and his entourage also visited the battle-field of Minden, fought by Brunswick in the wake of his defeat at Bergen. He was accompanied once more by Freytag, as well as his secretary Richard Grenville, and the German draftsman Anton Heinrich du Plat. The latter had provided detailed terrain mapping, and several battle plans of the Seven Years' War,[13] and now accompanied the prince, furnished with his own maps of the countryside, 'in order to explain to him the several particulars relative to that action, & to shew him the different positions of the two army's [sic] on that day'.[14] With both a veteran of the battle and an expert on the military geography of the campaign, Frederick studied both the tactics used in the battle itself and the wider campaign which had culminated in the clash of arms. He would have learned that after Brunswick withdrew from Bergen, Broglie had occupied Minden on 9 July, opening a route to Hanover. With the arrival of Marshal Louis Georges Érasme, Marquis de Contades, the French were able to field 60,000 men against Brunswick's 43,000. At Minden, though, on 1 August, Brunswick engineered a battle which reversed earlier French successes.

Contades had, according to the commander of the British cavalry contingent, Lord George Sackville, 'fortif[ied] himself in a camp which from its natural situation appears inaccessible'.[15] Brunswick split his forces in order to threaten the French lines of supply, and Contades took the opportunity to leave his strong position and move over to an offensive posture, believing his adversary to be overextended.[16] With the situation so fluid, Brunswick kept 'his army very alert'.[17] He had withdrawn to the west, but had deliberately left a large corps under General Georg August von Wagenheim apparently isolated at the river Wesser, near the village of Todtenhausen, north of Minden.[18]

It was here in 1781 that Frederick commenced his study of the battle-field. 'We came first to the place where Wagenheim's corps was encamped,' wrote Frederick, 'and so passed through one of the openings which were cut for His Column to march up to their ground though the rest of these openings are planted up, it is easy to perceive where they were as the trees are not yet come to their full growth.'[19] Contades had deployed Broglie against Wagenheim, who had actually gained a very strong position. Broglie unleashed a furious artillery bombardment, and Wagenheim gave the order for the allied infantry to kneel. At length, Wagenheim brought his guns into action, and the battle on the French right descended into stalemate.[20]

With Minden at his back, Contades deployed his army in an arc west from the river Wesser through the dwelling of Malbergen and then south-west, with his left flank anchored at Hahlen. He amassed his artillery in a grand battery in the centre at Malbergen, protected by his cavalry. Upon learning that Contades had decided to move, Brunswick had ordered his own force to march into the plain in front of Minden in eight columns, deploying into two lines, with the right anchored at a windmill near the village of Hahlen, and the left at the village of Stemmer, in communication with Wagenheim at Todtenhausen.[21] After viewing the battlefield from its opening stage, Frederick, Freytag and du Plat next moved 'to the place where the Great Battery of the French was and from thence to the Windmill where our right wing of cavalry was pitted in front of which is the Famous Fir Wood which could not have been above 100 paces long and fifty wide'.[22]

The wood to which Frederick referred was in front of the village of Hahlen and was the site of a famous misunderstanding between Brunswick and Hanoverian General Fredrich von Spörcken. The latter commanded six British regiments of foot and two Hanoverian battalions. As he reached the wood in front of the windmill at Hahlen, Spörcken deployed as instructed into two lines, then misinterpreted an order from Brunswick and advanced immediately without waiting for further orders. A prolonged firefight broke out, during which Spörcken's men sustained repeated attacks from the French cavalry and infantry. Despite sustaining severe losses, the Anglo-Hanoverian units held their ground. Contades was astonished. 'I never thought to see a single line of infantry', he wrote after the battle, 'break through three lines of cavalry, ranked in order of battle and tumble them to ruin.'[23]

By 9 a.m. on 1 August 1759, Contades gave the order to retreat. As this astonishing display of martial courage had been unfolding, Brunswick repeatedly exhorted Sackville to move his cavalry squadrons to support the infantry, but the latter refused, claiming he was unable to get through the wood without significant disruption to the cohesion of his force. Sackville's failure to move earned him a court martial and was evidently a subject of interest to Frederick during his tour of Minden. On inspecting the wood more closely, du Plat pointed out that 'with a place on each side of it over which our squadrons might have passed a breadth, and indeed the wood itself is so excessively thin, that it could have been no inconvenience to them. . . .'[24]

The lessons for Frederick were many and varied but were focused on the steadiness and discipline of the troops. Unsurprisingly, the episode confirmed in the young prince an appreciation of the Prussian system of drill. The effectiveness of rifled weapons may also have been noted, as he was particularly interested in innovative ideas. The tour concluded as the group 'passed along the side of the Morass, to the spot where the French had thrown their bridges over, and from thence going over the glacis of the town of Minden, we came to the place where the Grenadiers of France were so roughly handled'.[25]

Soldiers could therefore derive much that was of use from visits to historical battlefields, drawing lessons not just about decision making in war, but also on the character of war itself. Embarking on his own martial grand tour, one unnamed captain in the 10th Dragoons focused on the fortifications of Europe. At Breisach, he noted that the town 'lies so snug that you are almost on the fortifications before you even see them. This is reckon'd a very complete fortress. . . .'[26] At Strasbourg, he was grateful for the hospitality of Louis Georges Érasme de Contades, the celebrated marshal of France and commander of French forces at the Battle of Minden in 1759. 'I was very glad to see a man of whom I had heard so much in our last War in Germany,' wrote the captain. 'He received me very kindly, & invited me to dine with him whilst I stay'd,' though there is no record of the things the two officers might have discussed.[27]

The unnamed captain was principally interested in positional warfare: lengthy descriptions of fortifications and garrisons intersperse his social commentary on the odd fashions of German women, and the extraordinary ability of French soldiers to keep their hair in place in strong winds through the use of copious quantities of powder. By contrast, he missed the opportunity to visit the site of the Battle of Blenheim, which a short detour would have enabled him to view as he travelled between Ulm and Augsburg. Clearly, the anonymous captain was interested in studying the profession of arms insofar as it related to the popular themes of the period – notably that the main objectives of warfare were focused on the acquisition of enemy fortifications: set-piece battles were the product rather than an alternative to sieges. Our nameless officer was not alone in holding these views. Other similarly themed travel journals – grand tours with an obsession with military sightseeing – also focus on descriptions of fortifications. One journal writer travelled along the coast of Valencia and

Catalonia in 1754. As he passed through Morviedro, he commented on the huge castle overlooking the settlement: 'anciently Saguntum,' he wrote, 'so famous for its siege'.[28]

While some soldiers saw confirmation of ideas about the focus on fortifications, others identified lessons suggesting the increasing importance of manoeuvre in warfare. In 1766, Brigadier John Burgoyne had begun a tour of the continent. He visited some of the main battlefields of the Seven Years' War, often accompanied by veterans of the battle, and also conducted research into the military capabilities of the main European powers. He took every opportunity to visit the most important sites of military activity. 'Every step I have taken has been to a soldier classic ground, and I have wandered over it with enthusiasm,' he wrote to a friend. 'I have had the good fortune to go over many of the great scenes with very intelligent officers who were present in the actions; I have been assisted with the best plans, and have conversed with most of the principal actors on both sides.' While clearly interested in battles, Burgoyne also 'passed some days … tracing with extreme amusement the positions and marches of both armies during different periods of the late war'.[29] For Burgoyne, and many others, it was not just the tactics of the battlefield, but the manoeuvres of the campaign that interested him and guided him on his explorations.

*   *   *

Burgoyne had tentative plans to write a history of the Seven Years' War, with a view to finding innovative solutions to the problems facing the British Army in the eighteenth century. In addition to the study of the military geography of the previous war, Burgoyne also considered professional reading to be of central importance. He recommended 'a short space of time given to reading each day, if the books are well chosen and the subject properly digested, will furnish a great deal of instruction'.[30] Yet he was wary of adopting wholesale the views and ideas of continental thinkers and practitioners. In particular, he was hesitant about the value of European methods of drill and discipline. 'There are two systems which, generally speaking, divide the disciplinarians; the one is that of *training men like spaniels, by the stick*; the other, after the French, of *substituting the point of honour in the place of severity*,' he wrote while considering his approach to drill and training. 'The followers of the first are for reducing the nature of man as low as it will bear,' he continued. 'The admirers of the latter, who commonly argue more from speculation than practice, are for exalting rationality, and they are commonly deceived in their expectations.'

Instead, Burgoyne sought to encourage a degree of independent thought in his men. 'English soldiers are to be treated as thinking beings,' he argued. He therefore sought to achieve a balance between the excessively strict discipline of the Prussian service and the lax approach adopted by the French. 'The Germans are the best; the French, by the avowal of their own officers, the worst disciplined troops in Europe,' he wrote. 'I apprehend a just medium between the two extremes to be the surest means to bring English soldiers to perfection.'[31] Based on his own experience of the use of irregular tactics during his deployment to Portugal in 1762, Burgoyne was an advocate of the use of light infantry and operational manoeuvre.[32] Though he never wrote the history he had planned to, these conclusions guided his own thinking when he commanded an army in the next war.

Burgoyne was not alone in his perception of the importance of professional reading to the modern soldier and officer. As we have seen, James Wolfe also advised junior officers to read widely on the subject of war and military history, recommending works by Comte de Turpin, the 'King of Prussia's Regulations for his Horse and Foot', the 'Memoirs' of the Marquis de Santa Crus, Feuquières and Montecuccoli, and Folard's 'Commentaries upon Polybius'.[33]

Wolfe's recommendations balanced the traditional reading selections of British officers – namely classical and contemporary military history – with new concepts and thinking about war, produced largely on the continent. This reflected a shift in reading preferences, largely the result of the near-catastrophic and humiliating defeats inflicted on the British Army during the War of Austrian Succession and the opening stages of the Seven Years' War, both in America and Europe. Until then, tactical manuals had done little more than crystallise military thinking developed during Marlborough's campaigns in the War of Spanish Succession.[34]

The paucity of original thought on the art of war and the profession of arms illustrated that British officers were, prior to the calamities of the War of Austrian Succession and the Jacobite uprising, broadly satisfied with the organisation, command and tactical arrangements of the army. Ira Gruber, in his major study of the reading habits of British officers in the eighteenth century, has added weight to this conclusion. In *Books and the British Army*, Gruber intensively researched the reading habits of 42 officers, most of whom achieved the rank of colonel or above.

Fourteen of these officers served, and therefore made reading selections, before 1754, while the remaining 28 came to prominence during or after the Seven Years' War. Gruber's analysis concluded that the 14 officers who made their selection prior to 1754 preferred to read the classics – Vegetius, Polybius and Thucydides – and campaign histories rather than continental treatises on the art of war.[35] Add to this the fact that many officers selected recent successful campaign histories of the British Army, which easily recalled the glories of the most recent war, then it is evident that British officers saw themselves on a par with their classical heroes.

In the wake of the defeats of the 1740s and 1750s there was a discernible shift in the selection of professional reading by British officers, as illustrated by Wolfe's recommendations. Military history remained a popular choice, but officers now began reading continental treatises in much greater numbers. In part, this was owing to the fact that the French and Prussian armies had been seen to be more effective, so the obvious thing seemed to be to learn from them.

The first of Wolfe's recommendations, grounded in the reality of mid-century war, was Turpin de Crissé's *An Essay on the Art of War* published in 1754.[36] It was translated into English only in 1761, but had already gained a substantial following among French-speaking British officers. Although very much a reflection of his own experience of warfare, de Crissé's essay offered general rules for the conduct of warfighting, but allowed for considerable flexibility in their interpretation, provided the soldier appreciated the importance of intelligence, security and terrain.[37]

The wide-ranging treatise discussed campaign planning, logistical support and *petite guerre*. De Crissé's most enduring theories on the art of war likened the planning of an operation to that of a siege. 'The province, or country to be conquered, hath always some principal point, which it must be the general's endeavour to arrive at,' de Crissé argued. 'Therefore, when a general is advancing into a country, why may not he form a first parallel and a general magazine for subsistence . . . .'[38] A general who followed this advice, then, would ensure his logistics and communication were protected and guarded by a system of fortifications and magazines, which would provide him with strength in depth and allow lighter and more rapid movement. Inevitably, such an approach was labour-intensive and time-consuming. 'A general who proposes succeeding by such a method will find prudence more necessary than bravery,' de Crissé explained.[39] John Forbes was an advocate of de Crissé's ideas, and in 1758 based the operation against Fort DuQuesne on 'a project that I took from *Turpin's Essay Sur la Guerre* . . . If you will take the trouble of looking into this Book,' he advised Prime Minister William Pitt, 'you will see the Generall principles upon which I have proceeded.'[40]

De Crissé also discussed how to set and avoid ambushes and was an early advocate of both light infantry and light cavalry. De Crissé drew on his knowledge of military history and personal experience as a hussar officer in his exposition of *la petite guerre*, noting the tactical and operational flexibility which light infantry offered. 'It hath been to these troops, that the most warlike people have often been indebted for success,' he wrote. 'They rush into the midst of the enemy, and are in a manner sheltered from danger by their lightness and dexterity, while they serve to protect the army to which they belong, they discover the enemy's motions, render his ambuscades useless, and also form ambuscades themselves.'[41] English readers and reviewers were rather less impressed by de Crissé's comments on light infantry. In an appraisal published in *The Critical Review* in 1761, most chapters received detailed synopses and commentaries. Chapter two of the second book – namely that on tactics for setting and avoiding ambushes – is dismissed merely as 'very full, curious, and entertaining'.[42] This implies that the idea of irregular tactics was not taken particularly seriously, at least in Britain, despite clear evidence from recent campaigns in both Europe and America that irregular expertise would offer a competitive edge.

British readers were rather more enamoured with the writings of Frederick II of Prussia, whose recent exploits in Europe seemed to demonstrate the utility and effectiveness of well-disciplined massed infantry. Frederick himself was a proponent of wide-ranging professional reading as well as learning from history. 'Past events serve to feed the imagination and stock the memory,' Frederick had written. 'They are a fund of ideas which provide the raw material which can then be refined and tested by the exercise of judgment.'[43] Much attention was paid to the training and drill methods advocated by the Prussian king, with its emphasis on discipline and manoeuvrability.

Even Burgoyne, who was otherwise critical of the Prussian system, admired the way 'the art and beauty of it consist in making the utmost simplicity in the movement of small parts effect the finest and most complicated movements of great bodies'. This enabled 'the highest conceptions of the King of Prussia's mind' to be 'instantly executed by the most stupid part of mankind'.[44] By contrast, Charles, Earl Cornwallis, visiting Prussian encampments in 1785, observed 'two lines coming up within six yards of one another, and firing in one another's face till they had no ammunition left: nothing could be more ridiculous'.[45] Cornwallis, fresh from the experience of war in the terrain of North America, was reacting to the close-order tactical arrangement dominant in Europe.[46]

Beyond drill, discipline and tactics, though, the strategies and operational plans adopted by Frederick also proved to be of interest to British military readers. Frederick advocated concentration of forces in order to achieve speed and mobility to force a decisive battle, and this approach won him considerable success in the War of Austrian Succession. During the Seven Years' War, however, as his enemies adapted and reacted to his methods of warfare, he in turn was forced to adapt his approach. While he wrote about 'ridding myself of an enemy', in reality he accepted he could no longer achieve 'the total annihilation' of his adversaries. Rather, he made use of his armies to win himself more time and freedom of manoeuvre to find solutions to a deteriorating situation in another theatre. War became a series of interlinked operations that might result in decisive strategic victory, even if it failed to result in decisive tactical victory.[47] By and large, however, British officers used Frederick's writing to confirm their existing biases. Those looking for evidence of the decisiveness of tactical engagements found much to support this view in both his writings and experiences; likewise, those who would advocate indirect manoeuvres could draw on Frederick's later experiences to support their viewpoint.

Proponents of decisive battle rather than skilful manoeuvre could turn to the treatises by Jean Charles, chevalier de Folard, and Antoine de Pas, Marquis de Feuquières. In his *Abrégé des Commentaires de M. de Folard sur L'Histoire de Polybe*, published in 1727, Folard used his personal experience of fighting in the War of Spanish Succession (1701–1713) to analyse Polybius's *Histories*. He concluded that shock would always defeat firepower and argued that the relatively little used infantry column could be used to achieve decisive tactical success. Indeed, cavalry and infantry could be successfully integrated in the column formation, providing both offensive and defensive capabilities.[48]

Following his defeat at Yorktown in October 1783, Cornwallis became 'more and more convinced of the necessity of military reading', which he admitted to finding 'very agreeable'.[49] In particular, Cornwallis found Folard's arguments to be persuasive and particularly enjoyed his 'Traité de la Colonne', the essay in which he advocated for the use of infantry columns as superior tactical organisations to the line for use on the battlefield. In Folard's view, the shock action provided by the column would always defeat the firepower of infantry in line armed with muskets and supported by artillery, though he conceded well-positioned artillery could cause significant casualties to infantry columns.[50] Cornwallis claimed to be 'much amused by' Folard's 'Traité', finding the arguments to be 'stated with clearness and ingenuity', particularly those that drew on classical history, for which Cornwallis shared a fondness.[51]

More generally, Cornwallis might have found Folard's wider arguments and commentary persuasive. Folard was critical of his contemporaries for inactivity and avoiding battle. His instinct was to seize the initiative and seek a decisive battle early in a campaign. These were qualities which Cornwallis agreed with, but Folard also sounded a note of caution: military commanders should only seek to fight a decisive battle with strong justification and careful preparation, he argued. While he admired aggressive generals, he criticised rash behaviour, including any failure to assemble adequate supplies, and was unable to tolerate those who failed to learn from their mistakes and engage in the professional study of war. It must have been with a wry smile that Cornwallis read the 'Traité', recognising in himself many of the qualities that Folard criticised.[52]

In his *Mémoires*, Feuquières reflected on his experiences during the wars of Louis XIV. He argued that 'the principal View of a General in every Species of War . . . should always be to act on the Offensive, because this is a Form of War most easy to be sustained, at the same time that it produces the greatest advantage to the Prince'.[53] Like Folard, though, Feuquières argued that battle should only be offered in favourable conditions 'wherein the Benefits that will redound to his Prince, from a prosperous Event, will be much greater than any Disadvantages he can possibly sustain by a Defeat'.[54] As with Frederick, Folard and Feuquières were popular among British officers in the mid-eighteenth century, but it was easy for readers to draw conclusions that reinforced pre-existing biases.

Just like Cornwallis, Wolfe's personal experience of war – dominated as it was by large set-piece confrontations, such as those fought at Dettingen, Culloden and Lauffeldt – drove him to seek 'the grand object', a war of general engagements and decisive battle.[55] As he read these texts, he privileged certain arguments, such as those of Frederick the Great and Folard, over those of de Crissé and Feuquières. In so doing, he found evidence to support his preference for battle.[56] Other officers, with different experiences, looked for different lessons in the same books. Cornwallis likewise found evidence of the value of decisive battle, but his command in India suggests he did so only in favourable circumstances.

This explains how officers could read the same or similar selections of books, as well as visit similar battlefields and still derive completely different conclusions about the art of war. As the British emerged triumphant from the Seven Years' War, differing ideas about how to employ military power began to emerge. Though he had been killed at the moment of his greatest victory, Wolfe had sought relentlessly to achieve it, seeking the decisive battle which would deal a catastrophic blow to French power in North America. Others saw such an approach as filled with risk: an enormous military confrontation might well result in decisive defeat. Opposed to the quest for the decisive engagement were those who advocated for campaigns of manoeuvre, designed to outwit the enemy, and either drive them out of the war or set conditions such that victory in battle was all but certain. As he toured historical European battlefields in 1774, Henry Clinton evidently formed this view. The battle at Bergen had been fought unnecessarily in his view, and decisions to fight other battles were similarly criticised.

Clinton's reading preferences correlated closely with those of Wolfe, Burgoyne and Cornwallis – of whom the latter two were also close contemporaries. There was a mutual admiration for the most popular classics: Thucydides, Vegetius, Polybius and Caesar. They also both read more recent military histories, including the *Military Memoirs and Maxims of Marshal Turenne* and *The Military History of the Late Prince Eugene of Savoy, and of the Late John Duke of Marlborough*, as well as the campaign histories of Frederick the Great and Ferdinand of Brunswick. For a range of continental military thinking, Clinton likewise read Folard, Feuquières and Raimondo, Prince Montecuccoli, as well as Jacques François de Chasenet and the Marquis de Puységur.[57]

From at least 1760, Clinton kept detailed notes on his professional reading choices, leaving a trail of intellectual breadcrumbs that help reconstruct his personal thinking on the subject of war. His thoughts are recorded primarily in a series of disordered notebooks, while there are also fragments of commentary on the history and theory of war littering his papers and correspondence.[58] In contrast to Wolfe and Burgoyne, what emerged for Clinton from his reading was a marked hesitancy to commit to battle, unless it was the last resort, or in irrefutably advantageous circumstances.

His earliest thoughts on war, committed to paper as he prepared to deploy to Germany as the aide-de-camp to Charles, Hereditary Prince of Brunswick, are contained in a newly identified notebook held at the Library of the Society of the Cincinnati in Washington, DC.[59] The notebook is important because it also illustrates the evolution of Clinton's thinking on war over time. Keeping his original historical observations confined to the recto (right-hand page), Clinton left the verso (left-hand page) blank for later additions. This was a common practice in eighteenth-century society, as readers revisited notes seeking to contextualise and acquire explanations for important historical events unfolding around them.[60]

Eighteenth-century military officers were exposed to a period of almost unparalleled experimentation in the conduct of war throughout the second half of the century. This was reflected in Clinton's notebooks, but most acutely in the book he took with him as his military career began in earnest. He returned to the notebook intermittently in the years that followed, adding contemporary references and linkages at relevant points on the corresponding verso. The notebook thus offers us a glimpse not only of the evolution of Clinton's thinking, and the merging of historical and contemporary narratives, but how he sought to link the study of military history with a didactic pursuit of common theories about war.

It is easy to imagine Clinton referencing and amending this notebook throughout his life, in particular during the American Revolutionary War, when he commanded the British Army in the field. Like many readers, Clinton relied on conversations with peers and subordinates, as well as his wider social network, to discuss his thinking about war and what he had read.[61] He frequently highlighted geographical reference points in his notes, such as his brief analysis of the Battle of Entzheim (4 October 1674), in which Marshal Turenne was charged with defending Strasbourg. His adversaries were Field Marshal Alexander von Bournonville and General Raimondo Montecuccoli, commanding the Army of the Holy Roman Empire. Though he had secured Strasbourg, Turenne attacked Bournonville at Entzheim before the Imperial Armies could unite, but 'his left was broke, his center could not consequently avail itself of the advantage it had'.[62] The battle thus ended in stalemate. Clinton inferred in analysis added later that Turenne should not have attacked after having secured Strasbourg. The battle had been costly – both sides lost between three and four thousand men – and Turenne had finished the day in the same situation he had prior to the commencement of the battle.

Similar lessons were drawn by Clinton from his studies of the battles of Fleurus (1 July 1690), Blenheim (13 August 1704) and Staffarda (18 August 1690). He drew parallels between the latter and Hastenbeck, comparing Cumberland's selection of terrain in 1757 unfavourably with Savoy's tactical deployment in 1690. Clinton commented that if the Duke of Cumberland had 'placed his left on that part of the ridge best calculated to his numbers and his right to Hamelin' – which would have protected his flank – 'he would not have been beat'.[63]

Throughout, Clinton displayed a common interest in examining the reasons for defeat, in particular when commanders had left their flanks unnecessarily exposed, or conversely, when defeat was avoided by occupying a highly defendable position.[64] In this respect, Clinton referenced his own personal experience. In the wake of the Battle of Monmouth Courthouse (28 June 1778), Clinton reflected on his mistakes by looking to military history in order to better understand his experiences and place them in a broader context. He picked up the notebook he had begun in 1760 and read through his comments on the European campaigns a century earlier. As he reread his brief synopsis of the Battle of Seneffe, fought in Belgium in 1674 during the Franco-Dutch War, he noted similarities between the Duke of Orange's command decisions and those taken by Washington. In a crisp, youthful hand, Clinton had in 1760 written:

Seneff 1674 Condé & D'Orange. the latter retired with the usual precaution by neglecting to occupy the first defile to receive his armed[?] guard & it would have been more decisive had not D O occupied with his Cavalry a plain which perceived his armed[?] Guard & the Infantry of his Gros[?] took an unattackable position which prevented a general engagement.

Above this, in a much less clear, thicker hand, he added that *'Washington had that merit at Monmouth'*.[65]

These observations were likewise reinforced by Clinton's earlier personal experience of war. In 1762, Clinton had been serving as aide-de-camp to Charles, Hereditary Prince of Brunswick, who commanded a corps of the allied army under Ferdinand of Brunswick. Poor intelligence had resulted in Charles unnecessarily exposing his flanks. During this assault, Clinton sustained a severe wound to his shoulder,[66] which made him 'weak with loss of blood'.[67]

Clinton would seek to avoid similar circumstances in future, so looked for evidence to support this viewpoint in his reading. A constant theme is sensible selection of terrain. Battle should only be offered when in possession of an advantageous position, with secured flanks, and a means of escape. Linked to this, the ground selected needed to play to the strengths of the soldiers: all troops should be trained and thoroughly familiar with tactical drill and manoeuvre; cavalry should guard the flanks; light troops, where available, should be used to hold and make an advantage of rough terrain. Commanders needed to make accurate but swift decisions and for this needed not only sound intelligence but also a calm mind. All of this pointed to an inescapable conclusion that would dominate and, in some ways, constrain Clinton's thinking for his whole career: battle was the last resort and should only be offered in optimal circumstances after an adversary had been duly manoeuvred into a proportionately disadvantageous situation. But Clinton also understood the importance of battle and would seek to offer it when the right circumstances were present.

In thinking along these lines, Clinton was not alone. Accompanying him on his battlefield tour of Europe in 1774 was one of the few British military theorists, General Henry Lloyd. Lloyd was a soldier of fortune and his military career was distinctly unusual, but it offered him a unique insight into European warfare. In the 1760s, Lloyd worked on a history of the Seven Years' War and included in it an essay outlining what he perceived to be the principles of war. An updated version was produced in the early 1780s, and from then Lloyd's work became highly influential in the British Army.

*   *   *

Born in 1718 in the Welsh county of Merioneth, Lloyd attended Jesus College, Oxford, but, after his stepfather defrauded him of his inheritance, he was unable to purchase a commission in the British Army. In 1744, he entered a Jesuit College in Spain as a lay brother tutoring young soldiers in geography and military engineering. There he met with and became friends with Lord John Drummond, travelled with him to the Low Countries and conducted several meticulous surveys of the local geography, including the site at which the Battle of Fontenoy would be fought. Writing four decades later, Drummond recalled that 'no man ever was more correct with his eye' than Lloyd. 'He saw at once the advantages and disadvantages of ground; and his remarks were made with so much penetration and judgement, that all his observations were to be depended upon.'[68] When these surveys came to the attention of the commander of the French army, Marshal Maurice de Saxe arranged for Lloyd to receive a commission as an engineer.

In the wake of Fontenoy, Lloyd accompanied the forces sent to Scotland in support of Charles Stuart in his attempt to usurp the Hanoverian throne. After seeing action at the Battle of Prestonpans, Lloyd embarked on a secret mission to spread word of the uprising in Wales, and then, disguised as a clergyman, he went on to reconnoitre the south coast of England in preparation for a possible French invasion. After he was arrested as a suspected spy, Drummond secured his release and Lloyd returned to the continent where he served again as an engineer in the French Army during the siege of Bergen op Zoom in 1747.

The Seven Years' War would be a significant formative experience in Lloyd's military thinking. In 1756, Lloyd again sought service on the continent, this time on the general staff of the Austrian army under Lieutenant General Franz Moritz Graf von Lacy. In an interview with Lacy, Lloyd claimed to want to 'learn the profession of war'. Lacy offered him a position as aide-de-camp with a commission as first lieutenant.[69] Lacy had fashioned a highly professional staff that acted as the central nervous system of the Austrian army, gathering military and topographical intelligence and planning movements and operations. Lloyd quickly proved himself a motivated and intelligent officer capable of original thought, and accelerated up the ranks despite his lack of social status: Lacy valued merit and talent more than status.

In 1760, Lacy promoted Lloyd to captain in the *Feld-Jäger-Corps* – the Austrian light infantry. Distinguishing himself in this new role, Lloyd tracked the Prussian army throughout the 1760 campaign, but grew frustrated at the lethargy of the Austrian High Command, and the constant failure to take advantage of the intelligence he and other reconnaissance units were bringing them. He resigned his Austrian commission in February 1761, and later that year was offered and accepted a commission in the army of Duke Ferdinand of Brunswick. At some point in the next year and a half, Lloyd encountered Henry Clinton, and the two became friends, corresponding regularly with one another, frequently about professional matters.[70]

While serving in the armies of Austria and Brunswick, Lloyd collected as much information as he could about the operations and battles that he witnessed and fought in. He obtained first-hand accounts from other participants and made notes on his own experience as soon as possible after the battle concluded. For those battles he did not personally witness, he sought to visit and study the field on which it had been fought. Witnesses observed him studying battlefields from prominent geographic positions.[71] Geography was central to Lloyd's study of war. Without a complete appreciation of the limitations and challenges presented by the geography of the theatre war, Lloyd believed it impossible to possess a true understanding of the nature of the war itself.[72] To facilitate geographic and geopolitical understanding, he compiled a rigorous analytical study of the 'seat' of the Seven Years' War, which explained the geography of the European theatre through hand-drawn maps, and analysed the war aims and strategic situation of the various protagonists.[73] He then produced a history of the war, which he sought to base on empirical fact, derived from sources that he personally compiled, and which sought to explain the course of the war, rather than merely recount it. This, Lloyd described as a 'New Plan' for the study of military history, in order to 'give a clear, and exact account of the most essential transactions which have occurred, during the course of this important war'.[74]

Lloyd's approach to writing history was new and innovative. Rather than the deployment of a basic narrative of a campaign, which outlined the facts as they were then understood, in the order in which they were thought to have unfolded, Lloyd offered a critical analysis, which attempted to understand the decision-making process of the key commanders. Moreover, Lloyd also expanded on this analysis by positing a series of counterfactual questions which suggested alternative options that commanders might have pursued. Lloyd was not merely recording an event but encouraging a discourse with his reader which allowed critical analysis of the campaign: inspiring the reader to understand not just what happened but why it happened.[75] Such an approach invited the reader more fully to understand the progress of the war, and also presented the human face of command: decisions taken in the heat of battle or when an incomplete intelligence picture was available were easy to criticise with the benefit of hindsight. The reality which Lloyd exposed was that war was an intensely human endeavour.

Lloyd's analysis of the campaigns and battles of the Seven Years War allowed him to identify what he considered to be immutable principles of war. Zorndorf (25 August 1758) and Paltzig (23 July 1759) – both of which ended in stalemate – illustrated the need for speed of decision and early seizure of the initiative. Kolin (18 June 1757) – Frederick the Great's defeat at the hands of a superior Austrian Army during the siege of Prague – illustrated the need for prudence while on the offensive. Leuthen (5 December 1757) highlighted that an inferior army – in this case Frederick's force of 39,000 – could achieve decisive results against a superior adversary – Austria's 66,000 troops – if an isolated flank was attacked and defeated. Though Lloyd in general considered it a mistake for an inferior army to go on the offensive, he nevertheless recognised that in certain circumstances – where the aggressor possessed the benefit of surprise, reliable and actionable intelligence, and a suitable target of opportunity – it was possible to achieve victory over a superior adversary.

By and large, Lloyd believed the evidence of history demonstrated 'that no operation whatever should be attempted, or post attacked, unless the possession of it be absolutely necessary to facilitate some capital enterprise'.[76] For Lloyd, then, like Clinton, battle was the last resort. His own experience in the Austrian Army in 1758 – during which, despite superior intelligence and communication, the Austrian commander failed both to seize the initiative and identify suitable objectives – illustrated this point effectively. Manoeuvre was more important than battle, as a lost battle was calamitous, while judicious manoeuvre could gradually achieve strategic superiority.

This was evident in Lloyd's ongoing correspondence with Clinton, with whom he shared drafts of his work. Unsurprisingly, the written – and most likely verbal (for the two frequently saw one another) – conversation focused on Lloyd's discussion of manoeuvre versus battle. In one letter, for example, Lloyd noted that 'one of the great errors committed by all those who write and speak of manoeuvres is that they never think of the enemy, & always propose doing this, or that motion, without asking themselves what the enemy would or might do. . . .'[77] Clinton agreed that prudence was paramount in warfare decision making and planning, and both he and Lloyd used historical and geographical examples in support of this argument. Referring to Lloyd's 'General Principles of War', Clinton commented that 'there is no doubt but that the best possible disposition that can be made is that by which a number of men can move with *simplicity, safely* to transition and act with the greatest velocity to the front, rear & flanks'. When planning campaigns 'with respect to marches the first thing to be attended to is that to invade with all the celerity possible consistent with *safety*, the more columns you can march in the better'.[78] Clinton had become firmly of the view that direct confrontation was the last resort. Far better for an army to manoeuvre the enemy cleverly out of their positions than risk defeat in an unnecessary battle.[79]

All of these principles – initiative, surprise, intelligence and identifying and maintaining the strategic objective – could be achieved by soldiers and officers who were masters of the profession of arms, and this could be achieved if the basics were simplified and made more efficient in practice. Writing at a time when the Enlightenment catalysed education reform, Lloyd, first of all, advocated that military education needed to be improved for all ranks. Officers should master the motivations and mental inclinations of their soldiers through effective education, rather than through punitive discipline.[80] Thereafter, Lloyd suggested that drill manuals be simplified, reducing the number of steps in firing drill and streamlining marching practice. 'The army which marches the best', he argued, 'must, if the rest is equal, in the end prevail.'[81]

The commander of the army, meanwhile, needed a comprehensive knowledge of geometry and arithmetic. A general so educated would therefore be able to calculate, using the basic facts of how much space a soldier occupied (two feet from elbow to elbow) and how fast they marched (one pace every second, with a pace being equal to approximately 20 inches), how long it would take to execute any type of manoeuvre. This was as true for the campaign theatre as it was for the battlefield. In this vein, Lloyd channelled the thinking of de Crissé. 'It is a certain rule, from which a General ought never to depart,' Lloyd argued, 'to shorten continually as he advances his line of operation, by forcing new depots behind him,' while 'an army whose line of operation is considerably too long can execute no solid enterprise, though it be ever so powerful ...'.[82] Geography was therefore also essential for the education of a general. 'A little experience and a certain *coup d'œil*', Lloyd argued, 'will enable a man to judge with great precision, of the time and space necessary to execute any evolution whatever.'[83]

Lloyd published this work in 1766 as *The History of the Late War in Germany, Between the King of Prussia, and the Empress of Germany and her Allies*. This was accompanied by 'Reflections on the General Principles of War; and on the composition and characters of the different armies in Europe', an essay that captured Lloyd's thinking on the art of war. Despite an initially warm reception, the book failed to gain the traction Lloyd expected, and, in Lloyd's words, it 'lay unnoticed for a long while which discouraged the author from prosecuting it'.[84] In 1772, Lloyd accepted a commission in the Russian army of Catherine the Great and departed England to fight in the Russo-Turkish War, where he was destined to command a division under Field-Marshal Count Petr Aleksandrovich Rumianstev. Lloyd persuaded Clinton to accompany him as an observer, along with Thomas Pelham Clinton, the future Duke of Newcastle and Clinton's cousin, Richard Fitzwilliam, the future 7th Viscount Fitzwilliam, and Major Thomas Carleton of the 20th Regiment of Foot. En route, they planned to visit the battlefields of Europe.

In Clinton's words, as the party set out on their 2,500-mile journey to Moldavia, they looked 'a most ridiculous sight the Genl in his bear'skin Cap;

... green great coat, running footman's stick ... Carleton in a coat of the
year 1752. TPC & myself not better equipped, the courier having lost his
horse obliged to trudge in his heavy boots ...'.[85] The party arrived in
Ostend after a choppy crossing on 28 April, and headed straight for Bruges,
where the camaraderie between the collection of individuals was apparent
when the group 'put G[eneral] L[loyd's] patience to the trial by send[ing]
six different bands of musick to play before him as he walked in the street'.[86]

Over the next few weeks, the party made their way slowly to the
Balkans, the seat of the Russo-Turkish War. On their way, in addition to
Bergen, the party visited Lauffeldt (fought on 2 July 1747), which 'ought
not to have been fought at all', and Dettingen (fought on 27 June 1743).[87]
There, Clinton was critical of poor French decision making, a theme
which ran throughout his didactic study of history. 'Many are the circumstances of blunder and misfortune,' he commented in another notebook,
'from dispute in command, want of humanity & confidence.'[88]

The group reached Vienna on 12 May and were granted permission to
join the Russian camp near Silistria, where they arrived on 20 June. Clinton
now observed his friend command a Russian division in the siege of
Silistria, while Rumianstev pressed on to strike a decisive blow at Shumla.
Lloyd deftly commanded his forces, successfully defending against several
Turkish sorties. By the beginning of July, Lloyd was in a position to launch
a devastating artillery barrage, but the conclusion of peace negotiations on
16 July ended the war. Lloyd and Clinton had taken the opportunity to
observe Rumianstev's approach to warfighting, and it appeared to confirm
their own thinking: namely a focus on mobility and combined arms
designed to achieve local, and decisive, superiority. Like the lessons of the
historical battlefields, Lloyd and Clinton's observations of the current
battles of the Russo-Turkish War (1768–1774) illustrated the importance
of operational manoeuvre in order to achieve decisive victory.[89]

The following year, long-term discontent over perceived political
interference in the governance of the Thirteen North American Colonies
boiled over into revolution. Clinton found himself appointed to a senior
position in the army deployed to suppress the rebellion. The outbreak of
the American Revolutionary War helped to revive public interest in Lloyd's
theories. Since the original publication of his book, Lloyd had gradually
established himself as the premier British military thinker. On the outbreak
of war with Spain in 1779, Lloyd visited an old friend, Lieutenant General
George Augustus Elliott, who was now governor of Gibraltar. Lloyd had
first met Elliott in Prussia during the Seven Years War and had remained

in contact ever since. While at Gibraltar, Lloyd advised Elliott on his views
of the best means of defending the Rock from the inevitable siege.[90]
'Happy would an officer have been, who could have overheard the conversation of Elliott and Lloyd on the ramparts off Gibraltar,' wrote Lloyd's son
in a short memoir completed following the general's death, 'communicating their ideas and their views, the results of long study and profound
meditation . . . .'[91]

On his return to England later that summer, Lloyd penned a savage
critique of the political and strategic execution of the war in America. He
regretted the political interference which he felt hamstrung Clinton.
'Politics have not in the least contributed to bring this very important war
to its necessary conclusion, probably have retarded it,' he wrote. 'In
general, I have observed, that when [politicians] interfere with military
operations, they have rather retarded, than accelerated the war.' Lloyd
instead believed that military commanders who were well educated in the
limitations of geography should be left to plan and execute a campaign.
'When an Army is once in the field and the plan of the Campaign settled,
Let the General go on his own way,' he wrote. 'He is on the spot and with
the assistance of his Officers alone can determine what is to be done and
how it is to be done.'[92]

The criticism rang true, and with Britain facing seemingly insurmountable military challenges across the globe, interest gradually increased in the
few British military theorists who might feasibly offer solutions to difficulties posed in America. Lloyd's *History* and the accompanying essay on the
'General Principles of War', in particular, began to sell out. 'At length it
made its way in the world, and the whole edition has long since been sold
off,' Lloyd wrote. 'It was likewise translated into the German Language,
and several thousand copies sold in these last four years. Encouraged by
such marks of public approbation,' Lloyd published an updated version,
which included a new military system that sought to end the decades of
indecisive warfare which had dominated the eighteenth century.[93]

He proposed a significant disruption of the tactical and operational
organisation of an army, including the creation of what might be termed
mixed-order deployments, where skirmishers trained in light infantry
tactics, regular line infantry, artillery and cavalry were distributed in
regular intervals throughout the battlefield.[94] Such deployments might
offer a greater degree of tactical flexibility, and put the emphasis on
manoeuvrability and mobility, but at the expense of a general's ability to
mass firepower, and therefore create shock action, or maintain defensive

strength and cohesion. In France, Jacques Antoine Hippolyte, Comte de Guibert, was developing similar ideas, and Napoleon Bonaparte would deploy mixed-order tactical arrangements, and benefit substantially from the enhanced mobility of his units, resulting in overwhelming battlefield success by the beginning of the nineteenth century.[95]

Perhaps Lloyd's most enduring tactical innovation was the employment of light infantry in the general order of battle, the theoretical and formal embodiment of what had evolved in practice during the course of the French and Indian War. These troops, picked for their intelligence, strength and speed, would be highly trained in the light infantry tactical discipline emerging from North America in the wake of the French and Indian War, but likewise in regular infantry tactical drill, thus enabling the troops to fulfil multiple roles. On campaign, the light infantry would act to protect the army's flank and rear, as well as its logistics train. In battle, the light infantry would act as a skirmishing line, identifying attacking units, shielding the regular infantry for as long as possible from the oncoming attack and disrupting the enemy command. When battle was joined, the light infantry could fall back to support the regular infantry, act as a reserve and plug any emerging gaps in the line.[96] In essence, Lloyd defined the role of light infantry more than 20 years before it became a regular feature of the British order of battle.

The republication of Lloyd's essay on the 'General Principles of War' brought his theories on 'lines of operation' and manoeuvres to a larger audience. Lloyd's theory was easily mischaracterised. One historian claimed that Lloyd was 'obsessed by the eighteenth-century delusion that wars could be won without battles by the simple (and magic) occupation of decisive points'.[97] True enough, Lloyd preferred manoeuvre and believed that clever positioning of an army would negate the need for a battle by persuading an enemy to abandon the fight, but his comments on tactics suggest that he fully expected armies to fight battles, and that they were necessary to achieve decisive success. Indeed, he advocated for the reintroduction of the pike, in the belief that it would prove a superior weapon in close combat.[98] His operational arguments found currency very quickly outside Britain, heavily influencing Dietrich Heinrich von Bülow, a Prussian theorist, who would expand the ideas of lines of operations, manoeuvre and decisive points in his *Spirit of the Modern System of War*, which in turn would heavily influence the thinking of the resurgent school of Prussian military thought in the wake of their total defeat at the hands of Napoleon at the Battle of Jena-Auerstädt in October 1806.[99]

But it was Lloyd's comments on the strategic and political character of war that held most currency. His inspiration was drawn not only from his study of Greek, Roman and early European wars, but also from the theories and writings of his old mentor, Maurice de Saxe, who had commented on the strategic culture of an army itself. Saxe believed that human nature needed to be incorporated into the military model, rather than thrashed out through the rigorous training and discipline policies of the age. This was an argument with which Lloyd would come to agree. He elaborated on Saxe's ideas and developed the concept of 'national character'. In part, he used this argument to criticise the adoption by the British Army of the Prussian system of drill. 'Nature must be improved, not annihilated,' he cautioned.[100] Rather than merely adopt wholesale tactics, techniques and procedures that worked well for one army, Lloyd argued that a nation must find its own way in war.[101] For Britain, this was an ad-hoc informal response, driven by field-based innovation and the exchange of experience-based learning and military knowledge. This process might be slow and imperfect, often producing steep learning curves, but it was frequently stunningly decisive.

Lloyd defined this as the 'philosophy of war', and the concept would garner widespread interest after the publication of his revised history, arguing as it did for a meritocracy, and suggesting controversially that the social inequality endemic in Western Europe, despite the relative political liberty that had developed there in the last century, nevertheless still hindered military development. Lloyd's ideas found a wide readership within the British officer corps of the late eighteenth and early nineteenth century, and there is evidence his works continued to be preferred reading at least until the 1830s.[102] Early versions of his publications were recommended by Field Marshal Sir John Ligonier, prior to his death in 1770.[103] Captain George Smith, inspector of the Royal Military Academy at Woolwich between 1772 and 1783, recommended Lloyd's works to the cadets at the academy. As inspector, he was responsible for the direction of all instruction, had to accompany cadets when they left the academy for field exercises, maintain a military library and recommend 'such books ... as he might think best adapted to the several Capacities and a due Course of Military Knowledge'.[104] More generally, Smith compiled the *Universal Military Dictionary*, published in 1779, which defined 350 pages worth of military terminology, and included 'Some of the best BOOKS on the art of war, in English'. Lloyd's *History of the Late Wars* (a shortened version of the title) appeared here, in a list that was widely distributed throughout the British Army, alongside

Dalrymple's *Military Essays*, a translation of Turpin de Crissé's *Art of War* and *Military Instructions for Officers Detached in the Field*, published in 1770. Elsewhere in the dictionary, terms which Lloyd had coined were given new currency. 'There are two kinds of lines, viz. right lines and curve lines,' Smith explained. 'Right lines are all those which go to the nearest way to any given point. Curve lines are usually divided into geometrical and mechanical.'[105] In this sense, right lines were the lines Lloyd had conceived of as lines of operation – the shortest distance between two decisive points.[106]

Though no formal army-wide military education establishment existed until 1799 for officers outside the ordnance branch, recommendations such as those made by Smith and Ligonier carried weight. Bookshops that served military personnel picked up such recommendations and passed them on to their clientele. On 6 June 1796, a 28-year-old lieutenant-colonel of the 33rd Regiment of Foot, named Arthur Wesley, having recently received notice of his deployment to India, spent the not insubstantial sum of £58 2s 6d on a collection of books to accompany him on his voyage east. The young colonel bought the library on the advice of the trusted bookseller Mr. Faulder of Bond Street. Besides the classics, Frederick the Great's writings and less well-known books on the politics and military affairs of the subcontinent was Henry Lloyd's *History of the Late War in Germany*.[107] The young colonel was reasonably well-connected politically, but had yet to demonstrate any significant military prowess, besides learning 'what not to do' in the Low Countries the year before. That, like his name, was set to change while he was in India.

Elsewhere, Lloyd's arguments were exchanged in the professional networks of the junior ranks of the army. In preparation for his deployment to the Peninsula in 1811, Ensign Thomas Mitchell of the 95th Rifles kept copious notes of his education and training. Lloyd was the principal source on which Mitchell relied during his time in Portugal and Spain, and the theories on training and education, geography and politics, resonated with the young officer. He noted 84 maxims derived from Lloyd's *History*, including, for example, views on the manoeuvrability and order of troops in battle. 'The perfection of an order of battle consists of placing both cavalry & infantry into line', Mitchell noted, 'in such a manner that they may afford aid & support to each other, and that their efforts may be combined & directed to the same points. "It is the unit of action which can alone secure victory," . . . Lloyd apprehends.'[108]

Mitchell was seconded to the Quartermaster General's Department, where he, like Lloyd more than six decades earlier, produced sketches and maps of the terrain in which the army was to operate. For Mitchell, like Lloyd, 'Rivers, woods, ravines, mountains . . . together form the great book of war; and he who cannot read it must for ever be content with the title of a brave soldier, and never repair to that of a great general.'[109] If the physical space in which battles were fought provided practical examples of warfighting for later visitors, and books offered the conceptual underpinning for generation of new military knowledge, maps offered 'a form of instant shorthand and a lingua franca to the military officers of the period'.[110] Accessing and examining maps therefore became a universal means of learning from history, and these too underwent a significant transformation in the course of the eighteenth century.

* * *

As with the transformation in military thinking and the evolution in critical approaches to the construction of military history, map-making underwent a significant change from the middle of the eighteenth century. The introduction of common symbols, standard training for surveyors, colour-coding and the application of mathematical formulae, astronomical calculations and the latest scientific principles to the creation of maps meant that they were both more accurate and more readable. As a soldier who was profoundly interested in the professional study of war, the Duke of Cumberland acquired over the course of his career thousands of maps depicting battles and military campaigns.

In 1746, Cumberland had been appointed Ranger of Windsor Great Park, a position which carried with it the residence of Windsor Great Lodge, and maps and books of military significance were a prominent feature of its library. An observant visitor might have noticed hanging on the wall a plan of Dettingen, the battle fought in 1743 at which Cumberland's father, King George II, had commanded. A model of a Vauban-designed fortification and a scene from Culloden could be found elsewhere in the Lodge. Cumberland saw himself as a professional military officer and surrounded himself with what he perceived to be the greatest conveyor of military knowledge: maps. They were the universal language of the soldier. Cartography was one of the most common means of accessing military knowledge in the eighteenth century, and although there was growing interest in military history and treatises on the art of war, maps were instantly and universally recognisable. Most, if not all, military personnel would be able to glean something from them.

To that end, in 1747, Cumberland commissioned a huge renovation project for the Great Lodge. The library was redesigned to include purpose-built facilities for the display of a huge map collection. Visitors who were invited to inspect the collection sat on mahogany 'banister back chairs with black leather seats brass Nail'd', and around an extendable mahogany table designed to hold the largest of the maps. The table also came with specially adapted partitions for storage of the collection. If joint viewing was desired, there were two 'Mahog[any] Pillars with cross pieces to hang up Maps'.[111] The range of maps collected by Cumberland illustrated the breadth and diversity of his interest in the subject, and his eagerness to learn, and to foster in others the desire to learn, about the military profession. It also reflected the transformation in military cartography during the eighteenth-century Enlightenment.[112] Cumberland's map room, and the collection it housed, served as a catalogue of this transformation.

Maps could be used to convey different aspects of the military experience: pictorial or artistic maps helped the viewer understand the magnitude of the battle, the way in which the army interacted with terrain and how commanders made decisions. More detailed, symbolic maps often contained the full order of battle for each protagonist, as well as the deployment of various units in the precise locations on the fields. Where the pictorial but possibly inaccurate maps offered a glimpse of the art of war, the use of symbols and the emphasis on precision communicated its science. They also conveyed the progress of battle, with different dispositions indicating the evolution of the fighting.[113] Indeed, Cumberland's map collection contained information on every aspect of the profession of arms: from the planning of operations to tactical deployment on the battlefield; from the most suitable location for building supply depots to the most efficient arrangement of headquarters; from the optimum design of topographical plans to understanding arcs of fire.

The maps themselves also charted the changing character of warfare in the second half of the eighteenth century, with plans of fortifications dominating the collection dating from the first half of the eighteenth century.[114] Maps depicting mid-century wars, and those added to the collections after Cumberland's death, focused more on the tactical details of battle. Gradually campaign maps, which depicted the movements of armies toward battle, began to occur more frequently, reflecting the transition from positional, siege-focused warfare to campaigns based on manoeuvre that emphasised the mobility and flexibility of an army. Cartographic training, however, did not keep pace with these developments, and the focus on surveys prior to the outbreak of hostilities continued to be on fortifications and defensible locations until well into the second half of the century. Instead, it was the experience of warfare itself, as practised by the military engineers, surveyors and cartographers attached to the army, that helped transform the way maps depicted war, and with it, the developing archive of military knowledge.

Frustrated by the poor nature of the formal cartographical training output of the Royal Military Academy in Woolwich, George Townshend, Master General of the Ordnance from 1772, turned to the Drawing Room of the Tower of London as a means of furnishing the army with suitably trained draftsmen and map-makers. Established in 1717, the Drawing Room of the Tower of London was responsible for the drawing, compilation and storage of maps of Britain's military exploits. From 1752 it was gradually expanded in size and professionalised the role of military draftsmen. The training regimen included field visits which instructed the draftsmen in the merits of the French method of learning by doing, an approach increasingly admired within British military circles following French successes on the continent in the War of Austrian Succession. As a result of Townshend's training reforms, cadets who attended the Drawing Room had the knowledge and ability to create their own surveys and correct inaccuracies in the products of others. Nearly thirty draftsmen were trained at the Tower Drawing Room in 1759, rising to 48 by 1780. As many as a third of those who trained there obtained commissions in the army, and went on to furnish maps to British generals across the empire. The business of map-making for military purposes was therefore treated seriously.[115]

The reform of the education and training at the Drawing Room coincided with the emergence of a European cartographic tradition in the eighteenth century. Driven partly by new print technologies, improved education, economic diversification and the emergence of humanist culture as part of the Enlightenment, public, as well as political, interest in maps accelerated sharply in the eighteenth century. As a result, maps became the dominant vehicle for the transmission of ideas of geography, culture and the political interaction with newly discovered space.[116] Standardised symbols, colours and drawing techniques all allowed for a universal understanding of maps for the purposes of siegecraft, reconnaissance, route and encampment selection, campaign planning and coastal charting.[117] As understanding and perceptions of the use of colour evolved in the eighteenth century, and pigments became more affordable, manuals on military map colour-coding facilitated increasingly sophisticated map design and drawing.[118]

Eighteenth-century military cartographic education, then, and the maps produced as a result, became extremely powerful tools for political purposes, widely used in the extension and reinforcement of imperial power. Evidence suggests, however, that this was not so much the case for the application of military power. Despite the evident desire for maps for the purposes of campaign planning and decision making, the majority of maps were necessarily of static locations, such as forts, that could be besieged as part of a campaign. Map-making did not, therefore, maintain pace with the emergence of mobile warfare in the revolutionary era. Battles and campaigns were often fought on unmapped terrain and hasty sketches were completed as the campaign was in progress, rather than before its commencement. An experienced draftsman might be able to produce a detailed but inexact sketch of a battlefield in perhaps one day, but by then the battle was often over or had moved on. Maps were not, then, of much utility in campaign planning. Rather, it was for education and learning, as Cumberland envisaged with the creation of his map library in Windsor Great Lodge, that maps had most utility in the eighteenth century. Nevertheless, the surveys were also the product of the latest scientific endeavours and techniques, and they marked the intersection of military, scientific and imperial knowledge networks, which saw Britain overtake France as the pre-eminent scientific power in the second half of the eighteenth century. Combined, these elements illustrated Britain's global ambitions, at the centre of which was the British military.[119]

Nevertheless, the evolution of map-making in the eighteenth century was also closely linked with military operations and imperial expansion. The experience of the wars in North America between 1754 and 1781, and the concurrent expansion of British interests in South Asia, fundamentally transformed the character of map-making, and the use to which maps were put, both by the military and the state. War had 'incited us to survey', wrote Samuel Johnson in 1756, 'by stronger motives than mere science of curiosity could ever have supplied'.[120] Almost all aspects of military knowledge essential to the successful prosecution of a campaign could be captured and transmitted in a map, whether it be for logistical planning, siege works and defences or detailed road and river information to facilitate a campaign involving the movement of thousands of soldiers.

This was perhaps most clearly illustrated by the evolution of map-making in South Asia. The peace in North America between 1760 and 1775 had perpetuated a period of stagnation in both the thinking about war and in the creation of maps to aid in the preparation for war. British soldiers, and with them their cartographers, appeared to privilege the prospect of static and positional warfare, based on the capture of territory, rather than the emerging focus on the operational mobility of an army. This is perhaps unsurprising given the prevalence of siege warfare during the war against the French and Native Americans between 1755 and 1760, though the lessons of manoeuvre and rapid mobility were evident in the growing importance of light infantry to all aspects of military operations by the end of the war. In contrast, military cartography in India during the same period, where periods of peace were considerably more limited, evolved to produce maps that proved of immense value to military preparations, though here, as in America, the pathway to such innovations was by no means straightforward, a situation which historian Matthew Edney has termed 'cartographic anarchy'.[121]

During his second term of office in India, Robert Clive appointed James Rennell as surveyor general in 1767. Rennell had trained in the Royal Navy before securing a position in the Bengal army. He immediately set about compiling a comprehensive survey of the East India Company's possessions in Bengal. He drew on a variety of cartographic methods in drawing his maps. Starting with earlier maps, historical data and indigenous maps, he proceeded to measure distances along roads, establishing the coordinates of control points from which he could scale his drawings. He then created a 'graticule' or grid system to enable him to create his maps.[122] In 1775, as he prepared to depart India, Rennell submitted a complete set of provincial maps to the Governor General, with a scale of five miles to an inch.[123] Five years later, he published *A Bengal Atlas*, which would remain the standard administrative map of Bengal for almost five decades.[124]

Rennell's successor as surveyor general, Colonel John Call, focused his attention on the compilation of an atlas of the whole of India. His deputies commenced surveys of parts of the subcontinent that had so far remained poorly mapped. However, the outbreak of war with the Marathas in 1775, and Mysore in 1780, furnished a new opportunity for surveys to be conducted for specifically military purposes. At Madras, Lieutenant John Pringle was appointed to command a new 'Corps of Guides & Hircarrahs' and began compiling details of routes along which forces could be marched, and he 'measured & made his Remarks upon more than

600 miles of Roads, besides the actual Survey of Annacutty, &c'.[125] Here, in the close on-the-spot cooperation between army operational decision makers and their cartographers, is evidence of the production of maps of significant operational utility. During the Second Anglo-Mysore War, Pringle 'surveyed the marches of the army under Sir Eyre Coote' and 'has ascertained some interesting geographical positions ... and by this means extended very considerably the dimensions of what may be called the *Surveyed tract* ...'.[126] At the conclusion of the war, Pringle drew a map of the routes of Coote's army which attempted to depict in one map the major manoeuvres of the British force.[127]

Further maps of Mysore were completed during the Third Anglo-Mysore War (1790–1792). During the two-season campaign, Captain Alexander Beatson, who had succeeded Pringle in command of the Corps of Guides, made a meticulous 'Geographical Observation in Mysore ... with an examination of the Passes', to which he added 'some Military sketches of Hill Forts & of Seringapatam', the capital of Mysore. These were later described as a 'monument of great industry, skill, and minute accuracy'.[128] As Pringle had for the Second Anglo-Mysore War, at the end of the third, Beatson completed a map of the 'Marches of the British Armies in the Peninsula of India', which was published to illustrate Rennell's *Marches of the British Armies*. This was a work of military topographical history, which began to close the gap between the static military topographies prevalent in North America and the mobile warfare which had now emerged in the campaigns in India.[129]

Pringle and Beatson are significant because the maps and plans they drew illustrate the organic evolution of the character of warfare from static and positional confrontations to ones focused on increased mobility and manoeuvrability. Cartographers in North America had found it difficult to furnish maps with the sort of detail and information needed to facilitate such operations, but in India, the focus on the trappings of manoeuvre – roads, rivers, suitable encampment sites, supply depots and economic and social information – had been quickly integrated into map drawing, principally because of the close relationship between the map-makers and the decision makers. This evolution also matched the shift in the meaning of the term 'terrain' in military discourse throughout the eighteenth century. As historians Catriona Kennedy and Anders Engberg-Petersen have demonstrated, in the first half of the century, the term referred to the ground in the immediate vicinity of fortifications. By the end of the century, however, the term had evolved as a sort of 'shorthand for topographical space'.[130] Such detailed maps would also prove useful as tools for learning and understanding how to conduct manoeuvre warfare.

*　*　*

If North America proved to be a laboratory for the creation of and experimentation with new military knowledge and innovations in the British Army, and South Asia provided opportunities for further refinement and adaptation, it was to wars in Europe that personnel turned for more formal avenues of military education and learning. Officers with means and the inclination to do so could avail themselves of the opportunity to visit former battlefields, accompanied by veterans and informed by books and lavish maps.

Officers of more modest means, as well as the common soldier, were denied such opportunities. For them, the only option for formal military education, at least before 1799 and the establishment of the Royal Military College in High Wycombe, was infrequently organised military encampments. Such events were common occurrences on the continent. The future Duke of York frequently visited such encampments during his military education in Germany in the 1780s. At one in May 1783, he met Frederick the Great himself, 'a short and small but wonderfully strong man, not very well upon his legs', the young prince observed.[131]

After inspecting Prussian army units and observing examples of intensive infantry training, Prince Frederick was impressed by the resulting calibre of the soldiers, noting, for example, 'how exceedingly well they aim'.[132] Two years later, when visiting an encampment in Silesia, Frederick observed, and appeared impressed by, the tactical manoeuvring of the infantry.[133] On one occasion, this involved a mock battlefield simulation with a line of infantry numbering some 11,000 men drawn up in two lines, supported by 15 squadrons of cavalry.[134] This would confirm the future Duke as a great advocate for the discipline and tactics of Frederick the Great's Prussia. Based on his experience of the battlefields of Europe during the Seven Years' War, and his observations of modern Prussian infantry training, York came to believe that a standardised drill practice had 'the essential purpose' of promoting 'Uniformity in the Discipline of the Troops'.[135]

In Britain, however, encampments were more often hastily organised as war loomed. At the outset of the Seven Years' War, for example, Prussian tactical drill methods were demonstrated by Hessian battalions at the Blandford encampment in the summer of 1756.[136] James Wolfe, who was in attendance, was particularly impressed by 'their steadiness under Arms, & strict attention is worthy of imitation, and, the exact knowledge that every Officer has of his own part is exemplary'.[137] Indeed, Wolfe became increasingly convinced that the same approach to training and discipline needed to be adopted throughout the British Army, not least because, as he wrote to the Duke of Richmond, 'natural courage seldome prevails against experience & military knowledge'.[138] At a second encampment, held at Barham Downs in September 1757, General Sir John Mordaunt, commander of the British expeditionary force who ordered to attack French coastal positions, had adopted the alternate-fire system as standard. 'This is truly great and you have no idea how much it has already improved the other regiments,' wrote one enthusiast. 'This is all against order, and some persons are amazed that Sir John Mordaunt will undertake it. I admire him for it.'[139]

Military encampments, then, frequently served as sponsors of innovation. In the summer of 1774, Major General Sir William Howe, veteran of Quebec and Havana, staged one of the most realistic encampments for the purposes of training the British Army in the eighteenth century.[140] In the words of one participant, the exercise 'consisted of a set of manoeuvres for light infantry, and was ordered by his Majesty to be practised in the different regiments. ... The manoeuvres were chiefly intended for woody and intricate districts, with which North America abounds, where an army cannot act in line.' The explicit objective was to trial 'this excellent mode of discipline for light troops and render it general without delay',[141] by integrating the American version of light infantry into the regular order of battle of the British Army.[142] The encampment culminated on 3 October 1774 with a mock battle, held in the presence of King George III, at Richmond Park, London. Among various tasks, units of at least seven regiments were to perform various manoeuvres derived from Howe's experience in North America.[143] For example, they were to 'march thro' the wood in extended order, halt at the edge of it, Tree and Fire by Files'.[144] The verb, 'to tree' or 'tree-all', which had emerged in North America, was the practice of using trees as cover to aim and fire as accurately as possible, and reload sheltered from the enemy.[145]

The obvious success and adaptability of Howe's light infantry drill cemented his reputation as an innovative general, brave both in the face of resistance to reform at home and in battle against enemies abroad. 'His Majesty himself went to [Richmond] to see them, and was much pleased with their utility, and the manner of their execution,' noted Corporal Roger Lamb.[146] In the wake of the royal review, the War Office ordered light infantry drills be adopted across the Army, with expert companies training others in their brigade.[147] In so doing, knowledge and understanding of the tactics was disseminated from regiment to regiment. The 9th Regiment of Foot, for example, was trained by the 33rd (who themselves had been trained by one of the regiments that attended the camp at Salisbury). 'The 33rd was in a high state of appointment, and exceedingly well disciplined,' noted Lamb. 'I never witnessed any regiment that excelled it in discipline and military appearance.' Having attended the Salisbury camp himself, and having now also received training directly from the 33rd Regiment, Lamb became one of the experts in light infantry discipline in the 9th:

> After I had acquired a knowledge of the new discipline from the noncommissioned officers of the 33rd regiment, I was appointed to take charge of a squad of our regiment, and executed that important and laborious task to the best of my ability. The constant attendance and habit of exercise is almost every thing in the soldier's life; and it is indeed surprising to see how soon an awkward young man becomes well disciplined, performs his evolutions with a neat agility, and handles his arms with a graceful dexterity.[148]

By March 1775, these exercises were being practised in New England. On a visit to Boston, the American merchant Robert Honyman observed units from the British Army exercising. 'Some of the regiments were extremely expert in their exercises & the manoeuvres & manner of fighting of the Light Infantry was exceedingly curious,' he recorded in his diary on 2 March. 'Every regiment here has a company of Light Infantry, young active fellows & they run out in parties on the wings of the regiment where they keep up a constant & irregular fire.' In addition, Honyman noted that 'they secure their retreat & defend their front while they are forming; in one part of their exercise they ly on their backs & charge their pieces & fire on their bellies.'[149]

With tensions mounting between the British government and its colonies in North America, it is unsurprising that the commander-in-chief, General Sir Thomas Gage, instituted a training regimen designed to prepare new soldiers and remind veterans of the particular challenges of fighting in America. The British Army was never particularly good at maintaining tactical standards in periods of peace, but the evidence suggests that if it was not at the peak fighting condition it had achieved by 1763, the British Army in North America was more effectively prepared for the oncoming conflict than some historians have suggested.[150] More importantly, those officers with the greatest experience of fighting there were selected for the command in North America, theoretically at least ensuring the maintenance of relevant professional networks, and the continued exchange of military knowledge.

In June 1775, news had arrived in London that tensions in North America over taxation, quartering and territorial expansion had finally boiled over into violence.[151] Gage's tiny force of regular troops had been defeated at a running skirmish between the towns of Lexington and Concord. The news caused a degree of consternation in London, and the consensus appeared to be that Gage, who had succeeded Amherst as commander-in-chief in 1763, was not up to the job. 'I must lament that General Gage, with all his good qualitys, finds himself in a situation of too great importance for his talents,' wrote Lord George Germain, who was soon to be appointed Secretary of State for the American Colonies. 'The conduct of such a war requires more than common abilities.' William Howe was considered the obvious choice to succeed Gage, given his personal experience of war in America. 'The manner of opposing an enemy that avoid facing you in the open field is totally different from what young officers learn from the common discipline of the army,' Germain explained.

> Mr Braddock first suffered in the last war by a surprize from the Indians, and his little army sacrifiz'd without seeing an enemy, and by keeping together and firing in bodys, could neither defend themselves or annoy their opponents. Another discipline was then establish'd and all our light troops in America were taught to separate and secure themselves by trees, walls, or hedges, and became so formidable both to the Indians and Canadians that they were victorious upon all occasions, and ever protected the main body of the army from surprize or insult. Nobody understands that discipline so well as General Howe, who had the command of the light troops, and who will, I am persuaded, teach the present army to be as formidable as that he formerly acted with.[152]

On 18 April 1775, Howe set sail for North America aboard the *Cerberus*, accompanied by Henry Clinton and John Burgoyne. Howe was seen as a path-breaking innovator: a key proponent of light infantry, a highly experienced veteran of multiple theatres and a great leader of men. He carried with him a dormant commission to succeed Gage as commander-in-chief, should the latter resign or be incapacitated. Clinton was appointed third-in-command and would become Howe's deputy should the latter become commander-in-chief. Both Clinton and Burgoyne had demonstrated an acute professional interest in the military sciences, were widely read in the history of war, and in the latest theories emerging from the continent. They were consequently well known for their innovative views on the future direction of the British Army. There was little to indicate that under the command of these generals, the British Army would suffer calamitous defeat.

What might this trio of forward-thinking generals have discussed during the weeks-long voyage to America? Clinton kept records of some of the conversations. 'At first . . . I kept my distance', he wrote to his close friend and confidante, William Phillips. He 'seldom spoke until my two colleagues forced me out'. When the three eventually did discuss their views on how to prosecute the war, they found they agreed on little. 'We of course differ often in opinion,' he wrote, 'but in such a manner as, I am sure, I receive great benefit from.'[153] In reality, the personal and professional differences between these three men would derail British strategy. They were also indicative of a wider intellectual schism in the strategic thinking of the British Army.

CHAPTER 4

'No Idea of Any Other Than a Direct Attack'

WILLIAM HOWE IN AMERICA, 1774–1777

SHORTLY after their arrival in North America, Howe, Clinton and Burgoyne found themselves in the midst of the ongoing siege of Boston. The city was overlooked to the north and south by hills, command of either of which would offer the Americans the ability to bombard both the city and the harbour. General Sir Thomas Gage, the British commander-in-chief, had been preparing to occupy the Dorchester Heights, which commanded the harbour to the south of Boston, when news was received that the Americans were building a redoubt on top of Breed's Hill, which commanded the harbour to the north. Howe advocated landing at the base of the hill and launching a frontal assault on the redoubt as quickly as possible.

Clinton suggested outflanking the American position at Breed's Hill, but Gage dismissed the plan, thinking 'himself so well informed that he would not take any opinion of others, particularly of a man bred up in the German School, which that of America affects to despise'.[1] Howe argued he had insufficient high-sided landing craft to protect his men as they came within range of enemy musketry, so Gage agreed to Howe's frontal assault.[2] Clinton concluded that his colleagues had 'no idea of any other than a direct at[tack]'.[3]

Howe selected the light companies of the 5th and 38th Regiments for the initial assault, followed by soldiers from the 43rd and 52nd Regiments, who would land in a second wave.[4] Once ashore, the British formed three lines. As they approached the American position, 'it was clearly seen that the rebels were in force and strongly entrenched' in a 600-yard line running over the hill from Charlestown to the Mystik River.[5]

Realising he was too weak, Howe requested reinforcements which when they arrived increased his force to 2,200 troops, arranged in two rather than three lines; a disposition which Burgoyne described as 'extremely soldier-like; in my opinion it was perfect'.[6] As Howe prepared to open the attack, he addressed his men, reportedly telling them: 'I shall not desire one of you to go a step farther where I go myself at your head'.[7] Howe was as good as his word and led the main assault, which advanced 'slowly and frequently halting to give time for the artillery to fire'.[8]

As the troops advanced, they encountered obstacles which disrupted their cohesion. 'Their orders were executed ... with a laudable perseverance, but not with the greatest share of discipline,' Howe wrote privately to the Adjutant-General, Edward Harvey. The troops on Howe's left, commanded by General Sir Robert Pigot, also sustained casualties from musket fire from houses in Charlestown. As the advance stalled, 'there was *a Moment that I never felt before ...*' Howe exclaimed.[9] Although the British troops were evidently not trained to the standards Howe expected, it is difficult to argue that any infantry force, no matter how well-trained, could have overcome the obstacles faced by the British on Breed's Hill without incurring significant casualties. This was not a tactical or a training failure, but a command failure: the decision to launch a frontal assault overestimated the quality of the attackers and underestimated the quality of the defenders.

The battle began to turn in Howe's favour, however, after Clinton, who was observing from the sidelines, ordered Charlestown be set ablaze, forcing the Americans to withdraw from the left flank. Pigot pressed on to carry the Breed's Hill redoubt 'in a very handsome manner, at the *second* onset, tho' it was most obstinately defended to the last, thirty of the rebels having been killed by bayonets within it'.[10] After the breakthrough on the left, Howe's light infantry recovered and launched a second assault to complete the capture of the redoubt on Breed's Hill. 'The Rebels were then forced from other strong holds,' Gage reported in his account of the battle, 'and pursued till they were drove clear off the Peninsula, leaving five pieces of Cannon behind them.'[11]

Known as the Battle of Bunker Hill, after the adjacent hill, the first major action of what became known as the American Revolutionary War had been a desperately bloody affair. 'The Success', Howe wrote, was 'too dearly bought'.[12] The British suffered 160 rank and file killed and 300 wounded, along with 92 officers, among them Captain George Harris of the 5th Foot, who, as he entered the breach in the redoubt defences, received a severe wound 'when a ball grazed the top of my head, and I fell deprived of sense and motion'. He was carried unconscious to a field hospital, where 'the surgeons did not at first apprehend danger from the contusion, notwithstanding the extreme pain I felt' but after they observed

> symptoms of matter forming (which, had it fallen on the brain, must have produced instant death, or at least distraction), performed the operation of trepanning, from which time the pain abated, and I began to recover; but before the callous was formed, they indulged me with the gratification of a singular curiosity – fixing looking glasses so as to give me a sight of my own brain.[13]

Reflecting on the battle, Howe wrote 'when I look to the consequences of it . . . I do it with horror'.[14] There is little doubt that his personal experience of Bunker Hill, and the heavy losses his men sustained, had a significant impact on Howe's military thinking. The casualty rate arguably made him risk-averse, and in particular hesitant to launch frontal assaults on fortified positions. Howe's personal experience at the end of the previous war also supported this conclusion. Though successful, the siege of Havana between 7 June and 18 October 1762 had cost the British 5,366 casualties.[15] Howe had commanded a wing of the army deployed to lay siege to the Spanish stronghold, and would have noted the high costs of taking such fortifications. Nevertheless, both the capture of Havana and the capture of Quebec in 1759 illustrated how effective a set-piece military action could be. Howe's experience taught him that the capture of vital terrain could have a decisive impact on the course of a war, but that the cost of such activity was likely to be high. Any attempt to capture such targets would therefore need to be undertaken in extremely favourable circumstances, or when the benefits of doing so significantly outweighed the consequences. Attempting to identify the correct balance was extremely difficult, and would blight Howe's command in North America.

Besides ignoring Clinton's suggested outflanking manoeuvre, historians have criticised Howe for incorrectly using specialist and light troops as regular infantry for assaults on heavily fortified and defended positions,[16] but this overlooks the fact that he had trained light infantry troops to do precisely this at the Salisbury encampment the year before.[17] Superior tactics and discipline, however, would not protect troops from the surprisingly effective fire which the Americans had been able to bring to bear against the British. Indeed, innovative tactics would prove wholly less useful than innovative strategising. Howe might well have developed a justifiable aversion to frontal assaults, but he remained focused on the conquest of territory as a strategy for victory – an approach which had worked against France in the previous war but would prove unsuccessful in the war against the Americans. By focusing on terrain as his principle objective, Howe developed an approach which allowed him to capture objectives while avoiding large set-piece battles, where the risk of unsustainable casualties was high. But such a strategy allowed the American army to survive, and with it the rebellion.

In the wake of the bloodbath at Bunker Hill, the government acted on the increasingly widely held belief that Gage was not up to the job. He was recalled and replaced by his second-in-command. On paper at least, Howe assumed the command at a point when Britain had the best chance of defeating the American rebellion. Britain was encumbered by no other military commitments, and its only focus need be the restoration of royal authority in North America. But Howe was not an innovative strategist, and he would squander many opportunities to defeat the rebellion.

* * *

Howe now focused on remedying his concern that his army lacked sufficient training to prosecute the war, but in doing so neglected to take sufficient precautions for the safety of the British position in Boston. In March 1776, the Americans occupied the Dorchester Heights, which commanded the city, and with them in American hands, the British position became untenable. Howe was forced to evacuate Boston and withdraw to Halifax. Initially, at least, he remained convinced that the only way to bring about an end to the war was the defeat of the American army. 'The scene here at present wears a lowering aspect,' he wrote to Germain, 'there not being the least prospect of conciliating this Continent until its armies shall have been roughly dealt with.' He was apprehensive 'that such an event will not be readily brought about; the rebels get on apace, and knowing their advantages in having the whole country, as it were, at their disposal, they will not be readily brought into a situation where the King's troops can meet them upon equal terms'.[18]

Moreover, Howe had been called upon to make significant detachments to the south and north. First, Clinton had been sent to support a rumoured Loyalist uprising in North Carolina, and then five regiments were to be sent to help defend Quebec. 'If a respectable supply of Troops from Europe does not arrive soon in the Spring,' Howe warned, 'another

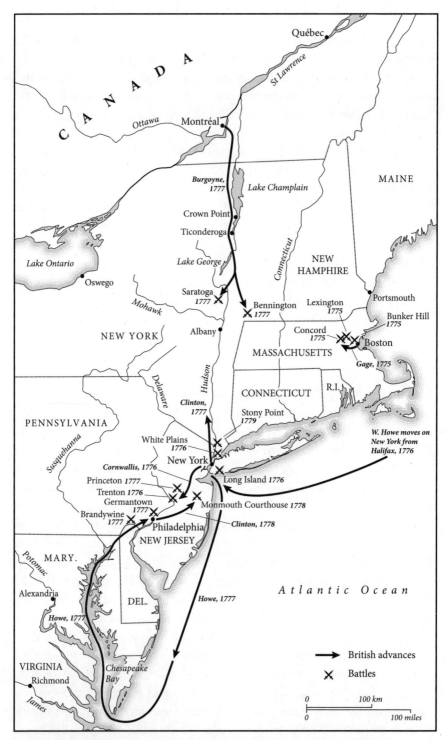

Map 3. British Campaigns in the American Revolutionary War, 1775–1779.

defensive Campaign, I conclude, will be the consequence.' In such circumstances, the Americans would 'have full Time to entrench in every strong position their Commanders may fix upon, in which case, tho' we should get possession of New York without resistance, we must not expect to carry their entrenched Camps but with considerable Loss'. Were he adequately reinforced, however, and able to deploy 'a proper army of 20,000 Men', he believed 'the present unfavourable appearance of things would probably wear a very different aspect before the end of the ensuing Campaign'. The British could then reasonably expect 'by rapid Movements [to] bring the Rebels to an Action upon equal terms', but 'with Fewer Troops, the success of any offensive operations will be very doubtful'.[19]

Howe valued experience and knowledge of the fighting methods employed in America, so he requested 'some old and experienced Officers upon this Duty'.[20] The government was at least able to scrape together a composite battalion of the Guards, whose troops were highly experienced, though not necessarily in the specifics of North America.[21] For the majority of the reinforcements, however, the government was relying on German mercenaries, but it was not until March 1776 that an agreement was reached to employ 12,200 Hessian troops in America.[22] As these forces would need to be first transported to England, and then onward to America, the prospects of them reaching Howe in the spring were negligible (indeed, the first Hessians did not arrive until 12 August). The delay contributed to frosty relations between Howe and Germain. The situation was not helped by evident strain between Howe and the Hessian commanding officer, Lieutenant General Philip von Heister, from the moment of the latter's arrival. Von Heister demanded a period of recuperation for his troops following their long journey, but Howe wanted them immediately in action. Their personalities clashed as well. Howe preferred informality, while von Heister was described by Howe's aide-de-camp as 'a stiff and completely militarily minded general'.[23] By the end of the year, Howe 'tremble[d] when [he thought Heister] may remain with us another campaign. He is exceedingly unsteady and so entirely averse to carry the Hessians into action, I must be very anxious for his removal'.[24]

Following the withdrawal to Halifax, Howe did at least take the opportunity to refresh his men's training. From mid- to late April, each regiment received one day of drill exercise, which Howe slightly amended to prepare the regular infantry for service in America. 'Regts when formed by Company's in Battn, or when on the General Parade, are always to have their File 18 Inches distant from each other,' Howe ordered, 'which they will take care to practice for the future, being the Order in w[hi]ch they are to Engage the Enemy.'[25] Though still six inches closer than the spacing regulated by Howe's Salisbury training manual, the increased distances between troops was a clear nod towards the challenges presented by the terrain in North America.[26] The light infantry companies, meanwhile, were separated from their parent regiments and reorganised into two battalions. Howe also ordered that they receive two days of exercise. In a related acknowledgement of the unique conditions faced in North America, marksmanship was also improved. 'The Commandg Officers of Corps to practice their Recruits & drafts in fireing at marks, and may, when they think it necessary, order the whole out for that purpose . . . .'[27]

None of this would matter, however, if Howe did not receive reinforcements. He had originally planned to begin the campaign in April, but already this ambition had slipped, and with it the extent of the objectives he considered feasible to achieve in 1776.[28] Having evacuated Boston, Howe's objective was the capture of New York. He also planned to use the troops formerly assigned to the garrison of Boston to capture Rhode Island, including the extensive harbour at Newport.[29]

Once New York was in British hands, Howe planned to turn his attention to the Hudson River. 'This Corps to be employed in opening a communication with Canada in the first instance, leaving five Battalions for the Defence of the city of New York.' In Canada, Howe anticipated an army of 7,000, including 4,000 Canadian troops. This force would strike south to link up the army from New York, and establish waterborne communications along the Hudson, severing those of the Americans between the middle colonies and New England. The Hudson strategy, as it has been dubbed, was designed to isolate what was perceived to be the epicentre of the rebellion from the rest of the colonies.[30] Either support for the rebellion would wither on the vine or the newly appointed commander-in-chief of the Continental Army, General George Washington, would be forced to seek a decisive battle to reopen these crucial communications.[31]

The merits of the strategy have been long debated, with several historians concluding that capturing the Hudson river and cutting American communications never held any prospect of success. Prominent Americans were nevertheless concerned. John Adams considered the Hudson to be 'a kind of key to the whole continent' and Thomas Jefferson believed that if the British captured the river, it would 'ruin America'. Washington, meanwhile, was equally concerned. 'The importance of the North [Hudson]

River in the present contest, and the necessity of defending it are subjects which have been so frequently and so fully discussed, and are so well understood, that it is unnecessary to enlarge upon them,' Washington argued. 'The possession of it is indispensably essential to preserve the communication between the eastern, middle and southern states; and further, that upon its security, in a great measure, depend our chief supplies of flour for the subsistence of such force, as we may have occasion for, in the course of the war....'[32]

The delayed arrival of the reinforcements, however, forced Howe to limit his objectives to the capture of New York and Rhode Island. He had to wait for Clinton's return from the south, where an attempt to capture the city of Charleston in South Carolina had turned into a debacle. With their arrival, along with the Guards and the Hessians from Europe, Howe began preparations for an attack in August. New York occupied the southern tip of Manhattan, or York Island, and was cut off from New Jersey to the west by the Hudson River (frequently referred to as the North River), and separated from Long Island by the East River. Outside the city, the terrain on Manhattan was rugged, rising to high ground at Harlem in the north. One British soldier observed that 'every advantage Nature gave, has been improved to the best advantage by those Scoundrels, who if they could fight as they work might defy any Power in the World'.[33] Howe himself described the country as 'so covered with wood swamps, and creeks, that is not open in the least degree to be known ... from accounts to be collected from the inhabitants entirely ignorant of military discipline'.[34]

The only physical connection between Manhattan and New Jersey was via two bridges at Westchester County, at the northern tip of the Island. Brooklyn Heights on Long Island overlooked the city, so these were fortified by redoubts and entrenchments. To protect against a landward assault, a further chain of entrenchments ran in front of the heights across the Brooklyn peninsula.[35] Surrounded as it was by navigable waters on all sides, and with the high ground in Brooklyn extremely vulnerable, Manhattan presented a defensive problem for the Americans. Washington recognised this and determined that if the British were going to capture it, they should do so at a high price.[36]

Howe was therefore deeply concerned about unsustainable losses. He recognised that the army was 'the stock upon which the national force in America must in future be grafted'.[37] Clinton also understood this perspective, and initially advocated focusing on the New Jersey bridges, either by landing on the northern tip of Manhattan or on the opposite shore where high ground could be used to command the bridges.[38] Howe seemingly misunderstood the significance of such a move, seeing it only as a means of interrupting the American supply line to Manhattan. He preferred, largely because his experience suggested it would work, a more direct assault on the enemy defences at Long Island, in order to facilitate a subsequent attack on Manhattan.[39]

He also had concerns about the discipline and reliability of his forces, which had not been tested in battle since their mediocre performance at Bunker Hill. Flanking manoeuvres were complex operations requiring the coordination of multiple detachments, all of which had to remain disciplined: any lapse could cause the whole plan to unravel. The British Army provided no professional training for planning such tasks, instead relying on the combination of experience and personal self-education. Warfare in North America presented few if any opportunities to study such operations. The combination of these factors – concern about unsustainable casualties, inexperience in conducting flanking manoeuvres, and a nagging worry that his army was not yet sufficiently disciplined in battle – caused Howe to become perhaps excessively risk-averse.

By contrast, Clinton, having served in Europe during the Seven Years War and studied European military history and theory extensively, was well informed on how to plan and execute a flanking manoeuvre, and, free from the political shackles of the chief command, was willing to be more innovative. 'Though most people think we should, I am clear we should not land' on Manhattan, 'and I am equally clear the island of New York may be ours without any loss', by turning the American flank and landing forces on Long Island. In so doing, the British would take possession of all the high ground overlooking Manhattan: the Americans would have no choice but to withdraw.[40] 'The Corps which turns this flank must be in very great force, for reasons obvious.'[41]

At headquarters, the initial reception was muted. Clinton was 'savouring too much of the German school' in proposing yet another turning movement. 'As the rebels knew nothing of turning a flank,' Howe purportedly (and ridiculously) responded, 'such a movement would have *no* effect.'[42] Fearful of the costs of a direct assault, and aware that time was of the essence, Howe eventually adopted Clinton's plan, despite his concerns. He stopped short, however, at seeking an engagement, preferring to chase the Americans out of their posts. His principal objective was the capture of the enemy positions, rather than the elimination of the enemy army.

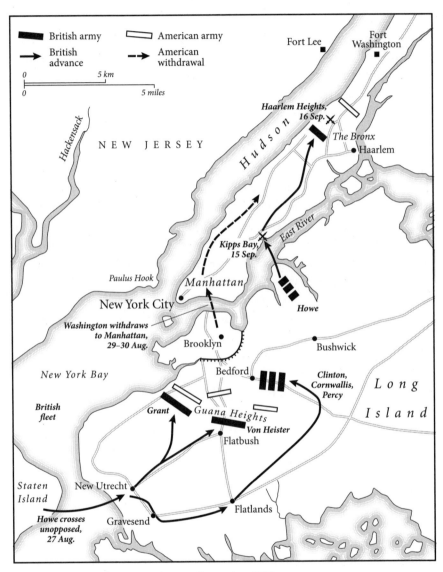

Map 4. New York Campaign, August–September 1776.

On 22 August, 15,000 redcoats landed on Long Island, with 7,000 Hessians arriving a day later. After reconnoitring the American position on Long Island on 24 August, Clinton realised that Washington had completed a second line of defensive works in front of those on Brooklyn Heights, on the Gowanus Heights, but there was an unguarded road through the heights at Jamaica Pass leading to the town of Bedford. Clinton advised that under cover of darkness, a substantial British force should move along this road in a wide right-flanking march and get behind the enemy positions, cutting off their avenue of retreat. Meanwhile, columns in the centre and on the left would launch diversionary attacks to draw the Americans forward, with the ultimate objective of encirclement.

On the evening of 26 August, Clinton led a column of 10,000 troops through the unguarded pass, arriving at Bedford at 8:30 p.m., whereupon the centre and left columns pressed their attacks forward, forcing the Americans from their defensive works straight toward Clinton's forces.[43] 'From this instant no appearance of a Stand, all confusion, they had lost their *direct* retreat, and their whole left was thrown back on its right,' recorded Clinton.[44] Fortunately for the Americans, the British left had not advanced as far or as fast as Clinton had expected, and Howe called off an unauthorised attack on an American position in Brooklyn, fearful that 'any considerable loss sustained by the army could not speedily, nor easily, be repaired'.[45] Two days later, making use of a summer storm as cover, Washington was able to withdraw his forces from Long Island across the East River to Manhattan.[46]

It was two weeks before Howe made his next move, during which time Washington had determined to evacuate New York, and reorganised his army so that it regained some of the confidence it had lost in the defeat at Long Island. Had Howe attacked immediately after Washington's withdrawal from Long Island, he might well have been able to inflict a decisive defeat on the Continental Army.[47] Instead, Howe selected Kip's Bay, a couple of miles north of New York City, to land his army on 15 September. Clinton disliked the plan. 'No diversion no demonstration, but what a child would see through,' he wrote in a scrawled note hours before the landing was due to take place. 'Little prospect of victory without buying it dear, some apprehension of receiving – what we might have given – a defeat *en detail*.'[48]

In the event, the landing operation was delayed by a few hours. Clinton learned that 'the tide ran so strong if we attempted to pass we should be carried up beyond Kipps Bay'. He therefore 'advised bringing up alongside the Transports till the tide slacked'. As luck would have it, 'the Rebels seeing this movement thought we waited for the Ebb and intended to land' further south toward the city, and 'they marched in force towards that place to oppose us'.[49]

When the transports eventually sailed, they found Kip's Bay weakly defended. 'The Ships began a terrible fire into the Woods which continued for some time till the Grenadiers & Light Infantry made good their landing which they did to the amazem[en]t of every one without the least opposition,' wrote Lieutenant Loftus Cliffe of the 46th Regiment.[50] The cannonade was like nothing the inexperienced militia stationed at Kip's Bay had ever experienced. Meanwhile, realising their mistake, the Continental troops turned about-face and tried to return to the bay, but were forced by gunfire from the British ships to make a substantial detour.[51] The whole army got ashore with very few casualties. 'You may conceive', wrote Cliffe to his brother, 'how much to the satisfaction of Gen: Howe this purchase was, when he layd it down cheap at 500 Men.'[52]

The expectation had been for heavier hand-to-hand combat once the landing was made, and Howe had given orders that his troops have 'an entire dependence upon their bayonets', which had proved highly effective during the battle for Long Island, 'even in the woods, where [the Americans] had thought themselves invincible'.[53] In the event, it took the British six hours to cut off all the roads north out of New York, by which time, Washington had managed to evacuate the city completely.[54] British officers 'seemed more intent upon looking out for comfortable quarters' raged one Hessian lieutenant, 'than preventing the retreat' of Washington's forces.[55] The following day, as the army moved north toward Harlem, a relatively minor skirmish escalated until several units were involved in a meeting engagement on Harlem Heights. Intervening to break off the action, Howe was 'extreamly displeased' with his brigade and battalion commanders.[56] His fears that his infantry were still too ill-disciplined to risk a set-piece battle appeared to be confirmed.

Four nights later, New York City erupted in flame, though a sudden change in wind direction prevented the entire city from being consumed. Washington had been explicitly forbidden by Congress from laying waste to New York, but he might well have attempted to orchestrate the destruction of the city in order to force Howe to look for a battle in which the Americans hoped to inflict maximum casualties. Bereft of winter quarters, supply depots and naval docking facilities, the British general might then have been forced to seek an early conclusion to the war before

winter set in. It seems this was Washington's hope when he occupied
Harlem Heights for several weeks after Howe withdrew his forces back
into Manhattan. But Howe had no intention of risking his army in such
a battle, and in any event, most of the city survived the fire. He viewed
Washington's position as 'too strongly posted to be attacked in front' while
'innumerable difficulties' hindered the planning and execution of a
flanking attack.[57]

It was not until 12 October that Howe made his next move, blaming
the delay on securing the British position in New York and collecting
intelligence on 'the face of the country to be possessed'.[58] When the
British eventually made their move, the plan was to outflank Washington's
position at Kingsbridge and Harlem, by landing north-east at Throgg's
Point. This entailed navigating the treacherous Hell Gate – narrow waterways flowing around islands in the East River before broadening out into
Long Island Sound. Here, 'if the stream catches a boat or vessel, it is
drawn into a kind of whirlpool or eddy where it is carried round several
times with great violence and then, if not sucked in, is thrown on the
adjacent rocks and dashed to pieces.'[59] As the British flotilla entered this
dangerous waterway, 'an exceeding great fog arose', but the excellent
seamanship of the Royal Navy pilots ensured few losses.[60]

Once through Hell Gate, Howe was badly let down by his intelligence
gathering, as Throgg's Point was found to be easily defensible, and a new
landing site had to be quickly located. Pell's Point, south of Rochelle, was
selected instead. Clinton once more led the advance guard and while the
landing was initially unopposed, he 'soon found the Rebels in some force
having exceeding strong walls in their front'. A unit of grenadiers had
been detached to open the right flank, but when Howe arrived, according
to Clinton, 'he ordered the Light Infantry to advance and drive them from
the Walls'. Clinton was incredulous. 'These walls are always to be turned,'
he reportedly said,[61] only for one of Howe's staff to deride the plan as
'German jargon'.[62]

For the third time in little more than a year, Clinton's ideas had been
summarily dismissed as being irrelevant to warfare in America. In the
event, the attack was 'attempted with very great spirit but too much loss',
Clinton wrote. 'Every inch of their ground was disputed,' he continued,
but 'the Rebels were soon drove off the Road'.[63] With a bridgehead now
established threatening Washington's communication with New England,
the Americans were forced to withdraw northwards. Howe once more
missed an opportunity to intercept the American retreat, focusing for

several days on 'getting up stores and provisions'.[64] When he moved, he found Washington waiting in a strong position at White Plains, about 20 miles north of Harlem Heights.

Having been gifted a week to prepare for a British attack, Washington had made full use of the time in establishing a strong defensive position on several hills, reinforced by solid entrenchments, anchored on the left by a lake and Chatterton's Hill on the right. Clinton and Howe reconnoitred the position and Clinton saw that the American right flank was vulnerable. 'I soon saw they might be forced from their position', Clinton wrote, 'by our left taking possession of a bald hill on our side of the Bronx.'[65] Howe ordered in the assault on 28 October, though he changed Clinton's plan to a frontal assault on the hill, which Clinton once again disagreed with. Howe paraded his entire army before the attack went in, hoping to undermine the apparent confidence of his adversary. The main attack was led by the Hessians, in a frontal assault reminiscent of Bunker Hill, and was only successful when the land grenadiers of Colonel Johann Rall's regiment took an unguarded hill to the east of Chatterton's Hill. Realising they were in danger of being outflanked, Washington withdrew to a secondary defensive line.

Faced with a particularly steep death toll – some 150 Hessians were killed or wounded in the assault – Howe declined to press his advantage, and instead planned another two assaults on 29 and 31 October, the first of which was delayed after discovering how much stronger the American line now was. Clinton again disagreed with his superior, citing 'the strength of the post, the difficulty of approach, the little protection from cannon, little chance of making a blow of consequence', and 'the risk after a tolerable good campaign of finishing it by a cheque'. Why risk all this, he argued, when there existed 'the moral certainty of a junction with Burgoyne next year'.[66] In the event, the second attack was thwarted by poor weather, which gave Washington time to withdraw, and Howe decided against a pursuit, publicly stating that he believed Washington to be deliberately avoiding a major battle.[67] Clinton, for once, agreed, seeing as 'there was no prospect of great advantage, I thought it advisable to run no great risks'.[68]

After the inconclusive battle at White Plains, Howe now turned his attention to clearing out the remaining Continental troops from Manhattan, where Fort Washington remained in the hands of the Americans, and sent Clinton, much to the disapproval of the latter, to capture Rhode Island. Positioned as it was in the Narragansett Bay, the island offered useful positioning for future raids of the American coastline, while the harbour at

Newport on the southern tip of the island was considered safer than New York. Major General Charles, Earl Cornwallis, meanwhile, was sent to New Jersey in pursuit of Washington. Any plans to envelop the Continental Army, strike north up the Hudson to sever American communications, or strike at its seat of power in Philadelphia, were suspended. Once Clinton successfully captured Rhode Island, Howe would go into winter quarters to await the campaign of 1777.

Focused though he might have been on capturing New York rather than eliminating Washington's army, Howe nevertheless came very close to achieving the latter. On 30 November, he issued a proclamation of conciliation, inviting the inhabitants of New Jersey to reaffirm their allegiance to the Crown, in return for which 'a free and general pardon' would be granted.[69] Washington's army began to disintegrate. The lack of any military success, the loss of New York and the looming expiry of commissions in the Continental Army resulted in near-catastrophic collapse in morale and support.[70] Intelligence received in December indicated that Washington commanded just 12,000 troops.[71] Washington needed a quick success to re-energise support for the rebellion. Just such an opportunity presented itself in late December.

In an effort to create an illusion of control and therefore encourage support for the proclamation, Howe had occupied a chain of posts throughout New Jersey, reaching as far as Trenton. Before his departure for England in December, Clinton had warned Howe that 'our chain has been extended too much'.[72] Howe, in part, agreed. 'The Chain, I own, is rather too extensive', he wrote to Germain, but he believed the levels of local loyalist support meant 'the Troops will be in perfect Security'.[73] Not for the last time, the British overestimated the levels of loyalist support.

Trenton was garrisoned by 1,400 Hessians, commanded by Colonel Johann Rall. On the morning of 26 December, Washington surrounded Trenton and Rall recklessly advanced to engage the Americans, whose disciplined fire shocked the Hessians and forced them to fall back in confusion and disorder. Despite firing off a couple of volleys, the Hessians were outgunned and surrendered. 'The Rebels will no doubt be much elated by their success,' Howe wrote in exasperation to Germain, 'which seems to have proceeded from Colonel Rall's quitting his post and advancing to the attack instead of defending the village, a measure nothing could induce him to take but a too despicable Opinion of those he had to oppose.'[74]

Rall, though, was not the only one to underestimate Washington. A week later, Cornwallis was sent to retaliate, but Washington eluded Cornwallis's main force and won a series of smaller victories over isolated detachments in and around Princeton. Howe was less critical of Cornwallis, but Archibald Robertson, an engineer at Princeton, observed that 'throughout this whole Expedition we certainly always erred in imprudently separating our Small Army of 6,000 men by far too much and must hope it will serve as a lesson in future never to despise any Enemy too much.'[75]

The combined American successes at Trenton and Princeton breathed new life into support for the military prosecution of the rebellion. Units across America reported revived morale upon learning of the victories, and many companies elected to extend their service instead of returning home.[76] Howe confessed to Germain that he thought 'their success will probably produce another campaign'.[77] Having captured New York, it appeared the next step was the completion of the Hudson strategy. A substantial army under General Sir John Burgoyne's command was preparing to make an attack on Ticonderoga and move on down the Hudson Valley where it would expect to link up with a similarly strong force sent north from New York. Howe, though, had other plans.

* * *

On 30 November, with Washington's army in full flight across the Delaware, and the British army in the ascendant, Howe had proposed an ambitious plan for 1777. First, Clinton would take command of an army composed of 10,000 troops at Rhode Island and move against Boston. Rhode Island would be defended by a garrison of 2,000 troops, which would also be employed to make 'small incursions ... upon the coast of Connecticut'. Meanwhile, a second army, again of 10,000 troops, would 'move up the North River to Albany', while 5,000 men held New York. Then, 8,000 men would act defensively in New Jersey, 'to keep the Southern Army in Check, by giving a Jealousy to Philadelphia, which I would propose to attack in Autumn, as well as Virginia'. Finally, 'South Carolina and Georgia must be the Objects for Winter.' In order to execute this plan, Howe requested a reinforcement of 15,000 troops, which 'would strike such Terror through the Country ...'.[78]

Less than three weeks later, Howe sent an amended version of the plan to Germain. News of the continued collapse in support for Washington's army had been received at Howe's headquarters, along with rumours of increased loyalist support in Pennsylvania. This news made him reconsider his options. Believing that a decisive move to capture Philadelphia would be successful, Howe was 'fully persuaded the principal army should act offensively on that Side, where the Enemy's Chief Strength will certainly be collected.'[79]

There was much to recommend the plan. It promised to capitalise on the successes of 1776 and would crush the remaining support for the rebellion, which had been so severely dented after the loss of New York. The offensive against Boston was put on hold, and the number of troops assigned to the execution of the Hudson strategy was reduced to 4,000. This was overly optimistic. Howe assumed that Philadelphia would be in British hands before Burgoyne reached Albany, meaning Howe would be free to support Burgoyne should he need it.[80]

All of this made sense if the strategic and operational picture on which Howe based these decisions remained unchanged. The British defeats at Trenton and Princeton, however, had a disproportionate effect on the fortunes of the rebellion. The British had been given a bloody nose, and Washington's men had been shown to be disciplined and capable in the field. By Howe's own measure, Philadelphia was no longer a viable objective, since it carried with it none of the original benefits Howe had outlined to Germain. Howe admitted as much to Germain on 20 January. 'The unfortunate and untimely defeat at Trenton has thrown us further back than was at first apprehended, from the great encouragement it has given to the rebels,' he wrote.

Inexplicably, though, Howe did not change his plans accordingly. Philadelphia was 'now the principal object'. It appears Howe believed there was no 'prospect of terminating the war, but by a general action, and I am aware of the difficulties in our way to obtain it, as the enemy moves with so much more celerity than we possibly can'.[81] If the British could not pin Washington's army down and force them to fight a battle, the only available option, in Howe's view, was the capture of important territorial objectives, in the hope that this either undermined the American will to fight or forced them to fight a battle to win their territory back. Howe never explained why Philadelphia was a more enticing territorial objective than the capture of the Hudson Valley.

Perhaps most extraordinarily, none of these decisions were made at the behest of Germain himself, whose response to the original 30 November plan still had not been received by Howe. When Germain's response finally arrived on 9 March, it served only to annoy Howe. Germain confessed that when he 'first read your Requisition of a Reinforcement of 15,000 Rank & File, I must own to you that I was really alarmed, because I could not see the least chance of my being able to supply you' with the requested troops. Germain then deliberately misinterpreted the number of troops available to Howe, choosing to count as being available for employment those highlighted in returns as either prisoners or wounded. Under Germain's calculations, he could bring Howe's force to near 35,000 by sending out seven or eight thousand reinforcements.[82] Calculated though this might have been to find a compromise, the move simply alienated Howe, who once again amended his plan. 'I find myself under the Necessity of relinquishing a principal part of the plan before proposed for an offensive Corps on the Side of Rhode Island' and 'from the Difficulties and Delay that would attend the Passage of the River Delaware by a march thro' Jersey, I propose to invade Pensilvania by Sea, and from this arrangement we must probably abandon the Jersies.'[83]

Philadelphia still remained the principal objective, while the corps in New York would act strictly on the defensive. The time it would take to evacuate New Jersey meant the opening of the campaign would be severely delayed. Moreover, 'the offensive Army will be too weak for rapid success,' Howe explained, despite the fact that he allocated 11,000 rather than the originally planned 10,000 troops to capture Philadelphia.[84] 'Restricted as I am from entering upon more extensive Operations by the Want of Force, my Hopes of terminating the War this Year are vanished,' Howe concluded.[85]

Nevertheless, Howe appeared convinced that the plan had been tacitly approved, even if it was not to be as well resourced as he would like; Germain had, after all, described the plan as 'well-digested' at the beginning of his correspondence. Later on Howe explained to Clinton that 'he had sent home his plan, it was approved & he would abide by it'.[86] By this point, Howe clearly considered the Hudson strategy to be a discreet operation executed solely by Burgoyne's army from Canada, lying outside Howe's command responsibilities. 'After taking Ticonderoga', Howe explained, Burgoyne, 'will, I fear, have little assistance from [New York] to facilitate their approach'. All that Howe would promise from New York was to 'endeavour to have a corps upon the lower part of the Hudson's River sufficient to open the communication for shipping through the Highlands'.[87]

Clinton was astonished when he learned of Howe's plans after returning to New York in July 1777, having spent the winter and spring in England. The subsequent arguments between Howe and Clinton, in which the latter tried to convince the former of his folly, were the most heated of their fractious relationship, and illustrate not only the complexity of strategic planning in North America, but also the diametrically opposed viewpoints the two held over the art of war. The debate was tinged with personal animus after Howe had learned that Clinton 'could not bear to serve under him, & had rather command 3 Companies by myself than hold my post I had done last Campaign in his Army'. Clinton said he had uttered the comment in the heat of the moment, but Howe continued to bear the grudge.[88]

From this position of weakness, Clinton tried on 8 July to convince Howe to abandon his Philadelphia plan, which would oblige him to 'act on the defensive in two places to enable him to act offensively in a third'. The only merit to it was 'the principle of raising friends' and even then, 'if he conquered ... he must afterwards keep which was impossible', as the British did not command the support or the resources to make a success of such a strategy. 'The better move', Clinton argued, 'would be to act upon the Hudson's River, form if possible the Junction [with Burgoyne] and then the 4 Provinces [of New England] were crushed.' Although he agreed, Howe affirmed that 'he thought if he could take P[ennsylvania], [New] Jersey would fall, & he should think it a good campaign'.[89]

A week later, Clinton tried a different approach, focusing on Washington's likely response to Howe's move on Philadelphia. 'I said that Washington had one of three things to do, – march in force against Burgoyne – Murder us in his Absence – or meet the General at his landing' in Pennsylvania. Clinton believed 'an Attempt upon [New York] most likely, as it was of most consequence'. He argued that 'it was worth Washington's while to risk everything to get this place that by it he finished the *War*'. Howe disagreed, believing New York to be of 'some little consequence'. Clinton, by contrast, argued that the Hudson Highlands were 'of so much consequence, that they never wou'd leave them unprotected, that they would ever be in very great force there'. Indeed, he continued, establishing control of the Hudson, along with the several strongly held forts that commanded it, would be impossible: 'there was no chance of ever opening that road with less than his whole Army'.[90]

The only point of moving on Philadelphia was to compel Washington to fight a decisive battle, but, Clinton argued, there was little to no chance of that. Howe 'would land, but not be opposed in force, that they would not risk a Battle to save Philadelphia, that they would retire to the Mountains beyond German Town with part of their Army, with the remainder pass the Susquehanna, over which he dared not follow them'. Again, although Howe agreed with the logic of the argument, he did not consider it sufficient to warrant abandonment of the Philadelphia operation. In the event the Americans withdrew from Philadelphia, 'his Operations would be finished, [and] he would reinforce [Clinton's] Army'. Finally, Clinton tried to persuade Howe that moving on Philadelphia jeopardised the security of Burgoyne's army, but Howe believed that Washington's whole army could not defeat Burgoyne.[91]

In a later conversation also witnessed by Sir William Erskine, Howe 'said he was not apprehensive of Washington's insulting Burgoyne'.[92] In any event, 'he said he hoped to see Burgoyne no further than Albany, and had wrote him word he could not Cooperate with him early'.[93] This, it seemed, was the crux of Howe's argument: he did not believe Burgoyne would encounter any significant resistance in his move down the Hudson Valley, and would make it to Albany unscathed. He therefore perceived any attempt to support him to be a waste of time and resources. As he prepared to sail on 7 July for the Chesapeake, however, it appears Howe had changed his mind. 'I do not suppose', he wrote to Germain, that the planned junction with the northern army 'can happen this campaign, as I apprehend General Burgoyne will find full Employment for his Army against that of the Rebels opposed to him'.[94]

Clinton persevered with his arguments until Howe departed for Philadelphia. The two clearly had deep personal differences, but the root of their disagreement was fundamentally different ways of thinking about the application of military power. Though they seemed to understand these differences, they perhaps never accepted them. Howe observed that the two 'never had agreed upon any single Question'. In response, Clinton 'told him that as our Military Education had been so different, it was not likely we should agree upon every one'.[95] Howe's approach was borne of experience in America, Clinton's was the product of his earlier experiences in Germany.

Simply put, Howe was focused on conquering territory, believing this to be the quickest way of subduing the rebellion. The approach he adopted in capturing New York in 1776 illustrated this point, as did his obsession with capturing Philadelphia in 1777. Though he remained risk-averse, he saw direct attacks as the most efficient way of achieving these terrain-based objectives. By contrast, Clinton's focus was Washington's army and the means by which it could supply itself. His approach was to manoeuvre the British army so that it cut off the Continentals from their supplies and thus either force a decisive battle or starve them into submission. In this estimation, Clinton was to be proved right. Territorial considerations were less important to the Americans than the continued ability to fight, and the only way this might be maintained was with the survival of the Continental Army.

The flotilla of 225 vessels carrying 13,000 troops eventually departed New York on 23 July. Clinton remained incredulous for several weeks after Howe's departure. 'I cannot believe my Ears, my Eyes, tho' every Letter from the CinC assures me he is gone to Chesapeake,' he wrote to his confidante Edward Harvey. 'I cannot scarcely credit it, the move elsewhere (up the Hudson) is so natural, & in my opinion so sure of being decisive.'[96] It was not until 28 August that Howe arrived at Head of Elk in Maryland. Upon disembarkation, Howe learned that Washington had been in the area. Indeed, on the 27th, Washington had dined at the house that now became Howe's headquarters.[97] It seemed the longed-for opportunity had arrived to confront the Continental Army in a general action, but Howe demurred, collecting his supplies before moving off. On 7 September, several deserters came in who 'all insisted that their General was in the intention to stand an action'.[98] Howe now at least seized the opportunity to attack his adversary.

At 4 a.m. on 11 September, he deployed General Wilhelm von Knyphausen with a force of about 3,500 to demonstrate in front of Washington, while Howe and Cornwallis with 7,500 men moved about 12 miles on the American right flank to the Brandywine River.[99] Washington, though, had learned of the flanking move at about noon and redeployed his force accordingly.[100] Howe 'found the Rebels posted on the Heights to oppose him', Major John André recorded in his diary.[101] Archibald Robertson observed that though 'the Rebels were Drawn up upon very Strong ground and seem'd determin'd to stand, ... the impetuosity of our Troops was irresistible'.[102] For Lieutenant Eyre Coote of the 37th Regiment of Foot, the troops behaved in a 'very gallant and spirited' manner, 'by repeatedly charging and routing under a very heavy fire, the enemy posted to the greatest advantage'.[103] The Americans were overwhelmed and 'we Drove them before us for two miles until fatigued and night came on we were obliged to stop'.[104]

The road to Philadelphia was now open, but Howe spent the next four days bringing his wounded to Wilmington and consolidating his strength. In an effort to learn as much about Washington's intentions as possible, he ordered 'all orderly books of the enemy whatever, which are or may hereafter be taken, to be given in to Headquarters as soon as possible'.[105] On 16 September, Howe received intelligence that the Americans were within five miles and could be trapped on the Delaware. He threw his force rapidly forward in two columns, 'but a most violent Fall of Rain setting in, and continuing the whole Day and Night without Intermission, made the intended attack impracticable'.[106]

Washington was able to escape in some disorder across the Delaware, and Howe had missed the last chance to defeat the Continental Army in 1777. En route to Philadelphia, Howe dispatched Major General Sir Charles Grey to attack a unit of American soldiers under the command of General Anthony Wayne, that had been harassing the British rearguard. Grey decided on a night-time attack, and in order to preserve the secrecy of his approach, acquired the nickname 'no flint Grey' when he ordered his troops – the 2nd Battalion Light Infantry, and the 42nd and 44th Regiments – to remove the flints from their weapons.[107] In the subsequent attack, Grey achieved total surprise, and 'killed and wounded not less than three hundred on the Spot'.[108] The incident became known as the Paoli Massacre – named for the nearby tavern – and deepened the animus between the Americans and the British.

Ten days later, Cornwallis marched into Philadelphia. Despite the American capital having been captured, the expected influx of loyalist support failed to materialise, and the Americans still controlled the Delaware, forcing supplies to be brought up overland from Chester. The British position would remain vulnerable until the Delaware could be cleared. It was while Howe was distracted attempting to open the river to waterborne communication that Washington decided to launch an attack on Howe's unguarded outposts at Germantown, early in the morning of 4 October. Shocked, Howe appeared initially to disbelieve the intelligence reports from his patrols that the Americans were launching an attack – 'that cannot be!' he reportedly exclaimed.[109] Nevertheless, the army was put on guard, and when the attack commenced at daybreak, the British were able initially to hold the line, but the strength of the attack forced the 2nd Light Infantry and the 40th Regiment to fall back. 'For shame, Light Infantry,' Howe allegedly cried, 'I never saw you retreat before, form! form!'

Shortly afterwards, Howe himself came under fire. One participant from the 52nd Regiment was 'pleased to hear the grape rattle around the commander-in-chief's ears after he had accused the battalions of having run away from a scouting party'.[110] The British managed to hold the line until Grey and Agnew arrived with the 3rd and 4th Brigades. Overwhelmed, the American position collapsed and their troops were 'pursued thro a strong country between four and five miles'.[111] Washington withdrew nearly 20 miles, having sustained by Howe's estimation between 200 and 300 casualties. Howe was left in unchallenged possession of Philadelphia. Celebrations were muted. Though social clubs reopened, theatre troops were re-established and lavish balls thrown, the difficulty of supplying the city pushed prices up and caused considerable disharmony. And then, on 16 October, rumours from the north struck like a hammer blow. Burgoyne and his army had surrendered at Saratoga.

* * *

Burgoyne had commenced his advance from Montreal on 20 June with 7,125 troops, more than a thousand short of the numbers he hoped to command. More worrying was the relatively tiny number of loyalists who volunteered for service – fewer than 10 per cent of the expected numbers. In addition, Burgoyne only received a third of his requested logistical support, and half the projected number of Native American warriors. This was a problem, as he had proposed that a 'Corps of savages, supported by detachments of light regulars, should be continually on foot' to reconnoitre and collect intelligence.[112] Burgoyne, however, was not worried: Native Americans were expensive allies, he believed the Americans would abandon the Hudson Valley once the British had captured Ticonderoga, and he expected to recruit hundreds of loyalists once he advanced south of Lake George. Local magazines would then fill any shortfall created by his imperfect supply line back to Canada.[113] Burgoyne's optimistic analysis entirely overlooked the difficulty of the terrain through which he proposed to march, and the fact that the New England militia comprised some of Britain's most inveterate enemies.[114]

The invasion force was divided into three columns. The leading edge was commanded by Brigadier General Simon Fraser, a highly experienced veteran of warfare in North America. Major General William Phillips, a grumpy artilleryman, commanded the left-hand column, which included the 138 artillery guns thought necessary to undertake the siege of Ticonderoga. The right, meanwhile, was composed of 3,000 Brunswickers and commanded by Major General Riediesel. Seven days prior to their departure, Burgoyne issued a proclamation in which he promised to sow 'Devastation, Famine and every concomitant Horror' unless the Americans abandoned 'the Phrenzy of Hostility'. This, combined with news of a speech Burgoyne had given to the Native Americans promising virtually unrestrained spoils of war, alienated many inhabitants of New York. Nevertheless, within 10 days, Burgoyne's army had reached Ticonderoga.[115]

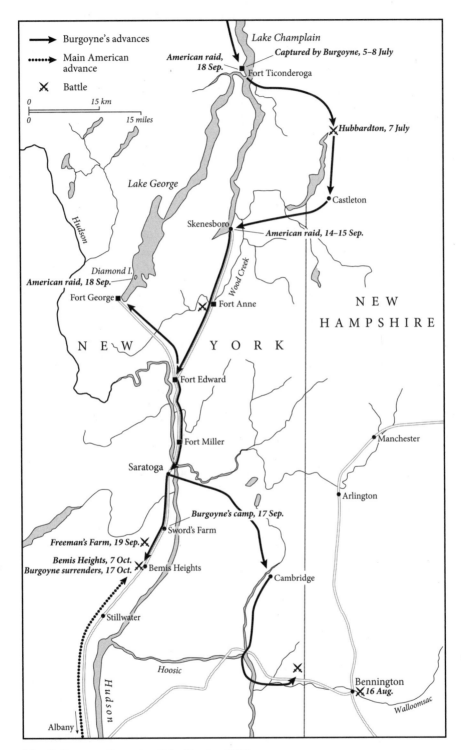

Map 5. Saratoga Campaign, July–October 1777.

Since capturing Ticonderoga in 1775, the Americans had strengthened its defences. Besides rebuilding the walls of the fort itself, a large star redoubt had been built on Mount Independence, across the lake to the east. Believing it to be inaccessible to artillery, however, the Americans had neglected to put any arms on Sugar Hill, the high ground to the south of Ticonderoga, which easily commanded the position. On the night of 5 July, Fraser's battalion of light infantry took Sugar Hill and work began on building an artillery battery there. The garrison commander saw this and, in a council of war, concluded that Ticonderoga was no longer defensible. That evening the garrison evacuated Ticonderoga, withdrawing as much of the stores across the lake as possible. 'The manner of taking up the ground at Ticonderoga convinces me that they have no men of military science,' wrote Burgoyne.[116]

Washington was understandably furious. 'The stroke is indeed severe and has distressed me much,' he wrote to General Schuyler, then in command along the Hudson. But there was something to be sanguine about, as Washington hoped that Burgoyne would become overconfident and 'hurry . . . into measures which will in their consequence be favourable to us',[117] Washington was right. Word of the fall of Ticonderoga was received with jubilation in England. Upon hearing the news, the king himself reportedly dashed into the queen's apartment crying 'I have beat them, I have beat all the Americans'![118] Once again, the mistaken belief that the capture of important terrain was the key that would unlock the rebellion was pervasive, not just among the generals in command in America, but also at the highest levels of government.

Burgoyne pursued the retreating Americans up Lake Champlain to Skenesborough, and then west to Fort Edward on the Hudson. This was perhaps an unnecessary detour, as the road passed through difficult terrain, and there was a more direct, though easily blocked, route from Lake George to the Hudson. As a result of the necessity to clear felled trees, and rebuild as many as 40 bridges, Burgoyne's advance slowed dramatically, taking some 20 days to advance as many miles. On 30 July, he at last reached Fort Edward, but was unable to advance any further as he now also needed to open the Lake George road to bring up his supplies, which he found to be moving at a glacial pace for lack of adequate waggons and drivers. Burgoyne also elected to bring up a huge quantity of heavy artillery – some 52 guns, which he believed necessary to capture entrenched positions and defend his own positions when they were established. As a result, his mobility was severely restricted. All these delays gave the

Americans plenty of time to concentrate what forces they could bring to bear in the Hudson Valley.

Finding it impossible to bring up adequate supplies, Burgoyne resolved to attack an American magazine at Bennington, 20 miles south-east of Fort Edward. There, on 16 August, the Americans inflicted severe casualties on the British detachment. Given that Burgoyne had already detached troops to garrison Ticonderoga and in an unsuccessful diversion to the Mohawk River, Burgoyne found himself severely under strength and with his flanks unprotected. By mid-September, the Americans had gathered nearly seven thousand troops in the Hudson Valley, now under the command of General Horatio Gates.[119] Moreover, the Americans had gained a reasonably clear picture of the state and intentions of Burgoyne's army, having interrogated several prisoners taken at Bennington.[120]

By 13 September, Burgoyne had collected sufficient supplies to facilitate a move forward; the question now remained as to whether or not he *should* move forward. His force was severely reduced, his flanks unprotected and vulnerable to hostile militia; his lines of supply were likewise vulnerable and the absence of the expected loyalist support severely constricted his ability to amass magazines in useful locations. His enemy, likewise, had concentrated in such numbers as to form an army at least equal to his own. Riedisel, though, was the only one among his general officers to make these points and he recommended retreating to Ticonderoga. In reality, Burgoyne was never going to retreat. During the Seven Years' War, he had won acclaim risking his force in raids deep into enemy territory in Portugal, and against enemy flanks on the French coast.[121] Speed, decision and tempo were his key command characteristics. Moreover, Burgoyne convinced himself that if he retreated, he would leave 'at liberty such an army as General Gate's to operate against Sir William Howe'.[122]

No sooner had Burgoyne commenced his advance than the Americans sprung their trap. On 18 September, General Benjamin Lincoln with 1,500 militiamen attacked Burgoyne's rear, capturing the British shipping on Lake George. Unaware of the danger behind him, the following day, Burgoyne attacked the Americans at Freeman's Farm. The position Gates had adopted was very strong. On the left, Brigadier-General Benedict Arnold commanded high ground above a deep ravine, while Gates commanded the right on a ridge of hills which ran above the banks of the Hudson. Gates had positioned two batteries to command the Hudson, while the base of the hills was protected by an abattis nearly a mile long. Dense wood covered the position to the north, inhibiting any outflanking move. Burgoyne advanced in three columns, commanding the centre himself, with Fraser on the right and Phillips and Riedesel on the left. The army advanced with little information about the enemy position, as its scouts and skirmishers had been driven in by American irregular troops. Burgoyne elected to attack Arnold, as his personal reconnaissance had convinced him that Gates's position was impregnable. As the British advanced, Arnold's forces also moved forward seeking to outflank Burgoyne's right.

The central column advanced and attempted to occupy Freeman's Farm but encountered a crack corps of riflemen under the command of Daniel Morgan who specialised in picking off British officers and artillerymen. One battery lost 36 of its 48 gunners. The British fell back, but Fraser had manoeuvred through the woods to avoid the ravine, and at 2 p.m. caught the American flank. After a sharp musketry battle, the Americans were 'routed' by the British light infantry. Morgan was reportedly devastated: 'I am ruined by G_d!'.[123] Burgoyne once more advanced to Freeman's Farm, and a general action commenced at 2 p.m. The British continued to sustain heavy casualties, with the three battalions in the central column – 20th, 21st and 62nd Foot – losing nearly half their number. Fraser maintained the British right flank, deploying light infantry units to plug emerging gaps.[124] At about 6 p.m., as the British line was beginning to buckle, Riedesel attacked from the British right, and the Americans were forced to withdraw.[125] Burgoyne was left in command of the field, but at great cost, some 556 killed and wounded, compared with just over two hundred American losses.[126]

Burgoyne planned to use the light infantry in Fraser's columns to spearhead a follow-on attack the following day, but a message from Clinton in New York gave him pause. 'I will make a push at Montgomery in about ten days,' Clinton wrote in a secret letter, 'but ever jealous of my flanks, if they make a move in force on either of them I must return to save this important post.'[127] Burgoyne believed that such a move would 'draw away a part of this force, & I will follow them close. Do it my dear friend'.[128] Burgoyne therefore elected to entrench at Freeman's Farm and wait for Gates to feel threatened by Clinton. It was the decision that lost America for the British.

* * *

After Howe's departure for Philadelphia, Clinton, who had been left defending New York, found himself both weak and uninformed. 'I am sorry to say that intelligence is so very defective', he wrote in exasperation to Howe, 'that what is asserted one day is contradicted the next.'[129] Moreover, he felt paralysed, able to muster only 7,700 troops, so moving north into the Hudson Highlands seemed impossible. 'I cannot leave an extended coast of near 200 miles altogether to less than 5,000 & with the other 3,000 attempt to break thro' such a country as the Highlands, opposed by double that number already there'.[130] He had written as much to Burgoyne, in a secret letter using an hourglass mask to hide its true content. 'I am left to command here with too small a force to make any effectual diversion in your favour,' he explained. 'I own I think Sir William's move at this time has been the worst he could have taken.'[131]

On 22 August, as he had predicted in his earlier conversations with Howe, the Americans took advantage of Clinton's isolation and made three simultaneous attacks on his outposts at Kingsbridge, on the eastern shore of Long Island, and on Staten Island. Clinton correctly deduced that the main assault was on Staten Island, and the other two were feints, and so he concentrated his defensive efforts there in time to witness the Americans crossing to the Jersey shore. A sharp firefight broke out, and the Americans were forced to withdraw.[132]

Clinton admired the speed, dexterity and coordination of the American attack, and believed a better supported attack might have seriously jeopardised his position. He expected a follow-on attack until he realised that Washington had turned his attention to fixing Howe in Pennsylvania, to give Gates greater freedom on the Hudson.[133] Tentatively, Clinton began to think about conducting demonstrations in an attempt to distract the Americans. In mid-September he moved into eastern New Jersey, but was too weak to distract Washington.[134] If he was to have any material effect on the campaign, he needed to try to capture the forts along the Hudson and threaten the American flank in the Highlands.

The opportunity to move against the Hudson forts arose when Clinton received news that General Isaac Putnam, the American commander in the Highlands, had concentrated his forces on the east bank of the Hudson, rather than around the forts themselves.[135] Combined with news that he was about to receive a small reinforcement from England, Clinton saw a chance, but he felt he could only move if Burgoyne's situation demanded it. Howe had made clear before he left for Philadelphia that the defence of New York was Clinton's primary objective. Clinton thus wrote his second secret message to Burgoyne, once again disguising the true contents using an hourglass mask, in which he offered to move against the forts, an operation which he expected would take 10 days to implement.[136] Though Burgoyne replied immediately, the note only reached New York eight days later. Clinton instantly swung into action. Having received his sought-after reinforcements on the 24th, by 3 October he had embarked 3,000 troops and appeared off Verplanck's Point on the eastern shore of the Hudson. He landed a small force and captured the battery there.

This was a feint to persuade Putnam – who was based a few miles north at Peekskill – that he was the target of the attack. Putnam fell for it and called away more reinforcements from the forts on the western shore. Clinton then landed the main body of his force on Stony Point, on the western shore and moved on Forts Montgomery and Clinton. 'After a very laborious march over mountains, precipices, and every difficulty we were in a situation to make two attacks on Forts Clinton and Montgomery,' Clinton wrote to Harvey.[137] The trails along which they marched were too rough to bring along the artillery. 'I never saw more gallantry and intrepidity shown on any occasion than on this,' wrote one participant. 'It is impossible to give ... an idea of the strength of the country we had to march through to this attack; well might they think it impregnable, for it certainly was so to any but British troops. But they took it even without cannon.'[138] After abandoning the forts, the Americans destroyed all the ships and stores in their vicinity.[139]

In the wake of this success, Clinton sent Vaughan up the Hudson 'with orders to feel for Genl Burgoyne, & if possible to assist his operations' and with 'provisions sufficient to supply Genl Burgoyne's Army for 6 months'. In the event, Vaughan was forced to turn back long before he reached Albany after witnessing American forces in considerable numbers on either bank of the Hudson. At this point, Clinton received new orders from Howe to send 4,000 reinforcements to Pennsylvania. Any hope of linking up with, or even sustaining, Burgoyne from the south now ended. 'Good God what a fair prospect blasted,' Clinton wrote.[140] He sent a message concealed in a musket ball notifying Burgoyne that he could advance no further.

As with his manoeuvres against New York, Clinton's planning and execution of the attacks on the Hudson forts give a glimpse of the sort of military campaign he would have preferred to execute: one based on manoeuvring designed to knock his adversary off balance and create considerable advantage for the British. Such manoeuvres demanded relative strength, excellent intelligence and superior confidence. By the end of the 1777 campaign, Clinton was distinctly lacking in all three. 'Still stronger reasons every day', he wrote to his sisters, 'determine me to quit this mortifying service,'[141] and Howe eventually granted him leave to return home. 'I have told him my resolution, and he has consented to my leaving this command in March,' he wrote. 'No man dreads the displeasure of his royal master more than I do', but Clinton was determined to resign.[142] News from Saratoga would soon change the situation.

In the time it took Clinton to execute his operations against the Hudson forts, Gates received substantial reinforcements from Washington, increasing his force to 11,000 troops. 'From the best intelligence', Gates knew that Burgoyne had 'not more than three weeks provisions in store; it will take him at least eight days to get Back to T[iconderoga], so that in a fortnight at farthest, he must decide whether he will rashly risqué at infinite disadvantage to force my Camp; or Retreat to his Den'.[143] Gates also knew that Clinton's move on the Hudson forts was nothing more than a well-orchestrated demonstration, as the courier carrying the message to Burgoyne concealed in a musket ball had been captured by the Americans.[144] 'On taking the bullets out of his pocket', one of his interrogators 'remarked the light weight of the pretended bullet, when the spy alarmed caught it out of his hand and swallowed it.' A doctor was called, and an emetic failing to produce the ball, 'he tried a medicine of an *opposite* character which had the desired effect. The ball was found to unscrew, and in it, written on a thin bank-bill paper' was the message from Clinton. 'I sincerely hope this little success of ours may facilitate your operations . . . I cannot presume to order or even advise, for reasons obvious. I heartily wish you success.'[145] Gates knew what Burgoyne did not: that Clinton could go no further, and that Burgoyne was on his own.

Gates did not have to wait long for Burgoyne to decide between attack and retreat. With his force dwindling to below 4,000 effectives, on 7 October, Burgoyne organised a reconnaissance in force to identify weak points in the American line, with a follow-up attack the next day.[146] He assigned 1,400 troops to this task, arranged in one continuous line, stretching nearly half a mile, while a company of rangers, Native Americans and loyalists would 'go to secret paths in the woods to gain the Enemy's rear, and by showing themselves there to keep them in check'.[147] As the British advanced, Gates, at about 2 p.m., took the opportunity to attack both the British right and left flank. Burgoyne was badly outnumbered, and his line quickly began to disintegrate. Nearly six thousand Americans were now advancing against the collapsing British line. Fraser tried to restore order, using the light infantry to form a second line, but he fell mortally wounded and the British line collapsed, fleeing to the entrenchments, where the light infantry fought a pitched defensive battle, eventually forcing the Americans to withdraw and focus on a different part of the British line. With his position badly compromised, Burgoyne fell back to Saratoga. His army had suffered over six hundred casualties. With fewer than three thousand effective troops, limited supplies, surrounded on all sides, and no prospect of relief, Burgoyne was forced to seek terms.

* * *

The repercussions of Burgoyne's surrender would entail a complete re-evaluation of British strategy in America. Howe was not to be the general to implement that strategy. His approach to the American war had proved to be catastrophically wrong. By focusing on capturing territory, both he and Burgoyne had been drawn into a campaign that was excessively costly for the British, while failing to prove terminal for the American cause.

Arguably, Howe's (and Burgoyne's) focus on territory as an objective was the product of their personal experience of war as well as the result of their tactical proficiency. Both were proponents of light infantry doctrine or the use of irregular approaches to warfighting. Both had demonstrated acute skills in exercising these tactics. In so doing, they had perhaps not had the opportunity, or been forced to think, about the strategic use of military power.[148] As a result, they looked for ways to employ their armies with decisive effect using the tactics which they knew to work.

In reality, only the destruction of the American army would put an end to the American Revolution, and the best, perhaps the only, chance to do this had been lost. Howe's successor, the infinitely prickly Sir Henry Clinton, had the right ideas, but would now have to implement those ideas with severely curtailed resources, and in the unspoken reality where North America as a strategic objective was less important than Canada, Florida and particularly the Sugar Islands in the West Indies.

Germain dispatched instructions to the new commander-in-chief on 8 March 1778. The government had hopes that a negotiated peace might be possible, but Burgoyne's surrender, and 'the unbroken State of the Rebel Force', wrote Germain, 'would make it necessary to have at least as great an Army in the Field to effect anything of importance in the next Campaign, as that which Sir William Howe commanded in the last'. To that end, 10–12,000 reinforcements were being sent from England, along with a couple of German regiments. With this considerably enhanced force, Clinton would be expected to send modest detachments to Canada and the Floridas, and should aim 'to bring Mr Washington to a general and decisive action early in the Campaign'.[149]

Germain finished the instruction by noting that should he see an opportunity to prosecute the war differently, Clinton should not be bound by the instructions. 'A private letter ... which came with my first instruction gave me hopes of being dealt with liberally, that I should not be tied down by instructions with those I received from L[or]d G[eorge] G[ermain]', Clinton wrote to Newcastle; 'I was satisfied.'[150] That satisfaction was short-lived. Barely a fortnight after Germain's original despatch was sent, France 'signed a Treaty of Amity and Commerce with the Rebel Agents at Paris'. Tantamount, as this was, to a declaration of war, French entry into the American struggle completely transformed its nature from a contained colonial civil conflict to a war with potentially global dimensions.

The government determined to launch 'an immediate attack upon the French possessions in the West Indies'. Inevitably, this meant Clinton would no longer be receiving the reinforcements Germain had so confidently promised.[151] Worse, Clinton was ordered to detach 5,000 troops to the West Indies, 3,000 troops to St Augustine in East Florida, and be ready to detach reinforcements to Canada at a moment's notice.[152] Retreat from Philadelphia was now inevitable. New York once more became the base of British operations, as it was 'so necessary to give dignity and effect to the [peace] negotiations', wrote Germain. Clinton's new instructions were merely to 'keep up an alarm on the sea coasts of the rebellious provinces'.[153]

Clinton was incredulous. Clearly, the Thirteen Colonies were no longer London's principal strategic concern. But there were likewise inconsistencies in Germain's new strategy. He wanted to negotiate an end to the war in the Thirteen Colonies, but, as Clinton pointed out, 'is it expected that America in her present situation will agree to terms when [this] army is avowedly retiring (for such are my instructions to propagate)?'[154] He continued, 'had I been left to my first instructions [of 8 March] – if America is still an object, she might possibly have been recovered, as it is I fear she will be lost. England had but one army, it was a good one, by late arrangements I fear a great part of it will be destroyed.'[155]

There was nevertheless little Clinton could do. Remaining in Philadelphia exposed the British to defeat both there and in New York. If he was to have any hope of success, he needed to evacuate Philadelphia, and concentrate his army in New York, but it would only be possible to embark the army 40 miles away at Newcastle. Not only would his flank be threatened during this movement, but if he 'should afterwards have been detained by contrary winds ..., Mr Washington might have seized the opportunity of making a decisive push at New York'.[156] Clinton therefore 'determined to move through Jersey, as that move saves N York, which by all accounts is threaten[ed], should W[ashington] put himself in my way, offense will then become defence and something may come of it'.[157]

The army evacuated Philadelphia by 3 a.m. on 18 June 1778, crossing the Delaware by 10 that morning. Washington was aware of the move, and quickly reoccupied the city. He sent advanced units to throw obstacles along Clinton's path, including felling trees and breaking bridges.[158] As he was marching through scorched countryside, Clinton needed to take an adequate supply of food, but this then produced an alarming vulnerability: his baggage train stretched as far as 12 miles behind the vanguard of his army. As a result, he was forced to split his force in two with a rearguard of 2,000 men under Cornwallis – the best troops in the army – protecting the train, and the balance of his force in the vanguard under General Knyphausen's command. 'As the Country is much intersected with marshy rivulets,' he wrote to Germain, 'the Obstructions we met with were frequent and the excessive Heat of the Season rendered the Labour of repairing the Bridges severely felt.'[159]

Skirmishes broke out as the army continued its march. On one occasion, Colonel Robert Abercromby's company of light infantry clashed with Daniel Morgan's riflemen. Abercromby 'ordered his troops to charge them with the bayonet; not one man of them, out of four, had time to fire,' recorded one memoirist, 'and those that did had not time given them to load again'. As a result, the Americans 'did not stand three minutes; the light infantry not only dispersed them instantly, but drove them for miles over the country: they never attacked ... our light infantry again, without a regular force to support them'.[160] The incident, one of several where riflemen were caught unsupported in opposition to well-trained troops armed only with muskets and bayonets, helped perpetuate a debate in the British Army of the relative merits of the Brown Bess musket over those of the significantly more accurate but cumbersome rifle. This debate would last at least for another three-quarters of a century.[161]

By 23 June, Clinton was at Allentown, east of Trenton. There, he 'received intelligence that Generals Washington and Lee had passed the Delaware with their Army' to the northwest. Clinton concluded that 'as I could not hope that after having always hitherto so studiously avoided a general Action, General Washington would now give into it against every Dictate of Policy, I cou'd only suppose that his views were directed against my baggage &c, in which part I was indeed vulnerable'. Consequently, Clinton decided to turn north-east for Sandy Hook.[162]

On 27 June, the British encamped at a clearing near Monmouth Courthouse in the village of Freehold. Here, Washington saw an opportunity to strike, as Clinton suspected, at the British baggage train, and deployed over 5,000 troops in three columns. His hope, it seems, was to cut off Cornwallis's rearguard and inflict a devastating blow on Clinton's army.[163] Cornwallis's division was composed of the assembled flank units of light infantry and grenadiers, as well as Colonel John Simcoe's Queen's Rangers. 'The Brigades', wrote one Lieutenant in the Grenadiers company of the 45th Foot, 'have been looked upon as nurseries only for the flank Corps.'[164] Capturing or inflicting severe casualties on this force would critically undermine the British ability to sustain the fight in North America.

Early in the morning of Sunday 28 June, General Charles Lee commanded the three columns as they advanced to contact, with the aim of outflanking Clinton's right and cutting off the British rearguard. The rolling and close terrain, which was bisected by three streams that formed morasses, hindered his advance. The British were encamped behind the third, or the east morass, but when he began his advance, Lee, having had no opportunity to reconnoitre prior to the commencement of his attack, had no idea about the ruggedness of the terrain. It was not until 10 a.m., then, that Lee was able to reach the east morass, by which time the heat of the day was starting to fatigue troops on both sides of the battlefield. Knyphausen had already moved off with the vanguard and baggage train, and Cornwallis had just begun to move. At this point, 'some General Officers of The Enemy were seen Reconnoitring on the Left Flank',[165] and Simcoe had dispersed militia scouting parties, though he had received a flesh wound in his arm during the skirmish.[166]

Lee managed to get his three columns into action and Clinton scrabbled to respond. He sent orders recalling Knyphausen, but the German general failed to respond fast enough.[167] Interpretations of the next few moments vary. Clinton is either portrayed as a decisive commander, redeploying Cornwallis and counterattacking in force,[168] or as impetuous and rash, 'galloping like a Newmarket jockey at the head of a wing of Grenadiers and expressly forbidding all form and order'.[169] In reality, Clinton needed to counterattack to prevent his rearguard from being outflanked, and the opportunity potentially to strike a severe blow on a significant portion of Washington's army was too good to overlook, but the manner in which he orchestrated the battle is open to criticism.

Clinton judged that Lee's misunderstanding of the terrain had isolated his detachment from the rest of Washington's army, and thus was exposed to defeat in detail. He therefore ordered the grenadiers on the British left to launch an immediate attack. 'Judge of my inexpressible surprise,' wrote Lieutenant Hale of the 45th shortly after the battle, 'Gen. Clinton himself appeared at the head of our left wing accompanied by Lord Cornwallis, and crying out "Charge, Grenadiers, never heed forming."' As the grenadiers advanced 'amidst the heaviest fire I have yet felt,' Hale recalled, 'it was no longer a contest for bringing up our respective companies in the best order, but all officers as well as soldiers strove who could be foremost . . .'.[170]

With his flanks collapsing and his centre under intense pressure, Lee was forced to withdraw to the west morass, where he collided with Washington and the main body of the American army. Shocked to see Lee withdrawing in some haste, Washington assumed command and decided to make a stand. 'They then took a . . . position,' recorded Clinton, 'with a marshy hollow in front, over which it would have been scarcely possible to have attacked them.'[171] At this point, some of the British units which had departed earlier in the morning returned and joined the battle. 'The 3d. Brigade came up after a very quick & fatiguing march of six or 7 miles, and leaving their Packs at the edge of the wood on their right,' wrote John Peebles, an officer in the grenadier company of the 42nd Regiment. 'They dash'd thro' that wood & a deep swamp, and came upon a Scatter'd Body of the Rebels whom the[y] drove before them . . . .'[172] After capturing a hill onto which the British could deploy artillery, the advancing British forces lost momentum.

The intense heat was starting to take its toll. 'With the thermometer at 96[°F] – when people fell dead in the street, and even in their houses – what could be done at midday in a hot pine barren, loaded with everything that [the] poor soldier carries?' asked Clinton in the aftermath to his sisters. 'It breaks my heart that I was obliged under those cruel circumstances to attempt.'[173] The heat was so intense that it now became difficult to manoeuvre, and the battle descended into a stalemate. The largest artillery duel of the American Revolutionary War now commenced. 'With some difficulty we were brought in a disorderly manner under the hill we had gained,' recalled Hale, 'and the most terrible cannonade . . . ensued and last[ed] for above two hours, at the distance of 600 yards.' The British troops, while sheltered from the fire of the American artillery, were nevertheless exposed without shelter to the afternoon sun. For Hale, the cannonade was almost preferable. 'Had my strength enabled me to have crawled so far I would most certainly have preferred the chance of dying by a cannon ball,' he wrote to his parents.[174] Clinton withdrew his forces to Monmouth Courthouse, rested them until the moon rose and then withdrew.[175] By 2 July, the British were at Sandy Hook, making arrangements with the Navy to withdraw to New York.

Clinton had had high hopes for a battle during the withdrawal from Philadelphia to New York, but the action of Monmouth Courthouse, though one of the largest of the war, and the only battle at which Clinton commanded the British Army as its commander-in-chief, was a disappointing affair. Hale, no fan of Clinton, was particularly critical. 'I know not whether from want of inclination or abilities,' he wrote subsequently, 'but none of our Generals have yet engaged more than three thousand of this Army at one time, and in the last action scarce half that number was opposed to the whole Rebel Army.'[176] The reality was that, even if Clinton had been able to get Knyphausen back in time to play a role in a battle, the terrain prevented the deployment of the whole army into battle, a not uncommon problem presented by the geography of North America.[177] More concerning was Clinton's apparent errors during the battle itself, which included mistiming the deployment of the grenadiers without first forming the unit. 'At Freehold indeed', wrote Hale, 'an attempt too late for success was made to employ them by General C. who seems to possess all the ideas, though it's feared not the abilities of a soldier.'[178]

Clinton himself now found a renewed respect for Washington's generalship, and the effectiveness of his army. 'I will do the rebels justice to say it was well-timed,' he wrote to his sisters.[179] It is perhaps too much to argue that his experience at Monmouth Courthouse made Clinton more risk-averse, but over the next few months, he gave serious consideration as to how to avoid battle unless in supremely advantageous circumstances for his army. In place of the 'direct attack' of which he was so critical, Clinton now sought to implement a new strategy in North America, which he dubbed 'indirect manoeuvres'. Partly the product of necessity, as his resources were now so limited, the strategy also chimed very closely with how he perceived war should be fought. Unfortunately for Clinton, Cornwallis, who became Clinton's deputy, disagreed as much with his commander as Clinton had with Howe.

CHAPTER 5

'Indirect Manoeuvres'

THE FAILURE OF HENRY CLINTON'S AMERICAN STRATEGY, 1775–1781

AFTER his return to New York, Clinton was obliged to send 6,000 of his best troops to the West Indies. He was initially unable to do so because of the presence of Admiral Charles Henri Hector, Comte d'Estaing's fleet of French battleships anchored outside the bar at Sandy Hook, but eventually d'Estaing was forced to withdraw to Boston, and in November the force was duly dispatched. 'The parting with such a corps of veterans was an agony like the separating of soul and body,' Clinton recorded miserably. 'Indeed, the body remained but the soul was gone and with it our hopes of ending the rebellion.'[1] Clinton observed that unless 'this Army is greatly reinforced it must remain on a most strict defensive'.[2]

Indeed, such were his instructions from London. In the wake of the withdrawal from Philadelphia, Clinton was to 'relinquish the Idea of carrying on offensive Operations against the Rebels within Land', and launch a series of raids against the 'Ports on the Coast from New York to Nova Scotia, and to seize or destroy every ship or Vessel ... destroy all Wharf and Stores and materials for shipbuilding, so as to incapacitate them from raising a Marine, or continuing their Depredations upon the Trade of this Kingdom'. Optimistically hoping the raids would be executed at the latest by October, Germain also instructed Clinton to detach an independent command to open a new front in Georgia and South Carolina. Intelligence suggested that the population of the southern colonies had a 'general Disposition to return to their allegiance'.[3]

The instructions signified a marked shift in strategy.[4] Rather than seeking to undermine the rebellion by destroying the Continental Army,

Clinton was to facilitate economic war against the Americans. If his raids and the conquest of the south were successful, Germain concluded, 'it might not be too much to expect that all America . . . would return to their Allegiance'.[5] The raiding strategy appealed to Clinton. It was, after all, the approach he had originally advocated, and it allowed him to employ military power indirectly against the Americans. But Clinton confessed that bereft of reinforcements and facing the loss of 8,000 of his regular troops, it would be difficult for him to prosecute anything meaningful.

With this constraint in mind, Clinton orchestrated a series of limited maritime raids. In September, he ordered General Grey to launch a raid on New London, which proved successful.[6] 'A favourable wind & every possible exertion and assistance received from the Navy, enabled us to land so rapidly yesterday evening about 6 o'clock, that the Enemy had a very few hours notice of our approach,' Grey reported to Clinton. 'The business was finished & the troops all re-embarked this morning by 12 o'clock.'[7] Grey followed up with equally successful raids on Bedford and Fair Haven.[8]

In early October, Clinton 'proposed taking a forward position with the Army' with a view to acquiring a new regular forage supply, as well as observing 'the motions of the Rebel Army'. On the back of this, he proposed an expedition to 'Egg Harbour', where 'the Enemy had a Number of Privateers & Prizes & considerable Salt Works'. The operation might force Washington to risk 'a General Action in a Country little favourable to him'.[9]

Meanwhile, Cornwallis and Grey launched a raid on Tappan and captured a body of militia and a regiment of light dragoons which had been sent to interrupt a British foraging expedition. Grey managed to get ashore undiscovered and 'made so good a disposition to surround the village of Old Taapan [sic] where the Regiment of Dragoons lay that he entirely surprised them, and very few escaped being either killed or taken'.[10] John Robert Shawe, a private in Cornwallis's regiment, could barely stomach the level of violence meted out to the Americans by the British. When Grey's troops approached Old Tappan, the advanced guard found the sentry asleep. 'One of the officers of the grenadiers instantly cut off his head, without a word. The 33rd Regiment, to which I belonged, was about three miles off when the cruel carnage began', Shawe wrote with evident disgust. 'Tongue cannot tell nor pen unfold the horrors of that dismal night. Some were seen having their arms cut off, and others with their bowels hanging out crying for mercy.'[11]

Separately, but at the same time, Patrick Ferguson undertook a raid on Egg Harbour. While there, '... an opportunity offered without interrupting our progress, ... to penetrate some miles into the country, destroy three salt works & raze to the Ground, the stores & settlements of a Chairman of their committees, a Capt of Militia & one or two other violent rebels,' reported Ferguson, 'who had all been remarkably active in fomenting the rebellion, oppressing the people & forcing them against their inclination & better judgement to assist in their crimes.'[12] The raiding strategy was at least in part a campaign of terror to dissuade the population from supporting the rebellion. Clinton explicitly hoped that the raiding strategy would 'serve to convince these poor deluded people that that sort of war, carried to a greater extent and with more devastation will sooner or later reduce them'.[13]

Germain approved of Clinton's approach. The instructions he issued at the beginning of 1779 prioritised attempts to seek a decisive general action against the Continental Army, but failing that Clinton should act to contain Washington's freedom of manoeuvre. 'It is imagined that with an army of about 12,000 men in the field under your immediate command,' Germain wrote somewhat optimistically, 'you may force him to seek for safety in the Highlands of New York or the Jerseies [sic].' Clinton could achieve this by splitting his meagre army into three. One branch of his army would hold New York, a second would 'act on the side of New England and New Hampshire and the other in the Chesapeake Bay', where they would conduct raids and destroy maritime infrastructure. Having failed to move south in the winter of 1778, Clinton was to launch a campaign in Georgia as the winter of 1779 approached and campaigning in the northern colonies became impossible.[14]

Inevitably, the instructions annoyed Clinton. Modest though they were compared to earlier directives, German's instructions were still overambitious. For a start, Germain had badly overestimated the strength of Clinton's meagre army, choosing to include in the list of available forces those already committed to vital garrison duty, or who were declared ineffective through sickness or injury sustained in the previous campaign. Nevertheless, Clinton resolved to find a way to execute his instructions. 'To force Washington to an action upon terms tolerably equal has been the object of every campaign during this war,' Clinton wrote. 'The difficulty of attaining that object in so strong a country' had proved impossible, 'even with the Force Sir William Howe had'. The force with which Clinton was to attempt to do the same thing 'is in my idea by no means equal to the task'.

Attacking Washington on grounds of his choosing was consequently out of the question, but a new plan suggested itself. 'It shall be my endeavour to draw Washington forward ... by indirect manoeuvres,' Clinton explained. The chances of success remained low, but Clinton promised that 'if he gives into my views, no effort shall be wanting to strike at him whilst he is in motion, but if he persists in keeping his present post, I must not flatter myself that it will be easy to gain any advantages over him'.[15] Clinton's new strategy bore the hallmarks of his friendship with Henry Lloyd, whose influence is evident, whether direct through the communication of his views on America, or indirect through the two Henrys' shared interest in new approaches to manoeuvre warfare. Lloyd had addressed this specific point in correspondence with Clinton more than a decade earlier. 'One of the great errors committed by all those who write and speak of manoeuvres is that they never think of the enemy,' explained Lloyd. They 'always propose doing this, or that motion, without asking themselves what the enemy would or might do ....'.[16]

By now, Clinton had learned what did and did not provoke a reaction from Washington. Seizing terrain itself rarely forced Washington to move, but this was not the case if Clinton threatened a vital line of communication. Lloyd agreed, and publicly argued that the British could only draw Washington into a decisive battle by acting in a line of operation from Boston to the Hudson River, and threatening American communications between the middle colonies and New England. In the face of these threats on such vital lines, the Americans would have no option but to act. 'It is evident that the more he advances on the line from Hudson's River towards Boston the more certain is his ruin,' Lloyd wrote.[17] Most of all, it was essential that the British 'cease those fruitless and unmeaning excursions in the American woods'.[18]

Clinton, like Lloyd, had identified that the Hudson was of critical importance to the Americans and chose now to focus his meagre army there in an effort to draw Washington out. 'To effect it there appeared to me only one method; the seizing the forts of Verplank's and Stony Point, which form the entrance of the Highlands,' he later explained to Germain. 'I have long been sensible of the importance of that Post and ever designed to possess myself of it ....'[19] He asked his friend Newcastle to 'look at the map', and 'you will see the importance of it (Verplank's & Stony Points) it forbids Washington's communication with the Eastern Provinces, except by a very circuitous route of 60 miles ... through the mountains, & much exposed to the Indians', he explained. 'My whole force on the contrary can in 24 hours be assembled on either side of the Hudson's River.'[20]

Having been promised a large but unspecified reinforcement, on 31 May, Clinton launched a lightning strike against the recently completed twin fortifications on either side of the Hudson river near the town of Peekskill about 50 miles north of New York. General Vaughan commanded British and Hessian Grenadiers, the 33rd and the 42nd Regiments, in the descent on the eastern bank, eight miles south of Verplanck's Point. Colonel Johnson commanded the 17th, 63rd and 64th Regiments landing three miles south of Stony Point on the western bank. 'On the Ships Coming in View the Rebels evacuated their Works, which were in some forwardness, and set fire to a large Blockhouse,' Clinton reported to Germain. 'As the Troops approached to take Possession, they made some Shew of Resistance by drawing up upon the Hills, but did not wait a Conflict.'[21] Captain Peebles, who was with the Grenadiers on the eastern shore, observed that 'on the other side of the River[,] Rocky point[,] & from the Gallies they threw some shot & shells into the little fort which surrender'd about noon two kill'd & 1 wounded in the work, about 60 taken prisoners of war'.[22]

That night Clinton brought the artillery ashore at Stony Point, which could then bombard Verplanck's Point. 'Their effect was soon perceived,' wrote Clinton. 'General Vaughan appearing at this Time in the Rear of the Fort prevented the Retreat which the Enemy were Concerting. Under these Circumstances they delivered themselves into our Hands upon the Terms of Human Treatment which I promised them.'[23] Clinton had high hopes for the wider operational and strategic impact of this tactical move. 'In the first place, I opened the Campaign three weeks before Washington expected, or was prepared for it,' he wrote to Newcastle. 'I seized his short communication with the Eastern provinces, by King's Ferry [the crossing between Stony and Verplanck's Points]. I did suppose he must either act directly to recover it, risking a general action on unfavourable terms, or put himself immediately behind the Mountains to save Fort Defiance &c &c at West Point.' Clinton admitted that the latter action was unnecessary, as 'without a fleet & very superior Army, it is not attackable, & for other motives, I should never form an idea of attacking it'.[24] There remained a prospect, then, that when the reinforcements arrived, 'something very important might have followed this move'.[25]

News soon arrived, however, that the promised reinforcement had been delayed, and had not sailed until 25 May, which meant Clinton could not 'expect it till the first week in September & when it comes, what will it be?'[26] This curtailed Clinton's ability to operate. 'Had the reinforcement arrived at the time I had right to expect it,' Clinton later explained, then he might well have been able to move against the Americans 'for Washington assembled his army many weeks sooner than he intended and marched behind the Mountains to New Windsor, where he is much distressed, I believe, & his army discontented'.[27]

Though Washington would not move to retake the King's Ferry, his lines of communication and supply to New Windsor were vulnerable. 'As I had an Army afloat ready to debark on either side, I could by a rapid & tolerably well combined march, have got hold of a strong position near Middlebrook,' Clinton explained to Newcastle, 'in which situation I should have been upon his Communications with Trenton, & nearer to his stores at Easton than he could be for some days.' Without the reinforcements, however, there was little Clinton could do. 'I fortified Stony Point & Verplanck's, leaving near 1,000 Men for their defence. I collected what troops could be spared from Rhode Island, & sent expeditions into Connecticut, hoping the strong motivations of that Province would have forced Washington to march to their assistance.' The move proved futile. 'Nothing however could draw him from New Windsor,' Clinton wrote despondently.[28] He judged that Washington would not risk a general action on terrain so unfavourable to the Americans.[29]

In the event, the Americans did make an attack on Stony Point on the night of 16 July. A column of infantry made a frontal assault, while a second stronger column stormed the upper works, with 'every person within them put to the Sword'.[30] Clinton had been unable to mobilise his forces from New York in time to retrieve the situation, but when he did arrive 'within sight of Stoney Point, the enemy abandoned it with precipitation & some circumstances of disgrace'.[31] Tossing the artillery into the Hudson, the Americans withdrew under instruction to avoid significant casualties. Clinton's attempt to draw Washington out by indirect manoeuvres had failed.

It is perhaps fair to argue that Clinton was the right general at the wrong time. Had he been in command earlier in the war, then his plans to manoeuvre Washington into a decisive action on unfavourable terms to the Americans might well have succeeded. Certainly, he demonstrated such potential at New York, when he advised manoeuvring to cut off Washington's line of retreat. The British Army was strong enough then to impose such an action on Washington. In 1779, Clinton lacked the manpower to bring his strategy to fruition. With the British foothold at Stony and Verplanck's Point tenuous at best, and with Washington showing no signs of taking the bait, Clinton felt 'hopeless of bringing him to a general action'.[32] With the campaigning season in the north drawing to a close, Clinton decided to withdraw from the Hudson and concentrate on the southern colonies.

The campaign there had begun successfully enough when an assault force numbering some 2,500 troops under the command of Lieutenant-Colonel Archibald Campbell and Commodore Hyde Parker arrived in the Savannah River in December 1778. They quickly confronted the defenders of the strategically important port of Savannah. Campbell managed to manoeuvre his light infantry units 'into the rear of Enemy's right Flank', whereupon as soon as the American defenders realised their position was turned, they lost cohesion and fled across the river into South Carolina.[33] A follow-up operation against Augusta in January 1779 was equally successful, but the British position there proved unsustainable and Campbell was forced to withdraw.

In September 1779, Campbell's replacement, General Augustine Prevost, managed to fend off a combined Franco-American attack on Savannah.[34] For Clinton this 'most critical cheque' appeared to confirm the viability of the so-called Southern Strategy.[35] It was with a considerable degree of confidence, then, that he assembled a formidable and highly experienced body of men with which to attack Charleston, the capital of South Carolina, and probably the most strategically important port in North America besides New York.

In total, Clinton assembled 8,708 troops, including five regular battalions, two of grenadiers, three of light infantry, six German units, Banastre Tarleton's British Legion and Patrick Ferguson's Rangers. When the force sailed on 26 December 1779, severe weather scattered the fleet, and it was not until the end of January that the first ships limped into Savannah. By the middle of February, Clinton had assembled his command, drawing extra forces from Prevost's garrison of Savannah, as well as 1,000 sailors.[36]

An abortive expedition in 1776 had illustrated to Clinton how difficult it was to approach Charleston by sea, so he selected a land attack instead. The city itself was on a small peninsula, which was connected to the mainland by a narrow isthmus. It was here that Clinton planned to conduct his siege and cut off Charleston from American support and reinforcements. With the Royal Navy in command of the waterways surrounding Charleston, the success of the siege was all but a foregone conclusion. The local American commander, General Benjamin Lincoln, realised there was little to do, and planned to escape with his substantial garrison, but the civilian administration demanded he stay and attempt to defend the town.

On 29 March, Clinton made his move. The naval commander, Admiral Mariot Arbuthnot, blockaded the outer harbour, though he remained unwilling to move his ships to the inner harbour, fearful they would come within range of the guns in Fort Moultrie which guarded the entrance. The move nevertheless succeeded in distracting the defenders' attention while Clinton landed his ground forces several miles north-west of the city. Before the Americans could react, Clinton gained control of the isthmus, started building siegeworks and commenced a bombardment on 10 April. Once the siegeworks on the isthmus were completed, Arbuthnot ran the gauntlet of Moultrie's guns and got his fleet into the Inner Harbour, further limiting Lincoln's options. All that remained was for Clinton to seal off the remaining routes into or out of Charleston. Indeed, Clinton saw this as the key to success. 'To secure the capture of all the rebel corps in Charleston', he wrote, 'had been from the first a very principal object with me, as I saw the reduction of the rest of the province in great measure depended upon it.'[37]

On 14 April, Clinton detached Banastre Tarleton and Patrick Ferguson to seize Monck's Corner and Biggin Bridge, which might have afforded Lincoln a means of escape and an American depot. Both were earning reputations as bold and decisive commanders, and they attacked Monck's Corner at night without fully appreciating its defences.[38] 'The order was executed with the greatest promptitude and success. The Americans were completely surprised' and 'many officers and men fled on foot to the swamps'.[39] A counterattack was similarly dispersed. The move seemingly illustrated that bold and aggressive offensive action would ultimately achieve success. In early May, Clinton attacked and captured Hobcaw Point and moved along the Wando River, sealing off Charleston.[40] By 25 April, the British parallels had reached almost to the base of the American defences on the isthmus, and on 8 May a closer bombardment was ready to commence. With the city now completely surrounded and facing bombardment on all sides, Clinton summoned Lincoln to surrender unconditionally. The latter, however, sought the 'Honours of War', in an effort to preserve the cohesion of his garrison. Clinton refused, and on 9 May, 'orders were given to fire on the city with red-hot shot, which set fire to several houses', recalled Captain Johann Ewald, 'and made the sight more terrible and melancholy'.[41] A two-day bombardment achieved the desired results, and on 12 May, Lincoln surrendered the city and its substantial garrison of 5,500 regular soldiers and 500 militia unconditionally.[42]

The loss of Charleston was the worst defeat suffered by the Americans during the Revolutionary War. Flushed with success, Clinton elected to return to New York and develop plans for operations in the Chesapeake Bay, leaving his deputy, Charles, Earl Cornwallis, in command in Charleston. Clinton expected Cornwallis to conduct a strategy similar to the one he had executed in the north, one focused on raiding to denude the Americans of support and supplies, bring succour to isolated loyalists and gradually smother the rebellion. He proposed to 'leave with ... Cornwallis a force equal to the defence of this province & that of Georgia and also to any further active measure' against the remaining American forces in the Carolinas.[43] Clinton expected great things from such an approach. Privately, he hoped he was 'not ... too sanguine in saying (if the reports from our friends in the back country are founded) we shall soon have nearly conquered both Carolinas in C[harles]Town'.[44]

However, the British estimation of the level of loyalist support in the back country of the Carolina's was wildly awry. Prior to his departure, Clinton made things worse by issuing a series of proclamations which alienated any nascent loyalist support by offering amnesty to all rebels who submitted once more to royal authority, and then alienated any wavering rebels by stating that those who had not sworn allegiance would be considered in an active state of rebellion. Indeed, 'nine out of ten' neutrals, noted one officer, 'are now embodied on the part of the rebels'.[45] Moreover, Cornwallis had no intention of pursuing a war by indirect manoeuvres. Although he would reorganise his army into a highly mobile and effective unit, his aim was a direct confrontation in order to bring about a decisive battle.

Like each of his peers to reach the highest levels of command in North America, Cornwallis took the profession of arms seriously.[46] At the outbreak of the Seven Years' War, Cornwallis had obtained special permission to travel through Europe, guided by a veteran of the War of Austrian Succession, Captain de Roguin. Their ultimate destination was Turin, where Cornwallis entered the military academy, and undertook several months of varied military study, including three hours a day taught by the master of arms, and a curriculum focused on mathematics and fortifications, ballroom dancing and language lessons. As the war in Europe escalated, Cornwallis volunteered to join the staff of Prince Ferdinand, where he served until British forces arrived in Germany. On 6 August 1758,

Cornwallis was appointed aide-de-camp to the Marquis of Granby, who, following Sackville's disgrace at Minden, would go on to command British forces in Europe.

Alongside Granby, Cornwallis learned much about the operational practice of war, while after his promotion on 1 May 1761 to lieutenant-colonel in the 12th Foot, he also gained experience of the tactical and logistical management of troops in battle. As his career progressed, Cornwallis became 'more and more convinced of the necessity of military reading'.[47] His military planning belied a fondness for the works of Turpin de Crissé, but his later interest in particular in Folard's arguments confirmed his opinion that the principal use for an army was to fight and win decisive battles.[48] The cumulative effect of Cornwallis's education and military experience produced, in the words of historian Stanley Carpenter, a personality that 'drove him to bold, risky, aggressive, and offensive-oriented warfare'. In America, he argued for a 'highly aggressive strategy of annihilation'.[49] In this key respect, Cornwallis differed with Clinton, and their relationship swiftly soured as a result.

Tensions between the two generals increased noticeably during the siege of Charleston. Clinton looked to their similar experiences in Europe in the hope of finding common ground. 'As our education had been the same, it was not extraordinary we should think alike,' he noted in a detailed account of conversations he had with Cornwallis during the siege. Indeed, Clinton believed he 'had been influenced a good deal by [Cornwallis's] opinions'.[50] Cornwallis, however, was frustrated by Clinton's defensive posture and indirect manoeuvres. Instead, Cornwallis developed a strategy of detachments, which would hunt down enemy units and destroy them. 'By acting distinctly,' wrote André, 'I apprehend he means to undertake particular points of attack or particular marches etc having with him branches of the different departments for his assistance.'[51]

Clinton became increasingly convinced that Cornwallis would 'play me false, I fear'.[52] As the campaign progressed, and Clinton watched from afar, largely powerless in New York, he became more and more concerned that Cornwallis's strategy was doomed to fail. Cornwallis's plan, he suggested, was 'to cover a country with small posts, by which he is sure that some will be affronted. And I think the whole may be beat in detail ...'.[53] Clinton was starkly illustrating the intellectual differences between himself and his deputy.

Clinton remained risk-averse and wanted to husband his resources until a decisive opportunity presented itself. Keen to maintain the initiative, however, Cornwallis felt it necessary to make detachments in order to facilitate his broader strategic mobility with the aim of tracking down and destroying the Continental regular force in the south. Here, then, was the root of strategic and operational dissonance in North America as the war of independence approached its conclusion: the intellectual battle between those who advocated the pursuit of decisive battle at all costs and those who sought to manoeuvre their enemy into defeat. The failure to resolve this dissonance largely explains the defeat of British arms in North America.

*   *   *

In the wake of the fall of Charleston, the strategic situation in the summer of 1780 looked very bright for the British forces. A series of conventional victories had, on the face of it, seen active support for the rebellion apparently collapse in South Carolina. In reality, however, brutal assaults such as that launched at the Waxhaws by Banastre Tarleton's British Legion, which resulted in the deaths of 113 Americans and the wounding of a further 150, set a bloody tone for the campaign. The Waxhaws massacre, as it became known, was to further alienate previously neutral southerners and crystallised American hatred of the British. In future, British soldiers trying to surrender were offered 'Tarleton's Quarter'.[54]

At the time, however, Cornwallis wrote enthusiastically of Tarleton's 'zeal, spirit, and abilities'.[55] The speed and decision of Tarleton's movement seemed to confirm Cornwallis's preference for an approach that was designed to bring about a decisive confrontation in which the superiority of British arms would prevail. Such an approach depended on a strong logistical network of local depots and magazines. The great limiting factor of swift and decisive manoeuvre in eighteenth-century warfare was the delays imposed by ensuring sufficient supplies existed to maintain the army in the field. Loyalist support was needed more for this purpose than for the limited tactical advantage their numbers offered on the battlefield. As he departed Charleston, commencing operations in the interior of South Carolina, Cornwallis was blissfully ignorant of the simmering discontent unleashed by the political and military missteps in the wake of the capture of Charleston.

He commenced his efforts to complete the pacification of South Carolina by adopting an approach probably derived from Turpin de Crissé's *Essai sur la guerre* and reminiscent of Forbes's plan of operations against Fort DuQuesne in 1758. Within weeks of the fall of Charleston he had established a chain of posts that extended in an arc some 140 miles north and north-west of the newly captured city, from Augusta, through the town of Ninety Six, Camden and to within 25 miles of the border with North Carolina. His 11,000-strong army was, as a result, thinly spread, meaning considerable local command authority had to be delegated to trusted subordinates like Patrick Ferguson, Banastre Tarleton and Francis Rawdon.[56]

Nevertheless, by the end of June, Cornwallis felt able to make plans go on the offensive. '[W]ith the force at present under my command . . . I can leave South Carolina in security', he wrote optimistically, 'and march about the beginning of September with a body of troops into the back part of North Carolina with the greatest probability of reducing that Province to its duty . . . .'[57] Within a month of Cornwallis writing this ambitious assessment, his units had collectively been attacked more than a dozen times by irregular bands of American partisans; storehouses were pillaged and destroyed, and convoys repeatedly ambushed. In just five weeks, casualties exceeded 400, principally centred on the Loyalist forces upon which the British depended. South Carolina was, Cornwallis wryly observed to Clinton, 'not so peaceable as when I wrote last' and was 'in an absolute state of rebellion'.[58]

In this atmosphere, intelligence began to trickle in that an American army, under the command of the hero of Saratoga, General Horatio Gates, was moving south, 'and making every appearance of attacking Lord Rawdon'.[59] The latter 'endeavoured to delay Gates as much as possible in his progress', but 'whensoever he threatened to pass round my flank and get between me and Camden, I was always obliged to fall back'. Eventually, Rawdon concentrated his force at Camden and prepared for an attack. 'Gates's army is called five thousand,' Rawdon reported to Cornwallis, 'but I do not believe they exceed three thousand five hundred.'[60]

In addition, however, Colonel Thomas Sumter's highly energetic band of irregular soldiers had been reinforced by Gates. Sumter now commanded 1,000 men, and planned to attack the British posts at Rocky Mount and Hanging Rock. Cornwallis was quick to react and deployed from Charleston in the direction of Camden late on 10 August. It was the excuse he had been looking for in order to justify an offensive operation. Cornwallis had convinced himself that the only way to subdue the rebellion in South Carolina was to cut it off from support by invading North Carolina.[61] He acknowledged that some 'doubted . . . whether the invasion . . . may be a prudent measure,' but continued, 'I am convinced it is a

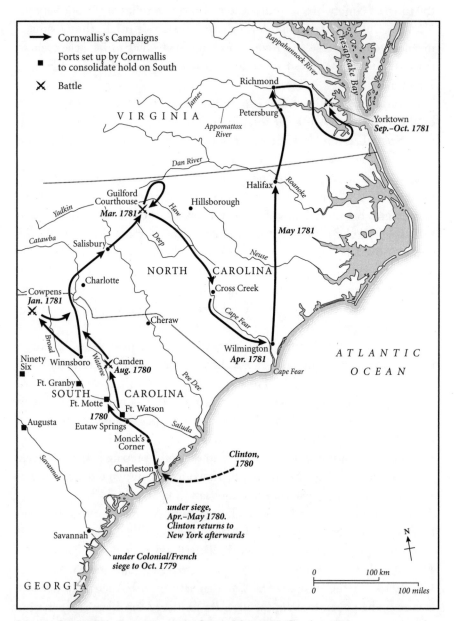

Map 6. Cornwallis's Campaign in the South, May 1780–October 1781.

necessary one, and that, if we do not attack that province, we must give up both South Carolina and Georgia and retire within the walls of Charlestown.'[62]

Cornwallis arrived at Camden on 13 August, bringing with him four companies of light infantry from Ninety Six. His total force exceeded 1,900 men, including more than 1,000 veteran redcoats, 500 men from Tarleton's Legion, a North Carolina provincial regiment, and 300 battle-hardened loyalists. The British were outnumbered by Gates, but Cornwallis agreed with Rawdon that the quality of his adversary's troops was low, while he also recognised that retreat was not an option, since it would irrevocably harm the already poor morale of North Carolina loyalists.

In darkness, on 15 August, Cornwallis put his combined forces in motion, blundering into Gates north of Camden. At dawn, Gates thought he perceived a last-minute reorganisation in Cornwallis's lines on the British right and ordered an immediate attack, just as Cornwallis himself ordered his right to begin an advance. 'In a few minutes the action was general along the whole front,' Cornwallis explained. With no wind in the air, the smoke from the weapons fire quickly 'occasioned so thick a darkness that it was difficult to see the effect of a very heavy and well supported fire on both sides'.[63] On the British left, the 33rd Foot sustained casualties as they came up against hardened American regulars, but on the right, the 23rd 'being opposed only by militia ... first broke the enemy's front line', and then turned 'on the left flank of the continentals, who were abandoned by their militia',[64] many of whom flew 'into such a panic that they threw down their *loaded* arms and fled, in the utmost consternation'.[65]

Unaware that the militia had collapsed, the American regulars fought on until their commanding officers were themselves shot and injured. According to Cornwallis, the redcoats displayed 'the cool intrepidity of experienced British soldiers, keeping up a constant fire or making use of bayonets as opportunities offered'. After barely an hour, as the American line began to disintegrate, Tarleton's Legion entered the fray and a general 'rout and slaughter ensued in every quarter'.[66] In the days that followed, Tarleton tracked down and surprised Sumter at Catawba Falls, all but eliminating his force and removing any threat to Cornwallis's lines of communication.[67]

In the wake of Camden, Gates's unit essentially ceased to exist as a coherent entity and Gates himself fled to Hillsborough, where he frantically tried to reassemble the Continental Army in the South. On the surface, at least, Cornwallis's strategy appeared rapidly to be bearing fruit, though he made the fatal assumption that military victory would auto-matically translate into political control.[68] Indeed, with 'the rebel forces at present being dispersed,' he wrote optimistically to Germain, 'the internal commotions and insurrections in the province will now subside.'[69] Cornwallis was not the first, nor would he be the last, army officer to make this mistake. While seeking to eliminate the conventional Continental Army as an effective adversary had evident merits, the British failed to understand that popular support for the rebellion was a political rather than military problem.[70]

In reality, British losses were also very troubling for Cornwallis. He had lost 324 of all ranks, but the losses sustained by his regulars were the most concerning. The 33rd, for example, lost 36 per cent of its fighting force, including half of its officers.[71] If he was to maintain an aggressive campaign designed to bring his adversary to decisive battles, Cornwallis could not sustain this rate of attrition for long. He was acutely conscious of this and appealed to Clinton for reinforcements. 'Our sickness is great and truly alarming,' he wrote towards the end of August.[72] Clinton, however, refused. Washington's army had been energised by recent rein-forcements from France, which he now estimated numbered nearly 18,000 troops.[73] Clinton therefore felt he could not afford to divert forces to support Cornwallis in his fight with 'a small body of ill armed peas-antry'.[74] As the campaign wore on, and casualties mounted, Cornwallis was quick to point out that 'the list of British officers and soldiers killed and wounded by' the American forces 'since last June proves but too fatally that they are not wholly contemptible'.[75]

Cornwallis, meanwhile, pressed on with his plans to invade North Carolina, though he was at this point by no means impetuous, as some historians have claimed.[76] 'It is difficult to form a plan of operations, which must depend so much on circumstances,' he explained to Clinton. 'It at present appears to me that I should endeavour to get as soon as possible to Hillsborough and there assemble, and try to arrange, the friends who are inclined to arm in our favour and endeavour to form a very large magazine for the winter of flour and meal from the country.'[77] As with his plans to spread British control in South Carolina, Cornwallis was extending de Crissé's 'war of posts' concept into North Carolina. He was painfully aware of how ambitious this plan was: he had only 2,200 reliable soldiers to execute the move to Hillsborough, and he was moving his army further and further from the coast and naval support. Moreover, rather than serving as a means of spreading British control in South

Carolina and into North Carolina, his 'war of posts' simply served to offer tempting targets to American partisans in search of employment.

Beset by sickness and harassed by partisan attacks, Cornwallis was unable to make it as far as Hillsborough. Bad news then arrived from the forces protecting his left flank, where Major Patrick Ferguson had been detached with loyalist militia.[78] Bands of irregulars, known locally as the over-the-mountain men, had begun to coalesce and move against Ferguson's position, sparking a confrontation over the control of the north-west corner of South Carolina and the border with North Carolina. On 30 September, Ferguson learned that as many as 2,000 American irregulars were bearing down on his position. He appealed to Cornwallis for reinforcements. '*2000 I cannot face*. I shall therefore probably incline *eastward.*'[79]

By 6 October, after a few days hard marching, Ferguson had reached a high point known as King's Mountain and chose to offer battle there, believing the steep-sided mountain offered a formidable challenge to his adversary. In fact, the dense woodland around the base of the hill and on its steep slopes afforded the highly trained American marksmen excellent cover from which to target the defenders. The loyalist troops soon began to lose cohesion, and although a 'little detachment of soldiers charged the enemy with success and drove the right wing of them back in confusion', the attackers used the thick foliage to return to the plateau and continue their devastating fire. By targeting their officers, the over-the-mountain men caused increased confusion and disarray among the provincials.[80] Ferguson was himself killed trying to rally his disintegrating command, shot no fewer than seven times in the chest. His body was dragged by his terrified horse across the battlefield. As the remaining loyalist soldiers were bottled into a piece of terrain that measured barely 60 yards by 40 yards, Captain Abraham DePeyster, upon whom command had now devolved, elected to surrender. Unable to contain their enthusiasm for assaulting the remnants of Ferguson's command, many of the Americans yelled 'Tarleton's Quarter' and continued to fire at point-blank range. The American officers eventually managed to restore order, but casualties were devastating. As many as 157 men lay dead while a further 123 would succumb to their wounds. As many as 700 were marched into captivity. The Americans suffered fewer than 100 casualties in total.

Ferguson's defeat and death dealt a severe blow to Cornwallis's plans. Besides rendering his left flank vulnerable, the loss of such a substantial body of troops undermined his offensive strategy and further subdued already hesitant loyalist support for the Crown cause. Though 'many of the inhabitants wish well to His Majesty's arms', Rawdon reported at the end of October, 'they have not given evidence enough either of their number or activity, to justify the stake of this province'.[81] Cornwallis withdrew to Winnsborough in South Carolina, and detached Tarleton to try to catch and destroy the partisans. This he managed to do at Blackstock's Plantation in November, but the Americans were again able to escape, while Tarleton suffered disproportionate casualties. Though Tarleton painted the events at Blackstock's Plantation as a Crown victory, continued American raids suggested a different story. Attacks throughout December on loyalist detachments at Long Canes, Halfway Swamp, Singleton's Mill and Hammond's Store, all near Ninety Six, demonstrated Cornwallis's tenuous control of South Carolina.

Faced with the continued failure to suppress the irregular forces in South Carolina, Cornwallis decided to recommit to his offensive strategy. If he could sweep aside the remaining regular Continental Army in North Carolina, then he might be able to invade Virginia and Maryland and even challenge Washington in a two-pronged attack in coordination with Clinton. His decision to pursue this strategy coincided with Gates's replacement with Major General Nathanael Greene.

An avid reader of military history and theory, Greene had proved himself a first-class quartermaster, and upon his appointment to command in the south began a systematic reorganisation of the army. He convinced another veteran of the Saratoga Campaign, Daniel Morgan, to return to the service, in command of the Virginia Continentals which had been sent to reinforce the southern army. Still, he recognised that his regular force was no match for Cornwallis and seeing 'little prospect of getting a force to contend with the enemy upon equal grounds', he decided to 'make the most of a kind of partisan war'.[82] Greene adopted a Fabian strategy designed to exhaust Cornwallis's army, while preserving the integrity and tactical mobility of the Continental force. In so doing, Greene made excellent use of the terrain of North Carolina, and led Cornwallis on a series of frustrating marches, which drew the British further from their supply bases. The irregulars, meanwhile, would interrupt the lengthening British supply lines.[83]

Faced with his own supply shortages, Greene elected to split his force in two, sending Morgan, with the Maryland and Delaware Continentals, the Virginia Riflemen and a unit of the Continental Light Dragoons, south-west toward Ninety Six with the objective of threatening Cornwallis's left flank. Greene himself, with the remainder of his army, moved south-east toward the Pee Dee River. He aimed to compel his 'adversary to divide his' force and leave 'him in doubt as to his own line of conduct'.[84] The plan worked almost exactly as Greene intended. Cornwallis amassed the majority of his force in an effort to counter Greene's move on his right flank, while Tarleton was detached to defend Ninety Six. In response, Morgan withdrew and Cornwallis 'directed Lt Colonel Tarleton ... to endeavour to strike a blow at General Morgan'.[85]

Tarleton commenced his pursuit on 1 January 1781, with a 1,000-strong force. He pursued his opponent with vigour, until Morgan eventually decided to make a stand on 17 January at Hannah's Cowpens, a relatively open wood, with little to disrupt Tarleton's use of cavalry. The opportunity was too good for Tarleton to pass up. 'An open wood was certainly a proper place for action', recalled Tarleton, 'America does not produce many more suitable'.[86] Deploying his force in three lines, Morgan ordered his jittery militia, in the front two lines, to fire off a couple of good volleys and retire, hoping this would disrupt Tarleton's attack sufficiently for the Continental regulars, deployed in the third line at the crest of a hill, to make a stand.

Tarleton ordered his infantry to deploy into two lines but commenced his attack without first resting his troops and having failed to conduct a reconnaissance of the field of battle. He assumed the American militia would panic, leaving his force to assault the Continentals unhampered. So keen was he to commence the battle that he ordered an advance before his infantry had finished falling into line. As the British advanced, they were surprised at the discipline exhibited by the militia, withholding their fire until the British were within 'thirty or forty paces'.[87] At this point, 'the front line ... poured in a close fire', the effect of which was 'considerable: it produced something like a recoil, but not to any extent'.[88] The British light infantry tried to charge the American riflemen but were repulsed with some loss. A second attempt was made after the militia had reloaded, but the British again sustained significant casualties. Some parts of the militia line managed to get off five volleys in three minutes, but with their weapons discharged and their ammunition spent, the militia, as planned, withdrew to their left. A charge by Tarleton's horse was itself disrupted by the Continental Light Dragoons.

The British infantry continued to advance, and now encountered the line of Maryland and Delaware regulars. They were steadier and better trained than the militia, and the sustained fire from the third American line stopped Tarleton's advance cold. Nevertheless, Tarleton sought to extend his attacking line in an effort to envelop the Continentals. Orders were given to counter this action, but the Americans misunderstood and commenced a well-ordered retreat. Realising an opportunity to draw Tarleton into a trap, Morgan encouraged the manoeuvre. Believing their adversaries to be in retreat, the British infantry commenced a charge that disrupted their own cohesion.

At this point Morgan gave the order to turn about face and the Americans 'made a perfect line' and 'commenced a very destructive fire, which' the British 'little expected, and a few rounds occasioned great disorder in their ranks'.[89] Meanwhile, the militia had made a complete circuit of the field, and were now rallied by Morgan himself. 'Form, my brave fellows,' yelled the Old Waggoner. 'Old Morgan was never beaten'. The militia 'made a half circuit at full speed and came upon the rear of the British line, shouting and charging like madmen ...'. At this point, 'the British line broke'.[90] The British flanks gave way first, before a charge by the American regulars precipitated the collapse of the rest of the line. Tarleton fled the battlefield, having burnt his baggage.

Tarleton would later blame the 'loose manner of forming which had always been practised by the King's troops in America'. He argued that 'if infantry who are formed very open, and only two deep, meet with opposition, they can have no stability ... when they experience an unexpected shock'.[91] The common practice of forming in two ranks and relying on superior firepower and marksmanship, heralded by Wolfe at Quebec and repeated since, was only effective if the British possessed the tactical advantage on the battlefield. Sustained resistance would weaken the infantry cohesion too quickly and terminally undermine its discipline. Writing several weeks later and having received numerous accounts of the battle, Clinton seemed inclined to agree. 'Tarleton's order of battle does not seem to have been a bad one,' he wrote in a confidential memorandum. 'I fear his first line after its success, in the charge, has advanced too much ... and the second has sustained too closely and probably too loose Order.' When the first met with a check, he continued, it was 'thrown back in confusion upon the second and the enemy I fear in better order has attacked them at that critical moment'.[92]

Other witnesses, however, preferred to blame '*that boy*' – Tarleton – for his arrogance, and, indeed, this was what Morgan had counted on.[93] He had drawn the British infantry into a trap and enveloped them with his militia. The Battle of Cowpens all but destroyed Tarleton's legion, and eliminated two regular battalions – the 7th and 71st Foot – as coherent fighting units for the foreseeable future. More than 100 British soldiers were killed including 39 of the 66 officers who started the battle. In addition, 200 were wounded and 525 taken prisoner. Morgan suffered 75 killed and wounded.[94] Cornwallis tried to dismiss the significance of Tarleton's defeat. 'It is impossible to foresee all the consequences that this unexpected and extraordinary event may produce,' he wrote to Clinton, 'but your Excellency may be assured that nothing but the most absolute necessity shall induce me to give up the important object of the winter's campaign.'[95]

Clinton was having none of it. He could not understand why Cornwallis would take such a risk in ordering Tarleton to follow Morgan 'unsustained for days till [he] falls back and gathers like a snowball'.[96] Indeed, following Ferguson's death, Clinton had begun to harbour grave doubts about Cornwallis's strategy. 'Why meet the enemy on their own terms?' he questioned. 'Their object is action en detail.' Now Tarleton's defeat seemed to confirm Clinton's worst fears. 'I tremble at this system of detachment,' he wrote.[97] The loss of two of his most experienced regiments and the lion's share of his light infantry had, indeed, dealt a grievous blow to Cornwallis's operational and tactical capabilities. Bereft of light infantry to conduct reconnaissance, he would now suffer from poor situational awareness, and would be unable to move as rapidly.

As he planned his invasion of North Carolina, then, Cornwallis sought to shape the breadth of his operations. He ordered Colonel Nisbet Balfour to detach a force from Charleston to occupy Wilmington on the North Carolina coast. The objective here was to establish a forward magazine on which the Crown forces would eventually be able to depend. Balfour sent Major Craig of the 82nd, who found Wilmington virtually unprotected, and occupied the city with ease on 28 January. Meanwhile, in the wake of the battle at the Cowpens, Morgan had marched west in an effort to avoid a further confrontation with the main British force, encamped 30 miles away at Turkey Creek. Cornwallis decided to pursue and defeat him before his force could rendezvous with Greene but received faulty intelligence and moved in the wrong direction. When he learned the truth, he set off in pursuit of his quarry, but it was by then too late. Morgan easily outran the British army, encumbered as it was by a lengthy supply train which moved slowly along the poor roads in the wilderness of western North Carolina. Having covered only 72 miles in seven days, when Cornwallis reached Ramsour's Mill on 25 January, he decided the only way to increase his mobility was to burn his baggage train.

Somewhat surprisingly, there were few desertions, even as 'all prospect of future rum and even a regular supply of provisions to the soldiers' went up in flames.[98] This was probably because Cornwallis ensured that his soldiers were not alone in facing this enforced destitution when he added his own possessions and those of his officers to the inferno. In so doing, Cornwallis essentially transformed his entire force into a 'light, highly manoeuvrable and agile striking force'.[99] The transition was not as challenging as might be imagined. As was the custom in North America, all troops had received rudimentary light infantry tactical training while encamped in Nova Scotia prior to deployment to New York in 1776.[100] 'In this situation,' on 28 January, 'without baggage, necessaries or provisions of any sort for officer or soldier,' wrote Brigadier Charles O'Hara of the Foot Guards, 'in the most barren, inhospitable, unhealthy part of North America, opposed to the most savage, inveterate, perfidious, cruel enemy, with zeal and with bayonets only, it was resolved to follow Greene's army to the end of the world.'[101]

Greene, however, had anticipated this strategy and chose to use the geography of North Carolina against Cornwallis. He realised that no matter how light Cornwallis's force was, it would be delayed in its movements if denied easy passage of the rivers that bisected North Carolina in a south-by-south-easterly direction. He therefore gave orders for sufficient numbers of boats to be gathered at each river to act as pontoon bridges, which could be easily built and dismantled. At the same time, he ordered his quartermaster to deny the same option to his adversary by collecting and withdrawing as many boats as possible and withholding them from the British. Greene also positioned supply magazines along the likely routes by which he would march, consuming those supplies as his army withdrew northwards toward Virginia, leaving nothing for the advancing British. Benefitting likewise from information readily provided by a friendly local population, Greene also planned his movements with much better situational awareness than the British.

Cornwallis nevertheless moved faster than Greene anticipated, crossing the Catawba river at Cowan's Ford on 1 February, before pursuing the Americans to the banks of the Yadkin. There, Greene's advanced preparations proved essential. The Americans were able to cross in the nick of time, but the lack of boats available to their pursuers forced Cornwallis to divert 50 miles north to a suitable ford. He then paused for two days at Salisbury to feed his bedraggled army. There, he learned that Greene had ordered Morgan and Huger to rendezvous with the main Continental army at Guilford Courthouse, 50 miles north-east of Salisbury. Cornwallis's attempts to defeat the American forces in detail had failed. But Greene decided against offering battle on the advantageous position at Guilford Courthouse: he remained concerned that his force of 1,400 Continentals and nearly a thousand militia were outmatched by Cornwallis's near three thousand regulars, both qualitatively and quantitatively.

Instead, he decided to continue his strategy of drawing Cornwallis ever further from his supply bases in Wilmington and Camden, and thus attriting British strength. Greene detached a light corps under the command of Colonel Otho Williams to delay, harass and misdirect Cornwallis. Williams headed northwest from Guilford on 8 February. As expected, Cornwallis assumed this to be the American rearguard and so began an immediate pursuit hoping to outflank Williams. Greene, meanwhile, departed Guilford two days later, heading for the River Dan in a different direction. Despite appalling weather conditions, the two armies made remarkable progress, covering up to 40 miles in one day. Skirmishes occurred frequently, but Williams handled his troops well, and inflicted more casualties on the British than they did on him. Four days into the pursuit, Cornwallis received word from Tarleton of Greene's true location, and shifted his march to the east, but it was too late.

On 15 February, O'Hara caught up with Williams just as the American colonel reached the north bank of the Dan. Greene had crossed four days earlier. 'I tried by a most rapid march to strike a blow either at Greene or Morgan before they got over the Dan, but could not effect it', Cornwallis wrote to Rawdon. Both armies had marched 230 miles in eight days. 'The fatigue of our troops and hardships which they suffered were excessive', he continued. With his troops exhausted and faced with a lengthy march upstream for a suitable ford, Cornwallis ended the pursuit and fell back to Hillsborough, where he arrived on 20 February.[102] As with earlier attempts, local loyalist recruitment fell short of either expectation or requirement, and demonstrated, in O'Hara's words, the 'fatal infatuation' the British had with the south.[103]

On 23 February, having received reinforcements from Virginia, Greene marched for Hillsborough. A game of cat and mouse now ensued, in which Cornwallis attempted to force Greene to accept battle, but the latter would not fight until favourable conditions could be gained. By 10 March, having received additional reinforcements, including 550 Continental regulars from Baron Friedrich von Steuben's command in south-eastern Virginia, Greene now commanded nearly 4,400 troops, although 2,800 were militia, some of whom Greene could not trust in a set-piece confrontation.[104]

Despite this concern, Greene now felt able to offer Cornwallis battle, and selected the same ground at Guilford Courthouse that he had vacated several weeks earlier. He deployed his army in a manner which reflected Morgan's successful deployment at Cowpens earlier in the year. In the frontline, Greene placed two brigades of North Carolina militia, his least reliable troops. Like Morgan, he hoped that the militia would be able to get off a few good shots and then withdraw. Some three hundred yards behind this line, in dense woodland, Greene positioned the Virginia militia, where he clearly expected the more seasoned troops to take advantage of the terrain to inflict losses on the advancing British regulars. Some five hundred yards behind the Virginians, Greene positioned the Maryland, Delaware and Virginia Continental regulars. The most experienced troops in the army therefore had an open field of fire. Greene wanted the first two lines of militia to wear down the British advance, leaving the Continentals to inflict devastating losses with their superior musketry and bayonets.

Cornwallis had very little understanding of the terrain in which he now prepared to fight. American prisoners captured by Tarleton offered 'no account of the enemy's order or position, and the country-people were extremely inaccurate in their description of the ground'.[105] As it approached the field of battle, Cornwallis deployed his army with the Hessians and the 71st on the right under Brigadier Alexander Leslie, supported by the 1st Battalion of the Brigade of Foot Guards. On the left, Colonel James Webster commanded the 23rd and 33rd, with the 2nd Battalion of Foot Guards in support. The composite units of light infantry, the German Jägers and Tarleton's dragoons held the British left flank. Cornwallis ordered the advance, and as the redcoats approached the American line, they observed the Carolinian militia with 'their arms presented and resting on a fence rail'. According to Sergeant Roger Lamb, 'they were taking aim with the nicest kind of precision'.[106] They opened fire at 40 yards, loosing off a 'most galling and destructive fire'.[107]

Accounts vary, but some militiamen managed to get off as many as three volleys. 'The part of the British line at which they aimed', noted one observer, 'looked like the scattering stalks in a wheatfield when the harvest man has passed over it with his cradle.'[108] Nevertheless, the redcoats persisted with their advance, firing several volleys and threatening a bayonet charge, which persuaded the Carolinian militia to flee the battlefield in panic. Attempts by their officers to rally them were unsuccessful: they suffered three killed, nine wounded and 549 missing.[109] Despite the collapse in the centre, the American flanks, where Greene had posted well-

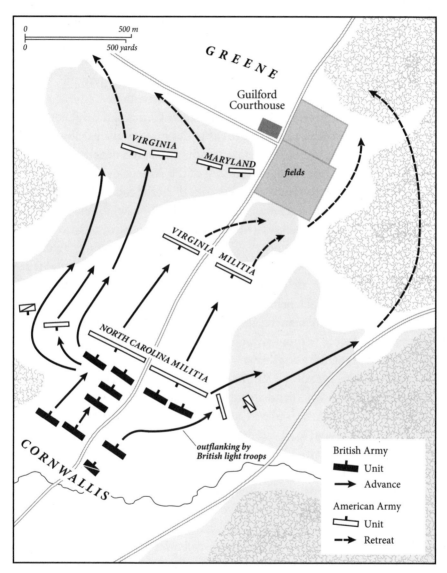

Map 7. Battle of Guilford Courthouse, 15 March 1781.

trained riflemen, held firm and opened fire on the British as they passed through the shattered line. Finding their flanks enfiladed, the British right had to turn and drive the Americans back at an oblique angle. Withdrawing in order, the Americans helped open a gap in the British right, which O'Hara advanced to fill with the Guards. Further gaps opened up as the British entered the woodland in which the second American line was posted. Leslie had to order forward the light infantry to help plug those gaps, resulting in the whole army now coming into action and leaving Cornwallis with no reserve to deploy later in the battle.

More experienced and disciplined than their Carolinian neighbours, the Virginian militia inflicted still more casualties on Cornwallis's army. As so often occurs during combat in close terrain, the battle degenerated into a melee where the superior marksmanship of the American riflemen exacted a devastating toll on the advancing redcoats.[110] In the confusion, Cornwallis himself had his horse shot from under him, but managed to find a remount and remained in the thick of the action.[111] American resistance was far from uniform, however, and the British demonstrated some benefit of their own significant experience of wilderness warfare. Fighting tenaciously and using the dense woodland to mask their movements, British troops managed to get behind some of the Virginian militia, 'throwing them into such confusion' recalled one American participant, that they 'instantly broke off without firing a single gun and dispersed like a flock of sheep frightened by dogs'.[112]

On the left, as part of the Virginian line disintegrated, Colonel Webster emerged from the woodland ahead of the main British line. Forming his battalions into line, he ordered an immediate advance upon the third American line, a couple of hundred yards ahead, deployed just in front of Guilford Courthouse. Greene's continental regulars waited until the British were within 40 yards and delivered a devastating volley of musket-fire before charging with fixed bayonets. The British were forced to retreat in some confusion. Greene, however, refused to order a general attack, fearful that his army would be unable to sustain the advantage. Shortly after, the rest of the Virginian line collapsed in the woodland and Cornwallis was now able to order a full assault on the line of Continental regulars. As the 2nd Guards battalion cleared the woodland, its commander likewise ordered an immediate assault.

The Guards found themselves advancing against the inexperienced 2nd battalion of Maryland Continentals. The sight of the highly disciplined troops terrified the Marylanders who fled the field. The Guards picked up the pace in an effort to exploit the gap created by the collapse, but as they did so, the much more experienced 1st battalion of Marylanders wheeled to enfilade the British column. 'This conflict between the brigade of Guards and the first Regiment of Marylanders was most terrific,' observed one American soldier. 'They fired at the same instant, and they appeared so near that the blazes from the muzzles of their guns seemed to meet.'[113] As the Guards fell back in disorder, the American cavalry under William Washington suddenly attacked their flank, causing more confusion.

John Eager Howard, commanding the 1st Marylanders, sensed an opportunity and ordered in a second bayonet charge. A bitter hand-to-hand contest now erupted between the two elite units of both armies, and for a short time the Guards seemed on the brink of collapse. Witnessing the imminent disintegration of the mainstay of his army, Cornwallis ordered the artillery to fire grapeshot to break up the American attack. 'This is a necessary evil,' he said to O'Hara, after the latter 'remonstrated and begged' him to avoid firing on the Guards who remained engaged in close combat with the Americans. Cornwallis was unrepentant; it was, he claimed, the only way to 'arrest impending destruction'.[114] The resultant barrage, as expected, caused casualties in both units, but successfully dispersed the Marylanders. Seeing an opportunity to advance and fill the gap left by the 2nd battalion of Marylanders, Cornwallis ordered an advance, but Greene had decided he had achieved his objective of inflicting severe costs on the British and ordered a withdrawal.

Cornwallis was left in command of the field, but his army had suffered 532 casualties, more than a quarter of the British contingent. Of these, 93 lay dead, while many of the most seriously injured would also succumb to their wounds. 'The cries of the wounded and dying who remained in the field of action during the night', wrote one observer, 'exceed all description.'[115] In contrast, Greene's army suffered just 78 killed and 185 wounded, though as many as 1,000 North Carolinian militia were missing.[116] Cornwallis, of course, portrayed the battle as a grand victory for the British, but O'Hara offered a more truthful account. 'Every part of our army was beat repeatedly,' he wrote. 'The Rebels were so exceedingly numerous, as to be constantly to oppose fresh troops to us, and to be in force to our Front, Flanks and Rear . . . .'[117]

Though the field was his, Cornwallis was in possession of little else. His army went without food for two days after the battle, and so he was forced once more to retreat, this time to Wilmington in order to re-establish contact with the sea, his lines of supply and communications with

Charleston, from where he hoped to receive reinforcements. In so doing, he left both Carolinas open to attack from Greene's forces. Only after arriving at Wilmington did Cornwallis write to Clinton with news that 'our military operations were uniformly successfull and the victory of Guildford, altho' one of the bloodiest of this war, was very complete'.[118]

Clinton was unconvinced. Guilford Courthouse proved the folly of the pursuit of decisive battle as an end in itself. Bereft of a wider strategy, in fighting a set-piece battle on his adversary's terms, even if he was successful, Cornwallis would gain no exploitable opportunities.[119] Instead, he should never have allowed himself to get drawn into a battle where 'the consequence of a defeat was destruction to his army' as well as 'the friends he called forth'; even 'victory', Clinton pointed out, 'had every consequence of a defeat'.[120] With his strategy in tatters, Cornwallis now sought to salvage something from the campaign. To his mind, he had invaded North Carolina as fighting a defensive war in South Carolina was impractical, so withdrawing to Charleston was never seriously considered. In the absence of active loyalist support in North Carolina, attempting to continue a campaign there also seemed ill-advised. 'The men and riches of Virginia', meanwhile, continued to provide 'ample supplies to the rebel southern army'. Cornwallis therefore concluded 'that until Virginia was to a degree subjected we could not reduce North Carolina or have any certain hold of the back country of South Carolina ...'.[121]

Clinton objected to the plan. 'Experience ought to convince us', he wrote, 'that there is no possibility of restoring Order in any rebellious Province ... without the hearty Assistance of numerous friends.' The loyalist support upon which British strategy in North America had rested 'are gone from us, and I fear, are not to be recovered'.[122] Moreover, he continued to refuse to send reinforcements. By his own reckoning, he faced Washington's 20,000-strong force with only 10,931 troops, but the intelligence picture was incomplete.[123] Though Washington advocated an attack on Clinton in New York, his French ally, General Jean Baptiste Donatien de Vimeur, Comte de Rochambeau, preferred to send forces south to support Major General Gilbert de Mortier, Marquis de LaFayette, in Virginia. The two eventually settled on the latter course of action, but Clinton only learned of the first option, and failed to understand the danger Cornwallis was in. He therefore recommended that 'as soon as you have finished the active operation you may now be engaged in, to take a defensive station in any healthy situation you chuse (be it at Williamsburg or York Town)'.[124]

Cornwallis was less than impressed by his new orders. 'What is our plan?' he wrote to his friend, Major General William Phillips, expressing his frustration at Clinton's strategy of indirect manoeuvres. 'Without one we cannot succeed, and I assure you that I am quite tired of marching about the country in quest of adventures. If we mean an offensive war in America, we must abandon New York,' he argued, 'and bring our whole force' into the southern campaign.

> We then have a stake to fight for, and a successful battle may give us America. If our plan is defence, mixed with desultory expeditions, let us quit the Carolinas (which cannot be held defensively while Virginia can be so easily armed against us) and stick to our salt pork at New York, sending now and then a detachment to steal tobacco.[125]

Nevertheless, having received intelligence on 23 April that Greene had marched for South Carolina, Cornwallis saw that the route to Virginia was free of opposition, and so marched north, crossing the Roanoke River on 13 May.[126] By early summer, Cornwallis had rendezvoused with the 5,304 troops under Phillips's command, though Phillips himself had died of typhus on 15 May. Cornwallis now commanded 7,200 troops, while Lafayette, who commanded the American contingent in Virginia, had half as many soldiers. Cornwallis began to establish what he hoped would be a suitable naval operating base at Yorktown, a small and formerly prosperous port on the south bank of the York River, and commenced Clinton's 'desultory expeditions'. Cornwallis established a force of 500 mounted hussars and light dragoons, which added 800 mounted light infantry as more horses were confiscated from the Americans. These mounted warriors were able to cover up to 70 miles in one day, and targeted American military stores and sought to devastate the Virginian economy by burning plantations and freeing the enslaved people confined on them. Many entered British service as spies, offering Cornwallis his best local situational awareness of the whole campaign.

Though this economic warfare strategy appeared to be bearing some fruit, the strategic situation was about to shift dramatically. In early June 1781, Rear Admiral François Joseph Paul, Comte de Grasse, sailed from Brest with 20 ships of the line. Though their destination was the West Indies, de Grasse's fleet was available to support Franco-American operations should the need arise. Intercepted despatches appeared to confirm that New York was the focus of those operations, so Clinton again refused to move in support of Cornwallis.[127] In fact, de Grasse was heading for the Chesapeake, while Washington and Rochambeau were heading south through New Jersey as early as 19 August. By the time Clinton received confirmation of this, it was impossible for him to send reinforcements. De Grasse had defeated British Admiral Thomas Graves at the Battle of the Virginia Capes on 5 September and obtained local control of the sea. Cornwallis was isolated in Yorktown.

Throughout August, he had constructed a series of fortifications that formed a crescent around the town. Ten redoubts formed strong points in the defensive lines, with the ninth and tenth redoubts dominating the left of the position controlling relatively level ground. Supplemented by 18-pounders brought ashore from frigates moored in the York River, Cornwallis's light artillery guns were organised into 14 batteries. Cornwallis commanded 7,500 troops. As soon as he learned of Washington's and Rochambeau's move south, Clinton promised to dispatch 4,000 reinforcements to Cornwallis the moment conditions permitted.[128] This news convinced Cornwallis to call off a breakout attempt on 6 September. 'If I had not hopes of relief,' he wrote in mid-September, 'I would rather risk an action than defend my half-finished works.'[129] Had Cornwallis attacked the Continental Army when they first arrived, he might have stood a chance, but the delay proved fatal. Washington and Rochambeau rendezvoused with Lafayette on the 21st and six days later the siege of Yorktown commenced. Washington commanded 5,000 Continental regulars and 3,200 militia from Virginia and occupied the territory to the south and south-east of Yorktown, while Rochambeau occupied the ground to the west with his left anchored on the river. On 28 September, Washington began moving his forces gradually closer to Cornwallis's defences.

By the night of 6–7 October, after a week of preparatory activity, in which the Americans sustained casualties from British defensive artillery fire, Washington was finally ready to commence work on the first parallel. Diversionary activity from the French attracted British attention, so the Americans were able to work unimpeded. At dawn on the 7th, a four-foot-deep trench ran for 2,000 yards from the centre of Washington's line to the riverbank; in places it came within 800 yards of the British defences. Two days later, the French batteries were completed, and the bombardment of Yorktown commenced. Many of the defensive works were soon damaged, and Cornwallis concluded 'we cannot hope to make a very long resistance'.[130]

The Americans completed their second parallel on 11 October and were now within 300 yards of the British defences. 'Upwards of a thousand shells was thrown into the works on this night, and every spot became alike dangerous,' wrote one participant. 'The noise and thundering of the cannon, the distressing cries of the wounded, and the lamentable sufferings of the inhabitants, whose dwellings were chiefly in flames, added to the restless fatigues of the duty ....'[131] On 14 October, two 400-men storming parties attacked Redoubts 9 and 10, capturing the positions in minutes. Washington installed artillery in the redoubts and began to bombard the British at point-blank range. In an attempt to forestall the inevitable, at dawn on 16 October, Cornwallis ordered Colonel Robert Abercromby to make a sortie against the French batteries on the British right, which succeeded in spiking 11 guns, though the bombardment of the British lines continued from the remaining batteries.[132]

With the defence of Yorktown clearly untenable, Cornwallis finally elected to make a bid to escape. The same night, he attempted to ferry his army across the York River to Gloucester Point, but a squall blew up and made the crossing impossible. Why Cornwallis waited so long to attempt this is unclear. Indeed, for a commander whose career thus far had been marked by decision and action, Cornwallis's management of the defence of Yorktown was strangely lacking in both. His behaviour surprised his opponent. 'Lord Cornwallis's conduct has hitherto been passive beyond conception,' wrote Washington. 'A few days must determine whether he will or will not give us much trouble.'[133] In fact, following his failed escape, and with ammunition running perilously short, Cornwallis wrote to Washington seeking terms. On 19 October, having sustained more than 50 per cent casualties, the remaining 3,500 soldiers in Cornwallis's army marched out of Yorktown and into captivity.

*   *   *

Though Clinton scrabbled to assemble a relief force, the fleet departed New York the day after Cornwallis surrendered.[134] In defeat, Clinton was 'a distress'd man, looking for friends and suspicious of all mankind'. He 'complains of the number of his enemies' and engaged in 'a desultory justification of his own conduct and censure of everybody else'.[135] For Clinton, of course, everyone else was to blame. The truth of this assertion has been debated since Yorktown effectively ended British military operations in North America, and all parties hold responsibility to some degree. The government, principally Germain, imposed a strategy that in no way corresponded with the reality of the situation; Howe squandered perhaps the only real opportunity to bring the Continental Army to battle and defeat it; from 1778 the Admiralty pursued a defensive strategy which denuded North America of sufficient naval power to support offensive land operations. Clinton implemented a military strategy which though designed to avoid catastrophic defeat and bring about the optimal circumstances for victory, served only to increase risk aversion and indecision; and Cornwallis pursued precisely the opposite agenda – the pursuit of decisive battle at all costs, with the resultant abandonment of all due regard for wider military strategy, logistics and naval support. In Clinton's mind, though everyone had some blame to carry, the lion's share rested with Cornwallis. In his post-war analysis of the campaign in the south, Clinton concluded that King's Mountain had turned the tide against the British. This defeat, which had alienated so much potential loyalist support, 'proved to be the first link in a chain of evils that followed each other in regular succession until they at last ended in the total loss of America'.[136]

Cornwallis returned to New York on parole in mid-November before returning to London. Clinton concluded that Cornwallis would salvage his own career by blaming him for the defeat. He was not wrong, and his increasing paranoia only served to alienate potential allies and prove his detractors correct. 'I pity him in his disgrace,' wrote one former friend. 'His jealousy and pride are excessive; they have ruined a mind that has soft affections and a prodigal liberality.'[137] After his resignation in 1782, Clinton returned to England, unaware that his active military service was at an end. He engaged in a correspondence war with Cornwallis in order, unsuccessfully, to try to clear his name. Consequently, Clinton, in the words of his biographer, came to be seen as 'an old soldier obsessed with his grievances and battling indefatigably to vindicate himself'.[138] Clinton never succeeded in rehabilitating his reputation in his lifetime, but the merits of his military thinking were not completely forgotten.

Defeat in America, however, did much to diminish the value of military knowledge gained in the course of the two wars fought there since 1754. On a very basic level, the size of the British army was reduced substantially. At the end of the American Revolutionary War, the army consisted of 35 cavalry regiments, three regiments of foot guards and 113 battalions of regular infantry; in all, this totalled 144,000 men at a cost of £2,000,000 per annum.[139] Initial plans saw every regiment of foot numbered above 65 disbanded; a total of more than 100,000 troops. The commander-in-chief, General Sir Henry Conway, estimated a total annual cost of £830,000. In April 1783, a new ministry took office and insisted the army's budget not exceed £700,000 per annum.[140] This would ensure that the post-1783 peace establishment would end up costing less than it had in 1750. Conway resisted the move. It was, he argued, not 'an Article of real economy ...'. 'The Danger arising from such Weakness', he continued, 'may either Tempt our ambitious Antagonists to begin a War or give them a clear Advantage in the outset of it.'[141] Conway was concerned that stripping out the internal composition of the remaining regiments would make future augmentations difficult and cause confusion at the commencement of a new conflict. In essence, the British government was jettisoning the body of military knowledge established in the last 30 years. Those lessons would need to be relearned, at the same, or perhaps greater, cost, when a new war broke out.

This prompted a rhetorical question in the House of Commons on 13 June from Colonel Richard Fitzpatrick, the new Secretary at War. 'Which ought to be preferred in a reduction?' he asked. 'Strong battalions thinly officered, or thin battalions strongly officered?' The decision for the latter had already been made, as 'the private soldier was very soon formed when placed among veterans, but . . . an officer was not so easily formed'.[142] And so, on 25 June, each battalion was reduced to only eight companies. With an abundance of officers, and few roles for them, the officer corps stagnated. The end of war in America, then, produced a paralysing effect on the exchange of military knowledge. Though peace had arrived in the Western Hemisphere, conflict still continued in the east, and reinforcements were promptly deployed to India. In 1786, a new governor-general was appointed with a mandate to reform the political administration of India. Having successfully deflected criticism of his conduct in North America, Charles, Earl Cornwallis, also demanded the role of commander-in-chief, and he set out to transform the military organisation of the subcontinent. From America, then, it was to India that the continued development of British military knowledge now moved.

CHAPTER 6

'Advance and Be Forward'

MILITARY KNOWLEDGE AND ADAPTATION IN INDIA,
1750–1790

I N darkness during the night of Monday 11 September 1786, Lieutenant
General Charles, the Earl of Cornwallis, alighted from his budgerow
– an oar-powered longboat – which had ferried him up the Hugli River,
and set foot in Calcutta for the first time. He had already spent the last
fortnight in India, at Madras, where he had enjoyed the company of the
governor of Madras and old comrade-in-arms, Sir Archibald Campbell.
Now, though, Cornwallis, in an unostentatious ceremony and attended
by a company of soldiers standing to attention, assumed the office of
governor-general of India. Nothing less than the political, military and
administrative reform of the British presence in the subcontinent
occupied his attention, and it was a task not easily undertaken.

Cornwallis had found himself preparing inconsistently for the role for the
past four years. The governor-generalship of India had been offered to him
in 1783, 1784 and 1785, but on each occasion, the failure of the British
government to combine the political duties of the governor-general with the
military duties of the commander-in-chief had dissuaded Cornwallis from
accepting. He could not 'abandon a profession to which I have from my youth
wholly turned my thoughts, and to which I have hitherto sacrificed every
consideration of advantage and happiness'. Nor could he accept the military
role alone, as 'without power or patronage, an officer could neither get credit
to himself, nor essentially serve the public'.[1] Only the joint position would
suffice, and when in 1786 it was finally offered, Cornwallis happily accepted.

His preparation had, like the role itself, a dual character. He remained
'convinced of the necessity of military reading',[2] and had familiarised

himself with recent military treatises on the art of war. But what of India itself? Cornwallis likewise spent a considerable amount of time reading the latest intelligence reports from India, forwarded to him by friends in the government. These included general intelligence estimates on the society, population and military strength of the increasingly disparate Indian political entities as the Mughal empire gradually fragmented,[3] as well as more specific information collected on local rulers and military states.[4] All of this helped to frame Cornwallis's understanding of the situation he could expect to find when he arrived in India. Military organisation and warfare on the subcontinent itself was undergoing something of a trans-formation in the second half of the eighteenth century, while Britain's position in relation to her indigenous rivals remained precarious. The history of the British military experience in South Asia would have been at the forefront of Cornwallis's professional preparations. In this respect, Cornwallis had at least one thing in common with his future adversary.

Britain's main opponent during Cornwallis's governor-generalship was Tipu Sultan of Mysore, against whom the British had in 1784 concluded an indecisive war. After his arrival in India, Cornwallis had been briefed on hopes that Mysore would act as a potential counterweight to the unpredictability and aggression demonstrated by the Maratha Confederacy. Cornwallis would later explain to his brother James, Bishop of Lichfield and Coventry:

> The political state of India is so much changed since the date of the orders which were read relative to the power of the Marathas, and Hyder's forming a barrier for us that a man might with as much propriety have said to the Elector of Saxony, in the middle of the Seven Years' War, – To be sure the Prussian troops are doing no great good in your country, but yet you are lucky to have such a neighbour as Frederick, he forms a noble barrier for you against the King of Sweden, whose power was very troublesome to your family in the beginning of the century.[5]

The comparison would prove apt.

In the wake of his conflict with the British, Tipu turned his attention to political, military, economic and social reform, building on the innovations commenced by his late father, Haidar 'Ali, and transforming Mysore into a powerful fiscal-military state.[6] While his economic reforms brought long-lasting new industries to Mysore, Tipu also championed religion and the arts, and saw the acquisition of knowledge to be a particular indicator of martial success. To this end, he celebrated his triumphs with the creation of breathtaking floor-to-ceiling murals in his elaborate teak-structured summer palace, the Daria Daulat Bagh, just outside the fortress walls of his capital, Seringapatam. Haidar 'Ali had begun construction of the palace in 1778, but Tipu oversaw its completion. He authorised several additions, and some of the murals Tipu commissioned depicted British defeats, while others depicted his cavalry on parade, resplendent in blue uniforms, sabres drawn in salute to their leader. The palace was a homage to Mysore's victories over the British in the last two wars. Besides the murals, ornaments and trinkets adorned the hallways and state rooms, including, famously, an organ set inside a tiger savaging a redcoated sepoy.[7]

This powerful sense of history as access to knowledge was also reflected in Tipu's extensive library, which was held in a 'dark room, in the S.E. angle of the upper verandah of the interior quadrangle' of the Daria Daulat Bagh.[8] Tipu added to the library throughout his reign by pillaging those of his defeated rivals, a kind of witness and testament to his martial prowess, and with it the superiority of his own intellect. Among the titles were no fewer than 118 works of history,[9] including the *Kholāset al Akhbār*, which narrated the history of south and central Asia to the reign of Tamerlane, and the *Tabkāt Nāssery*, which focused on the life and descendants of Genghis Khan.[10] Books on the art of war were uncommon, but there was at least one treatise on the modern use of artillery.[11] The library was Tipu's personal space. The binding of each book was marked with the motto of his government,[12] and the books themselves were not held on shelves. 'Instead of being beautifully arranged,' noted one commentator, 'the books were heaped together in hampers, covered with leather; to consult which, it was necessary to discharge the whole contents on the floor.'[13] Access to knowledge was by invitation and a necessarily immersive experience.

The combination of a detailed awareness of the military history of Mysore and of the wider history of the Indian subcontinent helped Tipu to transform his military. Whether or not Tipu personally consulted Western treatises on the art of war is unknown: none appeared in a catalogue compiled 10 years after the end of the fourth and final Anglo-Mysore War.[14] More likely, Tipu's familiarity with Western concepts of warfighting was obtained from the numerous French mercenaries who offered their services to train his army, as well as military confrontation with the British themselves.

The success of European armies employing Western infantry tactics over indigenous Indian armies had been evident for some decades. In October 1746, perhaps 350 French regular soldiers and 700 Indian troops trained in European tactics faced a Mughal army of 10,000 troops under the command of Mahfuz Khan. On paper, Khan should have swept all before him, but in 1742 the French commander, Joseph Dupleix, had undertaken to improve the French Compagnie des Indes's military capability. Within four years, Dupleix was able to field two regiments of 'cypahes' – soon Anglicised to 'sepoy': Indian troops that were formed, drilled, uniformed, armed and paid along European lines.[15]

At a battle on the estuary of the Adyar River on 24 October 1746, Khan's army was unable to defeat the French force sent to oppose it. The French had 'formed the soldiers and the sepoys into four divisions' and 'ordered each to engage a separate body of the enemy'. Khan responded by firing 'three rockets and four cannon', but 'their contents fell into the river, and caused no damage. The French', noted one eyewitness, 'then opened a volley of musketry on the enemy, killing numbers of them'. Khan's forces reportedly 'threw down their arms and fled, with dishevelled hair and dress. Some fell dead in the act of flight'.[16] Though Khan's defeat was as much the result of the poor discipline of his own forces, he and his father immediately concluded that the superior technology and discipline of their European adversaries would be essential to any future military exploits in India. Arguably, as news of this stark demonstration of the superiority of European weaponry, tactics and discipline spread across India, many became convinced of the need to adopt similar training and discipline.[17]

The reality of the situation was, of course, much more complex. European discipline had been a feature of Indian armies since at least the middle of the seventeenth century, when European observers of Mughal battles witnessed effective combinations of infantry, cavalry and artillery, using complex battlefield tactics and manoeuvres.[18] Moreover, Shivaji Bhonsle – known as the Maratha warrior king of the seventeenth century – clothed his troops in uniforms and drilled them in the tactics of conventional warfare.[19] Nor was this the first example of the use of locally recruited Indian troops trained in European tactics. At least as early as 1664, the directors of the East India Company had authorised the governor of Madras to train indigenous solders in European drill, 'arming them and such other of the inhabitants as may bee most useful unto you'.[20]

The Battle of Adyar, then, was less of a turning point than has been suggested by historians seeking to explain the subsequent success of

European powers in India, but it certainly impacted perceptions in South Asia, where European tactical training became increasingly in demand. Witnessing the success of the French employment of European tactics, the British followed suit, with 'orders to make yourselves as secure as you can against the French or any other European Enemy'.[21] Both the British and French began increasing sepoy recruitment and training, and sought to undercut each other's influence by offering mercenary support to local rulers as power struggles engulfed the collapsing Mughal empire.

The resultant series of wars, known collectively as the Carnatic Wars, saw the expansion of French and British powers, along with the personal enrichment of the individuals who directed these activities. Contemporaries reported the inherent weaknesses of the disintegrating Mughal administration. It was 'certain', wrote Thomas Saunders, the new governor of Madras, 'any European nation resolved to make war on them with a tolerable force may overrun the whole country'.[22] Some historians have seen this as evidence of the inherent superiority of European military capabilities, resulting in the imposition of European – principally British – power in South Asia.[23] The exchange of military knowledge was not one way, however. In turn, European powers began to adopt indigenous military assets that offered solutions to the specific environmental challenges they encountered in India.[24]

The dominance of European techniques was repeatedly illustrated over the succeeding years. At Plassey, on 23 June 1757, Robert Clive, in command of a small army of 750 Europeans and 2,100 sepoys, defeated the 55,000-strong army of Siraj ud-Daula, the Nawab of Bengal. Using the terrain to his advantage, Clive's men withstood a sustained artillery bombardment, and then deployed a devastating hail of disciplined musketry and artillery fire against the Nawab's cavalry.[25] The Europeans 'kept up a continual fire with their small arms', and the enemy's cohesion began to collapse.[26] 'On this, a general rout ensued, and we pursued the enemy six miles,' Clive reported, 'passing upwards 40 pieces of cannon they had abandoned.'[27] The Europeans enjoyed a substantial advantage offered by disciplined infantry and mastery of the use of the musket, but there was also some evidence of adaptation to the geographical situation, with Clive making use of the terrain to protect his small force.[28]

Likewise at Buxar, on 23 October 1764, the Nawab of Awadh's army, numbering some 30,000 troops, encountered 900 European soldiers and 7,000 sepoys under the command of Major Hector Munro. The British force withstood repeated cavalry assaults before charging the Nawab's left flank and turning his position. 'Regular discipline and strict obedience to orders', claimed Munro, were 'the only superiority that Europeans possess in this country'.[29] As a result of Munro's success at Buxar, the Nawab of Awadh came to terms with the British, granting the East India Company the land revenue of Bengal, Bihar and Orissa. The company was now in effective control of most of north-eastern India, generating an income which helped pay for the increasing size of the East India Company army.[30]

Tipu's father, Haidar 'Ali, had learned much from European success, and he intended to implement those lessons in his own army, while combining tactical reform with Indian innovation. The British initially saw Haidar 'Ali as a useful counterweight to the Marathas, but the Nizam of Hyderabad viewed him as a threat, and in late 1766 forged a loose alliance with the Marathas and the British to move against the outlying Mysore fortress at Bangalore. Haidar 'Ali burnt all in the invaders' path, and then offered the Marathas 35 lakhs of rupees (in modern currency, about £46 million) to abandon the fight. Haidar 'Ali then entered into secret negotiations with the Nizam, and persuaded him to change sides, with the promise of gaining renewed control of the Carnatic. Faced with the combined forces of the Nizam and Haidar 'Ali, the British commander, Colonel Joseph Smith, had no option but to withdraw. His force of just 800 European infantry and 5,000 sepoys faced, in his estimation, as many as 50,000 troops, though these numbers are disputable.[31] What was evident, however, was the quality of Haidar 'Ali's infantry, some 28,000 of which were formed into 20 battalions of sepoy infantry trained by French mercenaries. En route, he attacked Smith outside Trinamalai on 26 September 1767, but the British managed to fight off the assault with heavy losses, continuing to withdraw with no rest.

The battle was a bloody affair. Smith's army was badly prepared for the encounter, short of supplies and ammunition. In contrast, the Mysore army was in a much better state. Its logistic system, a mobile cattle park designed to enable swift deployment throughout Mysore, was altogether better suited to the challenges of warfare in India. The Mysore infantry also benefitted tactically from the quality of their weaponry, which was based on designs supplied by the French. The artillery, moreover, had a heavier bore and longer range than the company's guns.[32] Haidar 'Ali's cavalry was also markedly better than that possessed by other Indian armies encountered by the British. Camel-mounted soldiers had perfected the use of rockets which sowed widespread panic in adversary cavalry units.[33]

After recovering and receiving limited reinforcements, Smith was able to go on the offensive, but not before Haidar 'Ali had attacked and eliminated several British garrisons in the Carnatic. While Smith forced Haidar 'Ali to retreat, the latter had, in early 1768, sent Tipu to raid Madras. With matters in a tentative balance, the British persuaded the Nizam to renege on his deal with Haidar 'Ali, who was himself concerned that the Marathas were on the brink of attacking him. Having chased the British out of Mysore, Haidar 'Ali concluded a peace treaty which saw the return to the *status quo ante*.

Smith was lauded for his conduct of the campaign, with the discipline and steadfastness of his sepoy battalions credited with much of the success. Eyewitnesses did not fail to note, however, the tactical effectiveness, discipline and versatility of Haidar 'Ali's own forces. 'The progress that the natives make in the knowledge of the art of war', observed the directors, 'is becoming a very alarming circumstance.' Their response was to try to prevent 'letting any European officers or soldiers enter into the service of the country government', while also discouraging, 'as far as in your power, all military improvements among them'.[34] Whatever attempts were made to curtail the circulation of military knowledge in South Asia totally failed, as was illustrated by the effectiveness of Haidar 'Ali's forces when war was renewed in 1780.

Despite the receipt of intelligence that Haidar 'Ali was assembling an army at Bangalore, the Madras authorities made virtually no preparations. On 17 July, Haidar 'Ali invaded the Carnatic with nearly 100,000 men, 35,000 of whom were infantry trained in European methods of warfighting. In addition, he boasted one of the largest artillery trains in India, carrying 100 guns. In the words of one eyewitness, the army 'covered the plains like waves of an angry sea, and with a trail of artillery that had no end'.[35]

Moving first on Arcot, Haidar 'Ali calculated correctly that a siege of this important city would result in the desertion of large numbers of British sepoys whose families resided there. Bereft of supplies and ammunition, and with no prospects of reinforcements, garrisons across the Carnatic fell like dominos. It was only on 25 August 1780 that Sir Hector Munro was able to assemble 5,000 sepoys. Colonel William Baillie, based 25 miles north of Madras, was marching to meet him at Kanchipuram with a force of 2,800, composed of the 73rd Highland Regiment and a battalion of sepoys. A monsoon storm flooded the river Kortalaiyar, stranding Baillie for 11 days, and in that time, Tipu managed to block Baillie's route with 11,000 cavalry. Haidar 'Ali marched to support his son, while Munro refused to leave Kanchipuram, which he had fortified, though he did send 1,000 men to reinforce Baillie.

At daybreak on 10 September, Baillie began his march to rendezvous with Munro. As he descended a hill, he found his path blocked by Tipu's army at the village of Pollilur. Tipu 'had placed batteries to command every part of the road through which' the British 'troops must necessarily pass. In this situation exposed to a heavy cannonade of 30 pieces of cannon the troops were ordered to sit down'.[36] Formed hastily into square, and sheltered as much as possible, Baillie's troops sustained fire from 30 guns for over an hour, whereupon the situation worsened dramatically: Haidar 'Ali arrived with 30 battalions of infantry, 25,000 cavalry and 50 guns. He ordered in no fewer than 13 cavalry charges, which the disciplined troops in Baillie's square were able to fend off, prompting the deployment of the artillery at point-blank range. 'Our fate was for above an hour to be exposed', wrote Baillie's brother John, 'to the hottest cannonade that ever was known in India.'[37]

Haidar 'Ali ordered the combined use of grapeshot and his now-infamous rockets, which caused huge casualties. When two ammunition tumbrils were hit, the resulting explosion blew holes in the British lines, which the cavalry quickly exploited. 'The sepoys immediately threw down their arms and fled, while the little body of Europeans stood collected and firm, determined,' wrote one survivor 'to defend themselves to the last extremity.'[38] As the battle reached a climax, 'the last and most awful struggle was marked by the clashing of arms and shields, the snorting and kicking of horses, ... the glistening of bloody swords, oaths and imprecations,' noted one eyewitness, a lieutenant of the 73rd Regiment. It 'concluded with the groans and cries of mutilated men, ... the hideous roaring of elephants as they trampled about and wielded their dreadful chains amongst both friends and foes'.[39]

Despite attempting to surrender, with Baillie's deputy, Major David Baird, ordering the troops to drop their weapons, some sepoys continued firing which prompted the Mysore cavalry to continue their assault, now against largely disarmed men.[40] Of the 3,800 strong force, only 200 survived, all taken prisoner, including Baillie, who had lost a leg, and Baird, who had severe sabre wounds to his head.[41] They were to enter captivity in the dungeons of Seringapatam, the fortress capital of Mysore, until the end of the war. Baillie would not survive. His defeat was dramatically recreated in one of the ceiling-high murals Tipu commissioned to adorn his summer palace. Baillie's stranded redcoats are portrayed desperately fighting in square, outnumbered and surrounded by masses of Mysore cavalry. When news of Pollilur reached Munro, meanwhile, he abandoned his heavy guns and hastily withdrew to Madras.

The British government dispatched Major General Sir Eyre Coote, the uncle of the lieutenant serving at the same time in North America, to restore order. When he arrived in Madras, the British could muster only 6,000 infantry and 8,000 cavalry against Haidar 'Ali's huge army. The Madras army was 'altogether unequal' to its adversary, Coote declared in a report to Hastings.[42] It would take several months to sort out the training and transportation issues that had bedevilled the army during the last campaign. Worse still, Haidar 'Ali had resorted to the scorched earth policy that had worked well against the British during the First Anglo-Mysore War. Few, if any, supplies could be found, and local Banjara were unwilling to trade with the British.[43] Coote became dependent on supplies brought in by sea, which in turn was dependent on the British control of the coast. After reinforcing the Carnatic garrisons, Coote managed to draw Haidar 'Ali out at the end of June 1781 outside Porto Novo.

Having conducted a personal reconnaissance, Coote decided to try to use the terrain to his advantage. 'It was necessary to explore ... the ground on our right,' he explained, 'in hopes of it admitting to advance from that point, by which we should avoid the enemy's direct fire from their batteries, and have a chance of gaining the left of their posts to turn or other ways command them.'[44] Indeed, Haidar 'Ali had not yet completed preparations on his left. Coote sent his 7,000 infantry in two columns, flanked by a couple of hundred native cavalry, and they soon found themselves in the shadow of sand dunes that protected them from the Mysore artillery fire.

Haidar 'Ali redeployed his infantry in an attempt to frustrate Coote's movement through the sand dunes. The resultant fire fight frustrated but did not halt Coote's advance, and, growing impatient, Haidar 'Ali 'pushed a large body of cavalry and infantry to our left in order to come round the Sand Hills and attack our rear, but in this they were prevented by our second line', under Brigadier James Stuart's command, 'which occupied these hills. A very sharp contest ensued however for their possession', wrote one participant. 'They sustained very great loss in several repeated attacks, and their infantry engaged ours with great spirit for above half an hour.'[45]

Haidar 'Ali's counterattack was virtually annihilated by the accurate musketry of Hector Munro's infantry in the first line, and artillery fire from the second line, which had now also emerged from the sand dunes. There was a genuine danger that the British might successfully outflank Haidar 'Ali's position, and his advisors urged a withdrawal, which he only reluctantly accepted.[46] Coote was too weak in cavalry to pursue, but his force had prevailed and dealt a bloody nose to Haidar 'Ali, who, as a result of Coote's complicated tactical manoeuvring, had never been able to bring his strongest arm – his infantry – into the battle. By contrast, 'the spirited behaviour of our sepoy corps did them the greatest credit; no Europeans could be steadier', wrote Coote in his after-action report. 'They were emulous of being foremost in every service it was necessary to undertake.'[47]

A series of confrontations, notably at Pollilur on 27 August and Vellore on 26 September, followed a similar pattern, where the superiority of the British infantry led to tactical success but the absence of cavalry prevented any strategic gain. This run of important but indecisive victories did at least persuade some of Haidar 'Ali's local supporters to abandon him, and he reverted to a raiding strategy. Coote in turn responded by forming flying columns to respond to such raids, which proved tactically successful, but again led to little or no strategic gain. In this way, Coote remained on the offensive until he was forced to return to Madras on 22 November, his army virtually out of supplies.[48] 'One cannot, upon reflection, but seriously lament the unfortunate check which was invariably given to the ardour of General Coote in all his exploits,' commented one of his officers. 'He never was once provided with a sufficient quantity of provisions to render any one action decisive; for a victory was no sooner gained than he was forced to retire to Madras for a fresh supply of grain, a necessity which rendered battle fruitless and the successful support of war impossible.'[49]

The stalemate continued for the remainder of the war. News of Haidar 'Ali's death reached Tipu on 7 December, and though desultory operations continued for the remainder of the war, neither side was able to gain a strategic advantage. Coote's death from a stroke on 27 April 1783 left the abrasive Brigadier-General James Stuart in charge, but he faced the same difficulties. With the coming of peace between Britain and France, Tipu was forced to withdraw, and the Second Anglo-Mysore War ended indecisively with a treaty signed at Mangalore on 11 March 1784. For the British, the key lesson was the need for an effective and reliable supply system, which would enable sustained operations. For Tipu, the battles his father had fought had been indecisive because his infantry had proven to be no match for the British, despite their impressive training.

Tipu therefore initiated a substantial programme of military reform over the next six years. The most notable change was the reduction in the size of the cavalry component, and a corresponding increase in the size of the infantry. In 1780, Haidar 'Ali had at his service some 32,000 cavalry, along-side just 15,000 infantry. Despite facing repeated battlefield defeats, in which the superiority of the English infantry prevailed tactically, Haidar 'Ali was still able to impose strategic costs on the British by using his cavalry to disrupt their supplies and limit their mobility. By 1790, however, Tipu had reduced his cavalry force to 20,000 and increased his infantry component to no fewer than 50,000 troops. This rebalancing had paid dividends during Tipu's wars with other Indian powers. 'There can be no question', wrote Colonel Mark Wilks, the future British resident at Mysore, 'that this change in his military establishment was among the causes of that superiority which he attained over Indian adversaries, in the campaigns of 1786–7.'[50]

Tipu must also have concluded that, while a strong cavalry component had helped his father avoid defeat, no strategic victory would be possible until Mysore could match the British on the battlefield. Many suspected that Tipu had surrendered a critical advantage. 'Unprovided or scantily furnished with cavalry as we are and always have been,' wrote Major James Kirkpatrick, 'it is undoubtedly fortunate for us that the armies occasionally opposed to us are less capable than formerly of harassing us by desultory and predatory operations . . . .'[51] Nevertheless, Tipu's cavalry remained a formidable adversary. The 'velocity with which his large bodies of Cavalry change their situation, and the general rapidity with which his whole movements, from one place to another, are executed, operate strongly in his favour', noted one British observer. 'Unable to ascertain his position, it is dangerous for us to detach from the main body.'[52] One of Tipu's French advisors, meanwhile, concluded that his use of irregular cavalry to intercept supplies and communications might even force the British to retreat, as they had done in both the First and Second Anglo-Mysore Wars.[53]

By 1790, then, Tipu's principal fighting arm was his infantry. 'Tippo is the only Indian Prince, who has persevered in disciplining and arranging his Army, after a regular Plan,' noted company clerk William Macleod. 'In this respect he is perfectly unprejudiced and ready to adopt any change . . . for the Improvement of his Troops . . . .'[54] Trained to perform complex battle-field manoeuvres, Tipu's infantry were also armed with the latest weaponry, leading one British observer, Colonel Donald Campbell, to conclude that Tipu's 'troops are in higher order than the force of any Asiatic state we are acquainted with'.[55] Despite this evident improvement in quality, many on the British side saw an advantage. Tipu was now 'less able to avoid that sort of engagement in which order, superior discipline, and knowledge will always perhaps secure to us the most decided advantages'.[56]

Such optimism, however, was not entirely warranted, for Tipu had also invested heavily in updating and expanding his artillery. By 1790, Tipu's artillery was 'both larger and longer than' that used by the British, 'which enables him to commence a cannonade on our Baggage, or line, before our guns can be used with effect', reported one British observer. 'In his artillery he places his greatest Confidence and dependence – that corps is the best appointed in his service, and very far superior to those of any power in India.'[57] Besides artillery, Tipu continued his father's use of rockets. Haidar 'Ali had fielded between 3,000 and 7,000 rocket men,[58] which, according to one British eyewitness, 'harassed us extremely, doing everything in their power to impede our march'.[59] By 1790, Tipu had at his disposal some 5,000 rocket men, with 200 camels and 600 iron engines for throwing them in the field.[60] 'In open and level ground,' wrote a British observer in 1791, 'they are, altho' uncertain in their direction, destructive and galling to our men.'[61]

Finally, Mysore's supply systems were also superior to those of the British. Tipu was able to draw on 400,000 bullocks and 100,000 buffalos.[62] British attempts to replicate this proved problematic because they were unable to source draught animals with a tolerance for the humidity of South India, while those bred in Mysore were considered among the hardiest in the region.[63] This system ensured that merchandise was transported throughout Mysore quickly and efficiently, and, according to one British observer, 'gave a celerity to his motion which ours could not equal'.[64] Indeed, Tipu was reportedly able to cross the breadth of the peninsula of India itself in little over a month.[65] In this regard, Mysore outstripped British capabilities by a significant margin. With no navigable rivers in the interior of the Carnatic, and without a reliable means of overland supply, the British had been unable to sustain lengthy campaigns during the previous two wars.[66]

On the face of it, then, Tipu Sultan posed a substantial threat to the British position in South India. More mobile, and capable in turn of neutralising British mobility, armed with longer-range weapons, and benefitting from larger numbers of infantry trained in European methods of warfighting, Tipu outmatched the British in nearly every department. Add to this the corruption which had infected the British administration of India, along with the poor recruitment and training methods employed by the company for its military arm, and Cornwallis was presented with a considerable challenge on his arrival in September 1786.

* * *

While Tipu had adapted his forces to take advantage of European tactical effectiveness, there is evidence that the British incorporated Indian campaigning methods in what historian Kaushik Roy terms a military synthesis.[67] The need for some form of tactical adaptation was apparent during the First Anglo-Maratha War, when a relief force was sent in late 1778 to install the company's preferred candidate as Peshwa (chief minister) of the Maratha Confederacy in the capital, Poona.

This consisted of nearly four thousand troops, including some six hundred European infantry, and was commanded by the elderly and decrepit Colonel Charles Egerton, with John Carnac his second. New to India, Egerton was a veteran of the Seven Years' War in Europe, where he had witnessed the systematic and successful use of firepower by the disciplined ranks of Frederick the Great's Prussian Armies.[68] Carnac, by contrast, had seen significant service in India, including commanding at the infamous siege of Patna in 1764. He therefore had a different perspective on the use of military force in India. As the expedition made its way from Bombay in early 1779, Carnac voiced grave concerns about Egerton's tactical acumen. 'Colonel Egerton's military ideas seem to be wholly derived from the mode of practice he has seen observed during the short time he was in Germany,' Carnac wrote to his superiors in Bombay. 'He proceeds with the same precaution as if he had an European Enemy to deal with.'[69]

Carnac was willing to make reforms based on his experiences in India, but Egerton remained wedded to anachronistic tactics. The expedition had made paralysingly slow progress, rarely moving more than a mile a day, with its siege and supply train hauled through steep ghats (mountain passes) by nearly 20,000 bullocks.[70] 'If we continue as we have hitherto done, moving on slowly from post to post, it is hard to say when the campaign may be at an end,' Carnac continued, 'for advantage will be all on their side, the ground being throughout broken into gullies and covered with bushes and underwood where they find many lurking places.'[71] As the British advanced, their adversaries raided their supplies and picked off stragglers. 'The Marathas hover about us and from the hours of 11 to three in the afternoon, playing their Artillery and Rockets upon us,' Carnac wrote despondently. 'I do not think Colonel Egerton can hold out much longer.'[72] On 9 January, the British force had reached Talegaon, just 18 miles from Poona, but, bereft of supplies, with their troops – including Egerton – sickening, and intelligence that the Marathas planned to burn Poona if the advance continued, the decision was taken two days later to retreat.[73]

Despite beginning the withdrawal at night, the Maratha army surged forward and surrounded the beleaguered British force. Anticipating a frontal assault, the British formed their European troops into lines, but the attack, when it came, hit hardest in the British rear, where the sepoys held their ground against repeated cavalry and infantry assaults. Casualties were manageable, and reportedly the sepoys had to be restrained from counterattacking their adversaries.[74] The sizeable contingent of bullock drivers and camp followers were less certain of their safety, and as the British moved toward the cover offered by the village of Wadgaon, they panicked and disrupted the discipline of the carefully planned movement. The Maratha cavalry did not waste the opportunity and inflicted severe casualties on European and sepoy units. Though the increasingly desperate force had reached the comparative safety of Wadgaon, it was readily apparent that there were few options. Morale plummeted and desertions increased. The following day rumours spread that there was no avenue of retreat, and despite successfully withstanding an artillery bombardment and resisting an infantry assault, the British sought to begin negotiations for their surrender. On 19 January, the British signed the convention of Wadgaon, by which they agreed to withdraw all forces from Maratha territory.[75]

Carnac believed that 'the only method of ensuring success in this country is to advance and be forward',[76] but if this vision was ever to come to fruition, then something would need to be done about the British logistics system. Coote had likewise seen his operations repeatedly curtailed by a poor logistical infrastructure, as he was unable to sustain his forces in the field for any length of time. A solution based on the unique experience of warfare in India was needed. But sorting out the logistical challenges would not be sufficient. Reform was needed to the systems of recruitment, retention, training and command of the British and company armies in India. Happily, for the British, Cornwallis had arrived in India with a plan to reform the British army in India, and by 1790 he had achieved some, though by no means all, of his aims.

Cornwallis wielded more political power than any of his predecessors in India. The independence of the company had been significantly curtailed by Pitt's India Act 1784, which ensured Whitehall had the final say over the East India Company's political decisions through a new Board of Control, headed by a middle-ranking minister. Cornwallis, as governor-general, head of the Supreme Council and commander-in-chief, had acquired more authority than any of his predecessors, because the Supreme Council, based in Bengal, now had authority over the other presidencies, notably over their relations with their neighbours.[77] This set the scene for the future character of British political relations in India, but first Cornwallis needed to reform the army, which was six times the size it had been 20 years earlier: totalling 55,000 troops in Bengal, 50,000 in Madras and 15,000 in Bombay.[78]

Cornwallis had arrived in India with instructions to oversee 'the Consolidation of the European troops in India into one Service'.[79] Within a year of his arrival, however, the new governor-general and commander-in-chief had been convinced to abandon this plan. The European officers serving in the Company army, commanding sepoy battalions, were 'in general, the best and most deserving officers in the army', Cornwallis explained. 'They are acquainted with the language, manners, and religious customs of the Sepoys,' he continued, and 'it is the reward of the best captains and subalterns to be appointed to Sepoy regiments'. If the armies were consolidated, those officers would lose their commands, become the most junior officers in their new regiments and 'without interest or connexions ... could not expect to get a regiment in twenty years'.[80]

Instead, Cornwallis wanted to focus on improving pay, pensions and conditions for officers in the Company army, as well as a general improvement in the quality of European recruits sent out to India.[81] Cornwallis clearly valued the local experience and knowledge of European officers in company service, and successfully lobbied for those officers to be granted equal seniority to King's officers of the same rank.[82] This, however, was little more than a sticking plaster, barely compensating for the abysmal quality of company soldiers recruited in Britain for service in India, who Cornwallis concluded were 'not only without discipline, but without subordination'.[83]

The situation was particularly bad in light of the setbacks the British had experienced during the conflict with Haidar 'Ali. 'The loss of Colonel Baillie's, and of several other detachments during the late war, has', Cornwallis explained, 'removed some part of that awe in which the Natives formerly stood at the name of British Troops.'[84] This impression had to be reversed as soon as possible, as, Cornwallis argued, 'it must be universally admitted that without a large and well-regulated body of Europeans, our hold of these valuable dominions must be very insecure'.[85] Reliable and effective European soldiers were, for Cornwallis, essential for maintaining the discipline of the sepoys. Although 'the native Troops have on many occasions evinced great fidelity and attachment to your service; on several others from want of pay, or other causes, they have manifested tokens of dissatisfaction and revolt. When wavering in their allegiance', he pointed out to the Court of Directors, only the presence of 'a respectable body of Europeans would awe them to obedience'.[86] To this end, Cornwallis demanded 'a better quality ... of European recruits'.[87]

At present, the company were reliant on recruiting agents – known as crimps – to acquire sufficient numbers to meet their requirements. Lacking any formal recruiting and training structures in England, the crimps were often forced to utilise underhand methods to recruit only those 'who from some defect would not be received anywhere else, or who from their debauchery and profligacy are in danger of a Gaol'. As there were no officers to train the new recruits, they lacked 'the smallest tincture of military discipline, or ideas of subordination'. The crimps did 'not have . . . even the powers of putting arms in their hands'. By the time they arrived in India, after having been confined in England and then on the long voyage, the result was undertrained, malnourished soldiers, 'ten thousand times more corrupted in Body and Mind', carrying 'insolence, mutiny, debauchery, and disease into their Armies in India'.[88]

These problems were amplified in wartime. In the year leading up to the outbreak of the Seven Years' War, for example, 1,001 men had been recruited and sent to India from Britain, but this fell by more than 50 per cent the year after hostilities began, while at the height of the war, between 1759 and 1760, only 202 men were recruited for service in India.[89] A similar pattern emerged during the American Revolutionary War, when numbers fell from 2,047 before the war to just 777 in 1779. Of these, 252 were under 16, and 356 were under 5 foot 2 inches tall.[90] Many regular army officers, including Generals William Howe and John Burgoyne, were opposed to any substantial reform to recruitment practices, fearful that the prospects of company service would undermine recruitment to the regular army. 'Let them take the worst of men to die in India', argued Thomas Townshend in the *London Evening Post*. Otherwise, he continued, 'the very flower of our youth would be swallowed up in that sink'.[91] With the long shadow of Britain's poor military performance on the global stage, Cornwallis's initial efforts to reform recruitment practices were initially defeated in 1787. Only in 1797, after the government repeatedly denied the Company a recruiting licence in Britain, did the directors accept reforms, and agreed to the creation of a depot on the Isle of Wight, where recruits would be housed and trained in anticipation of their dispatch to India.[92]

Though only of limited success, Cornwallis's attempts to reform recruitment and retention of European soldiers and officers in the service of the East India Company illustrated a significant transformation in his view of the military in India. On arrival, the new commander-in-chief had been convinced that the company's army had to be merged with the king's, but had quickly realised that this would deny experienced officers the opportunity to advance to significant commands. Though he failed to introduce promotion based on merit, Cornwallis did at least recognise the value of experience and local knowledge above that of political connections. In the absence of more substantial administrative reforms in London, Cornwallis turned to making localised reforms to training and supply practices.

In some ways, the structure and composition of the army exacerbated the supply difficulties which the British faced. In 1790, the Madras-based company administrator, Thomas Munro, argued that the British were 'as unprepared as the year 1780 . . . for war. We have added to our numbers, but not to our strength, by bringing so many regiments from Europe', he argued. 'So great a number of Europeans serve only to retard the operations of any Indian army,' because they were less effective in the military environment of India, and presented significantly greater logistical challenges than locally recruited and trained units. Munro concluded that 'we have . . . made our army more expensive and numerous, though less calculated for the purposes of war'.[93]

Experience had shown that Mysore outperformed the British in maintaining a fast and efficient supply system. As the British expanded the numbers of European soldiers and adapted to the availability of resources, their armies were attended by ever-increasing numbers of camp followers. The army was supplied by travelling military bazaars and market traders – so-called *brinjarry*. When he marched overland from Bengal to Bombay in 1778, Colonel Thomas Goddard's force of 6,624 troops were supported by more than 30,000 camp followers and bazaar sellers.[94] During his abortive campaigns in southern India, Sir Eyre Coote's force of 12,000 troops was attended by as many as 40,000 camp followers.[95]

'Bullocks and rice, the great sinews of Indian warfare, were objects of indispensable importance,' noted Captain Alexander Dirom, aide-de-camp to Major General Sir Archibald Campbell.[96] Reliable transportation was the critical problem, and in some respects, the challenge appeared insurmountable. 'The tribe of supernumerary servants, sutlers, and taylors which follow a battalion in the field', noted Campbell, 'are certainly among the greatest curses attending the movements of an Indian army.'[97] The problem was a unique manifestation of European military activity in South Asia, where armies composed partly of European officers and soldiers acclimatised to certain facilities on campaign, attracted a micro-economy in the form of a travelling bazaar. This in turn required sustenance and more draught animals to transport them, which in turn required increased forage. The 'difficulties that a general has to surmount' in India, noted military cartographer, James Rennell, 'particularly in the article of feeding his army and its myriads of followers, and beasts of burden, are more than most European officers can readily conceive'.[98]

Possible solutions were provided by Tipu's own experience. His success appeared to rest on access to enormous numbers of draught animals, and Cornwallis sought to mimic this by contracting local suppliers to furnish the army with tens of thousands of bullocks. This outwardly elegant solution created as many problems as it seemed to solve, however. In the coming campaign, it created tensions with the Marathas, nominally allied to the British, who sought to purchase from the same stock. When the army eventually took to the field, the animals themselves appeared ill-suited to the terrain and climate, and fell foul of the conditions in their thousands. 'Such had been the mortality among the draft and carriage cattle, that the contractors', recalled Dirom, 'had lost near forty thousand . . . .'[99]

The British were able to sustain the campaign because of civil reforms made to the tax system in Bengal, which was now based on a permanently fixed amount of revenue levied on landholders and farmers. In the four years prior to the outbreak of the Third Anglo-Mysore War in 1790, company debt had been reduced, and the political administration in Bengal was able to increase short-term spending much more effectively than they had in the past. By 1785, net revenues of the Bengal Presidency had increased to £5,315,197 from just £1,705,278 in 1772.[100] This increased access to cash and loans allowed Cornwallis to ensure a steady supply of draught animals and keep his supply train moving; but the time taken to procure the bullocks and any replacements proved just as paralysing as the original supply problems. Munro continued to believe the solution to Britain's military problems in India lay in local recruitment. 'Had half the money, idly thrown away in sending . . . four additional regiments to this country', he pointed out, 'been employed in increasing the establishment of sepoys and cattle, we should then have had an army which, for its lightness and capacity for action, would have broken the power of our formidable rival.'[101]

When war broke out, Cornwallis also advocated the use of magazines to reduce the burden on the supply train of the army. Well-located and resourced magazines would reduce the amount of material the army would have to carry. Combined with good intelligence, Cornwallis believed his army 'to be capable of rapid movement', free of concern for the security of its flanks and supply lines.[102] Such plans needed to be made well in advance, however, and, as Munro pointed out, the British had

commenced 'the war under the disadvantage of a want of magazines ...
Since the conclusion of the late war, we have acted as if we have been to
enjoy a perpetual peace'.[103]

If Cornwallis experienced mixed success employing local Indian solutions to the supply difficulties he faced, the synthesis of Indian and
European fighting techniques continued to make the British sepoy battalions some of the most reliable and effective units in India. Cornwallis had
initially been unimpressed by the sepoy battalions in British service. The
sepoys were 'fine men and would not in size disgrace the Prussian ranks',
he wrote in November 1786 to the Duke of York, 'but from the little I have
hitherto seen of them I have no favourable idea of their discipline'.[104]
Having spent a year touring some of the major British garrisons in India,
Cornwallis concluded that 'a brigade of our Sepoys would easily make
anybody Emperor of Hindostan',[105] though he critiqued their parade
ground performance as 'dancing about in various forms to jig tunes'.[106]

To capitalise on this success, Cornwallis, in concert with Campbell, the
governor of Madras, sought to impose uniform manoeuvre and tactical
drill. Soon after his first inspection of the troops in the vicinity of Calcutta,
Cornwallis amended the drill book written by the adjutant general, Sir
William Fawcett, updating it to reflect aspects of Indian tactical practice.[107] He also updated infantry regulations, published them in the
Calcutta Gazette and took measures to ensure everything was distributed to
Madras and Bombay,[108] with the explicit objective of guaranteeing uniform
infantry training in all three presidencies.[109]

Some of these adaptations were the result of local practice, but
Cornwallis also employed his experience from America. This approach
was adopted by Campbell, who, since his arrival in Madras, had sought to
employ in India ideas, innovations and lessons learned from his experiences serving during the American Revolutionary War. On 27 May 1787,
for example, he sent to Cornwallis 'a sample of Cartridge Pouches' which
he found from 'Experience in America ... was much preferable to what is
generally used by the King's Troops as it is not only lighter, but ... effectual
in preventing the Soldiers ammunition from getting wet', as well as more
durable and cheaper, all of which were 'of great importance on Service'.[110]

Besides seeking to introduce weapon designs he had picked up while in
America, Campbell also initiated localised tactical reforms which were
designed to make infantry battalions better able to cope with the vicissi-
tudes of campaigning in unfamiliar and challenging terrain. He published
'two books of Regulations' with the principal aim to 'practice the

Manoeuvres' so 'that the whole may observe one uniform principle in their movements'.[111] The regulations themselves were strikingly reminiscent of Howe's 1774 light infantry manual, notably in the section that instructed marching by file.[112]

Ambitious though Cornwallis's army reform plans were when he arrived in Calcutta, by 1790, he had achieved only limited success. He sought to strike a balance between local experience and new ideas from America and Europe. On the one hand, British officers in the East India Company army serving alongside regular army officers could expect more equal treatment and greater acknowledgement of the value of their local knowledge. On the other, Cornwallis wanted to draw on the relevant experience of those who had served in America, in the hope of injecting fresh and innovative thinking into areas such as tactical reforms and the employment of fire-power: a synthesis of American, European and South Asian military experience. Only so much could be achieved in peacetime however, and Cornwallis encountered significant resistance from both the King's and Company armies.

As the political situation in South India deteriorated in 1789, Cornwallis prepared for war having only partially reformed the imperial and military administration of India. His attempts to reform recruitment had failed, and the pressures of a new European war further impacted on army recruitment for India. Though he had sought to reform the system of supply and make transportation contracts more cost effective, his plans for large-scale operations continued to be hampered by the size of his train. His tactical reforms were likewise met with scepticism, because the one thing the British army in India did not lack was warfighting experience. Even without conflict with one of the major military powers in India, the British and East India Company armies had had to perform a policing role, quell unrest, hunt down insurgents and pacify restive populations. All of these factors conspired to hamper Cornwallis's attempted reforms. When war broke out once more with Mysore in late 1789, the opportunity arose to test old and new ideas alike.

CHAPTER 7

'Decisive Victory Will Relieve Us from All Our Distresses'

THE LESSONS OF WAR WITH MYSORE, 1790–1803

ON 29 December 1789, in Cornwallis's own words, 'that mad barbarian' Tipu Sultan 'forced us into a war with him by attacking without any just provocation our ally the Rajah of Tranvancore'.[1] Though the move had been expected, the fact that Tipu appeared willing to risk another war with the East India Company suggested he was well prepared. It also changed the political dynamic in India. Tipu's attack on Travancore had exposed the limits of the company's strategic intelligence, and the assumptions made about the balance of political power in India. Having been allowed to build a well-trained infantry army, Cornwallis realised that Tipu presented perhaps more of a threat to the British position in India than Haidar 'Ali had a decade earlier.

Cornwallis therefore responded swiftly by despatching Colonel Robert Abercromby from Bombay with orders to attack Tipu's position on the Malabar Coast.[2] Abercromby was a veteran of the American Revolutionary War, having served under Cornwallis's command in the Yorktown campaign. He took with him four newly raised battalions of European infantry, which had been raised in England and trained and equipped in Bombay. The deployment illustrated the perseverance of European drill techniques, with the commander of the 75th Foot, Captain Robert Craufurd, in particular, adopting 'the old Prussian model,' where 'fear was the great principle of action'.[3] Craufurd's approach had raised eyebrows in Bombay, where he regularly drilled his men in the fierce heat of the midday sun, but the resultant discipline of the soldiers paid dividends in the forthcoming campaign.

Another veteran of the American Revolutionary War, William Medows, orchestrated an operation from Madras. Medows had served alongside Cornwallis in the Philadelphia campaign in 1777, and then commanded a brigade during the British attack on St Lucia the following year. In 1780, Medows had arrived at the head of the reinforcements for Coote's army during the last Anglo-Mysore War. He therefore had more experience of warfare in India than did Cornwallis. A sound tactician, Medows was nevertheless impulsive and frequently failed to think through the implications of his plans. Cornwallis, however, aware of how an interfering but poorly informed senior officer could corrode both the personal relationship and the attainment of wider military objectives, tried his best to give Medows as much latitude in decision making for the forthcoming campaign. 'I do not wish to direct your opinions, I know how dangerous it would be for myself, as well as for the public service,' he explained, 'but after receiving all the information you can get . . . I wish you to act from your *own* opinions, and when I know they are your *own*, I shall have confidence in the them.'[4]

In May 1790, Medows elected to commence a two-pronged attack on Mysorean territory. The aim was to relieve pressure on Travancore by marching one army from Trichinopoly across southern India, while a smaller force moved west from Madras into Baramahal in order to threaten Tipu's north-eastern flank. The main force, composed of 15,000 troops, would march 150 miles to Coimbatore, which promised to be a key source of supplies. The plan was designed to force Tipu to withdraw from Travancore by occupying key agricultural and strategic locations in southern Mysore.[5] Despite his promises to remain at arm's length, Cornwallis was sceptical of the plan from the outset. 'The more I reflect upon [your] plan of the whole army going to the Southward, and postponing all offensive operations until they can carry with them forty days provision and thirty thousand bullocks,' he wrote as early as March 1790, 'the more my mind misgives me as to the probability of your success.'[6] The reasons for his scepticism were many and varied.

Cornwallis was legitimately concerned that Medows would become bogged down at Coimbatore when the monsoon began, and expressed his doubts in a succession of letters sent in late March. In such circumstances, Cornwallis explained, 'it will not then be easy for an army incumbered as yours will be to stir; Tippoo will know this, and . . . He will then send his rabble of cavalry to watch and harrass you, and lead the flower of his army to the borders of the Carnatic'. Cornwallis believed the route to success lay

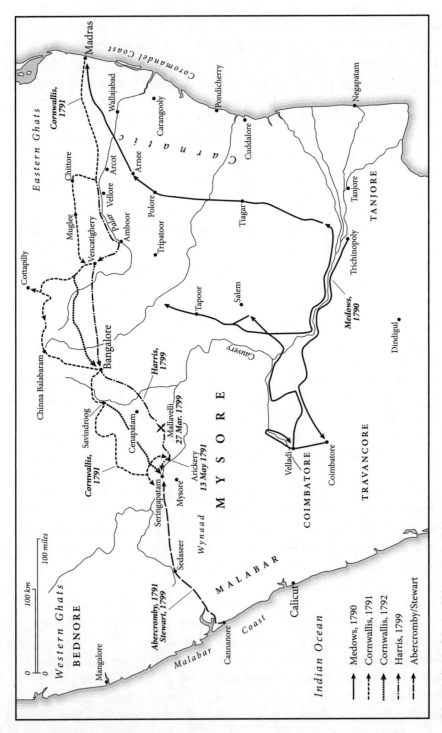

Map 8. Anglo-Mysore Wars, 1790–1799.

Madras

Coromandel Coast

Cornwallis,
1791

Wallajabad

Carangooly

Pondicherry

Negapatam

Eastern Ghats

Chittore

Arcot

Arnee

Cuddalore

TANJORE

Muglee

Vellore

Palar

Polore

Tiagar

Tanjore

Vencatigherry

Amboor

Tripatoor

Trichinopoly

Cottapilly

Tapoor

Salem

Medows,
1790

Chinna Balabaram

Bangalore

Dindigul

Harris,
1799

Savindroog

Cauvery

Cenapatam

Mallavelli
27 Mar. 1799

Cornwallis,
1791

Arickery
13 May 1791

Velladi

Coimbatore

COIMBATORE

TRAVANCORE

Seringapatam

Mysore

Wynaad

M Y S O R E

Abercromby, 1791
Stewart, 1799

Sedaseer

MALABAR

Western Ghats

BEDNORE

Calicut

Coast

Mangalore

Cannanore

Malabar

Indian Ocean

100 miles

100 km

Medows, 1790

Cornwallis, 1791

Cornwallis, 1792

Harris, 1799

Abercromby/Stewart

in maximising the mobility and manoeuvrability of the British force, so that it could launch a direct assault on the seat of Tipu's power in Mysore.

Medows's plan to take such a large supply train south imposed severe limitations on his ability to achieve any of these objectives. Invoking shared experience from their time together in America, Cornwallis confessed 'that this amazing proviant Train puts me in mind of the unfortunate and ruinous System which we pursued in America, when we thought it necessary to carry as much provision with us through the fertile plains of Pennsylvania, as if we had been to march from Aleppo to Bussorah'.[7] The indirect nature of Medows' plan also, unsurprisingly, concerned Cornwallis. 'I must confess it appears to me very like our going round by the head of Elke to conquer America', he explained, 'and I do not think our success on that occasion gives us much encouragement.'[8] The plan also failed to concentrate Medows' strength. 'You have as well as myself', Cornwallis wrote, 'so often seen the ill effects of hazarding small detachments and being beat in detail.' This would likewise leave his allies vulnerable and Cornwallis was worried about 'seeing the fatal effects which their being beat into making a separate peace must have upon our affairs'.[9]

In the event, Cornwallis was proven wholly correct. It took eight weeks for Medows to reach Coimbatore, by which point his army was severely undersupplied. Further delays were incurred securing local strongpoints, which, in the words of Major James Rennell, 'were intended for advanced *depots*, for the army, when it should move towards the Mysore country'.[10] As Cornwallis predicted, Tipu withdrew from Travancore, but capitalising on his superior mobility, he wrong-footed Medows by raiding Coimbatore before turning his focus to the smaller British force in Baramahal. Having failed to contain Tipu in Mysore, Medows' position at Coimbatore became vulnerable. Tipu evaded Medows' attempts to catch him by employing superior mobility, and repeatedly confounding Medows' intelligence network. Indeed, Medows' 'principal embarrassments', Cornwallis believed, 'have been occasioned by his almost total want of intelligence'.[11] With the British flanks exposed, Tipu took the opportunity to attack the Carnatic, getting within 80 miles of Madras by January 1791.[12]

Tipu had successfully evaded two British forces and had induced them to withdraw from Mysore. Though Medows had intended to establish magazines in Coimbatore, the need to divide his force, and the difficulty he had of bringing forward supplies, meant that he was never really able to seize the initiative. As Cornwallis had predicted, Medows got bogged down and his army sickened.[13] Though he could claim to have forced

Tipu to withdraw from Travancore, Medows retreated to Madras having achieved very little else. Cornwallis was unimpressed. In his view, only 'a decisive victory will relieve us from all our distresses, and little short of that will be of any essential use'.[14]

Cornwallis therefore decided to take personal command in December 1790. He sent ahead intelligence and logistics specialists with orders 'to obtain the most accurate information possible of the number and precise situation of the passes into Tippoo's country', including those suitable for artillery, and which were naturally defensible.[15] Cornwallis himself followed on 6 December, arriving in Madras nine days later after a stormy trip. Using the information gathered by his advanced party, by the time he was ensconced in Fort St George, Cornwallis had devised a plan to march his army into the heart of Mysore, striking at the seat of Tipu's power: the fortress capital itself, Seringapatam.[16]

Cornwallis did demonstrate that he had learned some lessons from the difficulties he experienced in North Carolina a decade earlier. He developed a much more extensive logistics plan, which aimed to resource his army with the necessary ammunition, equipment and supplies, while maximising mobility. 'We can only be said to be as nearly independent of contingencies as can be expected in war,' he wrote to Medows, 'when we are possessed of a complete battering train, and can move it with the army.'[17] To accomplish this, Cornwallis employed elephants for the first time by a British army in war, which were, in the words of Alexander Dirom, 'of such evident and essential advantage, that they will in future be considered of the first consequence in all operations'.[18] Besides, Cornwallis also understood the need to minimise the burden of his own supply train. 'Whilst we carry a large stock of provisions,' he explained to Medows, 'ample magazines shall be lodged in strong places in our rear at no great distance from the scene of our intended operations.'[19] In the event, this ambition proved the most difficult to achieve.

The army of 15,000 troops, 60,000 camp followers and 30,000 bullocks marched from Vellore on 11 February 1791 and, in an attempt to avoid an attack in the unfavourable terrain at the Amboor and Baramahal passes, Cornwallis chose to march north-west to the Moogla pass.[20] Meeting no opposition, the army thus entered the fertile tableland of Mysore, and with it access to plentiful supplies of grain and water. By 5 March, the army had reached Bangalore and commenced a siege of the outer walls of the town.

At this point disaster struck. Tipu drew the cavalry commander, Lieutenant Colonel John Floyd, into an ambush, killing 200 men and

300 horses. Despite this setback, Cornwallis determined to prosecute the siege, and not be drawn into a larger confrontation on Tipu's terms. On the 7th, the Pettah was stormed and captured, leaving the 'Siege of the fort which was rendered singularly arduous not only by the scarcity of forage and strength of its works and garrison, but also by the presence of Tippoo and his whole Army'. On 21 March, after several breaches were opened in the fort walls, Cornwallis ordered it to be stormed, 'in which the Killidar and a great number of his Garrison were put to the Sword'.[21]

The destruction of Floyd's squadron had severely curtailed Cornwallis's mobility. Tipu, meanwhile, 'took his measures with so much caution as to put it effectually out of my power to force him to risk an action'. Unable to pursue his adversary, Cornwallis turned north to rendezvous with the cavalry promised him by the Nizam of Hyderabad. This was not accomplished until 13 March. Cornwallis estimated the Nizam's cavalry amounted to 16,000, 'and tho' they are extremely defective in almost every point of military discipline, yet as the men are in general well-mounted' he was 'in great hopes that we should derive material advantage from their assistance'. Unfortunately for Cornwallis, he now found himself seriously undersupplied. Not only had he largely exhausted his existing supply train, but the reinforcements now added to the burden. He had no option but to return to Amboor, but there he found his plans in disarray after the bullock drivers had marched out.[22]

Struggling with only 20 days' supply, Cornwallis decided to make a run for Seringapatam. In a move reminiscent of the Guilford Courthouse campaign, to lighten the load, he 'requested the assistance of the officers, in reducing their baggage; and then sparing their surplus cattle for the purpose of carrying shot and stores for the siege'. As a result, '2,500 bullocks were transferred from private to public use'.[23] The delays, however, had cost Cornwallis his window of good weather. The onset of the monsoon rains in early May meant his army turned the roads into quagmires, while Tipu had scorched the terrain through which the British marched. Sickness bedevilled men and animals alike, and so many bullocks of the baggage and siege trains perished that sepoys had to haul the guns. The rains had likewise swollen the Cauvery, rendering it impassable, and as he searched for a ford at Arickery on 13 May, Tipu offered battle.

'Drawn up with their right to the river, and their left to a mountain of a very rugged and inaccessible appearance', Tipu's army was a mixture of regular and irregular infantry, supplemented by huge numbers of irregular cavalry.[24] In the opinion of James Rennell, 'Tippoo's judgement in choosing this post, is unquestionable ... from the nature of the ground itself, and that of the adjacent country.' As ever, it was the European-trained regular infantry that Cornwallis was most concerned about, though the cavalry presented a considerable threat to this flank. Cornwallis hoped to outflank his adversary, but the rains inhibited his movements and Tipu learned of the attempted manoeuvre. He drew 'out his army, and form[ed] it in several lines ... covering his right flank with the ravine', and 'his left with the shoulder of the ridge'. As Cornwallis reorganised his army, 'the troops were exposed to the whole artillery of the enemy', though 'a rocky eminence presented itself, and was taken advantage of: without which, the lines, whilst forming, would have been completely enfiladed'.[25]

Cornwallis nevertheless persisted with his outflanking manoeuvre, in order to 'force Tippoo to hazard an action on ground which I hoped would be less advantageous to him than that which he had chosen'.[26] He formed his infantry into two lines, with the first line composed of nine battalions of infantry under Medows' command, and the second line of four battalions under Colonel George Harris. Meanwhile, he despatched five battalions under Colonel Maxwell to capture the heights on Tipu's left. 'The ground on which our lines were formed', Rennell recorded, 'was a slope or ascent of the height, occupied by the enemy; the right wing standing on much higher ground that the left.'[27] Maxwell's infantry opened the battle by storming the heights on Tipu's left and capturing them at the point of the bayonet without firing a shot.

With his adversary's flank exposed, Cornwallis now ordered the remainder of his infantry to charge Tipu's main line. 'Their infantry on this occasion showed a much better countenance than usual, which perhaps may be principally attributed to Tippoo's own presence and exertions amongst them,' Cornwallis explained in his account of the campaign. 'In a short time', however, 'they began to waver, and soon after, upon the cavalry moving towards their right ... they entirely gave way.'[28] Tipu withdrew, but despite an active pursuit by Cornwallis's cavalry, managed to get back within the walls of Seringapatam.

Tipu had once again proven himself a capable general, selecting terrain that offered his disparate collection of infantry and cavalry the greatest possible advantages. Though evidently incapable of meeting the challenge presented by Cornwallis's own highly trained infantry, the methodical way in which Tipu's infantry managed the withdrawal of his guns to Seringapatam illustrated that this was a force that would not be easily beaten in conventional battle. Still, Cornwallis had illustrated his tactical prowess, selecting a plan of action that would mitigate Tipu's terrain-based advantages. The British infantry, both European and Indian, meanwhile, had demonstrated the continued superiority of their training, managing a battlefield transition across uneven terrain, and then forming for a conventional confrontation under heavy fire. Cornwallis's campaign plan was a product of his experience of warfare in America, but informed by the exigencies and limitations imposed by the character of conflict in South Asia and underpinned by traditional European discipline and tactics – a synthesis of military theory and practice on three continents.

Despite this victory, Cornwallis found himself unable 'to move forward a step ... without exposing this army to the certain state of perishing by famine', a situation made worse by the drain on his resources imposed by his allies and camp followers.[29] His best intelligence suggested that promised support from the Marathas was still more than 150 miles away. On 26 May, Cornwallis reluctantly blew up his battering train and began to withdraw to Bangalore. Abercromby, who had made it as far as Seringapatam, also withdrew. Unlike Cornwallis, who only had to go as far as Bangalore, Abercromby's men had to withdraw to the Malabar Coast, and did so through torrential rain, enduring severe shortages of fresh food. As they did so, they suffered continuous harassment from Tipu's irregular cavalry. Craufurd's well-disciplined 75th formed the rearguard, and maintained order in distressing circumstances. Abercromby came in for some criticism when news of the retreat reached London, and Craufurd's brother, Charles, offered a public defence. 'On such terrible roads and at such a season ... I believe you would find, if you trace their campaigns accurately, the King of Prussia and Prince Ferdinand doing the same thing and that in a more favourable climate ....'[30]

The following day, much to Cornwallis's annoyance, the Marathas arrived. Had they arrived 'three weeks sooner', he complained, 'I think we might have taken Seringapatam'.[31] Defeated once more by poor intelligence and insurmountable supply difficulties, rather than by enemy action, Cornwallis nevertheless had much to show for his exertions. Bangalore was in British hands, and the clearest topographical intelligence picture on Tipu's kingdom had been obtained. This complemented a detailed picture compiled by a number of officers with specific instructions to collect military intelligence on Tipu's army, by employing informants and spies and questioning local civilians.[32] Cornwallis now also had the chance to build up a supply network that would enable him to move with more decision and ease.

*   *   *

The end of the campaigning season afforded Cornwallis and his army some time to recover from the strains of the past months.[33] It also gave him the opportunity to implement the lessons he had learned. Unwilling to leave anything to chance, Cornwallis set about completely reforming the British system of supply. 'It is no easy task to feed between two and three hundred thousand men, on a hundred thousand horses, and twice that number of bullocks, besides elephants and camels, in a country which nature intended for a desert,' he wrote despairingly, 'and which Tippoo has, with the assistance of our friends the Mahrattas, rendered a complete one.'[34] Having suffered operational difficulties when the contracted bullock drivers abandoned the army after receiving no payment, he amended the contractual arrangements with the drivers to ensure their loyalty. They would henceforth be paid directly, frequently and regularly.[35]

This, however, would solve only half the problem. Cornwallis still could not feed the mass of camp followers from publicly funded supply lines. He therefore took measures to 'remove the only obstacle that could have materially defeated the effect of our other preparations'.[36] By the end of January 1792, Cornwallis expected 'to be joined by ... many thousand binjarries ...'.[37] Though the inclusion of what amounted to a privately funded travelling bazaar increased the size of Cornwallis's camp tremendously, the binjarries offered access to commodities which the army could not provide, and offered further transportation options.

In order to reduce the supply burden on the army's own transportation, Cornwallis reduced the food ration issued to sepoys and increased their pay, offering them the opportunity to buy what they wanted from the bazaars. 'The Sepoys bought coarser grain with the money they received for the half of their allowance of rice', noted Dirom, while 'the soldiers who preferred more liquor to the money might buy it in the bazars'. As a result, 'the public stores of grain and arrack were made to last double the time by this arrangement'.[38] In Cornwallis's view these were 'as necessary to the success of our operations as the fighting men, for without their assistance we could neither move our artillery, stores' or camp equipage'.[39] Within months, 'the department of military stores', was, according to one observer, 'complete in every respect and exhibits a capital display of the implements of war in an astonishing abundance'.[40]

Equipped with a reliable and effective supply system, Cornwallis next wanted to secure the chain of hill forts that commanded the roads between Bangalore and Seringapatam. The first two, at Ambajee-Durgum and Chillum-Cottha, surrendered with no resistance on 18 September. The next was a more challenging prospect. Nundydroog was the capital of a large, well-cultivated and therefore valuable district. The fortress was 'built on the summit of a mountain about one thousand seven hundred feet in height, three-fourths of its circumference being absolutely inaccessible'. Dirom observed that 'the only face on which it can be ascended was protected by two excellent walls, and an outwork which covered the gateway, and afforded a formidable flank fire'.[41] Dirom believed the obstacles 'surpassed whatever had been known in any former siege in India',[42] while another participant, Lieutenant Roderick Mackenzie, observed: 'it is highly probable that no degree of exertion in the troops . . . could have overcome the difficulties that intervened, but for the assistance of elephants.'[43] This was another of Cornwallis's adaptations. Having witnessed the strength of capabilities of the elephants used in the 1791 campaign, he increased the number of requisitions from 71 to 106 per month.[44]

Within two weeks, the British were able to build two batteries close enough to the fortress gates and establish a breach in the outer wall. The defenders maintained a constant fire, and the British 'were severely annoyed by ginjall, or wall pieces', observed Dirom, 'which are in general use among the native powers in the defence of forts, and throw a bullet of considerable size, with much accuracy, to a great distance'.[45] On 18 October, Cornwallis ordered the breach to be stormed by moonlight, but the defenders discovered the assailants and 'a heavy discharge of musquetry and rockets opened', recorded Mackenzie. In addition, 'stones of immense weight . . . rolling down from the works at the summit of the hill, with astonishing velocity were still more formidable to our troops than all the other defences'.[46] Despite sustaining some casualties, the British managed to break through the second gate before it was barricaded. A number of the garrison escaped 'by ropes and ladders over a low part of the wall', while the remainder surrendered.[47]

News of the fall of Nundydroog spread, and morale among the remaining garrisons began to collapse. At Sevendroog, a fortress of almost equal strength to Nundydroog, the garrison held out for four days under a heavy bombardment before fleeing after Cornwallis ordered another assault. As many as 200 jumped to their deaths. The remarkably swift success at Sevendroog compelled most other fortresses to surrender without resistance, though the garrison at Outradroog successfully escaped after causing a herd of wild bullocks to stampede the attackers. By February 1792, the captured hill forts offered Cornwallis a chain of magazines and depots between Bangalore and Seringapatam that were themselves no more than 12 miles apart.

With his supply lines secure, the way now lay open for Cornwallis's final march on Seringapatam.[48] To help prepare for the climax of the operation, Cornwallis gave orders for all officers commanding foraging detachments to report details of the roads and terrain. Local spies also brought in seemingly useful information about the structure and strength of Seringapatam and provided Cornwallis with a plan of the outworks of the fortress.[49]

Cornwallis made his move from Sevendroog on 25 January, arriving in the vicinity of Seringapatam on 5 February. During the march, Cornwallis received news that Abercromby, who had once more marched from the Malabar coast, was in a position to strike a surprise blow to the south-west of Tipu's fortress capital. He immediately sent instructions to Abercromby 'to hold his corps in readiness to move, lightly equipped in every respect, at the shortest notice', while he arranged for the Nizam's troops and the Madras battalions to be sent in support. The plan illustrated his use of ideas, adapted for the Indian context, which had previously been deployed, albeit unsuccessfully, when he commanded in America. As one of his subordinate officers during the southern campaign, Cornwallis could rely on Abercromby to execute his orders, confident he also understood his commander's intent. Knowledge gained in America was thus transferred and applied in South Asia.

Unfortunately, the plan exposed shortcomings in the quality and effectiveness of the forces under Cornwallis's command. He found the Nizam's forces unprepared for action and had to abandon the plan, ordering Abercromby instead to cross the Cauvery and rendezvous with the main British force on the north bank.[50] This was not the first time Cornwallis had been disappointed by the performance of his allies. Since the withdrawal to Bangalore the previous March, the Maratha cavalry had been conducting desultory operations, with limited success, against Tipu's detached forces, rather than offering the supply line protection Cornwallis had requested of them. Indeed, when joined in January 1792 by a substantial reinforcement of largely irregular troops under the command of the Nizam's son, and 'by many thousand binjarries ...; the latter', Cornwallis wrote, 'though not so high sounding, are at least as useful a reinforcement as the former'.[51]

On 6 February, having observed that Tipu had deployed his army outside Seringapatam, Cornwallis resolved to attack. In preparation, he questioned several 'hircurrahs [spies], who had been frequently sent to Tippoo's camp to make observations upon it; and on the following morning the whole position was carefully reconnoitred under cover of a strong detachment'. What he observed was a position which 'appeared to have been chosen with great judgement, and fortified with extraordinary care . . .'. Tipu's army of between 40,000 and 50,000 troops was deployed close to the north bank of the Cauvery, anchored by high ground on both flanks, with the main part of the line fortified by no fewer than six redoubts 'well-furnished with cannon'. In addition, the approach was 'rendered uncommonly difficult by a number of rice-fields, ravines and water-courses', while the entire position was covered by the guns in Seringapatam.[52] Fearing the casualties he would suffer if he attacked in daylight, Cornwallis settled on a night-time attack, and accepted that he would receive no support from either his own artillery or his allied cavalry. He elected personally to command the main part of the assault, on Tipu's centre, and believed that a strong attack here would compel his adversary to withdraw. Maxwell would begin the battle in command of a column of four battalions on Tipu's right, while Medows would launch a limited assault on his left, which was very strongly posted.

In the event, the first stage of the attack went according to plan. Maxwell's column opened the battle, which distracted the troops in the centre. Cornwallis ordered in his column which reached the line of redoubts with few casualties and continued the attack at the point of the bayonet. Outflanked on the right and facing a huge assault in the centre, Tipu's line collapsed and withdrew precipitately to Seringapatam. Medows, however, had misinterpreted his instructions and launched an attack on the strong redoubt on Tipu's left. His initial advance had been delayed by previously unidentified obstacles, but, having captured the fortification late with some casualties, Medows was unable to continue to advance.

Tipu recognised that Cornwallis's right flank was now exposed and launched an immediate counterattack. Cornwallis himself received a small wound in his right hand during the ensuing fighting, but nevertheless managed to rally his troops and retake the initiative, driving Tipu's counterattack from the field.[53] As dawn broke, Cornwallis's troops came under sustained and well-directed artillery fire, which forced him to withdraw to the cover provided by the high ground to his left. Throughout the day, Tipu launched five attacks to try to retake the redoubts. They all failed, and as night once more offered Cornwallis the cover he needed to relieve those positions, Tipu decided to withdraw from the field and focus on the defence of Seringapatam, the siege of which commenced the following day.

On 10 February, Abercromby arrived, adding 6,000 men to Cornwallis's force. The investment of the fortress was now complete, and Tipu's position largely hopeless. Cornwallis's own intelligence was found to be 'extremely incorrect and imperfect', but defections from Tipu's French mercenary officers offered a valuable corrective. Cornwallis therefore rearranged his siegeworks, moving from the north and east to the south and west of the fortress.[54] Though the result of the siege was inevitable, Tipu launched sorties on 22 February, which 'were repulsed and driven back'.[55] Two days later, Tipu sought terms and the guns fell silent.[56]

Many in the army were disappointed. 'This news damped the Spirits of every one who wished the downfall of the Tyrant,' wrote Lachlan Macquarie, an officer under Abercromby's command, and another veteran of the American Revolutionary War. He had 'hoped to have the satisfaction ... of storming his Capital'.[57] In the event, the peace terms, designed to try to avoid future conflict with Mysore, actually had the opposite effect. Though Cornwallis kept Tipu on the throne of Mysore, by seizing more than half his territory, including much of the Malabar Coast and the gateway to the Carnatic, the scene was set for Tipu to seek French aid in challenging British authority in southern India once more.

That Tipu accepted the terms demonstrated that Cornwallis had adapted to the character of warfare in India. European infantry tactics had again prevailed at the Battle of Seringapatam, but in all other respects the army that marched on Tipu's fortress capital was the product of the combination of military experience in America, Europe and India. Cornwallis had learned from failure in America, and those lessons had been implemented with Indian solutions. The logistical arrangements in particular were an evident synthesis of American, European and Indian thinking, while the methodical execution of the campaign that led to the encirclement of Seringapatam was a product of the European military theories Cornwallis had absorbed in advance of his deployment to South Asia, as well as specific responses to the experiences of the first two years of the campaign. Several memoirs of the campaign would be published in the next few years, including one by the staff officer, Major Alexander Dirom.[58] Though heavily biased against Britain's local allies, the detail proved essential for planning a new invasion, when another, largely inevitable war broke out in 1799.

*   *   *

Isolated and antagonised by the gradual expansion of British power in South India, Tipu turned once more to his former European ally, the

French, in the hopes of securing the support he needed, supposedly in his own words, 'to expel the British nation from India'. Given the circumstantial evidence of Tipu's attempts to reach alliances with the Nizam of Hyderabad, the Marathas and even Shah Zeman of Afghanistan, as well as the seeming penetration of French mercenaries into every indigenous army in South Asia, Governor General Richard Wellesley, Lord Mornington, concluded there was a 'strong argument ... in favour of an immediate attack'. He therefore gave orders for the assembly of armies 'upon the coasts of Coromandel and Malabar, and at Bombay'.[59]

Commanding the main British contingent at Madras, Major General Sir George Harris was concerned about the speed at which Mornington proposed launching a strike on Mysore. When he shared Mornington's direction with the Chief Secretary, Josiah Webbe, the latter was incredulous. 'I can anticipate nothing but a return of the shocking disasters', Webbe exclaimed, 'from a premature attack upon Tippoo in our present disabled condition.' Caught between military reality and political expediency, Harris opted to blame local allies for his inevitable inability to assemble a strike force against Tipu before the monsoons came in 1798.[60] 'The dilatoriness, indecision, and cowardice of our allies are beyond belief to those who have not been eye-witness to these qualities in them,' he wrote in July. They would, Harris argued, not act until the British had 'secured a position to cover their advance ... Thus they acted with Lord Cornwallis', he continued, 'and as that conduct was governed by principles which have undergone no change, a repetition of it must be expected'.[61]

Harris had served as an aide-de-camp to General Medows during the Third Anglo-Mysore War, and before that had served in North America and the West Indies during the American Revolutionary War. Despite the severe head injury he had sustained at Bunker Hill in 1775, he had accumulated a wealth of professional experience in a career that spanned the globe. He was therefore more than aware that the real reason he would be unable to move in line with Mornington's unrealistic timelines was because it was impossible to acquire the supplies he needed to sustain a march to and siege of Seringapatam. 'This difficulty', he concluded in his letter to Mornington, 'obliged Lord Cornwallis to relinquish the idea of besieging Seringapatam the first time he marched against it; and but for the almost despaired of co-operation of the Mahrattas, it would have been doubtful whether he would have ever been able to return to it again'.[62]

It was therefore unlikely that he needed the help and advice of Mornington's younger brother, Colonel Arthur Wellesley, in understanding the governor-general's wishes, but Harris was astute enough to recognise that Wellesley, though an intelligent and competent officer, was also a useful conduit to explain the true military situation to Mornington in a way the latter would understand. After spending five hours reviewing the plans, Wellesley wrote explaining Harris's concerns. 'The question of war or peace with Tippoo', Wellesley wrote, 'will depend upon your state of preparation,' as well as the financial health of the British government of India. Harris also needed to see detailed plans for the operations assigned to the Bombay and Madras armies, as well as an understanding of the strength of the reinforcement coming from Bengal.[63]

Indeed, Wellesley was himself deeply sceptical even that an army and its requisite supplies, along with a viable campaign plan, could be assembled quickly enough to attack Mysore in the following year. 'There is one circumstance however, of which I was not aware til lately, which has had great weight upon my mind,' he wrote. 'It is this: unless you can march from [Madras] early in January, you can't expect to do any good as the Malabar monsoon in May will oblige you to return from Seringapatam. Will you be able to march in January?' he asked rhetorically. 'Certainly not.'[64]

This, though, was exactly what Mornington, and eventually Harris and Wellesley, planned. Navigating the turbulent politics at Madras, Wellesley found himself working to convince Webbe and the experienced military secretary Colonel Barry Close that a swift and decisive campaign was possible. As ever, the most problematic element was the organisation of supplies and transportation. Wellesley relied on past experience to inform his own plans. Aware that war with Mysore was a real possibility, when he sailed for India in 1797, he had brought with him to read on the voyage Alexander Dirom's and Roderick Mackenzie's accounts of Cornwallis's campaigns.[65] He also, with Close's help, compiled a 'review of difference campaigns against Hyder Ali & Tipu Sultan', which informed his 'proposed plan for assembling an army'.[66] Close's personal experience – he had been present at the conclusion of the Second Anglo-Mysore War and served as Cornwallis's Adjutant General during the Third – also proved invaluable.

The combined weight of this experience, along with the evident military reality of the environmental conditions of South India, reinforced the importance of logistical planning and security. 'It is impossible to carry on a war in India without Bullocks,' Wellesley wrote, 'and yet the expense of an establishment at all adequate to the purposes for which it is intended is so great that I cannot recommend one.'[67] Indeed, by the end of October, Wellesley estimated that 40,000 bullocks would be needed to support the British invasion of Mysore, though he evidently found the method of contracting directly with their drivers suboptimal.[68] He orchestrated the acquisition of the minimum sufficient number of bullocks necessary to make the march to Seringapatam feasible. He also helped get the battering train to Vellore by early November 1798,[69] and ensured that the army had access to the right amount of grain and rice, a particularly important task, considering that there was general shortage in Madras in late 1798.[70] He helped make a few pieces of the complex jigsaw puzzle that was an army's logistics, but he did not put that jigsaw puzzle together. Indeed, by mid-December, logistical preparations were still under way, and far from complete.[71]

By January 1799, against all odds, half the needed bullocks had been requisitioned with promises of the remainder by the end of the month; the battering train had been brought forward and the troops were beginning to form. Wellesley had transferred to Vellore in mid-December and organised regular training and drill. But he remained sceptical. In addition to a general shortage of grain and money, there were doubts about the integrity of the Nizam's army, whether six battalions of sepoy infantry would make it to Vellore in time, and about the feasibility of the Bombay army supporting the invasion from the Malabar coast.[72]

That army, commanded by General James Stuart, who was himself a veteran of both America and Cornwallis's Seringapatam campaign, was, in fact, well positioned to launch a supporting attack. Serving once more on the staff of the Bombay Army was Lachlan Macquarie, now a major. 'Our little army is well equipped,' he wrote, 'and we shall be able to carry with us to Seringapatam at least Thirty days provisions for Twelve Thousand Men.'[73] Soon after they commenced their march, however, Tipu launched a surprise attack with 18,000 troops. Though Tipu attempted to outflank the British column, Stuart, by now experienced in Tipu's tactics, managed to fend off repeated assaults. Stuart's forces suffered just 143 casualties, while Tipu's 'dead and wounded are to be seen scattered on the Road and in the Jungle in great numbers'.[74]

At Vellore, meanwhile, by early February, Wellesley concluded that 'the ponderous machine', consisting of more than 20,000 solders, 5,000 of them European, as well as 60,000 camp followers and near 100,000 bullocks, 'is now nearly prepared, and all we have to do is to put and keep it in motion'.[75] Harris, who had arrived to take command on 26 January, was impressed by 'the very handsome appearance and perfect discipline of the troops', which he attributed to Wellesley's capable management.[76] Indeed, he believed 'wonderful exertions have been made to fit out the army', which was 'appointed beyond every expectation'.[77] He also complimented 'the judicious and masterly arrangements in respect to supplies, which', reliant once more on *brinjarries*, 'opened an abundant free market, and inspired confidence into dealers of every description'.[78] By way of reward, and in order to keep the governor-general's imperious younger brother at arm's length, Wellesley was given command of a detachment of British troops sent to support the Nizam's force, which was also rapidly approaching. The total size of that force was considerable – 1,000 European infantry, 5,000 sepoys and 10,000 irregular cavalry. Wellesley was, of course, delighted, but the move simultaneously alienated several more senior officers, including Major General David Baird, who, having fought in several campaigns against Haidar 'Ali and Tipu Sultan, felt he had earned the right to a semi-independent command.[79]

The remarkable speed with which the army and its supplies had been assembled was nothing short of extraordinary. Wellesley, an unusually competent and effective officer, carries much of the responsibility, but as he was fresh to India, he relied substantially on the support offered by Close, and on the previous written experience of those who had planned the 1791 and 1792 invasions. For this reason, Wellesley was also sceptical that Mornington's ambitious objectives, which included the capture of Seringapatam, could be accomplished in one campaign. As the army got under way, such scepticism would have been hard to dispel. 'The market of General Harris's army equals in extent . . . that of a populous city,' wrote one observer. 'The surrounding plains and downs appear to be in motion. Herds of cattle and flocks of sheep conceal the soil; the route of the troops is marked by the gleaming of their arms, and that of the battering train by a long slow-moving inky line.'[80]

As was the case for Cornwallis, Harris's army moved at a ponderous pace. It entered Mysore in early March, but because Tipu was attempting to eliminate the threat posed by Stuart on his western flank, the progress in the east was relatively unimpeded. This was fortunate, as the army quickly began experiencing logistical difficulties. By 10 March, 'our . . . movement showed a very serious deficiency in the Bullock department', Harris wrote to Mornington. The army was 'crippled in our movements from this cause, our marches have been tedious though short; our halts have been frequent and our progress has been slow'.[81] Wellesley found the pace frustrating. 'We have had much blundering and *puzzling*, and I have been present at many strong and violent discussions in the cabinet,' he wrote to Mornington as the army lurched forward.[82] Still, the situation was, at least initially, not as dire as it might have been. Distracted by

Stuart's advance from Malabar, Tipu had failed to replicate the scorched earth strategies that had served his father so well. 'Had he thrown his cavalry into the Barramahal,' Harris explained, 'I doubt much whether we could have proceeded before the next monsoon.'[83]

As the army continued its slow but inexorable progress, however, Tipu's forces began to harass the British column more effectively, picking off stragglers and flanking parties. Tipu's 'light cavalry, *looties* [local irregular horsemen], and others, are the best of the kind in the world', Wellesley explained.[84] Another participant noted that the further the army marched into Mysore, more 'towns and villages were in flames in every direction. Not one atom of forage or food could be procured . . .'.[85] Harris began to despair that the army would not be able to advance as far as Seringapatam. Many of the difficulties he had witnessed in 1791 were once more blighting his advance. Wellesley, though, was growing in confidence. 'There is not *now* a doubt that we shall bring that monstrous equipment to Seringapatam,' he wrote to Mornington, 'and, in that case, we shall certainly take the place.'[86]

Tipu attempted to arrest the British advance by offering battle at Mallavelli. 'Some of my staff urged me to march . . . against Tippoo very early,' Harris noted in his journal, 'but to this I gave a decided negative.' It is difficult to believe Cornwallis would have avoided the opportunity to fight a battle in such circumstances, but Harris had a clear idea of his political objectives and realised an unnecessary battle would only hamper his ability to achieve those ends. As the British continued their advance on 27 March, however, Tipu began an artillery bombardment. Realising he faced more than a mere detachment of the British army, he immediately ordered a withdrawal, and in the ensuing confusion a series of skirmishes broke out, the most serious of which was on Harris's right. Tipu's infantry 'were more than usually bold', Harris noted, for 'instead of retiring' they charged the British line 'to try the bayonet with us'.[87]

Once more the disciplined British infantry outmatched Tipu's forces, and after receiving a volley of musketry 'they ran off much too fast for me to allow our men to follow them'. The main force was caught for a short amount of time in a precarious situation. As they approached the enemy line, the light company of the 12th Regiment was charged by a large force of enemy cavalry, supported by 'two enormous elephants, having huge chains hanging on their proboscis, which they whirled about on both sides, a blow from which would have destroyed ten or twelve men at once'.[88] The timely arrival of a squadron of the Nizam's cavalry closed the gap, and Tipu's horsemen instead headed straight towards the front of the British line.

General Harris, who was at the rear of the line, ordered the troops to fire. Facing a cavalry charge drawn up in line was a terrible prospect, but fortunately for the British, Tipu's horsemen were undisciplined. If the 12th Regiment had fired when Harris told them to, the shots would have had little if any impact. According to Bayly, 'the men knew it was not the voice of their colonel, who, however, now gave the word, "Steady, 12th, I command. Wait until they are within ten yards; then singe the beggars' whiskers!"'[89] The volley of fire decimated the front ranks of Tipu's cavalry charge, and the arrival of two nine-pounders firing grapeshot completed the rout of the Mysorean right. Once again, disciplined British infantry firepower had been the decisive factor on an Indian battlefield. Tipu's defeat demoralised his army and left the road open to Seringapatam, before which the army arrived on 2 April.

Having conducted a reconnaissance with his engineers and intelligence officer, Captain John Malcolm, Harris concluded that 'the Western Angle is without doubt the weakest part of the Fort as it is ill-flanked, its strength consists solely in a rugged bed of a river not exceeding 200 yards broad.' But Malcolm noted in his journal of the campaign, 'General Harris thinks with Lord Cornwallis that the Grenadiers of his Army will force a passage anywhere.'[90] Harris's army would occupy the southern bank of the Cauvery, while Stuart, when his army completed its march from the Malabar Coast, would occupy the north bank. Over the next month, the British gradually dug trenches and built batteries in order to commence the bombardment of the western walls of the fortress. In return 'the Fort has fired very little', Malcolm noted with some surprise, 'and it would be impossible to suppose or believe that we were besieging the Capital of a Powerful Prince from the extreme quiet the Army enjoys.'[91]

The arrival of the Bombay army on 14 April caused Tipu to rethink his defence. Stuart's march had progressed relatively uneventfully, though the closer his army got to Seringapatam, the more 'the Enemy's Horse harrassed our Line', recorded Macquarie in his journal.[92] Harris sent Stuart north of the Cauvery to commence new siegeworks. On 20 April, troops from the Bombay army captured a deserted redoubt and began building a battery there on the north bank of the Cauvery. 'Whilst our Working Parties were busily employed in constructing the ... 4 Gun Battery,' Macquarie noted, 'the Enemy in great numbers came out of the Fort across the River about 12 o'clock at Night, and made a bold and spirited attack on our Covering Party and Advanced Post.' The working parties were briefly forced to withdraw until the infantry could counterattack and 'soon cleared it of the

Enemy, and maintained Possession of it during the remainder of the Night
...'.[93] Tipu's forces suffered in excess of 600 casualties as a result of this
abortive sortie. A second counterattack on 26 April was more successful in
causing British casualties, but Harris refused to withdraw, and the batteries
were completed and a bombardment commenced on 2 May, with a practicable breach established by the following evening.

Harris gave David Baird command of the initial assault. The 'Forlorn
Hope' was composed of volunteers from the 12th, 33rd, 73rd and 74th
Regiments, while supporting columns approached from the right and left.
On the right were the flank companies of the 73rd and 74th, dubbed the
Scotch Brigade; and on the left, were the flank companies of 75th and
77th, with the 12th and 33rd in reserve. The Forlorn Hope suffered badly.
Many lost their footing on the slippery riverbed, while the rest met stiff
resistance in the breach itself.[94]

Once through the breach, Baird discovered a second wall which, though
in a state of disrepair, offered an extra obstacle. 'Good God! I did not expect
this!' Baird reputedly exclaimed. Though the attackers were briefly held up,
the light infantry of the 12th managed to scramble over the wall and
engaged in fierce hand-to-hand fighting with the defenders. Tipu was killed
in the melee, attempting to defend one of the gates. By 3 p.m., the British
colours flew over the ramparts. Seringapatam had fallen. Harris's army
suffered a total of 1,531 casualties during the siege. Having proven himself
a competent administrator, Harris appointed Wellesley to quell the riot of
looting and pillaging that had ensued after the capture of the fortress.

A few days later, to Baird's considerable annoyance, Harris confirmed
Wellesley as the permanent governor of Seringapatam. Wellesley took as
his headquarters Tipu's opulent summer palace, the Daria Daulat Bagh.
As he settled into his new accommodations, he dwelt on the campaign
which had just concluded. It had, by any measure, been an outstanding
success, but it had come perilously close to failure on a number of occasions, all because of issues chiefly related to logistics. This was, for
Wellesley, an unsatisfactory situation, and an entirely different approach
to warfare was needed, one that was less reliant on supply trains and more
dependent on speed and manoeuvre.[95] 'In the wars which we may expect
in India in future,' wrote Colonel Arthur Wellesley, 'we must look to light
and quick movements; and we ought always to be in that state to be able
to strike a blow as soon as a war might become evidently necessary.'[96]

Wellesley's conclusion was not his alone, but the product of decades of
combined experience across the world, from America to India. Wellesley

was exposed to this wealth of military knowledge because of his interaction with complex formal and informal networks when he arrived in India. The formal connections are obvious: while laying the foundations of the Army's supply system, he worked closely with veterans of South Asian campaigns, such as Lieutenant Colonel Barry Close, the adjutant general; Lieutenant Colonel Sydenham, the auditor general; and a host of captains and majors.[97] All had extensive experience of military operations in India, what had worked and what had not. An extensive review was compiled of the earlier campaigns fought against Haidar 'Ali and Tipu Sultan to help ensure that the same mistakes were not made again.[98] This knowledge and experience would have been invaluable to Wellesley. In addition, he also read extensively on the military history of India, and, during his six-month voyage to India in 1797, consumed, among others, Alexander Dirom's *Narrative of the Campaign in India*, which provided an extensive account of Cornwallis's campaign planning, as well as Roderick Mackenzie's two-volume *Sketch of the War with Tippoo Sultan*.[99]

More informal networks, which would have exposed Wellesley to ideas born of warfighting experience in America, are more difficult to identify. Of those who had served in India, Cornwallis was the most prominent veteran of American service. The plan, if not the execution, of the 1791 and 1792 campaigns was clearly derived from Cornwallis's experiences in America, as demonstrated by his repeated reference to those campaigns. Adaptations to the environmental conditions in India, notably with the establishment of a large and unwieldy, but ultimately sustainable logistics system, helped the British overcome the supply difficulties that had simultaneously blighted both their operations in the southern colonies and against Mysore. Wellesley and Close largely replicated those adaptations when they helped organise the logistics for the 1799 campaign.

Moreover, though Cornwallis and Wellesley never served together, they were in the same regiment. The two corresponded prior to Wellesley's deployment, with Cornwallis decrying the lack of light infantry in the regular British army.[100] It is possible that the two met informally prior to Wellesley's deployment to India, though neither mentioned the meeting if one did take place. Such meetings frequently occurred: over dinner, at soirees and in other recreational pursuits, in which personal experience was the subject of conversation and discussion. There were also other more direct linkages between Wellesley and those with experience of war in America.

The commander of the Madras army itself, George Harris, had seen action throughout the American Revolutionary War, serving at Bunker

Hill and New York, before heading to the West Indies in 1778. Other veterans included the commander of the Bombay army, James Stuart, and several of the staff, such as Lachlan Macquarie, who had been delighted, when the Bombay army arrived at Seringapatam, to reacquaint with 'some of my old American Friends'.[101] The experience of warfighting in America suffused the army in which Wellesley served in 1799, and he would have been exposed to those experiences through informal discussions throughout the campaign. Indeed, as with his personal experiences gained in India, the collective experience of warfare in America impacted on his later thinking. 'In such countries as America, very extensive, thinly peopled, and producing but little food in proportion to their extent,' he would later comment, 'military operations by large bodies are impracticable, unless the party carrying them on has the uninterrupted use of a navigable river, or very extensive means of land transport, which such a country can rarely supply.'[102]

It was precisely this challenge that Wellesley sought to overcome in devising what he termed 'light and quick movements'. Besides being the result of personal interactions with those with experience of warfare in India and America, Wellesley's ideas were also the product of his own interest in his profession. Much of the genesis of the idea for 'light and quick movements' was derived from a close reading of military theorists such as Turpin de Crissé and Henry Lloyd. Lloyd's work was one of those that Wellesley had read during his voyage to India.[103] It is evident from his actions in India, and in his subsequent military career, that Lloyd's arguments had a profound effect on Wellesley's own military knowledge.

First and foremost, 'light and quick movements' were focused on the achievement of the strategic aims of the campaign. If this resulted in battle, then the army should be as well prepared for that eventuality as possible, but battle was not the end in and of itself. Lloyd had argued that 'no operation whatever, should be attempted, or post attacked, unless the possession of it be absolutely necessary to facilitate some capital enterprise'.[104] This was a principle which Lloyd's close friend, Henry Clinton, had employed, to much derision, in America, but those who had been critical of the approach had gradually accepted its wisdom. Harris, for example, had initially refused battle at Mallavelli on 27 March 1799, telling his staff that his 'object was to set down before Seringapatam as speedily as possible; that the pains I had taken to be ready to fight Tippoo was entirely with the hope it would enable me to avoid it: that nothing but his stopping the high road should make me seek him'.[105] Wellesley might have been critical of Harris's leadership, but as historian Rory Muir observed in his biography of Wellesley, 'Harris was not a brilliant general but Wellesley learnt as much from watching his *"puzzling"* as he would have from a far abler commander'.[106]

In addition to being prepared for the last resort of a battle, an army needed to be as well trained for the operation itself. 'The army which marches the best,' Lloyd argued, 'must, if the rest is equal, in the end prevail.'[107] This maxim lay at the heart of Wellesley's concept of 'light and quick movements', but in order for it to work, a suitably organised system of supply was essential, one which did not hinder the rapid movements of the army but helped facilitate them. Lloyd also had advice on this matter, derived from Turpin de Crissé and Folard, but nevertheless valuable to Wellesley. 'It is a certain rule, from which a General ought never to depart,' Lloyd counselled, 'to shorten continually as he advances his line of operation, by forcing new depots behind him', while 'an army whose line of operation is considerably too long can execute no solid enterprise, though it be ever so powerful . . .'.[108]

Rather than carrying the entirety of the army's supplies with them, Lloyd advised the establishment of depots upon which the army could draw to facilitate its more rapid and therefore decisive movements. In future, Wellesley would devote considerable political effort to building and maintaining supply depots prior to the commencement of military operations. The genesis of the concept of 'light and quick movements', then, was a combination of formal knowledge exchange as Wellesley helped prepare for the invasion of Mysore, the informal exchange of experiences and ideas derived from Britain's recent military history, and the theories and arguments of published military theorists. Some of these linkages can be illustrated through Wellesley's correspondence as well as that of the officers with whom he worked, while some are inferred from his reading prior to his arrival in India. Other linkages are inferred based on the contacts he had, the arguments he constructed, the decisions he made and the subsequent actions he took. Wellesley remade the military knowledge he accumulated prior to the 1799 Mysore campaign, and conceptualised a new approach to warfighting, one that was a true synthesis of the British experience of war in America, Europe and India. For Wellesley, the next challenge was turning a concept into an action.

*   *   *

Over the next two years, relations with the Maratha Confederacy gradually deteriorated, creating a situation in which Wellesley would have the opportunity to employ his concept of 'light and quick movements' against a highly effective adversary. War broke out in August 1803 between Britain and two of the most powerful chieftains in the Maratha Confederacy, Daulatrao Sindhia and Raghuji Bhonsla, the Rajah of Berar. The cause was British interference in the internal politics of the Confederacy, the culmination of Mornington's expansionist policies.[109] Arthur Wellesley, by now a major general, was offered command of a force which would operate in the Deccan, while the new commander-in-chief of British forces in India, Lieutenant General Sir Gerard Lake, took command of an army in Hindustan.

Wellesley underestimated his opponent from the outset. 'The Marathas have long boasted that they would carry on a predatory war against us,' he had written in 1801.[110] Based on his experience working with the Marathas in the campaigns against Tipu along with the evidence provided by Dirom and Mackenzie, Wellesley concluded that the 'Maratha army is principally composed of cavalry', while 'their plan of operations against a British army would be to endeavour to cut off its communications with its rear, and impede the junction of its supplies from the Mysore country'.[111]

This preconceived viewpoint was contradicted by the intelligence received from Lieutenant Colonel John Collins, the former British resident at Sindhia's court. Collins reported that while Sindhia's cavalry outnumbered Wellesley's infantry by more than two to one Sindhia also had under his command more than 7,700 European-trained infantry.[112] Collins reinforced this intelligence when he briefed Wellesley personally in late August. 'I tell you, General, as to their cavalry ..., you may ride over them wherever you meet them; but their infantry and guns will astonish you.' Wellesley, however, was disinclined to accept Collins's intelligence.[113] This assumption informed ongoing British intelligence collection efforts, and *hurkarrahs* sent to spy in Sindhia's camp were specifically directed to pay particular attention to the nature, strength and condition of the Maratha cavalry.[114] Faulty assumptions therefore impacted on the reliability of new intelligence, which only served to confirm the original assumptions.

After capturing the strategically important fortress of Ahmednagar, Wellesley instigated a pursuit of Sindhia's force, dividing his force into two columns. Based on the assumption that the Marathas would rely on the highly mobile cavalry, Wellesley warned his officers that 'he supposed, before ten days were over, we should leave our baggage behind; which he said would often happen'.[115] The army initially advanced slowly and methodically, relying on intelligence to identify and locate its adversary, before striking rapidly with overwhelming force in order to inflict a defeat in conventional battle.

Sindhia and Bhonsla were able to capitalise on the deficiencies in Wellesley's intelligence department. It was soon apparent that the British had very little idea where the Maratha forces were located. 'Where they are now I am not certain,' admitted Mountstuart Elphinstone, Wellesley's intelligence chief.[116] As the weeks unfolded, it became clear that the British had no idea where their adversary was, or what their intentions were. 'We made several marches and countermarches, owing, I believe, to the movements of a large body of cavalry which Sindhia and the Berar Rajah had detached to manoeuvre on our rear,' noted Captain Ralph Blakiston in his private journal.[117] Their objective was to distract the British to enable the infantry to withdraw further into Maratha territory, which Sindhia managed to do successfully.[118]

On 21 September, after reaching Budnapur, Wellesley finally received intelligence that the Marathas were 16 miles away. He sent his second-in-command, Colonel James and Stevenson north-west, while he moved north-east with the object of descending on the Maratha position.[119] In reality, the Marathas were much closer, near the village of Assaye, and it seemed as though they were offering battle. 'But who knows what a native will do,' wrote Elphinstone, 'perhaps they will give us the slip and get to the southward.'[120] Worried that Sindhia would indeed make a last-minute escape, Wellesley resolved to attack on 23 September before Stevenson could arrive with his reinforcements. The decision proved nearly calamitous. Blakiston believed that had Wellesley 'then possessed the experience he afterwards obtained of the discipline of Sindhia's infantry, and of the efficiency of his artillery, or had he relied sufficiently on the information given him by Colonel Collins, I much doubt whether he would have ventured on so hazardous a step'.[121]

As Wellesley commenced an attack designed to outflank the Maratha force, composed of over 10,000 troops, including 8,500 commanded by European mercenaries, members of his staff 'observed the enemy's infantry in the act of changing their front, and taking up a new position, with their right to the river Kailna and their left on the village of Assaye. This manoeuvre they were performing in the most steady manner possible'. Wellesley was clearly surprised as 'not supposing the enemy to be capable of such a manoeuvre in the face of an attacking force, he had ... already formed the infantry in two lines'.[122] In addition to the surprisingly well-trained infantry, the British were also confronted by a large and well-directed artillery barrage.

Wellesley ordered an immediate advance to seize the guns which had begun firing deadly cannister and chain shot.[123] Under sustained bombardment, confusion reigned in the British lines. On the right, the infantry advanced too far and became embroiled in close combat in the village of Assaye itself, where the fighting was notably intense. The Maratha infantry gave 'no quarter to any of our wounded, only cutting and shooting them as they came up with them'.[124] Wellesley was forced to deploy the 19th Dragoons, under the command of Colonel Maxwell, to prevent the British advance being outflanked.[125] Meanwhile, on the left, while also under an intense bombardment, the sepoys took 'advantage of . . . irregularities in the ground to shelter themselves from the deadly shower'.[126] The infantry of the 78th Regiment continued the advance, overwhelming the Maratha gunners, many of whom 'pretended to be dead', and 'when we passed on to the second line of guns, turned the guns we had taken upon us, which obliged us to return and again to drive them from them'.[127] With the village and the Maratha artillery in British hands, Sindhia ordered a retreat.

The battle was over; but victory had come at a high price: 428 dead, 1,138 wounded – a third of Wellesley's fighting force. The Marathas suffered four times as many casualties, and with the loss of their artillery and a significant portion of their European-trained infantry, Assaye was arguably a decisive victory for Wellesley, though he still needed to pursue the remnants of Sindhia's force, as well as the relatively unscathed army under Bhonsla's command. While his own army recovered, Wellesley sent Stevenson in pursuit of the Marathas. The hill forts of Burhanpur and Asirghar surrendered without a fight on 15 and 21 October, providing valuable new supply depots.

On 29 November, Wellesley and Stevenson found the Maratha army, consisting mainly of Bhonsla's infantry, offering battle on a three-mile-wide plain near the village of Arguam. Wellesley resolved once again to attack immediately, but as his infantry marched past the small village of Sirsoni, Bhonsla's artillery open fire. They had used the village to range their weapons in advance, so the fire was immediately and devastatingly accurate. Two battalions of Sepoys panicked and Wellesley had to rally the troops personally. Leading them back onto the battlefield, he ordered them to lie down, employing the methods he had observed used at Assaye. Under this cover, Wellesley formed his infantry into two lines and then commenced a steady and disciplined advance. 'It was a splendid sight to see such a line advancing, as on a field-day,' noted one participant, 'but the pause when the enemy's guns ceased firing, and they advanced in front of them, was an awful one.'[128] On this occasion, however, the Maratha infantry was no match for the disciplined ranks of the British, which targeted their adversaries with steady and sustained musketry. A second British victory forced Sindhia to reconsider terms, but Bhonsla continued the fight until his hill-top fortress of Gawilghur was captured by storm on 15 December.

Thus ended the war in the Deccan, and with it, Arthur Wellesley's Indian military career. After a short stint launching small-scale counterinsurgency operations, from the former Maratha stronghold of Ahmednagar, Wellesley opted to return to England, having 'understood as much of military matters as I ever have done ...'.[129] Assaye and Arguam had once again illustrated the superiority of European training in Indian warfare, but the adaptations made by Wellesley to the logistics system he had ultimately inherited from Cornwallis meant that his army had been considerably more mobile and manoeuvrable than those commanded by his predecessors. Despite the intelligence difficulties, this system, a further adaptation of the 'light and quick' concept, had allowed him to bring his adversary to battle on terms favourable to the British. Wellesley's innovations and adaptations demonstrated the importance of informal military knowledge exchange across generations of officers, as well as illustrating how officers could successfully synthesise new approaches by combining that knowledge with local ideas.

Four years after leaving India, Arthur Wellesley was appointed to command a small force sent to provide support to Portuguese resistance to a French invasion, but shortly after his arrival in Portugal, he learned he was to be superseded as much-needed reinforcements arrived. 'They removed me because they thought very little of anyone who had served in India,' Wellesley complained many years later to his friend John Croker. 'An Indian victory', he suggested, 'was ... actually a cause of suspicion.'[130] It would be easy to conclude, given Wellesley's seeming personal disdain for his own experience in South Asia, that the lessons learned about warfare in India did not return to Europe with him. Indeed, European ideas about warfighting had evolved significantly during the French Revolutionary War and in the early stages of the war against Napoleon. But far from irrelevant, the integration of ideas, experience and military knowledge from India, with the methods and means of fighting elsewhere in the empire as well as in Europe itself, would prove crucial to eventual British success. Arthur Wellesley was an important part of that story, but he capitalised on advantages and foundations laid by many others.

CHAPTER 8

'Totally Unfit for Service'

DEFEAT AND HUMILIATION, 1793–1799

ON the eve of British involvement in a war that would consume Europe for the next 23 years, Henry Clinton, veteran of the Seven Years War and the American Revolutionary War and now aged 62, travelled to Spa in the Austrian Netherlands, modern-day Belgium, to meet with the Duke of Brunswick, under whom he had served as aide-de-camp in Germany in 1762. It was August 1792, and Brunswick was commanding the Prussian army sent to fight the French Revolutionaries. The two discussed the oncoming war and what the prospects for success were.

Clinton was eager to impart lessons from his experiences against the Americans. He found plenty of 'sanguine Gentlemen at the Army', but warned Brunswick not to rely too heavily on the support of defectors from the French armies. Speaking of his experience with Benedict Arnold's defection and attempted surrender of West Point into British hands in 1780, Clinton commented that 'even with my Friend Arnold (when he offered to give up his Forts to me) I made such arrangements as removed every possibility of suspicion that there was any Collusion'. French Royalists, such as Georges Félix de Wimpffen, commandant of the fortified town of Thionville, would, Clinton argued, be 'glad of a good opportunity to have given up his Fortress, but such a Place could not surrender on simple summons, or without a Train in Battery against it, to save appearances'.[1]

On his return to England, Clinton discussed his trip in an audience with the Prince of Wales, convinced that Britain needed also to join the war, as 'intervention may not only operate in favour of what I must call the

common cause of sovereigns, but is absolutely necessary to our own
political security – nay, existence'.[2] The Prince of Wales, with whom
Clinton had developed a professional friendship, was interested in the
retired general's views and the conversations were subsequently elaborated
upon in a brief correspondence between 29 September and 27 October,
during which time news arrived of Brunswick's defeat at the Battle of
Valmy on 20 September.[3] Clinton accurately predicted in his first letter,
written prior to receiving news of the Prussian defeat, 'that a Conflict has
passed about the 20th between the United Forces of both armies'.
Referring to a map which the Prussians believed the French commander,
Charles François Dumouriez, was using, Clinton guessed that Valmy
would be the seat of battle, but he surmised incorrectly that Brunswick
would win the day, that he 'may have got possession of Rheims' and be
preparing for a move on Paris. By the time Clinton finished the letter,
news had arrived which did 'not seem to confirm my very humble opinions', though he discounted the reports, believing them to be forgeries to
protect the revolutionary French government.[4]

A month later, Clinton had received multiple reports of the battle, and
was ready to present a brief analysis.[5] The lessons which he identified
both resonated with his own experiences and highlighted the principle
issues the British army would face when it was hurriedly deployed to
confront the French Revolutionaries. First was the problem of sickness in
the army. Retreat seemed 'to have become necessary, to save a Fine Army,
reduced almost to incapacity by adverse Elements; An Enemy ... (as I
have often experienced) most to be dreaded tho' seldom thought of in
military calculations'. Second was the mismanagement of logistics.
Dumouriez had selected a position which offered him secure supply lines,
but the Prussians were overextended. 'Incessant rain, and bad weather,
badness of roads, tardiness of supply, but above all an incredible number
of sick, obliged [Brunswick] to retire to the Meuse', in order to 'shorten
his communications'. Third was the character of the French army, on
which Clinton could not yet offer a considered analysis. The Prussian
retreat had been slow, but 'the imposing manner in which it was made,
prove, that it was not done under the Pressure of a Foe, who tho' he might
be superior in number was greatly inferior in Discipline.' Clinton would
perhaps not realise it, but the mass which the French would be able to
bring to bear would overawe even the best disciplined troops. Finally,
Clinton had become aware of tensions and disagreements between the
allies. Reports seemed 'to imply Treachery somewhere or Tardiness or

Timidity in the Austrians . . .'.[6] Like Clinton's conversation with Brunswick at Spa, the correspondence with the Prince of Wales is an evident attempt to offer advice based on the experience of fighting one revolutionary army in preparation for war with another. His brief analysis touched upon all the major issues the British Army would face in the coming war, some of which were new, but many, as Clinton's ability to highlight parallels with America show, were not.

Clinton was not alone in drawing on his American experience in an attempt to inform and advise the British government. Major General John Money, who had been General John Burgoyne's quartermaster general at Saratoga, had served alongside his friend Charles Dumouriez in the French army under 'the unfortunate King's commission', and had witnessed first-hand the challenges presented by the French Revolutionaries. He produced an account of the campaign, which he published in 1793.[7] In that, and in a series of letters to government ministers and General Jeffrey Amherst, the newly appointed commander-in-chief, he tried to draw parallels between the geographical conditions in America and the Low Countries, where wide open spaces had, in the last century of agricultural and economic development, been transformed into a land of small fields, bounded by fences and hedgerows. These looked less like the plains of Germany, on which terrain the British army had based its training, and more like the backcountry of North America.[8] This, Money argued, had enabled the French Revolutionaries to make use of the large bodies of irregular soldiers which they had deployed during the 1792 campaign, and which allowed him to draw direct comparisons with his personal experience in North America. 'What was the army that captured General Burgoyne's but an army of Irregulars? What other appellation can be given to Militia untrained to any species of evolution, and undisciplined, but that of Irregulars?' Money later wrote in an open letter on the reorganisation of the British Army. 'At Saratoga the finest army in the world . . . laid down their arms to . . . an "undisciplined rabble": but they were all Woodsmen; that is, marksmen . . . .'[9]

The French Revolutionaries, Money argued, behaved in the same manner, with the employment of chasseurs who were 'indispensable with a great army, and particularly in an enclosed country, of which nevertheless some of our Generals have not the smallest conception. They tell me that our light infantry answers every purpose of chasseurs, but officers lately from the continent think with me, that there is no comparison between them'. Light infantry, Money contended, were trained to fire wherever he perceived an enemy to be, firing continuously 'as long as his ammunition lasts'.

By contrast, when a chasseur 'hears a ball whistle by him, he conceals himself immediately, peeps through the hedge and never fires till he sees an object to fire at, then he takes deliberate aim'. In so doing, 'he fires perhaps five or six shots in an hour with effect, when a light infantry soldier fires thirty without doing any execution.'[10] It was essential for the British army to counter this threat, or it would face insurmountable difficulties, not just on the battlefield, but on the march as well. 'My blood ran cold in my veins after that unhappy war' in America, 'when it occurred to my mind' that, 'notwithstanding the experience we have had in that war, ... we should not fight it over again in the same manner from the cheapness with which Riflemen and Irregulars are still held'.[11] Money's analysis, like Clinton's, was remarkably prescient.

For Britain, though the French Revolutionary War began on 1 February 1793 – it had perhaps become inevitable after the French victories over the Prussians at Valmy and over the Austrians as Jemappes on 6 November. Brussels fell just over a week later. One of the 'incontrovertible maxims of British policy' – namely the independence of the Low Countries – had succumbed to French expansionism.[12] If the French Revolutionaries had not declared war on Britain, London would have had no alternative but to intervene, for, as Edmund Burke argued, the Low Countries were 'as necessary a part of this country as Kent'.[13] The British army was to be deployed to the European continent for the first time in three decades, and there is some debate over whether it was sufficiently prepared for this deployment. The swingeing cuts imposed in the wake of the defeat in America resulted in an army that was 'wasted and thin', and unable to sustain a war in Europe.[14]

The events of the first two years of the war would seem to bear this argument out, but in reality, the army of 1793 was well balanced and positioned to meet the challenges of war on a global scale. In 1790, 12 of the 14 infantry battalions in the regular home force were complete, as were all 19 based in Ireland, all 10 deployed to Gibraltar, 11 of the 17 deployed to the West Indies, and all nine deployed to India. Only in North America were forces weaker than planned, with only three of the 12 deployed there reporting complete in 1790.[15] So the British Army was able to defend all of Britain's interests. Still, the onset of a new war, against an enemy whose true nature was not clearly understood, called for a rapid expansion of the army, and this brought with it difficulties associated with huge numbers of new and untrained recruits. Indeed, virtually complete though it may have been, the regular home force still numbered just 17,000, though some 52,000 militia and 40,000 fencibles might provide a sufficient basis on which to expand. The aim was to expand to a force of 175,000, allowing the government to assemble a contingent large enough to support Austria in a new attack on eastern France, to be deployed under the command of the Duke of York.[16]

The army was undoubtedly better organised in 1793. Ten-company battalions were reintroduced during the administrative reforms between 1783 and 1793, providing the infantry with much-needed tactical strength and resilience, while new corps were raised, archaic organisations abandoned and innovations incorporated into the main order of battle.[17] But administrative reforms hid a myriad of issues which ran deep and would take years to resolve adequately. The British state was ill-equipped to support an army at war in Europe, though it had proved itself capable of maintaining multiple deployments on a global scale. Recruitment had fallen short throughout the American war and great efforts were made to improve enlistment in the following decade of peace. This, however, gave rise to a largely complete, according to the peacetime complement, but inexperienced army: a problem compounded by high levels of desertion and officer absenteeism. As a result, the officer corps was poorly prepared to plan, manage and sustain complex operations in conjunction with allies.

The campaigns which took place between 1793 and 1795, against an innovative, adaptable and unpredictable new enemy, exposed the short-comings of Britain as a military power and the deficiencies of its army, which was subjected to a series of defeats that ruined its reputation.[18] Though it might have been prepared to fight, neither the army nor the British state was evidently sufficiently prepared for war. The defeats incurred in the first campaign against Revolutionary France, blame for which was often shouldered by the army's high command, more often than not exposed the inability of Britain to cope with a war against a state that mobilised the resources of its nation. They nevertheless produced sufficient humiliation and fear to engender a process of initially informal innovation and adaptation, based largely, though not entirely, on the confluence of unique ideas and experiences gained by an army which had wandered the world for the past half century.

* * *

The British government managed to assemble and deploy a small expeditionary force to Flanders. Frederick, Duke of York, the king's 29-year-old second son, was in overall command and the force was initially composed of one cavalry brigade, under the command of Major General Robert Laurie, and two infantry brigades, under Major Generals Gerard Lake and Ralph Abercromby. Later in the summer, this was reinforced with two further cavalry brigades. This meagre force, which in total amounted to 5,200 infantry and 1,300 cavalry, was supplemented by nearly 14,000 Hanoverian troops commanded by York's old mentor, Feldmarschall Wilhelm von Freytag, and 6,500 troops from Hesse-Cassel under the command of Generalleutnant Baron von Buttlar.[19]

York had considered William Howe and Henry Clinton for his brigade commanders, but realised that the two American veterans, though now on cordial terms, had previously had a fractious relationship.[20] Lake was seen as a younger, more dynamic officer, while Abercromby, on the cusp of 60, brought a wealth of experience and professional knowledge. He had joined the army just before the Seven Years' War broke out in Europe and served as an aide to General Sir William Pitt in Germany, where he had been impressed by the military machine built by Frederick the Great. He resigned his commission at the beginning of the American Revolutionary War because he personally disagreed with the government's policy towards the colonists, though he was likely apprised of events by his brother Robert.[21] Abercromby returned to the army when war broke out with France in 1793 and was then quickly selected for command, sailing for the continent on 21 March 1793.[22]

He soon realised that the troops over which he had taken command were 'comprised of nothing but undisciplined and raw recruits', who 'were in general totally unfit for service, ... inadequate to the fatigues of a campaign', and, according to Captain Henry Calvert, aide-de-camp to the Duke of York, 'worse than any I saw, even at the close of the American War'.[23] Abercromby had little time to resolve these issues, however, as the campaign commenced immediately. Training would have to be conducted on the march. In the event, drilled or not, the British would be unable to withstand the sheer numbers the French were able to throw at them, and the widespread use of *tirailleurs* – irregular troops trained in skirmishing – caused significant attrition in the British ranks.[24] As a result, though they performed relatively well in battle and other conventional actions, the British were unable to sustain this advantage in the wider campaign, which was filled with smaller-scale skirmishes.

The British were to support an Austrian plan to capture enemy frontier fortresses in an effort to contain French expansion. By July, the Austrians and British were besieging Valenciennes. After meticulous preparation, three mines were exploded on 25 July, and an attack made in three columns. Abercromby commanded one column of British infantry, while the Austrians commanded the other two. 'Nothing could exceed the courage and spirit with which the attack was made,' York wrote to his father.[25] The troops advanced, noted one participant, 'like the rushing of a flood, and carried all before them at the point of the bayonet'.[26] Valenciennes capitulated the following day. The garrison 'marched out with a sullen dignity', noted one British participant, a cavalry officer named John Le Marchant. 'Their Cavalry was fine, the regiment which marched out first was the one present at the beheading of their King, and who mounted themselves on His Majesty's horses.'[27] The campaign had got off to an impressive start, and much of the worries about the discipline of the British troops appeared unfounded. Elsewhere the Austrians captured Condé on 10 July and the Prussians captured Mainz on the 22nd. The combined armies briefly appeared to be working to a common objective. 'It was curious, at the same time magnificent, to see different nations, people of different dresses, manners and customs passing along, and all occupied in the same pursuit,' remarked Le Marchant. 'It appears to be a complete world in action.'[28] The cooperation was not to last long.

After suffering concurrent setbacks in the Mediterranean and in the Vendée, the French appointed Lazare Carnot to help restore French fortunes. On 23 August, he instituted the *levée en masse*, which mobilised the civilian population of France.[29] Meanwhile, internal divisions had prevented the allies taking advantage of the chaos in Paris. York was under orders to capture Dunkirk, while the Austrians focused on Quesnoy, and in the process dispersed their forces. York advanced on Dunkirk with his main force, leaving a cordon of Hanoverian troops under Freytag to protect his flanks. As York advanced, Carnot managed to slip 3,000 reinforcements into Dunkirk, bringing the garrison to a total of 8,000, while a force under General Jean Nicolas Houchard, numbering 40,000 by September, had gathered to threaten York's flank.

On 6 September, Houchard attacked Freytag's covering force, severely wounded the old Field Marshal and nearly captured him and his staff. On the 8th, the Hanoverians were defeated in a pitched battle at Hondschoote, while a sortie from Dunkirk prevented York from offering assistance. Here the devastating capabilities of the French skirmishers, or *tirailleurs*, was dramatically demonstrated. On receiving accurate and well-aimed fire from a body of French skirmishers, Freytag, an experienced light infantryman himself, had ordered his own troops to advance with the bayonet. As they did so, their opponents withdrew to a second enclosed position. The *tirailleurs*, exactly as described in the French drill regulations – the *Règlements* – issued in April 1792, were 'placed in small thickets, ditches or small rises according to the nature of the terrain ... benefiting from any feature that may afford them cover', enabling them to bring their superior marksmanship to bear against the tightly packed ranks of their enemy.[30] Taking unsustainable casualties, the Hanoverians withdrew, only to see the *tirailleurs* re-emerge from their cover and continue to pour fire into their ranks. At the end of the battle, the Hanoverians had sustained 2,650 casualties, while the French had got off relatively lightly.[31]

With his flank forces depleted by a third, and having made no appreciable progress in the siege, York decided to withdraw, abandoning his guns, and with a loss of 2,000 men killed and wounded. Failure was principally a result of delays getting the siege train to Dunkirk in time or to organise naval cooperation, both of which were outside York's control. Withdrawal ceded the initiative to the French, and the British were soon in retreat. The Austrians had more success, defeating Houchard at Courtrai, before moving on Menin. Houchard was relieved of command, charged with cowardice and guillotined. His replacement, Jean-Baptiste Jourdan, was tasked with stemming the Austrian advance, which he did at Wattignies on 15–16 October.

As the weather worsened, the campaign descended into stalemate, partly because the allies were unable to agree on a coherent plan and viewed each other with suspicion. In an effort to identify a common plan, York resolved to consult personally with the Austrian commander General Friedrich Coburg. He was painfully aware of the 'absolute necessity which there is that a well digested plan for the next campaign should be arranged and settled between the different Allied powers ... and in the great detriment which the want of such a plan was to the whole of the last campaign'.[32] In the event, York found Coburg unwilling to 'undertake anything', as the Austrians 'have hardly any magazines left, and that ... no arrangement is yet made for their magazines for the next campaign'.[33] The crux of the issue lay in the fact that neither Austria nor Prussia considered the Low Countries a strategic priority in the same way Britain did. While their strategic interests remained divergent, there were limited prospects for any successful military cooperation.

The first months of 1794 continued in the same vein, with high-level strategic wrangling disrupting military planning. A series of desultory operations and skirmishes brought the allies together for an attack on the

French at Turcoing on 16 May, where, it was hoped, the French might be driven from Flanders. The allies, who had mustered 62,000 troops to France's 82,000, divided into six columns and planned an elaborate encircling manoeuvre. Late arrival of orders, difficult terrain and challenging obstacle crossing, reduced coordination which meant that the attack, when it began, was poorly sequenced. York had managed to get into position and though he succeeded in capturing his objectives, his flank was badly exposed. An overwhelming French counterattack was launched at 3 a.m. and within three hours, York's position was in danger of being overrun. At 9 a.m., Abercromby ordered a withdrawal, and the remainder of the day was spent trying to prevent a complete rout.

Once more, British troops managed to maintain discipline and remain calm under fire, even as French sharpshooters took potshots at them as they retreated. York and Abercromby had been able to instil a degree of battlefield discipline, but this proved meaningless, as Austrian diplomat Baron Johan von Thugut observed, when in opposition to 'innumerable hordes who are in fact constantly defeated and repulsed, but our army is vastly weakened by these partial victories while the enemy repairs its losses with the greatest ease'.[34] Calvert observed that 'while the same loose, unconnected, unmilitary system is persevered in ... nothing but loss and disgrace can attend' the allied armies.[35]

Though the defeat was not decisive, it was enough to drive further wedges between the allies. Le Marchant was now anxious that the many and varied allied objectives would prove too great a challenge for the disunited armies. Recent battles had 'taught us, that in an inclosed country' the French 'are almost equal to disciplined soldiers, and if they are capable of bringing the *whole* of the combined army to so near an issue on our own ground, and within a mile of our camp', he wrote dejectedly to his wife. 'What are we to expect if we have to detach part of this army for the protection of Flanders?'[36] Just over a month later, Coburg's 54,000 Austrians attacked Jourdan's army of 70,000 at Fleurus, but failed to make a breakthrough and Jourdan turned the tables, inflicting a stinging defeat on Coburg. Austria and Prussia turned their attention to the partition of Poland – a much more significant strategic priority for them than Flanders – and allied strategic cooperation collapsed. An uncoordinated withdrawal commenced, which resulted in the British falling back in the hopes of staging a defence on the river networks of eastern Holland.

The complex river system afforded some hope to the beleaguered army, and the Duke of York aimed to use strong defensive lines on the rivers

Maas and Waal. Cavalrymen like Le Marchant were rather less optimistic. The withdrawal 'obliged us to shift our theatre of war from their country into our own', he wrote, 'which among other disadvantages, is so well wooded that our cavalry (the strength of the Allied army) is rendered utterly useless'.[37] The first of York's defensive lines on the Maas was outflanked when the French surprised and took a key British position at Boxtel on 14 September. A subsequent attempt to recapture the village failed, and the British were compelled to fall back on Grave and Nijmegen, taking up strong defensive positions on the River Waal. York's position on the Waal was undoubtedly strong. Nijmegen stood 'on a rising ground on the south bank of the river Waal, ... which is large, and runs with a very strong current'.[38]

The river was clearly the lynchpin of York's defence. 'We think it is impossible for them to cross the Waal,' noted one British soldier. 'The whole of the river is commanded by our guns, and batteries erected all along the dyke at convenient distances'. In addition, 'a road is made behind the dyke for guns, carriages, etc to pass and repass.'[39] According to one of his aides-de-camp, Captain Henry Clinton – son of the American veteran – York ordered his force to 'retire by the Bridge of boats', and once across 'the bridge was on fire in every part'.[40] In the absence of a bridge, it would take a great deal of time for the French to row individual boats across the river, under fire from the opposite bank, and in the strong current they would end up about a mile downstream of their starting point. By 21 November, York had 14 regiments on the northern bank of the Waal, spanning seven or eight miles of its length.

Lieutenant-Colonel Arthur Wesley and the 33rd were positioned at Tiel under the command of Major General David Dundas, seven miles from Nijmegen, and 20 from army headquarters in Arnhem.[41] The army, despite the depredations of the past months of retreat, seemed confident. 'I think it impossible for any troops (even the French)', wrote Wesley, 'to keep the field in this severe weather.'[42] It was the belief in headquarters, however, that the enemy planned 'to attempt the passage of the Waal', and it was the severe weather that was to provide the route to victory for the French. On 5 December, a severe frost set in. Two days later, the river was glazed with a sheet of ice; on the 8th, and again on the 10th, the French attacked, but on both occasions they were repulsed. Writing on Christmas Eve 1794, Dundas was wholly unable to mask his low spirits. 'At this early period a very severe frost has for these ten days set in,' he explained, 'which threatens immediately to close up the *Waal*, and to facilitate a passage that in its fluid state they would have found a very precarious undertaking . . . .'[43]

At the end of December, the French attacked again, this time in overwhelming force, puncturing the British defence in several places. On New Year's Eve, the British, now commanded by Lieutenant General Sir William Harcourt after York was recalled to London, attempted a counterattack, which managed to stem the French advance for a few days. A series of small skirmishes broke out along the line, in which the British infantry displayed considerable 'resolution & gallantry'.[44] Despite these tactical successes, which were familiar sights along the entire British line on the 'Island' between the Waal and Rhine rivers, the game was already up. Consideration was given to defending the dyke on the southern bank of the Rhine, but this was abandoned when the French managed to break through, cross the Rhine and position artillery on the Oosterbeek Heights. From there, according to Harcourt, they were apparently able to threaten the British headquarters at Arnhem.[45]

The third British defensive line was rendered untenable, and the army was again forced to retreat, first to Apeldoorn, and then headlong to the river Ems. On 17 January, Utrecht fell to the French, and the French set Amsterdam, already rebellious, in their sights. For the British, the campaign in the Low Countries was over, as it was for the Austrians, who had fled precipitately from Arnhem on the 7th, and the Prussians. The British were forced to withdraw to Germany, reaching the port of Bremerleche, from which they were evacuated on 24 April 1795.

York has shouldered the blame for the disastrous campaign of 1793–1795. The real reasons for failure, however, were threefold: the strategic inability of the allied powers to decide on a coherent set of war aims and to plan a sensible combined operation; the operational ability of the French to replenish losses sustained in battle; and the tactical deficit in irregular troops, while the French also proved to be the superior marksmen. According to the Duke of Brunswick, who had resigned the command of the Prussian army in frustration, 'the same causes will divide the Allied Powers which have hitherto divided them; the movements of the armies will suffer from them as they have suffered; their march will be embarrassed, retarded, prevented . . .'.[46] Until the great powers of Europe could decide on a coherent strategy, and reform their armies to meet the challenges presented by the revolutionaries, French power would continue to expand untamed.

There were, of course, plenty of military lessons from the campaign's many failures. Arthur Wesley, gaining his first experience of battle prior to his deployment to India and adopting Wellesley as his surname, famously said the campaign taught him 'how one ought not to do it', and 'that is always something'.[47] Dundas had likewise learned lessons during the campaign, though his were rather more specific and put to immediate use. Having 'put together some few Cavalry circumstances' while commanding a mounted brigade,[48] Dundas drafted the interim *Rules and Regulations for the Cavalry* later that year, and practised and revised them at an encampment in 1796. Designed to correspond closely with his earlier *Principles of Military Movement*, taken together, the two treatises offered for the first time a universal system of drill and training for the British infantry and cavalry.[49]

If Wellesley had taken nebulous and intangible lessons about effective command practices, and Dundas had rewritten the British drill, Abercromby had witnessed the importance of both, and the essential interaction of the military and political levels. 'A General who means to succeed, must follow his own ideas, command his army himself, and choose his own assistants,' he wrote when Henry Dundas asked him what in his view had gone awry in the campaign. 'Official men ought not on all occasions to act the general, and sometimes the politician; they ought to attend to their own business, and things would go better on.'[50] His experience during the Flanders campaign emphasised the need to maintain and improve conditions for the soldiers under his command, as well as the diversity of skills on which they were to rely. These were lessons he would seek to implement during his next deployment to the West Indies.

*   *   *

Strangulation of French trade with its colonies in the West Indies was a traditional British strategic approach in any eighteenth-century war with France and was once more adopted in 1793.[51] Geographical and environmental conditions imposed limitations on military decision making, and while the capital of the largest French colony, Saint-Domingue – just 100 miles from Jamaica and with 40,000 Europeans and half a million enslaved people – fell under British control in June 1794, it was to the eastern Caribbean that the British turned their attention.[52]

Martinique, with a population of 100,000 and over 300 sugar estates, lay in the middle of a chain of islands, with St Lucia to its south and Guadeloupe to its north. Barbados, site of Britain's eastern Caribbean naval base, was 100 miles to the south-east. Operations were only really possible between March and June, as the hurricane season between July and October precluded activity in the Caribbean and the prevailing west-erly gales in the North Atlantic restricted deployment and resupply from Britain between November and March. Still, occupation of the islands had proven an effective economic strategy in previous wars with France, while the islands were useful bargaining chips at the post-war negotiating table.

In November 1793, 7,000 troops under General Sir Charles Grey sailed with a fleet commanded by Admiral Sir John Jervis. Grey and Jervis had an excellent relationship and plentiful experience of combined operations. They arrived in Barbados in early January, and immediately commenced planning for an attack on Martinique. Grey, a hard-nosed military officer, was a veteran of the Seven Years' War in Europe, where he had served as aide-de-camp to Duke Ferdinand of Brunswick at Minden, and later attained a degree of infamy during the American Revolutionary War, where he advocated an unrestricted approach. He subsequently prosecuted a series of raids in September 1778, which desolated regions of New England, and now adopted similar strategies in the West Indies.

Troops were trained extensively in amphibious assault techniques, generally between 3 a.m. and 8 a.m., to avoid the heat of the day and in an effort to keep the army healthy. Grey also wanted to replicate some of the innovations that had led to considerable tactical success in earlier wars. In America, he had seen light infantry 'brought to such a height of perfection by constant practice' and now worried that 'a continuation of Peace for 11 years' had degraded understanding of this important capability.[53] He therefore ordered that three elite light infantry battalions be created for service in the West Indies.[54] These he trained 'for steadiness, coolness, rapid movements, judgement in taking up ground, gallantry & spirit' in the execution of operations. He appointed Major General Thomas Dundas, an 'officer of so much experience in actual Service in America',[55] to command the battalions.[56] He ordered each battalion commander to consult with Dundas so that he might 'point out & communicate to them the manner in which a variety of useful manoeuvres should be put into practice, so necessary for the rapid forming & movement of Lt Infy . . .'.[57] Grey delib-erately sought to utilise the lessons of the war in America, where consider-able tactical and operational, though not strategic, success had been facilitated by light infantry.

Grey prioritised marksmanship training for the light infantry, though he favoured the bayonet. As the army prepared to embark, Grey assured his troops that the coming assault 'would not be a contest . . . to be decided by fire or bayonet'. In keeping with his reputation, 'this last method is

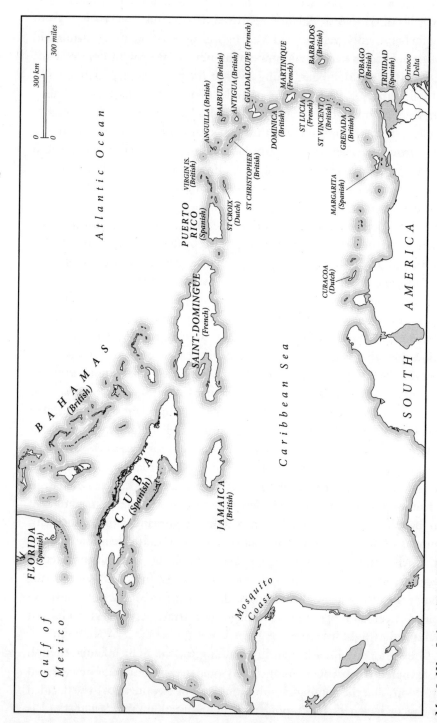

Gulf of
Mexico

Atlantic Ocean

FLORIDA
(Spanish)

B A H A M A S
(British)

C U B A
(Spanish)

JAMAICA
(British)

SAINT-DOMINGUE
(French)

PUERTO
RICO
(Spanish)

VIRGIN IS.
(British)

ST CROIX
(Dutch)

ST CHRISTOPHER
(British)

ANGUILLA (British)

BARBUDA (British)

ANTIGUA (British)

GUADALOUPE (French)

DOMINICA
(British)

MARTINIQUE
(French)

ST LUCIA
(French)

ST VINCENT
(British)

GRENADA
(British)

BARBADOS
(British)

MARGARITA
(Spanish)

CURACOA
(Dutch)

TOBAGO
(British)

TRINIDAD
(Spanish)

Orinoco
Delta

Caribbean Sea

Mosquito
Coast

SOUTH AMERICA

300 km
300 miles

0
0

Map 9. West Indies, 1793–1797.

always to be preferred,' Grey said, 'but much more so when acting against such bad troops as the army we are now to be opposed to.'[58] Grey went on to emphasise that 'in case of a night attack, ammunition and firing are totally out of the question, and the bayonet is ever to be preferred and made use of', as it 'conceals you and your numbers from the enemy'.[59]

The fleet sailed from Barbados on 3 February, arriving off Martinique on the 5th. Grey had excellent intelligence for his assault from French royalists recently escaped from the island. On the basis of this information, he and Jervis planned a three-pronged assault to create as much confusion among the defenders as possible and prevent them from concentrating against one landing. Martinique was dominated by a capacious bay on the west of the island, which was commanded by a large battery on a 60-foot-high rocky outcrop, known as Pigeon Isle. The main town, Fort Royal, was on the northern coast of the bay, itself commanded by the strong Fort Bourbon. The rest of the island was fairly mountainous, and there were several populated areas – in the south at Trois Rivières, in the north-east at La Trinité, and in the north-west at Saint-Pierre. Previous attacks on the island had focused on Case Navire, an accessible strip of beaches to the west of Fort Royal. Unsurprisingly, the French had constructed strong defences there.[60]

Grey planned the main landing at Trois Rivières and this commenced at 3 a.m. on 6 February. By 9 a.m., 2,500 troops were ashore with little opposition. With routes preplanned from excellent intelligence, Grey marched his men in gruelling heat eight miles over the heights separating his force from the southern coast of Fort Royal Bay.[61] On the way, the 3rd Light Infantry were detached to capture the coastal batteries and Pigeon Isle which they achieved by 11 February.[62] On the east coast, meanwhile, Dundas landed unopposed with the second brigade at La Trinité, after a navy sloop had destroyed the coastal batteries with a broadside. Lieutenant Colonel Eyre Coote, veteran of North America and nephew to General Sir Eyre Coote, commanded the 1st Battalion of the light infantry, who spearheaded the assault. Once ashore, the troops 'march'd under an extreme heavy fire on our front & left & about four in the evening we perceiv'd the enemy about 200 men drawn up'. Coote's men 'attack'd under a very heavy fire' and 'took possession of their very strong holds & hill. This Height Commands La Trinité which village the French burn'd in the night'.[63] With La Trinité in British hands, Dundas marched inland, aiming to link up with Grey outside Fort Royal.

Lastly, a third landing at Case Navire, commanded by Lieutenant General Sir Charles Gordon, sustained significant casualties and ground to a halt trying to outflank the strong defences along the heights of Sainte-Catherine. Nevertheless, the pressure on Gordon was relieved following the capture of Pigeon Isle, when Jervis sailed his fleet into Fort Royal Bay, outflanking the French coastal defences. With Grey and Dundas making good progress, the army was able to converge on a siege of Fort Bourbon. The remaining French stronghold, Saint-Pierre, a commercial centre on the north-west coast, was cleared in a combined army–navy operation by 17 February.[64]

A month-long siege of Fort Bourbon now commenced. Jervis bombarded the fort day and night, while artillery was dragged up the hill to establish batteries on the fort. Heavy rain made the activity burdensome. Coote, whose battalion of light infantry was 'in front & within about eight hundred yards of Fort Bourbon', was 'completely harassed' and found 'the situation ... most fatiguing'.[65] By 7 March, the batteries were complete and opened fire. Despite an intense bombardment, the French defenders held out, maintaining a constant counterfire. On 20 March, a combined army–navy operation was undertaken to force Fort Bourbon to surrender. A sloop deliberately grounded in order to get marines ashore, while Coote simultaneously attacked with the light infantry and grenadiers, and within three hours 'took possession of the town'.[66] With their access to resupply from the town cut off, the defenders of Fort Bourbon lost all morale and negotiated a surrender. On 25 March, the French garrison marched out with the full honours of war.[67]

Grey had needed a quick victory at Martinique if he was to capture successfully the remaining French strongholds in the eastern Caribbean before the climate made campaigning impossible and sickness ravaged his army. The French defence of Martinique had come close to wrecking his plans. He sustained 92 killed, 228 wounded and 500 sick. His effective line infantry now numbered fewer than 6,000. Martinique was nevertheless a considerable prize. 'The arsenal here is the best I ever saw,' he wrote, 'supplied with a profusion of every article ..., the finest harbour in the universe, where the largest fleet may ride in perfect safety during the hurricane months.'[68]

St Lucia, defended by a much weaker garrison, was the next target. The main port, Castries, was in a bay on the north-west tip of the island, and was likewise protected by a battery in the bay; a large fortified coastal battery, known as the Vigie; and a citadel, Morne Fortune, on high ground overlooking the port town. Grey's intelligence informed him that the French could muster no more than 1,200 defenders. As at Martinique, he planned another three-pronged assault.[69] The battery in the bay proved inadequate to its defence and was quickly overwhelmed. The 2nd and 3rd Light Infantry were successfully put ashore in two assaults north of Castries and cleared the coastal batteries before preparing for an attack on the Vigie battery, which was captured having been abandoned on 2 April. A separate landing force went ashore on the same day to the south of Castries and captured a battery protecting Morne Fortune. The bay was now unprotected and the fleet could sail in to support the army. Unwilling to risk another prolonged siege, Grey sought to shock the French defenders into submission. In the early hours of 3 April, Coote, with five companies of light infantry, stormed three outlying redoubts and 'put to the Bayonet about thirty of the Enemy'.[70] The attack made 'a deep Impression upon' the defenders, who were 'so compleatly terrified by this act of gallantry that they capitulated the next day', noted Coote in his private journal.[71]

Light infantry would likewise lead the assault on Guadeloupe. Here, the same shock tactics employed by Coote succeeded in capturing one of the main towns on the island. Time was running short, however, and 'finding the rainy season setting in, & the Troops getting very sickly', Grey determined to take the remaining stronghold by assault on 19 April. The attack nearly went awry, with the troops getting lost in 'such a Country as scarcely' could be 'travell'd thro',[72] but French morale soon collapsed, and they surrendered on 22 April.[73] The high point of British success in the West Indies was reached in early June, when longed-for reinforcements arrived and enabled Grey to complete the capture of Saint-Domingue in the western Caribbean.[74]

The tide, however, was already beginning to turn. The sickness, which Grey long expected, now ravaged his army. By 1 June 1794, his effective force was reduced to just 4,761; a day later, the unexpected arrival of 11,000 French reinforcements at Guadeloupe forced the British garrison from the productive agricultural areas. All the while, growing discontent at the behaviour of British troops among the population began to undermine Grey's position, and resistance to British control began to grow. Though Grey had concentrated on taking the main towns and ports of Martinique, St Lucia and Guadeloupe, he never adequately gained control over the less accessible mountainous countryside. This offered sanctuary to those who sought to undermine the British position. Meanwhile, slave revolts in Grenada, St Vincent and Jamaica challenged British control of their own Caribbean colonies and isolated their position on Saint Domingue. By July 1795, St Lucia and Guadeloupe were back in French hands.[75]

After the catastrophes in the Low Countries, the hopes of the British government lay in a breakthrough in the West Indies, and so a new expedition was assembled, this time under the command of Major General Ralph Abercromby. After researching the correspondence and accounts of Grey's campaigns and those of preceding wars, Abercromby concluded that the priority should be on the capture of Guadeloupe as this would limit French threats to the British islands.[76] The government now scrambled to assemble a force of sufficient strength and capability to reassert British dominance in the eastern Caribbean, but the Duke of York found the troops recently returned from the Low Countries to be badly understrength, 'without arms, and are likewise deficient in every other article of cloathing and accoutrements, and I am sorry to add, in exercise'.[77]

As the units began arriving in Southampton ready for embarkation, they were assembled at sites in Nursling and Netley, which became 'this very large camp', as the Prince of Wales observed, after visiting in late September, 'the largest of Regulars ever known in this country'.[78] Despite its size, however, Abercromby was disappointed to find 'in all regiments many old men and boys perfectly unfit for service',[79] while some regiments were so new that their officers and men were unaware even of how to set up camp.[80] Nor could morale have been high. As they prepared to embark at Southampton, soldiers overheard the residents of the port town muttering 'What pity such brave men should go to that West India grave!—to that hateful climate to be killed by the plague!'.[81]

When they were eventually ready to sail, horrendous storms prevented their departure, threatening to disrupt the expedition. Abercromby's force did not, therefore, arrive in the West Indies until March 1796, well behind schedule and in terrible shape. The fleet had got separated in the stormy voyage, so units arrived piecemeal, with much of their equipment missing, and large numbers of soldiers already sick. Unlike 1794, Abercromby suffered from a poor intelligence picture, though there were indications that St Lucia now had an enlarged garrison, with as many as 4,000 troops, large numbers of whom were formerly enslaved people.

Guadeloupe, meanwhile, had a garrison of 8,000, again including many formerly enslaved people, who, reports suggested, were 'well-disciplined', though Abercromby suspected this information was exaggerated.[82] Still, with his plan of operations now already delayed by more than a month, and with further delays expected as he awaited the arrival of 7,000 reinforcements from Portsmouth, Abercromby decided to focus on smaller, more attainable objectives before striking at Guadeloupe. His lack of confidence in the capabilities of his own troops, at least in part, also explains this decision.

St Lucia became the first target, before restoring the garrisons of St Vincent and Grenada. If there was time, he would move on to Guadeloupe. In the event, the needed reinforcements did not arrive until mid-April, whereupon Abercromby divided his force into two substantive brigades, commanded by Major Generals Alexander Campbell and William Morshead, and two regiments of German troops, commanded by Brigadier General James Perryn. Abercromby also planned a reserve, but these troops were yet to arrive, and would not do so until the army was embroiled in a brutal campaign on St Lucia.[83]

Supplementing his force, however, was a battalion of 'black native troops', 1,187 strong. The idea of recruiting a regiment of infantry from among the enslaved population of the West Indies had been suggested early in 1795, when French reinforcements had swung the strategic balance in favour of the French. The government had grudgingly accepted this plan, based on the observation that black people were more tolerant of the climate, could withstand the fatigues of military service in such conditions better than their white counterparts and had been demonstrably adept at pursuing insurgents supporting the French republicans.[84] Officers with 'knowledge ... of the habits and dispositions of the Negroes and Mulattoes, and of the nature of the operations for which they are destined' were selected to train the new battalion.[85]

Ready, but not confident, Abercromby began his campaign on 26 April 1796. Campbell managed to get two regiments of his first brigade ashore north of Castries, but difficulties elsewhere meant few supporting units managed to land. He had been ordered to advance quickly to capture key positions overlooking Morne Fortune, but Abercromby asked Campbell to pause his deployment. Brigadier John Moore, Campbell's deputy, argued that a swift march would catch the defenders off-guard. 'To re-embark was impossible; to put off the march ... till next morning, dangerous', argued Moore. A delay would allow the defenders to 'assemble, attack, and tease us upon our March', but if the British moved immediately, they might be able to surprise the French. He was right. Though he expected to be harassed, his troops encountered no resistance and in fact pushed the defenders into the outer works of Morne Fortune.[86]

The campaign had got off to a surprisingly successful start. Bringing the remainder of his force ashore, Abercromby now focused on clearing the positions outside Morne Fortune. He ordered Moore and Brigadier

John Hope to clear Morne Chabot, a promontory adjacent to the French fortress. Moore commanded 750 men, while Hope, who was to act on Moore's flank, commanded 550 men. The two agreed that surprise would again be essential, and to commence the attack at daybreak, which meant Moore had to get his forces into position in darkness. The route through the close terrain limited the speed of manoeuvre, and just before daybreak his advanced units came into contact with enemy outposts, forcing the British to fall back. His cover blown, Moore concluded that he 'could not wait in file in a wood in a country of which I was ignorant and with which the enemy were acquainted'. He therefore elected to attack immediately.[87]

As they began their attack, Moore's men came into range of enemy fire from the crown of the hill. Moore 'could not prevent our men from firing or induce them to advance with a bayonet'. Soon 'those in our rear began also to fire, so that no situation could be more distressing'. Eventually the British advanced and seized the hilltop, but in the aftermath, Moore remained concerned that his men 'showed great want of discipline and confidence in their officers ... A failure would have been destruction; through such a country there was no retreat'. Moore was acutely aware of the personal 'consequences of a failure ... it was my *coup d'essai* in an army where I was unknown, and by its success my character would be judged'.[88] The episode was a stark illustration of the need for a balanced, well-trained combined arms force, capable of meeting the challenges presented by enclosed terrain.

Having secured Morne Chabot at some cost, as dawn broke, Moore and Hope linked up and observed a second larger hill, known as Morne Duchazeau, which overlooked Morne Fortune. They took the opportunity to capitalise on their enemy's disarray and seize it to help link up with the southern flank of the British beachhead. In the event, this move was decisive, as Morne Duchazeau would become the location of the main British battery.

Abercromby, meanwhile, was shocked less by the strength of the enemy garrison than by the challenging nature of the terrain. 'The difficulty in reducing this island will be greater than I apprehended,' he observed in a dispatch to David Dundas on 2 May, 'not from any increased number of blacks in arms, but totally from the natural strength of the country.'[89] He initially sought to avoid a regular siege by attempting to capture the coastal batteries which formed the key to the defences south-west of Morne Fortune. Confusion and miscommunication between the units led to failure and the British sustained 150 casualties, many of them black recruits.[90]

1. The Duke of Cumberland, King George II's second son, had a deep interest in the profession of arms. Though he led the British to their worst defeat in half a century at Fontenoy, his innovations proved a great success at the Battle of Culloden the following year. In peacetime he studied the history of war at his map library in Windsor Great Lodge, often sharing conversations with favoured subordinates.

2. Cumberland commanded a coalition of British, Dutch and Austrian troops at the Battle of Fontenoy (11 May 1745). He personally led a huge infantry attack which broke through the French lines, but he had neglected to secure his flanks and was forced to retreat with heavy losses. The unexpected, catastrophic defeat ushered in a period of introspection and renewal.

3. The British suffered another disastrous defeat on the banks of the river Monongahela in the Ohio Valley (9 July 1755). A column of British regular infantry and American colonial troops were ambushed by irregular French and Native American warriors. The defeat sent shockwaves through the British Empire, and proved the British needed to re-evaluate their approach to warfare in North America.

LE MAJOR ROBERT ROGER
Commandant en Chef les Troupes Indiennes au Services des
Americains

4. Hand-picked by Cumberland to sort out the mess in North America, John Campbell, Fourth Earl of Loudoun was a highly experienced officer. Though he made several important administrative improvements to the functioning of the British Army, he was sacked after a series of defeats during his tenure before the fruits of his labour could properly be experienced.

5. Robert Rogers gained widespread notoriety for his command of the North American Rangers. Sanctioned by the British to conduct intelligence-gathering operations into enemy territory, Rogers often exceeded the limits of his authority, brutalising enemy population centres. His tactical instructions were based on his extensive experience and proved essential to the transformation of the British way of war.

6. Ticonderoga commanded the small land-bridge between Lakes George and Champlain, as well as strategic communications in North America. It was therefore heavily contested in both the French and Indian War and the American Revolutionary War. In 1758 the British, commanded by General James Abercromby, launched a doomed attempt to capture the fort by storm.

7. Identified by General Sir John Ligonier for his talent, Jeffrey Amherst was promoted to command at the Siege of Louisbourg in 1758, before taking over as commander-in-chief the following year. His masterful orchestration of a three-pronged descent on Montreal in 1760 illustrated the transformation of British warfare in North America.

8. James Wolfe's plan to land his army at the foot of cliffs overlooking the St Lawrence River, scale them, and form up on the Plains of Abraham outside Quebec was audacious and risky. The complete surprise with which he took his French opponents ensured its success. Though mortally wounded at the resulting battle, Wolfe lived long enough to learn of his victory.

9. Benjamin West took considerable artistic licence when constructing this image of James Wolfe's death. Every element of the army he commanded to victory at Quebec is depicted, including a Native American warrior, a Ranger and a Highlander. In the background to the left, the French commander, Montcalm, falls mortally wounded, whilst a British aide-de-camp rushes in with news of victory.

10. Henry Lloyd had acquired a wealth of diverse military experience after serving in the French, Austrian, Prussian and Russian armies. He applied this in his history of the Seven Years' War, which combined traditional story-telling with critical analysis. His theories on the art of war foreshadowed military thinkers of the nineteenth century and influenced British officers for several generations, among them Henry Clinton and Arthur Wellesley.

11. This engraving depicts every commanding officer of the American Revolutionary War. In the centre is Charles, Earl Cornwallis, and then clockwise from the top, General Thomas Gage, General Sir John Burgoyne, General Sir William Howe and General Sir Henry Clinton.

12. In 1768, cavalry officer Captain Edward Hamilton set out on a Grand Tour of Europe with his friend Sir Watkin Williams-Wynn. Together they visited many of the artistic and cultural centres of Europe. In pursuit of professional self-education, military officers frequently embarked on Grand Tours with a more martial flair, visiting battlefields and fortresses to improve their understanding of war.

13. Having successfully outflanked the Americans on Long Island in August 1776, General Sir William Howe launched an amphibious assault on Manhattan. A powerful naval bombardment preceded the landing at Kip's Bay. As luck would have it, a delay caused by the unexpected running tide confused the defenders who assumed a different landing location and left Kip's Bay relatively poorly defended.

14. This celebratory French engraving illustrates the complexity and confusion of the Siege of Yorktown. Cornwallis's hastily erected redoubts are evident outside the town, while the American and French armies prepare their assaults. American civilians watch the scene of growing devastation. At sea the French victory over the British is depicted, gaining them temporary control of local waters and sealing Cornwallis's defeat.

15. At Plassey, on 23 June 1757, Robert Clive commanded 750 European soldiers and 2,100 sepoys to victory against the 55,000 troops of Siraj ud-Daula, Nawab of Bengal. The battle illustrated the superiority of European tactical training; over the next three decades, military forces in India met the challenges they faced by adopting different tactics and techniques to suit the challenges of terrain and environment.

16. The British fought four wars with Mysore in the late eighteenth century. The military prowess of the leader of Mysore, Haidar 'Ali, and his son, Tipu Sultan, inflicted several defeats on the British before General Cornwallis combined Indian and European military methods to defeat and impose terms on Tipu in 1792. Never satisfied with the outcome, war resumed in 1799, resulting in Tipu's death whilst defending his fortress capital.

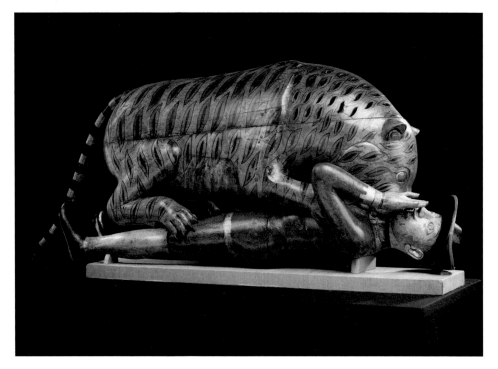

17. After its capture, Arthur Wellesley became governor of Seringapatam and took Tipu Sultan's summer palace, the Daria Daulat Bagh, as his headquarters. Adorned with floor-to-ceiling murals depicting famous British defeats, the palace also housed a huge library, as well as an ornamental organ of a tiger mauling a British redcoat.

18. In this print satirising the introduction of light infantry tactics into the regular order of battle of the British Army, an astonished King George III watches as his troops take flight and his artillery sprout wings. The notion that light infantry tactics, widely used in the closed terrain of North America, would be of use on the open plains of Europe, was widely derided.

19. Military encampments were the only occasion when several units could train and practice together. They were held infrequently in peacetime and as a result units were poorly prepared when war broke out. In 1774 General William Howe organised an encampment in Richmond Park in which a mock battle was fought to demonstrate the effectiveness of light infantry tactics.

20. Like his great uncle the Duke of Cumberland, Frederick, Duke of York was fiercely committed to the professional study of war. Famously ineffective in command, York's true skills emerged as a competent administrator of the British Army. He championed innovations such as the adoption of light infantry tactics, the creation of an experimental rifle brigade, and the opening of the Royal Military College.

21. Produced in 1797 and championed by the Duke of York, West's military figures could be used by newly commissioned officers to learn the rudimentaries of parade-ground drill. Each pack consisted of 10 regular companies, 2 flank companies, 12 non-commissioned officers, and a condensed version of the 18 parade ground drill commands.

22. Having failed to defeat Revolutionary France on the battlefields of the Low Countries, Great Britain turned its attention to the West Indies, where military success would, it was hoped, strangle France economically. Martinique was quickly captured, along with Guadeloupe and St Lucia, but success proved short-lived, and between 1794 and 1797 nearly 50,000 British soldiers died in the West Indies, most from tropical diseases.

23. In 1799 the renewal of the European war offered the British a new opportunity to assemble an expeditionary force and once more fight on the continent. Political pressure and poor planning meant the expedition to Den Helder in Holland was immediately beset with difficulties. Despite some early successes, the British force quickly got bogged down and was forced to withdraw later in the year.

24. Having failed in Holland, the British expeditionary force spent the next 18 months searching for targets of opportunity in the Mediterranean, before eventually focusing on the liberation of Egypt. During this time the little army was transformed into a highly trained and efficient fighting force. Despite encountering heavy resistance as it landed at Abukir Bay, the force went on to liberate Egypt in six months.

25. Every unit of the British Army that fought in Egypt is depicted in this highly stylised image, including Ottoman cavalry on the right and a sepoy on the left. The soldiers are seen hanging portraits of their commanding officers on an Egyptian ruin. At the top is General Sir Ralph Abercromby; Lieutenant-General Sir John Hely-Hutchinson and Sir Eyre Coote are below him. General John Moore is on the fourth row.

26. The Rifles were deployed to Portugal in 1808 where they helped achieve an unexpected victory over the French. With enemy forces seemingly in retreat, Moore, who had assumed command of the force in August, went on the offensive. Quickly outmanoeuvred by Napoleon, he was forced into a devastating retreat to Corunna, where he successfully fought a delaying action. Though his army was evacuated, Moore himself was mortally wounded.

27. In 1799, Lieutenant Colonel John Le Marchant, an officer known for creating and implementing key innovations in the British Army, submitted a proposal for the establishment of a Royal Military College at High Wycombe. The British Army's first 'Staff College' aimed to train and educate mid-career officers in the art of staff and command. During the Peninsular War, Wellington referred to its graduates as his 'Scientifics'.

28. Many in the British Army had been sceptical about the utility of the rifle. While slower to reload and requiring more training to use than the Brown Bess musket, the Baker Rifle was much more accurate. In 1803, on the advice of General Sir John Moore, the 95th Rifle Regiment moved to Shorncliffe in Kent and began training as part of an elite light infantry force.

29. Wellington is seen here surrounded by his key generals and staff officers in preparation for an unnamed battle. Appropriately enough, his quartermaster general, George Murray, is pictured poring over a map with Rowland Hill. Murray had been educated at High Wycombe and held a number of staff appointments before the Peninsular War where Wellington became increasingly reliant on him.

30. William Napier served in the 43rd Regiment throughout the Peninsular War. During the 1820s and 1830s, Napier published a multi-volume history of the war, which established him as the premier military historian of the age, though some veterans, notably George Murray, vociferously criticised the work. Napier's conservatism led him to question the widespread adoption of the rifle, preferring the tried-and-tested Brown Bess musket.

31. The failure to capture New Orleans illustrated the challenges the British still faced when conducting operations against a well-positioned enemy. British troops proved incapable of penetrating the multi-layered defences built by American General Andrew Jackson, whilst they also suffered horrendous casualties at the hands of American riflemen.

32. Like their predecessors at the Battle of the Monongahela, the soldiers of the 44th Regiment of Foot fought tenaciously in defence of their position at Gandamak during the retreat from Afghanistan in January 1842. Their eventual demise illustrated the limitations of the musket in opposition to the more accurate jezail rifle.

Abercromby was forced to resort to a regular siege, and the arrival of 5,500 reinforcements at least allowed him to fully man his operations. He ordered his quartermaster, Brigadier John Knox, to build a road from the coast to the Morne Duchazeau, in order to get the guns up to a new battery, but the defenders were able easily to penetrate the siege lines and disrupt British activity. To shorten his lines, Abercromby decided to seize the Vigie, a coastal battery which protected the main bay on St Lucia. The attack turned into another fiasco, however, after the defenders waited until the attackers were within point-blank range before firing a devastating hail of musketry. Over 200 redcoats were killed or wounded.

In conversation with Moore after the latest setback, 'Abercromby . . . was in low spirits . . . The attack was planned in a hurry', he said, 'and executed without spirit or judgement. The regiments in general are extremely bad; it is hard to say whether the officers or men are worse'. Moore argued that 'when it is determined that a post cannot be assaulted, but must be reduced by Canon, a certain time is required. That time, according to circumstances, must be greater or less. In a country so mountainous and difficult as this, it must be long'. He used examples from earlier in his career to justify his viewpoint. 'I told Sir Ralph that at the siege of Calvi the difficulties of the country were greater than here, that the siege therefore lasted upwards of two months . . . .' On St Lucia, meanwhile, 'the enemy had the advantage of position', Moore observed. 'We had to overcome that difficulty by labour and by superiority of fire. I took the liberty also of telling him, for I saw that nobody about him would, that his presence' at the front 'would infinitely forward the service. It would inspire zeal, and he would be ready to observe and take advantage of events on the instant'.[91]

Thus the siege continued, with the gradual establishment of parallels from Morne Duchazeau. The French, meanwhile, were suffering considerable supply difficulties themselves; their water, food and ammunition were all running low. On 24 May, Abercromby ordered Moore to clear an enemy advanced post commanding the outworks of the fortress. While Abercromby organised two diversions, Moore attacked with the light and grenadier companies of the 27th Foot. After initially gaining the stronghold, the French counterattacked twice, but Moore's troops were able to hold the line.[92] This proved to be a decisive moment. The capture of the outwork allowed a third parallel to be constructed, bringing the British siege guns to point-blank range. Virtually out of ammunition, the French garrison surrendered on 25 May. In total, the British took 2,066 prisoners, along with 261 women and 94 children.[93] The British had sustained 566 casualties.

Resistance continued in the interior of the island, however, so Abercromby had to leave Moore with nearly six thousand men to suppress what was a growing insurgency. Moore established a chain of posts throughout the countryside and ordered regular patrols between them. It was hoped that these would draw the insurgents out, and though they were regularly fired upon, the British found it difficult to pin down their adversary. Moore concluded that 'the Black troops are the only troops equal to scour the woods – the British are unequal to such service'.[94] Struck down by fever, Moore returned to England in 1798, where he advised the government that a garrison of not less than 1,800 troops, two-thirds of whom should be European, was sufficient to hold St Lucia.[95]

Abercromby, meanwhile, concentrated on St Vincent and Grenada, which proved altogether easier nuts to crack. He reinforced the latter first, before organising an operation to surround the French in their stronghold on St Vincent.[96] So well-orchestrated and executed was the operation on 9 June that the French surrendered by 5 p.m.[97] On Grenada, Abercromby's reinforcements had managed to secure the main town, but rebels still continued to undermine the British from a mountainous stronghold in the interior. Following his success on St Vincent, Abercromby returned to Grenada and once more orchestrated an operation to flush out the insurgents on the night of 18–19 June. As the weather broke, Abercromby concluded he had achieved all he could. Guadeloupe remained a French republican stronghold, but he lacked time and resources to do anything about it. Tropical illness once more swept through the army and by 1 January 1797, nearly 6,500 had succumbed to malaria and yellow fever.[98]

Attempts to rebuild the British West Indies contingent for a new campaign in 1797 proved largely ineffective. The forthcoming operation, to which Abercromby was again appointed commander, would now focus on Spain's colonies following the latter's alliance with France and subsequent declaration of war against Britain. In preparation for an assault on Trinidad in February, Abercromby gained valuable intelligence from Lieutenant-Colonel Charles Soter, who commanded a battalion of black soldiers, and who knew the Spanish island well.[99] In the event, the British found the Spanish defenders demoralised. Upon observing the arrival of the British fleet in Chaguaramas Bay on 16 February, the Spanish 'set fire to their ships and we were reduced to the necessity of remaining quiet spectators of the conflagration', observed John Hope.[100]

Likewise, the defenders of the main stronghold, Port of Spain, had no confidence. This was fortuitous for the British, as the landing was once again beset by chaos. Troops broke into plantations and got drunk on the rum they found. The Spanish troops behaved comparably, however, and the civilian population begged the governor to surrender. The island, a considerable prize, along with its garrison of 634 soldiers and 1,687 sailors, fell into British hands on 18 February. Abercromby had lost only seven men.[101]

By contrast, the Spanish defenders of Puerto Rico, at the other end of the string of Caribbean islands, were better prepared. The British assault got ashore, but found the defences insurmountable. Though Abercromby 'had occasion for his personal exertions during the siege ... it was observed that he could not keep his temper', noted Charles Stewart of the 53rd Regiment. 'He endeavoured to encourage the soldiers (*entre nous* they required it, their bravery was not conspicuous).'[102] The British soldiery were again the weak link. On 30 April, Abercromby decided to withdraw. This part of the operation was at least executed with skill and completed before the Spanish could react.[103]

Thus ended British offensive military operations in the West Indies. The campaigns had been attended by some operational success, but their strategic impact was limited. The toll, meanwhile, on the British army was profound. Of the 89,000 officers and men sent to the West Indies between 1793 and 1801, 62,250 – 70 per cent – were reported casualties. Of those, 45,250 lost their lives, the vast majority the result of disease rather than enemy action.[104] More generally, the West Indian campaigns exposed some serious flaws in the effectiveness and capabilities of the British redcoat. The veteran regiments had been ravaged by disease after the opening campaign and their replacements proved wholly unequal to the task. 'Against an enemy of experience,' Moore argued, 'we must have failed.'[105]

The campaigns in the West Indies had illustrated the enduring importance of the lessons learned in America: light infantry was essential for overcoming the challenges of terrain and an adversary capable of varied tactics. Training, refinement and practice would be essential if the British Army was to overcome its new challenges in Europe. Officers with experience of American warfare, and now campaigns in the West Indies, were eager to demonstrate the value of these ideas. Eyre Coote, for example, after returning from the West Indies, drafted in 1796 'Instructions to Officers of Light Infantry', designed to complement David Dundas's *Principles of Military Manoeuvre*, since the latter 'had paid little attention to the Service of the Light Infantry'.[106]

More generally, the campaigns which the British Army fought between 1793 and 1797 illustrated many of its inadequacies, as Henry Clinton had predicted when he had visited the headquarters of his old friend, the Duke of Brunswick. The terrain was 'most favourable to the French mode of making war', namely that practised by well-trained marksmen and light infantry. The British preference for the massed firepower of the musket and the shock of the bayonet charge was negated by the same terrain, and 'could not be injurious to troops scattered over an immense surface'.[107] One officer bemoaned the fact that the British light infantry, such as they were, seemed to be 'perfectly unacquainted with the system of sharp-shooting (and it is impossible not to lament the want of that species of warfare in our army)'.[108]

This, however, was not the only problem bedevilling British military operations. Poor intelligence and poor staff training blighted the actions of the British Army in the first years of the French Revolutionary War. So too did the mismanagement of logistics, sickness in the ranks and tensions between allies. Moreover, there was a serious disconnect between the political and military levels. Politicians did not understand war, and military officers had gone into the three most recent campaign theatres seeking decisive victory on the battlefield, and not recognising the wider strategic and operational context. For some, military victory became the end and not the means to the end desired. Henry Clinton's predictions, then, had become reality.

Only when the British were able to resolve this particular range of challenges would they be able to pose a reasonable challenge to the ascendancy of the French army. Nevertheless, the campaigns had illustrated that the British were willing to learn the lessons both of their recent military history and of the campaigns against the new and unexpected enemy they now faced. An opportunity was presented to apply those lessons in 1799, when war broke out between France and Austria, and Britain saw a new chance to deploy an expeditionary force to the continent. The next two years would see this force wander from the North Sea to the Mediterranean and up the Nile, and in the process, undergo a rebirth.

CHAPTER 9

The 'Wandering Army'

THE REBIRTH OF THE BRITISH ARMY, 1799–1801

'NEVER did so large and effective a force leave the ports of England,' wrote Major General Sir Eyre Coote in his journal on 2 October 1800, 'and never was a year so completely wasted away without advantages to the country. We must consider ourselves as a wandering Army, not knowing where to go or what progress to pursue.'[1] Coote made this observation in characteristic melodramatic fashion while serving as a brigade commander during the deployment of Britain's expeditionary force to the Mediterranean. He was frustrated at the slow pace of operations, the seeming interminable drifting around the Mediterranean, sometimes searching for targets of opportunity, but mostly cooped up aboard the flotilla of transports or spending time ashore in Gibraltar, Minorca or Turkey. His frustrations were widely shared, but in the course of the 18 months in which the force was deployed to the Mediterranean, the British army was reborn.

All the senior officers had served together, some for extensive periods of time. Subordinates began to understand their general's intent, anticipate his decisions and work towards a common objective. This group of officers, ranging from the senior staff to the leadership of various regiments, lived in close proximity to each other. As they got to know and trust one another more, knowledge exchange became more frequent. Those with extensive past experiences discussed their knowledge with their subordinates in a variety of settings – at dinner in the mess, on informal battlefield tours and during training encampments prior to deployment. As a result, informal adaptation and innovation in the field was encouraged, offering new solutions to the challenges posed by France's revolutionary armies.

* * *

The nucleus of this expeditionary force had been formed in 1799. British Prime Minister William Pitt and Foreign Secretary Lord Grenville had finally succeeded in assembling a new coalition of great powers, comprised of Great Britain, Russia and Austria, against Revolutionary France.[2] Attempts to draw in Prussia failed, but there remained the possibility that Berlin might call for France to withdraw from Holland. In order to facilitate this, Pitt, Grenville and Secretary of State for War Henry Dundas alighted upon the possibility of a combined Anglo-Russian attack on the Dutch coast. After the end of active operations in the West Indies and the successful conclusion of operations in Ireland after the 1798 rebellion, it was evident that an expeditionary element of the British Army was available for deployment to Europe.

General Sir Ralph Abercromby was appointed to command the initial British amphibious assault force, with the Duke of York taking over command when the foothold in Holland was established and Russian reinforcements had arrived. The army at his disposal was a mixture of veteran regiments, raw recruits and militia units drafted into the regular army. West Indies veterans dominated the command and staff, with Major Generals Eyre Coote and John Moore commanding two of the four brigades, Colonel John Hope serving as adjutant and Lieutenant Colonel Robert Anstruther appointed quartermaster general.

Having inspected his brigade after it assembled at Barham Downs in preparation for embarkation, Moore was not terribly assured about the prospects of success. 'The regiments of the Line are in general but poor, and', he wrote in his diary on 10 August 1799, 'few of them are formed or disciplined.'[3] Coote was equally concerned, having spent the last few months inspecting militia companies in the hopes of finding suitable recruits for the expedition. 'Greater attention has ever been paid to the shew than to the study of the more essential parts of their duty,' he wrote in a report intended for the Duke of York. 'To the general badness of the officers must be attributed the great disadvantage the Regiments labour under; the inaccuracy of their movements; badness of levelling; and inexperience of ball firing.'[4]

In addition to the army's tactical shortcomings, as the campaign plan took shape, it quickly became clear that it relied on a series of strategic assumptions which were not fully supported by the available evidence. In broad terms,

Abercromby's British units would deploy to the coast of Holland (specific location to be determined), establish a beachhead and drive the defending Franco-Dutch forces away from the coast. A contingent of Russian troops would then arrive to support the operation. Success was at least in part predicated on the ambitious expectation that, upon the arrival of the Anglo-Russian force, the inhabitants of Holland would rise up en masse and overthrow their French occupiers. Indeed, so expectant were the British of a large-scale popular rebellion against the French that Grenville was concerned that there might be a 'premature explosion' among the restive population, and it would thus be snuffed out before the British could deploy in its support.[5]

In reality, the expedition was rushed into execution because of the political necessity of acting in support of Austrian military operations in Italy.[6] When Grenville was informed that the British troops assigned to the expedition needed another three months training to reach the expected standard to fight the French successfully, the Foreign Secretary argued that the British would not have to fight in Holland, as the Dutch uprising would force the French to evacuate the Low Countries without a shot being fired.[7]

Grenville was convinced that if Abercromby prosecuted the campaign with sufficient vigour and tempo, then it would in turn generate an insurrection among the Dutch populace, a bow wave upon which the British army could ride to success. 'Look at the campaign of 1787,' he argued, referring to the successful Prussian invasion of the Netherlands to restore the Orangist regime. 'How little time it cost the Duke of Brunswick, with all his doubts, and hesitations, and cautions, and precautions, to march with 25,000 men (no more) from Wesel to Amsterdam; and then let any man tell me what there is in the present circumstances to stop British generals and British soldiers, with the country unanimously in their favour . . . .'[8] Grenville would not be the last politician to abuse history in support of his political aims.

Abercromby was not so confident. In an effort to obtain information on the prospective landing beaches, and to facilitate cooperation with the Dutch after a viable beachhead had been achieved, he requested 'a few Dutch officers . . . be directed to attend him for the purpose of intercourse with the inhabitants'.[9] No such support was forthcoming, however, as the British had discouraged emigration after the revolution, hopeful that they would form the core of resistance to French occupation.[10] The British therefore had virtually no intelligence on the terrain or enemy strength in any of the prospective targets.

Grenville was concerned that the seeming procrastination of the military leadership of the expedition was causing a paralysing loss of time that would have catastrophic repercussions. Delays were created only on 'the vague idea of insufficiency of force', Grenville grumbled, 'not calculated on any data of difficulties to be combated or of resistance to be surmounted, but merely on the general notion that it is safer to try the enterprise with 20,000 men than with 12,000'.[11] The Foreign Secretary was more effusive in private letters to his brother. 'They are disputing about force and losing in these stupid hesitations the very time and moment of action – I am sick of it.'[12]

Pitt agreed. 'All military difficulties are completely overruled,' he wrote on 2 August.[13] The expedition was ordered to sail without delay. Moore, by now one of Abercromby's most trusted brigade commanders, neatly summarised the nature of the political situation. While at dinner at Walmer Castle with Pitt and Dundas the evening before the expedition sailed, Moore learned that the island of Goeree rather than Walcheren was now the main objective. 'The information with respect to the force upon these islands, their state of defence etc, is extremely imperfect,' he recorded in his diary that evening. 'The expedition has undoubtedly been hurried beyond reason, but the country having been put to the expense of assembling it, it is necessary that we should be sent to attempt something.'[14]

The chief difficulty Abercromby faced was a complete lack of information of any reliability on where his force could land. There were three options: in the south at the mouth of the rivers Scheldt and Maas, on the islands of Walcheren and Goeree; in the north at the mouth of the river Ems; and finally at the mouth of the Texel, between the first two options. Intelligence received on the eve of deployment suggested that only Walcheren or the Texel were viable options. Abercromby received open final instructions to try his luck at the former, where the most significant strategic impact would be achieved, and if that seemed untenable, he could proceed with discretion to the Texel, an option he availed himself of immediately after learning of its light defences.[15] Moreover, the latter offered the possibility of capturing the Orangist-leaning Dutch Navy and a reliable supply base if the port of Den Helder could be secured.

A storm struck the fleet soon after it sailed and battered it until 20 August. Miraculously, it stayed together and approached the Dutch coast on the 21st. The garrison of Den Helder was summoned, but a fresh gale blew in and the fleet was forced to put to sea once more. Only on the 26th did the weather abate, and Abercromby prepared to land his forces on the 27th, by which time the French had been able to reinforce Den Helder to a garrison of 2,000, while a further 5,400 troops were positioned on the flanks of the landing beaches. A reserve force inland could be drawn on to boost numbers to 8,800. The element of surprise had been lost, but Abercromby chose a beach that was difficult to defend, and the enemy commander unaccountably chose not to resist the landing itself, but to fight the British further inland.

At 3 a.m. on 27 August, the landing craft cast off from the fleet under a protective naval bombardment. Sheltered behind the dunes, the French escaped unscathed, while the still intemperate weather scattered the landing craft. When they reached the shores, the British were in complete disorder. 'We landed with great confusion and irregularity,' recorded Moore. 'I was put on shore with not more than 300 men of my brigade, and these a mixture of every different regiment . . . .'[16] The invaders were badly outclassed by the apparent quality of the troops to which they were opposed. 'The enemy from the crests of the sand-dunes kept up a constant and destructive fire,' noted Captain Henry Bunbury, who participated in the landings. Meanwhile, 'the disadvantages under which the invaders fought necessarily exposed the three brigades . . . engaged to a serious loss of men; and a large proportion . . . fell under the aim of the . . . riflemen'.[17]

Moore was ordered to besiege Den Helder itself with three brigades, while Lieutenant General Sir James Pulteney, Abercromby's second-in-command, was given two brigades to hold off any French counterattack. As it turned out, it was this southern flank that encountered most resistance from the French, and a series of scattered battles developed among the sand dunes between French skirmishers and British grenadiers and light infantry. Pulteney was shot in the arm and relieved by Abercromby's timely arrival. Over the course of several hours, the British managed to force the French to withdraw and established a secure line at the village of Groote Keten. Abercromby was more than a little surprised at the quality of French resistance. 'They may be said to have behaved better than we expected,' he wrote to Dundas the following day. 'They certainly at times pushed our people with spirit and perseverance, as they returned several times to the attack.'[18]

His southern flank secured, Abercromby now ordered Moore to storm Den Helder. For both, no doubt exhausted by the day's action, the situation appeared grim. Moore described it as 'unpromising'. 'An enemy was on both our flanks,' he continued, 'and we were in a position which, however favourably it had been represented by maps, proved to be extremely bad.'[19] As he prepared his attack, however, he observed enemy movements within Den Helder and eventually realised the French were evacuating. By daylight the following morning, the British had secured a

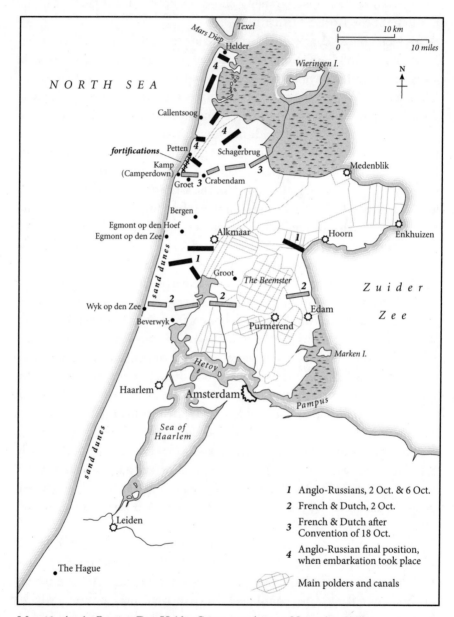

Map 10. Anglo-Russian Den Helder Campaign, August–November 1799.

supply base. Meanwhile, with Dutch pilots guiding the way, the fleet navigated the shoals at the entrance to the Zuider Zee. Confronted by the sudden appearance of the British line-of-battle ships at the entrance to their harbour, the Dutch fleet promptly surrendered. 'Thus the greatest stroke that has perhaps been struck in this war', wrote Moore, 'has been accomplished in a few hours, and with a trifling loss.'[20]

Abercromby did not receive any cavalry reinforcements until 31 August. Bereft, until then, of any reconnaissance force, he remained ignorant of French movements for several days. As soon as his first detachment arrived, he sent it out on reconnaissance duties, and the subsequent reports indicated that the local commander, Dutch revolutionary Herman Willem Daendels, had underestimated Abercromby's difficulties, overrated his strength and chose to withdraw from a strong defensive position on the Zijpe polder. As the British troops had been exposed to biting gales and driving rain, as well as dwindling supplies, Abercromby took the opportunity 'as much of necessity as of choice, to move forward'.[21]

The new position afforded the British troops shelter and supplies, and would be a formidable defensive barrier to any French counterattack. However, forward reconnaissance revealed that the country beyond the Zijpe polder 'is entirely intersected with ditches and canals'. Abercromby elected to hold this position until the arrival of the Russians, at which point he expected the French 'to quit their present position, probably without fighting'.[22]

This was an understandable decision: he had no wagons, horses or pack animals with which to move supplies. On 10 September, however, the French, now under the command of General Guillaume Brune, counterattacked; the attack fell on the British left. There was a brief moment of peril when the French 'pressed us most ... at a Battery' which was relatively weakly defended. Had it fallen, 'they must have cut off the retreat of half of us'.[23]

The British lines held firm, however, and the French suffered 1,000 casualties in the attack, compared to fewer than 200 British wounded and killed. 'The Troops behaved as well as I could wish, before the action was over they grew cool, reserving their fire, altho' full of ardour', observed Abercromby. 'The Militia Men, are I think a superior race of men, and a great acquisition to the army at this time. I reckon that the troops I have with me are made for this campaign, and up to anything, if they do not receive an unforeseen check.'[24]

Had this attack been met in the open countryside in front of the Zijpe polder, the story would have been a different one. 'It is possible that my

determination to remain on the defence until reinforced may not meet
with the approbation of His Majesty's Ministers or of Professional Men,'
observed Abercromby.[25] He was right. In Pitt's view, if Abercromby had
gone on the offensive before the arrival of reinforcements, 'there is great
reason to think that with his present force he might have succeeded. His
opinions about the disposition of the country, on the grounds he states, are
certainly worth very little'.[26]

Nevertheless, Abercromby was 'certain that I have acted right; the difficulties of the country in a military point of view are such that to gain any
advantage you must pay dear for it . . .'.[27] But Abercromby's concern about
the nature of the terrain was not the only evidence influencing his decision. Intelligence on both the Dutch army and population indicated that
Grenville's hopes of a spontaneous insurrection were wide of the mark.
Very few deserters had arrived in the British lines and there was no sign
of the expected uprising among the civilian population.[28]

Shortly after the French counterattack had been defeated, reinforcements in the shape of two Russian and one British contingent – the latter
composed chiefly of raw recruits – began arriving. Abercromby now
handed supreme command to the Duke of York, and preparations for a
breakout commenced. York proposed taking the offensive on 19 September.
The day before, he had received disturbing intelligence that '17,000
French had been ordered to march from Belgium into Holland', while a
further 20,000 troops were concentrating against the British and
Russians.[29] As the allied force was currently comfortably superior to the
present enemy strength, York decided on an immediate attack.

York's plan for what would become known as the Battle of Bergen on 19
September 1799 was to launch a four-pronged attack designed to envelop
the French. York reorganised the army into columns, loose operational
arrangements of brigades which foreshadowed the formal divisional
structure adopted 10 years later.[30] The Anglo-Russian right flank attack,
commanded by Russian General Johann Hermann, began successfully
enough, reaching their objectives despite sustaining significant casualties
from friendly fire. However, a French counterattack threatened the overextended position, and the allies were forced to retreat.

The two-column British advance in the centre, commanded by Pulteney
and General David Dundas was more successful though hampered by
watercourses and other terrain obstacles. Here, once again, the inadequacies of British light infantry, skirmishing and marksmanship training were
laid bare. 'We soon got into a smart fire from the enemy's riflemen, which

we found was the only description of troops ... that we had to contend with,' noted William Surtees. 'They had greatly the advantage over us in point of shooting, their balls doing much more execution than ours ....'[31]

Although the British forced the French and Dutch from their defences in the centre, albeit with significant loss, the debacle on the allied right forced the British to retreat to their starting positions. On the allied left, Abercromby's advance was virtually unopposed, but the terrain and the defences left by the French ensured that the outflanking manoeuvre was too circuitous to have the proposed effect. With news of the collapse on the right, Abercromby too, was forced to retreat to his starting position.

In the aftermath of the failure, the Duke of York was quick to pin the blame, albeit privately, on the Russians. 'I do the Russians full justice for bravery,' he wrote confidentially to Dundas, 'but it is owing to their conduct only that we were obliged to give up the advantages which we had gained.'[32] Another eyewitness observed that the Russian attack 'went in the greatest disorder possible'.[33] It was clear from the accounts of other participants, however, that the challenges posed by terrain and the lack of adequate training also played their part. 'The event of a battle is at all times doubtful,' wrote Abercromby, 'but in this country the difficulties that an attacking army has to surmount are not to be equalled in any country in Europe ... From the knowledge I have of the ground, as much was done, and as great advantages were gained as could have been expected.'[34] More specifically, Colonel Robert Brownrigg, serving in the quartermaster's department, observed that both the British and Russians had been surprised by the quality of the French and Dutch troops. 'Even General Hermann acknowledged ... that his defeat was owing to too great *hardiesse* on the part of the soldiers, and that he himself was not aware of the sort of troops he had to act against.'[35]

Despite the arrival of Russian reinforcements, poor weather prevented York from renewing the attack for another two weeks. By then, Dutch engineers had broken the dykes intersecting the terrain and inundated the surrounding countryside. This further hampered the allies and left just narrow strips of land through which to advance. The new plan of attack, which commenced at 6.30 a.m. on 2 October, saw Abercromby command the right wing, with instructions to outflank the French by marching down the beach. The incoming tide hampered this movement and forced the British to advance along a very narrow strip of dry sand. Exhausted and thirsty, the British sustained severe casualties, among them John Moore who was hit in the thigh and face by enemy sniper fire.[36]

As the British approached the French lines, they suffered further heavy casualties at the hands of French sharpshooters, before a French cavalry charge swept in and captured two British artillery pieces. British troops desperately fought to retake the guns, charging the position unsuccessfully four times, but the British cavalry, commanded by Henry Paget, eventually counterattacked, and 'soon dislodged them taking several prisoners'. Paget and his men found the guns 'loaded with canister', but the French 'had not time to make use of them'.[37]

On the right, meanwhile, Pulteney's column was instructed to fix the French at Bergen, while, in the centre, the Anglo-Russian column made slow but steady progress, fighting off a determined counterattack. By the end of the day, although Abercromby had outflanked Bergen, his troops were too exhausted to press home an attack. The French felt sufficiently threatened to withdraw from Bergen, however, and formed a new line with the village of Castricum in its centre. York notified the King of a success, though the 'loss I am affraid is considerable . . .'.[38]

This was effectively the high-water mark of the Anglo-Russian expedition. With the terrain inundated and virtually unnavigable, supplies running short and the health of the remaining troops in decline, an armed reconnaissance of Castricum on 6 October turned into an all-out attack when the Russians spied an opportunity. The French rushed reinforcements to the village, and the attack was beaten off with heavy losses. Overextended and exhausted, York convened a council of war and determined to retreat back to the Zijpe polder – the starting point on 19 September. Faced with the prospect of a winter siege, York approached Brune on 14 October proposing an honourable withdrawal. An armistice was agreed almost immediately, and the British and Russians given until 1 December to evacuate. They had done so by 19 November.

* * *

The government now found itself with a sizeable expeditionary force at its disposal but no real plans for its use. Brief proposals were made for an attack on Belleisle off the French west coast, in the hopes it would divert French forces from the war against Austria. These were eventually abandoned after the Austrian war effort collapsed. In early 1800, the decision was taken to divert the expeditionary force instead to the Mediterranean. York, for one, was reluctant to support the initiative. He observed that the majority of the battalions assigned to this force 'were entirely composed of volunteers from the English Militia . . . incomplete in Cloathing, arms and appointments, and without having undergone that preparation which is absolutely necessary for troops . . . proceeding on actual service'. Moreover, 'during any active campaign particularly during one so arduous as that sustained by the Army in Holland,' York observed, 'it must be evident that it is impossible to exercise troops or to ground them in the first rudiments of their business'.[39] Given the soldiers' limited formal training, any innovations which were to be formally incorporated into the regular order of battle would have to be tested and refined by officers in the field. Happily for the British, as its expeditionary force prepared to deploy to the Mediterranean, the body of officers now serving in its ranks had the accumulated military knowledge needed to achieve this.

In command, once more, was General Sir Ralph Abercromby. Lieutenant General John Hely-Hutchinson was appointed second-in-command. Abercromby and Hely-Hutchinson had been dispatched to Gibraltar in early 1800 along with John Moore, Abercromby's favoured brigade commander, and John Hope, his adjutant. Robert Anstruther once more took the role of quartermaster general, with George Murray as his deputy. The units which Abercromby found at Gibraltar comprised only half his force, however. Sir James Pulteney was bringing the balance of the force, having been dispatched earlier in an ultimately abortive operation to capture Belleisle.

Among Pulteney's brigade commanders was Eyre Coote, who would maintain a detailed journal of the expedition, as would Major Christopher Hely-Hutchinson, younger brother of John, and likewise en route to Gibraltar with Pulteney's corps. Hely-Hutchinson's journal offers a glimpse of the day-to-day life of a group of officers preparing for a major operation. He recorded details of conversations held at the mess table, during which earlier experiences were discussed and ideas exchanged. Conversation ranged from historical anecdotes to reviews of earlier campaigns.[40] What is revealed is a professionally orientated corps, profoundly interested in acquiring knowledge of military history and of likely scenarios which they might well encounter.

On the way to Gibraltar, Pulteney landed at El Ferrol on the north Spanish coast, only to re-embark almost immediately. The incident did not bode well for the future success of the expedition. 'It is perhaps unprecedented in the annals of the world', recorded Coote, once again rather melodramatically, 'that 12,000 men landed on one day, and embarked on the next, in an enemy's country, without losing one man.'[41] In fact, there were 59 casualties, but the point was forcefully made, and the fiasco at

El Ferrol was not the last time this expeditionary force would embarrass itself. On this occasion, the failure was the result of poor intelligence on the fortifications of El Ferrol, as well as the difficulties of disembarking sufficient siege artillery. The expeditionary force, along with its senior staff, still had much to learn. Happily, the open-ended nature of the deployment offered an opportunity to learn, adapt and innovate, a process which for the British was informal and took place in varying ways.

The expeditionary force remained at Gibraltar for several weeks, awaiting instructions, before moving to Minorca and then returning to Gibraltar. In this time, the officers and soldiers settled into the routine of what was essentially life in a mobile garrison. Hely-Hutchinson recorded in extensive detail the frequent occasions on which he dined with fellow officers, illustrating the intersection of different professional, patronage and friendship networks. At Sir Ralph Abercromby's dining table, for example, politics was the subject of discussion, at Moore's dining table, news of recent military campaigns – such as Pulteney's abortive descent on El Ferrol – while at a regimental dining table, close friends discussed earlier military experiences. One night in November, for example, Hely-Hutchinson 'dined at the 63rd mess . . .', where he 'Talked over the action of the 6th October last year in North Holland in front of Egmont op zie when this regiment was under my Brother who was then wounded . . .'.[42]

Such interactions, rarely the subject of record or comment in personal diaries and correspondence, were the spaces where informal learning and knowledge exchange and creation would take place. These interactions also illustrate the gradual formation of regimental bonds and an esprit de corps which would be essential for battlefield success. Shared experiences, and shared understanding of those experiences, helped build trust and confidence. They also afforded the more experienced officers the opportunity to pass on their knowledge and ideas, a process which saw them reach not only into their own career history, but into the larger scope of Britain's military history.

Major General John Moore, with considerable experience of warfighting ranging from Europe to the West Indies, was one such officer. He enjoyed a personal network of connections to officers with a much wider experience of warfare in North America, India and Europe. Having recently served in the West Indies, Moore had become a strong advocate for the development of light infantry battalions in the regular order of battle of the British Army, but it was not just his service there which suggested the importance of irregular troops to Britain's war effort. Following his return from the

Caribbean, Moore was assigned to serve under Sir William Howe's command in East Anglia during the 1797 French invasion scare. Howe had assembled a brigade consisting of a detachment of Royal Horse Artillery, two troops of light horse and two light companies.[43]

Moore observed these units in an exercise. 'I can conceive of nothing in higher order than this troop,' he wrote. 'It is a great improvement, and great advantage may be derived from the celerity with which they move.'[44] Howe believed that a successful defence hinged on the appropriate use of irregular troops to disorientate an enemy landing. He organised encampments and training sessions to help prepare selected soldiers for the challenges of action in the light infantry.[45] The approach he adopted to the raising, training and command of permanent light infantry units was therefore imbued with a combination of personal and collective experience, of professional reading and discussion, and of the latest thinking. Its foundation was the training and drill regime Howe had first developed in 1774, which was itself a distillation of his earlier experience in North America during the Seven Years' War.[46]

Moore was also an avid reader, and one of his earliest professional book selections was James Wolfe's *Instructions to Young Officers*, which he copied by hand in 1777 while deployed to Minorca as an ensign in the 51st Regiment of Foot, and which he inscribed as such on the title page.[47] Though published posthumously, and a loose assemblage of Wolfe's general orders, the book illustrated how officers could innovate and adapt to the conditions they faced on the ground, often in violation of formal constraints imposed by senior commanders. Wolfe famously altered Cumberland's preferred tactical drill in order to meet the challenges of the conditions he faced.[48] Moore would bear this in mind as he faced new challenges during the Mediterranean campaign. His professional experience was therefore supplemented by knowledge obtained directly or indirectly from veterans of past wars in America.

Moore would have passed on this knowledge in the course of professional discussions during the expedition to the Mediterranean, and there were several ways in which this knowledge exchange took place. The most common was in the mess, where there was no escape from discussion, and the conversation, as Hely-Hutchinson's diary indicates, was controlled by the senior officer present.[49] Professionally minded, at his dining table Moore was principally interested in discussing historical and contemporary military campaigns and how to plan and execute them. Conversations about history and the art of war were not uncommon in the mess and had been a feature of British military deployments since the Seven Years' War.[50]

But the mess hall was not the only place where such knowledge exchange took place; the historical battlefield tour also offered opportunities for professional discussion, the building of new relationships and the comparison of history and contemporary affairs. While in Gibraltar, Hely-Hutchinson took the opportunity to visit the armaments of the Rock, as well as the Spanish lines and the location where 'the battering ships 13th September 1782 were placed in a direction opposite the King's bastion near the Old Mole Algeciras ...'.[51] A discussion of the Spanish siege of 1782 followed. Similar exchanges took place on Minorca, where Hely-Hutchinson toured the military architecture of the town with Colonel Rowland Hill of the 90th Regiment, and then visited the assault beaches used by Charles Stuart two years earlier. On this occasion, he was accompanied by General Moore, Colonel Dyer and Captain Anderson.[52] There they might have discussed how Stuart's adjutant-general, Major Kenneth Mackenzie, had assembled an elite light infantry unit by joining the flank companies of five battalions.[53] Anderson, who was Moore's aide-de-camp, shared Hely-Hutchinson's interest in recent military history. As the flotilla sailed past Corsica, he described the military operations conducted there in 1794, clearly learned directly from Moore, who had served in the operation.[54] The discussion of history, the exchange of personal experience and wider ideas infused conversations between officers provided opportunities for informal learning and reflection. In this way, military knowledge was remade and tailored to specific challenges. As the expedition progressed, this new knowledge was applied and adapted in theatre.

*   *   *

In October, following the rendezvous at Gibraltar, the force launched an amphibious assault on the Spanish port of Cadiz. Little planning was done in preparation for the assault, and there were too few boats to embark the whole landing force – some 5,000 men. This was principally because of a lack of communication between the naval and military commanders – Admiral Lord Keith and Abercromby. Moore, who was in command of the reserve, had gone to explain the situation to Keith, but found him 'all confusion, blaming everything, but attempting to remedy nothing'.[55] Disagreements over the best place to land had undermined command cohesion. The assault force was recalled even before it had begun landing.

Coote was once more scathing of both Keith and Abercromby's command during the abortive operation. 'I am sorry to observe that there appeared to me too much indecision in the minds of the Commanders-in-Chief, as well as a want of preparation for immediate landing which should have taken place,' he complained. 'It is much to be lamented that upon the expeditions we undertook we do not pay more attention to obtain the best intelligence. So many and unsuccessful attempts made upon our enemies coasts only serve to lower us in the eyes of Europe.'[56] Hely-Hutchinson, meanwhile, blamed the politicians for ordering the operation and attempting to control events at a distance. 'I think Ministers in the first place highly censurable for ordering a thing to be attempted which even if succeeded in was an object in itself contemptible.' Even had they succeeded beyond their wildest expectations, Hely-Hutchinson wrote, it would 'not have affected anything against our present most formidable foe the French'.[57] The main objective of the operation was, of course, to attrit Spanish naval resources and capabilities, but the ineptitude with which it was planned suggested substantial training was needed to remedy the problems and difficulties facing the expeditionary force.

The fiasco at Cadiz compounded many officers' feelings of frustration that the expedition as a whole lacked an objective. In London, though, a decision had been reached on what to do with this force: Dundas had finally convinced his cabinet colleagues of the need to clear the French from Egypt. In 1798, Napoleon Bonaparte had escaped from Toulon with a large invasion force, causing widespread panic throughout the Mediterranean, in the West Indies and even in Britain where it was feared an attack might be planned. His destination, however, was Egypt, and soon after his arrival and disembarkation, Admiral Horatio Nelson had trapped and destroyed the French fleet in Abukir Bay on 1 August. Whatever grand plans, realistic or otherwise, Bonaparte might have had of conquering Egypt, traversing the country and then sailing through the Red Sea for India, sank with his fleet, but he nevertheless took the opportunity to subdue the Mamelukes, and invade Palestine and Syria. Dealt a bloody nose at Acre, Bonaparte took the opportunity to escape the Middle East and return to France where he was installed as First Consul in the coup of 18 Brumaire. He left his army in control of Egypt. Now Henry Dundas took advantage of the opportunity to make use of Abercromby's expeditionary force to liberate Egypt, and eliminate one potential threat to British control of India.[58]

The decision to launch an attack on French-occupied Egypt was grounded in worrying intelligence that having repulsed the French from Syria, the Turkish army would prove unable to deliver the knockout blow. It would then be very difficult to force the French through negotiation

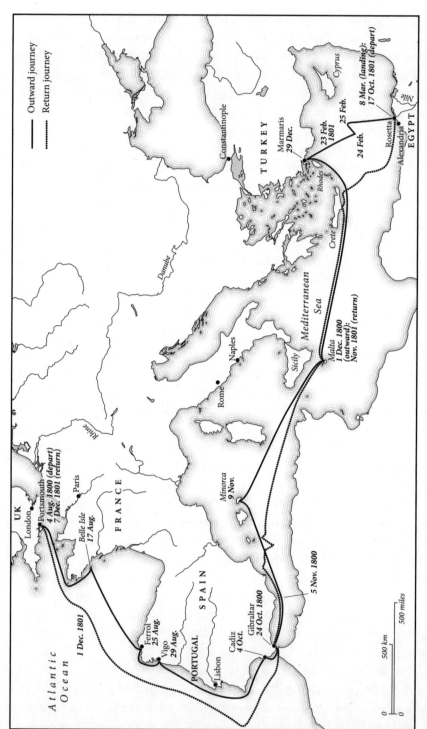

Map 11. Mediterranean Expedition, August 1800–December 1801.

alone to relinquish control of Egypt. 'It is unnecessary for me to point out … how material it is for this country to counteract the Enemy's intentions and not to rest our sole reliance for the attainment of an object so essential to our interests,' Dundas argued, 'on the chance of negotiation, or on the more precarious expectation of the struggle on the continent being ultimately decided in favour of the Allies.'[59] Dundas was essentially ceding the continental war to France, but peace could not be made if French troops remained in Egypt, where they represented a clear and present threat to the British position in India.

Dundas sent every available piece of intelligence to Abercromby, including a detailed report on the defences of Alexandria written a year earlier by the then commander of the French forces in Egypt, General Jean Baptiste Kleber, and subsequently obtained by British spies. Kleber himself had since been assassinated,[60] and succeeded by one of his divisional generals, Jacques-François Menou. On the back of this, Dundas was extremely confident of success. 'I have little doubt that with an Army of Fifteen Thousand Men, and the Command by Sea,' he wrote optimistically to Abercromby, 'it will be in your power to ensure the Surrender of the Place, as it appears impossible … that the French could bring against you such a force as would afford them the least prospect of disturbing you in the operations of the siege.'[61]

In comparison to his previous amphibious operations, then, Abercromby was extremely well informed. Meanwhile, Egypt offered a limited and contained operation. It would be very difficult for the French to get reinforcements there once the British had landed, and with the Turkish army theoretically friendly to the British, it would be relatively easy to maintain situational awareness once ashore. Dundas ordered Abercromby to make contact with the local naval commander, Sir Sydney Smith, and find the best anchorage at which to revictual, train, negotiate with the Turkish army and determine a 'Plan of attack, against the Common Enemy'. Dundas concluded, 'at this meeting you will endeavour to ascertain as nearly as possible the time at which it may be practicable and advantageous this attack should take place, and to adjust all the necessary arrangements for carrying it into execution, in concert with the Forces' of the Ottoman army.[62]

Abercromby's advance team, led by his quartermaster general, Robert Anstruther, went ahead to commence preparations. Smith recommended the secluded and sheltered Marmaris Bay on the southern coast of Turkey as a suitable location to train the force for the approaching campaign, and Abercromby, in command of an army totalling nearly 15,000 men of all arms, arrived there just after Christmas 1800.[63] The bay, sheltered as it was from the Mediterranean, offered an excellent opportunity for amphibious assault training, while preparations for the campaign were put in motion. George Murray and then Moore were dispatched to inspect the Ottoman army and decide on the best mode of cooperation. Their conclusions were not positive. 'The Turkish Empire is in fact no longer anything more substantial than a shadow,' Murray discovered. 'And of this Shadow the limbs are independent and distrustfull of each other.'[64] Smith, who had fought alongside these troops during Napoleon's invasion of Palestine and Syria, had warned that operating in conjunction with the Ottomans was 'impossible where there is no obedience, and the best among these troops (which are the Albanians) being only equal to what was called bush fighting in America, which can never be productive of any great result'.[65] The majority of the force was not in a fit state, both Murray and Moore concluded, to operate closely with the British. Instead, the Ottomans were encouraged to support the British by threatening Cairo.[66]

In total, the expeditionary force remained in the bay for six weeks, and despite the benefits an extended stay ashore had on the sick in the army, many could not escape the feeling that time was being wasted unnecessarily.[67] On 8 February, for example, 'it rained almost incessantly all the day', moaned Coote. 'Our stay in this bay is far from being serviceable to our cause.'[68] Coote had made similar remarks a few days earlier in the company of Major Christopher Hely-Hutchinson and General John Cradock. At 'dinner we had a dissertation on this expedition which', noted Hely-Hutchinson, 'would have been better withheld'.[69] Even the level-headed John Moore worried that the delay might have a detrimental impact on the operation whenever it commenced. 'Had we sailed straight from Malta to Alexandria, or after staying here a few days to water,' he wrote, 'we should certainly have taken the French unawares. They have now had time to prepare and to digest their mode of defence ....'[70]

The expedition's second-in-command, Lieutenant General Sir John Hely-Hutchinson, meanwhile, harboured similar concerns. On 9 February, he told Abercromby that he was 'strongly averse to the attempt'. In his opinion, 'with our present force there was no rational reason to hope for success'. Abercromby shared with him his orders from Dundas, and confided in him his plans once ashore, which were to divide his force in two, one to focus on Alexandria, the other to march to, besiege and take Cairo, though he did admit this seemed unlikely to succeed without reinforcements. Relieved to have raised the issue, Hely-Hutchinson admitted that he 'felt he had discharged his duty by his country and was satisfied'.[71]

Having learned from the command and control difficulties which had undermined the Cadiz operation the previous October, Abercromby adopted 'a kind of council of war' to instil collective decision making and ensure everyone with a stake in the campaign understood those decisions. The council was composed of Keith and three senior naval officers, including Smith, as well as Hely-Hutchinson, Hope, Anstruther and Moore.[72] It was decided, based on reconnaissance and spy reports, to land the army at Abukir Bay, which, though some distance from the initial objectives of the campaign, offered the best beaches for landing. The quartermaster general, meanwhile, had adopted the additional duties of intelligence gathering, reflecting the diversified nature of the department at the turn of the century. Reports on previous campaigns were distributed to help officers prepare for the challenges they faced.[73]

The time at Marmaris Bay offered the command team the opportunity to discuss the plans for the campaign and provided both soldiers and sailors with much-needed time to engage in the training which the Duke of York had been so concerned they lacked following the difficulties at Den Helder.[74] Captain Alexander Cochrane, appointed beach-master to coordinate the landings, had had time to plan the disembarkation of the troops in Abukir Bay and had liaised with Anstruther in doing so. Moreover, the troops themselves had had a rare opportunity to practise an assault landing.

On 21 January, for example, Coote's 'brigade with the reserve landed, and after having formed in line, fronting the country, and with the right towards Marmaris, re-embarked immediately. The whole', Coote commented in his diary, 'was well conducted and with very little confusion'.[75] A week earlier, part of Coote's brigade had some much-needed drill practice. On a 'fine plain' just behind the British encampment, 'sufficiently spacious to allow one or two brigades to manoeuvre at the same time', Coote 'saw the 1/54 . . . form square, four deep, at several different times, & filing from the right of companies, and afterwards forming line'.[76] Hely-Hutchinson likewise witnessed Coote's and Moore's brigades operating together. 'They landed about 11 o'clock and having formed line on the beach returned to their respective ships', noted Hely-Hutchinson in his private journal. 'I understand the whole amounted to something short of 5,000 men exclusive of seamen.'[77] The British had rarely had the opportunity to train such large numbers of soldiers in the complexities of amphibious tactics.

The six weeks spent in Marmaris Bay, then, were far from wasted. Though the French troops in Egypt were reported to be 'very tired of their conquest', severe resistance was nevertheless expected during the landing, and the subsequent campaign against Alexandria.[78] 'Every account states their number of effectives in Egypt to be about 13,000 or 14,000 French,' recorded Moore on 24 January. 'They will be able to spare 10,000 men, including the garrison of Alexandria, to act against us. Were they with this force to attempt to fight us, I should have little doubt of our success,' he continued. 'But they will probably rather employ it in harassing us, in intercepting our communications with the sea etc, and in this their superiority in cavalry will much assist them. I cannot but think the enterprise in which we are about to engage extremely hazardous and doubtful in its event.'[79] The General Orders reflected the possibility of irregular threat. The army was 'to march in columns of Brigades' while Abercromby 'gave the General Officers a certain latitude to take any advantage over the enemy without waiting'.[80]

Abercromby was sanctioning independent decision making and command, and adaptation to the circumstances presented. In this regard, his actions were in line with the experiences of his predecessors in the field, taking advantage of close-knit regimental cultures and structures. Indeed, 'bottom-up' adaptations and innovations had set the conditions for British success throughout the eighteenth century. Irregular and light infantry tactics and procedures had been adopted on an ad-hoc basis by British units in North America much earlier than the formal adoption of the system.[81] Individual regimental and battalion commanders frequently adapted training practices to better prepare their soldiers for the specific tactical challenges they faced, often making adjustments to tactical manuals. In the Bombay army, for example, musket-firing drill was modified by the inclusion of a fourth command, 'Load', in order to ensure that troops 'pause for precision'.[82]

Such practices frequently frustrated senior personnel. Cumberland complained, for example, of 'the Whim & Supposed Improvements of every fertile Genius', but the practice continued well into the nineteenth century.[83] As late as 1814, General Robert Ross added marginalia notes to his personal copy of Dundas's *Principles of Military Movement*,[84] reflecting the particular circumstances in which his forces were deployed during the campaign to capture the city of Washington during the War of 1812.[85] Soldiers in the field, meanwhile, made unsanctioned adjustments to their clothing and weaponry to suit the environmental conditions in which they fought.[86] Regimental culture, then, far from sticking rigidly to the practices prescribed by the highest echelons of the army, fostered a culture of adaptation and innovation in challenging circumstances. These relied on the accumulated military knowledge of the officers and soldiers serving in the regiment, often the product of direct experience, but frequently also the result of knowledge exchange with veterans of earlier campaigns.

Abercromby would come to rely on this military knowledge when his expeditionary force finally landed in Abukir Bay. The beach on which the troops were to land was sandy and steeply ascended from the surf, providing the French with cover and a dominating field of fire. From a 'distance of a mile and a half, the enemy opened a most tremendous & well directed fire upon our boats, and as we got closer, began to throw in showers of grape,' wrote Coote in his diary. 'Never was there a more trying moment for troops than this, exposed as they were to this galling and destructive fire, without the means of defending themselves or of returning it'.[87] For Moore, who commanded the reserve, the rain of grapeshot was just as severe. Despite this, 'as soon as the boats touched the land, the officers and men sprang out and formed on the beach ... I then ascended the sandhill with the Grenadiers and Light Infantry ... They never offered to fire until they had gained the summit, where they charged the French ...'.[88] The discipline exhibited by the troops under Moore's command stood in stark contrast with the newly raised troops he had commanded five years earlier in the West Indies.

No amount of practice could hasten the slow movement of artillery through shifting sand, however, and the French were able to escape. Abercromby was nevertheless impressed. 'It is impossible to pass over the good order in which the 23rd and the 42nd Regiments landed,' he wrote in his dispatch to Henry Dundas. 'The troops in general lost not a moment in remedying any little disorder, which became scarcely unavoidable in a landing under such circumstances.'[89] The naval support, as well, had gained Abercromby's gratitude. 'The arrangements made by Lord Keith', he wrote, 'were such as to enable us to land at once a body of six thousand men', while 'the honourable Captain Cochrane and those other captains and officers of the Royal Navy who were intrusted with the disembarkation ... have executed themselves in such a manner as to claim the warmest acknowledgement of the whole Army'.[90]

Over the next few days, Moore pushed the advanced guard of the army forward, occupying a small redoubt at Mandara. On 10 March, he performed another reconnaissance and encountered a 'considerable body of cavalry who endeavoured to push us back'. Moore was having none of it.

'As the ground was favourable to infantry, the Corsican [Rangers] were directed to disperse and post themselves,' he wrote in his diary the following day. 'By this means they forced the advanced guard of the cavalry back; but instead of being satisfied with this ... they followed the enemy, who led them close to their main body, and then turned upon them.'[91] Ten officers and men were captured, but the position at Mandara was maintained.

Meanwhile, the rest of the army moved forward to the line of the Mandara redoubt, advancing in two columns, fronted by the reserves. The training, drill and discipline instilled at Marmaris now paid dividends during the march. Moore recalled that 'though the ground over which the reserve marched was broken and intersected by brushwood and old ruins which obliged the companies frequently to file round, yet the general line was preserved, and the movement made with such steadiness that when we halted upon the new ground there was hardly any correction necessary'. This brought the enemy armies so close 'that it was evident that neither army could move without bringing on an action'.[92]

Consequently, Abercromby decided to attack the French in an attempt to turn them out of a strong defensive position, reorganising his army into five lines, with the 90th – commanded by Colonel Rowland Hill – and 92nd Regiments forming the advanced guard.[93] Hill's deputy, Major Kenneth Mackenzie, had spent considerable time and effort training the 90th as an elite light infantry unit, in all but name. The two regiments advanced quickly, and 'were attacked by the main body of the French, suffering severely before the columns [of lines] could deploy and come to their support. They, however, held their ground, and defeated a body of cavalry which attempted to charge them'.[94]

Thereafter, the rest of the army entered the fray. Coote's brigade was in the second line on the right, immediately behind Cradock's brigade. 'The object', Coote observed, 'was to turn the enemy's right, which was effected by ... Cradock's brigade in a most handsome and masterly style, forming from column into line under perhaps one of the heaviest and most destructive cannonade that was ever experienced.'[95] Moore recalled similar adversity. 'The men, though mowed down by the cannon, never lost their order,' he wrote after the battle. 'There was no period during the action or pursuit that I could not have halted the reserve and instantly wheeled to a flank without an interval.'[96] Hill was struck on the helmet by a spent musket ball which knocked him unconscious. He was later evacuated to Keith's flagship to recover.[97]

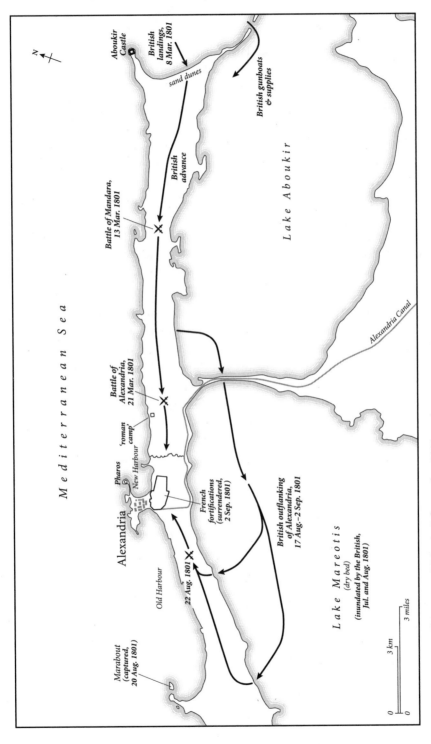

Map 12. Egyptian Campaign, 8 March–2 September 1801.

Having gained the original French position, the British force now advanced into an open plain, which was dominated by reinforced heights to the west, known as the Heights of Nicopolis. Moore realised that a direct attack on the heights would fail and halted the advance. While deliberations about whether to launch a flanking attack took place, the main body of the army came under a severe fire from French guns positioned on the heights. Coote recalled how his brigade 'remained from half past eleven until four, exposed all the time to the fire of their guns, which killed and wounded an immense number of our men'.[98] 'We were therefore destroyed by his artillery', noted Moore, 'without the power of retaliation.'[99] Abercromby, Hely-Hutchinson and Hope reconnoitred the French position and 'on finding that we were not prepared to occupy it, after it should be carried, prudence required that the troops who had behaved so bravely, and who were still willing to attempt anything however arduous, should not be exposed to a certain loss, when the extent of the advantage could not be ascertained. They were therefore withdrawn'.[100]

In the wake of the battle, Abercromby began bringing ashore heavy artillery and prepared his own dispositions for an attack on the French lines. He had occupied a position on a ridge overlooking Alexandria, with an open plain to the left, while his right was anchored on a set of Roman ruins known by the French as 'Caesar's Camp'. By 20 March, the preparations were complete and Abercromby was ready to attack at dawn the following morning.

The French beat him to it, beginning an attack on the British lines in the early hours of the 21st. 'The affair was warmest on the right and left of our position,' Murray explained to his brother. 'Menou's plan upon paper being to force these points ... and to drive the British Army into the Lake of Aboukir.'[101] The initial assault was against 'Caesar's Camp', held by Moore's reserve. Realising that if the French could drive his forces out of the ruins, the whole British line would become untenable, Moore brought up the 42nd and 23rd Regiments to reinforce the 28th and 58th, commanded by Colonel Edward Paget. It was the latter that first alerted Moore to an unexpected turning of his position. Somehow a column of French infantry had managed in the darkness and confusion to push through to the left of the ruins and form up in the British rear.

Faced with being outflanked, Moore was delighted to find elements of the 42nd had arrived. 'I ran to them,' he wrote, 'ordered them to face to the right about, and showed them the French completely in their power'. The tables were quickly turned, and every man in the French unit was killed or captured. Repeated infantry and cavalry charges were subsequently repulsed. 'There has seldom been more hard fighting,' Moore recalled. The French were stronger and their artillery was better positioned, but the British troops had 'no idea of giving way, and there cannot be a more convincing proof of the superiority of our infantry'. As daylight broke, and with ammunition for both muskets and the artillery expended, Moore could do little but place 'as many men under cover of the redoubt' as he could, such was the effect of the French artillery. 'Our artillery could not return a shot, and had their infantry again advanced we must have repelled them with the bayonet. Our fellows would have done it; I never saw men more determined to do their duty; but the French had suffered so severely that they could not get their men to make another attempt.'[102]

To the left of the ruins, meanwhile, a column of French infantry had 'made a very determined charge upon the Guards and Royals'. Once more the British infantry stood firm. With 'day breaking', recorded Coote, 'we perceived the column that had [attacked] us & which we had so warmly received retreating out of the range of our musketry'.[103] At the end of the battle, 1,361 British soldiers had been killed or wounded, including Abercromby and Moore, who had both remained at their commands having received shots in the leg; Abercromby's wound was to prove fatal. The French, meanwhile, received in the region of 4,000 casualties.[104] The battle illustrated the adaptability of the British infantry, along with the incorporation of mixed tactics to meet the challenges presented by both terrain and enemy.

After Abercromby's death, John Hely-Hutchinson took command. He now faced a difficult decision: Menou was holed up in Alexandria, but the Turks were reportedly advancing on Cairo, where a second French force, commanded by General Augustin-Daniel Belliard, was headquartered. Hely-Hutchinson had to decide whether to advance to support the Turks, and eliminate the threat Belliard clearly posed to his flank, or lay siege to and take Alexandria first. Both presented problems, and Hely-Hutchinson's meticulous analysis of them, and his equally meticulous planning when he decided to advance inland to Cairo, suggested to his detractors in the army that he lacked motivation and drive. Coote found Hely-Hutchinson's deliberations infuriating. 'Nothing can surely justify the great delay that has taken place,' he wrote in his journal. 'No, not even the most compleat success can warrant it ... The complete indolence & inactivity which has existed altogether since the 21 March, is beyond anything that can be conceived & in its consequence may be dreadful.'

Coote, open-minded though he was about light infantry, was thirsty for military victory. 'Egypt ought to have been ours a month ago', he moaned in July, 'had proper & active measures been taken.'[105] What he meant, of course, was decisive battle. Hely-Hutchinson, though, understood the wider strategic situation, and had much to consider. He was aware, unlike Coote, that Abercromby had planned to split the army, invest Alexandria and advance against Cairo, but he had no clear intelligence on the interior of Egypt.[106] 'It is vain to . . . refer you to maps,' wrote Robert Anstruther to his brother, attempting to explain the operational situation. 'There are none but what the French may now have that are not the greatest botch-pennies possible, and perfectly erroneous.'[107]

As a result of this, the British had no formed plan for the forthcoming advance. Supply lines would have to be organised and routes plotted. With Menou contained in Alexandria, Hely-Hutchinson knew that he could afford the time to plan an operation against Cairo carefully. Delaying an advance would not cede the initiative to the French, but rushing one might well knock the British off balance. There was concern, notably expressed by Keith, that French reinforcements, or an attack on the Ottoman Empire, were expected at any moment. In either event, the fleet would need to put to sea, leaving the army vulnerable.[108] When the army finally made its move, leaving a brigade under Coote, much to his annoyance, to keep an eye on Alexandria, the march was initially slow.

As the army advanced, in a move which echoed the learned experience of earlier wars, members of the Quartermaster General's Department moved 'forward to reconnoitre for the march of the army next day. Another assisted in taking up the group for the encampment. Another sketching the country'.[109] Not only did this facilitate a smooth advance, but it helped establish and maintain supply lines. Rosetta was captured on 19 April, and Rahmanieh on 9 May. Thereafter, the army could use the Nile to transport its supplies as it marched to Cairo, which was captured by capitulation on 22 June. A French garrison of no fewer than 13,000 troops, far stronger than any in the British camp had anticipated, had to be marched back to the coast for repatriation to France under the terms of their surrender. The scale of Hely-Hutchinson's success shocked many, and his critics were largely silenced. Colonel John Colborne, newly arrived from England with rein-forcements sent in the wake of the victory at Alexandria in March, remarked that Hely-Hutchinson was 'thought to have acted very politically'.[110]

Coote, however, still fumed at having been left hanging at Alexandria. The city itself lay on a narrow coastal isthmus, with the Mediterranean to the north, and the shallow Nile inundation of Lake Mareotis to the south. The British held the eastern entrance to the city, but were confronted by heavily entrenched French defensive works at the Heights of Nicopolis, which, Moore observed, were 'very formidable. Nature had made it strong, and they have added to it much by art'.[111] Coote had also long harboured concerns that the enemy had been able to bring in resupplies along the narrow neck of land to Alexandria from the west. After a reconnaissance found the French gunboats on Lake Mareotis severely undermanned, Hely-Hutchinson planned a two-front assault on Alexandria. A substantial force would move forward with siege works toward Nicopolis, while three brigades – about 4,500 men – commanded by Coote would be transported by the navy across Lake Mareotis to the western edge of Alexandria. It took until 13 August to put in place the necessary preparations, and at night on 16 August, the British made their move.

As Coote's force made their way to the western end of Alexandria, he saw that their initial landing area was heavily defended. He ordered Major General Finch, commanding the 2nd Brigade, to make a feint there, and went with the rest of the army two miles further down the coast. 'This movement perfectly succeeded and while the enemy was thus effectually kept in check,' he observed, 'I landed the remainder of our force ... without the slightest opposition.'[112] Meanwhile, Hely-Hutchinson ordered in a large demonstration at the Heights of Nicopolis to prevent Menou from rushing reinforcements to the western limits of Alexandria. This was successful, though Moore remained opposed to an all-out assault on the French lines. To the west, meanwhile, Coote was unable to move towards Alexandria without flank support from naval gunboats on both sides of the isthmus, and this was not possible until he had taken the battery on the small island of Marabout which commanded the entrance to the old harbour.

As Coote awaited two 24-pounders which were being laboriously dragged into position, by 20 August the light company of the 54th were 'placed in so advantageous a situation at the extremity of the neck of land near Marabout', Coote commented, 'that not a soul can show his head above the parapets of the fort without being fired upon. They are thus hindered from making any use of their guns against our battery, as every gunner is picked off, as soon as he appears'.[113] The following day, the British guns were in place, and by midday, the tower had been destroyed. The French garrison commander surrendered as the remaining companies of the 54th prepared to attack.

With the harbour open, British and Turkish sloops managed to gain entrance, and Coote was satisfied his flanks were secure. He 'immediately determined to move forward and take as advanced a position near the town of Alexandria as prudence & security would permit'. At daybreak on 22 August, Coote ordered his brigades to advance. In front acting as skirmishers were 150 of the rifle corps, which Hely-Hutchinson had sent over the evening before. The advance was an impressive feat of army–navy coordination. Ships of war in the harbour and gunboats on the lake coordinated with the advance to protect its flanks. Coote organised the advancing troops into three columns, with two nearer the lake shore, and a third close to the sea. Though the enemy had taken a strong position, 'the troops continued to move forward with the greatest coolness & regularity, being under a very heavy fire of cannon & musquetry ...'.[114]

The French had deployed a force of 1,200 troops on the narrowest part of the isthmus, but though they concentrated grapeshot from two batteries as well as the musket-fire of the infantry, the British advance could not be checked. 'Finding that a serious attack was intended,' noted one participant, 'and afraid of the bayonet, the enemy retired from their positions, abandoning the heavy guns.' They duly formed on a second ridge 'and maintained a galling fire of musquetry and grape'.[115] Having achieved his initial objective so easily, Coote ordered the advance to continue. 'Notwithstanding their very heavy fire,' recalled Robert Wilson, 'we drove the enemy over a space of four miles, and took post within a mile of the walls of Alexandria.'[116] Coote remained at the front for the whole advance. 'Never was there a grander or more superb spectacle than that which the affair of this morning offered,' he wrote in his journal that evening. 'The Army moving in separate & regular columns over the Isthmus, the fire of our guns and musquetry, the ships and gunboats keeping up a constant cannonade upon our right & left, & advancing gradually with our troops presented altogether with the fineness of the morning, a sight rarely to be seen & in beauty seldom to be equalled.'[117]

Some of his officers were concerned that Coote 'exposed his person as much as the most intrepid soldier of the army', and that 'he should not have done it so much',[118] but the fact remained that he felt he had 'to be as forward as possible ... that he might reconnoitre in person, ground with which every one was unacquainted'.[119] The following day, Hely-Hutchinson came over to inspect the ground. He and Coote concluded that the defensive works on the west were far weaker than at Nicopolis, so the focus of the siege shifted. With great effort, guns were brought forward to bombard the outworks of Alexandria, but were still too far away to have a material effect. On the evening of the 25th, Coote sent in the 20th Foot to capture a ridge just 600 yards from the French defences.

A night action developed after the French counterattacked, with brutal hand-to-hand fighting, at the end of which the British held the ridge.[120] By the following evening, two batteries had been built and the British were in a position to bombard the French lines from a dominating position. At Nicopolis, meanwhile, pressure was maintained with a furious bombardment. The next day, Menou asked for an armistice. Negotiations proceeded slowly, as Menou played for time in the hope of the arrival of either reinforcements or news of a general peace. Though the defences of the city were not yet compromised, and the garrison had sufficient food for maybe 30 days, morale had completely disintegrated. Defeat, they felt, was inevitable, and the terms would only get worse. On 2 September, Menou accepted what were reasonably generous conditions: he and his garrison would be evacuated with personal arms and property, and 10 pieces of artillery, back to France.[121] The liberation of Egypt from French domination had been achieved in less than six months.

*   *   *

Compared to their conduct earlier in the war, the redcoats had acquitted themselves well against an opponent that, despite achieving considerable military success, was now suffering from exhaustion and indiscipline of its own. Diarists and correspondents across the army all noted the impressive level of discipline and endurance demonstrated by the British troops, frequently while under severe fire. Historian Piers Mackesy cites this as evidence of the practical success of David Dundas's *Principles of Military Movements*, and it is hard to disagree with this conclusion. At Mandara, infantry, well formed in superior order and exhibiting, in Dundas's own words, 'regularity and weight of fire' had fended off both cavalry and infantry, while also reforming from column into line to mitigate the debilitating impact of artillery fire. 'It was the antithesis', Mackesy comments, 'of the old loose order of the "American" system.' At last, after years of failure and humiliation, caused by incompetence of command, administration and management, 'the British Army was beginning to come right'.[122]

But is this a fair or accurate conclusion? There are a number of circumstances and events during the first two weeks of the Egyptian campaign that suggest the importance of the 'American' school, rather than its decline. First, Britain had great experience of amphibious assault operations in

America and the West Indies, and Abercromby, Moore and Coote, as well as other brigade commanders in Egypt, such as John Hope, had all participated in campaigns in both theatres.[123] More importantly, during the 1790s, all had witnessed the effective use of light infantry in small-scale skirmishing actions that had an effect disproportionate to the size of the force used. As in America, the expeditionary army sent to Egypt demonstrated the value of a mixed-order formation, with soldiers fulfilling different roles on the march and in battle.

This was not implemented because of the formal adoption of a system of light infantry: indeed, the Duke of York had been forced to put on hold the creation of permanent elite light infantry units. Instead, the officers making decisions during operational planning and in battle itself either had direct experience of the use and effectiveness of light infantry and troops trained to perform multiple roles, or had learned of it through the exchange of military knowledge from elsewhere in the army, and had modified this knowledge for application in different scenarios. This new and remade knowledge had been derived from Britain's global experience of war in the eighteenth century. The successful informal application of new military knowledge, and with it, the triumph of the British Army in the expedition to Egypt cleared the way for the formal adoption of many of the adaptations and innovations employed during the campaign.

CHAPTER 10

The 'Universal Soldier'

SHORNCLIFFE AND THE LIGHT DIVISION, 1803–1812

I N May 1811, Ensign Thomas Mitchell, newly commissioned in the 95th Rifles, arrived in Portugal. In some ways, Mitchell represented what had been dubbed 'the universal soldier'.[1] Trained to perform regular infantry line duties, these members of the light infantry were also capable of more specialist skirmishing, reconnaissance and intelligence-collection duties. Mitchell was a case in point. A subaltern in the 95th with a thirst for knowledge of his profession, Mitchell had read widely before his deployment, including Henry Lloyd's *Philosophy of War*, from which he had extracted several maxims on the use of light infantry, and more general observations on the conduct of war.[2]

Mitchell had immersed himself in the military history of the British and European armies, had studied in some depth the campaigns of Marlborough and Frederick the Great and had attempted to link these to lessons pertinent to contemporary warfare. He used Lloyd's writings to frame these lessons. The concept of a 'universal soldier' was something Lloyd had alluded to, and which Mitchell picked up on in his notes. Worried about the 'imperfections' – inaccuracy and unreliability – of firearms, Lloyd recommended that a 'certain number of men should be armed with pikes'. Though he missed the mark with the choice of weapon, Lloyd was nevertheless alluding to the centrality of the bayonet to British tactical doctrine. 'This alone', Mitchell noted in his annotations of Lloyd, 'can enable us to form a number of men so that they shall have strength to resist the shock of an enemy, Horse & foot, & to act in every kind of ground with equal advantage.' The modern soldier 'must combine & unite the solidity of hand weapons with the advantage of firearms'.[3]

In the wake of the failures of the 1790s and the success of the campaign in Egypt, it became clear that the British Army needed to re-evaluate its order of battle. The Frederician tactics employed during the early campaigns against Revolutionary France had proved of limited value. They were central to success in conventional battle but were vulnerable to the expansion of the French light infantry arm. The British Army had been experimenting informally with the use of light infantry for decades, inspired by the experience of wilderness warfare in North America. Units had been formed from flank companies of regular battalions for special assignments, but the assumption had always been that those troops had limited utility, and once they had achieved their objectives, they were returned to their parent regiments. Moreover, the assumption remained that light infantry was only of use in the complex terrain of North America. Any attempt to import the concept to the regular order of the British Army was treated with derision.

Nevertheless, as had been seen in the campaign in Egypt, the military knowledge acquired in North America had been communicated across the army through personal, professional and regimental networks. Recent campaigns had not only illustrated the wider utility of irregular troops and light infantry discipline, but had demonstrated that the British Army was willing to adapt and adopt those tactics and techniques to meet new challenges. As the war continued with seemingly no end in sight, a variety of factors prompted the transformation of informal responses to the challenges presented by Revolutionary and Napoleonic France into formal, permanent solutions. The network of officers that made this happen had experience of warfare across the world, and the increased drive for the formalisation of these ideas resulted from those combined experiences. Soldiers like Thomas Mitchell were the eventual product of this process.

*   *   *

Deeply passionate about the profession of arms, from the outset of his appointment as commander-in-chief, the Duke of York was at the heart of the reform and modernisation of the British Army. His position enabled him to formalise the innovations and adaptations which officers and soldiers had adopted on an informal basis, many over the course of decades of military service. Having been educated in Prussia in the early 1780s, York had witnessed the famed military encampments of the Prussian army, at which modern and complex infantry tactics and discipline were impressively demonstrated. In May 1783, while visiting the elderly Frederick the Great at Berlin, York participated in the royal review of the Prussian army and observed the organisation of Prussian units, including the intense training regimen that each infantryman underwent. 'The Prussians never put a man into the rank til he has been a whole twelve months at the drill square,' York noted, during 'which time he is not allowed to receive a single visitor,' As a result, 'the order and discipline of them is ... very surprising, and one Regiment is so exactly like the other, that it strikes one very much'.

York also commented on the disciplinarian nature of the training regimen. 'During the exercises,' he wrote, 'you never saw a single blow given, the first serjeant of each company ... stands in the rear of the company and marks down each fault that is committed, those men who have made these faults are ... thoroughly thrashed.' Nevertheless, the soldiers were, in York's view, also treated very fairly. Noncommissioned officers were 'obliged to see that the men are properly fed and indeed it is wonderful the level of health which all the regiments have.... They seldom exercise more than two hours, by which means the men are never fatigued'. York was also clearly impressed by the focus on marksmanship. 'They are obliged to load and fire six times,' he observed to his father. 'They always say what is certainly very true that a man who knows how to fire fast can always make his fire slow, but that upon many occasions firing fast is very necessary particularly against cavalry, so that was done with regularity.'[4]

York continued to visit military encampments across Germany throughout his military education. In October 1785, while in Silesia, he admired the tactical acumen of the Prussian infantry. 'The nine and twenty Battalions marched in one line which never was attempted before and I suppose never will be again,' he wrote in some amazement to his father. 'The distance from one wing to the other was seven thousand six hundred and fifty six paces. It succeeded surprisingly well.'[5] Also present at the Prussian encampment in Silesia was Colonel David Dundas, who was at this time putting the finishing touches to his soon-to-be-published *Principles of Military Movements*.[6] He used descriptions of the manoeuvres performed at this encampment to illustrate the infantry drill he was proposing for the British Army, including the same manoeuvre that York had witnessed. 'The line of infantry of 11,000 men supported by 15 squadrons of Cavalry (each covering a Battalion) in 2 lines, and 10 squadrons on each flank', Dundas described. 'When about 600 yards from an Enemy, advanced to attack from the left in 4 echelons retired about 150 paces behind each other. The attack being repulsed, the Echelons fell back upon one another and upon the Right Flank which had remained on a favourable height.'[7]

Dundas based his *Principles* on his considerable 'service of many years in varied situations, of much regimental experience and of five campaigns in the war of 1760'.[8] He had spent years researching the work, studying the drill, tactics, techniques and procedures of European armies. In 1774, he toured the garrisons of the Low Countries, the lower Rhineland and northern France. He took detailed notes on the system of drill used by Austrian regiments based in Brussels, as well as the Prussian battalions based at Wesel. He studied the Dutch garrisons of Maastricht, Namur, Nijmegen, The Hague and Bergen op Zoom, as well as French practices at Metz and Lille. Along the way, he also found time to visit some of the nearby battlefields of the Seven Years War.[9] An abridged version of Dundas's *Principles* was adopted by George III in 1792 as the standard drill manual of all infantry battalions in the British Army. This represented the primacy of the European school of close-order infantry tactics over the American preference for loose order and flexibility. The adoption, however, of Dundas's *Principles* did not, as some of his critics have suggested, embody the 'Prussification' of the British Army.[10]

Indeed, Dundas was well aware of the utility of American ideas, as he had witnessed when he served in the West Indies during the siege of Havana in 1762. During an attempt by the British to seize a crucial position, the Spanish counterattacked with a cavalry charge. The British troops, which included a battalion of light infantry, 'with the greatest steadiness and presence of mind had faced about, wheeled forward, were in 2 lines, and in readiness to give them a fire of 500 muskets at a distance of 60 yards', Dundas recorded in a memorandum of the campaign. 'This checked their career, they ceased to advance, the troops reloaded, recommenced a fire, and the enemy went back as fast as they came.' The position fell to the British, but Dundas remained concerned that

> had this cavalry not pulled up, but persevered in the attack, that they would have discomfited this corps, which would have led to serious consequences in the beginning of our enterprise, for half the men (the light infantry) had left their bayonets on board ship; accustomed only to act in the woods, they never dreamt of such advantage in open ground.[11]

In making this observation, Dundas perceived the light infantry to be adding limitations rather than flexibility to the regular order of battle.

Instead, Dundas believed that light infantry should be 'considered as an accessory to the battalion', not 'the principal feature of our army'. Indeed, he was of the view that, while 'during the late war' in America, 'their service was conspicuous, and their gallantry and exertions have met with merited applause', the increasing centrality of the concept of light infantry to the British regiment since had contributed to the 'adopt[ion] of such partial methods as seem to each [regiment] convenient', which now meant there was 'no proper system laid down' for the army as a whole. His *Principles* was designed to remedy this problem. For Dundas, 'the showy exercise, the airy dress, the independent modes which' the light infantry 'have adopted, have caught the minds of young officers, and made them imagine that these ought to be general and exclusive'. As he wrote in the introduction to his book: 'The battalions, constantly drained of their best men, have been taught to undervalue themselves, almost to forget that on their steadiness and efforts, the decision of events depends, and that light infantry – yagers – marksmen – riflemen &c. &c. vanish before the solid movements of the line.'[12] Unsurprisingly, Dundas believed that this approach had hindered the training of the heavy infantry, on which the security of the army in a European battle would inevitably depend.[13]

The result was a 'very thin and extended order to make more show; an affected extreme of quickness on all occasions ... the forming and breaking on the move, the easier to cover and conceal lost distances and accidental lines, which otherwise would be apparent ... the different and false composition of columns'. With most infantry units trained to form two ranks rather than three, 'all idea of solidity seems lost'. In such circumstances, the British infantry would be unable 'to attack or repulse a determined enemy, but only to annoy a timid and irregular one'.[14] The insinuation was clear: the British infantry of the 1780s might be able to hold its own tactically against the asymmetric threat posed by adversaries in North America, but against the massed infantry and cavalry of a continental foe – the French – defeat beckoned. Towards the end of the first edition of *Principles*, Dundas appended his own brief sketch of the course of the Seven Years War in Europe. In his short description of Minden, Dundas noted how the British infantry 'highly distinguished themselves in withstanding and repelling the repeated attacks of the enemy's cavalry'.[15] Such a victory, Dundas implied, was impossible nearly three decades later.

Having visited Minden himself, York could not have failed to agree. It is unclear whether Dundas and York met while both were at the Prussian encampment in Silesia, but by the time the latter was commander-in-chief of the British Army, he was an advocate of Dundas's arguments. These, of course, had been written before the full effects of the so-called revolutionary approach to war practised by the French in the early 1790s had come fully to light. York and Dundas served together in Flanders 1793–1795, and York considered Dundas as 'a most excellent officer'.[16] By 1795, York had instituted a regular regimen of battalion inspections up and down the country. It was apparent that the 1792 edict to adopt Dundas's *Principles* as the standard drill manual across the army had not been universally observed. York therefore ordered that they were to be 'strictly followed . . . without any deviation whatever', with 'the essential purpose' being the promotion of 'Uniformity in the Discipline of the Troops'. Imposing some of the ideas he had witnessed employed to such great effect in Prussia, York demanded that 'Monday and Friday in every week' be devoted to battalion drill training, while on Tuesdays and Saturdays the troops were to be exercised 'by brigades'. Wednesdays would see the commanding general 'take out the whole Line, and make them perform such Movements, Manoeuvres or other Exercises as he may think proper'; while 'Thursday is to be set apart as a day of Repose for the whole'.[17]

York was also conscious that to be successfully taught across the army, junior officers – those responsible for instilling this discipline in the soldiers – would need to understand fully the 18 separate movements into which Dundas had distilled his *Principles*. To this end, York supported innovative endeavours to help educate those officers, including the creation of a set of 'Military Figures for the Practice of Tacticks'.[18] Easily mistaken for a children's toy, the 'Military Figures' came with an instruction booklet and consisted of eight regular companies, and one each of light infantry and grenadiers.

It was the author's hope that by using the figures to practise the drill manoeuvres, young officers 'will become expert in the business when in the field of exercise'.[19] Officially patronised by the Duke of York, the instructions offered readers the means to understand different battalion formations, and the 18 manoeuvres in their own time. As a means of knowledge transmission, the Military Figures offered a more portable medium than could be achieved in the drill square, and a more practical application than a book. It is unclear how many boxes were produced, but it appears the Figures were popular in the British Army as well as among its competitors. Reference to a set can be found in the correspondence of George Washington, and a complete set can be found in the military archive of General Henry Burbeck, an American artillery officer who served in the Revolutionary War.[20]

Even with such innovations, it was also evident from the experience of the Flanders campaign that, despite Dundas's prognostications, the Prussian approach on its own would not meet the challenge posed by the French, and that consideration would need to be given to the formation of permanent light infantry units. Part of the problem was the temporary nature of these units. Since the Seven Years' War, the British had formed elite battalions from the flank companies of regular regiments.[21] These had frequently played decisive roles in battlefield victories, but their formation denuded the regular regiments of the elite companies, demoralised the men and undermined cohesion. Moreover, the temporary formations were disbanded the moment they were no longer needed, preventing the development of any enduring esprit de corps.[22] In 1799, the military theorist General John Money argued that

> it is to this new system of bringing more Irregulars into the field than their opponents, that the French owe chiefly their success ... Let us learn to fight them by land in the manner they have found out and adopted; never let us be above or ashamed following the example of an enemy, when we see it is a good one.[23]

Indeed, after 'observing the superiority of the French system' when he returned to the Low Countries in 1799, York 'resolved to introduce ... the rifle practice into the British service'.[24] General John Moore was very supportive of the incorporation of light troops into the order of battle of the British Army. In 1798, he devised a brief drill manual for Irish militia trained as light infantry, and also advocated on behalf of the Corsican Rangers.[25] This unit had proven crucial during the Egyptian campaign, and were, in Moore's words, 'better adapted to the service of light troops than any, I shall venture to say, that we shall have. The Corsicans are naturally attached to the English. They are brave, intelligent and faithful'.[26] The decision to deploy the British expeditionary force to the Mediterranean in 1800 and on to Egypt in 1801 delayed these innovations, but the resulting campaign not only illustrated that the redcoats could master the rigid discipline of the Prussian system, but that they could implement loose-order tactics simultaneously to achieve a decisive advantage.[27]

* * *

Following his return from Egypt, and the end of the French Revolutionary War with the Peace of Amiens in 1802, General Moore was appointed to

command the Southern Military District of England, which was a position of some importance. In 1803, relations with France deteriorated and
war inevitably resumed. Napoleon assembled a vast army in the vicinity of
Boulogne, with the apparent express intention of embarking on a cross-
channel invasion. Moore, therefore, needed to prepare for the possible
descent of French forces, and he was concerned that the countryside of
southern England would play into the hands of the now-infamous French
light troops, the *tirailleurs*. One defence planner described Kent, Sussex
and Hampshire as 'so destitute of open plains and cut up by countless
hedges that' they were 'all so many impediments'.[28] York decided it was
essential to augment the numbers of trained skirmishers and light infantry
in the army, and consulted Moore on how best to achieve this aim.[29]

Moore was ideally placed, then, to implement a key reform which York
had become convinced was essential to the future of the British Army. At
Moore's fingertips was the latest modern thinking on light infantry tactics
and discipline, but he also drew on the rich history of informal light
infantry development in the British Army. The decision was taken to
convert the 52nd 'Oxfordshire' Foot into a battalion of light infantry. Moore
identified 'from sixty to seventy men who ought to be discharged, under the
Heads of Old, Short & Weak'. Of the remainder, there were those who 'may
be best selected from the two Battalions of the 52nd Regt so as to form one
Corps fit for the Service of Light Infantry', which would leave 'a body of
men fit for the Service of the Line'. In their stead, Moore wanted 'from the
96th, an equal number of Light Infantry, & men who, without being tall,
were young and active'. In his view, the 'Service of Light Infantry does not
so much require Men of Stature, as it requires them to be Intelligent, Hardy,
& Active and they should, in the first instance, be young, or they will
neither take to the Service, nor be easily instructed in it'.[30]

The precise nature of that instruction was yet to be decided, but as had
been the case for British light infantry in America, the men 'should be
practiced as marksmen, with the usual muskets, and instructed both in
light infantry manoeuvres and also to act when required as a firm
battalion'.[31] This would allow the army to maximise the skills and
attributes of all the soldiers in the army, as there were 'short active men
who act to great disadvantage when placed in the Centre of the Battalion
at Close Order, but are equally good, if not better, than the tallest men, to
skirmish & sharp shoot'.[32] This was likewise an approach favoured by
York, who, in May 1791, had been particularly impressed by the light
infantry in the Duke of Magdeburg's army. These 'very small men, know

perfectly the Light Infantry exercise, and at the same time can act in Line as well as any other Battalion'.[33] York was keen for the units he now designated as light infantry in the British Army to be trained in the same manner, an objective duly echoed by the instructions devised for light infantry training, which insisted that 'before the soldier is instructed in the manoeuvres of light troops, he must be taught how to hold himself, to mark, face, wheel etc. as in regular infantry'.[34]

In June 1803, the 52nd was ordered to relocate to Shorncliffe in Kent. A month later, York designated the 43rd 'Monmouthshire' Regiment the second permanent light infantry unit,[35] though they did not relocate to Shorncliffe for another year. Along with the Experimental Rifle Corps, the two new light infantry units made Shorncliffe the principal training camp for light infantry and skirmishers. The Rifle Corps had initially been proposed by Lieutenant-Colonel William Stewart, who, while attached to the Austrian headquarters as an observer, had witnessed the successful use of rifles during the 1799 Italian campaign.[36] Enthusiastic as ever for innovative ideas, York invited comment from across the army. 'The D[uke] of Y[ork] has ... asked my opinion on the formation of a corps of riflemen of 600 or 800 men in this country,' noted Cornwallis in February 1800, 'to be taken either from the Line or the Fencibles.' Worried about the impact on cohesion and effectiveness, Cornwallis recommended that 'only a tenth part of the corps should be armed with rifles, and that the others should be trained as light infantry'.[37]

Cornwallis was not alone in having reservations about the adoption of rifled weapons in the British Army. Weapons of greater complexity, they required more training to be used properly, and, though much more accurate, could not be fired at the same rate as the musket. As a result, riflemen caught in the open while reloading were extremely vulnerable to musketfire and the bayonet. One commentator noted, for example, the casualties sustained by American Daniel Morgan's riflemen at the hands of Robert Abercromby's bayonet-wielding infantry during the 1778 retreat from Philadelphia.[38] York initially considered the unit to be 'a Corps of Experiment and Instruction', though he believed that 'the progress it cannot fail to make ... will ensure a similar one being formed on a permanent footing'.[39]

Colonel Coote Manningham was appointed to command, with Stewart acting as Lieutenant Colonel. Like Stewart, Manningham had experienced the utility of light infantry, as well as the need for superior marksmanship when both had served in the West Indies. Orders were sent to 14 regiments of the line, requiring each of them to furnish four noncommissioned officers and 30 privates for training in the use of rifles and associated tactics and drill. They were to select 'such men as appear most capable of receiving ... instructions and most competent to the performance of the Duty of Riflemen'.[40] Initially, and perhaps inevitably, the regimental colonels took the opportunity to get rid of the worst men in their units, and it was not until the end of April 1800 that Manningham and Stewart were satisfied with the composition of the new unit. Their soldiers would be armed with the new Pattern Infantry Rifle, known as the 'Baker Rifle', designed by Ezekiel Baker after an experimental trial conducted by the Board of Ordnance at Woolwich Arsenal in February 1800.[41]

Training and education commenced at an encampment in Horsham before being relocated to Blatchington in Sussex. Despite York's continued reluctance to add the unit to the permanent order of battle, by April 1802, Manningham and Stewart were granted the authority to recruit soldiers directly into what was now the 95th Rifles. In late 1802, as he discussed retraining the 52nd as light infantry, Moore contacted Stewart with orders to march the 95th to Shorncliffe, where, he hoped, the encampment could be 'adapted, both to your Target practice and Field Movements'.[42] In late 1804, second battalions of the 43rd, 52nd and 95th were raised, joining the corps at Shorncliffe in early 1805.

The final unit brought to Shorncliffe was the 5th Battalion 60th Foot, the Royal American Regiment. Formed in 1797 from the several independent German units serving within the British Army, including Hompesch's *Jägers*, the 5/60th was dressed in green and equipped with rifles. It was commanded by Baron Francis de Rottenburg, a German soldier who had served in the French and Russian armies, before becoming a *Jäger* and deploying to the West Indies in the 1790s. In 1798, Rottenburg published *Regulations for the Exercise of Riflemen and Light Infantry*, translated at the Duke of York's request into English by the Adjutant General Sir William Fawcett. The *Regulations* proved to be one of the definitive training manuals for British light infantry, as a mixture of the latest thinking and experience, combined with the influence of decades of history. Rottenburg was most notably influenced by Johann von Ewald, a Hessian officer who had served under William Howe's command in the American Revolutionary War, as well as the more recent writings of French theorist Jacques Antoine Hippolyte, Comte de Guibert.[43]

Once regular infantry drill had been mastered, the focus shifted to the specific skills that defined the light infantry. Like his predecessors who had fought in wars across three continents over the last five decades, the nineteenth-century British light infantry soldier needed to learn to 'never fire without being sure of his man'.[44] Marksmanship training was central to Rottenburg's discipline, with the use of targets and competition for 'amusement in this practice'.[45] In this respect, Rottenburg's training regimen echoed the views of earlier theorists. Henry Lloyd, for example, argued that, while the regular battalions were 'to fire by ranks, the light troops' were to be formed 'obliquely along the enemy's line, choosing their time and object'.[46] Thereafter, soldiers were trained in basic skirmishing and light infantry drill, including a uniform way of extending frontage in order to cover the regular line.

Conscious of the vulnerability riflemen experienced in the field and learning from experiences during the American Revolutionary War, Rottenburg also insisted that at least one of the two soldiers in any file was ready to fire at any given moment, while 'never more than half a body of riflemen must be sent forward to skirmish, the other half remain formed and ready to support'.[47] The rest of the tactical system was based on these components, with instructions on how to conduct surveillance and reconnaissance, how to guard against surprise and how to manoeuvre in battle.[48] Rottenburg's *Regulations* were necessarily focused on the tactical application of the light infantry, but as had been seen throughout Britain's wars in North America, the arm offered advantages in the wider execution of a campaign. For advice on the operational utility of the light infantry, York ordered for distribution 'a small treatise upon the duties of officers of Light Infantry drawn up by General Jarré which appears to me to contain such very useful instructions'.[49]

The treatise in question was the *Instruction Concerning the Duties of Light Infantry in the Field*, by General François Jarry, a French émigré who had escaped with the British during the 1795 evacuation. The *Instructions* contained extensive discussions of *petite guerre* operations, including outpost duties, intelligence collection and surveillance and reconnaissance methods, as well as a wider discussion on the role light infantry were to play in regular operations. In Jarry's view, the role of light infantry was to protect the army, by giving 'timely warning' of an attack, and to keep as many options open as possible. Jarry recommended occupying churches, which were at the centre of many villages, and thus controlled 'the roads which lead into the village from the side of the enemy, as well as to the road which leads in a direct line to the camp'.[50] Controlling communications hubs and road networks would deny the enemy the operational initiative. Reconnaissance of the local terrain was essential to facilitate planning for all eventualities.

When battle was joined, light infantry were to be used to attack the enemy's flank. 'It is particularly by contriving to penetrate, by stealth, through neglected parts', wrote Jarry, 'that light infantry can ... contribute, materially, to the success of regular attacks, made in front by the troops of the line.'[51] In all circumstances, familiarity with the ground, with the commanders' plans and with the capabilities of the soldiers was necessary; in short, 'to study attentively every part of the service, which concerns the safety of an army'.[52] Like Rottenburg, Jarry was not only influenced by Guibert and von Ewald, but also borrowed from the theories of Henry Lloyd, who saw light infantry as a central and crucial element of a balanced regular force, and one which offered vital and decisive operational flexibility.[53] This was a theme that would be emphasised strongly at Shorncliffe, where the new system of training and education represented a marked change to the methods employed more generally in the British Army.

Rottenburg adopted a more enlightened approach to discipline, seeking to instil an esprit de corps. Preferring reward and positive reinforcement to punishment, he introduced a meritocratic system, which saw the finest marksmen rewarded. He avoided flogging his men, instituted a regular exercise regime and insisted on good hygiene. Jarry likewise believed that 'though the good will of the men is not to be obtained by the sacrifice of discipline ... the best manner of gaining the affections of the soldiers ... is by providing carefully for their wants'.[54] Rottenburg set an example by his own actions, and commanded his men in a 'patriarchal manner, more as a father would his children'.[55]

Rottenburg permitted men to choose their partners, fostering a sense of trust between the two soldiers in each file, which was particularly important given how closely these individuals would have to work together.[56] The light infantry officer, meanwhile, was encouraged 'to obtain a thorough individual knowledge of the men under his command, that he may employ them according to their intelligence and courage'.[57] This was the only way, both Rottenburg and Jarry believed, that the men would learn to operate in isolated detachments, where they were dependent on their own initiative. In such circumstances, in Jarry's words, 'everything that he wants he must find in himself, and, in many perilous situations of that so often insulated service, bravery, united to military knowledge, can alone extricate him with honour'.[58] Stewart adopted similar approaches, using history to illustrate the utility of professional knowledge. 'It has invariably been the object of great commanders to mingle authority with lenity, to inspire their troops with confidence in their own capacity, to call forth their enthusiasm, and to create a common feeling between the officer and the soldier. Upon these principles', Stewart wrote, 'Frederick, Suvarrov and the great Nelson acted ....'[59]

Coote Manningham, meanwhile, delivered a series of lectures in 1803 to the officers of the 95th, much of which was not only based on the writings of Rottenburg and Jarry, but also drew on recent historical experiences, notably from the American Revolutionary War, and Manningham's own experience in the West Indies.[60] This led Manningham to the conclusion that the light infantry officer needed to understand all levels of war in order to prosecute his role effectively. Echoing Jarry in particular, Manningham argued that in addition to an unimpeachable knowledge of the tactics, techniques and procedures of the light infantry, the officers should also understand how these 'are intimately connected with the grand operations of war'.[61] Therefore, the written work and training curriculum at Shorncliffe offered a combination of experience, innovation and theory, which, John Moore hoped, would help create a corps of light infantry capable of independent action, providing close support to regular infantry, and that promised to be an important addition to the regular order of battle.

When devising instructions for the unit of light infantry he trained as part of the Irish militia in 1798 and 1799, Moore attested to this multirole function, which he saw as unique to the British Army. 'Light infantry in the British service is a species of troops different to the light troops of every other nation', he wrote in the preamble to his drill instructions. European light infantry units 'seldom act in line', he continued, 'and are so little expected to use the bayonet, that it is not even given to them'. In contrast, British light infantry 'not only are employed as Yagers, but act in line and are selected upon every occasion to head attacks when enterprise, activity, and courage are peculiarly required. They are in fact a mixture of the Yager, and the Grenadier. Their discipline should therefore be adapted to the various service in which they are employed.' And so 'their first drill and instruction should, I conceive, be the same as that of the infantry. They should be confirmed in the exercise and movements of regular battalions, before they are taught those of any other'. Indeed, bespoke light infantry training should only commence 'when the men appear sufficiently expert at the other'.[62]

Unsurprisingly, Moore was eager that like-minded officers should promote these ideas at Shorncliffe, and draw together the range of knowledge and experience of theorists like Rottenburg and Jarry. In addition to Manningham and Stewart, then, Moore requested the appointment of Lieutenant Colonel Kenneth Mackenzie to command the 52nd at Shorncliffe.[63] Having joined the army in 1780, Mackenzie had seen extensive service in the West Indies, and then in 1794 joined Thomas Graham's newly raised 90th Regiment (dubbed the 'Perthshire Light Infantry') where he trained the corps in the methods of irregular and light infantry tactics he had learned by experience in the West Indies. In 1796, he became Sir Charles Stuart's adjutant-general during the campaign to retain Minorca, before volunteering for service in Egypt. There, his training and reorganisation of the 90th Regiment had particularly impressed Moore. He was therefore well placed to complement the training and education offered by Manningham and Stewart and offer a bespoke programme of learning for officers and soldiers in the 52nd and later the 43rd Light Infantry.

Moore 'never met with anyone so perfectly qualify'd to instruct officers and men in every part of his duty', whether in regular or irregular tactics, 'or as to steadiness and intelligence in the looser order requir'd of Tirailleurs ...'.[64] Soon after his arrival at Shorncliffe, he introduced an improved system of marching, platoon exercise and drill.[65] For Mackenzie, as well, universal understanding and knowledge were essential to success. 'The only way of having a regiment in good order was by every individual thoroughly knowing and performing his duty; and that if officers did not fully understand their duty, it would be quite impossible to expect that the men either could or would perform theirs as they ought,' Mackenzie reflected. He therefore advocated training officers first 'and when they became perfectly acquainted with the system, they could teach the men ...'.[66] He referred to this as the 'internal and moral system'.[67]

By the summer of 1804, Mackenzie had devised a new system of light movements and drill, which he expected officers to know inside out. 'The officer ... was not considered clear' recalled Captain Cooke of the 43rd, 'until he could put a company through the evolutions by word of command ... It generally took him six months ... at four times a day (an hour at each period) to perfect him and all he had to learn.'[68] Officers were also expected to know their men and be at all times respectful and considerate of their needs. 'The great thing that Sir John Moore and Colonel Mackenzie used to impress upon the minds of the officers was that our duty was to do everything in our power to prevent crime, as then there would be no occasion for punishment ....'[69] Training and drill were practised regularly. 'The corps paraded twice a week in heavy marching order,' noted Cooke, 'and the mess was equally well conducted, in a system of style and economy happily blended.'[70]

Specific marching techniques, designed to keep units moving swiftly for long periods of time, were also developed by Mackenzie. 'All flourishing of the feet and extreme distress of the knees are expressly prohibited as tending to render the body unsteady.'[71] The new instructions suggested that 'stiffness of the knees' would result in 'stamping against the ground'. This was to be avoided as 'highly improper'.[72] Instead, 'the feet should be brought down without any exertion, or straining or knocking against the ground, which may tend to shake the body'. It was 'better to practice them in an easy and steady, though perhaps not elegant, mode of marching', recorded one officer of the 52nd in his pocketbook.[73] By reducing the strain of heavy marching, the new techniques increased the speed of manoeuvre of the new light infantry units. The combination of these developments produced the most disciplined corps in the army. As a result, the Shorncliffe light regiments had 'the admiration of all, for their discipline, and the rapidity of their light movements ....'.[74]

In addition, like his colleagues at Shorncliffe, Mackenzie emphasised the importance of regular marksmanship training.[75] An adapted version of the musket, to help facilitate aimed fire, was trialled for use by the 52nd.[76] 'The Barrel' of this weapon 'shall be browned, a grooved sight shall be fixed at the breech end of the barrel, and a canvas cover, similar to that used by the Austrian troops, shall be provided for the purpose of covering and protecting the Butt and the Lock of each piece.'[77] Echoing George Howe's 1758 adaptations in North America, and though heavier than the Brown Bess, the new design musket was easier to aim, and the trial was successful.[78]

So successful was the training and education established at Shorncliffe, that in 1808 the 68th and 85th Regiments were also converted to light infantry, and 'assimilated with regard to their clothing, arming and Discipline to the 43rd and 52nd Regiments'.[79] The Light Infantry training programme overseen by Moore, and developed and implemented by Manningham, Stewart and Mackenzie, was the product both of the latest thinking on irregular tactics and of military historical experience, passed through knowledge networks within the British Army. All three had served for considerable periods with those with direct experience of light infantry developments stretching back to the French and Indian Wars. The power of informal knowledge exchange was therefore at least as important as contemporary experience in establishing new tactics and doctrine. Innovations and adaptations, such as the new approaches to discipline and the changes to marching styles, were clearly the result of military education and reactions to personal experience in the West Indies. The notion of a universal soldier, capable of fighting successfully in the line, as a skirmisher and in the light infantry role, was hardly new, however. James Wolfe,

George Howe and Jeffrey Amherst had all advocated for and implemented such innovations during their time in America, while William Howe, John Burgoyne, Henry Clinton and Charles Cornwallis had adopted similar arguments during their commands. Cornwallis, meanwhile, had been involved with several weapon adaptations that foreshadowed the suggested modifications put forward by Mackenzie.[80]

*   *   *

The conversion of two new light infantry battalions was ordered as a result of British intervention in the Iberian Peninsula. The French had invaded Portugal in 1807, and then attempted to extend control over Spain the following year. This had catalysed a widespread but fragmented rebellion. Four companies of the 2/95th, along with Rottenburg's 5/60th, were sent in a small expeditionary force under Major General Sir Arthur Wellesley to do what it could to support the Portuguese. The army got ashore unopposed at Figueira da Foz in the first week of August and marched south to confront the French forces under General Jean-Andoche Junot. At a minor action at Roliça on 17 August, in which the riflemen of the 5/60th and 95th moved 'on in extended order, under whatever cover the nature of the ground afforded',[81] Wellesley dealt the French a bloody nose. On 21 August, he fought and defeated Junot at Vimeiro, having received reinforcements, including the second battalions of the 43rd and 52nd the day before.

With those reinforcements came Wellesley's relief: he was too junior to command such a large force. The new commanders, Sir Hew Dalrymple and Harry Burrard, refused to pursue the retreating enemy and instead negotiated a humiliating convention at Cintra, under the terms of which Junot's entire army was returned to France, along with its arms and booty. Amid uproar in England, Dalrymple and Burrard were recalled to face a court of enquiry. Wellesley went with them to answer questions about his role in the affair, leaving the expedition under the command of General Sir John Moore, who had arrived with further reinforcements after a failed military assistance operation in Sweden.

Facing political pressure to act, and with the French army surprisingly in retreat behind the river Ebro in north-east Spain after a series of unexpected defeats at the hands of the Spanish, Moore felt compelled to move forward to strike a blow in conjunction with Britain's new allies. He reorganised his army into brigades, including, for the first time, a light brigade, under the command of General Robert Craufurd, which was composed of the 5/60th, and the second battalions of the 43rd, 52nd and 95th. Moving

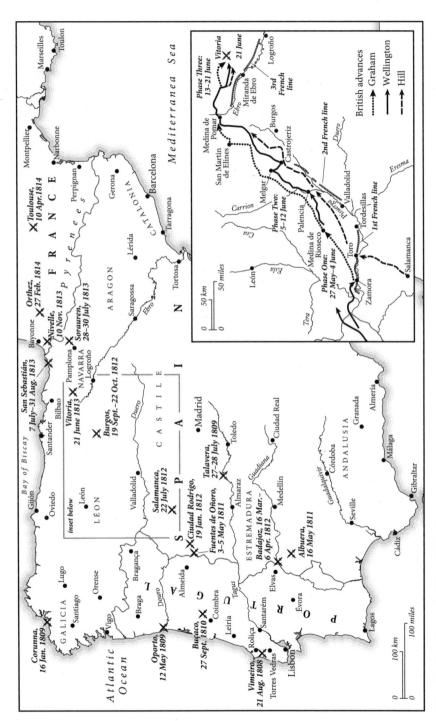

Map 13. The Peninsular War, 1808–1814.

in two columns towards Salamanca and then on toward Valladolid and Burgos, Moore was wrong-footed when the arrival of massive reinforcements under Napoleon's personal command swept aside the Spanish army under the command of General Francisco Javier Castaños and retook Madrid.[82] With his southern flank now threatened, Moore was forced to retreat. 'To the sensible mortification of the whole army, the following morning commenced a retreat which in point of fatigue and privation and hardship stands almost without a parallel in the military annals of Britain,' recorded Henry Clinton, son of the American veteran, on 23 December.[83]

The army withdrew in bitter winter conditions. By marching hard and fast, Moore managed to keep his army ahead of the French. 'Many ... would have straggled from the ranks, and perished, had not Craufurd held them together with a firm rein,' recalled Rifleman Benjamin Harris of the 95th. 'Thus we staggered on, night and day, for about four days ...' before an opportunity to rest was granted.[84] On New Year's Eve, Moore split his force in two: the light brigade was directed to march to Vigo, from where they were evacuated on 21 January 1809. Moore, with the rest of his force, meanwhile, marched to Corunna, but as conditions worsened, the army began to disintegrate, resulting in acts of horrendous brutality and depravity against the local population.

Moore's army reached Corunna on 12 January 1809, pursued by Marshal Nicolas Soult, whose command was now badly strung out over the Cantabrian mountains. Recognising that Moore was a competent general, whose army, even in the battered condition it was in, was not to be taken lightly, Soult declined an immediate attack. Contrary winds prevented the British transport fleet from entering Corunna harbour for two days, giving Soult the opportunity to bring up his army. By now, Moore had been able to resupply his command from the depots at Corunna and select a suitable defensive position from which he could fight a delaying action while his army embarked. On the 14th, the winds changed and the transport fleet was able to get into harbour. The evacuation commenced immediately. Seeing this, Soult decided on an attack on the 16th, forcing Moore to fight the delaying action he had anticipated.

He posted 15,000 troops on the ridges of Monte Mero, overlooking Corunna, south of the town. If he was to break through, Soult had to capture this ridge. He first decided to bring up artillery on a ridge adjacent to Moore's position, which had an immediate effect. 'Such was the advantage of their position', recalled Clinton, 'that almost every shot took effect

& claimed a heavy loss . . . .'[85] Soult then attacked the British right, where, among others, the 42nd Black Watch were posted. He perceived a weakness in the line that would allow him to trap the British on the coastline while he cut off their access to the harbour. In this estimation he was mistaken. A captured picket gave away the attack on the British right, and reserves were thrown in to counter the assault.[86] Through intense fighting, the British managed to cling on to their positions on the right, thwarting Soult's attempt to capture the ridge and cut off Moore's final line of retreat to the port. On the British left, attempts to capture the village of Piedralonga were defeated in an intense close-order combat, involving a bayonet charge 'which struck consternation into the enemy (tho' it is supposed they imagined it a general attack)'.[87]

Moore was fatally wounded directing the reserves in the battle, after a cannonball tore away his left shoulder and mangled his chest. The wound was so severe that his military secretary, John Colborne, thought 'from the profuse gushing out of the blood . . . he would have instantly expired', but Moore survived long enough to learn that his army had held the French off, and was able to embark in safety.[88] The Corunna campaign had cost the British army in the Peninsula a fifth of its strength: 5,000 men had died during the retreat, and another 800 were killed and wounded in the battle at Corunna, compared with 1,500 French casualties. Huge numbers of guns, ammunition, gunpowder and stores fell into French hands, while the cavalry slaughtered their own horses to prevent the same fate.[89]

The horrors of war were made startlingly apparent for the public when the tattered remnants of Moore's army disembarked at Portsmouth and Plymouth. 'Now indeed the miseries of war have been brought home to our doors,' noted *The Times*. 'The scenes are beyond any pen to describe . . . The wounds of the many men some of whom have never been dressed while others are dying for want are everywhere.'[90] The wisdom of the war in the Peninsula was publicly questioned, both in parliament and the press. Arthur Wellesley, however, his name cleared after the embarrassments of the convention of Cintra, argued that Lisbon, a valuable strategic position, could be defended at minimal cost by a small British field force that would reorganise the Portuguese army along British lines. Its officer corps and staff would be composed of British officers, and a vigorous programme of training and drill would be instituted. A core of an Anglo-Portuguese army would be ready quickly and effectively to take to the field against the French. In total, Wellesley estimated, this would cost the government no more than £1 million on top of the war expenditure it was already committed to. This was nothing, Wellesley argued, compared to the long-term gains the British would make in repulsing the French in Iberia.[91]

* * *

Wellesley's scheme won approval and in April 1809 he returned to Lisbon, this time in overall command of the army. His first objective was to clear the French from Oporto, which had been seized by Soult following his failure to prevent Moore's escape. In a daring cross-river raid on 12 May, Wellesley's army outflanked the occupying army and forced them to withdraw precipitately. Wellesley now found himself short on cash and lacking permission to march his considerable force into Spain. He took the opportunity to reorganise his army into a divisional structure, each composed of two or three infantry brigades. Divisional commanders would now liaise with Wellesley and his staff, streamlining decision making and communication, and enabling – theoretically at least – independent activity. Though Wellesley was the first British general officially to reorganise his command in such a fashion, and designate the formations with the term 'division', there were at least two precedents, albeit short-lived and informal. York had referred to groupings of several brigades as 'columns' during the expedition to Holland in 1799,[92] while during the Mediterranean expedition, Abercromby had referred to similar organisations as 'lines'.[93] Cathcart had temporarily reorganised his army during the 1807 Copenhagen expedition into divisions, and Moore had adopted a similar structure in 1808, but Wellesley's organisational reform was permanent, with a specifically appointed general officer commanding, rather than the senior brigadier, as had been the case until then.

Under Wellesley's reforms, each division was composed of 3–4,000 troops, though the First Division complement was set at 6,000. He attached a company of the 5/60th to each brigade, enhancing skirmishing abilities and providing each division with a body of light troops which could be organised into a reserve.[94] William Beresford was appointed to command the Portuguese army and in February 1810, once he had completed a substantial reorganisation and retraining programme, a brigade of Portuguese soldiers commanded by a British officer was attached to each division, increasing the complement of all to 6,000.[95] Continued expansion saw the number of divisions increase gradually over the next two years, and in total, Wellesley would command eight infantry divisions over the next six years, as well as two cavalry divisions. The divisional restructuring was, in many ways, the key to British success during the Peninsular War. Each divisional headquarters was organised along identical lines, which improved communication speeds. Divisional commanders also took on much of the work that the commander-in-chief of the army would have normally undertaken. By 1810, for example, they were organising intelligence networks and providing analysed intelligence reports, based on their specific localised knowledge. These were then passed to headquarters, where the newly ennobled Lord Wellington consumed them and integrated them into his decision-making process.[96]

As the war progressed, each division acquired a reputation and identity. The First and Third Divisions became known as the Fighting Divisions, for their tactical prowess at the battles of Talavera in 1809 and Salamanca in 1812, respectively. The Second Division, commanded by Wellington's most trusted subordinate, General Sir Rowland Hill, became known as the Observing Division, famed for their flank support, intelligence collection activities and independent operations, such as the seizure of the bridge at Almaraz, which secured Wellington's flank for the advance on Salamanca in May 1812. Perhaps the most famous was the Light Division, which, under the command of General Robert Craufurd – a harsh, but effective, disciplinarian – became the premier fighting unit of Wellington's army.

Craufurd joined the British Army in 1779, and served in Bombay under the command of General Robert Abercromby, where he earned plaudits as a strict disciplinarian in command of the 75th foot during the campaign against Tipu Sultan in 1792. After returning to Europe, he joined his brother Charles at the Austrian headquarters in the opening campaigns of the French Revolutionary War, observing Austrian staff practices and the character of the new war against France.[97] In 1797, he was appointed deputy quartermaster general in Ireland and helped prepare defences against the expected French invasion. In 1799, he resumed his secondment with the Austrians, but when the British army deployed to Holland, he joined York's headquarters as deputy quartermaster general.[98] In 1800, Craufurd married and in 1802 took a seat in Parliament which he held until 1806, when he resigned in order to resume his military career. Put in command of a newly formed light brigade, he found himself attempting to secure the British position in Buenos Aires.

British failure at Buenos Aires owed more to command deficiencies than to any tactical or training shortcomings on the part of the troops. Indeed, Craufurd's brief command of an ad-hoc assembly of light infantry units brought considerable success, opportunities which were squandered by the hesitancy and indecision of the commander-in-chief, Lieutenant General John Whitelocke. On 6 July 1807, having missed an opportunity to take it unopposed, Whitelocke ordered an assault on the city. In bitter street fighting, the British attack collapsed. Craufurd's light brigade had managed to seize its objective, a convent which, had the other objectives been captured, would have helped secure the city, but they were 'completely surrounded by the great body of the enemy's forces'. Forced 'to confine [them]selves to the defence of the convent', recalled Craufurd in his testimony at Whitelocke's court martial, his unit's 'defence consisted chiefly of the fire of the riflemen from the [roof]top'.[99] With the supporting attacks foundering, Craufurd was forced to surrender. Despite the humiliation of defeat, he came away from Buenos Aires with a fierce respect for the utility of light infantry, and notably the value of aimed fire.

It was a connection which would last the remainder of Craufurd's military career, and see him devise a series of standing orders, focused on operational conduct and divisional management, that would make the Light Division the most reliable of Wellington's units in the Iberian peninsula.[100] The standing orders were characterised by Craufurd's own staff training and his 'scientific' approach to war, learned alongside his brother at the Austrian headquarters in the early campaigns against Revolutionary France. As a result of this training, Craufurd was able to 'calculate to the minute the time his whole division ... would take to arrive at any given point, no matter how many days' march'.[101] This mirrored the views of Henry Lloyd, who demonstrated the importance of such skills when planning operations.[102] Craufurd almost certainly read Lloyd's work, as he had maintained an interest in the campaigns of the Seven Years' War and, with his brother, had translated *An Account of Some of the Most Remarkable Events of the War Between the Prussians, Austrians, and Russians, from 1756 to 1763*, which included *a Treatise on Several Branches of the Military Art*, by noted Saxon military theorist Johann Gottlieb Tielke.[103]

Craufurd was widely read both in the practice of tactics and the art of operations. His military library included the works, among others, of Vauban, Saxe and Guibert.[104] He appreciated both the science and art of war, and he instilled this appreciation by example in his men as well as his officers. 'He proved to [his troops] ... on true mathematical principle, that with the numbers of obstacles usually encountered on a day's march, it made a difference of several hours in their arrival at their bivouac for the night. That in indulging by the way, they were that much longer labouring under their load of arms, ammunition, and necessaries.' Craufurd did not share the outlook toward discipline practised by his contemporaries in the light infantry, however, and he enforced his orders 'in the first instance, with unnecessary severity'.[105] Indeed, shortly after the retreat from

Talavera, the troops of the light brigade 'paraded ... when we got volleys of abuse and blasphemous language from that infernal scoundrel Brigadier Robert Craufurd', at the end of which the men 'lay down to sleep at nine o'clock but not without offering hearty prayers for the discomfiture of our cursed commander'.[106] The hostility to Craufurd continued for much of the remainder of the year, but once the troops experienced the benefits of Craufurd's system both in battle and on campaign, they grudgingly accepted the capability and skill of their commander, and 'the system, once established, went on like clockwork'.[107]

In the wake of the precipitate retreats to Corunna and Vigo, Craufurd returned to the Peninsula in July 1809 once more in command of a brigade composed of the light infantry battalions of the 43rd, 52nd and 95th. Receiving incomplete reports of a battle near Madrid, Craufurd marched his troops 62 miles in 26 hours, reaching Talavera too late to participate in the battle, but in time to cover the withdrawal of the British contingent back to the Portuguese border as Soult's army, recently ejected from Oporto, threatened British communications. Initially, Wellington incorporated the light brigade into the Third Division. In February 1810, in anticipation of another French invasion of Portugal, this time commanded by Marshal André Masséna, Wellington removed the light brigade from the Third Division and announced that 'the 1st and 2nd battalions of a Portuguese Chasseurs (Caçadores) are attached to the Brigade of Brigadier-General Craufurd, which is to be called the *Light Division*'.[108]

Craufurd was to guard the Portuguese frontier east of the border fortress of Almeida, the most likely entry point for any French invasion. This involved establishing a chain of outposts from which his troops could observe enemy movements, organise regular reconnaissance patrols, conduct topographical survey work and compile accurate, reliable and timely intelligence reports.[109] So extensive were his duties that he was 'obliged to sleep', Craufurd jested, 'with one eye open'.[110] In order to achieve his objectives, Craufurd split his units into companies and deployed them throughout the expanse of territory for which he was responsible. Each unit was deployed in accordance with the instructions devised and taught by Jarry, with two layers of sentries designed to guard against surprise.[111] Craufurd frequently moved them around to increase overall familiarity and establish as wide an intelligence net as possible. Locals were interrogated to find out information on French movements, and this information was then integrated with intelligence from other sources to provide a reliable picture of events.[112]

Craufurd relied on strict adherence to his standing orders for marching to ensure his troops could concentrate for action rapidly. As anticipation grew for a new invasion, the troops were ready to move at a moment's notice. In drills and exercises, as Captain William Napier of the 43rd observed, they managed to deploy with

> a promptitude and intelligence the like of which had seldom been known. Seven minutes sufficed to get under arms in the night, a quarter of an hour, night or day, to gather them in order of battle at the alarm posts, with baggage loaded and assembled at a convenient distance in the rear; and this not upon a concerted signal and as a trial, but at all times certain and for many months consecutively.[113]

Craufurd's overall success in guarding the Portuguese frontier owed much 'to his own admirable arrangements, and the surprising discipline of his troops', which enabled him to 'maintain a position which was no position, for three months, within an hour's march of . . . a brave, experienced, and enterprising enemy'.[114] The evident benefits of well-trained light infantry also prompted other officers to demand more of their regular soldiers. 'It must be allow'd by all, that the system of modern warfare requires a much larger proportion of light troops, or at least of men, *acquainted with the true principles of acting as such* than formerly,' wrote General Sir Thomas Graham to the adjutant-general, 'and that in point of fact we possess none that deserve to be so class'd, *as so instructed* except that Brit[ish] Regt's formerly in our friend Sir J. Moore's Brigade at Shorncliffe . . .'.[115]

As envisaged by Moore's concept of a universal soldier, the light infantry also became an important and integral aspect of Wellington's tactical arrangement on the battlefield. Deployed forward in the traditional role expected of skirmishing units, the rifles and light infantry had the specific objective of suppressing the French *tirailleurs* and denying them the ability to reconnoitre the main army, which was often hidden behind a hill. This was particularly effective at the Battle of Bussaco, on 27 September 1810. Having monitored the French invasion plans, Wellington had gradually withdrawn into Portugal. His ultimate objective was to fall back behind the Lines of Torres Vedras, a multilayered set of defensive positions which his and the Portuguese engineers had been building since late 1809.

As his army gathered in the vicinity of the town of Coimbra, Wellington reconnoitred a steep eight-mile long ridgeway known as the Serro de Bussaco. 'We have an excellent position here,' he wrote to his cavalry commander, Stapleton Cotton, on the evening of 21 September, 'in which I am strongly tempted to give battle. Unfortunately . . . there is a road upon our left by which we may be turned and cut off from Coimbra. But I don't yet give up hopes of discovering a remedy for this last misfortune.'[116] In many ways, the ridgeway on which the Battle of Bussaco was fought was a classic piece of terrain selection by Wellington for a defensive battle. Steep sloped to wear out the attackers, and with plenty of obstacles to disrupt their march and offer the riflemen of the 95th the opportunity to pick off the officers, the terrain offered substantial shelter for the Anglo-Portuguese forces from French artillery fire, while they remained hidden from French view on the reverse slope of the ridgeway. The selection of similar ground would determine success at many of Wellington's set-piece battles. It was, unquestionably, an extension of his experiences in India.

As Masséna's infantry columns went up the hill to the attack, their advance was disrupted by the targeted fire of the 95th. On the British centre right, Thomas Picton's Third Division repulsed repeated attacks from General Reynier. 'The attack was made with great impetuosity and en masse,' Picton wrote a month after the battle, 'but nothing could exceed the determined bravery of the troops who repulsed them with the Bayonet'.[117] In the centre left, meanwhile, General Loison sent in a column of infantry to seize and silence a strongly posted artillery battery. The French column 'ascended with a wonderful alacrity, and though the light troops plied it unceasingly with musketry, and the artillery bullets swept through it from the first to the last section, its order was never disturbed nor its speed in the least abated', wrote Napier. Though it remained composed, Loison's division had already sustained heavy casualties, for it had faced no fewer than 2,000 rifles during this perilous attack.[118]

'Craufurd ... had been intently watching the progress of this attack, and now with a shrill tone ordered the two regiments in reserve' – the 43rd and 52nd – 'to charge! The next moment a horrid shout startled the French column and eighteen hundred British bayonets were sparkling over the brow of the hill.'[119] Shocked though they were, the experienced French troops continued their attack, but the delivery of three volleys of musketfire at virtually point-blank range, halted their advance. A bayonet charge delivered after three cheers forced the French to withdraw in disorder. 'The instant the attacking columns were turned back, they were exposed to the fire of our whole division,' wrote Jonathan Leach of the 95th. 'Our battalion and some caçadores were ordered to pursue, and to give them a flanking fire.' Panic set in and French soldiers were seen 'trampling each other to death in their great haste to escape. Men, muskets, knapsacks, and bayonets, rolled down the side of the mountain in such a confused mass'.[120]

Craufurd's units suffered just 23 casualties in the battle. The soldiers of the Light Infantry had lived up to Moore's concept, proving capable of irregular and skirmishing action prior to a battle, and fighting as regular line infantry during a battle. Lieutenant Ralph Blakiston would later comment that he 'never saw such skirmishers as the 95th ... They possessed an individual boldness, a mutual understanding and a quickness of the eye in taking advantage of the ground, which ... I never saw equalled'.[121] While such ideas were derived from Britain's long experience in America, Wellington's deployment at Bussaco, meanwhile, had been inspired by his experience in India. The troops were sheltered from the worst of the French artillery fire and were well hidden from view. The arrangement prevented the French from deploying from column into line at the culmination of the attack, further exposing the narrow frontage of the column to the devastating and well-directed fire of the redcoats.

Though this was a startling tactical victory for the British, Wellington's position was eventually outflanked, and he continued his withdrawal to Torres Vedras. There, the French advance ground to a halt and finding the Lines impenetrable attempted to lay siege. The Royal Navy managed, just, to keep the population of Lisbon and the Anglo-Portuguese army sufficiently supplied through a tough winter, while the French half-starved to death outside the Lines. On 14 March 1811, Masséna withdrew into Spain. In May, he made a last-ditch attempt to reverse his misfortune and attacked Wellington at Fuentes d'Oñoro, on the Portuguese border with Spain. The move very nearly succeeded after Masséna turned the British flank. Caught in an exposed position, the newly raised Seventh Division – another unit composed entirely of light troops, but not yet as well trained as Craufurd's men – were in real danger of being wiped out. Wellington sent Craufurd's Light Division, which had been acting as a reserve, to stabilise the situation.

Craufurd's men found the two battalions of the Seventh Division 'opposed, with their conspicuous red dresses, to the old trained French tirailleurs', according to Costello. 'It is no wonder that the gallant 85th should have suffered so severely.'[122] They were able to extract the Seventh, but now found themselves exposed and vulnerable to attack. Wellington had reorganised his line, but it was two miles away, across a large plain.[123] 'The mass of French cavalry, with artillery, continued to advance along the plain, threatening to cut off the Light Division from the position on the heights,' explained Captain Leach. 'We were, therefore, directed to ... form squares of battalions, and to fall back over the plain ....'[124] As the

Light Division extracted itself, a company of riflemen was nearly cut off and 'had to run for their lives into a square formed by the Fifty-Second'.[125]

The Light Division would remain under constant threat of cavalry attack during its withdrawal. However, when formed in square, 'it is difficult to move in that order, even for a short distance', explained Colonel Neil Campbell in his 1807 *Instructions for Light Infantry and Rifles*.[126] Craufurd therefore ordered his battalions into close column of companies. In this formation, the light infantry could form square simply by halting and facing outwards to form an all-round defence. Craufurd also arranged the battalions *en echelon* so that the men would be able to fire volleys at the oncoming French cavalry without causing friendly casualties. Lieutenant Dobbs of the 52nd explained that this 'was done by alternate squares under a heavy cannonade, the balls sometimes hopping in and out of the square'. The operation was tactically challenging, as 'marching in square' was 'a most difficult operation, as, if the correct line is not kept by the front or rear faces, or the sides in file marching not locked up or well covered, the square must be broken'.[127]

Once again, however, the extensive training conducted at Shorncliffe and by Craufurd while deployed paid off. 'The execution of our movements presented a magnificent military spectacle,' remembered Kincaid. 'While we were retiring', he continued, 'with the order of a common field day', the French cavalry 'kept dancing around us and every instant threatening a charge, without daring to execute it'.[128] Wellington's new line was very strong, and Masséna declined to attack. Instead, the battle continued in the village of Fuentes itself, which was hotly contested. The fighting here illustrated the limited success the British had introducing greater tactical flexibility into the regular soldiers' training regime. 'The place was strewn about with' the bodies of the 79th Highlanders, who 'had not been used to skirmishing,' observed Costello, 'and instead of occupying the houses in the neighbourhood, and firing from the windows, they had exposed themselves by firing in sections'.[129]

In the wake of Fuentes d'Oñoro, Masséna was replaced in command of the French army of Portugal by Marshal Auguste de Marmont. Wellington hoped to secure a breakthrough by capturing the twin border fortresses of Ciudad Rodrigo and Badajoz, but the combined strength of Marmont's army and that of Soult, based in Seville, prevented him from carrying on siege operations. In the winter of 1811, Napoleon began withdrawing forces from Spain in preparation for his fateful invasion of Russia. The gradual weakening of French strength on the Portuguese frontier gave

Wellington the opportunity he was looking for, and on 8 January 1812, he commenced siege works outside Ciudad Rodrigo. Batteries were established on a hill overlooking the fortress, and by the 13th, the bombardment of the fortress walls commenced. It took six days to make two breaches in the walls. The largest was located on the northwest corner, while a smaller breach was established 250 yards to the east.

On the night of the 19th, two columns of British infantry, composed of men from the Third and Light Divisions, prepared to storm the fortress. 'Calling out, "Now Lads, for the breach!", General Craufurd led the way,' recalled Costello, who had volunteered to be part of the storming party at the lesser breach. 'As we neared the breach, canister, grape, round-shot and shell, with fire-balls to show our ground, came pouring ... around us, with a regular hailstorm of bullets. General Craufurd fell almost immediately, mortally wounded.'[130] Despite the loss of their commander, the troops pressed on, but were held up by a deep ditch before the main wall. 'In mounting the breach,' recalled one participant, 'we found great difficulty in ascending from the loose earth slipping under our feet at every step', with 'the enemy at the same time pouring their shot amongst us from above'.[131] Eventually ladders were brought forward and 'up we mounted to attack the breach', continued Costello. 'The fire kept up there was most deadly, and our men, for some minutes, as they appeared in small bodies, were swept away. However, they still persevered, and gradually formed a lodgement.'[132] From here, the troops of the Light and Third Divisions managed to link up and push along the fortress walls, pursuing the French into the city.

The French commandant surrendered to Lieutenant John Gurwood, of the 52nd, who had led the Light Division's 'Forlorn Hope'. Thrilled to have succeeded, those troops that survived the assault now set about plundering the town, and it was only the 'voice of Sir Thomas Picton, with the power of twenty trumpets' who succeeded in restoring order by the following morning. As the victorious soldiers left the town, the Fifth Division formed on the side of the road, presented arms and cheered. Some of the troops 'were dressed in Frenchmen's coats, some in white breeches, and huge jack-boots, some with cocked hats ...'. As they passed by, Wellington demanded to know 'Who the devil are those fellows?' They were, he was told, his elite Light Division.[133]

Ciudad Rodrigo had been captured in just 11 days. In the course of the siege, 1,100 casualties had been sustained, 568 in the assault, of which 125 were killed. Craufurd lived another four days, in great pain. A musket ball had shot through his arm, pierced a lung and lodged near his spine. He passed in and out of consciousness, but when awake he was lucid and asked his close friend, Charles Stewart, for news of the storming and of the enemy. Wellington likewise visited his sickbed, and the two discussed the campaign so far. When Craufurd died, Wellington bitterly regretted the loss of such an able commander of light troops.[134]

Like Moore, Craufurd left a powerful legacy: a division of light troops capable of complex tactical actions, manoeuvring on campaign, conducting skirmishing activities and commanding and controlling large swathes of territory. The officers and soldiers were trained in a variety of tasks, including the collection and analysis of intelligence, map-drawing and route planning. They were Wellington's troubleshooters and were frequently deployed to achieve the most difficult and challenging of objectives. This was once again evident during the siege of Badajoz, where the Light Division led one of the main assaults, this time at much greater expense. There, the Light Division alone sustained 1,000 casualties, while the overall toll was 4,650.

Wellington could ill-afford such losses. His little Anglo-Portuguese army depended on manoeuvre and speed, defying their superior French adversaries to concentrate against them. Siege warfare fixed Wellington's army in place and allowed the French to concentrate and manoeuvre to threaten his lines of supply and communication. His army, particularly elite units like the Light Division, was capable of operational manoeuvre that could outwit the French, but such activity was complex and highly risky. While light infantry offered him the 'light and quick' option, this alone was insufficient. Wellington needed a staff capable of undertaking complex strategic and operational planning. Happily, the men of his staff had exactly those capabilities, and for this they could thank decades of diverse military experience leading to the establishment of a formal system of staff training and education.

CHAPTER II

'The Scientifics'

HIGH WYCOMBE AND THE BRITISH WAY OF
WARFARE, 1803–1815

O N 11 March 1821, a decade after he first arrived in Portugal, and only two years since he left, Thomas Mitchell was in his study in the Royal Military College at Sandhurst in Camberley, pouring over maps he had drawn of the Peninsular War battlefields. He was expecting a visit from the Duke of Wellington, accompanied by his old friend Sir George Murray, who two years earlier had been appointed governor of the college. Mitchell had become one of Murray's best map-makers, having toured Portugal and Spain between 1815 and 1819, making extensive trigono-metrical surveys of the terrain over which the British, Portuguese, Spanish and French armies fought for six years between 1808 and 1814. When he inspected the maps, Wellington was evidently impressed, and as one of few first-hand accounts of Wellington's reflections on the battles of the Peninsular War, it is worth quoting Mitchell's diary entry recalling the meeting at some length.

His Grace said Salamanca ground was very correct & the view very like the town, he thought the Arapiles had been further distant from each other. He liked the Fuentes d'Oñoro sketch very much & looked at the view. He was well satisfied with Busaco & enquired further [of the] country between that & the Alva & up to the mountains which he said was very important ground: – He looked for the high hill he stood on at Talavera which I showed him. He said the Lines [of Torres Vedras] were a great work; enquired for the forts, and the direction of the second line etc. On showing the sketch of the Battle of Pamplona, he enquired if we had all the mountains between that and France, which Sir G[eorge Murray] also showed him (done by me during the War). He looked at my view of the position of Guarda, & observed that it was very strong ground. We looked at a plan of Toulouse. He observed to me that this hill on our flank was very strong ground, and that if the enemy had got it he never would have beat them. He also looked at the ground where the battle was fought at Pamplona, when I showed the hill His Grace stood on. He then traced with his finger the road he came with great facility.[1]

As well as being a rare personal record of a conversation in which Wellington expressed opinions about the campaigns in the Peninsula, Mitchell's account illustrates that Wellington thought not just about the battles, but the operations that led to, and arose from, those battles. He admitted to mistakes he made interpreting the ground while conducting a reconnaissance near the village of Los Arapiles, shortly before the Battle of Salamanca commenced on 22 July 1812. He reviewed not just the features of tactical importance in Busaco, Sorauren – to which he referred as Pamplona – and Toulouse, but also traced the routes by which his army manoeuvred to those battles. In creating a cartographic record of his campaigns, Wellington wanted to privilege the operational as well as the tactical detail. His victories were based as much on operational manoeuvre as on tactical acumen. Indeed, by the end of the war, Wellington had achieved much of his successes in carefully orchestrated campaigns that did not necessarily have to result in large set-piece battles.

Instead, his forces were relying on superior planning, which accounted for all eventualities, speed of manoeuvre, which allowed the British to seize and keep the initiative, and a close link between tactical and strategic objectives. While Mitchell had read Henry Lloyd for the advice offered by the theorist on the importance and use of light troops, it is impossible to overlook the fact that Lloyd was also a strategic theorist, and a proponent of understanding military geography. As well as consuming the tactical suggestions made by Lloyd, Mitchell, very much aspiring to be a 'universal soldier', was just as interested in the operational and strategic argument. His notebooks are filled with closely written notes, mostly focusing on Lloyd's theories, and in particular on the formation of lines of operation, which for Lloyd was the central element of military planning. His advice ranged from planning to execution.

According to Lloyd, when planning a campaign, the selected line of operation needed clearly defined objectives, and to have security on its flanks. Once operations were under way, 'no army, however strong, can keep its ground if you advance against it in front and at the same time send a powerful corps to act on its flank and rear'. To achieve this, the commanding officer needed to understand the difference between what was possible and probable, 'and take his measures accordingly ...'. When 'all the data are clearly given and known, the respective forces are easily calculated, from whence a probable opinion may be formed and some certain object fixed and determined on'. It was, in Lloyd's opinion, essential that the commander 'pursued without any deviation' the selected objective.[2] For a general to make such a plan, reliable intelligence and maps were needed. Only then could a complex operation be planned to outflank and force an enemy army to retreat. Here as well, Mitchell excelled. An outstanding draughtsman, he was quickly spotted by Murray who, after a brief trial, made him a map-maker. By 1813, Mitchell was helping to plan Wellington's manoeuvres.

For Wellington, who had also read Lloyd's work, defeat of the enemy's forces in battle was an objective only if it aided the army in achieving wider strategic objectives. In the Peninsular War, these were the defence of Portugal, the liberation of Spain and the security and survival of the British army itself.[3] In essence, the resulting operations were a recreation of Wellington's 'light and quick movements', first developed and implemented in India, and clearly informed by Lloyd's ideas, including his arguments about operations and battles and so-called 'indirect manoeuvres'.[4] A knowledge network, based on experience, reading and personal connections, which linked the most senior and some of the youngest and most junior officers in the army, helped Wellington to develop these ideas.

*   *   *

The story of how Wellington and his staff officers were able to plan a series of increasingly ambitious and complex military campaigns in Spain and Portugal began with an innovative colonel from Guernsey. While Moore, Manningham, Stewart and Mackenzie worked to develop an effective training and education regime for the light infantry, John Gaspard Le Marchant sought to do the same for the cavalry. The son of a veteran of the Seven Years' War and his French wife, Le Marchant had commissioned into a regiment of Wiltshire Militia before transferring to the regular army in 1783. After serving in the First Regiment of Foot, he purchased a commission in the 6th Dragoons, and in 1789, after attracting the attention of the king when he commanded the royal escort from

Dorchester to Weymouth, Le Marchant was promoted to lieutenant in the 2nd Dragoon Guards. The royal encounter would facilitate Le Marchant's career on more than one occasion. On the outbreak of the French Revolutionary War, he was captain in the same regiment. In the campaign in Flanders, he served under the command of General William Harcourt and then David Dundas but returned home in September 1794 to take up a majority in the 16th Light Dragoons. During his time on the continent, Le Marchant had spent a considerable time with the Austrian army. Like many of his peers, he was impressed by the technical proficiency of the Austrian cavalry. 'I have ... paid particular attention to the mode of training of the Austrian cavalry in the use of the Sabre, in which their superiority over us is incredible,' he wrote excitedly to his wife, Mary, in November 1793.[5]

In particular, Le Marchant observed that the sword drill used by the British cavalry in combat was proving inadequate to the task. Not only was the practice ineffective against enemy cavalry and infantry, but surgeons were reporting that many injuries suffered by cavalrymen in combat could only have been self-inflicted.[6] After studying Austrian techniques, Le Marchant concluded that the problem was a combination of inappropriate weapon design, ineffective drill and inadequate horsemanship training. Only a completely new system of exercise would remedy these issues. Le Marchant developed a new drill and exercise routine, perfecting it with 20 men selected from his regiment, the 16th Light Dragoons. This obliged the cavalrymen 'to think for themselves, and to act independent of each other; which on service are, in a body of light troops, inestimable qualities'.[7] He designed a new weapon, based on the 'scimitar blades of the Turks, Mamalukes, Moors and Hungarians' who had 'proved that a light sword, if equally applicable to a cut or a thrust, is preferable to any other'.[8] By 1796, a manuscript of the new code of instruction was put before a board of general officers and approved for addition to the permanent regulations of the cavalry.

A 90-page manual, *Rules and Regulations for the Sword Exercise of the Cavalry*, was published in December 1796 and sold out its first print run in six weeks. Le Marchant was ordered to teach the drill at speedily convened centres around the country, to which various regiments would send detachments of an officer and 20 men. At schools established at Tunbridge Wells, Newmarket, Newcastle and Bradford, Le Marchant, along with his brother-in-law, Cornet Peter Carey and six sergeants and corporals, trained batches of 100 men in two weeks' concentrated schooling.

In the months that followed, Le Marchant expanded on the battle drill with instructions on the challenging duties of scouting and reconnaissance in 'The Duty of Officers on the Outpost'. The Duke of York rewarded Le Marchant with a lieutenant-colonelcy in Hompesch's Hussars, then serving in the West Indies, but the king, who was just as impressed by Le Marchant's industriousness, intervened and appointed him to a different, more senior regiment. So sudden was the appointment, that Le Marchant only learned of it as he waited to be presented to the king, and was therefore wearing the wrong uniform. 'How can you be so little of a martinet as to appear at Court in the wrong dress?' jested George III when Le Marchant was presented to him. 'You may now wear the 7th coat, as I have this morning appointed you lieutenant-colonel in the 7th Dragoons ... I wish you to know that whatever merit there is in it rests entirely between me and you, for no one else is concerned in it.'[9]

Le Marchant, then, was an innovator, and he hoped to improve his new regiment through the implementation of these new ideas. However, he was initially disappointed by the 'very so-so set' of officers and men in his new regiment, and hoped to 'weed the regiment of the black sheep'.[10] This he did over the course of a year, turning the resentment of his new unit into an appreciation of military knowledge, forming what was essentially a regimental school for officers. He paid particular attention to providing specific instruction to the subalterns 'in the same way that the marine officer is taught navigation on entering the Navy' and lectured the rest of the officers of the regiment three times a week on tactics and techniques on campaign. By October 1798, 'the officers are becoming like gentlemen', he wrote to his wife.[11]

With the 7th Light Dragoons gaining a reputation as an elite unit, Le Marchant began exploring the ways in which his system of training and education could be expanded to include other regiments. He initially proposed a 'Plan for establishing Regimental Schools for Officers throughout the Service', in which he envisaged regimental lieutenant-colonels taking responsibility for the delivery of a curriculum of tactical exercises. This, however, was limited by the deficiencies in the knowledge of the art of war which most officers in that station possessed. 'At present when an army goes upon service,' wrote Charles Craufurd, older brother of Robert, and a close friend of Le Marchant's, 'we are so destitute of officers qualified to form the Quartermaster-General's department and an efficient corps of aides-de-camp, and our officers in general, have so little knowledge of the most essential parts of their profession, that we are obliged to have recourse to foreigners for assistance or our operations are constantly liable to failure in their execution.'[12] Encouraged to think on a grander scale, Le Marchant proposed a national establishment for the education of officers. The Duke of York liked the idea, but in January 1799 was sceptical of gaining public support for such a move. He therefore asked for 'stronger arguments than those you have laid before me'. Le Marchant spent the next three months putting together the 'Outlines of a Plan for a Regular Course of Military Education'.[13]

Le Marchant's plan called for the creation of three departments and a 'Legion' responsible for the military education of future and serving officers at different stages of their careers. The 'Legion' would furnish the sons of selected ordinary soldiers with a basic education with a view to them entering the army and eventually serving as noncommissioned officers. Similarly, the 'First Department' would educate young men who wished to obtain a commission as an officer, while the 'Second Department' offered similar opportunities for 'cadets', who needed more education to become officers. The 'Third Department' would seek 'the improvement of the staff' and was 'intended only for officers of experience in the duties of regimental services', of more than four years' service.[14] Having been presented in a robust and well-researched report, Le Marchant's plan was adopted nearly wholesale. The Legion became the Royal Military Asylum at Chelsea; the First and Third Departments were renamed 'Junior' and 'Senior'. Only the Second Department was not adopted, although elements were integrated into the Junior Department.[15]

The idea of providing education to new officers prior to their commission was not particularly controversial, but the notion that serving officers, often with considerable field experience, needed further education in their profession was not widely accepted and the concept met with resistance from supporters of the prevalent system of military patronage.[16] This was a problem Le Marchant willingly recognised. 'Though no reluctance is felt in acknowledging inexperience while in subordinate stations,' he wrote in his outline of the plan, 'yet, having once arrived at rank, enquiry after information too naturally ceases, from a dread of ridicule, or the galling imputation of incapacity.'[17]

The Senior Department opened on 4 May 1799 in the inadequate, though oddly appropriate, accommodation of the Antelope Inn, High Wycombe, 'a village in a narrow valley upon the great road from London to Oxford', as described by one of the first students at the college.[18] It would take two years for the department's specific objectives to be laid out in a

Royal Warrant. Rather than, as Le Marchant had originally planned, 'to qualify officers to become aide-de-camps, and fill other staff appointments with the ability due to their high importance',[19] the Royal Military College would instead be limited 'for the purpose of instructing officers in the scientific parts of their profession, the duties of the Staff, particularly those that belong to the Quartermaster-General's Department in the Field'.[20]

Nevertheless, Le Marchant's concept was revolutionary. It promised to formalise the process of self-education with which professionally interested officers had been engaged throughout the eighteenth century. 'The immediate purpose of this institution is', Le Marchant wrote, 'to lead progressively from minutiae to a knowledge of military operations, upon those principles which direct the great scale of war, and thereby to expand the genius, that responsibility may not precede information ....'[21] Indeed, officers serving on the staff would be expected to have a generalist knowledge of all aspects of war and army organisation. 'Their instructions shall not be confined to military theories alone, but be made as universal as the mind shall be capable of embracing,' Le Marchant continued, 'for it is evident that the operations of war in the conduct of armies are interwoven with general knowledge which combined the military and political history of Europe, the habit of judging correctly of men and measures, by placing in a true point of view the influence of national prejudice active under the pressure of local circumstances.'[22]

Military theorists had been arguing for such an approach for decades. Henry Lloyd, in the preface to the first volume of his *History of the Late War in Germany*, argued that a generalist education was one of the fundamental laws, or principles, of the art of war. 'A soldier', he wrote, must 'be taught every thing that is absolutely necessary for him to know, in every case that may happen'.[23] British officers had been compensating for the lack of a formal military education throughout the century, via informal means such as recommended reading, and accessing historical knowledge through maps and battlefields. They also attended European military academies, such as those in Strasbourg, Turin and Geneva, where they studied a basic curriculum of riding, fencing and dance designed to encourage 'a strong military spirit' and prepare 'men's bodies for war'.[24]

Le Marchant wanted to create a more specific curriculum, which would 'treat of the great principle which should regulate command, and the policy requisite to high authority, in order to maintain discipline, inspire energy in the troops, and insure a perfect cooperation in every branch of the service'. Moreover, the importance of logistics and intelligence was not to be overlooked. The curriculum 'will point out generally the resources of

an army, in the various means of procuring supplies of forage and provisions; the power of influencing the good disposition and support of the
natural inhabitants of a country that may be the theatre of war; through
whose means intelligence of the enemy can be obtained …'.[25] Le
Marchant's personal experience of observing military operations in Europe
convinced him that 'the officers of the most distinguished talents shall be
sent annually … to visit the several courts of Europe'. There they would
'become acquainted with the interior discipline and conduct of Foreign
armies, to view with a military eye country rendered memorable by having
been the theatre of brilliant achievement in war; and by directing their
enquiries to points of useful knowledge they will acquire that intelligence
which will best qualify them for military command'.[26]

Though he had been initially hesitant, the Duke of York threw his
backing behind the plan. Pitt likewise 'promised to support the Plan, and
come forward with the necessary supplies'.[27] In the event, the French
émigré General François Jarry had proposed, alongside his treatise on light
infantry, a similar though less ambitious plan, and York suggested the two
should unite their thinking so 'that we might complete the institution
together'. Jarry was, Le Marchant explained to his wife, 'a man of great
merit, so that we shall be useful to each other',[28] and, indeed, he was highly
experienced, particularly in planning and executing military operations.
He had been taught by, and served under the leadership of, Frederick the
Great during the Seven Years' War. In the aftermath of that conflict, he had
served as the head of the École Militaire in Berlin, only leaving office when
Frederick died in 1786. At the invitation of General Charles Dumouriez,
Jarry had then joined the French army, but disagreements over the way the
campaign was being prosecuted, including the escalating brutality of the
war, convinced him to defect to the allies. After becoming acquainted with
Quintin Craufurd, the uncle of Charles and Robert, at Brussels, Jarry
began to win recognition from the supporters of reform in the British army
and state.[29] As a result, when the Royal Military College opened, Jarry
became the Director of Instruction, while Le Marchant was appointed
commandant.

The generalist curriculum consisted of classes in languages and mathematics. Thereafter, students would study survey techniques, including
cartography and sketching, before moving on to operational education,
such as the methods of planning and calculating the movement of troops,
and other tactical training.[30] This curriculum was interspersed with Jarry's
personal instruction, including lessons covering subjects such as 'marches

and movement of armies and light infantry, ... castrametation', namely the laying out of military camps, 'Grand Guards', or the protection of an encamped army, 'and Reconnaissance'.[31] Despite Le Marchant's and Jarry's ambitions for a broad generalist education in staff work, it quickly became clear that many officers, despite significant regimental experience, lacked a common foundation on which this could be built. According to his successor, Howard Douglas, 'Jarry soon found that the rudiments of military science in the British Army were not sufficiently known to enable all the students to profit by his instruction'. He therefore 'recommended that mathematical, and fortification, and other classes, should be established' to bring all attendees to a common level.[32] As the officers' education in these fundamental subjects gradually improved, so the curriculum began to link with other aspects of advanced military staff work. Language education was a prerequisite for successful intelligence collection, while more advanced mathematics, as taught by the leading mathematician Isaac Dalby[33] helped officers to undertake trigonometrical surveys to produce accurate mapping.[34]

The course culminated by linking the study of terrain and operations. Jarry had long experience of the 'absolute necessity of maps and military plans for the assistance of operations', which, he believed, 'had been recognised and proved in all periods of modern warfare'. However, maps alone were insufficient. A commander needed to be able to relate the ground to an operation. 'If ... it should be asked of what avail is a good plan of ground,' asked Jarry during one of his lectures, 'we would reply by another question, of what avail is ground itself?' Basing his teaching on his experiences serving under Frederick the Great, Jarry argued that staff officers would need to conduct what he described as 'graphical reconnaissances taken simultaneously with the movements of armies'.[35]

Aware that the production of detailed accurate mapping would take months, Jarry instead preferred 'sketching', which required a combination of descriptive views with mapping detail of important features. Using techniques also delivered at the Woolwich academy,[36] sketching was taught to delineate perspective, before applying that 'perspective in practice' through the use of light and shade, and preferably from the aerial perspective.[37] This facilitated a methodical process 'for obtaining in the field sketches of the immediate scene of operations, by the rapid and combined labour of a number of staff-officers and other draughtsmen'.[38] But a true understanding of the operational situation, Jarry explained, could only be achieved with effective reconnaissance. 'An essential part of these instructions consists in reconnoitering the situation', as it was essential to be 'timely informed of the movements of the enemy; in order to employ against them correspondent measures, by the adoption of which we may be able to avail ourselves of the advantages of ground'.[39]

From these two fundamentals, survey and reconnaissance, in Jarry's view, stemmed the other elements of success – logistical management, route planning and encampment. Soldiers needed food and materiel, they needed a road of sufficient size to march to their objective, and they needed a place large enough to encamp while on campaign. Jarry's ideas invoked Lloyd's lines of operation, the fundamentals of which were geographical knowledge and intelligence, and without which successful campaigns of manoeuvre would be impossible to undertake.[40] While the 'art of war comprehends many other branches ... this course of instruction', Jarry explained, was 'calculated to give to many officers in succession the practical knowledge of the principle operations of a campaign, so as to enable them to carry into effect the other dispositions, of General Officers ...'.[41] These principles were imparted to a total of 184 officers between 1799 and 1809. Limited though this number may seem, those officers passed on their knowledge to like-minded officers unable to attend, officers such as Thomas Mitchell, trained by Philip Bainbrigge, who had himself commenced studies at the Royal Military College in 1809, and would go on to serve throughout the Peninsular War in a variety of staff positions in Wellington's army.

Having 'witnessed upon service what it was for an army to act under the direction of a disorganised staff',[42] Le Marchant argued in an 1801 paper that a 'General Staff to the Army' was needed, consisting largely of the graduates of the Senior Department of the Royal Military College at High Wycombe. In the field, the staff, which was part of the Quartermaster General's Department, would be expected to do all the things Jarry had instructed. Moreover, to facilitate communication and management across the Army, a divisional structure should be created, with its own local staff system in place.[43]

Although the plan was warmly greeted by both York and Dundas, there remained limited support for its implementation. Le Marchant was frustrated by the seeming reluctance to adopt the wider administrative reforms he had proposed. In 1806, he wrote to his friend, Colonel William Stewart, who was by then training light infantry at Shorncliffe, complaining that 'at present the British Army ... knows of no other formation than the regiment or brigade. The advantage of formations into divisions with their component parts is as yet not understood'. This was despite the evident success of the divisional structure in the French and Austrian armies. 'We shall never be successful in our military operations (unless by accident) until these points are arranged,' he remonstrated. 'How can we be so absurd as to oppose that, neglecting as we do all instruction and the aid of science in our military enterprises, we are to be victorious over troops that possess those advantages in the highest degree of perfection?'[44]

When seen in combination with the curriculum taught at the Royal Military College, the ideas put forward by Le Marchant in the plan for a general staff were all designed to provide a commanding officer with the skilled personnel needed to plan and execute a campaign of manoeuvre, and to build an army that was capable not just of defeating an adversary in battle, but of manoeuvring that adversary into a position of disadvantage. Le Marchant was formalising the British approach to warfighting which had gradually evolved throughout the second half of the eighteenth century. This approach had so far met with limited success, in part because even if the commanding officers had ambitious plans, his staff were frequently incapable of executing them. As Henry Clinton argued when he was appointed to be Howe's second-in-command in North America, until then, he 'never had occasion to form a plan of operations for campaigns; my utmost merit, if that is one, has been to obey as an aide-de-camp the manoeuvres of my generals'.[45]

The seeming reluctance of the military establishment to adopt his recommendations frustrated Le Marchant, whose short temper often alienated those for whom he depended for support. Reflecting on this aspect of his character when he was deployed to the Peninsula, he regretted that he had 'been all my life squabbling and quarrelling, and unable to get out of troubled waters'. His friends by contrast saw this 'was not so much from defect of temper ... as from expecting all men to be as eager and able to do their duty as himself, and treating them, in case he happened to be disappointed, as if they were the very reverse of what he had supposed them'.[46] By the time he was in the Peninsula, of course, Wellington had essentially adopted the blueprint for a staff which Le Marchant had devised in 1801.

In the absence of any sustained interest in his suggestions for a general staff, Le Marchant remained associated with the Senior Department of the Royal Military College for nearly a decade. In 1801, when his old mentor, Sir William Harcourt, was appointed governor, Le Marchant had become lieutenant-governor and superintendent-general. In May 1802, the Junior Department was formally opened, with Lieutenant-Colonel James Butler as superintendent. Though Le Marchant had oversight of both departments, his relationship with Butler deteriorated, and he found 'the old humdrum routine' frustrating. 'I am heartily tired of it,' he complained in December 1808, though 'it must be borne with for nine good reasons – a wife and eight children'.[47] Indeed, when in July 1811 he was placed back on the active list and deployed for service to the Peninsula, he worried about 'great pecuniary difficulties'.[48]

Still, he had reason for pride in his achievements. 'At the Senior Department above 200 officers have already been educated to the duties of the General Staff,' he wrote to the Duke of York. 'At present the Quartermaster General of Lord Wellington's army, as well as Marshal Beresford, and most of their assistants, have received their instruction at the College ... At the Junior Department not less than 1,500 young persons have been sent into the Army as Regimental Officers, whose service has been favourably spoken of.'[49] The *Royal Military Chronicle* agreed. 'Marlow and Wycombe are rapidly affecting a change, not only by the numerous accomplished officers they produce,' pronounced its editorial in June 1811, 'but in the desire of knowledge which has thereby been disseminated through the Army.'[50] Le Marchant had set in motion the institutionalisation of formal military education in the British Army but, as had been the case prior to his intervention, military knowledge was still exchanged through informal networks across the army; the difference now was that the basis of that knowledge exchange was a standard curriculum.

Shortly after arriving in Lisbon in late summer 1811, Le Marchant received news of the death of his wife as a result of complications arising from the birth of their tenth child. Le Marchant was devastated, the news made him 'truly wretched'. 'I have now', he wrote to his son, Denis, 'little to look forward to.'[51] His brother-in-law stepped in to take care of the children, eager Le Marchant should be allowed to make a name for himself in the Peninsula, and though he threw himself into his new duties – Wellington appointed him president of the Board of Claims – Le Marchant appeared deeply unhappy. At Christmas time, he was able to visit Wellington's headquarters in Freneda, and there he must have witnessed first-hand the product of his success at High Wycombe, for many of the officers serving on Wellington's staff had been educated there. He also reconnected with many of his oldest friends, including, among others, Robert Craufurd. Conversations of past experiences must have filled many evenings. As Le Marchant's son observed in his memoir of his father, 'no persons after a long separation can have more to say to each other than military men of rank'.[52]

Three weeks later, Craufurd was dead. Le Marchant, with Wellington, observed the storming of Ciudad Rodrigo, which he described as 'the most spirited enterprise that has been undertaken this war ... Nothing', he said, 'could exceed the good order and judgement with which it was conducted'.[53] Le Marchant went with Wellington to Badajoz, and he and his brigade of heavy cavalry was deployed under Thomas Graham's command toward Seville to prevent Marshal Soult from launching a counterattack against the siege. Gradually, Le Marchant was regaining his drive and spirit, and rigorously trained his men for action. 'I am in command of what is considered the finest brigade of cavalry in the army,' he had written earlier in the year. 'Rely upon it, they will make a hole wherever their exertions are directed.'[54] Shortly after the fortress fell, Le Marchant's actions proved decisive in the defeat of a French cavalry unit at Villa Garcia on 11 April. He was delighted with his brigade's performance, he said afterwards, and was 'perfectly satisfied that no cavalry of double its numbers could stand against it'.[55] Le Marchant's sword drill was demonstrated to be particularly effective. Indeed, one observer had commented that 'the prisoners were dreadfully cut ... A French dragoon had his head nearer cut off that I ever saw before; it was by a sabre cut at the back of the neck'.[56]

In May, Wellington moved to capitalise on his early success and invaded Spain with a view to bringing Marshal Auguste de Marmont and the army of Portugal to battle. After several weeks of indecisive manoeuvre in the environs of Salamanca, Wellington had decided on retreat, and reorganised his army in preparation. Marmont thought he perceived an opportunity to outflank his adversary, and during the morning of 22 July, in undulating terrain south of the city, ordered his army to outflank the Anglo-Portuguese army. One division, commanded by the over-eager General Jean Guillaume Barthélemy Thomières, overextended the line. Marmont was injured before he could recall Thomières, and the resulting command paralysis gave Wellington the opportunity to strike. Quickly reorienting his army, he ordered Edward Pakenham with the Third Division, which had been sent some distance to the west to cover the expected retreat, to face about and attack Thomières's division. He then ordered General Andrew Leith and the Fifth Division to attack the next French division, that commanded by Antoine Louis Popon de Maucune. Once these attacks were under way, the Fourth Division, under Lowry Cole, was to attack the French centre. Le Marchant was ordered to capitalise on any success achieved by Pakenham and Leith. 'You must then charge', Wellington told him, 'at all hazards.'[57]

In preparation for the charge, Le Marchant sent Lieutenants Colonel Charles Dalbaic and William Light 'to the front and to the right, to reconnoitre the ground over which the heavy brigade would have to advance, and to drop videttes where impediments, if any, should be found'.[58] They selected terrain which protected the cavalry from French artillery fire. As Le Marchant's men prepared to move, two of Thomières's three brigades had collapsed after the unexpected and devastating attack delivered by Pakenham's division. Leith, meanwhile, was advancing with his division and would strike Maucune's men as they were in the process of manoeuvring into square. One fresh brigade, sent by Taupin, had also arrived in an effort to restore Thomières's position.

Le Marchant's brigade, composed of eight squadrons, advanced in two lines, presenting a frontage of about 600 yards. As they commenced their charge, the centre and right of the brigade came up behind the leading edge of Pakenham's division, who though they were initially startled, quickly opened gaps in the line through which the cavalry could pass.[59] The cavalry swept through the remnants of Thomières's division, which essentially ceased to exist as a fighting unit. 'We quickly came up with the French Columns and charged their Rear,' wrote William Bragge, three days after the battle. 'Hundreds threw down their Arms, their Cavalry ran away, and most of the Artillery jumped upon the Horses and followed the Cavalry.'[60]

The left of the cavalry brigade, meanwhile, swept into Maucune's division, which had just been broken by Leith's advance. Inspired by this success, the brigade coalesced into a single solid line, sweeping onwards toward the leading elements of Taupin's division, who were likewise broken and fled the field in disorder. Having swept away the remnants of two divisions, and inflicted heavy losses on a third, the charge inevitably descended into some confusion. 'One or two charges mixed up the whole Brigade,' explained Bragge, 'it being impossible to see for Dust and Smoak.'[61] Le Marchant, however, wanted to exploit the energy his men exhibited and joined half a squadron of the 4th Dragoons in charging a small French square, who surprisingly held their fire until the British cavalry were at point-blank range. Le Marchant was hit in the groin; he fell from his horse, dead.

Le Marchant's cavalry charge was one of the most decisive of the war, sealing the defeat of the French left wing, and crippling their ability to regroup. Despite difficulties experienced by Cole's Fourth Division in the centre, Henry Clinton's Sixth Division pressed home the Anglo-Portuguese advantage. The Battle of Salamanca ended late in the evening, with the

French army of Portugal retreating in some disorder. Although the Light Division – still relatively fresh – pursued them, the remnants of Marmont's army were able to escape across an unguarded bridge at Alba de Tormes, much to Wellington's fury. In his despatch detailing the events of 22 July, Wellington lamented 'the loss of a most able officer'. When news of Le Marchant's death reached Horse Guards, the Duke of York reportedly wept.[62]

*   *   *

In the wake of his victory at Salamanca, Wellington ordered the Anglo-Portuguese army, in combination with supporting Spanish units, to liberate Madrid. The combined armies marched into Madrid on 12 August, but this was the start of a few fraught weeks of decision making. The move compelled Marshal Soult to withdraw his forces from Andalusia. He marched across southern Spain with the aim of converging at Valencia with the troops – which were nominally under Joseph Bonaparte's command – recently withdrawn from Madrid, and General Louis Gabriel Suchet's army of Catalonia. General Bertrand Clausel, meanwhile, had taken command of the remnants of the army of Portugal and was busy reorganising it in northern Spain, drawing support from the French Army of the North. As Wellington knew it must, a major victory over one French army would compel the others to combine their forces in an attempt to defeat and kick the British out of the Iberian Peninsula.

In an effort to delay this eventuality long enough to force a pause in operations for winter, Wellington sent General Hill and the Second Division south of the Tagus river to try to delay Soult's march to Valencia, while he took a detachment of 22,000 troops north to track down and defeat Clausel's army. Having failed to achieve this, he turned his attention to the citadel of Burgos, which commanded the great road to France. If he could capture this, there was a reasonable chance the French would be forced to winter east of the Ebro and south of the Tagus. Unfortunately, the detachment he took with him carried just three heavy guns, which proved no match for the heavily fortified walls of Burgos.[63] After more than a month of frustrating siegeworks, and several failed and costly attempts to storm the fortress, Wellington was forced to withdraw when Soult, after a successful rendezvous with Joseph and Suchet, moved north with as many as 73,000 troops at his disposal.[64] Despite Hill's attempt to curtail his advance, Soult managed to cross the Tagus, and threaten the allied supply and communication lines with Portugal.[65] The Anglo-Portuguese army was forced to retreat with some difficulty, back to Ciudad Rodrigo.

What had gone wrong? There was some inevitability to the unsuccessful conclusion to Wellington's 1812 campaign. Although French strength had been reduced sufficiently to allow him to break out from the Portuguese border, the total strength of the French armies in Spain still outnumbered Wellington's force by more than three to one. Though Wellington tried to balance the odds with clever manoeuvring in order to force the French to separate rather than concentrate their strength, the fact remained that the more of Spain that had been liberated by allied action, the less the French had to control, and the more troops were freed for operations against the Anglo-Portuguese army. Combine this with Wellington's key vulnerability – the length of his lines of supply and communication – and there was always a real possibility that he would be forced to withdraw or face the same catastrophe that had befallen Moore in late 1808.[66]

The further Wellington marched into Spain, the longer his line of operation became, to put it in terms Henry Lloyd had coined half a century earlier. Given that the main transportation routes in Spain were commanded by powerful fortifications, then any allied advance would immediately lose momentum as soon as the need for a siege arose. This would afford the French the opportunity once more to concentrate their forces to raise the siege, as had occurred on multiple occasions in 1811. Wellington could not afford to engage in set-piece battles on the enemy's terms, but at the same time, if denied possession of key fortifications, he would be unable to manoeuvre far from his original base of operations.

Henry Lloyd had foreseen this scenario. 'It will be always found, that . . . a frontier can be attacked only in a few points, and that these points are fixed and determined by the nature and position of the countries at war.' These points, Lloyd explained, were the fortresses which housed the supply depots, and the roads along which any army could march. 'An army, like a traveller, must necessarily depart from a given point, and proceed to a given point in the enemy's country. The line which unites these points, I call *the Line of Operation*.' The longer a line of operation extended, the more vulnerable it became. 'The magazines formed in the country which attacks may for some time supply the invading army,' Lloyd explained, 'until by a victory it is enabled to take some capital fortress, and secure a tract of the enemy's country sufficient to form a new *dépôt* to support the whole, or a great part of the troops . . . .' This Wellington had tried and failed to do at Burgos. 'If this cannot be executed,' Lloyd had written, 'it is evident the attacking army must, after a fruitless campaign, return to its own country.' Indeed, 'in proportion as an army advances into the enemy's country, new *dépôts* must be continually formed, and these as near as possible; for when they are at considerable distance, the convoys arrive slow, require strong escorts, and are so precarious, that the army can neither move nor act, especially if the country is close and the enemy active.'[67]

Wellington's only hope, according to Lloyd, at least, was shorter lines of operation. This had a number of predictable but not uncomplicated consequences. Since Wellington could not achieve this by laying siege to and capturing fortresses like Burgos, as Lloyd had suggested, he needed a new line of operation, and for that a new supply base was needed. As luck would have it, in August 1812, Sir Home Popham had suggested Santander 'as the best position for all communications'. Indeed, in a letter to Wellington shortly after its capture, Popham had expressed 'no doubt but it will be made your port of communication, it is very superior indeed to the Tagus'.[68] Wellington had no time to transfer his supply base in the summer of 1812. 'I should doubt the practicability of the plan at any time on account of the want of the means of transport in the neighbouring country,' he replied to Popham, 'but it certainly would not answer till the Army should be fairly well established on the Ebro or probably farther on.'[69] To borrow a phrase Wellington famously used later in his career, he kept the idea in his pocket.

Back in Ciudad Rodrigo, with many of the gains achieved in a hard-fought campaign seemingly reversed, Wellington began planning the transfer of his supply base from Lisbon to Santander. Effective interservice cooperation between the British Army and the Royal Navy would be needed to execute the move, while it would also be necessary to move the army itself, now numbering in excess of 80,000 troops, nearly 450 miles fuelled only by the supplies it could carry with it. As the main road was commanded by the citadel of Burgos, the army would have to find an alternative route to avoid getting bogged down in an attritional siege. The resultant plan was informed by Wellington's personal experience in India, but there are also hallmarks of Lloyd's theories, while the avoidance of battle until Wellington was absolutely certain of success was reminiscent of the 'indirect manoeuvres' practised with somewhat less success in America by Sir Henry Clinton. There, the plans had failed because Clinton was unable to inspire his subordinates to adopt the same approach and lacked a staff with sufficient competence and capabilities to turn complex plans into reality. In the Iberian Peninsula, thanks in large part to the formalisation of staff training by Le Marchant, Wellington had an extremely competent and efficient staff at his disposal.

Almost everything was in place. Wellington only lacked an effective quartermaster general. George Murray, who had held that position until 1811, had resigned, frustrated at the absence of the prospect of promotion while holding a staff appointment. Both his deputy, William De Lancey, and his eventual replacement, James Willoughby Gordon, had proved disappointments in Wellington's eyes. To Henry Torrens, the military secretary at Horse Guards, Wellington complained that 'you think he has some talents; whereas I am quite certain [Gordon] has none, excepting those of Clerk at his Desk ... He is no more fit to be QMG of the Army, than he is to be King of England. De Lancey, who is the Idlest fellow I ever saw, did the business much better'.[70] Murray, meanwhile, was 'rather inclined to seek the Command of troops in preference to returning to the Staff',[71] as the position of quartermaster general 'has too little connections with the troops to be long pursued, after one has attained a Rank that gives claims to Command'.[72] Wellington was horrified. 'I can only hope that you relinquish your situation with as much regret,' he wrote in May 1812, 'as I feel upon losing your assistance.'[73] By September, Wellington felt that 'every day I have fresh reason to regret your departure'.[74]

Indeed, Murray had vast experience of the sort of activities that Wellington now planned. After returning from Egypt, Murray had briefly attended the Royal Military College at High Wycombe, where he had been very happy. 'My chief pleasure arises from having abundance of employ-ment. The more I can force myself to application,' he had written in 1802, 'the more satisfaction do I feel, and nothing makes me so happy as the thought that were several hours added to the day, I should still find occupa-tions sufficient for them all.'[75] His stay there was curtailed in June 1802, when he was recalled to service in the West Indies. He had not been at High Wycombe sufficiently long to complete the course of instruction, and though his French had markedly improved, he remained, in the words of one of his officers during the Peninsular War, 'unacquainted with the nature of military drawing'.[76]

After a brief stay in the West Indies, Murray was recalled to Horse Guards upon the outbreak of the new war with France. On his arrival in London, he was told by the quartermaster general, Sir Robert Brownrigg, that he was to be assistant quartermaster general and 'a scientific and intelligent assistant',[77] assigned to the newly formed Depot of Military Knowledge. Another innovation championed by the Duke of York, the Depot had four branches. Murray was to head the 'plans branch', and was responsible for the 'direction of the confidential correspondence ... for the purpose of collection of Military Knowledge'. Murray was also instructed to collect 'such plans as have been acted upon and the preparing of others most likely to be useful in future cases of Home and Foreign Service'.

Once this information was properly analysed, the 'movements branch' would use the resulting intelligence to prepare maps, route plans and movements of armies in the field. The third section, a military library, was 'intended to expose the course of past events', with analysis of manuscripts and documents related to former campaigns, 'with a view to future utility by showing the causes which have led to former success, or which may have occasioned the failure of Military operations'.[78] The final section was to be known as the 'topographical branch', and was designed for 'the arrangement and preservation of maps and plans; the direction of a drawing room for making copies of the same to be given out to officers destined for particular services, also for reducing or extending the scale or otherwise improving rough drafts & manuscript maps'.[79]

As a centralised organisation responsible for the management of intelligence and mapping, the Depot had considerable potential to transform the way in which Britain prepared for and executed military operations in the future. Unlike the Royal Military College and Shorncliffe, the innovation never reached its full potential. 'The chief obstacle has been a want of sufficient accommodation', York wrote to Castlereagh, 'to place in security and to arrange in order the valuable materials which were to be collected.'[80] Murray was also preoccupied with planning for and anticipating an invasion of southern England by the forces of Napoleon Bonaparte, then gathering at Boulogne. 'The preparations for receiving in a suitable manner, the First Consul of France, engross all our time,' Murray wrote to his sister in July 1803. 'If he does us any mischief it must be from our own bad management. Indeed, if we cannot defend ourselves with all the advantages we enjoy, we are extremely unworthy of being any longer an independent nation.'[81]

Nevertheless, Murray's brief experience at the Depot cemented the need for as broad a professional knowledge of military operations as possible. Prior to his deployment to the Peninsula, he had compiled a range of reports describing battles and campaigns fought by the French Army,[82] as well as detailed historical accounts of the previous campaigns fought by Britain in Portugal and Spain – notably the campaign led by the Earl of Loudoun in 1762.[83] His experience at the Depot also clarified the relationship between military and topographical intelligence: the successful planning and execution of operations and campaigns would be impossible without both.

This was reflected in Murray's 'Instructions to Officers of the Quartermaster Generals' Department', which he compiled and distributed when he took command of the department in 1809. 'One of the first Duties', he explained, 'of the Quarter Master Generals Department is to acquire a Knowledge of the Country which is the Theatre of the Operations of the Army.'[84] Murray's 'great object' was 'to gain an accurate report of a country, its roads, soil, rivers, etc., and the means it possesses of affording shelter for the Army'. Indeed, 'the primary object is with him moving the Troops and Artillery, and afterwards a complete knowledge of the local situation of the Villages, etc., with reference to Cantonment'.[85] To that extent, Murray preferred detailed maps, rather than the sketches which were taught by Jarry at High Wycombe. 'The Style of Drawing of our Wycombe Eléves is in general very bad,' he wrote in late 1810, 'and few if any of them are at all acquainted with surveying'.[86]

Murray looked for more precision in drawings produced by his map-makers and tested those recommended for secondment in order to identify the appropriate skills. When he arrived in Portugal in October 1811, Thomas Mitchell was recognised for his brilliant draughtsmanship, but Murray still wanted to ascertain the extent of Mitchell's skills. He was commissioned to draw nine maps of the French retreat from Torres Vedras the previous March.[87] Murray wanted sketches which included, for example, 'the situation of the French Army after it had passed through Pombal, and that of the Allied Army when it was intended to have attacked the Enemy ...'.[88] Mitchell produced detailed sketch maps, which identified important terrain features, and the locations of dwellings and roads. He also complemented the maps with views of the terrain, with specific features marked and cross-referenced with the maps. When appropriate, he also located French and allied army units, as Murray had requested.[89]

Mitchell was capable of producing in his maps both the exacting detail that Murray required and the type of sketch maps which could be used easily by officers and soldiers on the march. Though not himself educated at High Wycombe, Mitchell demonstrated the same natural talent as other officers who had attended and became one of Murray's most reliable map-makers. While Murray was in England, Mitchell was trained by Captain Philip Bainbrigge, who had himself demonstrated considerable natural talent, and together they helped produce reliable mapping for the sieges of Ciudad Rodrigo and Badajoz. Bainbrigge even reconnoitred and sketched part of the terrain over which the Battle of Salamanca was fought. Sketch mapping became particularly important during extended operations, when it was vital to convey topographical intelligence quickly and effectively to units in the field. During the retreat from Burgos, Bainbrigge proved to be essential to the identification of suitable routes, such as practicable river crossings.[90]

In this way, the work of Murray's map-makers complemented that of other intelligence-collection organisations in the Peninsula. One of the most important was the Corps of Guides, formed by then Captain George Scovell in 1808 from a group of French soldiers who had deserted after the Battle of Vimeiro. 'The first object was to use them as interpreters for the staff officers, as they all spoke French, and had acquired a good deal of Spanish and Portuguese,' Scovell recalled in a memorandum drafted in 1854. 'They were also used in procuring guides to accompany officers or Dragoons sent with despatches.' Though the original corps was disbanded after the withdrawal from Corunna, Murray asked Scovell to reform the Guides in April 1809, eventually reaching a complement of 200. The Guides adopted a wide variety of responsibilities, including maintaining communication between Wellington's headquarters and his divisions, with a postal route of 'regular stages of some ten or twelve miles each'.[91] They also took responsibility for route reconnaissance, language translation 'between the common village guides ... and the leaders of columns of troops', and even timely intelligence on the enemy.[92]

The information from Scovell's guides would have been meaningless without the support of an extraordinarily extensive and effective tactical and operational intelligence network. As with other innovations employed by Wellington and Murray in the Peninsular campaigns, the intelligence organisation that they adopted was the product of a combination of received wisdom, personal experience and a contingent response to the specific situation they faced. Timely and reliable intelligence was, of course, known to be such an 'Essential a part of the Service', as the Duke of Marlborough had explained to Parliament in 1712, 'that no War can be conducted successfully without early and good intelligence'.[93] Saxe had considered it of such value that it was 'cheap at any price'.[94] And plenty of advice was available on how to collect intelligence: from the employment of spies to the use of codes to facilitate secure transmission. 'Secret Correspondence' was to be conducted, advised one mid-eighteenth-century military treatise, 'either by Cyphers, or certain Compositions used in Place of Ink'.[95]

In the Peninsula, Murray recruited and deployed 'observing officers' on specific intelligence, reconnaissance and surveillance missions. These individuals often volunteered for the role and equipped themselves for their duties. In 1809, Captain Charles Cocks, of the 16th Light Dragoons, offered his services to Wellington as an observing officer. He wrote to his cousin asking him to send out 'a two-foot portable military telescope ... a pocket compass' and the 'largest maps of Spain and Portugal done on canvas and folding in a case'.[96] By frequently putting themselves in considerable danger, Cocks and his fellow 'observing officers' collected intelligence which complemented information brought to headquarters from much further afield. Following his appointment in March 1810, Charles Stuart, the British minister to Portugal, had organised a network of agents who spied on behalf of the British government. Though basic in nature, the intelligence they collected offered early warning of French movements. One network of agents brought regular updates from the Franco-Spanish border, where a spy disguised as a cobbler literally counted the number of French troops crossing into Spain.[97] Again, the staff of the quartermaster general's department proved essential interlocutors, helping to link Stuart's intelligence with that brought to headquarters by locally based sources.[98]

The challenge was not really how to collect reliable intelligence, or even to get it into the hands of decision makers in a timely fashion. Rather, the challenge lay in how to analyse the quantity of information available. In this respect, the military treatises of the eighteenth century were largely silent. Wellington, though, had had considerable experience of the difficulties of sorting reliable and unreliable intelligence during his service in India. There he had established 'three distinct departments for intelligence ... the head of each of which communicated directly' with Wellesley, and 'reported immediately on its arrival, the intelligence received', allowing him to compare and contrast the different accounts and to determine the most likely course of action.[99]

In the Peninsula, Murray served to analyse the intelligence at headquarters, but he also increasingly relied on the divisional staffs to provide finished intelligence reports. He was therefore able to incorporate the latest and most up-to-date information on French movements into his campaign planning.[100] In 1812, Wellington missed Murray's sage advice – and this helps explain some of the difficulties in the execution of the Burgos campaign. As the year drew to a close, he was expressing his 'earnest wish ... that you should return to your old situation upon the Peninsula'. York, meanwhile, had recognised 'the active course of your profession which will undoubtedly lead to any elevation as a soldier which your ambition might suggest'.[101] Satisfied that continued service as quartermaster general would not inhibit his career, George Murray returned to

Portugal, arriving at Freneda, much to Wellington's relief, in March 1813, to complete preparations for the forthcoming campaign.

There was much to do: divisions needed to be moved into position, the right equipment needed to be brought up, maps drawn, river-crossing points identified, routes of march planned. Murray worked tirelessly. His daily routine commenced with a morning walk and a breakfast of 'tea, Toast, Butter and Marmalade', during which he sorted through the 'packet of letters and papers' which invariably arrived 'early in the morning ... I open and read and sort those that are to be answered or attended to by my assistant'. He then 'set to work upon my own share of business. Between 10 and 11 o'clock generally I go to Lord Wellington, and after seeing him I return to complete my business of the day. After that is over, I mount my horse and ride till sunset'.[102]

It was vital for the success of the campaign that when it began the French should be taken by surprise: everything needed to be completed in the utmost secrecy. Wellington only confirmed the scope of the operation to the Earl of Bathurst nine days before it was launched. 'I propose on this side to commence our operations by turning the enemy's position on the Douro, by passing the left of our army over that river within the Portuguese frontier', he wrote. Wellington would use the right wing of the army to threaten the French left. He planned to 'move with it myself across the Tormes, and establish a bridge on the Douro below Zamora. The two wings of the army will thus be connected, and the enemy's position on the Douro will be turned. The Spanish army of Galicia', meanwhile, 'will be on the Esla on the left of our army at the same time that our army will be on that river'.[103]

If all went to plan, the French army of Portugal – already badly reduced by troop withdrawals to try to stem the losses suffered after Napoleon's disastrous invasion of Russia the previous year – would be forced to withdraw. It was not until 20 May, a month later than planned, that all the preparations had been made. The success of the campaign, that would become known by the enormous battle that concluded it at Vitoria in north-eastern Spain, was the result of a combination of the skills and capabilities of the British and Portuguese troops, of the ingenuity of the plan devised by Wellington, of superior intelligence organisation, and of the work completed by George Murray and the staff of the Quartermaster General's Department prior to the commencement of and during the operation. All of this was also the product of decades of varied military experience across the globe, and the translation of that experience into unique military knowledge which enabled the British to respond to new and near-overwhelming challenges in an innovative and ultimately successful fashion.

* * *

Between 20 May and 21 June 1813, the Anglo-Portuguese army, supported by a division of Spanish troops, had outflanked three French defensive positions, and fought and achieved a decisive victory at Vitoria, just one month after leaving Portugal. In that time, 80,000 troops had marched nearly 450 miles. Thereafter, the army had continued its advance to the French border, successfully defended against attempted French counterattacks on 25 July and 31 August, besieged and captured the fortress at San Sebastián and starved that of Pamplona into submission. Throughout, Wellington and Murray worked closely together. The operations in the foothills of the Pyrenees proved especially challenging, and great efforts were made to record previously unmapped terrain. In late August, Judge Advocate Francis Larpent 'found Lord Wellington . . . busy with all the Spanish staff and General Murray, with a dozen great Spanish drawings and plans of the mountains about them . . .'.[104]

The capture of San Sebastián offered Wellington the opportunity he needed to mount the invasion of France. On 7 October, he and Murray had orchestrated a crossing of the river Bidassoa, the first of a three stage assault. A month later, on 8 November, they stood together near the advanced posts of the Light Division, on top of a mountain called La Rhune, in the foothills of the Pyrenees. From the hilltop, the two officers were able to make out the location of the French lines. While Wellington's army was still stationed in Spanish territory, their adversary now defended France itself. The two officers were planning a huge attack. 'These fellows think themselves invulnerable,' he said to the commander of the 52nd, Colonel John Colborne, 'but I will beat them out, and with great ease.'

'That we shall beat them,' responded Colborne, 'when your lordship attacks, I have no doubt, but for the ease —.'

'Ah, Colborne, with your local knowledge only, you are perfectly right,' Wellington replied mischievously. 'It appears difficult, but the enemy have not men to man the works and lines they occupy. They dare not concentrate a sufficient body to resist the attacks I shall make upon them. I can pour a greater force on certain points than they can concentrate to resist me.' Wellington then turned to Murray and began a 'very earnest conversation'. Colborne and the other staff officers present prepared to take their leave. 'Oh, lie still', Wellington told them. One of those present, Colborne's brigade-major, Captain Harry Smith, recorded in later life his recollection of that conversation:

> After he had conversed for some time with Sir George Murray, Murray took out of his sabretache his writing-materials, and began to write the plan of attack for the whole army. When it was finished, so clearly had he understood the Duke, I do not think he erased one word. He says, 'My lord, is this your desire?' ... As Murray read, the Duke's eye was directed with his telescope to the spot in question ... When Sir G. Murray had finished, the Duke smiled and said, 'Ah, Murray, this will put us in possession of the fellows' lines'.[105]

Though Smith wrote his autobiography decades after the Peninsular War, the strength of the relationship between Wellington and Murray was a powerful memory. The operation which they were planning was the crossing of the Nivelle River. It would conclude with the Anglo-Portuguese army establishing a toehold in French territory, having driven them from their defences without fighting a set-piece battle. A month later, a further river crossing, this time of the Nive, would bring the allied army to the gates of Bayonne.[106]

The 1813 campaign had been a triumph of staff work and organisation. Murray was 'the life and soul of the army next to Lord Wellington ... it is thought that without him we could never have done what we have'. But in its genesis the plan was the product of decades of combined experience and ideas. Wellington had conceived of the idea as a grand version of the 'light and quick movements' he had developed in India, but the genius of the plan rested not in its culmination at Vitoria, but in the avoidance of culmination until Vitoria. The influence of Henry Lloyd is apparent, alongside the breadth of experience that helped the development of those ideas. Finally, Wellington was only able to implement this plan because of the dexterity and flexibility of his own army, as exemplified by the Light Division, itself the product of informal ideas and knowledge brought from America.

The wandering army was now a professional army, reliant not just on chance and bravery, but on the professional knowledge of its officers, on a scientific understanding of war as taught at High Wycombe, and on independence of thought as instilled at Shorncliffe. This was only possible because informal knowledge networks, the product of an accidental military enlightenment, had allowed diverse ideas and experiences to be exchanged throughout the army. So long as they existed, the British would continue to learn the lessons taught by war, even if the formal structures of education and knowledge sharing were dismantled. But in the wake of ultimate victory, and faced with the need for a peace dividend, the British army was dramatically reduced in size. In so doing, the British inadvertently dismantled the informal knowledge networks themselves, and hamstrung the army's ability to learn from experience.

CHAPTER 12

'The Dread of Innovation'

From Enlightenment to Ignorance, 1815–1856

WHEN news reached him that Napoleon had invaded the Low Countries in June 1815, William Napier was immersed in studies at the Royal Military College, which had recently relocated to Farnham. He had joined his brother Charles, and there the two hoped to broaden their extensive practical military experience into a more general understanding of war. 'A man ... cannot learn his profession without constant study to prepare, especially for the higher ranks,' Charles wrote, 'because he there wants the knowledge and experience of others improved by his own.' Officers who obtained high rank 'with an empty skull', he argued, were 'too late to fill it'.[1] Nevertheless, if an officer wanted to progress his career, formal education remained an inadequate alternative to battlefield success, and when news reached Farnham that a showdown outside Brussels seemed imminent, William had rushed to join the allied forces gathering in the area. He managed to secure passage from Dover and sailed the morning of 18 June. How frustrated he must have been to have missed the decisive battle. He joined the army as it marched on Paris, learning of the violence and brutality of the action at Waterloo from the survivors.

'Lord Wellington's luck predominates over Bonaparte's,' Napier wrote to his wife. 'As it is I believe that a nearer thing never was; the loss in men I should think pretty equal. Bonaparte lost about 40,000 ... We lost with the Prussians about 35,000.'[2] Among the papers that Napier collected was the eyewitness testimony of Horace Churchill, whose experience of the 'Battle of the Giants' – as he dubbed it – was rather typical. A Guards officer,

Churchill was Lord Hill's aide-de-camp. He observed the opening stages of the battle from the British right flank. What stood out from his lengthy description of it was its attritional character. At noon on 18 June 1815, 'the enemy began a cannonade from 250 pieces upon the front of our position'. The bombardment was, Churchill wrote, 'the most tremendous I believe ever known in the annals of war . . . the butchery was terrible'.[3] Wellington himself could not fail to agree. 'Hard pounding this, gentlemen,' he reportedly remarked to his staff, 'but we will see who can pound the longest.'[4] There is a sense from Wellington's private correspondence that he was somewhat disappointed at the way the battle had unfolded. 'Never did I see such a pounding match,' he wrote to his old comrade, Marshal William Beresford. 'Both were what the boxers call gluttons. Napoleon did not manoeuvre at all. He just moved forward in the old style, in columns, and was driven off in the old style.'[5]

In the course of the battle, Churchill had three horses shot from under him and, in his words, did his 'best to be killed, but Fortune protected' him. 'I had rather have fallen that day as a British infantry-man, or as a French cuirassier', he later wrote, 'than die ten years hence in my bed.'[6] This sentiment was commonly felt. The victory over Napoleon's forces at Waterloo was seen as the end of an era. Those unable to reach the scene of battle experienced frustration at being denied a final opportunity for glory.[7] Napier, meanwhile, an ardent Francophile, was 'much annoyed at finding how completely the French nation has lost all sense of shame'. In a further letter to his wife, on 9 July, this time from Paris, he noted that his 'admiration of Bonaparte is increased tenfold when I find what very contemptible stuff he had to work with'. He reported rumours that 'Napoleon is in Paris' and had watched the entrance of Louis XVIII into the city. 'It does not appear certain that the war is yet over,' Napier concluded, perhaps a little too hopefully.[8]

Napoleon, of course, was not in Paris, but had long since fled to Rochefort. After briefly entertaining the hope of fleeing across the Atlantic, he surrendered to the British aboard HMS *Bellerophon*. His captors now pondered what to do with the fallen emperor. The British prime minister, Lord Liverpool, initially favoured trial and execution as a rebel, but was persuaded out of this stance by his foreign secretary, Viscount Castlereagh. Instead, the Cabinet held 'strongly to the opinion that the best place of custody would be at a distance from Europe', and ultimately, they decided to banish him to the tiny island of St Helena in the South Atlantic.[9]

The Napoleonic Wars were finally at an end. After three years of occupation, in 1818 allied forces were withdrawn and, in Britain at least, demobilised.[10] The British Army had reached a pinnacle of professionalism and innovation, through a combination of interrelated factors: intellectual innovation and adaptation in the face of global military challenges; the concurrent circulation of military knowledge gained through the global experience of warfare; and networks that spanned the globe and facilitated the exchange of experience, ideas and military knowledge across space and time. Together, these factors enabled Britain's accidental military enlightenment. But in the wake of ultimate victory at Waterloo, the relationship between innovation, global challenge and knowledge circulation began to disintegrate.

Intellectual innovation, such as it was, was stymied by the seeming lessons presented at Waterloo, which had seen the traditional attritional approach to decisive battle triumph over the concept of manoeuvre and mobility that had emerged with such success in the years before. Despite the advent of steam and the telegraph revolutionising transportation and communications, and the increasing performance of rifled weapons rendering conventional tactics obsolete, attempted transformation to keep pace was hampered by Wellington himself, who 'opposed every project for major reforms of military administration'.[11]

Among those military writers who championed conservative thinking was William Napier, and he deployed the successes of the Peninsular War to confirm these perceptions. In contrast, as one proponent of change, Colonel John Mitchell argued that 'in no profession is the dread of innovation so great as in the army. No sooner is an officer looked upon as a theorist and innovator than he is set down as an unhappy person', whose ideas could be safely ignored and marginalised. 'The imperfect manner also, in which military history has, for the most part, been written', wrote Mitchell, 'is another cause of the slow progress of military science.' In Mitchell's opinion, 'a superficial view of every campaign, war, or battle, gives rise to new and fashionable doctrine, that are followed and upheld till some melancholy and unexpected catastrophe lays bare the feeble foundations on which they had been raised.'[12] Mitchell was echoing earlier theorists, such as Henry Lloyd, who had sought to challenge historical assumptions.

The informal knowledge networks, which had allowed ideas and experience from across the world to inform the development of the British Army during the Napoleonic Wars, were another important check on these assumptions. Though new regular military publications entered the market, such as the *United Service Journal* (founded in 1827) and the *Naval and Military Gazette* and the *United Service Gazette* (both founded in 1833), these could not replicate the informal exchange of knowledge created by the movement of regiments around the world. Despite the fact that those regiments could expect to spend between two-thirds and three-quarters of their service abroad, that service tended now to be limited to fewer places. New military knowledge was generated in remote colonies, shared infrequently with Horse Guards, and rarely with other colonies.

Yet in the decades after Waterloo, Britain fought at least 10 large-scale colonial conflicts, and it was in the defence and expansion of empire that Britain now expended its military effort. On the one hand, the expanding empire – the percentage of the world's land mass controlled, formally or informally, by the British Army rose from 5 per cent in 1750 to 20 per cent in 1900 – placed insurmountable burdens on the British Army,[13] such that, in Wellington's words, there were barely enough troops 'to relieve the sentries on duty in different parts of the world'.[14] On the other hand, the monotony of colonial garrison duty fostered intellectual stagnation. When Thomas Seaton went to India as an infantry cadet, he remarked that 'no care was in any way taken of us. We were neither sent to drill, not taught our duty, nor encouraged to study the native languages'.[15] While there is evidence that some officers sought to follow the example set by John Moore and create a system of discipline based on encouragement rather than punishment,[16] the reality was that regiments became intensely inward-looking.[17] The circulation and exchange of knowledge produced by the physical movement of personnel around the world all but ended. Despite impressive, localised reforms that illustrated progressive thinking on systems of discipline and professionalisation, Wellington, and a cadre of conservative officers in Horse Guards, prevented any attempts to render these peripheral developments in the centre. The Army itself remained unreformed, while its regiments, away on colonial garrison duty across the globe, frequently in contact with unpredictable and culturally diverse enemies, adapted at varying speeds to the emergence of new ideas and thinking.[18] Arguably, the Army was more a conglomeration of detachments scattered across the world, than a cohesive force.[19]

Finally, the British sought to dismantle the knowledge networks themselves. British officials were deeply apprehensive about the character and strength of their likely colonial enemies, which, as had been the case with the armies of Tipu Sultan of Mysore and the Maratha Confederacy, were trained in modern infantry tactics by European mercenaries. Indeed, by

1837, the Sikh army, the *Khalsa Dal*, was the most formidable army on the subcontinent. When the British commander-in-chief, Sir Henry Fane, visited Lahore for the wedding of Sikh leader Ranjit Singh's grandson, he was treated to an awe-inspiring display of Sikh military power. He estimated the Khalsa's strength as between 60 and 70 battalions, 700 artillery pieces and a large cavalry contingent of possibly 4,000 men.[20] Moreover, the European drill demonstrated by the Sikh warriors, in particular by the *Fauj-i Khas* – the Royal Bodyguard – heightened concerns that in a conflict with the Sikhs, the East India Company army would prove unequal to the task of extending British control over the Punjab.[21]

With such formidable armies, the British sought to prevent their enemies from learning about British and European tactics. French and Italian mercenaries were arrested, and British ones prevented from taking employment in Ranjit Singh's army.[22] Despite localised adaptations and innovations to counter specific threats, the informal knowledge networks that had previously allowed the transmission of ideas and experiences between theatres were severed. Whereas ideas and practices had previously been transmitted across continents, the British now sought to stymie this flow of information.

As a result, while the British might have curtailed the transmission of ideas to indigenous foes, the localised ideas and practices which had been the key to innovative responses in the past were transmitted from the periphery to the centre only in a fragmentary manner. In an atmosphere that sought to curtail knowledge transmission and innovation in an adversary's army, the principal outcome was merely that knowledge transmission and innovation was stymied within the British Army. This meant new thinking seldom challenged prevailing assumptions, and what debates occurred almost always developed in a binary context which pitted classic continental thinking against fresher but often regionally specific knowledge. With intellectual innovation stagnating, circulation of new ideas curtailed and networks of knowledge exchange dismantled, the British Army in the early nineteenth century quickly moved from military enlightenment to ignorance.

* * *

The influence of the Napoleonic War reached long into the nineteenth century. William Napier, who had trained under John Moore at Shorncliffe and seen action throughout the Peninsular War in the 43rd Regiment of Foot, retired on half-pay in 1819, and began to write on military theories.

He first started by commenting and critiquing the works of emerging continental theorists like Baron Antoine-Henri de Jomini.[23] In an article for the *Edinburgh Review*, Napier validated Jomini's arguments for the need to operate the mass of an army against a decisive point. Capitalising on his natural interest in military history, Napier used the campaigns of Frederick the Great as well as Napoleon's to illustrate the value of operating on interior lines. He related these lessons to both Moore and Wellington, with the Battle of Salamanca being a particularly 'beautiful application' of the principle of concentration of effort on a decisive point.[24] There was nothing particularly revelatory about this. Jomini was heavily influenced by Dietrich Heinrich von Bülow's *Spirit of the Modern System of War*, which had reflected many of Henry Lloyd's theories.[25]

In 1823, Napier commenced work on a history of the Peninsular War. It took him five years to conduct research on the documents to which he managed to obtain access. These included some of Wellington's official correspondence, as well as that of Joseph Bonaparte, Napoleon's older brother, found in the French baggage train captured after the Battle of Vitoria. In Paris, Nicolas Soult provided access to his own private correspondence and facilitated admission to the archives of the Bureau de la Guerre. In addition, Napier collected the private correspondence and journals of numerous officers, French and British, though both Wellington and Murray declined to provide access to their private papers. The first volume was published in 1828, with one reviewer commenting that 'in depth of thought, eloquence, and military skill and knowledge, it is altogether unrivalled by any other military work in our language'.[26] Others were less generous, particularly those, and the supporters of those, whom Napier saw fit to criticise, notably Generals Picton, Craufurd and Beresford. In contrast, French officers who had shown particular tactical skill received favourable coverage and Napoleon himself was lionised.

Though some of Napier's conclusions about policy and strategy, as well as the decision making of the British government, were questionable, his description of the campaigns and battles was authoritative and based on widespread and comprehensive research, which attempted to offer balanced analysis. It would be nearly a century, and only after the release of previously undisclosed archival materials, before Napier's history's was surpassed. The history became the premier source for the military education of new officers entering the Royal Military Academy at Sandhurst, particularly after Thomas Mitchell's Atlas was held up in preproduction squabbles with the publisher.[27] With the publication of these volumes,

Napier secured a reputation as the pre-eminent British military thinker of the first half of the nineteenth century.

Despite this, Napier declined, when asked, to write a book on the philosophy of war. 'What an overwhelming labour!' he wrote when explaining his decision in 1848. 'There is no work on the "Philosophy of War", I believe in any language. I have often heard literary men regret this; but I believe they have not considered the subject, and have not seen the reason.'[28] Evidently, unlike many of those whom he chose to criticise, Napier had not read Lloyd's essay on the philosophy of war in the latter's history of the Seven Years' War, nor had he read *Vom Krieg* by Prussian staff officer and veteran Carl von Clausewitz, recently published posthumously though only in German. Napier perhaps subscribed to the notion, as evinced in an essay on the 'Regeneration of the Army', published in 1849 in the *United Services Magazine,* that 'theorising never has been the characteristic of Englishmen', for it was 'perhaps, held in too great disrepute ... The English mind,' the author argued, 'is totally unfitted for such a study. Practice is all he cares for.'[29]

Indeed, 'how can a man who has never commanded an army in the field dare to dogmatise on such a subject?' Napier asked. 'A great and successful commander may do so safely, no other person can.'[30] Napier's observations on the changing character of war in the nineteenth century were therefore rooted solely in the history of the most recent European campaign in which the British Army had fought. Unlike Lloyd, who had successfully blended historical study with new theories on the art of war, Napier declined to do the latter, preferring instead to highlight the successes of the past as suggestions of how to conduct operations in the future.

For Napier, British success in the Peninsular War could be attributed to two things: the genius of the command and the excellence of the army. Though 'practice and study may make a good general as far as the handling of troops and the designing of a campaign', more than professional skill was required to produce a great general. 'Genius begins where rules end,' Napier wrote. Wellington was successful largely 'because he modified and reconciled the great principles of art with the peculiar difficulties' of the situation he found himself in.[31] In this way, Wellington modified the tactical doctrine first established by Dundas, and thus nurtured the natural brilliance of the British Army.

Though French columns might have proved effective against other continental armies, 'against the British it must always fail, because the English infantry is sufficiently firm, intelligent, and well disciplined to wait calmly in lines for the adverse masses, and sufficiently bold to close upon them with the bayonet'.[32] None of this would have been possible, however, without 'that queen of weapons', the musket.[33] Combined with the unbreakable effectiveness of the thin red line, the musket offered the British soldier everything he needed to achieve success on the battlefield. In part, this was due to the innate martial character of the Englishman, who, despite inadequate peacetime preparation, 'six years of uninterrupted success had engrafted on their natural strength and fierceness a confidence which rendered them invincible'.[34]

But this did not excuse the need for peacetime training and education. Indeed, Napier observed that 'in the beginning of each war, England has to seek in blood for the knowledge necessary to ensure success'.[35] This was because there was no adequate peacetime training system. In Napier's view, only 'when completely disciplined, – and three years are required to accomplish this,' the British soldier is 'observant, and quick to comprehend his orders, full of resources under difficulties, calm and resolute in danger, and more than usually obedient and careful of his officers in moments of imminent peril'.[36] In some respects, Napier was ahead of his time in recommending that a trained standing army be permanently raised, and it would not be until the Cardwell reforms of the 1870s, where anything like what he envisaged in 1828 would be realised.[37] In other respects, however, Napier represented the stagnation of military thought in Britain in the first half of the nineteenth century. He opposed the introduction of new weapons, which he said, favoured armies with superior numbers, and risked undermining the key strength of the British Army, namely the discipline and steadfastness of the infantry. New, more accurate weapons, 'which at 800 yards will enable its handler to knock down a man with tolerable certainty, must paralyse the action of cavalry against infantry, and of artillery within that range'. As a result, 'battles will be more confusedly arranged, more bloody, and less decisive'.[38]

Although the first volume of Napier's *History* did not sell particularly well, interest in the subsequent volumes gradually increased and by the mid-1830s, Napier had secured a reputation as the premier military historian of the age. The books, however, were divisive. Napier's vibrant Francophilia annoyed many readers, while his misunderstanding of the military situation riled many, particularly George Murray.[39] Upon publication of the fifth volume, Murray called it a 'pompous, flagitious, and shallow *History*', criticising Napier for 'a marked partiality for the French', and of a 'general and indiscriminating discontentment with whatever does not harmonize with his own prejudices and passions'. These factors combined 'to disqualify Colonel Napier for writing history'.[40]

Murray took exception to Napier's historical analysis. In volume two, for example, Napier referred to Napoleon's network of communications as the 'keystone' of his military system.[41] 'If it could be shown that he was ever the slave of a system,' Murray responded, 'it would be extremely difficult to prove that the "*key-stone*" of that system was the securing of his lines of communication.' In actual fact, Murray argued, Napoleon 'had the hardihood to put it aside sometimes without disadvantage, when he was aiming at great immediate results', and that on occasion this 'led to some of his greatest reverses'. Elsewhere, Murray criticised Napier for discounting the contribution made by the Spanish to the war effort. 'There never was displayed, perhaps, in any war, more diligence, more fidelity, or more disinterestedness', he wrote, 'than was shown by the Spaniards in procuring information respecting the enemy.'[42]

Napier's poor historical judgement, however, was nothing compared to 'the very superficial character of [his] military opinions, or *strategical doctrine*', because 'the plan which Colonel Napier had laid down for himself in writing his book has rendered it not only a history of the war in the Peninsula, but also a *treatise upon military science*'.[43] While Murray never committed his own military treatise to paper, his response to Napier's argument reveals what this might have looked like. He chose to highlight the differences between the two, by critiquing Napier's analysis of Wellesley's 1809 campaign.

In the second volume of his *History*, Napier implicitly criticised Wellesley for his decision, upon resuming command of the British army in Lisbon in April 1809, to move first against Soult in Oporto rather than Victor in Spain. 'In a *strategic point of view*', Napier wrote, 'to fall upon Victor was best, because he was the most *dangerous neighbour to Portugal*.'[44] Murray was so infuriated by this claim that he was prompted to outline some of what he considered to be the principles of war. First, clearly echoing Lloyd's concept of 'lines of operation', Murray stated that

> One of the most general and established principles of the art of war is, that in every military movement the base from which it proceeds, and the communications with that base, ought to be secured. The only exceptions to this principle are when the object of the movement contemplated is to form a new base; or when final success is so certain, or so probable, as to justify the neglect of the principle.

Had Wellesley moved first against Victor, then he would have left his supply and communications base exposed to a flank assault from Oporto.

A second 'important principle in the art of war', Murray continued, 'is to prefer a definite to an indefinite object'. Victor was not fixed in position, so would have been able to manoeuvre, forcing Wellesley to overextend his lines or fight on detrimental terms. Soult, by contrast, was fixed. The move against Oporto was therefore a limited and sustainable operation, whereas one against Victor was potentially open-ended. Finally, 'a third principle of war', Murray concluded, 'is that when two enterprises of equal, or nearly equal, importance present themselves, that enterprise should be undertaken first, the accomplishment of which will most favour the successful issue of both'. Forcing Soult from Oporto would secure the British position in Portugal, force a reorientation of the strategic balance in Spain and set the conditions for success against Victor. The same argument could not be made in favour of moving first against Victor.[45]

Elsewhere, Murray repeatedly criticised Napier's misreading of the military situation. Napier's geographical understanding of the theatre of war was shown to be at best incomplete, at worst inept. Rivers in Portugal were said to be fordable, and thus presenting no real obstacle to a French invader. Murray was at pains to point out that even if the rivers were fordable, which most were not, then the steep embankments and broken nature of the countryside through which they flowed rendered them significant geographical obstacles. This had the effect of forcing the French to choose one of three routes for invasion, which offered considerable advantages to the defender of Portugal, rather than, as Napier claimed, leaving 'no defensible frontier'.[46] The experienced military professional, Murray wrote, 'should receive another hint as to the real value of his much-vaunted local information'. The general reader, meanwhile, 'should be cautioned against relying implicitly upon our military historian's professional opinions'.[47]

Though Murray was perhaps the most senior officer to criticise Napier overtly, the latter responded with a well-crafted but vitriolic counterpoint published in the *London and Westminster Review*.[48] The opinions of a senior member of Wellington's staff could not be easily discounted, not least because Murray had a far better and more nuanced understanding of war. Nor was Murray alone in his views. Colonel John Mitchell also considered Napier to be a poor historian. In his view, Napier's *History* 'does not, from first to last, contain a single new idea or original thought upon war, or the science of arms'. This, perhaps, was the biggest problem with Napier's work. As with the military histories and treatises published in the decades after Marlborough's victories, Napier perpetuated false assumptions and lessons from victory in the last war. Writing in the middle of the nineteenth century, Mitchell echoed the mid-eighteenth-century malaise. The science of war, he said, quoting Maurice de Saxe, was 'a science covered with darkness'. Mitchell did, however, agree with Napier insofar that he questioned why military improvement must be 'constantly purchased by a boundless waste of human blood'.[49]

Mitchell bemoaned the absence of 'a single work on military science in the English language', a fact which he blamed on the persecution of military thinkers. Quoting Bülow, Mitchell argued that 'military writings which are found to contain truth, novelty, and originality, or to bear proofs of genius and talent, invariably exclude their author from all promotion and employment'. Such was the case with Folard, Puysegur, Berenhorst, Lloyd and Bülow himself. As a result, Mitchell exclaimed, 'learning and knowledge are but secondary objects to a military man'. In the absence of a British voice on the subject, Mitchell was keen to recommend Carl von Clausewitz's 'very able, though lengthy, and often obscure book on War'.

Mitchell's interpretations of Clausewitz were, however, at best simplistic and at worst dangerous. 'Even the greatest of the Continental battles lasted entire days,' Mitchell wrote. 'They were fought for the possession of posts or villages on which the world's fate seemed to depend . . . one bold contest would have been worth all this strategy a hundred times over.'[50] Mitchell's interpretations of Clausewitzian principles suggested that he believed the primary aim of an army should be to fight and do so with all available resources. In essence, a decisive battle should be sought and joined as rapidly as possible. He, along with other thinkers and writers in the period, overlooked Clausewitz's argument that policy, means and national character were intimately linked in the development of a national strategy.

Though he misinterpreted Clausewitz, Mitchell was eager to encourage new military thinking. 'The British army may at all hours be called upon to take the field in any quarter of the globe,' he wrote in his introduction to *Thoughts on Tactics*. 'They may again have to encounter the drilled soldiers of Europe, the riflemen of America, the fierce hordes of Central Asia, or the cunning savages of the Polynesian Islands; there is no situation of difficulty in which they are not liable to be placed . . . .' Despite such circumstances, 'the country has done nothing to improve the art of war – to facilitate for its soldiers the attainment of victory, and to render the necessary contents less destructive and less burdensome to the nation at large'. As a result, the British armed 'the soldier with a clumsy, unhandy musket, which, posted as he is in the ranks, he can never use to great advantage, and which he is besides never taught to use with skill . . . accurate marksmanship is therefore totally out of the question . . . last, but not least, modern tactics teach us to fix bayonets and to charge the enemy'.[51]

Military historians, including most prominently Napier, had advocated that this approach remained extant. Instead, Mitchell argued, it was vital to focus on mobility, marksmanship and more flexible formations. This had been the key to success under Wellington's command in the Peninsula, but

no sooner was his Grace's hand withdrawn from direct control than disaster again followed our last American contest. Nor did mismanagement cease here, for as late as 1841 a small British force, termed an army, was, in defiance of the very first and most evident principles of strategy, left at Cabool, far removed from assistance and support, exposed, without an open line of retreat or stronghold on which to fall back, to the assaults of the wild hordes of Central Asia.[52]

Mitchell wanted the British Army to take advantage of the knowledge gained from the military challenges Britain faced across the world, as had been the case since the middle of the eighteenth century, when Saxe and Lloyd had tried to lift the cloak of darkness shrouding military science. He complained:

We have no book that gives an account of the relative power of the different arms; of the best mode of using and combining the action of Infantry, Cavalry and Artillery; nothing to show what they can effect against each other, singly or collectively; nothing about marches; about the proper modes of acting on level plain, broken ground, behind temporary defences or regular ramparts. All knowledge on these points must come to us by direct inspiration.[53]

Insofar, then, that a debate took place on the page, military historians and practitioners agreed that some attention needed to be paid to the art of war in terms of operations and strategy, as well as to the art of winning battles. In practice, however, the focus of theoretical and empirical debate was driven to the lowest common denominator, the thing which all soldiers could understand: tactics. Attempts were made to capture the latest British approach to warfighting. In 1824, Henry Torrens published the *Field Exercise and Evolutions of the Army*. This was little more than a revision of Dundas's *Principles of Military Movement* which, Torrens acknowledged, aimed to re-establish uniformity after the informal incorporation of improvements 'suggested, by practical experience, during the late eventful war'. These, 'although important and essential in the abstract', he argued, 'were partially adopted, without adherence to any general or fixed principle of formation', and resulted in an incoherent approach which was 'at once desultory, and disunited'.[54]

The reality had, of course, been that the informal practice of developing innovative solutions and adapting prescribed techniques for particular circumstances had allowed the British Army to meet unexpected challenges across the globe. However, uneven adoption of the new practices meant that when it was required to do so, the Army had difficulty operating as a cohesive whole, as had been demonstrated early in the French Revolutionary War. Dundas's *Principles* had taken many of these ideas and, along with further developments sanctioned by the Duke of York at Shorncliffe and High Wycombe, had formalised them. The conduct of the Napoleonic War had prompted further adaptations and innovations, which now needed to be either formally integrated into the regular order of battle or discarded.[55] Torrens proposed a light revision to Dundas's *Principles*, but despite a promise to 'unite simplicity with utility, and precision with celerity', military interest tended to focus on the former at the expense of the latter.[56]

Torrens's comments on the role of light infantry, and the subsequent focus of debate between the emergent 'continental' and 'colonial' schools of thought, illustrated this problem most clearly. Light troops were expected to 'be thoroughly versed and well grounded in the prescribed exercise and movements of a battalion of the line', while the line infantry once 'in perfect order in all the detail of line movements, it is essential that they should be practised in certain extended formations'.[57] This essentially sought to formalise the arrangement which had evolved over the last seven decades, where commanding officers from Loudoun to Wellington had expected the light infantry to act as line infantry during set-piece battles, and for line infantry to be capable of rudimentary light infantry tactics if the need arose.

Some saw this as an erosion of the effectiveness of regular drill, which had, in the words of one conservative, become 'unnecessarily lax and disjointed'.[58] Though Torrens had sought to capture the successful conclusion of this evolution, further developments of tactics, techniques and procedures nevertheless persisted. Drill continued to evolve despite the publication of Torren's 1824 *Field Exercise*, and a further update in 1833, culminating in a formal revision in 1854. But while Torrens had tried to capture both the tactical and operational value of light infantry, it was on the tactical elements that debate focused, spurred on by the experience of colonial warfare, and the widespread emergence of increasingly reliable rifles as the weapon of choice of some of Britain's fiercest adversaries.

* * *

As early as the War of 1812 with the United States of America, the need for further adjustments to the tactics and techniques of the British Army had become evident. From the outset, there was some concern that the British would not be able to meet the challenges presented by extra-European conflict. On his arrival in theatre in 1807, the new commander of British forces in Upper Canada, Brigadier Isaac Brock, a veteran of the 1799 expedition to Holland, worried that the few men he had under his command were 'scattered along an extensive line of four or five hundred miles, unarmed and totally unacquainted with every thing military'. As a result, Brock doubted 'whether, in the event of actual war, this force could assemble in time, and become useful'.[59] Brock was also deeply concerned about American fighting capability. 'The Americans will probably draw their principal force', he had written in December 1811 to the Governor of Canada, General George Prevost, 'either for offence or defence, from the Ohio, – an enterprising, hardy race, and uncommonly expert on horseback with the rifle.'[60]

Though American attempts to invade Canada had been successfully resisted in 1812 and 1813, mixed success elsewhere persuaded the British to launch a last-ditch attempt to seize New Orleans in late 1814. They hoped that the loss of this strategically vital city, with its large stockpiles of sugar, tobacco, cotton and hemp, would force the Americans to the negotiating table. The untimely death of the expedition's commander during an abortive attempt to seize Baltimore in September had derailed British planning. Wellington's brother-in-law, Major-General Sir Edward Pakenham, was appointed as the new land commander, but he only arrived in theatre on Christmas Day, having missed all planning discussions. American forces on the Gulf Coast, meanwhile, were commanded by the extremely competent and headstrong Andrew Jackson, who, anticipating an attack on New Orleans, had captured Pensacola, 200 miles to the east, to prevent the British from performing a wide outflanking manoeuvre. This enabled him to plan and prepare a frontal defence of the city, which included the placement of obstacles and gun batteries along the riverine access from the Gulf, including 28 guns at Fort St Philip, 60 miles south of New Orleans. He also positioned gunboats as a further obstacle to British advance.[61]

Sailing up the Mississippi in mid-December, the British managed to get 1,800 troops ashore on 22 December, but the dense and swampy terrain hampered movement. 'The troops were therefore obliged to pass over the boats as a bridge for a mile and a half,' noted the brigade commander, Major-General Sir John Keane, 'which necessarily took a considerable time.'[62] Unable to move any further, the British encamped just seven miles from New Orleans, but the delay gave Jackson the opportunity to launch a counterattack, sending a schooner and a column of 3,000 men downriver to bombard the British encampment. An intense hand-to-hand fight eventually saw the Americans repulsed when British reinforcements began to arrive.

Further deterred from launching a serious attack against Jackson, Keane elected to wait for more reinforcements. When Pakenham arrived on Christmas Day, eager to move against Jackson, the terrain and impressive defensive works hampered British efforts. It was thus not until 8 January that Pakenham was in a position to launch a new attack. By then, Jackson had increased his force to 3,500 regulars, militia and Kentucky riflemen. In addition, he had been able to construct three entrenched lines of defences, two of which were composed of earthworks anchored by redoubts and gun emplacements, while the third was composed of a 'ditch of twelve feet broad and six feet deep, cut expressly'. In the words of a British engineer sent to review the defensive structures after the conclusion of the war, the defence of New Orleans was 'one of the strongest possible by nature'.[63]

On the 8th, Pakenham split his force into three. Keane was to assault the American right-central position, while newly arrived Major-General Sir Samuel Gibbs commanded a column against the American left. General John Lambert would command the reserve with the 7th Fusiliers and the 43rd Light Infantry. Just as dawn broke, the order was given to commence the attack. By insisting on advancing in column, Pakenham allowed the Americans to maximise the impact of their artillery and musket fire. On the American left, Jackson had posted the Kentucky riflemen, who were well hidden in the dense cypress trees. 'The whole

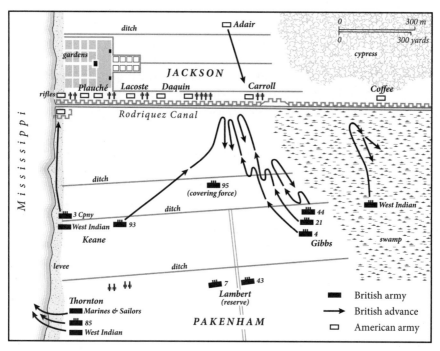

Map 14. The Battle of New Orleans, 8 January 1815.

right of the British column was mowed down by these invisible riflemen, and their front was exposed to the fire of both our batteries,' recalled one American observer.[64]

Standing with Lambert's reserve, Harry Smith, Pakenham's assistant adjutant, watched with increasing unease. 'Sir Edward Pakenham galloped past me with all his Staff, saying, "That's a terrific fire, Lambert,"' Smith turned to Lambert and reportedly said, 'In twenty-five minutes, General, you will command the Army. Sir Edward Pakenham will be wounded and incapable, or killed. The troops do not get on a step. He will be at the head of the first Brigade he comes to, and what I say will occur'.[65] On the right, the attack was faltering. 'Now and then, as the smoke rose we could see them flying, throwing away musket and fascine,' recorded the American observer, 'while a staff-officer, mounted on a black-charger, strove to drive them back with the chapeau which he held in his hand. At last, riddled by bullets, he fell backwards from his horse, and a soldier caught him and bore him away. We learned in the evening that it was General Pakenham in person.'[66]

Lambert, now in command as Smith had purportedly predicted, moved forward in an effort to stop the increasing disorder, but finding the weight of American artillery fire too great, and requiring substantial reinforcements to follow up meagre successes on the left, he decided to end the battle. With 291 dead, including Pakenham, 1,262 wounded and 484 missing, compared to just 120 American casualties, Lambert decided to withdraw to the fleet on 18 January. While an abundance of caution had perhaps hampered British military planning at the commencement of the war, overconfidence blighted its conclusion. At the outset, Brock had voiced concerns that the British would prove inadequate to the challenge posed by the superiority the Americans possessed in riflemen, though their true impact was not felt until Jackson had judiciously combined them with well-directed artillery fire and extremely well-prepared entrenchments.

The British defeat at New Orleans was a calamity. John Mitchell believed that alongside 'the Duke of Wellington's Lines at Torres Vedras; General Jackson's entrenchments at New Orleans, show how much benefit may, at times, be derived from such works. But', he continued, 'we suspect that they are rather out of fashion just now, and military history is ready with a hundred good examples, to prove that they are absolutely worthless'.[67] British troops experienced similar difficulties overcoming entrenched defensive positions throughout the nineteenth century, including, notably, during the Second Taranaki War in New Zealand, where the Māori countered superior British weaponry and numbers by constructing trenches and bunkers designed to withstand artillery bombardment.[68]

Nor were these the only century-wide comparisons. By the middle of the nineteenth century, British military writers were explicitly linking eighteenth- and nineteenth-century bush-fighting experiences. In his memoir of the Taranaki War, Colonel James Alexander made explicit reference to bush-fighting techniques taught at the Royal Military College, and perfected in the field in South Africa, where 'it was not the custom to encumber the troops with much baggage ... that paths would be found in the bush, that attacks at early dawn were best, and that much was to be done by the intelligence department, in ascertaining the position and strength of the enemy ...'.[69] Alexander's experiences became a touchstone for soldiers preparing to deploy to New Zealand when the second Māori war broke out. As he prepared to deploy, Ensign Spencer Nicholl of the 43rd Regiment of Foot read Alexander's *Incidents of the Maori War*, which he liked 'very much' as he felt it gave 'one a very good idea of the kind of fighting that one would have out there and also the kind of country'.[70] Following the conclusion of the Māori wars, Alexander published a second volume, entitled *Bush Fighting Illustrated by Remarkable Actions and Incidents of the Maori War in New Zealand*, in which he crystalised the commonality of experience in North America, South Africa and New Zealand.[71]

Mitchell, though, was correct. These conflicts were seen as sideshows, offering lessons relevant only to warfare in the periphery of empire, and which bore little relation to the experience of war in Europe. The accompanying fact that the Battle of New Orleans itself had been completely unnecessary, taking place just days after the Peace of Ghent was signed, ending the war between Great Britain and the United States, meant that any lessons could be easily swept aside.

Even where the colonial experience pointed to the need for a combination of mobility, manoeuvrability and marksmanship, the resultant military knowledge lacked the impact to drive home the need for scrutiny and debate on how this could be achieved. The reality was that the lessons of extra-European warfare were considered either relevant only to the theatre of war in which they were originally learned, or were rarely communicated beyond the theatre owing to the limited circulation of British units. As a result, the networks that had helped develop British military knowledge in the eighteenth century were effectively dismantled in the early nineteenth century. Thus, when Lachlan Macquarie launched a series of campaigns

against the Aboriginal peoples of New South Wales in the 1810s, although
he employed lessons learned and ideas gained in India in the 1790s, the
resultant new and remade military knowledge was not shared with the
army more widely. This, despite the fact that Macquarie's forces had to
adapt to a new style of warfare which developed in response to the expansion of British territorial acquisition in New South Wales.

In the early nineteenth century, there was a prevailing assumption that
the Aboriginal peoples of New South Wales preferred traditional weaponry to the firearms used by the British, for reasons that were both
cultural – a perceived preference for the spear as weapon of choice – and
technical – the evident unreliability of the musket. In reality, the
Aboriginal peoples of New South Wales had limited means of obtaining
access to firearms: the British were the only colonial power in Australia
and were therefore able to constrain the supply of weaponry across the
frontier, while the Aboriginal economy did not produce commodities in
sufficient numbers to facilitate large-scale trade.[72] The Aboriginal peoples
of New South Wales thus fought the British with the same weapons that
they had previously used to fight each other.[73] This forced them to adapt
tactically rather than technologically. In the face of land seizures, the
Aboriginal response was to raid the settlers' lands in an effort to impose
excessive costs on the British, which had no precedent in earlier forms of
warfare in Australia.[74]

In the 1790s, raiding by one Aboriginal community, the Darug, along
the Hawkesbury–Nepean river, became so intense that the British launched
a punitive response which escalated the situation and resulted in a permanent garrison at Hawkesbury. Despite this, the Darug continued to raid
settler farms, stealing corn and burning wheat, often in large groups, and
with increasing sophistication. Indeed, the Darug began to time the
rhythm of their attacks based on their knowledge of 'how little use a
musket was when once discharged', which 'effectually removed that terror
of our fire-arms with which it had been our constant endeavour to inspire
them'.[75] They became so successful that they could live off the spoils,
perpetuating the activity. On balance, the cost of building, maintaining
and defending settlements along the lower Hawkesbury compared with
the meagre returns persuaded the British to abandon settlements along the
lower Hawkesbury in the mid-1800s, illustrating that the tactical approach
adopted by the Darug could be successful when applied in locations where
they enjoyed topographical advantage. At the same time, the Darug
numbers declined as a consequence of internecine warfare and disease.

The Hawkesbury–Nepean frontier was therefore relatively quiet until May 1814, when the Darug formed fragile alliances with the neighbouring Darawal and Gandangara peoples in response to the establishment of British settlements along the Nepean river. Corn raids escalated in both frequency and intensity, and the British were forced to send 'arm'd parties ... to scower the country', though they complained of 'the Velocity with which these people Remove from One place to another'.[76] Bereft of local knowledge, the British could not match their adversaries in speed or dexterity. Using a combination of local geographical knowledge, and an understanding of the tactical limitations of the musket, the Darug, Darawal and Gandangara were able to inflict some losses on the British. 'The natives would fall down as soon as the men would present their muskets at them', noted one settler, Samuel Hassall, 'and then get up and dance',[77] rushing the soldiers 'with a promptitude that put it out of their power to reload'.[78] As the situation escalated, Macquarie 'ordered *three Separate Military Detachments* to march into the Interior and remote parts of the Colony, for the purpose of Punishing the Hostile Natives, by clearing the Country of them entirely, and driving them across the mountains'.[79]

In an attempt to neutralise the advantages held by the Aboriginal peoples, Macquarie borrowed ideas he had seen implemented with some success during his deployment to India, and later Egypt. He organised a strike force of 70 soldiers, composed of light infantry and grenadiers, split into three detachments, and facilitated by mounted messengers, 'proper Guides of Europeans and friendly Natives', and a small baggage train,[80] sending them to what he described as 'very rough and intricate country'.[81] Though Macquarie ordered the men to 'use every possible precaution to save the lives of the Native Women and Children', this objective proved functionally impossible to achieve, as the only means by which the soldiers could track down their adversaries was by surprising them at night. In several instances, the detachments tracked down and attacked Aboriginal encampments, killing and wounding several men, and in one instance inadvertently driving several survivors over a cliff.[82]

In contrast, when in pursuit, the British were unable to catch up with their adversaries, who were able to escape. After a month, Macquarie recalled the detachments, content that his troops had 'inflicted exemplary Punishment on the Hostile Natives'. One of the detachment commanders, Captain James Wallis, praised his grenadiers for 'their steadiness and patient endurance of long marches & privations of every kind'.[83] The expedition achieved its objectives. By April 1817, 'all Hostility on both

Sides has long since Ceased'.[84] Light infantry and elite units had proved
essential for achieving specific colonial objectives. Macquarie had had to
fashion his light detachments out of the flank companies of the regular
46th regiment of foot stationed at Sydney, and then had been barely able
to meet their relatively modest objectives. This was a problem widely
reflected across the empire, where light infantry were best suited to the
challenges presented by indigenous adversaries, but only flank companies
were available to meet those challenges.[85]

A further divide began to emerge in the way the army thought about
war, which deepened the focus on tactical adaptation at the expense of
operational innovation. There were those who saw light infantry as the elite
elements of the regular army, and thus separate. A leading proponent of
this school of thought, based on his experience in the Peninsula, was
George Murray, who believed the talents of light infantrymen were in the
main the result of natural attributes rather than training. In the view of
these officers, to expect all infantry to act as light troops 'seems very like
expecting that a dray horse and a racer would run well in a curricle, or
compete in a race'.[86] In opposition, there were those who thought there was
'only one sort of infantry, and in the modern system of warfare every foot
soldier is required to perform every sort of military service'.[87] By and large,
those with more colonial experience saw the wisdom of this argument,
among them Harry Smith, who wrote a memorandum on the subject after
his experience in South Africa and India, in which he argued that all
infantry should be trained 'for cover or for assault'.[88]

Tactical adaptation nevertheless continued in response to the specific
challenges presented in colonial conflicts. In his instructions for young
officers while stationed in Poona, Lord Fitzclarence advised that the best
time to learn the 'mechanical portion, or ABC' was 'in time of peace on the
level surface of the parade ground, with a view of applying such knowledge
in broken undulated ground'.[89] He drilled all his soldiers in light infantry
tactical doctrine and ordered that the men nearest the enemy always
pushed forward to perform a skirmishing role, giving time for the main
force to realign appropriately.[90] This offered the British considerable
tactical advantage during the operations around Multan in the Second
Anglo-Sikh War, where the 32nd Regiment was able to utilise three of
its regular companies in a skirmishing role; and at the Battle of Gujerat
(21 February 1849), when the 24th Regiment utilised regular companies
in a similar fashion.[91] In South Africa, during the eighth of a sustained
series of guerrilla wars with the Xhosa, the 74th Highlanders utilised light

infantry tactics to make use of 'everything that afforded shelter', in order to survive an ambush on 8 September 1851 in the Kroomie Forest.[92] At one stage, the soldiers were engaged in intense hand-to-hand fighting with warriors of the Gcaleka Xhosa under their chief, Maqoma, while marksmen of the Cape Mounted Rifles provided aimed fire. Despite the intensity of the skirmish and being severely outnumbered, the regiment sustained only 15 killed and 15 wounded.[93]

The collective experience of colonial warfare in the nineteenth century, therefore, pointed to the need for a more agile and better trained marksman, capable of both skirmishing capability against irregular opponents and parade-ground drill in which mass firepower could be brought to bear. The principal impediment to the achievement of this objective was the inaccuracy and limitations of the musket, which, after all, had been the principal arm of the British infantry since the days of Marlborough. With limited range, clunky reloading techniques, many pieces suffering from poor workmanship and difficult to use in inclement weather, the musket was ripe for an upgrade.[94]

In 1835, Sir Hussey Vivian was appointed master-general of the ordnance. He believed strongly that if all soldiers could become effective marksmen, their morale and confidence in battle would be substantially enhanced.[95] The need for more reliable and effective weaponry was illustrated within a few years during the so-called Opium War in China in 1841. There, in a battle which the British would not normally have found problematic, 'a company of sepoys, armed with flintlock muskets, which would not go off in heavy rain, were surrounded by some thousand Chinese, and were in eminent peril, when two companies of marines', reported the *London Gazette*, 'armed with percussion-cap muskets, were ordered up, and soon disposed of the enemy with great loss'.[96] The following year, the inadequacy of the musket was further and dramatically demonstrated during the closing stages of the First Anglo-Afghan War.

Britain had invaded Afghanistan in late 1839, the result of a series of diplomatic missteps arising from competing strategic demands emerging in the north-west frontier of India. The invasion itself had been a spectacular success. The British had exploited the fragmented nature of the Afghan polity, and the capital, Kabul, had quickly fallen. If British forces had withdrawn immediately, it was possible that wider strategic objectives might have been achieved, but opposition to the British and their puppet government gradually began to solidify, culminating in the assassination of the British resident and his deputy in late 1841, and the isolation of the British garrison. Though the British managed to negotiate a withdrawal to Jellalabad in January 1842, they were forced to commence their retreat immediately.

A column of 700 European soldiers and cavalry, 3,800 sepoys and nearly 14,000 camp followers commenced the treacherous retreat on 6 January. In an illustration of the breakdown of British trust of local military knowledge and intelligence, specific information that the garrison was marching into a trap was ignored.[97] The Afghans were armed with jezail rifles, which easily outranged the musket. Even before the British arrived at the designated encampment on the first night of the retreat, panic began to spread as camp followers started falling, picked off by marksmen hidden in the surrounding terrain. As the column entered the Khord Kabul pass, its discipline severely disrupted by a combination of enemy action and desperately cold weather, the Afghans sprung a perfectly timed ambush. Well-prepared earthworks had been constructed to protect the Afghan marksmen, who had been able to range their weapons for maximum effect.[98] 'The scene of slaughter was dreadful,' wrote one survivor. 'We had to run the gauntlet of the whole length of this fearful defile, a distance of about 5 miles. All baggage was abandoned. The enemy not only poured in a murderous fire from every rock and cave in the heights on each side, but descended into the Pass and slew man, woman and child.'[99]

By 11 January, the British had sustained more than 12,000 casualties. Nearly the entirety of the senior command of the British force had been captured or killed. On the morning of 12 January, 20 officers and 45 privates of the 44th Regiment of Foot, having made it as far south as the village of Gandamak, found themselves surrounded. 'Every hut had poured forth its inhabitants to murder and plunder,' wrote Captain Thomas Souter. Forming square, they exhausted their ammunition, 'driving the Affghans several times down the hill', and then fought hand-to-hand with the bayonet. Only nine prisoners were taken, including Souter, who had been wounded.[100] Famously, only one man, Dr William Brydon, made it to Jellalabad, wounded and close to death. Though the commander of the Jellalabad garrison, General Robert Sale, whose wife was among those captured during the infamous retreat, sent out search parties, 'to scour the plains . . . they only found . . . bodies'.[101] News of the unprecedented defeat quickly spread. 'Dr Brydon's tale struck horror into the hearts of all who had heard it,' wrote Captain Thomas Seaton in his private journal. 'The whole army had been destroyed, one man alone escaping to tell the fearful tale.'[102]

* * *

The 44th Regiment has the ignominious glory of having had a battalion all but destroyed twice in its history. The first was on the banks of the Monongahela on 9 July 1755. The second was at Gandamak at the foot of the Khoord Kabul pass on 12 January 1842. In both confrontations, the troops of the unfortunate regiment were armed with the same weapons and faced an enemy that used irregular tactics, and weaponry which surpassed the effectiveness of British arms. In both confrontations, the well-trained troops used European tactics which allowed them to survive for some time but offered no hope of success. The humiliation of the first confrontation prompted 70 years of military innovation and adaptation which allowed the British Army to respond to the challenges it faced across the world. This period culminated at the Battle of Waterloo, where the 44th again suffered severe casualties, but where a victory was achieved in the toughest of circumstances. The crowning glory of the British Army at Waterloo fostered a period of intellectual stagnation which, as had been the case following Marlborough's successes, led to repeated and cata-strophic failures.

Here, again, the vocal veterans of the last conflict were to blame. Despite the evidence of the need for new approaches, Charles and William Napier, and a sizeable clique of like-minded officers, rubbished the idea. 'In an age essentially theorising and experimental,' exclaimed one editorial in the *United Services Magazine* published in 1852, 'it is natural that young and inexperienced officers, devoted to their profession, and anxious to secure the utmost efficiency, should be led away by meretricious novelties, and regard every plausible invention as an improvement.' This, the author added, was to be commended, but, he continued, 'let us not discard, as mere useless and impracticable lumber, all the experiences, the lessons, and the deductions of the past'. The views of Charles Napier confirmed the point, and are worth quoting at length.

> I do not altogether enter into the new inventions. I fought in '*The Bush*' in America: so thick it was, that we could hardly pierce its denseness; my regiment was opposed to Kentucky *riflemen*. We had *muskets*, and we beat them. We had *red coats* – they had brown coats; yet we slew more of them than they did of us. We are told that, at the Cape, the *Kaffirs* lie hidden till our soldiers come within a *few feet*! Then what do we want with a *rifle*? The Cape corps were armed with short carbines, *not* with rifles and are said to have done better service than any other corps, while the men were

faithful ... The old spirit of the British soldiers was to *close with their enemy*, not to keep at the distance of two miles from him! '*The bayonet! the bayonet!*' was their cry, under strong hearts and strong arms of Britons bore down in closer array upon the enemy! But now that system seems changed. The strong hearts and strong bodies are forthcoming; so is the proud *red* uniform of England; so is the British musket and bayonet: but some of our anonymous writers are trying to drive all these from the field, and turn our main battle into skirmishers, fighting the enemy at a vast distance! Perhaps they are right, but I do not think so. I think it will make men fearful of getting too near the enemy, and of closing with a bayonet. Some of these writers would almost make one believe that victory depended on *dress* and *rifles*, not on *discipline* and *stern soldiers*! If soldiers be constantly told that their arms are good for nothing, and their dress as bad as their arms (although in that dress and with those arms they carried England's glory to its greatest height), they will soon lose all confidence in their own superior physical powers. One laughs at the exaggeration of men who see danger only in an enemy's arms, and fancy our own harmless. A jezail will kill you, if it hits you in the right place, and you must expect to be killed in battle and when mounting steep rocks in face of jezails, or even of pocket-pistols; but you are not to forget that your own musket kills its man as well, and kills more men too! These gentlemen who want to have battles with the killing all on one side; and their '*tales of terror*' about jezails and matchlocks, and such rubbish, alarm the soldiers.[103]

Sir Charles had systematically dispelled the notion that lessons could be learned from Britain's wars in America, Australia, Africa and Asia. His brother was just as resistant. 'The Minié rifle seems to be established by experiment as a real improvement on fire-arms', William wrote in the *Naval and Military Gazette* in 1853, 'and is likely to supersede the old musket. I am sorry for it; not sorry that the better weapons should be adopted, but sorry that the improved weapon should have been invented.'[104] The Minié had been shown in trials to be 20 per cent more effective than the musket when fired at a target 100 yards away, 37½ per cent more effective when the target was 200 yards away and 48 per cent more effective when then target was 400 yards away.[105] The Napiers could not prevent the introduction of new weapons, but their continued resistance to such innovations helped suppress innovative thinking, and meant that the British were chronically unprepared for the challenges presented during the wars of the mid-nineteenth century. This was evident when Britain went to war with Russia in 1854. Though the Minié rifle had been adopted in 1851, its capabilities had not been incorporated into tactical and drill training manuals. Soldiers had no idea of the effectiveness of the weapon they carried; their commanders had no concept of how it might be used in battle. At the Alma (20 September 1854), the British had been formed into lines two ranks deep, which their adversaries found to be extraordinary. 'We had never before seen troops fight in lines of two deep,' wrote one Russian participant, 'nor did we think it possible for men to be found with sufficient firmness of morale to be able to attack in this apparently weak formation our massive columns.'[106] Unsurprisingly, the forward elements of the British attack at the Battle of the Alma, headed by the Light Division, suffered horrendous casualties. The follow-up attack, spearheaded by the Highland Brigade of the Guards Division, was ordered by its commander, Sir Colin Campbell, to hold their fire until they were 'within a yard of the Russians', and then charge with the bayonet. Disrupted by the retreat of the Light Division, the Guards advanced in disorder toward a Russian-held redoubt. 'Suddenly the Russians seemed to line the redoubt again,' recorded one participant in his private journal, 'and their fire grew hotter.'[107]

They were unable to sustain the advance, so the order was given to withdraw and the Grenadiers and Coldstream Guards were ordered to advance instead. But they refused to do so, having discovered the accuracy and effectiveness of their new weapon. Instead the 2,000-strong brigade formed into two lines and fired 14 volleys of Minié rifle shot at the Russian infantry, who were some 1,200 paces away, and themselves carried weapons with a range of just 300 paces. The effect was devastating and battle-winning. 'Left to themselves to perform the role of sharpshooters, the British troops did not hesitate under fire and did not require orders or supervision,' recorded Russian military engineer Eduard Totleben, in his history of the Crimean War. 'Troops thus armed were full of confidence once they found out the accuracy and immense range of their weapon.' The British avoided close combat, withdrew when pressed until out of range of their adversaries and opened 'a murderous fusillade', obliging the Russians to withdraw.[108]

As had been the case a century before, the process of innovation and adaptation was prompted once more by the experience of battle, and generated not by senior officers, but by soldiers and junior officers. The effectiveness of the Minié rifle would not be effectively incorporated into the training and tactics of the British infantry in time to help secure a decisive victory over the Russians, but the process of reform commenced. The British Army, however, did not need to wait until the shock of the war in the Crimea to adapt and innovate in the face of new military challenges. The evidence for reform and how to do it had been presented in the colonial experience of warfare throughout the nineteenth century. Reform-resistant veterans, wedded to the tactical practices of a bygone age, hindered transformation, while the breakdown in the global networks of military knowledge exchange prevented the value of local colonial expertise reaching Horse Guards. Military ignorance once more resulted in defeat and humiliation, which in turn prompted a new period of military enlightenment, one marked by the industrialisation of warfare.

Conclusion

'Every Fertile Genius':
Britain's Accidental Military Enlightenment
Explained

THE eighteenth-century military enlightenment was a period of experimentation, innovation and development for European armies. The British Army, though separated by a different strategic outlook, was not isolated from it. The phenomenon was, for the British, both accidental and asymmetric. Accidental because the phenomenon itself was the product of defeat and humiliation on the battlefield which prompted a period of self-reflection. This coincided with the opportunistic imperial expansion of the late eighteenth century, which facilitated a process of knowledge exchange based on a unique experience of war on a global scale. A dynamic relationship between military thought, experience and knowledge exchange was therefore facilitated. It was asymmetric because the experience of the military enlightenment was an uneven and sometimes contradictory process.

There were a variety of reasons for a mid-eighteenth-century interest in the professional development of the Army. For some, it was a matter of survival. Soldiers fighting in the American wilderness broke convention and adapted their uniforms and weaponry to increase their chances of survival and success; sometimes they were castigated, sometimes their adaptations and innovations were adopted more widely by forward-thinking officers. Usually widely read and with a curiosity in the art of war, these officers transferred those innovations, ideas and experiences to other theatres of war, establishing informal networks of military knowledge exchange. More often than not, these new approaches were successfully applied and then abandoned, discarded as irrelevant, victims of cost-cutting and the entrenchment of tradition, as existing structures and processes reasserted themselves. Organisational inertia stymied change but, as with any organisation, there were those who championed innovation, and they had a disproportionate impact on the development of the British Army throughout the eighteenth century.

Britain's own experience of the military enlightenment was also an accident of agency; the captain-general of the British Army at the time of the emergence of increasingly enlightened thinking about war happened to be the Duke of Cumberland, a man who actively promoted professional learning and vibrant discussion of the nature and conduct of war. 'It is every man's duty as commander-in-chief', he wrote in December 1756, 'to ask the opinion and advice of those who can give him new lights from their Experience and knowledge of the country and service.'[1] Cumberland invited opinion and advice, and created opportunities to share experience in a variety of ways, whether it was among his staff while on campaign or in the confines and comforts of his map library at Windsor Great Lodge.[2]

There were, inevitably, limits to Cumberland's willingness to entertain the opinions of his subordinates. Should their arguments 'not convince, the Person commanding ought certainly to follow his own opinion, as it still appears to him the best, after having heard other opinions'.[3] Moreover, once he had arrived at his decisions, Cumberland frowned very heavily on 'the Whim & Supposed Improvements of every fertile Genius'.[4] Though the possibility of influencing Cumberland was limited only to those who enjoyed his patronage, in promoting an atmosphere of discussion and debate in helping to formulate new military knowledge Cumberland helped set the conditions of Britain's own military enlightenment.

As the eighteenth century progressed, many British officers and even some soldiers pondered the peculiar qualities that ensured martial prowess and debated the cost of war on both a political and individual level. Debates about moral methods in the execution of war, and what implications these ideas had for the honour, discipline and professionalism of the British Army, began to emerge during the Seven Years' War and continued for the remainder of the eighteenth century. This *esprit philosophique* was not only rooted in the literature of the period but was also informed by practical experience. Officers and soldiers, often deployed in unfamiliar and challenging environments, became adept at seeking technical adaptations and innovations that would offer a small advantage over their adversaries.[5]

Often the aggregate of these marginal gains, the product of Britain's global experience of war in the eighteenth century, amounted to what for the British became a leading edge in the conduct of war. As, however, with Cumberland's personal willingness to accept intellectual challenge from subordinates, so too were there limits on the philosophical and technical progress evident in the late eighteenth century. Conservative reactionary elements within the Army continued to stymie the formal exchange of new methods of fighting from across the globe. Knowledge and experiences of war in one theatre were viewed with suspicion and considered irrelevant elsewhere.

A constant theme throughout this period, however, was the fact that Britain's military enlightenment was also asymmetric, and this created different challenges threatening the exchange of knowledge and the development of innovations. The eighteenth century was a period in which writers and thinkers endeavoured to 'increase the well-being of humanity' through a process of enlightenment. As a result, beliefs and traditions which blinded people to their own interests were challenged, and the power of institutions which promoted those beliefs and traditions opposed.[6] However, as has been evident throughout this book, many of the advances in thinking about compassion and restraint in war were only applied for the benefit of a selected minority. Compassion and humanity, insofar as this existed on the battlefield, were offered only to other professional European adversaries; comparatively little was offered to Britain's non-European enemies. Brutality, meanwhile, was frequently justified by those practising it.

During the siege of Louisbourg in 1758, the French commandant, Augustin de Boschenry, chevalier de Drucour, offered the services of his personal surgeon to treat British officers in the siegeworks. The commander of British troops, Major General Jeffrey Amherst, sent through the lines to Drucour's wife a gift of West Indian pineapples, complimenting her on her courage after British troops witnessed her firing three cannon shots every day. Madame Drucour returned the favour by sending through a tub of fresh butter and a case of wine.[7]

Four years later, during the siege of Havana, having learned that 'seamen ... under my command have been barbarously treated when taken prisoners by the Spaniards', the British naval commander, Admiral George Pocock, wrote to the governor, Don Juan de Prado, that he believed such treatment 'entirely unbecoming the usage that ought to subsist between two Christian nations that unfortunately are now at war and have ever carried it on, as far as such a state would admit of, agreeable to the principles of humanity'. Indeed, Pocock hoped that 'we shall never deviate from the constant practice of civilized countries, which I shall make the rule of my actions, during the unhappy state we are embarked in'. Pocock trusted that the governor was 'in the same way of thinking' as he was.[8]

In October 1778, when the corps of 5,000 British regular soldiers sent from New York arrived at St Lucia, the commander of the reserve, Brigadier Sir William Medows, reminded his troops 'that clemency should go hand in hand with bravery; that an enemy in our power is an enemy no more, and the glorious characteristic of a British soldier is to conquer and to spare. Acting on these principles, they can never fail doing honour to themselves, their king, and the country they serve'.[9] During the ensuing battle, British soldiers noted the brutality of the conflict and its effect on their enemies. Witnessing the after-effects of an artillery bombardment, one participant noted 'the mangled portions of the human frame lay scattered round on every side. The dying were confounded with the dead, and added to the scene their piercing agony and groans, which even by the roughness of the British soldier's nature could not be resisted, nor beheld without concern'. The redcoats promptly 'forgot they were their country's enemies; and we, the officers, who half an hour before could behold with joy a cannon-ball take effect, and sweep away a rank of men, were shocked at the various examples, now before our eyes, of the calamities to which mankind are liable in the events of war'.[10]

These were all high-stakes operations which threatened the very existence of the French, Spanish or British empires in the Western Hemisphere; yet, in all cases, humanity and compassion existed between the adversaries. The sentiments stand in stark contrast to the brutal activities perpetrated by royal troops against indigenous adversaries or rebellious colonial subjects, and vice versa. While exchanging gifts with the French garrison of Louisbourg in 1758, for example, British troops simultaneously regarded their Native American adversaries outside the walls as 'barbarians',[11] and 'the only Brutes & Cowards in the Creation who were ever known to exercise their cruelties upon the fairer Sex & to Scalp & Mangle the poor sick Soldiers & defenceless Women'.[12] In revenge, British troops 'cut them to pieces wherever we found them, in return for a thousand acts of cruelty and barbarity'.[13]

This remained the case throughout the remainder of the Seven Years' War in America. In 1763, during what became known as Pontiac's War in the American backcountry, the then commander-in-chief, General Sir Jeffrey Amherst, advocated virtually unrestricted warfare and brutality against an enemy for whom he clearly had no respect. The war, he said, would 'bring Certain & Inevitable Ruin on the Whole Race of the Indians',[14] and after a punitive raid against the restive Cherokees in the Carolinas resulted in no fewer than 15 villages being burnt to the ground, Amherst remarked that 'never was Chastisement more justly necessary to any set of villains or more duly paid'.[15] In the event of battle '*no Prisoners*' were to be taken. This was a sentiment that was shared across the army. After the Battle of Bushy Run (6 August 1763), a Highlander captured a Native American and was escorting him to camp 'and after a little Examination' recorded the *Pennsylvania Gazette*, 'he received his Quietus'.[16] Famously, of course, it was during this conflict that Amherst advocated what was possibly the first attempt at a rudimentary form of biological warfare. 'Could it not be contrived to Send the *Small Pox* among those Disaffected Tribes of Indians?' he asked of the local commander. 'We must, on this occasion, Use Every Stratagem in our Power to Reduce them.'[17]

It should be no surprise that the British viewed their European adversaries as their moral and social equals, while Native American peoples, people of colour, whether free or enslaved, and South Asian troops were seen in very different ways. Disparaging commentaries emerged about Indian sepoys, for example, whom were described, using racial bias against peoples of African descent, as 'the country's negroes'. They were seen as undisciplined, militarily ineffective and weak. Their behaviour on the battlefield suggested cowardice. 'Fifty thousand' Europeans, noted one French observer, 'could rout six hundred thousand' sepoys. In the late 1760s, Dutch ethnographer Cornelius de Pauw published a dissertation on Native Americans. 'The American, strictly speaking, is neither virtuous nor vicious,' de Pauw explained. 'The timidity of his soul, the weakness of his intellect ... the powers of superstition ... all lead him far wide of the possibility of improvement ... he is revengeful through weakness, and atrocious in his vengeance.'[18] Europeans who spent a sustained amount of time in America would themselves, De Pauw believed, slowly but inevitably degenerate.[19]

Such viewpoints were not unheard of within the British Army and led some officers to use exposure to Native American practices as justification for extreme violence directed against Europeans. James Wolfe believed, for example, that the French use of Native American warriors, as well as Canadian irregulars, in asymmetric roles against the British, had fundamentally 'changed the very nature of the war', driving the British, as he had written to Amherst in 1758, 'to a deterring and dreadful vengeance'.[20] As he set sail for Quebec in May 1759, Wolfe had written to Amherst.

'Trust me,' he wrote, 'they shall feel us'.[21] Wolfe believed 'the American war' to be 'different from all others', and that the brutalisation of the population of New France was justified after the 'unheard of, and unprecedented, barbarities exercised by the French, Canadians and Indians upon such of our people as had the misfortune to fall into their hands'.[22] Although Wolfe blamed the French for the brutality of the war, he saw their actions as the product of fighting in America, and therefore sought to exact revenge on the population.

During the siege of Quebec, Wolfe deliberately developed a campaign of terror against the civilian population in order to undermine support for the French. On 12 July 1759, for example, Wolfe had commenced an artillery bombardment of Quebec City that lasted several weeks, and was indiscriminate in the selection of targets for his artillery batteries. 'We have been so successful as scarce to leave a house in the place that is not battered down by our guns', recorded one artillery officer, 'or burnt to ashes by our mortars.'[23] The town's inhabitants were unsurprisingly 'terrified', recorded one observer, 'in particular the women and children who were gathered in a big group by the citadel, crying, lamenting and praying continually, huddled in small cliques to recite prayers using their beads'.[24]

Wolfe's apologists have sought to justify such actions as being a proportionate response and in line with the era's laws of war because Quebec was a legitimate military target and the British believed the civilian population had been evacuated.[25] This was patently untrue, and Wolfe admitted as much, when he stated that 'the business of an assault would be little advanced by' an artillery bombardment.[26] Nor was the surrounding countryside spared Wolfe's vengeance. On 24 July, he ordered 'our out-parties . . . to burn and lay waste the country for the future, sparing only churches, or houses dedicated to divine worship', though 'women and children are not to be molested on any account whatsoever'.[27] While he sought to spare them the direct brutality of war, in destroying their capacity to survive Wolfe sought to ensure that they abandoned their support for the French.[28] He believed that 'their army is kept together by the violent strong hand of the Government and by the terror of the savages, joined to a situation which makes it difficult to evade'. The civilian population, meanwhile, he believed to be 'a disjointed, discontented, dispirited peasantry, beat into cowardice by Cadet, Bigot, Montcalm, and the savages'.[29] The bombardment of Quebec and the concurrent campaign of terror was clearly punitive, but it also combined messages of deterrence and compellence to the population.[30]

Nevertheless, Wolfe failed to drive a wedge between the civilian population, the army and the French administration. The viciousness of the war only continued to escalate. In 'almost daily skirmishes with these savages', the British tended to prevail, 'but not without loss'.[31] Throughout August, a campaign of terror, aimed at burning dwellings to the ground, destroying crops, rounding up livestock and taking civilians as hostages, failed either to persuade the population to abandon support for the French, or Montcalm to offer an opportunity for a decisive battle. Instead, he threatened that 'if the English did not desist from burning and destroying the country, he would give up all the ... prisoners in his power to the mercy of the Indian savages'. Wolfe purportedly countered by threatening sexual violence against the women in British captivity. 'All the French ladies, without distinction,' he supposedly threatened, 'should be given up to the delicate embraces of the English Tars.'[32] There is limited evidence this threat was ever made, and none that it was executed, but the presence of such contemporary reports from the Army suggested that the brutality of the war was spreading, and the threat of extreme violence against civilians was being normalised. Wolfe, nevertheless, did see the families of the Canadians as useful hostages. 'The Canadians have no affection for their government,' he wrote to his close friend, Ralph Burton, 'nor no tie so strong as their wives and children.'[33]

A range of emotion was evident in the response of the soldiery to the brutal actions they were being asked to undertake. On the one hand, there were officers who, though they saw 'these acts of hostility' as being 'warrantable by the laws of nations and rules of war, yet, as humanity is far from being incompatible with the character of a soldier, any man, who is possessed of the least share of it, cannot help sympathising with ... the miseries of his fellow-creatures, even though his enemies'.[34] Brigadier George Townshend had 'never served so disagreeable a Campaign as this', and looked on with increasing horror as 'Our unequal Force has reduced our Operations to a Scene of Skirmishing Cruelty & Devastation', he declared. 'It is War of the worst Shape.'[35] On the other hand, there were those who believed such brutality was 'not the temper of Britons, whose natural humanity forbids their sporting with real distress. Some severity became necessary to curb the pride of an insulting enemy, and to convince them that we were actually in earnest'.[36]

The British adopted similar approaches during the American Revolutionary War. As he prepared for the invasion of New York from Canada in 1777, General John Burgoyne promised to sow 'Devastation,

Famine and every concomitant Horror' unless the Americans abandoned 'the Phrenzy of Hostility',[37] a message which only served to galvanise support for the rebellion. Likewise, in June 1778, as the British prepared to withdraw from Philadelphia, there was a serious debate about whether or not the city should be destroyed 'upon the principle of its being just to extend the ravages of war in a country which declares itself at all events determined to become an accession to the strength of France'.[38] Similar justifications were used to explain away other atrocities committed by the British during the war.

In the wake of a British raid on Connecticut in November 1779, the British minister Lord George Germain could not help 'lamenting . . . that the Behaviour of the Rebels, in firing from their Houses upon the Troops, rendered it necessary to make use of Severities, that are ever painful to British Soldiers to inflict'. Nevertheless, these actions 'were justified, by the Rules of War, and by the General practice of all Nations upon like occasions, and in the present instance, it was not only a Chastisement which the Rebels justly deserved, but it appears to have been a measure absolutely necessary for the safety' of the British troops on the expedition.[39] Indeed, the increasing brutality of the raiding strategy – designed to deny supplies, port facilities and maritime capabilities to the Americans – was justified in similar terms. Clinton hoped that the brutality of the action would 'serve to convince these poor deluded people that that sort of war, carried to a greater extent and with more devastation will sooner or later reduce them'.[40]

Americans were certainly not alone in suffering brutal treatment at the hands of the British. As recent work has pointed out, British forces in India treated indigenous enemies with similar disdain, often justified as recriminations for the brutal tactics adopted by those forces in battle.[41] After the collapse of the Maratha infantry line at the climax of the Battle of Delhi (11 September 1803), the British cavalry, composed of the 27th Light Dragoons and the 2nd and 3rd Bengal Native Cavalry, pursued their fleeing adversaries 'into the Jumnah, and hundreds of them were destroyed in endeavouring to cross it. The Flying Artillery was up,' commented one participant, Grenadier John Pester, 'and the river appeared boiling by the fire of grape kept up on those of the enemy who had taken to the river. It was literally, for a time, a stream of blood . . .'.[42] At least one British observer was disgusted, in particular, at the behaviour of the British cavalry. 'Many attempted to make their escape by swimming but whenever an unhappy wretch showed his head above the water a dozen pistols were levelled at it. An old man with a child on his shoulders stood in the water afraid to proceed. A dragoon, untouched by remorse, shot him and the child, I suppose, must have drowned.'[43]

Likewise in the West Indies, British soldiers were quick to highlight the martial and physical differences between white European soldiers and black enslaved and former enslaved people serving as soldiers. After the French surrender of Martinique in March 1794, for example, British officer George Colville watched as the garrison marched into captivity, 'the regiment of Turenne leading them, very weak in numbers but in general well looking men. The mulattos and blacks next followed', he noted, 'in every respect a most despicable enemy, half naked and half starved. Between 6-700 souls marched out and a most pitiful appearance did they make'.[44] Two years later, as he prepared his force for an attack on St Lucia, which was garrisoned by 4,000 soldiers, many of them also formerly enslaved people, General Sir Ralph Abercromby pointed out:

> It is never wise to despise the enemy, at the same time there can be no doubt in the present war, if the British soldier will preserve his presence of mind, will disregard the shouts of savages and will be on his guard against surprises, that he will possess infinite advantages over the enemy and that he is certain of success.[45]

The inference was clear. British soldiers who could remain calm and disciplined in the face of the most stubborn enemy would prevail against the underhand tactics employed by their 'savage' foes.

Despite this initial dim view of black soldiers, over the course of his first campaign in the West Indies, Abercromby grew to be impressed by the regiments of black soldiers recruited to British ranks. They had proved to be excellent light infantry troops, and more effective in certain scenarios. As a result, he came to think of them as a potential solution to an intractable problem of warfare in the West Indies. Aghast at the toll tropical diseases were taking on his troops, Abercromby advocated recruitment from among the enslaved population of the West Indies on a much larger scale than so far enacted. He wrote 'in the strongest manner' of 'the great advantage which [the] service has derived already from the free Black Corps which has been employed, and the great saving of British soldiers which may be made should a certain number of Blacks be constantly kept in ... Service'.[46] He suggested 5,000 be enlisted into the British Army, 'and to form them into Battalions of eight Companies of five Hundred men each'.

Abercromby had intended that the men be recruited in return for their freedom after a period of service, but this aspect of his suggestion was quickly overruled. The colonial legislatures resented Whitehall's interference in the regional labour market and resisted the move. 'As it is found impossible to enlist them, and as the Islands do not seem disposed to give them,' wrote the Duke of York in support of the plan, 'it is necessary that they should be bought.'[47] From then on, the British Army bought newly arrived enslaved people straight off the slave ships; between 1795 and the end of the Atlantic slave trade in 1808 13,400 men of 195,000 were brought forcibly against their will to the British Caribbean. This was a significantly cheaper option than replacing white soldiers. The average cost of transporting a soldier to the West Indies was £70 each. On average each of these would need to be replaced every two years. In contrast, the average price of an enslaved person ranged from £56 in 1795 to £77 in 1801, and they became permanent additions to the fighting strength of the British units in the West Indies.[48] For this reason, the British Army became the leading purchaser of enslaved people arriving in the West Indies in the final decade of the slave trade.[49]

The principles of the military enlightenment, insofar as they extended to notions of compassion and restraint in war, were therefore a subjective concept for the British. Against the French or the Spanish armies – traditional European adversaries, with their similar professional, cultural and competitive strategic outlook – there was an expectation that enemy soldiers would be treated in a compassionate manner. On occasions where individual soldiers violated this principal, they faced repercussions within their own regiments. During the closing stages of the siege of Alexandria in August 1801, British soldiers captured a piece of high ground which gave them a line of direct bombardment into the city. The French quickly counterattacked and hand-to-hand fighting broke out, in the course of which the French were once more forced back. 'One poor old grey-headed French man,' a sergeant was told, 'not being able to keep up with the rest, fell on his knees and begged for mercy, but an English soldier, more like a savage than a man, ran him through with the bayonet.' Though this was an action taken in the heat of battle, 'our soldiers all cried "shame" at him'.[50]

The situation was manifestly different if the enemy was an indigenous foe, had been seen to have been overtly influenced by an indigenous foe or had in some way betrayed Britain or the principles for which the British Army stood and fought. Wolfe's escalating violence against the French army and civilian population of New France suggested that

European armies seen to have adopted savage practices would be subject to indiscriminate violence. Against the American army, meanwhile, whose very existence was a betrayal, there also appeared to be no such requirement to treat enemy combatants and the wider civilian population humanely, and if there was, the bar for violating these principles was very much lower than it was for the French or Spanish.[51]

All of this is important because it highlights the contradictions inherent within the emergence of a British military enlightenment. Brutality was a feature of British military activity against non-European adversaries throughout the eighteenth century, while enlightened ideals gradually began to change the perception of European enemies. Indeed, the very activity of fighting outside Europe, in challenging geographies and climates, led, in the opinions of some soldiers, to inhuman behaviour. Yet the British actively learned lessons from extra-European experiences and applied those lessons in European campaigns and battles. This contradiction at the heart of Britain's military enlightenment was itself explained by some of the underpinning philosophies that drove the Enlightenment itself, and also helps explain how British soldiers thought about the process of learning in war. While the emergence of humanity in war emphasised the need for compassion and restraint, the same philosophies suggested that an emotional response could be achieved by the imposition of physical effects. Officers like Wolfe could simultaneously demonstrate compassion in war and justify unrestricted violence against civilian populations in order to achieve the same ends. By the same token, lessons could be learned while also decrying the character of the campaign.

The British experience in Canada between 1759 and 1760, as well as the reaction to Pontiac's uprising in 1763, strongly suggested that this was an effective strategy. In the wake of the escalating indiscriminate violence sanctioned by Wolfe during the siege of Quebec, French Governor Vaudreuil warned the inhabitants of Canada that they faced similar treatment at the hands of the British. It was, Vaudreuil argued, a choice between 'whether they should be free men or slaves in bondage to the hard and exacting English'.[52] Instead, General James Murray, commanding the British advance from Quebec to Montreal in the summer of 1760, adopted a more conciliatory policy, encouraging the civilian population to swear new oaths of loyalty to the British Crown. Rather than the promised cruelty, the population were surprised to be treated well by the advancing British. 'We might thank our humanity more than our arms,' wrote one participant in the British advance, 'for so great an acquisition in allusion to Mr Murray's Expedition up the River.'[53]

These perceptions reflected the ways in which Enlightenment philosophers thought learning took place. The civilian population had initially resisted the British advance in 1759, been subjected to indiscriminate violence and, by accepting surprisingly humane and generous terms from the British in 1760, had been able to avoid more suffering. This appeared to confirm the concepts of sensationalism prevalent at the time: the infliction and experience of pain changed behaviour. Such notions were, of course, deeply flawed. The British advance on Montreal in 1760 was successful mainly because the wider British maritime strategy had strangled the French economy and their ability to maintain supplies to Canada. With the collapse of the French government in Canada, the prospect of stability under the British seemed more appealing.[54] Attempts to enact similar policies during the American Revolutionary War failed completely, partially because the British neglected to implement a similar economic strategy, and partly because the population were politically invested in the future of an America independent from Britain. Sir Henry Clinton had argued as early as February 1776 that the British must 'gain the hearts and subdue the minds of America', but by 1781 had realised that 'we have not their hearts' and as a result the British 'may conquer [but] shall never keep'.[55]

These sensationalist Enlightenment principles, flawed as they were, were also strongly evident and enduring in the area of discipline and training and help explain the changing learning process of the British soldier in the late eighteenth century. Fundamentally new ideas about how to train soldiers began gradually to emerge, though here more than anywhere else, the scale of conservative reaction was extreme. Across Europe, the belief was that 'armies must inevitably be composed of the filth of the nation, and everything which is useless and harmful to society'.[56] Looked down upon by the elite officers, the common soldier had no '"love of country" or "inclination toward military service"' but a 'love of idleness, a horror of any useful trade, ... inclination toward debauchery'.[57] Only rigorous drill and discipline would be successful in imposing order in such chaos, and, as we have seen, this proved successful, to some extent at least, on the battlefields of Europe.[58]

The wars in North America and India, however, illustrated that this approach to training was fundamentally limited, since it failed to prepare soldiers and officers for the challenges of fighting in difficult and unusual terrain. Britain's military enlightenment was therefore also a product of interconnected responses to these challenges. On the one hand, officers and soldiers needed to adapt to the conditions they encountered in the field, while on the other, military theorists wrote about these experiences and intersected their thinking with emerging philosophies on how soldiers might be trained more effectively.

In reality, British soldiers had always needed to demonstrate a degree of initiative, adaptation and innovation in order to be able to meet the unexpected challenges they encountered on any battlefield. Moreover, this points to the fact that soldiers in the British Army were not merely motivated by fear and greed, but also by pride in the profession of arms, personal honour, esprit de corps and small unit cohesion.[59] In the wake of the capture of Crown Point in 1759, Sergeant Roger Lamb explained why soldiers did their duty in combat. 'Personal bravery, hope of reward, and fear of punishment' were the three principal factors which ensured soldiers stayed on the battlefield in often terrifying circumstances.[60] Personal bravery, itself a subjective concept, was the combination of private and public satisfaction, the latter in relation to fellow soldiers. More often than not, soldiers remained in the field, fought with discipline and obeyed orders because not to do so risked the lives of their comrades, and ostracism from the networks of loyalty and acceptance within the soldiering community.[61]

Ancien régime military culture conveniently chose to ignore these facts since the small acts of initiative and bravery by common soldiers seldom translated into operational or strategic success. For the British in North America, however, the impact of adaptation and innovation by soldiers and individual officers was much more profound, leading to significant operational victories, and arguably overall strategic success. Thus the cumulation of adaptations to uniforms, changes to drill practices and the use of cover to protect individuals from ambuscades, all of which were designed to ease movement through and fighting in dense terrain, along with an increasing emphasis on marksmanship training, facilitated a considerable local shift in the art of war. To paraphrase Cumberland, 'every fertile genius' did in fact have a material impact on the course of war. Transmission and exchange of these ideas from America to Europe was facilitated by soldiers and officers who felt these lessons were useful outside North America.[62] As a result, the principles of the military enlightenment and sensationalism were instigated not just as theories, but in practice as well.

In turn, practice went on to be reflected in theory. In the mid-eighteenth century, sensationalist philosophers argued that the power of education was unlimited and could not be contained by accidents of birth. Since all knowledge was the product of experience, for sensationalists, the mind was a blank canvas, a *tabula rasa*, which if properly educated could achieve anything. These ideas permeated the military enlightenment, as publication of military memoirs, treatises and periodicals became more widespread, along with newly established centres of learning, such as the Royal Military Academy in Woolwich and later on the Royal Military College in High Wycombe. As a popular military theorist, Henry Lloyd was of increasing importance to the development of British thinking about training, particularly in the wake of the American Revolutionary War. Lloyd was influenced by sensationalist philosophy and his starting point was his own varied experience of military training and the shared experience of his peers. He argued that 'fear of, and an aversion to pain, and the desire for pleasure are the spring and cause of all actions, both in man and other species of animals'. Equipped with this knowledge, a general could achieve a much greater degree of control over the motivation and initiative of his soldiers, allowing him to dispose 'of their forces with unlimited authority'.[63]

In Lloyd's view, a general 'cannot create action in individuals; He cannot force men to act. He can only *persuade* and *direct*', which, Lloyd continued, 'can be done only by offering such motives to the troops as are most calculated to raise their courage, when depress'd, check and calm their passions, when violent and furious, in such a manner as to render himself absolute master of their inclinations ...'. This was Lloyd's 'Philosophy of War', which in his opinion was 'the most difficult, and sublime part of this or of any other profession, where the human heart is concerned. It supposes a perfect knowledge of the passions, because it is from that fountain only he must draw his arguments, to persuade or dissuade, as circumstances may require'.[64]

Lloyd linked the passion of the human heart to the political nature of war. In despotic states, such as those Lloyd had experienced when he served in Catherine the Great's army against the Turks, and where the population (and by extension those called upon to serve in the Army) had no voice, the power of persuasion rested on discipline and punishment. In monarchies and republics, where the population had acquired a degree of political liberty, the power of persuasion instead rested on the linkage between the population and the state itself. Military effectiveness, Lloyd therefore argued, increased in proportion to the degree of political liberty experienced by the population. This was a pointed reference to Lloyd's own military career, hamstrung as it had been by social inequality and the absence of political patronage.[65] Most importantly, however, Lloyd persuasively suggested that soldiers could be trained and educated to perform their duty in a thoughtful and innovative fashion, reflecting the practical realities the British had experienced in the wars of the second half of the eighteenth century, and fighting not through fear of the repercussions if they did not do so, but because they wanted to. In other words, rather than the coercion to fight that had been evident up to the first half of the eighteenth century, Britain's military enlightenment facilitated the co-optation of the common soldier.[66]

The key was perhaps identifying the crucial motivating factor that persuaded men to fight. Within the British Army, this was evidently the relationship that developed between the men themselves.[67] Whether in America, India or Europe, British soldiers faced many of the same difficulties: harsh weather and terrain; poorly organised supply systems which often led to them being poorly fed; disintegrating uniforms and shoes that wore through; long periods of boredom, interspersed with intensive training, lengthy marches and occasionally pitched battles in which the chances of death or severe, life-changing injury considerably increased.

Veterans experienced the latter with increasing levels of emotional detachment. 'Men who are familiarized to danger, approach it without thinking,' wrote Sergeant Lamb of his experience in America during the Seven Years' War, 'whereas troops unused to service apprehend danger where no danger exists.'[68] Over the course of a campaign, besides the intense physical endurance which soldiers experienced together, they also suffered extreme psychological trauma. This perspective was reflected by George Hennell, a private serving in the Peninsular War. 'When the balls began to whiz I expected every one would strike me,' he recorded during the siege of Badajoz in April 1812. 'As they increased I minded them less. I viewed calmly the town & to the whizzing of the balls soon became accustomed.'[69]

The relationship between the soldiers themselves was central to their ability to survive these challenges. As a result, as historian Ed Coss has argued, soldiers found themselves with a 'deep-seated need to belong' to a group, which would offer emotional support and camaraderie. In this way, rules and norms of acceptable behaviour were gradually established, which governed individual conduct both on and off the battlefield. These rules included sharing food while on the march or encamped and maintaining discipline during a battle. Failure to adhere to these rules – such as stealing food or fleeing the line of battle – would result in social condemnation and, ultimately, ostracism from the group.[70] Soldiers were co-opted not as a result of the imposition of strict forms of discipline, but the fear of social isolation, vital to survival in the campaign environment. Sensationalist philosophers would recognise the interlinkage of personal experience, emotion and social organisation in the behaviour of soldiers. These factors profoundly affected how officers and soldiers remembered war, how they viewed other participants in war and how they created military knowledge.

Traditional narratives of British military development in the eighteenth century assume the generation of military knowledge in the metropolitan centre – either at Horse Guards, by regimental commanders or by officers on home duty. Periodically, during a process of centralisation designed to enforce a degree of commonality and uniformity across the army, this knowledge was translated into training and education manuals and sent to regiments, which by the end of the eighteenth century were deployed across the world, with instructions to enact new systematic approaches to fighting and campaigning. In reality, the generation of military knowledge in the British Army of the eighteenth century was a largely informal process, a product of the physical and emotional experience of war in addition to a range of global influences transmitted around the periphery of the empire, and to the metropole in a complex web of networks. The resultant global military knowledge was itself a complicated product, based on the interaction of traditional formal military culture with informal innovations and adaptations borne of experience and learning derived from new ideas and thinking.[71]

Soldiers and officers themselves formed Britain's global military knowledge networks. While some had greater influence than others, all made or remade military knowledge as they experienced warfare throughout the eighteenth century. Their writings and correspondence offer a glimpse of the way in which their experiences translated into new military knowledge and help chart the progress of this knowledge around the world. Soldiers, as well as officers, wrote frequently of their experience of war, though letters to worried family members and loved ones were often sanitised, with the true horror of battle elided from the narrative of events.[72] Such details were often replaced with tactical and technical detail. In part, this helped soldiers to differentiate themselves morally from civilians.

The military enlightenment and sensationalist philosophical prioritisation of physical experience as the root of knowledge translated into an increasing belief that only those with experience of combat could truly understand its reality.[73] Such beliefs produced the notion that only soldiers were qualified to think and write about war, and by extension were worth reading. In turn, when they wrote about war, they had to be able to illustrate that the profession of arms required expertise and skill to practise effectively. This frequently led civilian observers, such as Walter Scott, to lament that soldiers focused 'too much upon the *tactique* to regard the picturesque'. He claimed no 'soldier could give me an idea of battle . . . The technical phrases of the military art, too, are unfavourable to convey a description of the concomitant terror and desolation that attends an engagement'.[74] The focus on the technical at the expense of the picturesque, as Scott put it, meant there was at least a commonality of language in the description of war, which helps illustrate knowledge networks and the exchange of ideas and experience.

This was further complicated by the emergence of different schools of thought which developed around officers and soldiers whose predominant experience of warfare was the result of fighting in one theatre of war or another. Those who had seen extensive service in America, for instance, argued that lessons learned there – such as the development of light infantry – should be integrated into the general order of battle of the British Army as a whole. To that end, then, did Major General Sir William Howe devise his 'Discipline for Light Infantry operating in Battalion'. Taught and drilled at the military encampment at Salisbury in August and September 1774, its incorporation into the regular order of battle of the British Army seemed to be confirmed when the new drill was successfully demonstrated in front of King George III at a simulated battle in Richmond Park on 4 October the same year.[75] The failure of that approach to secure strategic success during the American Revolutionary War, despite evident tactical and even operational victories, persuaded the British to set aside the incorporation of light infantry into the regular order of battle of the British Army.

Colonel David Dundas famously excluded light infantry drill from the first draft of his *Principles of Military Movement*, which drew heavily on the author's experience of warfighting in Europe, and from his regular attendance at Prussian military encampments in the 1780s.[76] This produced a backlash among officers with American experience who went on to serve in Europe, such as Major-General Sir Eyre Coote. In 1796, he drafted 'Instructions to Officers of Light Infantry', a counterpoint to Dundas who, in Coote's view, 'had paid little attention to the Service of the Light Infantry'.[77] When Coote went on to serve in Egypt in 1801, he found officers of the 'European School' referring to light infantry tactics as 'what was called bush fighting in America, which can never be productive of any great result'.[78] Indeed, though the American war offered, in the words of one contributor to the *Royal Military Chronicle* in 1811, 'an infinite variety as to scene of operation', being 'a war of surprises; of woods, and morasses', it was, as a result, 'not calculated to form an officer to European tactics'.[79]

The experience of the French Revolutionary War, with repeated defeats at the hands of apparently innovative French *tirailleurs* and *chasseurs*, persuaded the British to reconsider, and only because once more at the head of the Army was a reform-minded commander-in-chief. The Duke of York, like his great uncle, the Duke of Cumberland, championed innovation and was able to authorise the formation of centres for experimentation in light infantry training. Here again, the influence of informal knowledge networks persisted. York appointed John Moore, a veteran of the West Indies, and a professionally minded officer who drew extensively on his personal study of recent military campaigns to support his plans.[80] His appointment of similarly minded officers drew further on connections to Britain's wars in America. The result, by 1810, was a division solely composed of light infantry, on which Arthur Wellesley, by then Lord Wellington, could draw to manoeuvre rapidly, monitor his adversary and achieve tactical and operational superiority over the French. The informal military knowledge network that helped produce this result consisted of loose connections stretching to the middle of the eighteenth century and was the consequence of Britain's accidental military enlightenment.

To convert this tactical and operational success into strategic victory, the British drew on related informal knowledge networks. If light infantry produced necessary mobility, the strategic employment of this force was influenced by the concurrent debate about the pursuit of decisive battle. While many in the British ranks saw the principal utility of an army as to close with and destroy its main adversary, a parallel line of thought suggested that this was only desirable if it facilitated wider strategic and political ends. Here the competing American and European schools of thought once more suggested different conclusions. When he suggested a wide-flanking movement to cut off the American army at Bunker Hill in July 1775, Henry Clinton was reportedly mocked. The then commander-in-chief, General Sir Thomas Gage, considered 'himself so well informed that he would not take any opinion of others, particularly of a man bred up in the German School, which that of America affects to despise'.[81] Clinton's aim remained the defeat of the Americans, though he proposed a plan which might achieve that result without a battle of attrition. Gage, by selecting a frontal assault, made one inevitable.

Again, Henry Lloyd was instrumental in the development of the concept, which his friend, Clinton, called 'indirect manoeuvres'. As with light infantry, the failure to achieve a decisive result in the American Revolutionary War suggested that Clinton's approach was unachievable. Critics saw it as the avoidance of battle, rather than setting the conditions for success. Nevertheless, the approach persisted, continuing to draw criticism. The 'character of the American war will account for some peculiar traits which may be observed in officers who have been formed in it,' wrote one commentator, 'that is to say, a peculiar caution and tardiness'.[82] The experience of the French Revolutionary War, once again, proved to be the prompt needed to reassess this conclusion.

The absence of suitably qualified staff officers in the British Army to plan and conduct operations and campaigns prompted the Duke of York to agree to the creation of the Royal Military College under the direction of John Le Marchant. Through an intense curriculum, officers were trained in the art of war, not at the tactical level but in the realm of operations. Complex manoeuvres, previously beyond the capabilities of all but the most skilled officers, became possible with large armies. In 1813, then, Wellington was able to plan, with a staff system headed by his quartermaster general George Murray, and previously unavailable to his predecessors, a complex operation designed to force the French to withdraw from Spain. The battle that concluded the operation was a product of its success, not its original aim. Again, the loose and informal military knowledge network facilitated this, with connections existing between Lloyd, Clinton, York, Moore, Le Marchant and Murray.

Britain's accidental military enlightenment thus facilitated a transformation in the tactical, operational and strategic application of military power by the British Army in the second half of the eighteenth century. This was the product of Britain's 'wandering army'; not just of the emergence of Enlightenment thinking, but of the simultaneous experience of war on a global stage and facilitated by unique military knowledge networks. Enlightenment thinking helped to galvanise those networks and facilitated the incorporation of experiences previously thought relevant only to specific theatres and regions. The success of the British Army in the Peninsular War was the result of the combined experience of wars in America and India, as well as Europe. In the wake of ultimate victory at Waterloo in 1815, the collapse of those networks, alongside the simultaneous end of Britain's military enlightenment, once more forced those experiences into silos, curtailed the exchange of military knowledge and stymied innovation and adaptation for the next 50 years, even as technological advancement demanded new thinking. The British Army thus lurched from a period of enlightenment to one of ignorance.

Notes

Introduction: 'A Science Covered With Darkness'

1. Rex Whitworth, *Field Marshal Lord Ligonier: A Story of the British Army, 1702–1770* (Oxford: Oxford University Press, 1958), 102–103.
2. British Library, London (BL) Add MS 35354, Yorke to Hardwicke, 26 May 1745.
3. Ibid.
4. Adam Williamson, *Military Memoirs and Maxims of Marshal Turenne; Interspersed with Others, Taken from the Best Authors and Observation, with Remarks* (London: Knapton, 1740), v. See also J. A. Houlding, *Fit for Service: The Training of the British Army 1715–1795* (Oxford: Oxford University Press, 1981), 186–187.
5. J. W. Fortescue, *A History of the British Army*, 12 vols (London: Macmillan, 1899–1927), 2:62–72.
6. Kent History and Library Centre (KHLC) U1350/O1/1, Amherst Personal Journals, May 1741–October 1744, Wednesday June 26 NS 1743.
7. Library and Archives of Canada (LAC) MG18/L5/3/1, Wolfe to his father, 4 July 1743.
8. Royal Archives, Windsor Castle (RA) Papers of the Duke of Cumberland (DCP), OB6 General Order, 14 March 1745, ff. 116.
9. Houlding, *Fit for Service*, 358.
10. Earl John Russell, *Memoirs of the Affairs of Europe: From the Peace of Utrecht*, 2 vols (London: John Murray, 1829), 2:204.
11. KHLC U1350/O1/2, Amherst Personal Journals, April 1741–August 1746, 11 May 1745.
12. National Library of Scotland (NLS) Yester MS 7801, Hay to Tweeddale, 17, 22, 24 May 1745.
13. The National Archives of the United Kingdom, Kew (TNA) WO 87/17, Evidence of Captain John Forbes to the court martial of Brigadier Ingoldsby.
14. Fortescue, *History of the British Army*, 2:119.
15. BL Add MS 35354, Yorke to Hardwicke, 26 May 1745.
16. Maurice, Comte de Saxe, *Reveries, or Memoirs Concerning the Art of War* (Edinburgh: Sands, Donaldson, Murray and Cochran, 1759), 114. For a more general discussion of the life of Saxe, see Jon Manchip White, *Marshal of France: The Life and Times of Maurice de Saxe* (London: Hamish Hamilton, 1962).
17. For an expansion of this discussion, see Adam Lindsay Storring, 'Frederick the Great and the Meanings of War, 1730–1755' (Unpublished PhD Thesis, Cambridge

University, 2017); and Arthur Khule, 'War without contact: Berenhorst, Bülow, and the avoidance of violence as the core paradigm of military science', *War in History* (May 2020), 1–26.

18. See Christy Pichichero, *The Military Enlightenment: War and Culture in the French Empire from Louis XIV to Napoleon* (Ithaca: Cornell University Press, 2017). See also Eugene Miakinkov, *War and Enlightenment in Russia: Military Culture in the Age of Catherine II* (Toronto: University of Toronto Press, 2020); and Armstrong Starkey, *War in the Age of Enlightenment, 1700–1789* (London: Praeger, 2003).

19. Madeleine Dobie, "The enlightenment at war", *PMLA*, 124/5 (October 2009), 1851–1854. See also Pichichero, *Military Enlightenment*, 1–24; John Lynn, *Battle: A History of Combat and Culture from Ancient Greece to Modern America* (New York: Basic Books, 2003), 111–144; Starkey, *War in the Age of Enlightenment*, Chapter 2: 'The Military Enlightenment'; and Christopher Duffy, *The Military Experience in the Age of Reason* (New York: Atheneum, 1988), 3–34.

20. Ira D. Gruber, *Books and the British Army in the Age of the American Revolution* (Chapel Hill: University of North Carolina Press, 2010) explores the books read by a variety of British officers, records of whose libraries remain intact. Gruber charts the changing reading preferences of those officers, linking these changing preferences with Britain's evolving approach to war. For a more general review of the literature accessed by British officers, see Houlding, *Fit for Service*, 153–256. Matthew McCormack explores the literature used by the militia in 'Liberty and Discipline: Militia Training Literature in Mid-Georgian England', in Catriona Kennedy & Matthew McCormack (eds), *Soldiering in Britain and Ireland, 1750–1850: Men of Arms* (Basingstoke: Palgrave, 2013), 136–158. See also Mark Towsey, *Reading History in Britain and America, c.1750–c.1840* (Cambridge: Cambridge University Press, 2021), 45, 57, 67 for evidence of similar usages made on a more general basis by the wider reading public.

21. Brig. Richard Kane, *Campaigns of King William and Queen Anne; From 1689 to 1712. Also a New System of Military Discipline, for a Battalion of Foot on Action; with the Most Essential Exercise of the Cavalry* (London: J. Millan, 1745).

22. Kane, *Campaigns*, Editor's Preface; Houlding, *Fit for Service*, 185.

23. Library of the Society of the Cincinnati, Washington, DC (LSC) MSS L2008F48, Wolfe to Townshend, 18 July 1756.

24. The period is the subject of considerable debate. For arguments suggesting that the eighteenth century was a period of limited development leading to indecision, see, for example, David Chandler, *The Art of Warfare in the Age of Marlborough* (London: Batsford, 1976), 19–20; and Russell F. Weigley, *The Age of Battles: The Quest for Decisive Warfare from Breitenfeld to Waterloo* (Bloomington: Indiana University Press, 1991), 539. For a more recent discussion of the problems with this analysis, see Jeremy Black, *European Warfare, 1660–1815* (London: Yale University Press, 1994), 67–87; Charles J. Esdaile, *The Wars of the French Revolution, 1792–1801* (Abingdon: Routledge, 2019), 35–62; and Alexander Mikaberidze, *The Napoleonic Wars: A Global History* (Oxford: Oxford University Press, 2020), 18–43.

25. See Anthony Page, *Britain and the Seventy Years War, 1744–1815* (Basingstoke: Palgrave, 2015). Accounts of the British Army in this period have largely focused on its institutional evolution or its role within a wider British strategy. See also H. C. B. Rogers, *The British Army in the Eighteenth Century* (London: Allen & Unwin, 1977); Jeremy Black, *Britain as a Military Power, 1688–1815* (London: UCL Press, 1999); Stephen Conway, *The British Army, 1714–1783: An Institutional History* (Barnsley: Pen & Sword, 2021); and Saul David, *All the King's Men: The British Soldier from the Restoration to Waterloo* (London: Penguin, 2012) and *Victoria's Wars: The Rise of Empire* (London: Penguin, 2006). Bruce Collins, *War and Empire: The Expansion of Britain, 1790–1830* (London: Routledge, 2010) analyses the expansion of British power in a similar period illustrating the importance of the army to both regional and global

success. More recently, Jeremy Black has argued that the British Army deserves more attention in the debate about Britain's rise as a global power, though his arguments in *How the Army Made Britain a Global Power: 1688–1815* (Oxford: Casemate, 2021) do not make the same differentiation between informal and formal learning which the present volume does. A more general discussion of war in this period can be found in Duffy, *Military Experience in the Age of Reason*; and Roger Chickering & Stig Förster (eds), *War in an Age of Revolution, 1775–1815* (Cambridge: Cambridge University Press, 2010).

26. Alan Lester, *Imperial Networks: Creating Identities in Nineteenth-Century South Africa and Britain* (London: Routledge, 2001), 5–6.

27. Pichichero, *Military Enlightenment*, 8.

28. These ideas are discussed in detail in Yuval Noah Harari, *The Ultimate Experience: Battlefield Revelations and the Making of Modern War Culture, 1450–2000* (London: Palgrave, 2008), 129–196.

29. George Robert Gleig, *The Subaltern: A Chronicle of the Peninsular War* (London: T. Cadell, 1825), 161.

30. Quoted in Charles Taylor, *Sources of the Self: The Making of Modern Identity* (Cambridge, MA: Harvard University Press, 1989), 328.

31. Harari, *Ultimate Experience*, 137.

32. See Tony Ballantyne, *Webs of Empire: Locating New Zealand's Colonial Past* (Wellington: Bridget Williams Books, 2014), in particular, 'Introduction: Relocating Colonial Histories'; loc. 818/12348.

33. See David Lambert & Alan Lester (eds), *Colonial Lives Across the British Empire: Imperial Careering in the Long Nineteenth Century* (Cambridge: Cambridge University Press, 2006), 1–31. For more on knowledge exchange and circulation, see Zoe Laidlaw, *Colonial Connections, 1815–45: Patronage, the Information Revolution and Colonial Government* (Manchester: Manchester University Press, 2012), Chapter 2: 'Networking the Empire'; David Lambert & Peter Merriman (eds), *Empire and Mobility in the Long Nineteenth Century* (Manchester: Manchester University Press, 2020), 1–28; Lester, *Imperial Networks*; Claude Markovits, Jacques Pouchepadass & Sanjay Subrahmanyam (eds), *Society and Circulation: Mobile People and Itinerant Cultures in South Asia, 1750–1950* (London: Anthem Press, 2006); and Ulrike Hillemann, *Asian Empire and British Knowledge: China and the Networks of British Imperial Expansion* (Basingstoke: Palgrave, 2009).

34. For evidence of the subject of conversations in the mess, see, for example, Trinity College Dublin Library (TCD) Donoughmore Papers E/10c, Diaries of the Hon Christopher Hely-Hutchinson during the Expedition to Egypt, ff. 47–48. For more on the nature of knowledge networks in the British army, see Huw J. Davies, 'Military Print Culture, Knowledge and Terrain: Knowledge Mobility and Eighteenth-Century Military Colonialism', in Lambert & Merriman, *Empire and Mobility*, 29–49. Lindsay O'Neil, *The Opened Letter: Networking in the Early Modern British World* (Philadelphia: University of Pennsylvania Press, 2014), explores the development of correspondence networks in the late seventeenth and early eighteenth centuries. In so doing, O'Neil unearths the nature of knowledge exchange through correspondence and writing. Mark Towsey, *Reading History*, offers detailed analysis of the ways in which the British and Americans read and made use of history in the long eighteenth century. Towsey shows that not only was history used to confirm a national identity, but readers, including military personnel, used history as a means of understanding contemporary events. Sarah Goldsmith, *Masculinity and Danger on the Eighteenth-Century Grand Tour* (London: University of London Press, 2020), demonstrates the importance of European travel and study to the development of eighteenth-century conceptions of masculinity, including that of the military. In Chapter 2, 'Military Mad: War and the Grand Tour', 77–110, Goldsmith analyses the use made of battlefield visits, garrison tours and military academy destinations to the development of the military mind.

Developments in cartographical historiography point to an increasingly complex relationship between the generation of knowledge and the production of maps. See, for example, J. B. Hartley, Barbara Bartz Petchenick & Lawrence W. Towner, *Mapping the American Revolutionary War* (Chicago: University of Chicago Press, 1978). In particular, J. B. Hartley's chapter 'The Map User in the Revolution', 79–110 explores how Continental Army officers made use of maps during the war. Albeit from an American perspective, the arguments point to a general transformation in the drawing and use of maps during this period. More general discussions of the relationships between maps and knowledge can be found in J. B. Hartley, *The New Nature of Maps: Essays in the History of Cartography* (Baltimore: The Johns Hopkins University Press, 2001), 51–82. S. Max Edelson, *The New Map of Empire: How Britain Imagined America Before Independence* (Cambridge, MA: Harvard University Press, 2017), is an excellent exploration of the use of maps to visualise and contextualise space, and how that space can be used and occupied. In research currently under way, Bénédicte Miyamoto explores the development of map drawing in the eighteenth century, and how use was made of certain pigmentations to ensure consistent map creation. See, for more, Louisiane Ferlier & Bénédicte Miyamoto, *Forms, Formats and the Circulation of Knowledge: British Printscape's Innovations, 1688–1832* (Leiden: Brill, 2020), 1–24.

35. A. G. Doughty & G. W. Parmelee (eds), *The Siege of Quebec and the Battle of the Plains of Abraham*, 6 vols (Quebec: Dussault & Proulx, 1901), 'Journal of the Particular Transaction during Siege of Quebec, 12–13 September 1759', 5:188.

36. S. R. Lushington, *The Life and Services of General Lord Harris GCB, During his Campaigns in America, the West Indies and India* (London: John W. Parker, 1845), 82–3.

37. National Records of Scotland, Edinburgh (NRS) GD1/6/17, Narrative of the 2nd War with Hyderally.

38. William Dalrymple, *The Anarchy: The East India Company, Corporate Violence and the Pillage of an Empire* (New York: Bloomsbury, 2019), 251–256.

39. Ralph Blakiston, *12 Years Military Adventure in Three-quarters of the Globe . . .* (London: Henry Coulburn, 1840), 200–202.

40. See Huw J. Davies, *Wellington's Wars: The Making of a Military Genius* (London: Yale University Press, 2012), 65–68; W. H. Springer, 'The Military Apprenticeship of Arthur Wellesley in India, 1791–1805' (PhD Dissertation, Yale University, 1965), 152; Randolf G. S. Cooper, *The Anglo-Maratha Campaigns and the Contest for India: The Struggle for Control of the South Asian Military Economy* (Cambridge: Cambridge University Press, 2004), 127–128.

41. NRS GD1/6/17, Narrative of the 2nd War with Hyderally. See also Alexander Dirom, *A Narrative of the Campaign in India, which Terminated the War with Tippoo Sultan, in 1792* (London: Bulmer & Co., 1793).

42. NRS GD1/6/5/1, Campbell to Cornwallis, 16 December 1788

43. National Army Museum, Chelsea (NAM) MS 6807/157/6, Discipline established by Major General Howe for Light Infantry in Battalion, Sarum, September 1774.

44. NRS GD1/6/14 Observations humbly submitted to Major General Sir Archibald Campbell KB on his System of Manoeuvres by Files.

45. William L. Clements Library, University of Michigan, Ann Arbor (WCL) Clinton Papers (CP) 52/4, Campbell to Clinton, Savannah, 16 January 1779.

46. Philip Guedella, *The Duke* (London: Hodder & Stoughton, 1931), 54–65. See also Rory Muir, *Wellington: The Path to Victory, 1769–1814* (London: Yale University Press, 2013), 46.

47. Jean-Charles de Folard, *Nouvelles découvertes sur la guerre* (Brussels: Foppens & Tilliard, 1726), 11.

48. Starkey, *War in the Age of Enlightenment*, 540–577/3622.

49. See Harari, *Ultimate Experience*, 129–159.

1 'Grasping in the Dark'

1. *New York Mercury*, 26 July 1756, quoted in Guy Frégault, *Canada: The War of Conquest* (Oxford: Oxford University Press, 1969), 122.
2. William Smith, *An Historical Account of the Expedition Against the Ohio Indians ... Under the Command of Henry Bouquet* (Philadelphia: W. Bradford, 1766), 19.
3. For a general account of the Jacobite uprising, see Christopher Duffy, *Fight for a Throne: The Jacobite '45 Reconsidered* (Solihull: Helion, 2015).
4. Hugh Mackay, *Memoirs of the War Carried on in Scotland and Ireland* (Edinburgh: Privately Published, 1833), 51. See also David Blackmore, *Destructive and Formidable: British Infantry Firepower, 1642–1745* (Barnsley: Frontline, 2014), 109–110.
5. NRS RH4/213, The Reverend Alexander Duncan's Journal of the Rebellion of 1745.
6. Patrick Crichton, *The Woodhouselee MS. A Narrative of Events in Edinburgh and District During the Jacobite Occupation* (London: W. & R. Chambers, 1907), 38–9.
7. Henry E. Huntington Library, San Merino (HEH) Loudoun Papers (LO) 11785, Loudoun to [unnamed] colonel, Berwick, 23 September 1745.
8. 'Essay on regular and irregular forces', *The Gentleman's Magazine*, XVI (1746), 30–2.
9. Thomas I. Rae, 'The Loudoun Scottish Papers in the Huntington Library', *Scottish Historical Review*, 49/148 (October 1970), 227–231.
10. Andrew MacKillop, *'More Fruitful Than the Soil': Army, Empire and the Scottish Highlands, 1715–1815* (East Lothian, Tuckwell Press, 2000), 29, 39–40.
11. Quoted in John Grenier, *The First Way of War: American War Making on the Frontier* (Cambridge: Cambridge University Press, 2005), 107.
12. Quoted in Peter E. Russell, 'Redcoats in the wilderness: British officers and irregular warfare in Europe and America, 1740–1760', *William and Mary Quarterly*, 35/4 (October 1978), 637.
13. Charles Winchester (ed.), *Memoirs of the Chevalier de Johnstone*, 3 vols (Aberdeen: Wyllie & Son, 1871), 2:110–111.
14. HEH LO 11789, Loudoun Papers, Loudoun to Cope, Dornick, 12 March 1745/6.
15. Lewis Walpole Library, Yale University, Farmington CT (LWL) Weston Papers, MS 3, Campbell to Harrington, Appin Camp, 1746.
16. KHLC U1350/O2/2, Amherst Military Journals, November 1745, Litchfield, 30 November 1745. Manner of engaging the Rebels. See also Blackmore, *Destructive and Formidable*, 110.
17. Duffy, *Fight for a Throne*, 426.
18. Blackmore, *Destructive and Formidable*, 112–13. John Marchant, *The History of the Present Rebellion* (London: Hyndshaw & Thompson, 1746), 398–399.
19. Duffy, *Fight for a Throne*, 455.
20. Anonymous, *Observations on Mr Home's Account of the Battle of Culloden* (Exeter, 1802), 32.
21. Duffy, *Fight for a Throne*, 457–461.
22. 'Extract of a letter from Inverness', *The Gentleman's Magazine*, XVI (1746), 271.
23. BL Add MS 35354, Yorke to Hardwicke, Camp of Inverness, 18 April 1746.
24. Historical Manuscripts Commission (HMC) *Report on the Laing Manuscripts Preserved at the University of Edinburgh*, 3 vols (London, 1925), Anonymous draft letter, Edinburgh, 22 April 1746, 2:367.
25. Anonymous, *Observations on Mr Home's Account*, Daniel Hamilton, 'Account', 17.
26. Duffy, *Fight for a Throne*, 466–467.
27. Robert Wright, *The Life of Major-General Wolfe* (London: Chapman & Hall, 1864), Wolfe to William Sotherton, Inverness, 17 April 1746, 84–85.
28. TNA SP 54/30/21A, Cumberland to Newcastle, 18 April 1746.
29. George Townshend, *A Brief Narrative of the Late Campaigns in Germany and Flanders in a Letter to a Member of Parliament* (London: J. Lion, 1751), 44.
30. For more on the Battle of Lauffeldt, see Whitworth, *Ligonier*, 150–152; Alistair Massie & Jonathan Oates (eds), *The Duke of Cumberland's Campaigns in Britain and the Low Countries, 1745–1748: A Selection of His Letters* (Stroud: The History Press,

2018); Stephen Brumwell, *Paths of Glory: The Life and Death of James Wolfe* (London: Hambledon Continuum, 2006), 78.

31. Townshend, *Narrative of the Late Campaigns*, 58.
32. See KHLC U1350/02/5, Memorandum, 2 July in 'Orders 19 June to 13 September 1747'.
33. For background see Lawrence Gipson, *The British Empire Before the American Revolution*, 15 vols (Idaho & New York: Caxton & Knopf, 1936–1970), specifically volume 6 *The Great War for the Empire: The Years of Defeat, 1754–1757* (1948) and volume 7 *The Great War for Empire: The Victorious Years, 1758–1760* (1950). See also Douglas Edward Leach, *Arms for Empire: A Military History of the British Colonies in North America, 1607–1763* (New York: Macmillan, 1973); Howard H. Peckham, *The Colonial Wars, 1689–1762* (Chicago: University of Chicago Press, 1964); Ian K. Steele, *Warpaths: Invasions of North America* (Oxford: Oxford University Press, 1994); Jeremy Black, *Fighting for America: The Struggle for Mastery in North America, 1519–1871* (Bloomington: Indiana University Press, 2011); Fred Anderson, *Crucible of War: The Seven Years' War and the Fate of the British Empire in British North America, 1754–1766* (New York: Knopf, 2000); and Daniel Baugh, *The Global Seven Years War, 1754–1763* (Harlow: Longman, 2011). More specific treatments can be found in Stanley Pargellis, *Lord Loudoun in North America* (New Haven: Yale University Press, 1934); and more recently in Stephen Brumwell, *Redcoats: The British Soldier and War in the Americas, 1755–1763* (Cambridge: Cambridge University Press, 2002); Guy Chet, *Conquering the American Wilderness: The Triumph of European Warfare in the Colonial Northeast* (Amherst: University of Massachusetts, 2003); Michael N. McConnell, *Army and Empire: British Soldiers on the American Frontier, 1758–1775* (Lincoln: University of Nebraska, 2004); Matthew Ward, *Breaking the Backcountry: The Seven Years' War in Virginia and Pennsylvania, 1754–1765* (Pittsburgh: University of Pittsburgh Press, 2003); and George Yagi, *The Struggle for North America, 1754–1758: Britannia's Tarnished Laurels* (London: Bloomsbury, 2017).
34. Stanley Pargellis (ed.), *Military Affairs in North America, 1748–1765: Selected Documents From the Cumberland Papers in Windsor Castle* (New York: Appleton-Century, 1936), 'Sketch for the Operations in North America', 16 November 1754, 45.
35. See David Preston, *Braddock's Defeat: The Battle of the Monongahela and the Road to Revolution* (Oxford: Oxford University Press, 2015), particularly 269–322.
36. Albert & Shirley Small Special Collections Library, University of Virginia, Charlottesville (SSCL) MS 10034/1/9, St Clair to Napier, Hampton, 15 February 1755, ff. 29–30.
37. Charles Hamilton (ed.), *Braddock's Defeat: The Journal of Captain Robert Cholmley's Batman, the Journal of a British Officer, Halkett's Orderly Book* (Norman: University of Oklahoma Press, 1959), 45.
38. SSCL MS 10034/1/9, St Clair to Napier, Fort at Willis's Creek, 22 July 1755, ff. 123–125.
39. BL King's MS 212, Journal of Robert Orme, 1755, ff. 102–109.
40. Ibid.
41. HEH LO 685, Dunbar/Gage Statement on Monongahela, Albany, 21 November 1755.
42. Hamilton, *Braddock's Defeat*, 50–52.
43. HEH LO 685, Dunbar/Gage Statement on Monongahela, Albany, 21 November 1755.
44. HEH LO 606, Orme to Dinwiddie, Fort Cumberland, 18 July 1755.
45. Ibid.
46. BL King's MS 212, Journal of Robert Orme, 1755, ff. 102–109.
47. HEH LO 605, Washington to Dinwiddie, Fort Cumberland, 18 July 1755.
48. HEH LO 687, John Hale to John Calcraft, Fort Sackville, 27 November 1755.
49. HEH LO 685, Dunbar/Gage Statement on Monongahela, Albany, 21 November 1755.

50. Ibid.
51. Preston, *Braddock's Defeat*, 323–332.
52. Houlding, *Fit for Service*, 374–376.
53. 'Essay on regular and irregular forces', *The Gentleman's Magazine*, XVI (1746), 30–32.
54. Pargellis, *Military Affairs*, 'Sketch for Next Year's Campaign in North America', 6 September 1755, 133–136.
55. *Pennsylvania Gazette*, 25 December 1755, quoted in Frégault, *Canada*, 120.
56. HEH LO 1522, Loudoun to Fox, Albany, 19 August 1756.
57. HEH LO 1341, Loudoun to Lawrence, 24 July 1756.
58. Anderson, *Crucible of War*, 135.
59. HEH LO 1341, Loudoun to Lawrence, 24 July 1756.
60. HEH LO 1414, Loudoun to Webb, 4 August 1756 & LO 1403, Loudoun to Mercer, 3 August 1756.
61. HEH LO 1414, Loudoun to Webb, 4 August 1756.
62. HEH LO 1424, Loudoun to Bunton and Montressor, 5 August 1756.
63. HEH LO 644, William Johnson to Shirley, Camp at Lake George, 9 September 1755.
64. Pargellis, *Military Affairs*, Franklin to Fawkener, New York, 27 July 1756, 185.
65. HEH LO 1414, Loudoun to Webb, Albany, 4 August 1756.
66. Frégault, *Canada*, 127–9.
67. E. B. O'Callaghan & B. Fernow (eds), *Documents Relative to the Colonial History of the State of New York*, 15 vols (Albany: Argus & Co., 1853–1887), (*NYCD*), Letter from an officer, Camp at Chouagen [Oswego], 22 August 1756, 10:456.
68. Frégault, *Canada*, 134.
69. HEH LO 1525, Loudoun to Cumberland, Albany, 20 August 1756.
70. Pargellis, *Lord Loudoun*, 211–227.
71. Daniel J. Beattie, 'The Adaptation of the British Army to Wilderness Warfare, 1755–1763', in Marten Ultee (ed.), *Adapting to Conditions: War and Society in the Eighteenth Century* (Huntsville: University of Alabama Press, 1986), 63.
72. Pargellis, *Lord Loudoun*, 298–99.
73. HEH LO 1414, Loudoun to Webb, Albany, 4 August 1756.
74. See Chet, *Conquering the Wilderness*, 100–141; Beattie, 'Adaptation of the British Army to Wilderness Warfare', 56–83, Pargellis, *Lord Loudoun*, 104–131.
75. Ward, *Breaking the Back Country*, 59–90.
76. Pargellis, *Lord Loudoun*, 301.
77. Benjamin Church, *Diary of King Philip's War, 1675–1676* (Little Compton: Little Compton Historical Society, 1975), 106. See also Lisa Brooks, *Our Beloved Kin: A New History of King Philip's War* (New Haven: Yale University Press, 2018).
78. See Richard R. Johnson, 'The search for a usable Indian: An aspect of the defense of Colonial New England', *Journal of American History*, 64/3 (1977), 623–651.
79. Grenier, *First Way of War*, 33–34.
80. James Phinney Baxter (ed.), *Collections of the Maine Historical Society, Second Series, Documentary History of the State of Maine, Vols. 4, 9–12, Containing the Baxter Manuscripts* (Portland: Maine Historical Society, 1889–1916), William Bollan to the Duke of Newcastle, 17 August 1747, 11:387–388.
81. WCL Gorham MS 1/3, Gorham to Shirley, 4 October 1746.
82. 'Readers Questions', *Journal of the Society of Army Historical Society*, 32 (1954), 45. This is confirmed by Horatio Gates in his Journal of September 1750. See New York Historical Society (NYHS) MS 240, Journal kept on the expedition sent by Cornwallis, Governor of Nova Scotia, to dislodge the French and Indians from Chignecto, and the building of the fort etc. 10 September to 8 October 1750. Entry for 16 September 1750.
83. For more on this, see Wayne E. Lee, 'Fortify, fight, or flee: Tuscarora and Cherokee defensive warfare and military culture adaptation', *Journal of Military History*, 3/68 (July 2004), 713–770.

84. NYHS MS 240, Journal kept on the expedition sent by Cornwallis . . . 10 September to 8 October 1750. Entry for 16 September 1750.
85. HEH LO 2262, Loudoun to Cumberland, New York, 22 November 1756.
86. See, for example, *Boston Gazette*, 13 October 1755.
87. Stephen Brumwell, *White Devil: A True Story of War, Savagery, and Vengeance in Colonial America* (Cambridge, MA: Da Capo Press, 2004), 76.
88. HEH LO 1090 and 1091, Shirley to Winslow, New York, 30 April 1756.
89. HEH LO 4701, Methods used by Captain Robert Rogers in disciplining the Rangers of his Command, 25 October 1757.
90. HEH LO 2704, Robert Rogers, Journal of a Scout, Island near Fort Edward, 25 January 1757.
91. Robert Rogers, *Journals of Major Robert Rogers* (Albany: Joel Munsell's Sons, 1883), 55, 57.
92. HEH LO 1060, 'Exercises for the American Forces', approved by His Royal Highness, 18 April 1756.
93. Rogers, *Journals*, 55, 57.
94. See Julie Flavell, *The Howe Dynasty: The Untold Story of a Military Family and the Women Behind Britain's Wars for America* (New York: Liveright, 2021), for an original examination of the Howes including the early life and death of George Howe.
95. Rogers, *Journals*, 79–80.
96. Fortescue, *History of the British Army*, 2:323.
97. Ann Grant, *Memoirs of an American Lady*, 2 vols (London: Longman, Hurst, Rees & Orme, 1809) 1:199–200.
98. Dr Richard Huck to Jan Ingenhousz, 18 May 1758, quoted in Daniel J. Beattie, 'General Jeffrey Amherst and the Conquest of Canada, 1758–1760' (Unpublished PhD Thesis, Duke University, 1976), 126.
99. Fort Ticonderoga Archive (FTA) 02M/2162, Monypenny Orderly Book, June–July 1758.
100. HMC, *Report on the Manuscripts of Mrs. Stopford-Sackville of Drayton House, Northamptonshire*, 2 vols. (London, 1910), Wolfe to Sackville, Halifax, 24 May 1758, 2:259–260.
101. HEH LO 2263, Loudoun to Fox, Albany and New York, 22 November 1756.
102. HEH LO 2043, Rogers to Loudoun, Fort Edward, 19 October 1756.
103. Grenier, *First Way of War*, 115–145.
104. HEH LO 2263, Loudoun to Fox, Albany and New York, 22 November 1756.
105. Pargellis, *Lord Loudoun*, 300–306.
106. Pargellis, *Military Affairs*, Cumberland to Loudoun, St James's, 2 December 1756, 255.
107. HEH LO 1525, Loudoun to Cumberland, Albany, 20 August 1756.
108. SSCL Forbes Headquarters Papers, MS 10034/1/29, Abercromby to Forbes, 30 November 1757.
109. BL Add MS 73648, 'Capitulation d'un Regiment Suisse & Allemand pour le Service de la Grand Bretagne levee parmy les Gens de cette Nation Sujets de Sa Majeste', n.d.
110. Alexander V. Campbell, *The Royal American Regiment: An Atlantic Microcosm, 1755–1772* (Norman: Oklahoma University Press, 2010), 21–24.
111. HEH LO 2421, Loudoun to the Commanding Officers of the Royal American Regiment, 28 December 1756. See also Pargellis, *Loudoun*, 299–300.
112. TNA WO 71/130, Courts Martial Records, 9 July 1757.
113. SSCL Forbes Headquarters Papers, MS 10034/1/31, Abercromby to Forbes, 14 December 1757.
114. Russell, 'Redcoats in the Wilderness', 637–638.
115. Rogers, *Journals*, 33–34.
116. *New York Gazette*, 13 September 1756. Quoted in Frégault, *Canada*, 137.

117. Pargellis, *Lord Loudoun*, 211; Frégault, *Canada*, 137.
118. Pargellis, *Military Affairs*, Loudoun to Webb, HMS Sutherland, 20 June 1757, 371.
119. *New York Gazette*, 2 May 1757; and *Boston Gazette*, 16 May 1757. Quoted in Frégault, *Canada*, 148.
120. HEH LO 2766 Pitt to Loudoun, 4 February 1757.
121. HEH HM 1717/1, Loudoun Memorandum Book, January–June 1757.
122. HEH LO 3576, General Orders, 3, 24 July 1757.
123. John Knox, *An Historical Journal of the Campaigns in North America for the Years 1757, 1758, 1759, and 1760*, 3 vols (Toronto: The Champlain Society, 1914), entry for 24 July, 1:20.
124. RA DCP Evidence enclosed with Loudoun to Holdernesse, 1 September 1757.
125. Houlding, *Fit for Service*, 347.
126. HEH LO 4073, Loudoun to Holdernesse, Halifax, 5 August 1757.
127. Pargellis, *Military Affairs*, Loudoun to Webb, HMS Sutherland, 20 June 1757, 372.
128. For the intelligence, see HEH LO 2704, Robert Rogers, Journal of a Scout, Island near Fort Edward, 25 January 1757; and LO 4020, Webb to Loudoun, Fort Edward, 1 August 1757.
129. I. Minis Hays, 'A journal kept during the siege of Fort William Henry, August 1757, *Proceedings of the American Philosophical Society*, 37/157 (January 1898), 143–150.
130. Anderson, *Crucible of War*, 197–198.
131. Frégault, *Canada*, 155.
132. Yagi, *Struggle for North America*, loc. 1117.
133. Pargellis, *Lord Loudoun*, 346–350.
134. Houlding, *Fit for Service*, 375–376.
135. HEH LO 5066, Proposal for raising a Reg^t of Light Armed Foot, 22 December 1757.
136. SSCL Forbes Headquarters Papers, MS 10034/1/32, Orderly Book, New York, December 1757, f. 12.
137. NRS RH4/86/2, Unsigned memorandum concerning Gage's proposed regiment [c. December 1757].
138. HEH HM 1717/4, Loudoun Memorandum Book, New York, 13 December 1757.
139. Ibid., 11 December 1757.
140. Houlding, *Fit for Service*, 376.
141. Pargellis, *Lord Loudoun*, 300–306.
142. HEH HM 1717/4, Loudoun Memorandum Book, New York, 23 December 1757.
143. Ibid., 7 January 1758.
144. HEH LO 5515, Plan of Operations on the Mississippi, Ohio & Ca[nada], New York, 1 February 1758.
145. Irene Stewart (ed.), *Letters of General John Forbes relating to the Expedition Against Fort Duquesne in 1758* (Pittsburgh: Allegheny County Committee, 1927), Forbes to Pitt, 20 October 1758, 61.
146. S. K. Stevens, Donald H. Kent & Autumn L. Leonard (eds), *The Papers of Henry Bouquet*, 6 vols (Harrisburg: Pennsylvania Historical and Museum Commission, 1951), (*PHB*) Forbes to Bouquet, 27 June 1758, 2:135–137.
147. *PHB*, Forbes to Bouquet, 27 June 1758, 2:135–137.
148. NRS RH4/86/2, Unsigned memorandum concerning operations in North America [c. December 1757].
149. Stewart, *Letters of General John Forbes*, Forbes to Pitt, 20 October 1758, 61.
150. Alfred Proctor James, *Writings of General John Forbes Relating to his Service in North America* (Menasha, WI: The Collegiate Press, 1938), Forbes to Pitt, Philadelphia, 17 June 1758, 116–119.
151. Stewart, *Letters of General John Forbes*, Forbes to Pitt, 20 October 1758, 61.
152. James, *Writings of Forbes*, Forbes to Pitt, Philadelphia, 17 June 1758, 116–119.

153. Lancelot Turpin de Crissé, *An Essay on the Art of War. Translated from the French by Captain Joseph Otway*, 2 vols (London: Johnston, 1762), 2:110.
154. *PHB*, Grant to Forbes, 17 September 1758, 2:499–504.
155. HEH Abercromby Papers (AB) 436, Abercromby to Pitt, Camp at Lake George, 12 July 1758.
156. HEH AB 591, Bradstreet to Abercromby, Oswego, 31 August 1758.
157. FTA M/6008/9, Charles Lee to Sir William Bunbury, Niagara, 9 August 1759.
158. Anderson, *Crucible of War,* 338–339.
159. HEH AB 436, Abercromby to Pitt, Camp at Lake George, 12 July 1758.
160. FTA M/6008/9, Charles Lee to Sir William Bunbury, Niagara, 9 August 1759.
161. FTA 03M/2170, Monypenny Orderly Book, July–August 1759, Camp at Lake George, 17 July 1759.
162. New York Public Library (NYPL) MssCol NYGB 18231, Journal and Orderly Book of John Herbert.
163. Beckles Willson, *The Life and Letters of James Wolfe* (London: William Heinemann, 1909), Wolfe to Sackville, 24 May 1758, 366–369.
164. Brumwell, *Redcoats*, 191–226.
165. See Pargellis, *Lord Loudoun*, 253–278; and Yagi, *Struggle of North America*, loc. 610–1145/7041.

2 'I Was Come to Take Canada'

1. HMC, *Stopford-Sackville Manuscripts*, Wolfe to Sackville, Halifax, 24 May 1758, 2:259–262.
2. Reginald Savory, *His Britannic Majesty's Army in Germany During the Seven Years War* (Oxford: Clarendon Press, 1966), 27–38.
3. KHLC U1350/C19/6, Amherst Private Letters (Journal).
4. McCord Museum, C-173/A/1-3, James Wolfe to Walter Wolfe, 15 September 1755. http://collections.musee-mccord.qc.ca/en/collection/artifacts/C173-A_1-3/?msg=1 [Accessed 28 June 2021].
5. For more on the military thought and actions of Frederick the Great, see Christopher Duffy, *Frederick the Great: A Military Life* (London: Routledge, 1985); Christopher Duffy, *The Army of Frederick the Great* (London: David & Charles, 1974); Tim Blanning, *Frederick the Great: King of Prussia* (London: Allen Lane, 2015); and, more recently, Storring, 'Frederick the Great and the Meanings of War'.
6. Rex H. Whitworth, 'Some unpublished Wolfe letters, 1755–1758', *Journal of the Society for Army History Research*, 53/214 (Summer 1975), 73.
7. Brumwell, *Paths of Glory*, 112–113. See also Houlding, *Fit for Service*, 318–321.
8. James Wolfe, *General Wolfe's Instructions to Young Officers* (London: Millan, 1768), 50.
9. HMC, *Bathurst Manuscripts*, Duke of Richmond to Lord George Lennox, Barham Downs Camp, 9 September 1757, 679–681.
10. Whitworth, 'Some unpublished Wolfe letters', Wolfe to Richmond, Newport in the Isle of Wight, 23 August 1757, 83.
11. Willson, *Life and Letters of Wolfe*, Wolfe to Major Walter Wolfe, Blackheath, 18 October 1757, 336.
12. Ibid., Wolfe to Rickson, Blackheath, 5 November 1757, 335–339.
13. HMC, *Stopford-Sackville Manuscripts*, Wolfe to Sackville, Halifax, 24 May 1758, 2:259–262.
14. Willson, *Life and Letters of Wolfe*, Wolfe to Sackville, Halifax, 12 May 1758, 363–364.
15. Ibid.
16. HEH AB 303, Brigadier Charles Lawrence, Order for the Attack on Louisbourg, May 1758.
17. TNA WO 34/54, Ensign James Miller's Memoir.

18. Houghton Library, Harvard, MS Eng 509, Reminiscences of the Hon. Henry Hamilton, 1758–1762, f. 8. https://colonialnorthamerica.library.harvard.edu/spotlight/cna/catalog/990086015440203941 [Accessed 28 June 2021].
19. HMC, *Stopford-Sackville Manuscripts*, James Cunninghame to George Sackville, *Ludlow Castle* at sea, 30 May 1758, 2:262.
20. W. A. Gordon, 'Journal of the Siege of Louisbourg from a MS in the Royal United Service Institution', *Journal of the Royal United Services Institute*, 60:439 (1915), 121.
21. Beattie, 'Amherst and the Conquest of Canada', 62–63.
22. Hugh Boscawen, *The Capture of Louisbourg, 1758* (Norman: Oklahoma University Press, 2011), 153–154.
23. Knox, *Journal*, Amherst's General Orders, *Namur*, 4 June, 1:215.
24. Quoted in Brumwell, *Paths of Glory*, 147.
25. John C. Webster (ed.), *The Journal of Jeffrey Amherst* (Chicago: University of Chicago Press, 1931), 8 June, 50.
26. I. M. McCulloch, *Sons of the Mountains: The Highland Regiments in the French and Indian War, 1756–67*, 2 vols (New York: Purple Mountain, 2006), 1:71–72.
27. HEH AB 291, Journal of the Proceedings of the Fleet and Army, Enclosed in Monckton to Abercromby, 23 June 1758.
28. National Maritime Museum (NMM) Adm/L Lieutenants' Logs, Vol. D/106B (*Diana*: Lt Atkins), 8 June 1758.
29. Anonymous, *An Authentic Account of the Reduction of Louisbourg, in June and July 1758, by a Spectator* (London: W. Owen, 1758), 13.
30. Webster, *Journal of Jeffrey Amherst*, 8 June, 50.
31. Gertrude Selwyn Kimball (ed.), *Correspondence of William Pitt When Secretary of State with Colonial Governors and Military and Naval Commissioners in America*, 2 vols (New York: Macmillan, 1906), Amherst to Pitt, Camp before Louisbourg, 23 June 1758, 1:283.
32. Willson, *Life and Letters of Wolfe*, Wolfe to Walter Wolfe, Camp before Louisbourg, 27 July 1758, 384–386.
33. Kimball, *Pitt Correspondence*, Amherst to Pitt, Camp before Louisbourg, 6 July 1758, 1:293.
34. John C. Webster (ed.), *Journal of William Amherst in America, 1758–1760* (London: Butler & Tanner, 1927), 15–16.
35. HEH LO 5573, Captain George Scott to Loudoun, 14 July 1757.
36. Webster, *Journal of William Amherst*, 24.
37. Willson, *Life and Letters of Wolfe*, 380.
38. LAC MG18/K7, Montcalm Papers, 'Chevalier de Poilly à sa famille', n.d.
39. Willson, *Life and Letters of Wolfe*, Wolfe to Walter Wolfe, Camp before Louisbourg, 27 July 1758, 384–385.
40. TNA WO 34/54, Ensign James Miller's Memoir.
41. Beattie, 'Amherst and the Conquest of Canada', 83.
42. Willson, *Life and Letters of Wolfe*, Wolfe to Walter Wolfe, Camp before Louisbourg, 27 July 1758, 384–385.
43. Ibid., Wolfe to his father, Louisbourg, 11 August 1758, 385–396.
44. Brumwell, *Paths of Glory*, 161.
45. HEH LO 6975, Bell to John Calcraft, Louisbourg, c. 27 July 1758.
46. See, for example, FTA 02M/2162, Monypenny Orderly Book, June–July 1758; and NYPL MssCol NYGB 18231, Journal and Orderly Book of John Herbert.
47. See Rogers, *Journals*, 79–80; and Grant, *Memoirs*, 1:199–200.
48. HEH LO 5573, Captain George Scott to Loudoun, 14 July 1757.
49. HEH AB 303, Brigadier Charles Lawrence, Order for the Attack on Louisbourg, May 1758.
50. J. Mackay Hitsman, 'Order Before Landing at Louisbourg, 1758', *Military Affairs*, 15 (1958), 146–148.

51. Willson, *Life and Letters of Wolfe*, Wolfe to Walter Wolfe, London, 20 January 1759, 417–418.
52. Ibid., Wolfe to Captain Parr, Salisbury, 6 December 1758, 404–405.
53. Ibid., Wolfe to Walter Wolfe, London, 20 January 1759, 417–418.
54. Beattie, 'Amherst and the Conquest of Canada', 91–111.
55. TNA WO 34/17, Amherst to Whitmore, 29 May 1759, f. 179.
56. TNA WO 34/46B, Amherst to Wolfe, Albany, 6 May 1759, f. 310.
57. Webster, *Journal of Jeffrey Amherst*, 20–25 May 1759, 110–112.
58. See Rogers, *Journal*, 127–134.
59. TNA WO 34/46A, Description of Fort Carillon, Lieutenant Diedrich Brehm, March 1759.
60. WCL Amherst Papers (AP) MS 4, Amherst to Gage, Fort Edward, 6 June 1759.
61. TNA WO 34/30, Amherst to De Lancey, Camp of Lake George, 23 June 1759, f. 52.
62. LAC Amherst Papers P58, General Orders, 13 December 1758.
63. TNA WO 34/46A, Gage to Amherst, 24 February 1759.
64. TNA WO 34/79, Amherst to James Furnis, 5 May 1759; Rogers, *Journal*, Roger Townshend to Robert Rogers, 26 February 1759, 97–98.
65. Beattie, 'Amherst and the Conquest of Canada', 132–133.
66. Webster, *Journal of Jeffrey Amherst*, 26–27 July 1759, 146.
67. Ibid., 4 August 1759, 151.
68. Beattie, 'Amherst and the Conquest of Canada', 170–171.
69. TNA WO 34/46A, Amherst to Gage, 1 August 1759.
70. WCL AP MS 4, Amherst to Gage, Camp at Ticonderoga, 28 July 1759.
71. TNA WO 34/46A, Amherst to Gage, Camp of Crown Point, 21 September 1759, ff. 182–183.
72. TNA WO 34/46A, Gage to Amherst, Camp of Oswego, 2 October 1759, ff. 51–52.
73. TNA WO 34/64, Amherst to Loring, Camp of Crown Point, 15 September 1759, ff. 212–213.
74. Webster, *Journal of Jeffrey Amherst*, 9 August 1759, 178.
75. TNA WO 34/45, Amherst to Stanwix, Camp at Crown Point, 9 October 1759, f. 235.
76. Webster, *Journal of Jeffrey Amherst*, 12 October 1759, 180–181.
77. Beattie, 'Amherst and the Conquest of Canada', 181–184.
78. KHLC U1350/O/35/13, Amherst to Ligonier, Camp of Crown Point, 22 October 1759.
79. Thomas Hutchinson, *The History of the Province of Massachusetts Bay from 1749 to 1774* (London: John Murray, 1778), 78.
80. Willson, *Life and Letters of Wolfe*, Wolfe to Walter Wolfe, Louisbourg, 19 May 1759, 427–428.
81. *Gentleman's Magazine*, 1759, Wolfe to Pitt, Headquarters at Montmorenci, in the River St Laurence, 2 September 1759, 467.
82. Willson, *Life and Letters of Wolfe*, Wolfe to Walter Wolfe, Louisbourg, 19 May 1759, 427–428.
83. Brumwell, *Paths of Glory*, 194–198.
84. *Gentleman's Magazine*, 1759, Wolfe to Pitt, Headquarters at Montmorenci, in the River St Laurence, 2 September 1759, 467.
85. Willson, *Life and Letters of Wolfe*, Wolfe to Walter Wolfe, Louisbourg, 19 May 1759, 427–428.
86. LAC MG18/L5/5, Journal of James Wolfe, 27 June 1759.
87. BL Add MS 45662, Journal of Richard Humphrys, ff. 28–33.
88. LAC MG18/L5/5, Journal of James Wolfe, 1 July 1759.
89. Knox, *Journal*, 1:438.
90. Willson, *Life and Letters of Wolfe*, Wolfe to Amherst, 1 July 1758, 379.

91. A. G. Doughty, 'A new account of the death of Wolfe', *Canadian Historical Review*, 4:1 (March 1923), 47–48. Original French: 'Voilà mon cher Holland, ce sera ma Derniere Rescource mais il faut avant que mes autres projects travailent, et manquent. Je vous parle en confidance; en attendant, il faut deguiser mon intention à qui que ce soit et tachez de faire croire l'impossibilité de montez.'

92. Pargellis, *Military Affairs*, Extract of a Letter from an Officer in Major Genl Wolfe's Army, Island of Orleans, 10 August 1759, 433–434.

93. Doughty & Parmelee, *Siege of Quebec*, Townshend's Journal, 5:253–254.

94. Ibid., 'An Accurate and Authentic Journal of the Siege of Quebec 1759 by a Gentleman in an Eminent Station on the Spot', 4:286–287.

95. Ibid., Townshend's Journal, 5:253–254.

96. LAC MG18/C366, Northcliffe Collection, xxi, 'Return of the Kill'd, Wounded and Missing, at the attack of the Enemys Works, on the 31st of July'.

97. LAC MG40/Q17/A-1715, Robert Monckton Fonds, Wolfe to Monckton, Montmorency, 22 August 1759.

98. Doughty & Parmelee, *Siege of Quebec*, 'An Accurate and Authentic Journal', 4:286–287.

99. *NYCD*, 'Extract of a Journal', 10:1024.

100. Ibid., 10:1033–1035.

101. LAC MG18/L5/5, Journal of James Wolfe, 7 August 1759.

102. For evidence of the punitive activities, see Doughty & Parmelee, *Siege of Quebec*, John Montresor to his father, Montmorency, 10 August 1759, 4:318–319; and LAC MG18/C366, Northcliffe Collection, xxi, Gorham to Wolfe, *Beaver* transport, 19 August 1759.

103. *Gentleman's Magazine*, 1759, Wolfe to Pitt, Headquarters at Montmorenci, in the River St Laurence, 2 September 1759, 468.

104. Doughty & Parmelee, *Siege of Quebec*, Wolfe to his brigadiers, Headquarters Montmorency, 27 August 1759, 2:237–239.

105. LAC MG18/N45/A-652, Paulus Aemilius Irving Fonds, Journal of an officer on Wolfe's Staff.

106. Kimball, *Pitt Correspondence*, Saunders to Pitt, *Stirling Castle*, off Point Lévis, 5 September 1759, 2:161.

107. Doughty & Parmelee, *Siege of Quebec*, Letters of a Volunteer, Addressed to Mr. J. W., Sterling Castle, in the River St Lawrence, 2 miles below the City of Quebec, 2 September 1759, 5:19.

108. Ibid., Answer of the Brigadiers to General Wolfe, 30 August 1759, 2:239–240.

109. *Gentleman's Magazine*, 1759, Wolfe to Pitt, Headquarters at Montmorenci, in the River St Laurence, 2 September 1759, 469.

110. Wright, *Life of Wolfe*, Wolfe to his mother, Banks of the St Lawrence, 31 August 1759, 553.

111. Doughty & Parmelee, *Siege of Quebec*, Journal of Major Moncrief [Mackellar], 10 September 1759, 5:48–49.

112. Ibid., Letter of Admiral Holmes, Lowestoft off Foulon in the River St. Laurance, above Quebec, 18 September 1759, 4:295–296.

113. Ibid., Journal of the Particular Transaction during Siege of Quebec, 12 September 1759, 5:186.

114. Knox, *Journal*, 2:96.

115. Doughty & Parmelee, *Siege of Quebec*, Memoirs of the Quarter Master Sergeant, 5:107.

116. Brumwell, *Redcoats*, 254–255.

117. Knox, *Journal*, 2:101.

118. Doughty & Parmelee, *Siege of Quebec*, Memoirs of the Quarter Master Sergeant, 5:104.

119. Ibid., Journal of Major Moncrief [Mackellar], 13 September 1759, 5:53.

120. NAM MS 7808/93/2, Henry Brown to his father, Louisbourg, 17 November 1759.
121. LAC MG18/N45/A-652, Paulus Aemilius Irving Fonds, Journal of an officer on Wolfe's Staff.
122. Kimball, *Pitt Correspondence*, Pitt to Amherst, Whitehall, 7 January 1760, 2:238.
123. KHLC U1350/O/14, Amherst Personal Journal, Extract of Instructions to Brigadier-General Governor Murray, New York, 15 April 1760, f. 72.
124. TNA CO 5/58, Murray to Amherst, Quebec, 30 April 1760, ff. 192–194.
125. R. O. Alexander, 'The capture of Quebec: A manuscript journal relating to the operations before Quebec from 8th May 1759 to 17 May 1760 kept by Colonel Malcolm Fraser', *Journal of the Society for Army Historical Research*, 18/71 (Autumn 1939), 166.
126. TNA WO 34/4, Murray to Amherst, Quebec, 23 May 1760, ff. 19–23.
127. TNA WO 34/65, Loring to Amherst, Off Grand Island, 23 July 1760, ff. 22–23.
128. Richard Middleton (ed.), *Amherst and the Conquest of Canada* (Stroud: Sutton Publishing, 2003), xliii–xliv; Douglas R. Cubbison, *All Canada in the Hands of the British: General Jeffrey Amherst and the 1760 Campaign to Conquer New France* (Norman: University of Oklahoma Press, 2014), 72.
129. KHLC U1350/O/14, Amherst Personal Journal, Extract of Instructions to Brigadier-General Governor Murray, New York, 15 April 1760, f. 72.
130. Knox, *Journal*, 2:468.
131. Cubbison, *All Canada in the Hands of the British*, 74–77.
132. G. D. Scull (ed.), *The Montresor Journals* (New York: New York Historical Society, 1882), Letter to Lieutenant Colonel James Montresor, Quebec, 16 December 1760, 235.
133. Kimball, *Pitt Correspondence*, Murray to Pitt, Contrecour Nine leagues from Montreal, 24 August 1760, 2:322.
134. Chevalier de Johnstone, *The Campaign of 1760: A Narrative Attributed to Chevalier Johnstone* (Quebec: Literary and Historical Society of Quebec, 1887), 31.
135. Kimball, *Pitt Correspondence*, Murray to Pitt, Contrecour Nine leagues from Montreal, 24 August 1760, 2:322.
136. TNA WO 34/52, Amherst to Haviland, Albany 12 June 1760, ff. 48–50.
137. Rogers, *Journals*, 206.
138. J. M. Bradbury, 'Military Journal, April 1760 to August 1762', in *Bradbury Memorial* (Portland, MN, 1890), 279.
139. Johnstone, *Campaign of 1760*, 24.
140. Webster, *Journal of Jeffrey Amherst*, 15 July–9 August 1760, 219–225.
141. Ibid., 18 August 1760, 233.
142. Dunnigan, Brian Leigh (ed.), *Memoirs on the Late War in North America Between France and England* (New York: Old Fort Niagara Association, 1994), 313–314.
143. Webster, *Journal of Jeffrey Amherst*, 1–4 September 1760, 242–244.
144. Ibid., 8–10 September 1760, 247.
145. Beattie, 'Amherst and the Conquest of Canada', 216.
146. Webster, *Journal of Jeffrey Amherst*, 8–10 September 1760, 247.
147. Knox, *Journal*, 2:418.
148. Emmerich de Vattel, *The Law of Nations: Or Principles of the Law of Nature Applied to the Conduct of Nations and Sovereigns*, 2 vols (London: Sweet & Maxwell, 1834), 2:49. See also Pichichero, *Military Enlightenment*, 1–24; and Geoffrey Plank, *Rebellion and Savagery: The Jacobite Rising of 1745 and the British Empire* (Philadelphia: University of Pennsylvania Press, 2006), 161.

3 The 'Great Book of War'

1. WCL CP MS 286, Memoranda Book 1774, f. 83.
2. Savory, *His Britannic Majesty's Army in Germany*, 118–151.

3. See, for example, LSC MSS L1997F170, Notebook describing mistakes of tactics employed in various battles in Europe between 1645 and 1755, c. 1760. Author identified as Henry Clinton, f. 11.

4. WCL CP MS 286, Memoranda Book 1774, f. 83.

5. RA GEO/MAIN/43611–4, York to George III, 24 October 1783.

6. Goldsmith, *Masculinity and Danger*, 79.

7. Ibid., 82, 86.

8. LAC MG18/L5/3/1, Wolfe to his father, Inverness, 17 October 1751.

9. Goldsmith, *Masculinity and Danger*, 79, 83–84.

10. Rosie Dias, 'Memory and the Aesthetics of Military Experience: Viewing the Landscape of the Anglo-Mysore Wars', in Tate Papers, no.19, Spring 2013, www.tate.org.uk/research/tate-papers/19/memory-and-the-aesthetics-of-military-experience-viewing-the-landscape-of-the-anglo-mysore-wars [Accessed 27 August 2020].

11. Karen E. Till, *The New Berlin: Memory, Politics, Place* (Minneapolis: University of Minnesota Press, 2005), 8.

12. RA GEO/Main/43446–7, Duke of York to George III, Hanover, 30 July 1781.

13. RCIN 732019, Anton Heinrich du Plat, Minden, Dankersen and Holzhausen, 1757. https://militarymaps.rct.uk/the-seven-years-war-1756-63/minden-dankersen-and-holzhausen-1757 [Accessed 7 August 2020].

14. RA GEO/Main/43460, Richard Grenville to George III, Mont Brillant, 11 September 1781.

15. WCL Germain Papers (GSGP) MS 2, Sackville to Bute, 24 July 1759.

16. Harold Carmichael Wylly, *History of the King's Own Yorkshire Light Infantry from 1755 to 1914* (London: P. Lund, Humphries & co., 1924), 41.

17. WCL GSGP MS 2, Sackville to Bute, 24 July 1759.

18. Walter Evelyn Manners, *Some Account of the Military, Political, and Social Life of the Right Hon. John Manners, Marquis of Granby* (London: Macmillan, 1899), 75.

19. RA GEO/Main/43456–7, Duke of York to George III, Hanover, 3 September 1781.

20. Wylly, *History of the KOYLI*, 41.

21. Ibid., 40.

22. RA GEO/Main/43456–7, Duke of York to George III, Hanover, 3 September 1781.

23. Quoted in Wylly, *The History of the KOYLI*, 43.

24. RA GEO/Main/43456–7, Duke of York to George III, Hanover, 3 September 1781.

25. Ibid.

26. LWL MS55 European Military Tour Journal 1770, ff. 22.

27. Ibid., ff. 21.

28. Beinecke Rare Book and Manuscript Library, Yale University (BRBML), Osborn c200 European Travel Diary 1754–5, ff. 2.

29. Edward Barrington de Fonblanque, *Political and Military Episodes in the Latter Half of the Eighteenth Century: Derived from the Life and Correspondence of the Right Hon. John Burgoyne, General, Statesman, Dramatist* (London: Macmillan, 1876), Burgoyne to Ellyott, Headquarters of the Bohemian Army at Teutchbrod, 9 September 1766, 59–61.

30. Fonblanque, *Political and Military Episodes*, 19.

31. Ibid., 17.

32. Ibid., 'Observations and Reflections Upon the Present Military State of Prussia, Austria, and France, 1766', 62–82.

33. LSC MSS L2008F48, Wolfe to Townshend, 18 July 1756.

34. Houlding, *Fit for Service*, 179–180.

35. Gruber, *Books and the British Army*, 31–34.

36. LSC MSS L2008F48, Wolfe to Townshend, 18 July 1756.

37. Houlding, *Fit For Service*, 201.

38. Crissé, *Essay on the Art of War*, 2:98–108.

39. Ibid., 2:99–106.
40. Stewart, *Letters of General John Forbes*, Forbes to Pitt, 20 October 1758, 61.
41. Crissé, *Essay on the Art of War*, 2:110.
42. *The Critical Review, Or, Annals of Literature*, 11:311.
43. J. D. E. Preuss (ed.), *Œuvres de Frédéric le Grand*, 30 vols (Berlin: Impr. Royale, 1846–56), 4, 15, 17; quoted in Duffy, *Frederick the Great*, 301.
44. Fonblanque, *Political and Military Episodes*, 'Observations and Reflections Upon the Present Military State of Prussia, Austria, and France, 1766', 62–82.
45. Charles Ross (ed.), *Correspondence of Charles, First Marquis Cornwallis*, 3 vols (London: J. Murray, 1859) (*CC*), 1:212.
46. Stephen Conway, 'The British Army, "military Europe," and the American War of Independence', *William and Mary Quarterly*, 67/1 (January 2010), 69–100.
47. Preuss, *Oeuvres*, 27:79–80, quoted in Duffy, *Frederick the Great*, 302.
48. See 'Traité de la Colonne' in Jean-Charles de Folard, *L'Esprit de Chevalier Folard, Tiré de ses Commentaires sur l'Histoire de Polybe* (Paris: Jean Marie Bruyzet by La Compagnie des Libraires, 1760), 1:xxii–c, 7. Quoted in Gruber, *Books and the British Army*, 41–42.
49. *CC*, Cornwallis to Ross, Mansfield Street, 13 November 1783, 1:149.
50. Gruber, *Books and the British Army*, 41.
51. *CC*, Cornwallis to Ross, Brome, 5 September 1783, 1:146.
52. Gruber, *Books and the British Army*, 41.
53. Antoine de Pas Feuquières, *Mémoires de M. le Marquis de Feuquière*, 4 vols (London: P. Dunoyer, 1740), 1:152.
54. Ibid., 2:163.
55. See Andrew C. Thompson, *George II* (London: Yale University Press, 2011), 160.
56. See Towsey, *Reading History*, 45.
57. For evidence of the range of professional reading recommended and consumed by Wolfe and Clinton, see LSC MSS L2008F48, Wolfe to Townshend, 18 July 1756; MSS L1997F170 Notebook describing mistakes of tactics employed in various battles in Europe between 1645 and 1755, c. 1760. Author identified as Henry Clinton; WCL CP MS 245/6, Extract from Polien; 284/A-C, Military Notebooks; 285/A-C, Military Notebooks; and John Rylands Library, University of Manchester (JRL) Clinton Papers CP MS 185/1, Journal, c. 1760–1761.
58. See Ira D. Gruber, 'The education of Sir Henry Clinton', *Bulletin of the John Rylands University Library of Manchester*, 72, 1990, 131–53.
59. LSC MSS L1997F170 Notebook describing mistakes of tactics.
60. Towsey, *Reading History*, 30.
61. Ibid., 45.
62. LSC MSS L1997F170 Notebook describing mistakes of tactics, ff. 3–5.
63. Ibid., f. 11.
64. JRL CP MS 185/1, Journal, c. 1760–1761, in particular the sections on the Battle of Minden.
65. LSC MSS L1997F170 Notebook describing mistakes of tactics, f. 3.
66. WCL CP MS 1/31, Clinton's journal of his role in the campaign of the Hereditary Prince against the Prince de Condé ending in the Battle of Friedberg [Nauheim] in which Clinton was wounded, 21–30 August 1762.
67. WCL CP MS 1/32, Fragment of a Journal, 30 August 1762.
68. Henry Lloyd, *A Political and Military Rhapsody, on the Invasion and Defence of Great Britain and Ireland . . . To Which is Annexed, a Short Account of the Author* [signed: John Drummond], *and a Supplement by the Editor*. The fourth edition. With additions, etc. (London: Edgerton, 1795), xii.
69. Patrick J. Speelman, *Henry Lloyd and the Military Enlightenment of Eighteenth-Century Europe* (Westport: Greenwood Press, 2002), 41–42.
70. See, for example, WCL CP MS 1/40, Lloyd-Clinton [1762].

71. Germain Hyacinthe de Romance de Mesmon, *Mémoires militaires et politiques du Général Lloyd, servant d'introduction à l'histoire de la guerre . . .* (Paris: Magimel, 1801), 'Précis sur la Vie et le Caractère de Henri Lloyd', xxxviii.

72. Henry Lloyd, *The History of the Late War in Germany, Between the King of Prussia, and the Empress of Germany and her Allies (HLWG)* (London: Privately Published, 1766), 2–3.

73. *HLWG*, i–xii, xiii–xxxix.

74. Ibid, 3.

75. Neil Ramsey, 'Military History and Eighteenth Century Print Culture', unpublished paper delivered at New Direction in War and History Conference, Canberra, Friday 5 February 2016.

76. Henry Lloyd, *Continuation of the History of the Late War in Germany, Between the King of Prussia, and the Empress of Germany and Her Allies, Part II (CHLWG)* (London: Hooper, 1781), 2.

77. WCL CP MS 3/23, Lloyd to Clinton, Windsor, 29 March 1767.

78. JRL CP MS185/14 1791–1792.

79. Gruber, 'Education of Clinton', 143.

80. Harari, *Ultimate Experience*, 167–168.

81. *CHLWG*, 'Reflections on the General Principals of War; and on the composition and characters of the different armies in Europe', 17; *HLWG*, 15.

82. *CHLWG*, 89, 157–158.

83. *HLWG*, 17.

84. Hannibal Lloyd, *Memoir of General Lloyd* (Printed for Private Circulation, 1842), 12.

85. WCL CP MS 286, Memoranda Book of Henry Clinton, f. 82; and JRL CP 185, Notebook 3, 1768–1776; 1778–1779.

86. WCL CP MS 286, Memoranda Book of Henry Clinton, ff. 82–83.

87. Ibid.

88. JRL CP MS 185/3, Notebook. c. 1768–1776 Observations from Caesar's Comm^s by Col. Edmunds, 1655.

89. Speelman, *Henry Lloyd and the Military Enlightenment*, 84–87.

90. Ibid., 88–89.

91. Hannibal Lloyd, *Memoir*, 12.

92. Fitzwilliam Museum, Cambridge (FMC), Henry Lloyd Manuscripts (HL MS), Draft 'On America'.

93. FMC HL MS, "This Day are Published in 2 Vols in Quarto . . .'.

94. Speelman, *Henry Lloyd and the Military Enlightenment*, 106–109.

95. See Brent Nosworthy, *Battle Tactics of Napoleon and His Enemies* (London: Constable, 1995), 23–34. See also Jonathan Abel, *Guibert: Father of Napoleon's Grande Armée* (Norman: University of Oklahoma Press, 2016).

96. *CHLWG*, 41.

97. Guedella, *The Duke*, 54–65. See also Muir, *Wellington*, 46.

98. Speelman, *Henry Lloyd and the Military Enlightenment*, 39–60.

99. Khule, 'War without contact', 1–26.

100. *CHLWG*, 'Reflections', 310.

101. See Speelman, *Henry Lloyd and the Military Enlightenment*, 39–60.

102. John Mitchell, *Thoughts on Tactics and Military Organization: Together with an Enquiry into the Power and Position of Russia* (London: Longman, 1838), 11.

103. Gruber, *Books and the British Army*, 96–98.

104. George Townshend, *Rules and Orders for the Royal Military Academy at Woolwich* (London: Bullock & Spencer, 1776), quoted in Gruber, *Books and the British Army*, 117–122.

105. George Smith, *A Universal Military Dictionary* (London: J. Millan, 1779), entries under B and L.

106. *CHLWG*, 134.

107. Guedella, *The Duke*, 54–65. See also Muir, *Wellington*, 46.
108. State Library of New South Wales, Sydney (SLNSW) C11 Mitchell Fieldnotes 1811, ff. 4 and 6.
109. SLNSW C11 Mitchell Fieldnotes 1811, f. 5.
110. Hartley et al., *Mapping the American Revolutionary War*, 1.
111. RA DCP Descriptions of Cumberland Lodge are derived from 'Inventory of Household Furniture of His Late Royal Highness The Duke of Cumberland at Windsor Great Lodge' [1765–1766].
112. Douglas W. Marshall, 'Military maps of the eighteenth-century and the Tower of London Drawing Room', *Imago Mundi*, 32 (1980), 21; see also John Harwood Andrews, *Maps in Those Days: Cartographic Methods before 1850* (Dublin: Four Court Press, 2009).
113. See, for example, RCIN 729096, François Hancko, Plan General de l'attaque de l'armée Françoise pres de Fontenoy, 11 May 1745 or later, https://militarymaps.rct. uk/war-of-the-austrian-succession-1740-8/battle-of-fontenoy-1745-plan-of-the-attack [Accessed 29 June 2021].
114. See, for example, RCIN 725041, Anonymous, Plan von Landau, 1704 or later, https://militarymaps.rct.uk/war-of-the-spanish-succession-1701-14/landau-1704-plan-von-landau-nebst-der [Accessed 4 August 2020].
115. Marshall, 'Military maps', 25–26.
116. Matthew Edney, *Mapping an Empire: The Geographical Construction of British India, 1765-1843* (Chicago: Chicago University Press, 1990), 17–18.
117. Marshall, 'Military maps', 33.
118. Liliane Hilaire-Perez & Catherine Verna, 'Dissemination of technical knowledge in the Middle Ages and the Early Modern era: New approaches and methodological issues', *Technology and Culture*, 47/3 (2006), 536–565.
119. See Tony Ballantyne, 'Empire, Knowledge and Culture: From Proto-Globalization to Modern Globalization', in A. G. Hopkins (ed.), *Globalization in World History* (London: Pimlico, 2002), loc. 2987–3675.
120. Samuel Johnson, *The Works of Samuel Johnson*, 15 vols (London: Knapton, 1789), 15:454, quoted in Edelson, *New Map of Empire*, 65.
121. Edney, *Mapping an Empire*, 17–18.
122. Ibid.
123. Stephen S. Clark Map Library, University of Michigan, James Rennell, A map of Bengal, Bahar, Oude & Allahabad: with part of Agra and Delhi, exhibiting the course of the Ganges from Hurdwar to the sea, 1786. https://apps.lib.umich.edu/online-exhibits/exhibits/show/india-maps/item/5140 [Accessed 2 August 2020].
124. See James Rennell, *A Bengal Atlas: Containing Maps of the Theatre of War and Commerce on That Side of Hindostan* (London: Privately Published, 1781).
125. R. H. Phillimore, *Historical Records of the Survey of India*, 4 vols (Dehra Dun: Survey of India, 1945), 1:95.
126. James Rennell, *Memoir of a Map of Hindoostan: Or, The Mogul Empire: with an Introduction, Illustrative of the Geography and Present Division of that Country: and a Map of the Countries Situated Between the Heads of the Indian Rivers, and the Caspian Sea* (London: W. Bulmer & Co., 1793), 264.
127. RCIN 734059, John Pringle, 'Plan of the Route of the Grand Army in the Carnatic, 25 August 1780 to 7 June 1783', 1785, 1787. https://militarymaps.rct.uk/other-18th-19th-century-conflicts/carnatic-1780-83-plan-of-the-route-of-the-grand [Accessed 2 August].
128. Phillimore, *Historical Records of the Survey of India*, 1:110.
129. James Rennell, *The Marches of the British Armies in the Peninsula of India During the Campaigns of 1790 and 1791* (London: Bulmer & co, 1792). See also RCIN 734111, Alexander Beatson, The Marches of the British Armies, in the Peninsula of India During the Campaigns of 1790, 1791, 1792, https://militarymaps.rct.uk/miscellaneous/

india-1790-91-the-marches-of-the-british-armies-in-the-peninsula-of [Accessed 2 August 2020].

130. Catriona Kennedy, 'Military Ways of Seeing: British Soldiers' Sketches from the Egyptian Campaign of 1801', in Joseph Clarke & John Horne (eds), *Militarized Cultural Encounters in the Long Nineteenth Century: Making War, Mapping Europe* (Basingstoke: Palgrave, 2018), 197–222; and Anders Engberg-Petersen, *Empires of Chance: The Napoleonic Wars and the Disorder of Things* (Cambridge, MA: Harvard University Press, 2015), 43–44.

131. RA GEO/Main/43578–81, Duke of York to George III, Hanover, 6 June 1783.

132. Ibid.

133. RA GEO/Main/43745–6, Duke of York to George III, Hanover, 5 October 1785.

134. BL Add MS 27600, Colonel David Dundas, Principles of Military Movement, ff. 10v.

135. TNA WO 3/28 Adjutant General's Circular Letter to General the Marquis Townsend, the Duke of Richmond, Sir William Pitt, KB, Lord A Gordon, Lord George Lennox, Marquis Cornwallis ad Major General Musgrave, 16 May 1795.

136. Willson, *Life and Letters of Wolfe*, Wolfe to his father, 1 September 1756, 302–303.

137. Whitworth, 'Some unpublished Wolfe letters', Wolfe to Richmond, Devizes, 23 June 1756, 73–75.

138. Ibid.

139. HMC, *Bathurst Manuscripts*, Duke of Richmond to Lord George Lennox, Barham Downs Camp, 9 September 1757, 679–681.

140. Houlding, *Fit For Service*, 337.

141. Roger Lamb, *A Memoir of His Own Life* (Dublin: J. Jones, 1811), 89–90.

142. NAM 6807/157/6 Discipline established by Major General Howe for Light Infantry in Battalion, Sarum, September 1774.

143. The units in attendance included the light infantry companies of the 3rd, 11th, 21st, 29th, 32nd, 36th and 70th Regiments of Foot.

144. NAM 6807/157/6 Discipline established by Major General Howe for Light Infantry in Battalion, Sarum, September 1774.

145. Brumwell, *Redcoats*, 191–226.

146. Lamb, *A Memoir of His Own Life*, 89.

147. TNA WO 5/58, Circulars from the Secretary at War to 14 regiments, 14 July & 4 October 1774.

148. Lamb, *A Memoir of His Own Life*, 90, 94–95.

149. HEH/HM/818, Robert Honyman's Journal, 1775, f. 72.

150. The American Revolutionary War benefits from a wealth of excellent historical scholarship deeply rooted in extensive archival holdings. A broad understanding of the British experience of the war is provided by Piers Mackesy, *The War for America: 1775–1783* (Lincoln: University of Nebraska, 1964), while specific analysis of different challenges the British faced is in Matthew H. Spring, *With Zeal and Bayonets Only: The British Army on Campaign in North America, 1775–1783* (Norman: University of Oklahoma Press, 2008). A good account of the American perspective can be found in John Ferling, *Almost a Miracle: The American Victory in the War of Independence* (Oxford: Oxford University Press, 2007); and Howard H. Peckham, *The War for Independence* (Chicago: University of Chicago Press, 1958). John Shy offers a seminal account of the impact of the British Army on the destabilisation of the American colonies in *Toward Lexington: The Role of the British Army in the Coming of the American Revolution* (Princeton: Princeton University Press, 1965). Biographical accounts of the principal British protagonists are provided in Andrew O'Shaughnessy, *The Men who Lost America: British Command During the Revolutionary War and the Preservation of Empire* (New Haven: Yale University Press, 2013); David Smith, *William Howe and the American War of Independence* (London: Bloomsbury, 2015); Ira D. Gruber, *The Howe Brothers and the American Revolution* (Chapel Hill: University of North Carolina Press, 1972); William B. Willcox, *Portrait of a General: Sir Henry*

Clinton in the War of Independence (New York: Knopf, 1962); and Franklin & Mary Wickwire, *Cornwallis and the War of Independence* (London: Faber & Faber, 1971).

151. See John Gilbert McCurdy, *Quarters: The Accommodation of the British Army and the Coming of the American Revolution* (Ithaca: Cornell University Press, 2019), 165–200.
152. HMC, *Stopford-Sackville Manuscripts*, Germain to Suffolk, 16 June 1775, 2:2.
153. WCL CP MS 10/4, Clinton to Phillips[?], 13 June 1775. William B. Willcox (ed.), *The American Rebellion: Sir Henry Clinton's Narrative of His Campaigns, 1775–1782, with an Appendix of Original Documents* (New Haven: Yale University Press, 1954), xvii; Willcox, *Portrait of a General*, 44.

4 'No Idea of Any Other Than a Direct Attack'

1. WCL CP MS 282, *Narrative*, Vol III. Loose Note on description of Bunker Hill. See also CP MS 201/5, Memorandum, 13 April 1785.
2. Flavell, *Howe Dynasty*, 168.
3. WCL CP MS 241/12, Memoranda, Autumn 1775.
4. TNA CO 5/92, Gage to Dartmouth, 25 June 1775.
5. HMC, *Stopford-Sackville Manuscripts*, William Howe to Richard Howe, 22 June 1775, 2:3–4.
6. '"Bunker's Hill", extracted from a private letter written by Gen. Burgoyne', in *The United Service Journal and Naval and Military Magazine*, 1830/2, 504–505.
7. J. Clarke, *An Impartial and Authentic Narrative of the Battle Fought on the 17th of June 1775, between His Britannic Majesty's Troops and the American Provincial Army, on Bunker's Hill* (London: J. Millan, 1775), 4.
8. TNA CO 5/92, Gage to Dartmouth, 25 June 1775.
9. John Fortescue (ed.), *The Correspondence of King George the Third, From 1760 to December 1783*, 6 vols (London: Frank Cass, 1967), Howe to Harvey, 22 & 24 June 1775, 3:220–224.
10. HMC, *Stopford-Sackville Manuscripts*, William Howe to Richard Howe, 22 June 1775, 2:3–4.
11. TNA CO 5/92, Military Dispatches, North America, 1775, Gage to Dartmouth, 25 June 1775.
12. Fortescue, *Correspondence of King George III*, Howe to Harvey, 22 & 24 June 1775, 3:220–224.
13. Lushington, *The Life of Harris*, 41–42.
14. Fortescue, *Correspondence of King George III*, Howe to Harvey, 22 & 24 June 1775, 3:220–224.
15. David Syrett (ed.), *The Siege and Capture of Havana 1762* (London: Navy Records Society, 1970), xiii–xiv; Anderson, *Crucible of War*, 497–502; Elena A. Schneider, *The Occupation of Havana: War, Trade and Slavery in the Atlantic World* (Chapel Hill: University of North Carolina Press, 2018), 113–120.
16. See Mark Urban, *Fusiliers: How the British Army Lost America but Learned to Fight* (London: Faber & Faber, 2008).
17. See NAM 6807/157/6 Discipline established by Major General Howe for Light Infantry in Battalion, Sarum, September 1774.
18. HMC, *Stopford-Sackville Manuscripts*, William Howe to George Germain, 26 April 1776, 2:30–31.
19. TNA CO 5/93, Howe to Dartmouth, 16 January 1776.
20. TNA CO 5/92, Howe to Dartmouth, 9 October 1775, ff. 311–316.
21. TNA CO 5/93, Germain to Howe, 1 February 1776, ff. 17–20.
22. Ibid., 28 March 1776, ff. 69–76.
23. Friedrich Ernst von Muenchhausen, *At General Howe's Side, 1776–1778: The Diary of General William Howe's Aide de Camp, Captain Friedrich von Muenchhausen* (Monmouth Beach, NJ: Philip Freneau Press, 1974), 62.

24. HMC, *Stopford-Sackville Manuscript*, Howe to Germain, 31 December 1776, 2:53–55.
25. Benjamin Franklin Stevens (ed.), *General Sir William Howe's Orderly Book: At Charlestown, Boston and Halifax, June 17, 1775 to 1776, 26 May* (London: B. F. Stevens, 1890), 29 February 1776, 222.
26. Smith, *William Howe*, 42–43.
27. Stevens, *Orderly Book*, 20 January 1776, 201.
28. Smith, *William Howe*, 45–47.
29. TNA CO 5/92, Howe to Dartmouth, 9 October 1775, ff. 311–316.
30. George C. Daughan, *Revolution on the Hudson: New York City and the Hudson River Valley in the American War of Independence* (New York: W. W. Norton, 2016), 34–43.
31. TNA CO 5/92, Howe to Dartmouth, 9 October 1775, ff. 311–316.
32. Quoted in Daughan, *Revolution on the Hudson*, 4–5.
33. WCL Loftus Cliffe Papers (LCP) MS 4, Loftus Cliffe to Jack Cliffe, Camp York Island, 21 September 1776.
34. W. Howe, *The Narrative of Lieut. Ge. Sir William Howe, in a Committee of the House of Commons, on the 29th of April, 1779, Relative to His Conduct, During His Late Command of the King's Troops in North America* (London: H. Baldwin, 1780), 6.
35. Smith, *William Howe*, 63–64.
36. John H. Rhodehamel (ed.), *Washington: Writings* (Washington: Library of America, 1997), Washington to John Augustine Washington, 31 March 1776, 218–223.
37. TNA CO 5/93, Howe to Germain, 6 August 1776, ff. 228–230.
38. WCL CP MS 13/38a, Remarks on New York, 8 February 1776.
39. TNA CO 5/93, Howe to Germain, 7 & 8 July 1776, ff. 214–216; 217–218.
40. WCL CP MS 13/38a, Remarks on New York, 8 February 1776.
41. WCL CP MS 18/5, Plan of attack for battle of Long Island.
42. Quoted in Willcox, *Portrait of a General*, 105.
43. Ferling, *Almost a Miracle*, 131–137.
44. WCL CP MS 29/24, Narrative of New York Campaigns of 1776–1777, with postscript on Rhode Island move.
45. Howe, *Narrative*, 5.
46. Ferling, *Almost a Miracle*, 131–137.
47. Ibid., 137–9.
48. WCL CP MS 18/19, Observations, 15 September 1776.
49. WCL CP MS 29/24, Narrative of New York Campaigns of 1776–1777, with postscript on Rhode Island move.
50. WCL LCP MS 4, Loftus Cliffe to Jack Cliffe, Camp York Island, 21 September 1776.
51. WCL CP MS 29/24, Narrative of New York Campaigns.
52. WCL LCP MS 4, Loftus Cliffe to Jack Cliffe, Camp York Island, 21 September 1776.
53. HEH/HM/615, Orderly Book Of Lord Howe's Army, New York, August–September 1776, f. 40.
54. Ferling, *Almost a Miracle*, 140.
55. Bruce E. Burgoyne (ed.), *Enemy Views: The American Revolutionary War as Recorded by the Hessian Participants* (Westminster, MD: Heritage Books, 1996), Diary of Lieutenant von Bardeleben, 80.
56. WCL LCP MS 4, Loftus Cliffe to Jack Cliffe, Camp York Island, 21 September 1776.
57. Quoted in Ferling, *Almost a Miracle*, 143.
58. Howe, *Narrative*, 5.
59. Frederick Mackenzie, *Diary of Frederick Mackenzie*, 2 vols (Cambridge, MA: Harvard University Press, 1930), 1:85.
60. WCL CP MS 29/24, Narrative of New York Campaigns of 1776–1777.
61. Ibid.
62. Quoted in Willcox, *Portrait of a General*, 105.
63. WCL CP MS 29/24, Narrative of New York Campaigns of 1776–1777.
64. Howe, *Narrative*, 6.
65. WCL CP MS 29/24, Narrative of New York Campaigns of 1776–1777.

66. WCL CP MS 18/43, Opinions on continuance of operation, 30 October 1776.
67. Smith, *William Howe*, 86.
68. WCL CP MS 18/43, Observations, 30 October 1776.
69. Smith, *William Howe*, 63–108.
70. Gruber, *Howe Brothers*, 153–154.
71. TNA CO 5/94, Howe to Germain, 20 December 1776, ff. 15–19.
72. WCL CP MS 20/5, Clinton to Harvey, 4–7 January 1777.
73. TNA CO 5/94, Howe to Germain, 20 December 1776, ff. 15–19.
74. Ibid., ff. 29–30.
75. Harry Miller Lydenberg (ed.), *Archibald Robertson, Lieutenant-General Royal Engineers, His Diaries and Sketches in America, 1762–1780* (New York: New York Public Library, 1930), 120–1.
76. Gruber, *Howe Brothers*, 154–157.
77. TNA CO 5/94, Howe to Germain, 29 December 1776, ff. 29–30.
78. TNA CO 5/93, Howe to Germain, 30 November 1776, ff. 304–307.
79. TNA CO 5/94, Howe to Germain, 20 December 1776, ff. 20–21.
80. Ibid.
81. J. Stockdale (ed.), *Parliamentary Register* (London: J. Almon, 1775–), Howe to Germain, 20 January 1777, 10:377–378.
82. TNA CO 5/94, Germain to Howe, 14 January 1777, ff. 2–6.
83. TNA CO 5/94, Howe to Germain, 2 April 1777, ff. 143–146.
84. *Parliamentary Register*, Distribution of His Majesty's Troops, British and Foreign, from the Campaign of 1777, 10:390.
85. TNA CO 5/94, Howe to Germain, 2 April 1777, ff. 143–146.
86. WCL CP MS 21/29, Conversation with General [Howe], 8 July 1777.
87. *Parliamentary Register*, Howe to Carleton, 5 April 1777, 10:389–390.
88. WCL CP MS 21/26, Conversation with G[eneral] H[owe], 6 July 1777.
89. WCL CP MS 21/29, Conversation with General [Howe], 8 July 1777.
90. WCL CP MS 21/42, Conversation with G[en] H[owe], 13 July 1777.
91. Ibid.
92. WCL CP MS 21/46, Memorandum of Conversation with Sir Wm. Erskine, Lord Cornwallis and General Howe, 16 July 1777.
93. WCL CP MS 21/42, Conversation with G[en]. H[owe], 13 July 1777.
94. TNA CO 5/94, Howe to Germain, 7 July 1777, ff. 260–262.
95. WCL CP MS 21/26, Conversation with G[eneral] H[owe], 6 July 1777.
96. WCL CP MS 23/8, Clinton to Harvey, 18 August 1777.
97. Henry Cabot Lodge (ed.), *André's Journal: An Authentic Record of the Movements and Engagements of the British Army in America from June 1777 to November 1778 ...* (Boston: Bibliophile Society, 1903), 28 August 1777, 73.
98. Lodge, *André's Journal*, 7 September 1777, 82.
99. WCL ECP MS 22/4, Regimental order book of the 37th regt, 9 September–3 October 1777.
100. TNA CO 5/94, Howe to Germain, 10 October 1777, ff. 318–326.
101. Lodge, *André's Journal*, 11 September 1777, 84–88.
102. Lydenberg, *Robertson Diaries and Sketches*, 146–147.
103. WCL Eyre Coote Papers (ECP) MS 22/4, Regimental order book of the 37th regt.
104. Lydenberg, *Robertson Diaries and Sketches*, 146–7.
105. WCL ECP MS 22/4, Regimental order book of the 37th regt, 9 September–3 October 1777.
106. TNA CO 5/94, Howe to Germain, 10 October 1777, ff. 318–326.
107. O'Shaughnessy, *The Men Who Lost America*, 83–122.
108. TNA CO 5/94, Howe to Germain, 10 October 1777, ff. 318–326.
109. Joseph P. Tustin (ed.), *Diary of the American War: A Hessian Journal of Captain Johan Ewald, Field Jäger Corps* (New Haven: Yale University Press, 1979), 92.

110. W. H. Wilkin, *Some British Soldiers in America* (London: H. Rees, 1914), 12.

111. TNA CO 5/94, Howe to Germain, 10 October 1777, ff. 318–326.

112. K. G. Davies (ed.), *Documents of the American Revolution, 1770–1783*, 21 vols (Shannon: Irish University Press, 1972–1981), 'Thoughts for Conducting the War from the Side of Canada' by Lieut-General John Burgoyne, London, 28 February 1777, 14:41–46.

113. Ferling, *Almost a Miracle*, 204–241.

114. Mackesy, *War for America*, 123.

115. Henry Steele Commager & Richard B. Morris (eds), *The Spirit of '76: The Story of the American Revolution as Told by Participants*, 2 vols (Indianapolis: Bobbs-Merrill, 1958), Proclamation, 23 June 1777, 1:547–548 and 1:545–547.

116. Fonblanque, *Political and Military Episodes*, 247.

117. Ibid., 253.

118. A. Francis Steuart (ed.), *The Last Journals of Horace Walpole During the Reign of George III from 1771–1783*, 2 vols (London: The Bodley Head, 1910), 2:42. Fonblanque, *Political and Military Episodes*, 248.

119. NYHS MS 240, Gates to Washington, 28 August 1777.

120. Ibid., Narrative of the Information obtained from English Army Prisoners at Benningtown, undated.

121. See Fonblanque, *Political and Military Episodes*, 40–51; HEH LO 10645, Loudoun to Bute, 11 October 1762; and Richard Middleton, 'British Coastal Expeditions to France, 1757–1758', *Journal of the Society for Army History Research*, 71/286 (Summer 1993), 74–92.

122. Fonblanque, *Political and Military Episodes*, 291–292.

123. James Wilkinson, *Memoirs of my Own Times*, 3 vols (Philadelphia: Abraham Small, 1816), 1:237–238.

124. James M. Hadden, *A Journal Kept in Canada and Upon Burgoyne's Campaign in 1776 and 1777* (Albany: Munsell's, 1884), 166.

125. Marvin L. Brown (ed.), *Baroness von Riedesel and the American Revolution: Journal and Correspondence of a Tour of Duty, 1776–1783* (Chapel Hill: University of North Carolina Press, 1965), 150.

126. Brian E. Hubner, 'The Formation of the British Light Infantry Companies and Their Employment in the Saratoga Campaign of 1777' (Unpublished MA Thesis, University of Saskatchewan, 1986), 129.

127. WCL CP MS 23/40, Clinton to Burgoyne, 10 September 1777.

128. WCL CP MS 24/12, Burgoyne to Clinton, 21 September 1777.

129. WCL CP MS 23/29, Clinton to Howe, 1 September 1777.

130. WCL CP MS 23/8, Clinton to Harvey, 18 August 1777.

131. WCL CP MS 23/1, Clinton to Burgoyne, 18 August 1777.

132. TNA CO 5/94, John Campbell to Henry Clinton, 23 August 1777, ff. 337–338v.

133. Willcox, *Portrait of a General*, 172.

134. WCL CP MS 23/32, Clinton to Howe, 4 September 1777.

135. WCL CP MS 24/50, Clinton to Harvey, Fort Montgomery, 9 October 1777.

136. WCL CP MS 23/40, Clinton to Burgoyne, 10 September 1777.

137. WCL CP MS 24/50, Clinton to Harvey, Fort Montgomery, 9 October 1777.

138. Willcox, *Portrait of a General*, 180–181.

139. WCL CP MS 24/50, Clinton to Harvey, Fort Montgomery, 9 October 1777.

140. WCL CP MS 25/6, Clinton to Elizabeth & Martha Carter, 13 October 1777.

141. WCL CP MS 25/6, Clinton to Elizabeth & Martha Carter, 13 October 1777.

142. WCL CP MS 29/26, Clinton to Elizabeth & Martha Carter, End of 1777.

143. NYHS MS 240, Gates to Washington, 5 October 1777.

144. WCL CP MS 24/50, Clinton to Harvey, Fort Montgomery, 9 October 1777.

145. NYHS MS 240, 'Curious Relic of the Revolution – The Silver Ball', Newspaper Clipping, 7 February 1843.

146. John Burgoyne, *A State of the Expedition From Canada as Laid Before the House of Commons* ... (London: J. Almon, 1780), 49; Brown, *Riediesel and the American Revolution*, 169.

147. George F. Stanley (ed.), *For Want of a Horse: Being a Journal of the Campaigns Against the Americans in 1776 and 1777 Conducted from Canada by an Officer who Served with Lt. Gen. Burgoyne* (Sackville, NB: Tribune, 1961),161.

148. See Jeremy Black, *Military Strategy: A Global History* (London: Yale University Press, 2020), 25–35.

149. WCL CP MS 31/48, Germain to Clinton, 8 March 1778.

150. WCL CP MS 35/4, Clinton to Newcastle, 23 May 1778.

151. WCL CP MS 32/23, Germain to Clinton, 21 March 1778.

152. WCL CP MS 32/24, George III to Clinton, 21 March 1778.

153. WCL CP MS 32/23, Germain to Clinton, 21 March 1778.

154. WCL CP MS 35/18, Draft Memo by Clinton, 6 June 1778.

155. WCL CP MS 37/6, Clinton to Newcastle, 11 July 1778.

156. WCL CP MS 35/30, Clinton to Germain, 5 June 1778.

157. WCL CP MS 35/18, Draft Memo by Clinton, 6 June 1778.

158. Ferling, *Almost a Miracle*, 299–300.

159. WCL CP MS 36/29, Clinton to Germain, 5 July 1778.

160. George Hanger, *A Letter to ... Lord Castlereagh ... from G. H. ... proving how one hundred and fifty thousand men ... well disciplined ... may be acquired in the short space of two months* (London: Privately Published, 1808), 74–75.

161. See, for example, 'Sir Charles Napier on National Defence' By the Editor, *United Service Magazine*, 1:1852, 424.

162. WCL CP MS 36/29, Clinton to Germain, 5 July 1778.

163. See Mark Edward Lender & Garry Wheeler Stone, *Fatal Sunday: George Washington, the Monmouth Campaign and the Politics of Battle* (Norman: University of Oklahoma Press, 2016), 184–199.

164. Wilkin, *Some British Soldiers in America*, Hale to parents, Camp at Kingsbridge, 21 July 1778, 265–268.

165. WCL CP MS 35/49, Journal of the British Army's march through New Jersey, 18 June to 1 July 1778.

166. John Graves Simcoe, *A Journal of the Operations of the Queen's Rangers from the End of the Year 1777 to the Conclusion of the Late American War* (Exeter: Privately Published, 1787), 39–41.

167. WCL CP MS 36/10, Lt Forbes Champagne to Rawdon, 29 June 1778.

168. Willcox, *Portrait of a General*, 211–259.

169. Wilkin, *British Soldiers in America*, Hale to parents, New York, 14 July 1778, 262–265.

170. Ibid., Hale to parents, Camp at Neversunk, 4 July 1778, 257–261.

171. WCL CP MS 36/29, Clinton to Germain, 5 July 1778.

172. Ira D. Gruber (ed.), *John Peebles' American War: The Diary of a Scottish Grenadier, 1776–1782* (London: Stackpole Books, 1998), entry for 28 June 1778, 194.

173. WCL CP MS 36/33, Clinton to Mary & Elizabeth Carter, 6 July 1778.

174. Wilkin, *British Soldiers in America*, Hale to parents, Camp at Neversunk, 4 July 1778, 257–261.

175. WCL CP MS 35/49, Journal of the British Army's march through New Jersey, 18 June to 1 July 1778.

176. Wilkin, *British Soldiers in America*, Hale to parents, Camp at Kingsbridge, 21 July 1778, 265–268.

177. Spring, *With Zeal and Bayonets Only*, 57–60.

178. Wilkin, *British Soldiers in America*, Hale to parents, Camp at Kingsbridge, 21 July 1778, 265–268.

179. WCL CP MS 36/33, Clinton to Mary & Elizabeth Carter, 6 July 1778.

5 'Indirect Manoeuvres'

1. WCL CP MS 47/14, Clinton Memorandum, November 1778.
2. WCL CP MS 41/25, Clinton to Germain, 15 September 1778.
3. WCL CP MS 31/48, Germain to Clinton, 8 March 1778.
4. For a concise account of British military strategy in the American Revolutionary War, see Jeremy Black, 'British Military Strategy', in Donald Stoker, Kenneth J. Hagan & Michael T. McMaster (eds), *Strategy in the American War of Independence: A Global Approach* (London: Routledge, 2010), 58–72.
5. WCL CP MS 31/48, Germain to Clinton, 8 March 1778.
6. WCL CP MS 40/31, Clinton to Grey, 2 September 1778.
7. WCL CP MS 41/21, Grey to Clinton, 6 September 1778.
8. WCL CP MS 41/39, Clinton to Germain, 21 September 1778.
9. WCL CP MS 43/3, Clinton to Germain, 8 October 1778.
10. WCL CP MS 43/4, Cornwallis Report on Taapan Raid, 8 October 1778.
11. John Robert Shawe, *John Robert Shawe: An Autobiography of Thirty Years, 1777–1807* (Athens: Ohio University Press, 1992), quoted in Don Hagist, *British Soldiers of the American War: Voices of the American Revolution* (Yardley: Westholme Publishing, 2012), 26.
12. WCL CP MS 44/16, Ferguson to Clinton, 10 October 1778.
13. WCL CP MS 41/41, Clinton to Carter, 21 September 1778.
14. WCL CP MS 51/20, Germain to Clinton, 23 January 1779.
15. WCL CP MS 58/10, Clinton to Germain, 14 May 1779.
16. WCL CP MS 3/23, Lloyd to Clinton, Windsor, 29 March 1767.
17. FMC HL MS, 'Of America'.
18. Hannibal Lloyd, *Memoir*, 9.
19. WCL CP MS 61/17, Clinton to Germain, 18 June 1779.
20. WCL CP MS 61/22, Clinton to Newcastle, 18 June 1779.
21. WCL CP MS 61/16, Clinton to Germain, 18 June 1779.
22. Gruber, *John Peebles' American War*, entry for 1 June 1779, 266.
23. WCL CP MS 61/16, Clinton to Germain, 18 June 1779.
24. WCL CP MS 65/45, Clinton to Newcastle, 14 August 1779.
25. WCL CP MS 61/16, Clinton to Germain, 18 June 1779.
26. WCL CP MS 65/45, Clinton to Newcastle, 14 August 1779.
27. WCL CP MS 61/16, Clinton to Germain, 18 June 1779.
28. WCL CP MS 65/45, Clinton to Newcastle, 14 August 1779.
29. WCL CP MS 65/8, Clinton Memorandum, July 1779.
30. WCL CP MS 63/32, Lawrence Campbell to Clinton, 24 July 1779.
31. WCL CP MS 64/1, Clinton to Germain, 25 July 1779.
32. WCL CP MS 66/13, Clinton to Germain, 21 August 1779.
33. WCL CP MS 52/4, Campbell to Clinton, Savannah, 16 January 1779.
34. Library of Congress, Washington, DC (LOC) MS 1213 Regimental Orderly Book Siege of Savannah 1779.
35. WCL CP MS 80/1, Clinton to Eden, 11 December 1779.
36. John S. Pancake, *This Destructive War: The British Campaign in the Carolinas, 1780–1782* (Tuscaloosa: University of Alabama Press, 2003), 57–60.
37. Willcox, *American Rebellion*, 164.
38. The operation was initially suggested by Ferguson. See Howard H. Peckham (ed.), *Sources of American Independence: Selected Manuscripts from the Collections of the Williams L. Clements Library*, 2 vols (Chicago: University of Chicago Press, 1978), Ferguson to Clinton [Charleston], 31 March 1780, 2:356–358.
39. Banastre Tarleton, *A History of the Campaigns of 1780 and 1781, in the Southern Provinces of North America* (London: Cadell, 1787), 16.
40. Stanley D. M. Carpenter, *Southern Gambit: Cornwallis and the British March to Yorktown* (Norman: University of Oklahoma Press, 2018), 50–94.
41. Tustin, *Journal of Captain Johan Ewald*, 237.

42. Carpenter, *Southern Gambit*, 50–94.
43. WCL CP MS 98/23, Clinton to Germain, 14 May 1780.
44. WCL CP MS 97/42, Clinton to Newcastle, 12 May 1780.
45. TNA PRO 30/11/2, Rawdon to Cornwallis, Camden, 7 July 1780, ff. 252.
46. See Richard Middleton, *Cornwallis: Soldier and Statesman in a Revolutionary World* (London: Yale University Press, 2022), for a new assessment of Cornwallis's military career.
47. *CC*, Cornwallis to Ross, Mansfield Street, 13 November 1783, 1:149.
48. See 'Traité de la Colonne' in Folard, *Commentaires sur l'Histoire de Polybe*, 1:xxii–c, & 7. Quoted in Gruber, *Books and the British Army*, 41–42.
49. Carpenter, *Southern Gambit*, 103–104.
50. WCL CP MS 90/45, Memorandum by Clinton on a conversation with Cornwallis, end of March 1780.
51. WCL CP MS 91/21, André Memo on Cornwallis, 1780.
52. *CC*, Clinton to Phillips, New York, 26 April 1781, 1:435–440.
53. WCL CP MS 126/25, Clinton Memorandum, 20 October 1780.
54. Carpenter, *Southern Gambit*, 85–90.
55. TNA PRO 30/11/72, Cornwallis to Clinton, Camp at Beach Creek 20 miles from Camden, 30 May 1780, ff. 15.
56. Pancake, *This Destructive War*, 91.
57. TNA PRO 30/11/72, Cornwallis to Clinton, Charleston, 30 June 1780, ff. 18.
58. Ibid., Cornwallis to Clinton, 14 July 1780, ff. 26; and 6 August 1780, ff. 36.
59. Ibid., Cornwallis to Clinton, 10 August 1780, ff. 40.
60. TNA PRO 30/11/63, Rawdon to Cornwallis, Camden, 11 August 1780, 11 at night, ff. 34.
61. TNA PRO 30/11/72, Cornwallis to Clinton, 10 August 1780, ff. 40.
62. Ibid., Cornwallis to Clinton, 6 August 1780, ff. 36.
63. TNA PRO 30/11/76, Cornwallis to Germain, Camden, 21 August 1780, ff. 9.
64. Tarleton, *Campaigns*, 107.
65. William Johnson, *Sketches in the Life and Correspondence of Nathanael Greene*, 2 vols (Charleston: Privately Published, 1822), 'A Narrative of the Campaign of 1780, by Colonel Otho Holland Williams, Adjutant General', 1:495.
66. Tarleton, *Campaigns*, 107.
67. TNA PRO 30/11/76, Cornwallis to Germain, Camden, 21 August 1780, ff. 9.
68. Carpenter, *Southern Gambit*, 120.
69. TNA PRO 30/11/76, Cornwallis to Germain, Camden, 21 August 1780, ff. 9.
70. Carpenter, *Southern Gambit*, 123.
71. Pancake, *This Destructive War*, 107.
72. TNA PRO 30/11/72, Cornwallis to Clinton, Camden, 23 August 1780, ff. 42.
73. WCL CP MS 126/35, Clinton Memorandum, c. 20 October 1780.
74. WCL CP MS 262/4, Clinton to Cornwallis, New York, 11 June 1781, ff. 268–273.
75. TNA PRO 30/11/74, Cornwallis to Clinton, Williamsburgh, 30 June 1781, ff. 18A.
76. Wickwire, *Cornwallis and the War of Independence*, 195.
77. TNA PRO 30/11/72, Cornwallis to Clinton, Camden, 23 August 1780, ff. 42.
78. TNA PRO 30/11/64, Ferguson to Cornwallis, Gilberton, 14 September 1780, ff. 60.
79. Ibid., Ferguson to Cornwallis, 30 September 1780, ff. 128.
80. TNA PRO 30/11/3, DePeyster to Cornwallis, Camp near Gilbert Town, 11 October 1780, ff. 210.
81. TNA CO 5/101, Rawdon to Clinton, Camp between Broad River and Catawba, SC, 29 October 1780, ff. 43.
82. Quoted in Terry Golway, *Washington's General: Nathanael Greene and the Triumph of the American Revolution* (New York: Henry Holt, 2005), 232.
83. See Donald Stoker and Michael W. Jones, 'Colonial Military Strategy', in Stoker et al., *Strategy in the American War*, 5–34.

84. Richard K. Showman (ed.), *The Papers of Nathanael Greene*, 13 vols (Chapel Hill: University of North Carolina Press, 1976–2005), Greene to unknown, Camp on the Pee Dee River, South Carolina, n.d., 7:175.
85. TNA PRO 30/11/5, Cornwallis to Clinton, Camp on Turkey Creek, Broad River, 18 January 1781, ff. 47.
86. Tarleton, *Campaigns*, 215–223.
87. Quoted in Lawrence E. Babits, *A Devil of a Whipping: The Battle of Cowpens* (Chapel Hill: University of North Carolina Press, 1998), 91.
88. Robert E. Lee (ed.), *The Revolutionary War Memoirs of General Henry Lee* (New York: Da Capo Press, 1998), 257.
89. Henry Lee, *The Campaign of 1781 in the Carolinas* (Philadelphia: E. Littell, 1824), 97–98.
90. Thomas Young, 'Memoir of Thomas Young', *Orion*, 3 (October 1843), 294–295.
91. Tarleton, *Campaigns*, 221.
92. WCL CP MS 146/18, Clinton draft Memorandum, written after 16 February 1780.
93. Lee, *Campaign of 1781*, 98.
94. Pancake, *This Destructive War*, 135–138.
95. TNA PRO 30/11/5, Cornwallis to Clinton, Camp on Turkey Creek, Broad River, 18 January 1781, ff. 47.
96. WCL CP MS 146/18, Clinton draft Memorandum, written after 16 February 1780.
97. WCL CP MS 126/25, Clinton Memorandum, 20 October 1780.
98. TNA PRO 30/11/5, Cornwallis to Germain, Guildford, 17 March 1781, ff. 281.
99. Carpenter, *Southern Gambit*, 175–178.
100. Spring, *With Zeal and With Bayonets Only*, 253.
101. Suffolk Record Office (SRO), Grafton Papers, Acc. 423/191, O'Hara to the Duke of Grafton, Wilmington, North Carolina, 20 April 1781.
102. TNA PRO 30/11/85, Cornwallis to Rawdon, Hillsborough, 21 February 1781, ff. 9.
103. SRO, Grafton Papers, Acc. 423/191, O'Hara to the Duke of Grafton, Wilmington, N.C., 20 Apr. 1781.
104. Showman, *Papers of Nathanael Greene*, Greene to Jefferson, Near the High Rock Ford, N.C, 10 March 1781, 7:419.
105. *CC*, Cornwallis to Germain, 17 March 1781, 1:521.
106. Lamb, *Memoir*, 361.
107. John Buchanan, *The Road to Guilford Courthouse: The American Revolution in the Carolinas* (New York: Wiley, 1997), 375.
108. David Schenck, *North Carolina, 1780–'81: Being a History of the Invasion of the Carolinas by the British Army Under Lord Cornwallis in 1780–'81* (Raleigh: Edwards & Broughton, 1889), 352.
109. Pancake, *This Destructive War*, 179.
110. Wickwire, *Cornwallis*, 300.
111. Schenck, *North Carolina*, 360–361.
112. St George Tucker, 'St George Tucker to Francis Bland Tucker, 18 March 1781', *Magazine of American History*, 7 (September 1881), 39.
113. Thomas Baker, *Another Such Victory: The Story of the American Defeat at Guildford Courthouse That Helped Win the War for Independence* (New York: Eastern Acorn Press, 1981), 65.
114. Schenck, *North Carolina*, 366.
115. Charles Stedman, *The History of the Origin, Progress, and Termination of the American War* (London: J. Debrett, 1794), 2:385.
116. Wickwire, *Cornwallis*, 308–309.
117. SRO, Grafton Papers, Acc. 423/191, O'Hara to the Duke of Grafton, Wilmington. NC, 20 April 1781.
118. TNA PRO 30/11/5, Cornwallis to Clinton, Camp near Wilmington, 10 April 1781, ff. 209.
119. Wilcox, *Portrait of a General*, 381.

120. WCL CP MS 208, Notes on Tarleton's *History* [end of 1787].
121. TNA PRO 30/11/74, Cornwallis to Clinton, Williamsburgh, 30 June 1781, ff. 18A.
122. WCL CP MS 262/4, Clinton to Cornwallis, New York, 11 June 1781, ff. 268–273.
123. TNA PRO 30/11/68, Clinton to Cornwallis, New York, 8 June 1781, ff. 11.
124. WCL CP MS 262/4, Clinton to Cornwallis, New York, 11 June 1781, ff. 268–273.
125. *CC*, Cornwallis to Phillips, Wilmington, 10 April 1781, 1:87.
126. Carpenter, *Southern Gambit*, 213–214.
127. Benjamin Franklin Stevens, *The Campaign in Virginia, 1781: An Exact Reprint of Six Rare Pamphlets on the Clinton-Cornwallis Controversy*, 2 vols (London: Privately Published, 1888), 1:43.
128. TNA PRO 30/11/68, Clinton to Cornwallis, New York, 2 September 1781, ff. 77.
129. *CC*, Clinton to Cornwallis, 6 September 1781, 1:118; and Cornwallis to Clinton, 16 September 1781, 1:119.
130. *CC*, Cornwallis to Clinton, 11 October 1781, 1:124.
131. J. K. Laughton & J. Y. F. Sullivan (eds), *The Journal of Rear-Admiral Bartholomew James, 1752–1828* (London: Navy Records Society Publications, 1896), entry for 11 October 1781, 122–123.
132. Hugh Wodehouse Pearse, *Memoir of the Life and Military Services of Viscount Lake, Baron Lake of Delhi and Laswarree, 1744–1808* (London: Blackwood, 1908), 60–61.
133. John C. Fitzpatrick (ed.), *The Writings of George Washington from the Original Manuscript Sources, 1745–1799*, 39 vols (Washington: Government Printing Office, 1931–1944), Washington to Thomas Sim Lee, Head Quarters, Before York, 12 October 1781, 23:210.
134. French Ensor Chadwick (ed.), *The Graves Papers and Other Documents Relating to the Naval Operations of the Yorktown Campaign, July to October 1781* (New York: De Vinne Press for the Navy History Society, 1916), Graves to Philip Stevens, London at sea, 29 October 1781, 137–139.
135. I. N. Phelps Stokes, *The Iconography of Manhattan Island, 1498–1909*, 6 vols (New York: Robert H. Dodd, 1915–1928), 5:1140.
136. Willcox, *American Rebellion*, 261.
137. NYPL MssCol 2796/7, William Smith Jr Papers, Historical Memoirs, 21 December 1780–12 November 1783, entry for 13 May 1782.
138. Willcox, *Portrait of a General*, 463.
139. John L. Pimlott, 'The Administration of the British Army, 1783–1793' (Unpublished PhD Thesis, University of Leicester, 1975), 6.
140. TNA HO 50/1, North to Conway, 27 April 1783, ff. 138.
141. TNA HO 50/1, Conway to North, 22 May 1783, f. 163.
142. *Parliamentary Register*, Colonel Richard Fitzpatrick, House of Commons, 13 June 1783, 10:165.

6 'Advance and Be Forward'

1. *CC*, Cornwallis to Sydney, Culford, 4 August 1784, 1:173.
2. *CC*, Cornwallis to Ross, Mansfield Street, 13 November 1783, 1:149.
3. See, for example, TNA PRO 30/11/7, 'Observations on the English Possessions in India, their government, population, cultivation, produce and commerce, privately communicated to the right honoble Henry Dundas', ff. 267–308.
4. See, for example, BL Add MS 29209, 'Histories of the Two Maratta Wars & of the Rise & Declension of the House of Sewajee', ff. 309–310. Cornwallis continued to provide intelligence updates in this vein once he had assumed his dual-hatted role. See, for example, HEH DUN 6, 'An Account of Tippoo Sultan, his Family, the Revenues of his country and of his Army', 14 December 1789.
5. *CC*, Cornwallis to Bishop of Lichfield and Coventry, Camp near Bangalore, 13 July 1791, 2:98.

6. See Kaveh Yazdani, 'Mysore at War: The Military Structure During the Reigns of Haidar 'Ali and Tipu Sultan', in Ravi Ahuja & Martin Christof-Füchsle (eds), *A Great War in South India: German Accounts of the Anglo-Mysore Wars, 1766–1799* (Berlin: De Gruyter, 2020), 17–54.

7. Victoria and Albert Museum, London, 'Tipu's Tiger', 1780s or 1790s, Mysore, India. Museum no 2545 (IS). https://www.vam.ac.uk/articles/tipus-tiger [Accessed 10 November 2020].

8. David Price, *Memoirs of the Early Life and Service of a Field Officer on the Retired List of the Indian Army* (London: Wm. H. Allen & Co., 1839), 445.

9. Joshua Ehrlich, 'Plunder and prestige: Tipu Sultan's library and the making of British India', *South Asia: Journal of South Asian Studies*, 43:3 (May 2020), 484.

10. Charles Stewart, *A Descriptive Catalogue of the Oriental Library of the Late Tippoo Sultan of Mysore* (Cambridge: The University Press, 1809), 4–7.

11. Zain-ul-Abidin Shustari, Fath-ul-Mujahidin (1782/3), MS C210, Victoria Memorial Hall, Kolkata; cited in Ehrlich, 'Plunder and prestige', 482.

12. BL Asia, Pacific & Africa Collection (APAC) Mss Eur C10, Munshi M. Qasim (trans.), 'Account of Teepoo Sooltan's Hall of Public Audience', 209–10, quoted in Ehrlich, 'Plunder and prestige', 483.

13. Price, *Memoirs*, 445.

14. See Ehrlich, 'Plunder and prestige'; and Stewart, *Catalogue of the Library of Tippoo Sultan*.

15. Randolf G. S. Cooper, 'Culture, combat and colonialism in eighteenth and nineteenth century India', *International History Review*, 27/3 (September 2005), 537–538.

16. J. F. Price & K. Rangachari (eds), *The Private Diary of Ananda Ranga Pillai, Dubash to Joseph François Dupleix*, 12 vols (Madras: Government Press, 1904–1928), 3:9.

17. Dalrymple, *Anarchy*, 52.

18. François Bernier, *Travels in the Mogul Empire, AD 1656–68*, ed. A. Constable, trans. I. Brock (London: Constable, 1891), 47–48.

19. BL Add MS 29209, 'Histories of the Two Maratta Wars & of the Rise & Declension of the House of Sewajee', ff. 309–310.

20. D. F. Harding, *Small Arms of the East India Company*, 4 vols (London: Foresight, 1999), 4:150–151.

21. Charles Robert Wilson (ed.), *Old Fort William in Bengal: A Selection of Official Documents Dealing with its History*, 2 vols (London: John Murray, 1906), Court of Directors to the Governor of Fort William, London, 17 June 1748, 1:205–212.

22. Quoted in G. J. Bryant, *The Emergence of British Power in India, 1600–1784: A Grand Strategic Interpretation* (Woodbridge: Boydell Press, 2013), 9.

23. See Geoffrey Parker, *The Military Revolution: Military Innovation and the Rise of the West, 1500–1800* (Cambridge: Cambridge University Press, 1988), in particular 115–145. For a refutation of the thesis, see Jeremy Black, 'A Military Revolution? A 1660–1792 Perspective', in Clifford J. Rogers (ed.), *The Military Revolution Debate: Readings on the Military Transformation of Early Modern Europe* (Boulder: Westview Press, 1995), 95–116.

24. See Cooper, 'Culture, combat, and colonialism', 534–549.

25. National Archives of India, New Delhi (NAI), Home Misc of Ancient Records, 1757, 19:120–128, 26 July 1757.

26. Harold Carmichael Wylly, *A Life of Lieutenant-General Sir Eyre Coote* (Oxford: Clarendon Press, 1922), 41–42.

27. NAI, Home Misc of Ancient Records, 1757, 19:120–128, 26 July 1757.

28. T. A. Heathcote, *The Military in British India: The Development of British Land Forces in South Asia, 1600–1947* (Barnsley: The Praetorian Press, 2013), 26–27.

29. Quoted in Penderel Moon, *The British Conquest and Dominion of India* (London: Duckworth, 1989), 111.

30. Heathcote, *Military in British India*, 28–29.

31. Moon, *Conquest of India*, 138.

32. Dalrymple, *Anarchy*, 243.
33. For details of the rockets, see Linda Colley, 'Going native, telling tales: captivity, collaborations and empire', *Past & Present*, 168 (August 2000), 190.
34. K. D. Bhargava & S. N. Prasad (eds), *Fort William–India House Correspondence*, 20 vols (New Delhi: National Archives of India, 1949–1975), Letter from the Court of Directors to the Council in Bengal, 27 April 1765, 4:96.
35. Ghulam Hussain Khan, *Seir Mutaqherin*, 3:125, quoted in Dalrymple, *Anarchy*, 251.
36. NRS GD1/6/17 Narrative of the 2nd War with Hyderally.
37. BL APAC IOR/H/223, John Baillie's Account of Pollilur, ff. 160–166.
38. NRS GD1/6/17 Narrative of the 2nd War with Hyderally.
39. Alan Tritton, *When the Tiger Fought the Thistle: The Tragedy of Colonel William Baillie of the Madras Army* (London: Radcliffe Press, 2013), 271–272.
40. BL APAC IOR/H/223, Captain Muat's Account of the Defeat at Pollilur, ff. 83–85.
41. Dalrymple, *Anarchy*, 253.
42. Moon, *Conquest of India*, 203.
43. Mesrob Vartavarian, 'An open military economy: the British conquest of South India reconsidered, 1780–1799', *Journal of the Economic and Social History of the Orient*, 57:4 (2014), 486–510.
44. Wylly, *Life of Coote*, 225.
45. NRS GD1/6/17 Narrative of the 2nd War with Hyderally, Letter, 1 July 1781.
46. Fortescue, *History of the British Army*, 3:457–462.
47. Wylly, *Life of Coote*, 227.
48. Fortescue, *History of the British Army*, 3:465–469.
49. Wylly, *Life of Coote*, 245.
50. Mark Wilks, *Historical Sketches of the South of India in an Attempt to Trace the History of Mysoor*, 3 vols (London: Longman, 1817), 3:260.
51. Jadunath Sarkar & G. S. Sardesai (eds), *English Records of Maratha History: The Poona Residency Correspondence* (Bombay: Modern India Press, 1936–1951), (*PRC*), Kirkpatrick to Cornwallis, Fathgarh, 14 September 1787, 1:254.
52. BL APAC IOR/H/436, Captain Taylor, On the state of affairs in India … 1791, 142
53. Archives Nationales (AN), Paris, C/2/291: Defresne, À pondichery le 27.7.1790, 55.
54. Tamil Nadu State Archives, Chennai (TNSA) Military Sundries, vol. 101: William Macleod, of Tippo's Military Force in October 1794, 93.
55. Parveen Rukhsana, 'Military administration under Tipu Sultan – A study', *Quarterly Journal of the Mythic Society*, 93:1 (2002), 71.
56. *PRC*, Kirkpatrick to Cornwallis, Fathgarh, 14 September 1787, 1:254.
57. BL APAC IOR/H/436, Captain Taylor, On the state of affairs in India …, 1791, 141–142.
58. NAI Foreign Department Secret Proceedings, 2 October–9 November 1775: The Verbal Narration of Aly Navauz Cawn, 2212.
59. BL APAC MS Eur F128/142, Letters, 1785–1786, from and about Robert George Latham as prisoner of Hyder Ali.
60. TNSA Military Sundries, vol. 109 A: General Return of Ordnance, Ammunition, Military Stores found in the Fort and Island of Seringapatam by the Committee appointed for that purpose, 20 May 1799, 242–244.
61. BL APAC IOR/H/436, Captain Taylor, On the state of affairs in India …, 1791, 144.
62. BL APAC IOR/H/251, Particulars regarding Tipu's Revenues and Army in 1788.
63. Jean Deloche, *Transport and Communications in India Prior to Steam Locomotion; Volume 1: Land Transport* (Delhi: Oxford University Press, 1993), 242–243.
64. William Thomson, *Memoirs of the Late War in Asia, with a Narrative of the Imprisonment and Sufferings of our Officers and Soldiers, by an Officer of Colonel Baillie's Detachment*, 2 vols (London: John Murray, 1788), 1:198.
65. Deloche, *Transport and Communications in India*, 1:242.

66. Bryant, *Emergence of British Power*, 295.
67. Kaushik Roy, 'Military synthesis in South Asia: armies, warfare, and Indian society, c. 1740–1849', *Journal of Military History*, 69 (July 2005), 651–690. For a wider discussion of knowledge and the means by which it was transmitted and communicated in South Asia, see C. A. Bayly, *Empire and Information: Intelligence Gathering and Social Communication in India, 1780–1870* (Cambridge: Cambridge University Press, 1996); Bernard S. Cohn, *Colonialism and its Forms of Knowledge: The British in India* (Princeton: Princeton University Press, 1996); and Michael H. Fisher, *Indirect Rule in India: Residents and the Residency System, 1764–1858* (Oxford: Oxford University Press, 1991).
68. James Grant Duff, *A History of the Mahrattas*, 3 vols (London: Longman, 1826), 2:362.
69. BL APAC IOR/P/D/63, John Carnac to the Bombay Council, 1 January 1779, f. 132.
70. Dalrymple, *Anarchy*, 242–243.
71. BL APAC IOR/P/D/63, John Carnac to the Bombay Council, 1 January 1779, f. 132.
72. Ibid.
73. Duff, *History of the Mahrattas*, 2:368–369.
74. Ibid., 2:371–373.
75. Stewart Gordon, *The Marathas: 1600–1818* (Cambridge: Cambridge University Press, 1993), 164.
76. BL APAC IOR/P/D/63, John Carnac to the Bombay Council, 1 January 1779, f. 132.
77. Collins, *War and Empire*, 155.
78. Raymond Callahan, *The East India Company and Army Reform, 1783–1798* (Cambridge, MA: Harvard University Press, 1972), 70–103.
79. TNA PRO 30/11/127, Yonge to Cornwallis, April 1786.
80. *CC*, Cornwallis to Yonge and Pitt, 7 March 1788, 1:344–345.
81. Franklin & Mary Wickwire, *Cornwallis: The Imperial Years* (Chapel Hill: University of North Carolina Press, 1980), 105.
82. TNA PRO 30/11/123, 'Extract of a general letter from the Honble the Court of Directors to the Governor General in Council in the Secret and Military Department', 20 August 1788, ff. 3–4.
83. *CC*, Cornwallis to York, Calcutta, 20 July 1797, 1:264–265.
84. *CC*, Cornwallis to the Secret Committee of the Court of Directors, On the Ganges, 19 August 1787, 1:275–277.
85. *CC*, Cornwallis to the Court of Directors, On the Ganges, 18 August 1787, 1:523–525.
86. BL APAC IOR/E/4/45, Cornwallis to the Court of Directors, 16 November 1786, ff. 14–15.
87. *CC*, Cornwallis to the Court of Directors, On the Ganges, 18 August 1787, 1:523–525.
88. Letter of "A. B.", *The Public Advertiser*, 12 March 1771, quoted in Arthur N. Gilbert, 'Recruitment and reform in the East India Company Army, 1760–1800', *Journal of British Studies*, 15:1 (Autumn 1975), 93.
89. BL APAC IOR/L/Mil/9/85, Farrington Recruiting Figures. Quoted in Gilbert, 'Recruitment and reform', 93–94.
90. BL APAC IOR/L/Mil/9/85, Farrington Recruiting Figures; and IOR/L/Mil/103/7, Recruitment Figures, 1778–1784, quoted in Gilbert, 'Recruitment and reform', 99.
91. *London Evening Post*, 16–18 April 1771.
92. Quoted in Gilbert, 'Recruitment and reform', 107–108.
93. G. R. Gleig, *The Life of Sir Thomas Munro*, 2 vols (London: Colburn & Bentley, 1830), Munro to his father, Ambore, 17 January 1790, 1:79–83.
94. See Rennell, *Marches of the British Army in . . . India*, 99.
95. See H. H. Dodwell, 'Transport and the Second Mysore War', *Journal of the Society for Army Historical Research*, 3 (1924), 266–272.
96. Dirom, *A Narrative of the Campaign in India*, 17.
97. TNA PRO 30/11/118 Campbell to Cornwallis, 6 May 1787, ff. 80–90.
98. Rennell, *Marches of the British Army*, 8–9.

99. Dirom, *Narrative*, 17.

100. Collins, *War and Empire*, 156–157.

101. Gleig, *Life of Munro*, Munro to his father, Ambore, 17 January 1790, 1:79–83.

102. TNA PRO 30/11/174, Cornwallis to Medows, 24 March 1790, ff. 53–55.

103. Gleig, *Life of Munro*, Munro to his father, Ambore, 17 January 1790, 1:79–83.

104. *CC*, Cornwallis to York, 10 November 1786, 1:225.

105. *CC*, Cornwallis to York, 10 December 1787, 1:316.

106. TNA PRO 30/11/194, 'Memorandum for the Commanding Officers at the Stations of Cawnpore and Futtyghur', 28 October 1787.

107. TNA PRO 30/11/159, Cornwallis to Campbell, 12 January 1787, ff. 27–29.

108. *Calcutta Gazette*, 6:152, 25 January 1787.

109. TNA PRO 30/11/159, Cornwallis to Campbell, 6 February 1789.

110. NRS GD1/6/5/1 Campbell to Cornwallis, 27 May 1787.

111. Ibid., 16 December 1788.

112. NAM MS 6807/157/6 Discipline established by Major General Howe for Light Infantry in Battalion, Sarum, September 1774; and NRS GD1/6/14 Observations humbly submitted to Major General Sir Archibald Campbell KB on his System of Manoeuvres by Files.

7 'Decisive Victory Will Relieve Us From All Our Distresses'

1. *CC*, Cornwallis to Lansdowne, Calcutta, 15 April 1790, 2:20–21.

2. *CC*, Cornwallis to Abercromby, 3 May 1780, 2:24.

3. Quoted in Ian Fletcher, *Robert Craufurd, The Man and the Myth: The Life and Times of Wellington's Wayward Martinet* (Oxford: Pen & Sword, 2021), 21.

4. TNA PRO 30/11/174, Cornwallis to Medows, 24 March 1790, ff. 53–55.

5. Collins, *War and Empire*, 155–170.

6. TNA PRO 30/11/174, Cornwallis to Medows, 24 March 1790, ff. 53–55.

7. Ibid.

8. TNA PRO 30/11/174, Cornwallis to Medows, 30 March 1790, ff. 59–60.

9. Ibid., 27 June 1790, f. 98.

10. Rennell, *Marches of the British Army*, 23–28.

11. TNA PRO 30/11/269, Cornwallis to York, 20 November 1790, ff. 43–46.

12. Collins, *War and Empire*, 155–170.

13. Dalrymple, *Anarchy*, 323–326.

14. TNA PRO 30/11/174, Cornwallis to Medows, 27 June 1790, f. 100.

15. *CC*, Cornwallis to Captain Alexander Kyd, Fort William, 9 November 1790, 2:500.

16. TNA PRO 30/11/173, Cornwallis to Medows, Fort St. George, 15 December 1790, ff. 11–16.

17. TNA PRO 30/11/173, Cornwallis to Medows, Fort St. George, 4 January 1791, ff. 43–46.

18. Dirom, *Narrative*, 113.

19. TNA PRO 30/11/173, Cornwallis to Medows, Fort St. George, 4 January 1791, ff. 43–46.

20. TNA PRO 30/11/40, 'List of stores dispatched to Fort St. George since the departure of the Right Honble the Governor General and Commander in Chief', f. 567; and PRO 30/11/204, Casualty List Siege of Bangalore, ff. 1–2.

21. TNA PRO 30/11/155, Cornwallis to the Court of Directors, Camp at VenKettigherry, 20 April 1791, ff. 18–19.

22. TNA PRO 30/11/155, Cornwallis to the Court of Directors, Camp at VenKettigherry, 20 April 1791, ff. 18–19.

23. Rennell, *Marches of the British Army*, 75–76.

24. *CC*, Cornwallis to the Directors, 7 September 1791, 2:516–518.

25. Rennell, *Marches of the British Army*, 84–93.

26. *CC*, Cornwallis to the Directors, 7 September 1791, 2:516–518.

27. Rennell, *Marches of the British Army*, 94.

28. *CC*, Cornwallis to the Directors, 7 September 1791, 2:516–518.

29. TNA PRO 30/11/181, Cornwallis to Abercromby, 21 May 1791, ff. 55–56.

30. Quoted in Fletcher, *Craufurd*, 31–32.

31. TNA PRO 30/11/178, Cornwallis to Oakley, 31 May 1791, ff. 43–44.

32. See Wilks, *Historical Sketches of the South of India*, 2:449 for evidence of Cornwallis's commitment to intelligence collection; and TNA PRO 30/1147 for Cornwallis's intelligence papers.

33. *CC*, Cornwallis to Bishop of Lichfield and Coventry, Camp near Bangalore, 13 July 1791, 2:98.

34. HMC, *Report on Manuscripts in Various Collections*, 8 vols (London, 1909), Cornwallis to Commodore William Cornwallis, Camp 13 miles west of Bangalore, 5 July 1791, 6:373.

35. TNA PRO 30/11/178, Cornwallis to Oakley, 12 September 1791, ff. 105–106; Wickwire, *Imperial Years*, 155–156.

36. *CC*, Cornwallis to Dundas, Camp between Bangalore and Oossore, 24 October 1791, 2:128–129.

37. *CC*, Cornwallis to Dundas, 13 January 1792, 2:140–141.

38. Dirom, *Narrative*, 88.

39. *CC*, Cornwallis to Dundas, Camp between Bangalore and Oossore, 24 October 1791, 2:128–129.

40. *Calcutta Gazette*, 16:416, 16 February 1791, quoted in Wickwire, *Imperial Years*, 158.

41. Dirom, *Narrative*, 43.

42. Ibid., 43–44.

43. Roderick Mackenzie, *A Sketch of the War with Tippoo Sultan*, 2 vols (London: Sewell, 1793), 2:145.

44. TNA PRO 30/11/52, Lt. William Sandys to Cornwallis, June 1792, ff. 227–231. Quoted in Wickwire, 156.

45. Dirom, *Narrative*, 44.

46. Mackenzie, *Sketch of the War*, 2:149.

47. Dirom, *Narrative*, 46–47.

48. Wickwire, *Imperial Years*, 159–161.

49. TNA PRO 30/11/47, Translation of a Memorandum sent by Read and supposed to have been written about 31 December 1791, ff. 40–41.

50. *CC*, Cornwallis to Directors, Camp before Seringapatam, 4 March 1792, 2:529.

51. *CC*, Cornwallis to Dundas, 13 January 1792, 2:140–141.

52. *CC*, Cornwallis to Directors, Camp before Seringapatam, 4 March 1792, 2:530.

53. Mackenzie, *Sketch of the War*, 2:213.

54. *CC*, Cornwallis to Directors, Camp before Seringapatam, 4 March 1792, 2:533.

55. SLNSW MS A768, Macquarie Journal, No. 1, 15 December 1787–24 March 1792, 22 February 1792, ff. 355–367.

56. *CC*, Cornwallis to Directors, Camp before Seringapatam, 4 March 1792, 2:533.

57. SLNSW MS A768, Macquarie Journal, No. 1, 15 December 1787–24 March 1792, 24 February 1792, ff. 355–367.

58. See, for example, Dirom, *Narrative*, and Mackenzie, *Sketch of the War*.

59. Montgomery Martin (ed.), *The Dispatches, Minutes, and Correspondence of the Marquess Wellesley, K.G., During his Administration in India (RD)* (London: John Murray, 1836–7), Minute of the Governor-General in the Secret Department, Fort William, 12 August 1798, 1:159–208.

60. Lushington, *Life of Harris*, 118–119.

61. Ibid., Harris to Mornington, Madras, 6 July 1798, 120–121.

62. Ibid.

63. University of Southampton, Hartley Library (USL) Wellington Papers (WP) 1/8, Wellesley to Mornington, Fort St George, 15 September 1798.

64. USL WP 1/8, Wellesley to Mornington, Fort St. George, 19 September 1798.
65. See Dirom, *Narrative;* and Mackenzie, *Sketch of the War.*
66. BL APAC MS Eur/D/1053, Review of Different Campaigns Against Hyder Ali & Tipu Sultan with Proposed Plan for Assembling an Army, n.d.
67. 2nd Duke of Wellington (ed.), *Supplementary Dispatches and Memoranda of Field Marshall Arthur Duke of Wellington, 1797–1818 (SD)*, 14 vols (London: John Murray, 1858), Memorandum Respecting Collecting an Army in the Baramahal, July 1798, 1:55–8.
68. *SD*, Arthur Wellesley to Henry Wellesley, Fort St. George, 31 October 1798, 1:125–126.
69. Ibid.
70. TNSA PC231/1723, Minutes of Public Consultation, Fort St. George, 12 December 1798, ff. 4404–4013.
71. TNSA MC246/1741, Minutes of Military Consultation, Letter to the Military Board, Fort St. George, 15 December 1798, ff. 7831–7838.
72. *SD*, Arthur Wellesley to Henry Wellesley, Camp near Wallajah-Nuggur, 2 January 1799, 1:152–159.
73. SLNSW MS A790, Macquarie to Cliffe, Camp at Seedepore in the Coorga Country, 15 March 1799.
74. Ibid.
75. *SD*, Wellesley to Mornington, Camp near Vellore, 4 February 1799, 1:191–193.
76. Lushington, *Life of Harris*, Harris to Mornington, Camp near Vellore, 2 February 1799, 181.
77. Ibid., Harris to Robinson, Camp Moodoor, 26 February 1799, 188–189.
78. Ibid., Harris to Mornington, Camp near Vellore, 2 February 1799, 181.
79. Theodore Hook, *The Life of General, the Right Honourable Sir David Baird*, 2 vols (London: Bentley, 1832), 1:174–175.
80. H. M. Vibart, *The Military History of the Madras Engineers and Pioneers, From 1743 up to the Present Time*, 2 vols (London: W. H. Allen, 1888), 1:295.
81. *RD*, Harris to Richard Wellesley, Camp before Seringapatam, 5 April 1799, 1:514–7.
82. *SD*, Wellesley to Mornington, Camp, 2 miles west of Seringapatam, 5 April 1799, 1:208.
83. Lushington, *Life of Harris*, Harris to Robinson, Camp Moodoor, 26 February 1799, 188–189.
84. *SD*, Wellesley to Mornington, Camp, 2 miles west of Seringapatam, 5 April 1799, 1:208.
85. Ralph Bayly, *Diary of Colonel Bayly, 12th Regt, 1796–1830* (London: Army and Navy Cooperative Society, 1896), 72.
86. *SD*, Wellesley to Mornington, Camp near Allagoor, 25 March 1799, 1:206.
87. Lushington, *Life of Harris*, 199–201.
88. Bayly, *Diary*, 73.
89. Ibid.
90. BL Add MS 13664, Journal kept by Captain John Malcolm, serving in the Nizam's contingent in the expedition against Tippoo Sultaun, 6 January–May 1799, entry for 4 April 1799.
91. Ibid., Malcolm's Journal of the Campaign Against Tipu Sultan, entry for 13 April 1799.
92. SLNSW MS A790, Journal of the Operations of the Bombay Army, entry for 13 April 1799.
93. Ibid., entry for 21 April 1799.
94. See *RD*, Harris to RW, Seringapatam, 7 May 1799, 1:569; Bayly, *Diary*, 92; and Alexander Campbell, 'Letter from Lt Alexander Campbell, 74th Foot, to his brother Lt Frederick Campbell, RA, dated Seringapatam, 20 June 1799, describing the battle there', *Journal of the Royal Highland Fusiliers*, 6/1 (June 1969), 80.

95. *SD*, Wellesley to Sydenham, Seringapatam, 16 January 1800, 1:433.
96. Ibid.
97. TNSA MC246/1725, Minutes of Military Consultation, Letter to the Military Board, Fort St. George, 12 December 1798, ff.7811–7821.
98. BL APAC MS Eur/D/1053, Review of Different Campaigns against Hyder Ali & Tipu Sultan with Proposed Plan for assembling an Army, n.d.
99. See Dirom, *Narrative*; and Mackenzie, *Sketch of the War*. For an in-depth study of the Anglo-Maratha campaigns and the influence on British development before their commencement see Cooper, *Anglo-Maratha Campaigns*.
100. See, for example, *CC*, Cornwallis to Wesley, Whitehall, 23 February 1798, 2:333–334.
101. SLNSW MS A768, Macquarie Journal, No. 1, 15 December 1787–24 March 1792, 355–367, 16 & 20–21 February 1792.
102. Quoted in Piers Mackesy, 'What the British Army Learned', in Ronald Hoffman & Peter J. Albert (eds), *Arms and Independence: The Military Character of the American Revolution* (Charlottesville: University Press of Virginia, 1984), 200.
103. Guedella, *The Duke*, 54–65. See also Muir, *Path to Victory*, 46.
104. *CHLWG*, 2.
105. Lushington, *Life of Harris*, 199–200.
106. Muir, *Path to Victory*, 75.
107. Lloyd, 'Reflections' 173, *HLWG*, 15.
108. *CHLWG*, 89, 157–8.
109. For more on Mornington's expansionist policies, see John Severn, *Architects of Empire: The Duke of Wellington and his Brothers* (Norman: University of Oklahoma Press, 2007), 65–91.
110. *PRC*, Arthur Wellesley to Collins, Camp at Ahmednagar, 15 August 1803, 10:126–127.
111. John Gurwood (ed.), *The Dispatches of Field Marshal the Duke of Wellington During His Various Campaigns in India, Denmark, Portugal, Spain, The Low Countries and France*, 13 vols (*WD*) (London: John Murray, 1852), Memorandum upon Operations in the Maratha Territory, December 1800, updated January 1801, 1:357–365.
112. NAI Secret Department SD MS25/08/03 No. 90, Collins to Wellesley, 25 July 1803, ff. 9354–9355.
113. Blakiston, *12 Years Military Adventure*, 145.
114. See USL WP 3/3/84, Stevenson to Wellesley, four miles north of Aurungabad, 9 August 1803.
115. Thomas Edward Colebrook, *The Life of the Honourable Mountstuart Elphinstone*, 2 vols (London: John Murray, 1884), Elphinstone to Strachey, Camp at Ahmednuggur, 17 August 1803, 1:51.
116. Colebrook, *Life of Elphinstone*, Elphinstone to Strachey, Camp near Peepulgaon, 11 September 1803, 1:59.
117. Blakiston, *12 Years Military Adventure*, 150–151.
118. *PRC*, Close to Webbe, Poona, 6 October 1803, 10:151–153.
119. *SD*, Wellesley to Munro, Camp at Cheedkair, 1 November 1803, 4:210–211.
120. Colebrook, *Life of Elphinstone*, Elphinstone to Strachey, Camp 12 miles from Midgaon, 22 September 1803, 1:63.
121. Blakiston, *12 Years Military Adventure*, 154.
122. Ibid., 161.
123. *SD*, Letter by Lieutenant Campbell relative to the Battle of Assaye, written at the time of the transaction, 4:185.
124. NAM MS 8207/64, Account of the Battle of Assaye by Sgt Thomas Swarbrook, 19th Dragoons.
125. *SD*, Wellesley to Munro, Camp at Cheedkair, 1 November 1803, 4:210–211.
126. Blakiston, *12 Years Military Adventure*, 165.
127. *SD*, Letter by Lieutenant Campbell relative to the Battle of Assaye, written at the time of the transaction, 4:184–187.

128. James Welsh, *Military Reminiscences: Extracted from a Journal of Nearly Forty Years Active Service in the East Indies*, 2 vols (London: Smith, Elder & Co., 1830), 1:191.

129. Philip Henry Stanhope, *Notes of Conversations with the Duke of Wellington, 1831–1851* (London: John Murray, 1889), 130.

130. Louis J. Jennings (ed.), *The Croker Papers: The Correspondence and Diaries of John Wilson Croker*, 3 vols (London: John Murray, 1884), 1:342.

8 'Totally Unfit for Service'

1. RA GEO/MAIN/38742-38743, Clinton to Prince of Wales, 29 September 1792.

2. WCL CP MS 214, Clinton to Prince of Wales, August 1792; Clinton to Gloucester, 1 September 1792.

3. Michael Rowe, 'Lessons from the American Revolutionary War: Sir Henry Clinton's Analysis of the Allied Invasion of France, 1792', Georgian Papers Programme Blog, https://georgianpapers.com/2019/03/06/lessons-from-the-american-revolutionary-war-sir-henry-clintons-analysis-of-the-allied-invasion-of-france-1792/ [Accessed 29 January 2021].

4. RA GEO/MAIN/38742-38743, Clinton to Prince of Wales, 29 September 1792.

5. Wilcox, *Portrait of a General*, 484–486.

6. RA GEO/MAIN/38760-38761, Clinton to Prince of Wales, 27 October 1792.

7. John Money, *The History of the Campaign of 1792, Between the Armies of France Under General Dumourier, Valence etc, and the Allies Under the Duke of Brunswick* (London: E. Harlow, 1794), 287.

8. Money, 'Open Letter to William Windham', 35, quoted in Richard Glover, *Peninsular Preparation: The Reform of the British Army, 1795–1809* (Cambridge: Cambridge University Press, 1963), 124.

9. John Money, *To the Right Honourable William Windham on a Partial Reorganization of the British Army* (London: T. Egerton, 1799), 16–26.

10. Money, *Campaign of 1792*, 292–293.

11. Money, *Partial Reorganization*, 26–27.

12. Cyril Matheson, *The Life of Henry Dundas, First Viscount Melville, 1742–1811* (London: Constable, 1933), 182.

13. Quoted in T. C. W. Blanning, *The Origins of the French Revolutionary Wars* (London: Routledge, 1986), 158–159.

14. Glover, *Peninsular Preparation*, 215.

15. Pimlott, 'Administration of the British Army', 407–412.

16. Collins, *War and Empire*, 66.

17. Pimlott, 'Administration of the British Army', 352–353.

18. Keith John Bartlett, 'The Development of the British Army During the Wars with France, 1793–1815' (Unpublished PhD Thesis, University of Durham, 1998), 21–23.

19. Steve Brown, *The Duke of York's Flanders Campaign: Fighting the French Revolution, 1793–1795* (Barnsley: Frontline, 2018), 285–291.

20. Wilcox, *Portrait of a General*, 486–487.

21. See NYPL MssCol 6446 and 6447 for evidence of collected correspondence within a network that included the Abercromby brothers.

22. Carole Divall, *General Sir Ralph Abercromby and the French Revolutionary Wars, 1793–1801* (London: Pen & Sword, 2019), 16.

23. See Fortescue, *History of the British Army*, 4:80–81; Harry Varney (ed.), *The Journals and Correspondence of General Sir Harry Calvert . . . Comprising the Campaigns in Flanders and Holland in 1793–4* (London: Hurst & Blackett, 1853), 52, 67–68.

24. See Jordan R. Hayworth, *Revolutionary France's War of Conquest in the Rhineland: Conquering the Natural Frontier, 1792–1797* (Cambridge: Cambridge University Press, 2019), for the latest thinking on the French Revolutionary Army.

25. A. Aspinall (ed.), *The Later Correspondence of George III*, 5 vols (Cambridge: Cambridge University Press, 1966), (*LCG*), York to George III, Camp before Valenciennes, 26 July 1793, 2:66.

26. Brown, *Duke of York's Flanders Campaign*, 54.

27. R. H. Thoumine, *Scientific Soldier: A Life of General Le Marchant, 1766–1812* (Oxford: Oxford University Press, 1968), Le Marchant to his wife, Jemappes, 4 August 1793, 20.

28. Ibid., Le Marchant to his wife, Meuve, near Cambrai, 9 August 1793, 21.

29. See Hayworth, *Revolutionary France's War of Conquest*, 97–144.

30. *Règlement provisoire sur le service de l'infanterie en campagne du 5 avril 1792* (Paris: Magimel, 1792), 124.

31. David Gates, *The British Light Infantry Arm, c.1790–1815* (London: Batsford, 1987), 52.

32. *LCG*, York to George III, Ghent, 17 December 1793, 2:135.

33. *LCG*, York to G3, Ghent, 25 December 1793, 2:137.

34. Quoted in Karl A. Roider, *Baron Thugut and Austria's Response to the French Revolution* (Princeton: Princeton University Press, 1987), 152–154.

35. Varney, *Journals and Correspondence of Calvert*, 217.

36. Denis Le Marchant, *Memoirs of the Late Major General Le Marchant* (London: Samuel Bentley, 1841), 40.

37. Ibid., 40.

38. Jennings, *Croker Papers*, 5 October 1794, 1:197.

39. Robert Brown, *An Impartial Journal of a Detachment from the Brigade of Foot Guards Commencing 25th February 1793 and Ending 9 May 1795 by Robert Brown, Corporal in the Coldstream Guards* (London: John Stockdale, 1795), 24 October 1794, 203.

40. BRBML OSB MS 168-16-6, Journal of Henry Clinton, 1794. Entry for 8 September 1794.

41. Stanhope, *Conversations*, 181.

42. USL WP 1/2, Wesley to his brother, Thiel, 19 November 1794.

43. A. Aspinall (ed.), *The Correspondence of George, Prince of Wales 1770–1812*, 8 vols (*CPW*) (London: Cassell, 1964), Dundas to the Prince of Wales, Thiel, 24 December 1794, 2:526.

44. BL Add MS 46702, Dundas to Walmoden, Tuil, 31 December 1794.

45. Ibid., Beckwith to Don, British HQ, Apeldoorn, 7 January 1795.

46. Varney, *Journals and Correspondence of Calvert*, 396.

47. Stanhope, *Conversations*, 182.

48. *CPW*, Dundas to Prince of Wales, Diepholtz, 1 May 1795, 3:59–60.

49. Houlding, *Fit for Service*, 388–397.

50. NLS MS 3835, Abercromby to Dundas, 4 December 1794, f. 121.

51. See Michael Duffy, *Soldiers, Sugar and Seapower: The British Expeditions to the West Indies and the War Against Revolutionary France* (Oxford: Clarendon Press, 1987), 41–58.

52. Collins, *War and Empire*, 94–95.

53. WCL ECP MS 23/6, General Order book of the expedition to the West Indies headquartered at Barbados, 7 January–22 February 1794.

54. University of Durham Library (UDL) GRE/A200, 'Return of Strength of the Several Corps Composing the Army Commanded by General Sir Charles Grey, Embarked at Barbados on the Expedition against Martinique, 1 February 1794'.

55. WCL ECP MS 23/6, General Order book of the expedition to the West Indies headquartered at Barbados, 7 January–22 February 1794.

56. TNA CO 318/13, Grey to Dundas, 7, 15, 20 January, 2 February, 1794.

57. WCL ECP MS 23/6, General Order book of the expedition to the West Indies headquartered at Barbados, 7 January–22 February 1794.

58. Cooper Willyams, *An Account of the Campaign in the West Indies in the Year 1794* (London: T. Bensley, 1796), Grey, General Orders, Head Quarters, Barbadoes, 22 January 1794, A1–A6.

59. Willyams, *Account of the Campaign*, Grey, Further Orders before Embarkation, Barbadoes, 24 January 1794.
60. UDL GRE/A/192a Mémoire sur la deffense de la Martinique, with an English translation at GRE/A/192c.
61. UDL GRE/A246, Grey to Dundas, St Lucia, 4 April 1794.
62. UDL GRE/A196/9, Grey's landing instructions to Whyte, 1 February 1794.
63. WCL ECP MS 28/1, 'A journal kept by Lt.-Col Coote of 70th Regt when embarked at Cork 1793'.
64. See Duffy, *Soldiers, Sugar and Seapower*, 59–88.
65. WCL ECP MS 28/1, 'A journal kept by Lt.-Col Coote of 70th Regt when embarked at Cork 1793'.
66. Ibid.
67. Quoted in Duffy, *Soldiers, Sugar and Seapower*, 87.
68. TNA CO 318/13, Grey to Dundas, 25 March 1794.
69. UDL GRE/A238, Plan for the attack of St Lucia, undated.
70. WCL ECP MS 28/1, 'A journal kept by Lt.-Col Coote of 70th Regt when embarked at Cork 1793'.
71. WCL ECP MS 23/7, 'General Order book of the expedition to the West Indies headquartered at Guadelope', 20 February–14 May 1794.
72. WCL ECP MS 28/1, 'A journal kept by Lt.-Col Coote of 70th Regt when embarked at Cork 1793'.
73. TNA CO 318/13, Grey to Dundas, 22 April 1794.
74. David P. Geggus, *Slavery, War and Revolution: The British Occupation of Saint Domingue, 1793–1798* (Oxford: Oxford University Press, 1982), 108.
75. Collins, *War and Empire*, 95–96.
76. TNA PRO 30/8/107, Abercromby to Pitt, 14 July 1795.
77. *LCG*, 2:396–398, York to G3, London, 1 September 1795.
78. *CPW*, 3:104, Prince of Wales to the Queen, Brighton, 29 September 1795.
79. NLS MS 3835, Abercromby to Dundas, 4 September 1795.
80. NRS GD225/33/21, Garden to Hay, 2 August 1795.
81. George Pinkard, *Notes on the West Indies*, 3 vols (London: Longman, 1806), 1:16.
82. TNA WO 1/85, Return of black troops, 10 March 1796.
83. Duffy, *Soldiers, Sugar and Seapower*, 221–220
84. TNA WO 6/131, Dundas to the Duke of York, 16 April 1795.
85. TNA WO 1/83, Dundas to Vaughan, 17 April 1795.
86. J. F. Maurice (ed.), *The Diary of Sir John Moore*, 2 vols (London: Edward Arnold, 1904), entries for 26 and 29 April, 1:199–200.
87. Maurice, *Diary of Moore*, entry for 29 April 1796, 1:201–202.
88. Ibid., 1:201–203.
89. NLS MS 3835, Abercromby to Dundas, 2 May 1796.
90. BL Add MS 37876, Perryn to William Windham, 2, 4, 7 May 1796; NLS MS 3835, Abercromby to Dundas, 2 May 1796.
91. Maurice, *Diary of Moore*, entry for 18 May 1796, 1:213.
92. Ibid., entry for 25 May 1796, 1:216–217.
93. TNA WO 1/85, Abercromby to Dundas, 22, 30, 31 May 1796.
94. BL Add MS 57320, Moore to his father, 10 January 1797.
95. Janet MacDonald, *Sir John Moore: The Making of a Controversial Hero* (Barnsley: Pen & Sword, 2016), 74–75.
96. NLS Murray Papers, Adv MS 46.1.3, Orders, 8 June 1796.
97. TNA WO 1/85, Abercromby to Dundas, 21 June 1796.
98. Duffy, *Soldiers, Sugar and Seapower*, 257.
99. TNA WO 1/86, Abercromby to Dundas, 20 February 1797.
100. NRS GD364/25/1032, J. Hope to A. Hope, 20 February 1797.

101. TNA WO 1/86, Abercromby to Dundas, 20 February 1797.
102. NRS GD225/33/22/48, Stewart to Leith, 14 June 1797.
103. TNA WO 1/86, Abercromby to Dundas, 2 May 1797.
104. Duffy, *Soldiers, Sugar and Seapower*, 332.
105. Maurice, *Diary of Moore*, entry for 29 April 1796, 1:201–203.
106. WCL ECP MS 28/2, Instructions to Officers of Light Infantry.
107. John Watkins, *A Biographical Memoir of His Late Royal Highness Frederick, Duke of York and Albany* (London: Henry Fisher, 1827), 364.
108. C. G. Gardyne, *The Life of a Regiment: The History of the Gordon Highlanders*, 2 vols (Edinburgh: Douglas, 1901–1903), 1:67.

9 The 'Wandering Army'

1. WCL ECP 28/6, Journal of Sir Eyre Coote, 2 October 1800.
2. See Piers Mackesy, *Statesmen at War: Strategy of Overthrow, 1798–1799* (London: Longman, 1974).
3. Maurice, *Dairy of Moore*, entry for 10 August, 1:339.
4. WCL ECP MS 4/38, Observations of various militia regiments, Dover 15 April 1799.
5. HMC, *The Manuscripts of J. B. Fortescue, Preserved at Dropmore*, 9 vols (London, 1892–1912), Dutch Affairs. Minute of Lord Grenville, 23 July 1799, 5:175.
6. Mackesy, *Strategy of Overthrow*, 89–101.
7. HMC, *Dropmore Manuscripts*, Grenville to Dundas, Dropmore, 27 July 1799, 5:203.
8. Ibid., 30 July 1799, 5:207–209.
9. HMC, *Dropmore Manuscripts*, Dundas to Grenville, Wimbledon, 29 July 1799, 5:206.
10. Ibid., Grenville to Dundas, Dropmore, 30 July 1799, 5:209.
11. Ibid.
12. HEH Stowe Papers (SP) 317, Lord Grenville to Thomas Grenville, 2 August 1799.
13. HMC, *Dropmore Manuscripts*, Pitt to Grenville, Teston, 2 August 1799, 5:224–225.
14. Maurice, *Diary of Moore*, 1:340.
15. HMC, *Dropmore Manuscripts*, Dundas to Abercromby, Walmer Castle, 10 August 1799, 5:273–5; and Dundas to Grenville, Walmer Castle, 11 August 1799, 5:270–272. See also Mackesy, *Statesmen at War*, 173, 187.
16. Maurice, *Diary of John Moore*, 1:341.
17. Henry Bunbury, *A Narrative of the Campaign in North Holland, 1799* (London: Boone, 1849), 3.
18. HMC, *Dropmore Manuscripts*, Abercromby to Dundas, Klein Ketten, near the Helder, 28 August 1799, 5:333.
19. Maurice, *Diary of Moore*, 1:342.
20. Ibid, 1:343.
21. HMC, *Dropmore Manuscripts*, Abercromby to Dundas, Headquarters, Schagen Brug, 4 September 1799, 5:357–9.
22. Ibid.
23. HEH Townshend Papers (TP) 75/26, Horatio Townshend's account of the Expedition to Holland, 1799.
24. RA GEO/Main/9327–8, Sir R Abercromby to Henry Dundas, Schengen, 11 September 1799.
25. Ibid.
26. HMC, *Dropmore Manuscripts*, Pitt to Grenville, Walmer Castle, 10 September 1799, 5:379–81.
27. RA GEO/Main/9327–8, Sir R Abercromby to Henry Dundas, Schengen, 11 September 1799.

28. HMC, *Dropmore Manuscripts*, Abercromby to Huskisson, Schagenbrug, 4 September 1799, 5:359.
29. TNA WO 1/180, York to Dundas, Headquarters, Schagerbrug, 18 September 1799, ff. 113–117.
30. *LCG*, York to G3, Zyper Sluys, 4 October 1799, 3:274. See also Glover, *Peninsular Preparation*.
31. William Surtees, *Twenty-five Years in the Rifle Brigade* (London: T. Cadell, 1833), 16–17.
32. HMC, *Dropmore Manuscripts*, York to Dundas, Schlagen Bruch, 20 September 1799, Secret and Confidential, 5:417.
33. HEH TP 75/26, Horatio Townshend's account of the Expedition to Holland, 1799.
34. HMC, *Dropmore Manuscripts*, Abercromby to Dundas, Schlager Bruck, 20 September 1799, 5:427.
35. Ibid., Brownrigg to W. Huskisson, Schagen Brug, 26 September 1799, 5:425.
36. Watkins, *Biographical Memoir*, 361.
37. HEH TP 75/26, Horatio Townshend's account of the Expedition to Holland, 1799.
38. *LCG*, York to G3, Zyper Sluys, 4 October 1799, 3:274.
39. RA GEO/Main/9515–22, Duke of York to Henry Dundas, Horse Guards, 28 February 1800.
40. TCD Donoughmore Papers E/10c Diaries of the Hon Christopher Hely-Hutchinson during the Expedition to Egypt, ff. 47–48.
41. WCL ECP 28/6, Journal of Sir Eyre Coote, 27 August 1800.
42. TCD Donoughmore Papers E/10c Diaries of the Hon Christopher Hely-Hutchinson during the expedition to Egypt, ff. 47–48.
43. NRS GD364/1/1085, Draft instructions by Sir William Howe to general officers under his command in the Eastern District, 1798.
44. Maurice, *Diary of Moore*, 1:263.
45. NRS GD364/1/1085, Draft instructions by Sir William Howe to general officers under his command in the Eastern District, 1798.
46. NAM 6807/157/6 Discipline established by Major General Howe for Light Infantry in Battalion, Sarum, September 1774.
47. LAC/MG18/L5/8/1, Wolfe's Instructions for Young Officers, Fair Copy inscribed J. Moore, Ensign 51st Regiment, Minorca, 21 June 1777.
48. Wolfe, *Instructions to Young Officers*, 50.
49. TCD Donoughmore Papers E/10c Diaries of the Hon Christopher Hely-Hutchinson during the Expedition to Egypt, ff. 47–48.
50. See Willson, *Life of Wolfe*, 380; BL Add MS 21649, Gordon to Bouquet, 4 September 1763; WCL Bouquet Papers, Bouquet's Expedition Against the Indians, Volume 1, General Orders, January–July 1764; John Pester, *War and Sport in India, 1802–1806: An Officer's Diary* (London: Heath, Cranton & Ouseley, 1913), 27 July 1803, Shikobad, 134; and SLNSW MS A768, Macquarie Journal, No. 1, 15 December 1787–24 March 1792, 355–367, 16 & 20–21 February 1792.
51. TCD Donoughmore Papers E/10c Diaries of the Hon Christopher Hely-Hutchinson during the expedition to Egypt, 10 June 1800, f. 12.
52. Ibid., 18 August 1800, f. 29.
53. Piers Mackesy, *British Victory in Egypt: The End of Napoleon's Conquest* (London: Routledge, 1995), 36.
54. TCD Donoughmore Papers E/10c Diaries of the Hon Christopher Hely-Hutchinson during the Expedition to Egypt, 6 July 1800, f. 18.
55. Maurice, *Diary of Moore*, 1:377–8.
56. WCL ECP 28/6, Journal of Sir Eyre Coote, 6–8 October 1800.
57. TCD Donoughmore Papers E/10c Diaries of the Hon Christopher Hely-Hutchinson during the expedition to Egypt, 9 October 1800, ff. 38–39.

58. See Roger Knight, *Britain Against Napoleon: The Organization of Victory, 1793–1815* (London: Allen Lane, 2013), 144–151, 176–211.

59. TNA WO 6/21 Expeditions Pt 2 1799–1807, Dundas to Abercromby, Downing Street, 6 October 1800.

60. Ibid., Kleber to Sanson, au Caire, le 23 Vendemiaire an 8.

61. Ibid., Dundas to Abercromby, Downing Street, 6 October 1800.

62. Ibid.

63. Mackesy, *British Victory in Egypt*, 70–1.

64. NLS Murray Papers, MS 21102, Murray to Patrick Murray, Bay of Macri, 21 November 1800.

65. (TNA) WO1/344, Smith to Koehler, HMS Tigre off Alexandria, 27 July 1800, f. 281.

66. William Wittman, *Travels in Turkey, Asia-Minor, Syria, and Across the Desert Into Egypt During the Years 1799, 1800, and 1801, in Company with the Turkish Army, and the British Military Mission* (London: R. Phillips, 1803), 304.

67. TNA WO 1/345, Abercromby to H. Dundas, HMS Kent, Marmarice Harbour, 21 January 1801.

68. WCL ECP 28/6, Journal of Sir Eyre Coote, 8 February 1801.

69. TCD Donoughmore Papers E/10c Diaries of the Hon Christopher Hely-Hutchinson during the expedition to Egypt, 19 January 1801, f. 79.

70. Maurice, *Diary of Moore*, 1:399.

71. TCD Donoughmore Papers E/10c Diaries of the Hon Christopher Hely-Hutchinson during the expedition to Egypt, 9 February 1801, ff. 91–92.

72. Maurice, *Diary of Moore*, Marmaras Bay, 24 January 1801, 1:379.

73. Ibid., Moore's 'Notes Occasioned by Reading General Regnier's Account of the Egyptian Campaign', 2:54.

74. RA GEO/Main/9515–22, Duke of York to Henry Dundas, Horse Guards, 28 February 1800.

75. WCL ECP 28/6, Journal of Sir Eyre Coote, 21 January 1801

76. Ibid., 14–18 January 1801.

77. TCD Donoughmore Papers E/10c Diaries of the Hon Christopher Hely-Hutchinson during the expedition to Egypt, 22 January 1801, f. 80.

78. NLS Murray Papers, MS 21102, Murray to Patrick Murray, Bay of Macri, 21 November 1800.

79. Maurice, *Diary of Moore*, Marmarice Bay, 24 January 1801, 1:398–399.

80. WCL ECP 28/6, Journal of Sir Eyre Coote, 17 February 1801.

81. See, for example, NYPL MssCol 2861, Fort Stanwix orderly book, f. 1; MssCol NYGB 18231, Journal and Orderly Book of John Herbert; and FTA 01M/2164, Monypenny Orderly Book, May–June 1759. For a wider discussion see Houlding, *Fit for Service*, 366.

82. Maharashtra State Archives (MSA), Goa Envoy's Records Diary, no. 3a/606 of 1803–09, Pt. III. Quoted in Cooper, *Anglo-Maratha Campaigns*, 385, n.37.

83. Pargellis, *Military Affairs*, Cumberland to Barrington, Head Quarters at Rothenburg, 28 August 1757, 398.

84. LSC L2019F68, David Dundas, *Rules and Regulations for the Formations, Field-Exercise and Movements of His Majesty's Forces* (London: J. Walter, 1798), Marginalia amendments on 68, 145, 184–185; 241; 255.

85. See John McCavitt & Christopher T. George, *The Man who Captured Washington: Major General Robert Ross and the War of 1812* (Norman: University of Oklahoma Press, 2016), 116–138.

86. See FTA 01M/2164, Monypenny Orderly Book, May–June 1759; and Cecil C. P. Lawson, *A History of the Uniforms of the British Army*, 5 vols (London: Norman, 1961), 3:76–87.

87. WCL ECP 28/6, Journal of Sir Eyre Coote, 8 March 1801.
88. Maurice, *Diary of Moore*, 2:3–4.
89. TNA WO 1/345, Abercromby to Dundas, Camp before Alexandria, 16 March 1801.
90. Ibid.
91. Maurice, *Diary of Moore*, 2:5.
92. Ibid., 2:6–7.
93. TNA WO 1/345, Abercromby to Dundas, Camp before Alexandria, 16 March 1801.
94. Maurice, *Diary of Moore*, 2:7.
95. WCL ECP 28/6, Journal of Sir Eyre Coote, 13 March 1801.
96. Maurice, *Diary of Moore*, 2:8.
97. Joanna Hill, *Wellington's Right Hand: Rowland, Viscount Hill* (Stroud: Spellmount, 2011), 30.
98. WCL ECP 28/6, Journal of Sir Eyre Coote, 13 March 1801.
99. Maurice, *Diary of Moore*, 2:9.
100. TNA WO 1/345, Abercromby to Dundas, Camp before Alexandria, 16 March 1801.
101. NLS Murray Papers, MS 21102, Murray to Patrick Murray, Egypt, 25 March 1801.
102. Maurice, *Diary of Moore*. 2:14–16.
103. WCL ECP 28/6, Journal of Sir Eyre Coote, 21 March 1801.
104. Mackesy, *British Victory in Egypt*, 131.
105. WCL ECP 28/6, Journal of Sir Eyre Coote, 21 March 1801.
106. TCD Donoughmore Papers E/10c Diaries of the Hon Christopher Hely-Hutchinson during the expedition to Egypt, 9 February 1801, ff. 91–92.
107. Quoted in Mackesy, *British Victory in Egypt*, 86.
108. C. C. Lloyd (ed.), *The Keith papers*, 3 vols (London: Navy Records Society, 1950–1955), 2:300, 306–307.
109. Quoted in Thoumine, *Scientific Soldier*, 79.
110. Mackesy, *British Victory in Egypt*, 207.
111. Quoted in Mackesy, *British Victory in Egypt*, 215.
112. WCL ECP 28/7, Journal of Sir Eyre Coote, 17 August 1801.
113. Ibid., 20 August 1801.
114. Ibid., 22 August 1801.
115. R. T. Wilson, *A Narrative of the Expedition to Egypt, Under Sir Ralph Abercrombie* (London: Dutton, 1803), 147–148.
116. Herbert Randolph, *Life of General Sir Robert Wilson*, 2 vols (London: John Murray, 1862), 1:204.
117. WCL ECP 28/7, Journal of Sir Eyre Coote, 22 August 1801.
118. Randolph, *Life of General Sir Robert Wilson*, 1:204.
119. Wilson, *Narrative of the Expedition to Egypt*, 148–149.
120. Dacombe, M. R. & B. J. H. Rowe, 'The adventures of Serjeant Benjamin Miller during his service with the 4th Battalion, Royal Artillery, from 1796 to 1815', *Journal of the Society for Army Historical Research*, 7/27 (January 1928), 34.
121. Mackesy, *Victory in Egypt*, 222–224.
122. Ibid., 100–101.
123. See WCL ECP 23/5, General Order Book of the Expedition to the West Indies, 5–23 June 1794, and Maurice, *Diary of Moore*, 1:89–220.

10 The 'Universal Soldier'

1. BL Add MS 57321, Instructions given to the Battalion of Light Infantry of Irish Militia under my command in Ireland in 1798 and 1799.
2. SLNSW C11 Mitchell Fieldnotes 1811.
3. Ibid.
4. RA GEO/Main/43578-81, Duke of York to George III, Hanover, 6 June 1783.
5. RA GEO/Main/43745-6, Duke of York to George III, Hanover, 5 October 1785.

6. Glover, *Peninsular Preparation*, 118–121.
7. BL Add MS 27600, Colonel David Dundas, Principles of Military Movement, ff. 10v.
8. David Dundas, *Principles of Military Movements* (London: T. Cadell, 1788), iii.
9. BL King's MS 240, Memoranda relative to the Austrian, Prussian, Dutch, and French Troops, 1776, ff. 1–30.
10. Glover, *Peninsula Preparation*, 118–122.
11. Syrett, *Siege and Capture of Havana*, no. 529, Lieutenant-General David Dundas's Memorandum on the Capture of Havana, written in 1800, 316–317.
12. Dundas *Principles of Military Movements*, 12.
13. Houlding, *Fit for Service*, 240–241.
14. Dundas *Principles of Military Movements*, 9–14.
15. Ibid., 222.
16. *LCG*, York to George III, 6 May 1794, 202.
17. TNA WO 3/28, Adjutant General's Circular Letter to General the Marquis Townsend, the Duke of Richmond, Sir William Pitt, KB, Lord A. Gordon, Lord George Lennox, Marquis Cornwallis and Major General Musgrave, 16 May 1795.
18. LSC L2019F54, West's Military Figures for the Practice of Tacticks.
19. Ibid., Short Instructions to Officers . . . calculated to Accompany the Military Figures invented for Elucidating the Theory and Facilitating the Practice of Army Tackicks (London, 1803).
20. As illustrated by the General Henry Burbeck Military Archive. https://historical.ha.com/itm/autographs/military-figures/general-henry-burbeck-military-archive-total-6-items-/a/6057-35050.s [Accessed 7 July 2021].
21. See, for example, FTA 02M/2162, Monypenny Orderly Book, June–July 1758; and NYPL MssCol NYGB 18231, Journal and Orderly Book of John Herbert.
22. Gates, *British Light Infantry Arm*, 64–65.
23. Money, *Partial Reorganisation*, 55.
24. Watkins, *Memoir of York*, 364–365.
25. BL Add MS 57321, Instructions given to the Battalion of Light Infantry of Irish Militia under my command in Ireland in 1798 and 1799.
26. Maurice, *Diary of Moore*, 2:62.
27. RA GEO/Main/9515–22, Duke of York to Henry Dundas, Horse Guards, 28 February 1800.
28. TNA WO 30/72, *Memoir militaire sur l'Angleterre*; J. H. Rose and A. M. Broadly, *Dumouriez and the Defence of England Against Napoleon* (London: J. Lane, 1909).
29. James Carrick Moore, *The Life of Lieutenant-General Sir John Moore*, 2 vols (London: John Murray, 1834), 2:4–6.
30. BL Add MS 57547, Moore to Brownrigg, 17 January 1803.
31. Moore, *Life of Sir John Moore*, 2:5.
32. BL Add MS 57547, Moore to Calvert, 30 January 1803.
33. RA GEO/MAIN/43949–50, York to George III, 4 June 1791.
34. Baron Francis de Rottenburg, *Regulations for the Exercise of Riflemen and Light Infantry: Instructions for Their Conduct in the Field* (London: T. Egerton, 1803), 1.
35. TNA WO 3/36, Calvert to Smith, 12 July 1803.
36. William Stewart, *The Cumloden Papers: The Correspondence of Lieutenant-General Sir William Stewart* (Edinburgh: Privately Published, 1871), 22.
37. *CC*, Cornwallis to Ross, Dublin Castle, 4 February 1800, 3:177.
38. Hanger, *A Letter to . . . Lord Castlereagh*, 74–75.
39. TNA WO 3/32, Calvert to Manningham, 9 May 1800.
40. TNA WO 3/21, Circular to fourteen regiments from Calvert, 9 January 1800.
41. See Ezekiel Baker, *Remarks on Rifles and Guns* (London: T. Egerton, 1803).
42. BL Add MS 57547, Moore to Stewart, 2 October 1802.
43. See Gates, *Light Infantry Arm*, 95–96.

44. Gibbes Rigaud, *Celer et Audax: A Sketch of the Services of the Fifth Battalion Sixtieth Regiment (Rifles) During the Twenty Years of Their Existence* (Oxford: Pickard Hall, 1879), 20.
45. Rottenburg, *Regulations*, 13.
46. SLNSW C11 Mitchell Fieldnotes 1811.
47. Rottenburg, *Regulations*, 20.
48. Gates, *Light Infantry Arm*, 97–98.
49. RA GEO/MAIN/10343, York to George III, 13 August 1801.
50. François Jarry, *Instruction Concerning the Duties of Light Infantry in the Field* (London: A Dulau & Co., 1803), 46.
51. Ibid., 201.
52. Ibid., ii–iv.
53. *CHLWG*, 5–6.
54. Jarry, *Instruction*, vi–vii.
55. Rigaud, *Celer et Audax*, 5.
56. T. H. Cooper, *A Practical Guide for the Light Infantry Officer* (London: Robert Wilks, 1806), 14–16.
57. Jarry, *Instruction*, iv–vi.
58. Ibid., ii–iv.
59. William Stewart, *Outlines of a Plan for the General Reform of the British Land Forces* (London: T. Egerton, 1806), 10–11.
60. Gates, *Light Infantry Arm*, 109.
61. Coote Manningham, *Military Lectures Delivered to the Officers of the 95th (Rifle) Regiment at Shorn-Cliffe Barracks, Kent* (London: T. Egerton, 1803), 2.
62. BL Add MS 57321, Instructions given to the Battalion of Light Infantry of Irish Militia under my command in Ireland in 1798 and 1799.
63. BL Add MS 57547, Moore to Brownrigg, 17 January 1803.
64. NLS MSS 8028, Graham to Calvert, 15 October 1811, f. 33.
65. J. Philippart (ed.), *Royal Military Calendar*, 5 vols (London: T. Egerton, 1820), 3:184–185.
66. Tim Saunders & Rob Yuill, *The Light Division in the Peninsular War, 1808–1811* (Barnsley: Pen & Sword, 2020), 10.
67. W. F. P. Napier, *The Life and Opinions of General Sir Charles James Napier*, 4 vols (London: John Murray, 1857), 1:59.
68. Captain Cooke, *Memoirs of the Late War: The Personal Narrative of Captain Cooke of the 43rd Regiment, Light Infantry*, 2 vols (London: Colburn & Bentley, 1831), 1:32–33.
69. W. C. E. Napier, *The Early Military Life of General Sir George T. Napier* (London: John Murray, 1886), 14.
70. Cooke, *Memoirs of the Late War*, 1:32–33.
71. Officer Notebook, 'Peculiarities in the Drill of the 52nd', Block House Museum, Wellington, Ontario, Canada. Quoted in Bartlet, 'The Development of the British Army', 178.
72. John Cross, *A System of Drill and Manoeuvres as Practised in the 52nd Light Infantry Regiment* (London: T. Egerton, 1823), 8.
73. Officer Notebook, 'Peculiarities in the Drill of the 52nd'. Quoted in Bartlet, 'The Development of the British Army', 178.
74. Cooke, *Memoirs of the Late War*, 1:5.
75. NLS MSS 8028, Mackenzie to Moore, 28 January 1808, f. 17.
76. Cambridge University Library (CUL) GBR/0012/MS Add.9340/1, John Moore Letterbook 1803–1805, Moore to Calvert, 30 January 1804.
77. TNA WO 3/152/56, Calvert to RH Crewe, 27 July 1803.
78. CUL GBR/0012/MS Add.9340/1, Moore to Calvert, 22 January 1804.
79. TNA WO 40/29, Secretary at War to the colonel of the 68th and 85th Regiments, 10 September 1808.

80. See NRS GD1/6/5/1 Campbell to Cornwallis, 27 May 1787; and RA GEO/MAIN/43751, York to G3, 20 October 1785.
81. Christopher Hibbert (ed.), *Recollections of Rifleman Harris* (London: Archon Books, 1970), 23.
82. NLS MS 21261, Stuart to Moore, Aranjuez, 27 October 1809.
83. BRBML OSB MS 168/18/5 Journal of Henry Clinton 1808–9, entry for Sahagun, 22 December 1808.
84. Hibbert, *Recollections of Rifleman Harris*, 23.
85. BRBML OSB MS 168/18/7 Journal of Henry Clinton 1808–9, entry for Corunna, 16 January 1809.
86. Anonymous, *The Personal Narrative of a Private Soldier who Served in the Forty-Second Highlanders for Twelve Years During the Late War* (London: John Murray, 1821), 114–117.
87. NAM MS 6807/148, Papers and Correspondence of Ensign Augustus Dobree, 14th Regiment, 16 January 1809.
88. NAM MS 6807/452, Colbourne to his sister, Mrs Duke Yonge, February 1809.
89. NAM MS 8009/50, Journal of Captain Commissary John Charlton, Corps of Royal Artillery Drivers.
90. *The Times*, 2 February 1809.
91. *WD*, Memorandum on the Defence of Portugal, London, 7 March 1809, 4:261–3.
92. *LCG*, York to George III, Zyper Sluys, 4 October 1799, 3:274.
93. TNA WO 1/344, Abercromby, 19 May 1800.
94. Charles Oman, *Wellington's Army, 1809–1814* (London: E. Arnold, 1913), 165.
95. *SD*, General Order, Abrantes, 18 June 1809, 6:288–289.
96. See Huw J. Davies, *Spying for Wellington: British Military Intelligence in the Peninsular War* (Norman: University of Oklahoma Press, 2018), 71–90, 123–155.
97. William Rudolf Fletcher, '"Scientifics" and "Wycombites": A Study of the Quartermaster General's Department of the British Army, 1799–1814' (Unpublished PhD Thesis, King's College London, 2019), 102–103.
98. R. Gleig, *A Memoir of the Late Major-General Robert Craufurd Reprinted from the Military Panorama of October 1812 with an Account of his Funeral* (London: Private Impression, 1842), 5–6.
99. Quoted in Ian Fletcher, *Craufurd's Light Division: The Life of Robert Craufurd and his Command of the Light Division* (Tunbridge Wells: Spellmount, 1991), 43.
100. See Fletcher, *Craufurd's Light Division*, Craufurd's Standing Orders, 206–231.
101. W. F. P. Napier, *History of the War in the Peninsula and in the South of France from the Year 1807 to the Year 1814*, 6 vols (London: Thomas and William Boone, 1847), 2:136.
102. *CHLWG*, 128–132.
103. See C. Craufurd & R. Craufurd, *An Account of Some of the Most Remarkable Events of the War Between the Prussians, Austrians, and Russians, from 1756 to 1763, and a Treatise on Several Branches of the Military Art. With Plans and Maps, Translated from the Second Edition of the German Original of J.G. Tielke, by Captain C. Craufurd and Captain R. Craufurd*, 2 vols (London: J. Walter, 1788).
104. Fletcher, '"Scientifics" and "Wycombites"', 103.
105. John Kincaid, *Adventures in the Rifle Brigade and Random Shots from a Rifleman* (York: Leonaur, 2010), 194–195.
106. Jonathan Leach, *Rough Sketches of the Life of an Old Soldier* (London: Longman, 1831), 87–103.
107. Kincaid, *Adventures in the Rifle Brigade*, 195.
108. William Scarth Moorsom, *Historical Record of the Fifty-second Regiment (Oxfordshire Light Infantry) from the Year 1755 to the Year 1858* (London: Bentley, 1860), 117.
109. *WD*, Wellington to Craufurd, Viseu, 8 March 1810, 5:553–554.
110. Kincaid, *Adventures in the Rifle Brigade*, 196.
111. See Gates, *British Light Infantry Arm*, 159.

112. For more on interrogation and intelligence collection, see Davies, *Spying for Wellington*, 91–122.
113. Napier, *War in the Peninsula*, 2:404–405.
114. Kincaid, *Adventures in the Rifle Brigade*, 200.
115. NLS MSS 8028, Graham to Calvert, 15 October 1811, f. 33.
116. *WD*, Wellington to Cotton, Convent of Busaco, 21 September 1810, 6:459–460.
117. NAM MS 9404/476, Picton to Marryat, 31 October 1810.
118. Gates, *Light Infantry Arm*, 170.
119. Napier, *War in the Peninsula*, 3:26.
120. Leach, *Rough Sketches*, 166.
121. Blakiston, *Twelve Years Military Adventure*, 2:344–345.
122. Edward Costello, *The Adventures of a Soldier; or Memoirs of Edward Costello* (London: Henry Colburn, 1841), 95.
123. *WD*, Wellington to Liverpool, Villa Formosa, 8 May 1811, 7:528–37.
124. Leach, *Rough Sketches*, 213.
125. Costello, *Adventures of a Soldier*, 122–123.
126. See Neil Campbell, *Instructions for Light Infantry and Riflemen: Founded Upon the Regulations for the Exercise of Riflemen and Light Infantry in Close Order, and the Regulations for the Exercise of Riflemen and Light Infantry* (London: T. Egerton, 1807, reprinted 1813). See also, Saunders & Yuil, *Light Division in the Peninsular War*, 298, n.8.
127. John Dobbs, *Recollections of an Old 52nd Man* (Waterford: T. S. Harvey, 1859), 25.
128. Kincaid, *Adventures in the Rifle Brigade*, 75–76.
129. Costello, *Adventures of a Soldier*, 124.
130. Ibid., 14–17.
131. Joseph Donaldson, *Recollections of an Eventful Life, Chiefly Passed in the Army* (Glasgow: W. R. McPhun, 1824), 150–151.
132. Costello, *Adventures of a Soldier*, 14–17.
133. Quoted in Muir, *Path to Victory*, 443.
134. Fletcher, *Craufurd's Light Division*, 200–201.

11 'The Scientifics'

1. SLNSW Mitchell Papers C27, Mitchell Diaries 1819–1821. Entry for 11 March 1821.
2. SLNSW C11 Mitchell Fieldnotes 1811.
3. For more on Wellington's strategy in the Peninsular War, see Davies, *Wellington's Wars*, 99–125.
4. *CHLWG*, 133–137.
5. Thoumine, *Scientific Soldier*, Le Marchant to Mary, Tournai, 26 November 1793, 30.
6. Le Marchant, *Memoirs of Le Marchant*, 44.
7. Quoted in Thoumine, *Scientific Soldier*, 46.
8. J. G. Le Marchant, 'Notes on Sword Construction', quoted in Thoumine, *Scientific Soldier*, 44.
9. Quoted in Thoumine, *Scientific Soldier*, 53.
10. Ibid., 56.
11. Hungerton Letters; Guildford, 10 October 1798, quoted in Thoumine, *Scientific Soldier*, 57.
12. Le Marchant, *Memoirs of Le Marchant*, Craufurd to Le Marchant, 1798, 83.
13. Ibid., 65, 70.
14. Ibid., 70–77. See also Fletcher, '"Scientifics" and "Wycombites"', 116–117.
15. Fletcher, '"Scientifics" and "Wycombites"', 116–117.
16. Glover, *Peninsular Preparation*, 187–213.
17. Le Marchant, *Memoirs of Le Marchant*, 77.

18. NLS Murray Papers, MS 21103, Murray to Augusta, High Wycombe, 22 April 1802.
19. Le Marchant, *Memoirs of Le Marchant*, 77.
20. Supreme Board of Commissioners Royal Military College, Report draft of Royal Warrant, 14 October 1801, Royal Military Academy Sandhurst Archive, RMC WO 99/2, Box 3. Quoted in Fletcher, '"Scientifics" and "Wycombites"', 122.
21. Le Marchant, *Memoirs of Le Marchant*, 77.
22. J. G. Le Marchant, 'An Outline of a Plan for a Regular Course of Military Instruction', quoted in Thoumine, *Scientific Soldier*, 64.
23. *HLWG*, 7.
24. Goldsmith, *Masculinity and Danger*, 87–91.
25. Le Marchant, *Memoirs of Le Marchant*, 78.
26. J. G. Le Marchant, 'An Outline of a Plan for a Regular Course of Military Instruction', quoted in Thoumine, *Scientific Soldier*, 64.
27. Hungerton Letters, 8 March 1799, quoted in Thoumine, *Scientific Soldier*, 68.
28. Ibid.
29. Fletcher, '"Scientifics" and "Wycombites"', 124–125.
30. Ibid., 133–134.
31. Draft Royal Warrant, 14 October 1801, RMASA, RMC WO 99/2, Box 3. Quoted in Fletcher, '"Scientifics" and "Wycombites"', 134.
32. House of Commons, *Report from the Select Committee on Sandhurst Royal Military College* (London: HMSO, 1855), Howard Douglas's evidence, 15 May 1855, 157.
33. See Isaac Dalby, *A Course of Mathematics, Designed for the Use of Officers and Cadets, of the Royal Military College* (London: W. Glendinning, 1807).
34. As evidenced by Thomas Mitchell's map-making in the Peninsula. See, for example, SLNSW Mitchell Diaries C18, Field Notebook of the Battlefield of Fuentes d'Onoro 1811 (Surveyed in 1814).
35. Anonymous, 'Military Surveying No. III', *United Service Journal and Naval and Military Magazine*, 2/1320 (1830), 487–488.
36. Letter by Robert Brownrigg, 12 January 1805, RMASA, RMC WO 99/19, Box 23. Quoted in Fletcher, '"Scientifics" and "Wycombites"', 140.
37. See Glover, *Peninsular Preparation*, 211–213, Syllabus of the Royal Military Academy Woolwich in the early 1790s from W. D. Jones, *Records of the Royal Military Academy* (Woolwich: Royal Military Academy, 1851).
38. Anonymous, 'Military Surveying No. III', 487.
39. 'Having been favoured with the Perusal of the following Instructions relative to the Military School at High Wycombe, we present the same to our Readers, as containing important Information', *British Military Library or Journal*, 2/17 (February 1800), 161–163.
40. *CHLWG*, 133–137.
41. 'Instructions relative to the Military School', 161–162.
42. Le Marchant to Stewart, 18 June 1806, RMC Letterbooks, 3, 124. Quoted in Thoumine, *Scientific Soldier*, 104.
43. See J. G. Le Marchant, *An Outline for the Formation of a General Staff to the Army: To His Royal Highness Frederick Duke of York Field Marshal; Commander in Chief of His Majesty's Forces &c. &c. &c.* (High Wycombe: Royal Military College, 1802), Royal Military Academy Sandhurst Central Library, quoted in Fletcher, '"Scientifics" and "Wycombites"', 110.
44. Le Marchant to Stewart, 18 June 1806, RMC Letterbooks, 3, 124. Quoted in Thoumine, *Scientific Soldier*, 104–105.
45. WCL CP MS 10/4, Clinton to Phillips[?], 13 June 1775.
46. Le Marchant, *Memoirs of Le Marchant*, 177–178.
47. Le Marchant to Long, 4 December 1808, Sandhurst Papers, 8(a), No. 1. Quoted in Thoumine, *Scientific Soldier*, 127.
48. Thoumine, *Scientific Soldier*, 142–143.

49. Le Marchant to York, 23 July 1811, RMC Letterbooks, 6. Quoted in Thoumine, *Scientific Soldier*, 140–142.
50. *Royal Military Chronicle*, 'Course of Tactics' (June 1811), 40–46.
51. Le Marchant, *Memoirs of Le Marchant*, Le Marchant to Colonel Birch, March 1812, 201–202.
52. Le Marchant, *Memoirs of Le Marchant*, 177.
53. Ibid., Le Marchant to Colonel Birch, March 1812, 201–202.
54. Ibid.
55. Le Marchant to R. B. Long, 7 May 1812, Sandhurst Papers, 28(a), No. 2. Quoted in Thoumine, *Scientific Soldier*, 172.
56. William Tomkinson, *The Diary of a Cavalry Officer in the Peninsular and Waterloo Campaigns, 1809–1815* (London: Swann Sonnenschein, 1894), 151.
57. Le Marchant, *Memoirs of Le Marchant*, 289.
58. H. A. Bruce, *Life of General William Napier*, 2 vols (London: John Murray, 1864), 1:275, Dalbiac to Napier, Ripon, 17 December 1834.
59. William Grattan, 'Reminiscences of a subaltern: Battle of Salamanca', *United Services Journal* (June 1834), 185.
60. S. A. C. Cassels (ed.), *Peninsular Portrait, 1811–1814. The Letters of Captain William Bragge Third (King's Own) Dragoons* (London: Oxford University Press, 1963), 63–64.
61. Cassels, *Peninsular Portrait*, 63–64.
62. Le Marchant, *Memoirs of Le Marchant*, 307.
63. For a detailed account of the siege of Burgos, see Charles Esdaile & Philip Freeman, *Burgos in the Peninsular War, 1808–1814: Occupation, Siege, Aftermath* (London: Palgrave, 2015), 84–125.
64. *SD*, Thomas Sydenham to Henry Wellesley, Villa Toro, 10 October 1812, 7:447–54.
65. BL Add MS 35060, Wellington to Hill, Villa de Toro near Burgos, 21 September 1812.
66. Davies, *Wellington's Wars*, 146–170.
67. Henry Lloyd, 'A Rhapsody on the Present System of French Politics: on the Projected Invasion, and the Means to Defeat It' (1779), reproduced in Patrick J. Speelman (ed.), *War, Society and Enlightenment: The Works of General Lloyd* (Leiden: Brill, 2005), 347–348.
68. USL WP 1/348, Popham to Wellington, Santander, 4 August 1812.
69. BL Loan 57/108, Wellington to Popham, Villatoro, 17 October 1812.
70. USL WP 1/351, Wellington to Torrens, Rueda, 31 October 1812.
71. NLS Murray Papers, MS 21102, Murray to Patrick Murray, London, 13 February 1812.
72. Ibid., Murray to Thomas Graham, London, 10 May 1812.
73. *WD*, Wellington to Murray, Fuente Guinaldo, 28 May 1812, 9:181.
74. Ibid., Valladolid, 7 September 1812, 9:398.
75. NLS Murray Papers, MS 21103, Murray to Augusta, High Wycombe, 22 April 1802.
76. John Harding-Edgar, *Next to Wellington. General Sir George Murray: The Story of a Scottish Soldier and Statesman, Wellington's Quartermaster General* (London: Helion & Co., 2018), 64; Captain Tyron Still to Le Marchant, Torres Vedras, 28 October 1810. Sandhurst Papers, 2(a), No. 1. Quoted in Thoumine, *Scientific Soldier*, 110.
77. Ward Draft, Ch. III, 31–32. Quoted in Harding-Edgar, *Next to Wellington*, 70.
78. TNA WO 43/292, Brownrigg to Duke of York, Horse Guards, 26 June 1803.
79. Ibid. The Depot was based on the Austrian Imperial Archive, details of which had been sent the Duke of York in 1799. See NRS GD364/1/1120 Remarks on the Imperial Archive at Vienna, by the Austrian General Gomez (translated from the German), obtained by Alexander Hope and forwarded to the Duke of York.
80. TNA WO 43/292, York to Castlereagh, 3 August 1805.
81. NLS Murray Papers, MS 21103, Murray to Augusta, Horse Guards, 16 July 1803.

82. NLS Adv MS 46.1.21, Miscellaneous Papers Acquired by Murray before he went to Spain, consisting of letters and reports describing battles and campaigns etc.

83. NLS Adv MS 46.6.2–3, Previous Campaigns in Portugal and Spain, 1762, 1793, 1796.

84. NLS Adv MS 46.5.1, Lt Col Cathcart's Copy of 'Instructions to Officers of the Quartermaster Generals' Department'.

85. Captain Tyron Still to Le Marchant, Torres Vedras, 28 October 1810. Sandhurst Papers, 2(a), No. 1. Quoted in Thoumine, *Scientific Soldier*, 110.

86. NRS GD364/1/1196, Murray to Lindenthal, Cartaxo, 8 December 1810.

87. SLNSW A290 Mitchell Correspondence 1711–1818, Murray to Mitchell, Freneda, 3 October 1811, ff. 65–71.

88. Ibid.

89. SLNSW C14 Mitchell Diaries – Torres Vedras Fieldbook 1811.

90. *Colburn's United Service Magazine, and Naval and Military Journal*, 1863, 272–273.

91. NAM MS 8202/65, Notebook belonging to George Scovell, dealing with the formation of the Staff Provost Corps about 1854.

92. For more on the Guides, see Mark Urban, *The Man Who Broke Napoleon's Codes: The Story of George Scovell* (London: Faber, 2001). See also *WD*, Wellington to Bathurst, Freneda, 24 February 1813, 10:140.

93. John Churchill, Duke of Marlborough, *The Case of his Grace the D— of M— . As Design'd To be Represented by him to the Honourable House of Commons, in Vindication of Himself from the Charge of the Commissioners of Accounts In Relation To the Two and Half per Cent Bread and Bread Waggons* (London: A. Baldwin, 1712), 16.

94. Saxe, *Reveries*, 156.

95. *Essay of the Art of War: in which the General Principles of All the Operations of War in the Field are Fully Explained. The Whole Collected from the Opinions of the best Authors* (London: A. Millar, 1761), 207.

96. Julia Page (ed.), *Intelligence Officer in the Peninsula: Letters & Diaries of Major The Hon. Edward Charles Cocks, 1786–1812* (London: Spellmount, 1986), Cocks to Somers Cocks, Villa Vicosa, 5 September 1809, 39. Stockdale's map was not particularly accurate. Lopez's map was utilised widely by the army, and even this was considered somewhat inaccurate. See R. J. B. Muir and C. J. Esdaile, 'Strategic Planning in a Time of Small Government: The Wars Against Revolutionary and Napoleonic France, 1793–1815', in C. M. Woolgar (ed.), *Wellington Studies I* (Southampton: University of Southampton Press, 1996), 1–90.

97. Davies, *Spying for Wellington*, 71–90.

98. See, for example, Arquivo Histórico Militar, Lisbon (AHM) MS 1/14/199/24, Stuart to D'Urban, Lisbon 31 May 1810.

99. *SD*, Memorandum on the system for regulating the Intelligence Department in the Army under the Command of Major General the Hon. A. Wellesley, November 1804, 2:464–465.

100. Davies, *Spying for Wellington*, 91–122.

101. TNA WO 3/604, Torrens to Murray, London, 26 December 1812, ff. 9–11.

102. NLS Murray Papers, MS 21103, Murray to Augusta, Freneda, 14 April 1813.

103. *WD*, Wellington to Bathurst, Freneda, 11 May 1813, 10:372.

104. F. S. Larpent, *The Private Journal of F.S. Larpent, Esq. Judge Advocate General of the British Forces in the Peninsula attached to the Headquarters of Lord Wellington during the Peninsular War from 1812 to its Close*, 3 vols (London: Richard Bentley, 1853), 28 August 1813, 3:246.

105. G. C. Moore (ed.), *The Autobiography of Lieutenant-General Sir Harry Smith* (London: John Murray, 1901), 140–151.

106. For more on this campaign, see Ian Robertson, *Wellington Invades France: The Final Phase of the Peninsular War, 1813–1814* (London: Greenhill, 2003).

12 'The Dread of Innovation'

1. Quoted in Bruce, *Life of General Sir William Napier*, 1:174.
2. Quoted Ibid., 1:180–181.
3. Horace Churchill to his father, La Câteau, 24 June 1815. Quoted in Bruce, *Life of General Sir William Napier*, 1:175–180.
4. Quoted in John Bew, 'Waterloo: Beyond the Battlefield', *History Today*, 63/9, 2013. https://www.historytoday.com/archive/waterloo-beyond-battlefield [Accessed 29 March 2021].
5. *WD*, Wellington to Beresford, Gonesse, 2 July 1815, 12:529.
6. Horace Churchill to his father, La Câteau, 24 June 1815. Quoted in Bruce, *Life of General Sir William Napier*, 1:175–180.
7. For an analysis of the enduring memory of the Battle of Waterloo, see Alan Forrest, *Waterloo* (Oxford: Oxford University Press, 2015).
8. Quoted in Bruce, *Life of General Sir William Napier*, 1:181–182.
9. Charles Vane (ed.), *The Memoranda and Correspondence of Robert Stewart, Viscount Castlereagh*, 12 vols (London: Henry Coulburn, 1848–54), Liverpool to Castlereagh, Fife House, 15 July 1815, 10:430.
10. For an in-depth examination of the allied occupation of France in the wake of Napoleon's final defeat, see Christine Haynes, *Our Friends the Enemies: The Occupation of France After Napoleon* (Cambridge, MA: Harvard University Press, 2018).
11. Michael Howard, 'Wellington and the British Army', in Michael Howard (ed.), *Wellingtonian Studies* (Aldershot: Privately Published, 1959), 89.
12. John Mitchell, *Thoughts on Tactics and Military Organization: Together with an Enquiry into the Power and Position of Russia* (London: Longman, 1838), 11.
13. Jeffrey A. Auerbach, *Imperial Boredom: Monotony and the British Empire* (Oxford: Oxford University Press, 2018), 110.
14. Quoted in Jay Luvaas, *The Education of an Army: British Military Thought, 1815–1940* (London: Cassell, 1964), 4.
15. Thomas Seaton, *From Cadet to Colonel: The Record of a Life of Active Service*, 2 vols (London: Hurst and Blackett, 1866), 1: 8–9.
16. See Hew Strachan, *Wellington's Legacy: Reform of the British Army, 1830–54* (Manchester: Manchester University Press, 1986).
17. Luvaas, *Education of an Army*, 4.
18. Hew Strachan, *From Waterloo to Balaclava: Tactics, Technology, and the British Army 1815–1854* (Cambridge: Cambridge University Press, 1985), vii–viii.
19. Luvaas, *Education of an Army*, 4.
20. Bikrama Jit Hasrat, *Anglo-Sikh Relations, 1799–1849: A Reappraisal of the Rise and Fall of the Sikhs* (New Delhi: V.V. Research Institute Book Agency, 1968), 150–151. See NAI SD37/1/133, Wade to Macnaghten, Ludhiana, 12 April 1837, for evidence of the considerable alarm that Ranjit Singh's forces were causing the British.
21. See Jean-Marie LaFont, *Fauj-i-Khas: Maharaja Ranjit Singh and His French Officers* (Amritsar: Guru Nanak Dev University, 2002).
22. Benjamin D. Hopkins, *The Making of Modern Afghanistan* (Basingstoke: Palgrave, 2008), 61–81. See Punjab Archives Lahore (PAL) MS 115/79, Prinsep to Wade, 14 May 1831, for evidence of British attempts to arrest or curtail the movements of mercenaries.
23. Luvaas, *Education of an Army*, 9–11.
24. 'Traité des grandes opérations militaires, contenant l'histoire critique des campagnes de Frédéric II., comparées à celles de L'Empereur Napoléon; avec Recueil des Principes généraux de l'art de la guerre', *Edinburgh Review*, 35 (1821), 377–409, in particular 338, 379–381, 396, 400–401, 404–405. See also Luvaas, *Education of an Army*, 10–11.
25. For more on the linkages between Bülow and Lloyd, see Khule, 'War without contact', 1–26.
26. James Shaw Kennedy, *Notes on the Battle of Waterloo: With a Brief Memoir of His Life and Services and Plan for the Defence of Canada* (London: John Murray, 1865), 11–12.

27. For more on Mitchell's publishing tribulations, see J. H. L. Cumpston, *Thomas Mitchell: Surveyor General & Explorer* (Oxford: Oxford University Press, 1965).

28. Napier to Lord Frederick Fitzclarence, Blackheath, 1848. Quoted in Bruce, *Life of General Sir William Napier*, 2:277–279.

29. 'The regeneration of the army', *United Service Magazine*, 1:1849, 1.

30. Napier to Lord Frederick Fitzclarence, Blackheath, 1848. Quoted in Bruce, *Life of General Sir William Napier*, 2:277–279.

31. Quoted in Luvaas, *Education of an Army*, 27–28.

32. Napier, *War in the Peninsula*, 1:183–184.

33. Ibid., 4:65.

34. Ibid., 5:214.

35. Ibid., 3:90–91.

36. Ibid., 1:20–21.

37. For more on the Cardwell reforms, see Edward M. Spiers, *The Late Victorian Army, 1868–1902* (Manchester: Manchester University Press, 1992).

38. Bruce, *Life of General Sir William Napier*, 2:377–378.

39. 'Napier's *History of the War in the Peninsula* (Article Third)', in *Quarterly Review*, 57 (1836), 492–529. Murray was identified as the author of the article in Samuel Smiles, *A Publisher and his Friends: Memoir and Correspondence of John Murray, With an Account of the Origin and Progress of the House, 1768–1843*, 2 vols (New York: Dossier Press, 1904), 2:284.

40. 'Napier's *History of the War in the Peninsula* (Article Third)', 513, 529.

41. Napier, *War in the Peninsula*, 2:9.

42. 'Napier's *History of the War in the Peninsula* (Article Third)', 498, 501.

43. Ibid., 507–508, 510.

44. Napier, *War in the Peninsula*, 2:263–264.

45. 'Napier's *History of the War in the Peninsula* (Article Third)', 526, 527.

46. Napier, *War in the Peninsula*, 2:126.

47. 'Napier's *History of the War in the Peninsula* (Article Third)', 526, 529.

48. See William Napier, 'Reply to the Third Article in the Quarterly Review on Colonel Napier's History of the Peninsular War', *London and Westminster Review*, 26 (1837), 543.

49. Mitchell, *Thoughts on Tactics*, 1–3.

50. Ibid., 120. Quoted in Strachan, *Waterloo to Balaclava*, 9.

51. Mitchell, *Thoughts on Tactics*, 1–24.

52. See John Mitchell, *Biographies of Eminent Soldiers of the Last Four Centuries* (London: William Blackwood, 1865).

53. Mitchell, *Thoughts on Tactics*, ix.

54. Henry Torrens, *Field Exercise and Evolutions of the Army* (London: William Clowes, 1824), 1–2.

55. Strachan, *Waterloo to Balaclava*, 16–19.

56. Torrens, *Field Exercise*, 1–2.

57. Ibid., 217–218.

58. NLS MS 1848, Cochrane to Brown, 23 July 1852, f. 55.

59. Ferdinand Brock Tupper (ed.), *The Life and Correspondence of Major-General Sir Isaac Brock* (London: Simpkin, Marshall & Co., 1845), Brock to Gordon, Quebec, 6 September 1807, 64–65.

60. Ibid., Brock to Prevost, York, 2 December 1811, 123–130.

61. See LOC RG 107/M221/R63, Jackson to Monroe, 27 December 1814 for Jackson's defence preparations.

62. *SD*, Keane to Wellington, May 1815, enclosing 'A Journal of the Operations against New Orleans', 10:396.

63. George Wrottesley, *Life and Correspondence of Field Marshal Sir John Burgoyne*, 2 vols (London: Richard Bentley, 1873), 1:301–304, Harry D. Jones, 2nd Captain Royal Engineers, Dauphin Island, 30 March 1815.

64. Vincent Nolte, *Fifty Years in Both Hemispheres: Or, Reminiscences of the Life of a Former Merchant* (New York: Redfield, 1854), 221.
65. Moore, *Autobiography of Harry Smith*, 226–247.
66. Nolte, *Fifty Years in Both Hemispheres*, 221–222.
67. Mitchell, *Thoughts on Tactics*, 11–12.
68. See James Belich, *The New Zealand Wars and the Victorian Interpretation of Racial Conflict* (Auckland: Auckland University Press, 1998), 293–298.
69. James E. Alexander, *Incidents of the Maori War, New Zealand in 1860–1861* (London: Richard Bentley, 1863), 296–297.
70. Alexander Turnbull Library, Wellington, (ATL) MS–1712, Journal of Spencer Perceval Nicholl 15 October 1863 to 31 December 1864, f. 25.
71. James E. Alexander, *Bush Fighting Illustrated by Remarkable Actions and Incidents of the Maori War in New Zealand* (London: Low, Marston, Low & Searle, 1873), 1–19.
72. John Connor, *The Australian Frontier Wars 1788–1838* (Sydney: University of New South Wales Press, 2002), 19–20.
73. SLNSW MS A1597, Harris, 20 May 1791. Quoted in Conner, *Australian Frontier Wars*, 20.
74. Peter Dennis, Jeffrey Grey, Ewan Morris & Robin Prior (eds.), *Oxford Companion to Australian Military History* (Oxford: Oxford University Press, 2008), 5.
75. Dennis Collins, *An Account of the English Colony of New South Wales, 1788–1801*, 2 vols (London: T. Cadell, 1802), 1:383.
76. Quoted in Connor, *Australian Frontier Wars*, 47.
77. SLNSW MS A1677/4, Samuel Hassall to Thomas Hassell, 16 March 1816.
78. *Sydney Gazette*, 14 May 1814.
79. SLNSW MS A773 Macquarie Diary, 10 April 1816.
80. Ibid.
81. Stephen Gapps, *The Sydney Wars: Conflict in the Early Colony, 1788–1817* (Sydney: University of New South Wales Press, 2018), 230.
82. Connor, *Australian Frontier Wars*, 51.
83. National Library of Australia, Canberra (NLA) MS 202, Macquarie to Schaw and Wallis, 30 April 1816.
84. Commonwealth of Australia, *Historical Records of Australia: Series I: Governors' Despatches to and from England*, 37 vols (Sydney: Library Committee of the Commonwealth Parliament, 1917), Macquarie to Bathurst, 4 April 1817, 9:365–366.
85. Strachan, *Waterloo to Balaclava*, 20.
86. John Le Couteur, *The Rifle: Its Effects on the War; Or National Military Organization; and Preparation for Defence* (London: Parker, Furnival & Parker, 1855), 54.
87. *Naval and Military Gazette*, 9 April 1842, 230.
88. TNA WO 135/3, Memo by Smith, 24 February 1844, f. 86.
89. Frederick Fitzclarence, *Memoranda by Lieut.-General Lord Frederick Fitzclarence, for the Use of Young Officers Assembled in Poona During the Period of Exercise in December 1853, Including Instructions Applicable to a Combination of the Three Arms* (London: Parker, Furnival & Parker, 1854), 2.
90. Frederick Fitzclarence, *Suggestions for Brigade and Light Infantry Movements* (London: Parker, Furnival & Parker, 1851), 17–19.
91. See John Ryder, *Four Years' Service in India by a Private Soldier* (Leicester: W. H. Burton, 1853), 117; and Christopher Thomas Atkinson, *The South Wales Borderers, 24th Foot, 1689–1937* (Cambridge: Cambridge University Press, 1937), 302.
92. *Royal Military Magazine*, 1852, 1:83. Quoted in Strachan, *Waterloo to Balaclava*, 20–21.
93. For more on British and European campaigns of conquest in Africa, see Bruce Vandervort, *Wars of Imperial Conquest in Africa, 1830–1914* (London: UCL Press, 1998), 56–112.

94. Daniel R. Headrick, *The Tools of Empire: Technology and European Imperialism in the Nineteenth Century* (Oxford: Oxford University Press, 1981), 83–96.

95. Strachan, *Waterloo to Balaclava*, 33.

96. Lieut. Gen. Lord Viscount Gough to *London Gazette*, 8 October 1841. Quoted in Headrick, *Tools of Empire*, 87.

97. NAI Foreign, Secret Consultations, Memorandum by Mohan Lal, 28 December 1841, ff. 480–482.

98. For evidence of the methods employed to counter the technological advantages of European invaders in Afghanistan, see Louis Dupree, *Afghanistan* (Princeton: Princeton University Press, 1973), 343–413.

99. Quoted in William Dalrymple, *Return of a King: The Battle for Afghanistan, 1839–42* (London: Bloomsbury, 2013), 373–374.

100. NAM MS 6912/6, Thomas Souter to his wife, Describing the retreat from Kabul, 1842.

101. NAM MS 8301/60, Diary of Surgeon-Major William Brydon, entry for 13 January 1842.

102. Seaton, *From Cadet to Colonel*, 186.

103. 'Sir Charles Napier on National Defence', By the Editor, *United Service Magazine*, 1:1852, 424.

104. Quoted in Bruce, *Life of General Sir William Napier*, 2:377–378.

105. Luvaas, *Education of an Army*, 34.

106. Quoted in Orlando Figes, *Crimea: The Last Crusade* (London: Allen Lane, 2010), 211.

107. NAM MS 7606/10, Crimean Journal, 1854, ff. 54–55.

108. Quoted in Figes, *Crimea*, 215.

Conclusion

1. Pargellis, *Military Affairs*, Cumberland to Loudoun, St. James, 2 December 1756, 253.

2. RA DCP Descriptions of Cumberland Lodge are derived from 'Inventory of Household Furniture of His Late Royal Highness The Duke of Cumberland at Windsor Great Lodge' [1765–1766].

3. Pargellis, *Military Affairs*, Cumberland to Loudoun, St. James, 2 December 1756, 253.

4. Pargellis, Military Affairs, Cumberland to Barrington, Head Quarters at Rothenburg, 28 August 1757, 398.

5. Miakinkov, *War and Enlightenment in Russia*, 6.

6. Richie Robertson, *The Enlightenment: The Pursuit of Happiness, 1680–1790* (London: Allen Lane, 2020), xv.

7. Beattie, 'Amherst and the Conquest of Canada', 79–80.

8. Syrett, *Siege and Capture of Havana*, No. 289, Pocock to Governor Don Juan de Prado, 15 June 1762, 192.

9. Lushington, *Life of Harris*, 78–79.

10. Colin Lindsay, 'Narrative of the Occupation and Defence of the Island of St Lucie against the French, 1779', in Alexander, Lord Lindsay (ed.), *Lives of the Lindsays; Or, A Memoir of the Houses of Crawford and Balcarres*, 3 vols (London: John Murray, 1858), 3:346.

11. Webster, *Journal of William Amherst*, 15–16.

12. HEH AB 303, Brigadier Charles Lawrence, Order for the Attack on Louisbourg, May 1758.

13. Willson, *Life and Letters of Wolfe*, Wolfe to Walter Wolfe, Camp before Louisbourg, 27 July 1758, 384–386.

14. James Sullivan (ed.), *The Papers of Sir William Johnson*, 14 vols (Albany: University of the State of New York, 1921–1965), Amherst to Johnson, 16 June 1763, 4:149.

15. WCL AP MS 2/94, Amherst to Gage, Albany, 1 August 1761.

16. *Pennsylvania Gazette*, 18 August 1763, quoted in David Dixon, *Never Come to Peace Again: Pontiac's Uprising and the Fate of the British Empire in North America* (Norman: Oklahoma University Press, 2005), 313.

17. *PHB*, Amherst Memorandum, 7 July 1763, 4:301. See also Elizabeth A. Fenn, 'Biological warfare in eighteenth-century North America: beyond Jeffrey Amherst', *Journal of American History*, 86 (1999–2000), 1552–1580.

18. Quoted in Leah Hochman, *The Ugliness of Moses Mendelssohn: Aesthetics, Religion and Morality in the Eighteenth Century* (New York: Routledge, 2014), 91.

19. Pichichero, *Military Enlightenment*, 47.

20. Willson, *Life and Letters of Wolfe*, Wolfe to Amherst, 1 July 1758, 379.

21. Ibid., 1 May 1759, 425.

22. P. L. Carver (ed.), 'Wolfe to the Duke of Richmond: unpublished letters', *University of Toronto Quarterly*, 8/1 (1938), Wolfe to Richmond, 28 July 1758, 23.

23. 'Extract of letter from a military officer', in *Boston News-Letter*, 6 September 1759.

24. Jean-Félix Récher, *Journal du siège de Québec en 1759* (Quebec: Societé historique de Québec, 1959), entry for 13 July 1759, 18.

25. Brumwell, *Paths of Glory*, 208–209.

26. *Gentleman's Magazine*, 1759, Wolfe to Pitt, Headquarters at Montmorenci, in the River St Laurence, 2 September 1759, 469.

27. Knox, *Journal*, 1:438.

28. For more on Wolfe's campaign of terror, see Francis Jennings, *Empire of Fortune: Crowns, Colonies & Tribes in the Seven Years War in America* (New York: W. W. Norton, 1988), 420–421.

29. Wright, *Life of Wolfe*, Wolfe to Burton, 'Sutherland' above Carouge, 10 September 1759, 568–570.

30. Dan Snow, *Death or Victory: The Battle for Quebec and the Birth of Empire* (London: Harper Collins, 2010), 177.

31. *Gentleman's Magazine*, 1759, Wolfe to Pitt, Headquarters at Montmorenci, in the River St Laurence, 2 September 1759, 469.

32. Doughty & Parmelee, *Siege of Quebec*, Extract from Another Letter Addressed to Mr. M. P., Sterling Castle, in the River St. Lawrence, 2 miles below the City of Quebec, 2 September 1759, 5:20.

33. Wright, *Life of Wolfe*, Wolfe to Burton, 'Sutherland' above Carouge, 10 September 1759, 568–570.

34. Knox, *Journal*, 1:443.

35. HMC, *The Manuscripts of the Marquess Townshend* (London, 1887), Townshend to Lady Ferrers (his sister, Charlotte), Camp Levi, 6 September 1759, 308–309.

36. Doughty & Parmelee, *Siege of Quebec*, Extract from Another Letter Addressed to Mr. M. P., Sterling Castle, in the River St. Lawrence, 2 miles below the City of Quebec, 2 September 1759, 5:20.

37. Commager & Morris, *Spirit of '76*, Proclamation, 23 June 1777, 1:547–548.

38. WCL CP MS 33/32, Francis Rawdon, Memorandum on the situation of the British Army and what the reasons are for the retreat from Philadelphia, 5 June 1778.

39. WCL CP MS 73/43, Germain to Clinton, 4 November 1779.

40. WCL CP MS 41/41, Clinton to Carter, 21 September 1778.

41. See, for example, Dierk Walter, *Colonial Violence: European Armies and the Use of Force* (London: Hurst, 2017).

42. Pester, *War and Sport in India*, 167.

43. NAM MS 9204/121, Stuart's Diary.

44. Quoted in Duffy, *Soldiers, Sugar and Seapower*, 87.

45. NLS Murray Papers, Adv. MS 46.1.3. General Orders 23 March–30 April 1796.

46. RA GEO/Main/8253, Duke of York to George III, Horse Guards, 12 November 1796.

47. Ibid.

48. Roger Buckley, *Slaves in Red Coats: The British West India Regiments, 1795–1815* (New Haven: Yale University Press, 1979), 55.
49. Ibid., 55–56; and Collins, *War and Empire*, 97. See also Roger Buckley, *The British Army in the West Indies: Society and the Military in the Revolutionary Age* (Tallahassee: University Press of Florida, 1998).
50. Dacombe & Rowe, 'The adventures of Serjeant Miller', 34.
51. For a larger discussion, see Wayne E. Lee, *Barbarians and Brothers: Anglo-American Warfare, 1500–1865* (Oxford: Oxford University Press, 2011).
52. George McKinnon Wrong, *The Fall of Canada: A Chapter in the History of the Seven Years' War* (Oxford: Clarendon Press, 1914), 132–133.
53. Scull, *Montresor Journals*, Letter to Lieutenant Colonel James Montresor, Quebec, 16 December 1760, 235.
54. See William R. Nester, *The French and Indian War and the Conquest of New France* (Norman: University of Oklahoma Press, 2014), Chapter 10.
55. WCL CP MS 13/36, Report of conversation with Lord James Drummond and William Tryon, 7 February 1776.
56. Claude-Louis Saint-Germain, *Mémoires de M. le comte de Saint-Germain* (Amsterdam: M. M. Rey, 1779), 200–201.
57. Quoted in Christopher Duffy, *The Army of Maria Theresa: The Armed Forces of Imperial Austria, 1740–1780* (London: Hippocrene Books, 1977), 48–49.
58. See Harari, *Ultimate Experience*, 161–162.
59. Ibid., 164.
60. Lamb, *Memoir*, 175–177.
61. Ilya Berkovich, *Motivation in War: The Experience of Command Soldiers in Old-Regime Europe* (Cambridge: Cambridge University Press, 2017), 195. See also Edward J. Coss, *All for the King's Shilling: The British Soldier Under Wellington, 1808–1814* (Norman: University of Oklahoma Press, 2010), 191–210.
62. See, for example, NAM MS 6807/157/6 Discipline established by Major General Howe for Light Infantry in Battalion, Sarum, September 1774.
63. Quoted in Azar Gat, *The Origins of Military Thought: From the Enlightenment to Clausewitz* (Oxford: Oxford University Press, 1989), 71–72. See also Franco Venturi, 'Le avventure del generale Henry Lloyd', *Rivista Storia Italiana*, 151, 1979, 369–433.
64. FMC HL MS, Part the Second: On the Philosophy of War
65. Speelman, *Henry Lloyd and the Military Enlightenment*, 100–101.
66. Harari, *Ultimate Experience*, 165–168.
67. Coss, *All for the King's Shilling*, 191–110.
68. Lamb, *Memoir*, 175–176.
69. Michael Glover (ed.), *A Gentleman Volunteer: The Letters of George Hennell from the Peninsular War, 1812–1813* (London: Heineman, 1979), George Hennell, before Badajoz, 5 April 1812, 19.
70. Coss, *All for the King's Shilling*, 6–7.
71. Richard Price, *Making Empire: Colonial Encounters and the Creation of Imperial Rule in Nineteenth-Century Africa* (Cambridge: Cambridge University Press, 2008), 154.
72. See Catriona Kennedy, *Narratives of the Revolutionary and Napoleonic Wars: Military and Civilian Experience in Britain and Ireland* (Basingstoke: Palgrave, 2013), 69–91.
73. Harari, *Ultimate Experience*, 190–192.
74. Quoted in Simon Bainbridge, *British Poetry and the Revolutionary and Napoleonic Wars: Visions of Conflict* (Oxford: Oxford University Press, 2003), 124.
75. NAM 6807/157/6 Discipline established by Major General Howe for Light Infantry in Battalion, Sarum, September 1774.
76. See BL Add MS 27600, Colonel D. Dundas, Principles of Military Movements (Draft).
77. WCL ECP MS 28/2, Instructions to Officers of Light Infantry.

78. TNA WO 1/344, Smith to Koehler, *HMS Tigre* off Alexandria, 27 July 1800, f. 281.
79. *Royal Military Chronicle*, 'Biography of Sir Eyre Coote', March 1811, 326–327.
80. See, for example, BL Add MS 57321, Instructions given to the Battalion of Light Infantry of Irish Militia under my command in Ireland in 1798 and 1799.
81. WCL CP MS 282, *Narrative*, Vol III. Loose Note on description of Bunker Hill. See also WCL CP MS 201, Memorandum, 13 April 1785.
82. *Royal Military Chronicle*, 'Biography of Sir Eyre Coote', March 1811, 326–327.

Bibliography

Primary Sources

Archives

Albert & Shirley Small Special Collections Library, University of Virginia, Charlottesville
  MS 10034, Headquarters Papers of Brigadier John Forbes
Alexander Turnbull Library, Wellington
  MS-1712, Journal of Spencer Perceval Nicholl 15 October 1863 to 31 December 1864
Archives Nationales, Paris
  C/2/291: Defresne, À pondichery le 27.7.1790
Arquivo Histórico Militar, Lisbon
  MS 1/14, Papers of Benjamin D'Urban
Beinecke Rare Book and Manuscript Library, Yale University
  OSB MS 168, Correspondence, Papers and Diaries of William and Henry Clinton
  Osborn c200, European Travel Diary 1754–1755
British Library, London
  Manuscripts
    Add MS 13664, Journal kept by Captain John Malcolm, serving in the Nizam's
      contingent in the expedition against Tippoo Sultaun, 6 January–4 May 1799
    Add MS 21649, Papers of Colonel Henry Bouquet
    Add MS 27600, Colonel David Dundas, Principles of Military Movement
    Add MS 29209, Memoirs and papers relating to the history, geography, and trade of
      India
    Add MS 32852-32954, Newcastle Papers
    Add MS 35059-35067, Hill Papers
    Add MS 35354, Hardwicke Papers
    Add MS 37876, Windham Papers
    Add MS 41142, Townshend Papers
    Add MS 45662, Blechynden Papers
    Add MS 46702, Don Papers
    Add MS 57320-57332, Moore Papers
    Add MS 57701-57716, G. North America Maps of Military Engagements (1700–1899)
    Add MS 73648, Barrington Papers
    MS Loan 57/1-108, Bathurst, Lennox and Melville Papers

Asia, Pacific and Africa Collection
  IOR/E/4, Correspondence with India (1704–1858)
  IOR/H/223, Madras Military Papers
  IOR/H/436, Papers of Captain John Taylor
  IOR/H/251, Third Mysore War
  IOR P/D/63, Bombay Proceedings
  Mss Eur D1053, Sir Barry Close Papers
  Mss Eur F128, Papers of Brigadier John Carnac and of Sir Henry Strachey
  Mss Eur A101, Allen Bayard John Diary, 1849
  King's Manuscripts
    King's MS 212, Journal of Robert Orme, 1755
    King's MS 240, Memoranda relative to the Austrian, Prussian, Dutch, and French Troops, 1774
Cambridge University Library
  GBR/0012/MS Add.9340/1, John Moore Letterbook 1803–1805
Fitzwilliam Museum, Cambridge
  Henry Lloyd Manuscripts
Fort Ticonderoga Archive, Ticonderoga
  02M/2162, Monypenny Orderly Book, June–July 1758
  03M/2170, Monypenny Orderly Book, July–August 1759
  M/6008/9, Papers of Charles Lee
Henry E. Huntington Library, San Merino
  MSS AB Papers of General James Abercromby
  MSS DUN Papers of Henry Dundas
  MSS LO Papers of General John Campbell, Fourth Earl of Loudoun
  MSS SP Stowe Papers
  MSS TP Townshend Papers
  HM 615 Orderly Book of Lord Howe's Army, New York, August–September 1776
  HM 818 Robert Honyman's Journal 1775
  HM 1717 Loudoun Memorandum Books
Houghton Library, Harvard University, Cambridge, MA
  MS Eng 509, Reminiscences of the Hon. Henry Hamilton, 1758–1762
John Rylands Library, University of Manchester
  CP 185 Papers of General Sir Henry Clinton
  GB 133 ENG MS 198, John Pringle & B. Jones, Copy of John Pringle's Survey of Roads in the Carnatic, 1793
Kent History and Library Centre, Maidstone
  U1350 Amherst Papers
Lewis Walpole Library, Yale University, Farmington
  MS3 Weston Papers
  MS55 European Military Tour Journal 1770
  MS83 Military Correspondence of Henry Seymour Conway
  MS84 Correspondence of Henry Seymour Conway
Library and Archives of Canada, Ottawa
  H3/300/1761–1763 Survey of the St. Lawrence, 1761
  MG16/N45 Paulus Aemilius Irving Fonds
  MG18/C366 Northcliffe Collection
  MG18/K7 Montcalm Papers
  MG18/L5 Wolfe Papers
  MG40/Q17 Robert Monckton Fonds
  P58 Amherst Papers
Library of Congress, Washington, DC
  G3922.S3 1780 .C3 Vault, Archibald Campbell, Sketch of the northern frontiers of Georgia, extending from the mouth of the River Savannah to the town of Augusta, 1780.

G5100 1761 .C3 Vault, Archibald Campbell, Sketch of the coast round the island of Dominique, 1761.

MS 1213 Regimental Orderly Book Siege of Savannah 1779

RG 107/M221/R63, Papers of Anthony Jackson, 1814–1815

Library of the Society of the Cincinnati, Washington, DC

L2019F54, West's Military Figures for the Practice of Tacticks with *Short Instructions to Officers . . . calculated to Accompany the Military Figures Invented for Elucidating the Theory and Facilitating the Practice of Army Tacticks* (London, 1803)

L2019F68, David Dundas, *Rules and Regulations for the Formations, Field-Exercise and Movements of His Majesty's Forces* (London: J. Walter, 1798), amended by Robert Ross.

MSS L1997F170, Notebook describing mistakes of tactics employed in various battles in Europe between 1645 and 1755, c. 1760. Author identified as Henry Clinton

MSS L2008F48, Wolfe to Townshend, 18 July 1756

McCord Museum, Montreal

C-173/A/1-3, James Wolfe to Walter Wolfe, 15 September 1755

National Archives of India, New Delhi

Foreign Department Secret Proceedings

Home Misc of Ancient Records

Secret Department

National Archives of the United Kingdom, Kew

Colonial Office

CO 5 Secretary of State Correspondence

CO 318 West Indies Correspondence

CO 323 Board of Trade Correspondence

CO 700 Canada

Home Office

HO 50 Home Office: Military Correspondence

Private Papers

PRO 30/8 Chatham Papers

PRO 30/11 Papers of Charles, Earl Cornwallis

State Papers

SP54 State Papers Scotland Series II

SP87 Secretaries of State: State Papers Foreign, Military Expeditions

Maps and Plans

MPG 1/139; 328–334

War Office

WO 1 Secretary of State, Commander-in-Chief: In-Letters

WO 3 Commander-in-Chief: Out-Letters

WO 5 Secretary-at-War: Marching and Military Orders

WO 6/21 Expeditions 1799–1807

WO 6/131 Commander-in-Chief, 1794–1801

WO 30 Defences of Great Britain

WO 34 Papers of Jeffrey Amherst Commander-in-Chief

WO 40 Selected Unnumbered Papers

WO 43/292 Depot of Military Knowledge

WO 46 Ordnance Office: Out-Letters

WO 55 Plans and Drawings

WO 71 Courts Martial Proceedings

WO 87 Judge Advocate General's Office

WO 135 Papers of Harry Smith

Wills and Letters of Administration

PROB 11/1089/146, 'Will of Gamaliet Massiot of Plumsted, Kent'

National Army Museum, Chelsea

MS 6807/148, Papers and Correspondence of Ensign Augustus Dobree

MS 6807/157/6 Discipline established by Major General Howe for Light Infantry in Battalion, Sarum, September 1774

MS 6807/452, Colbourne Papers

MS 6912/6, Thomas Souter to his wife, Describing the retreat from Kabul, 1842

MS 7411/11/101, Hawley-Toovey Papers

MS 7606/10, Crimean Journal, 1854

MS 7808/93, Henry Brown Papers

MS 8009/50, Journal of Captain Commissary John Charlton, Corps of Royal Artillery Drivers

MS 8202/65, Notebook belonging to George Scovell, dealing with the formation of the Staff Provost Corps about 1854

MS 8207/64, Account of the Battle of Assaye by Sgt Thomas Swarbrook, 19th Dragoons

MS 8301/60, Diary of Surgeon-Major William Brydon

MS 9204/121, Major Charles Stuart's Diary

MS 9404/476, Thomas Picton Papers

National Library of Australia, Canberra

MS 202, Lachlan Macquarie, Letters 1799–1824

National Library of Scotland, Edinburgh

Advocates Manuscripts

Adv MS 46 Papers of General Sir George Murray

Manuscripts

MS 1848, Cochrane Papers

MS 2969 Forbes of Culloden Papers

MS 3835 Melville Papers

MS 7081 Yester Papers

MS 8028 Lynedoch Papers

MS 21102-21103 Murray Papers

MS 21261 Stuart de Rothesay papers

National Maritime Museum, Greenwich

Adm/L Lieutenants' Logs

National Records of Scotland, Edinburgh

GD 1/6 Campbell Papers

GD 225 Hay Papers

GD 364 Hope of Luffness Papers

RH 4/213 The Reverend Alexander Duncan's Journal of the Rebellion of 1745

RH 4/86 Brigadier-General John Forbes North American papers

New York Historical Society, New York

MS240 Papers of Horatio Gates

New York Public Library

MssCol 2796/7, William Smith Jr. Papers

MssCol 2861, Fort Stanwix orderly book

MssCol 6446-6447, Abercromby Correspondence

MssCol NYGB 18231, Journal and Orderly Book of John Herbert

Punjab Archives, Lahore

Lahore Residency Correspondence

Royal Archives, Windsor Castle

Papers of King George III

Papers of the Duke of Cumberland

Royal Collection, Windsor Castle

RCIN 725036, Nicolaas Visscher II, Nieuwe Kaart, van't Land Donawert, en Hochstett &c., 1704 or later

RCIN 725038, Pierre Husson, La Battaille de Hoechstedt, le 13 Aout 1704, 1704 or later

RCIN 725041, Anonymous, Plan von Landau, 1704 or later

RCIN 729096, François Hancko, Plan General de l'attaque de l'armée Françoise près de Fontenoy, 11 May 1745 or later

RCIN 730130, Plan de la Battaille de Laffelt, 1747

RCIN 731061.a-f, Six plans of Braddock's marches, camps and campaign in 1755

RCIN 731064.a, Patrick Mackellar, No. 1, A Sketch of the Field of Battle of the 9th July upon the Monongahela . . ., c. 1755

RCIN 731064.b, Patrick Mackellar, No 2, A Sketch of the Field of Battle &.c shewing the Disposition of the Troops about 2' a Clock when the whole of the main Body had joined the advanced . . ., c.1755

RCIN 731085, Patrick MacKellar, Plan of Oswego with its Forts as Besieged by the Marquis of Montcalm August 1756, c. 1756

RCIN 732019, Anton Heinrich du Plat, Minden, Dankersen and Holzhausen, 1757

RCIN 732025, Georg Joshua du Plat, Plan de la Position de L'Armée de sa Maj.té: Britnque: du 24 Juil.t 1757. près de Hastenbeck, 1757

RCIN 732028, Anonymous, Hastenbeck, 1757

RCIN 732069, Charles Rivez, A Map from the landing place to Ticonderoga, c. 1758

RCIN 732071, John Cleeve Pleydell, Plan of the Environs, Fort and Encampment of Raystown, 1758 or later

RCIN 732072, John Cleeve Pleydell, Plan of the Retrench'd Camp at Fort Ligonier, 1758 or later

RCIN 732099, Thomas Jeffreys, An Authentic Plan of the River St. Laurence from Sillery, to the Fall of Montmorenci, with the Operations of the Siege of Quebec, 1760

RCIN 732102, Patrick Mackellar, Plan of the south side of the River St Laurence from Point Levi to Point des Peres &c. c.1759

RCIN 732103, Patrick Mackellar, Plan of the Encampment upon the west End of the Isle of Orleans from 3–8 July, c.1759

RCIN 732104, Hugh Debbieg, Plan of Montmorency Camp taken possession of ye 8th July at night c.1759

RCIN 732111.a, William Roy, To Prince Ferdinand of Brunswick, This Plan of the Battle of Thonhausen gained 1 August 1759, 1760

RCIN 732114, Anonymous, Plan of the Battle Near Minden, 1759

RCIN 732115.a, Anonymous, Plan of the Battle Near Minden, 1759

RCIN 732120, Patrick Mackellar, Plan of the Battle fought upon Abraham Plains near Quebec on 13 September 1759, c.1759

RCIN 732122, Patrick Mackellar, Plan of the Encampment of the British Army upon Abraham-Plain before Quebec 13–18 September 1759

RCIN 733001, John Cleeve Pleydell, Plan of the Battle of Wandewash, 22 January 1760, 1760 or later

RCIN 733077, Anonymous, Plan des tapfern Angriffs und vollkommenen Sieges der Russisch Kayserlichen Waffen über die Turkische und Tattarische Armée an der Large in der Moldau, c.1770–1779

RCIN 733078, Anonymous, Plan der Schlacht und des vollkommenen Sieges, den die Armee Ihro Kayserlichen Maiestæt über die vom Grossvizier selbst angefürte Turckische Armee in Bessarabien am Fluss Kagul, 1770 or later

RCIN 734021, William Faden, A Plan of New York Island, with part of Long Island, Staten Island & East New Jersey, with a particular Description of the engagement on the Woody Heights of Long Island, 1776

RCIN 734059, John Pringle, 'Plan of the Route of the Grand Army in the Carnatic, 25 August 1780 to 7 June 1783', 1785, 1787

RCIN 734069, Sebastian Bauman, Plan of the investment of York and Gloucester, 1782.

RCIN 734111, Alexander Beatson, The Marches of the British Armies, in the Peninsula of India During the Campaigns of 1790, 1791, 1792

RCIN 735003, Colin Mackenzie, Battle of 15 May 1791 fought by the British Army Commanded by The Right Honourable Earl Cornwallis, K.G. and the Army of Tippoo Sultan Bahauder, 1791

State Library of New South Wales, Sydney
    Papers of Lachlan Macquarie
        A768, Journal No. 1, 15 December 1787–24 March 1792
        A768, Journal No. 2, 26 March 1792–28 December 1794
        A773, Macquarie Diary April 1816
        A790, Macquarie Letterbook 3 August 1797–22 November 1802
        A790, Journal of the Operations of the Bombay Army
    Papers of Thomas Mitchell
        A290, Correspondence 1711–1818
        C11, Fieldnotes of Thomas Mitchell, 1811
        C14, Diary of Thomas Mitchell, 1811
        C27, Diary of Thomas Mitchell, 1819–1821
        C28, Diary of Thomas Mitchell, 1821
    Papers of Samuel Hassall
        A1677, Correspondence, March 1816

Stephen S. Clark Map Library, University of Michigan, Ann Arbor
    James Rennell, 'A map of Bengal, Bahar, Oude & Allahabad: with part of Agra and Delhi, exhibiting the course of the Ganges from Hurdwar to the sea', 1786

Suffolk Record Office
    Acc. 423/191, Papers of the Duke of Grafton

Tamil Nadu State Archives, Chennai
    Military Consultations
    Military Sundries
    Public Consultations

Trinity College Dublin Library, Dublin
    E/10c Donoughmore Papers, Diaries of the Hon Christopher Hely-Hutchinson during the Expedition to Egypt

University of Durham Library
    GB-0033-GRE-A Papers of the 1st Earl Grey

University of Southampton, Hartley Library
    Wellington Papers

Victoria & Albert Museum, London
    Museum no 2545, 'Tipu's Tiger', 1780s or 1790s, Mysore, India

William L. Clements Library, University of Michigan, Ann Arbor
    Journal of Stephen Cross, 1756–1757
    Papers of Colonel Henry Bouquet
    Papers of General Sir Eyre Coote
    Papers of General Sir Henry Clinton
    Papers of General Sir Jeffrey Amherst
    Papers of General Sir Thomas Gage
    Papers of George Sackville, Lord Germain Papers
    Papers of James Gorham
    Papers of Loftus Cliffe
    Papers of the Earl of Shelburne

Printed Sources

Alexander, James E., *Incidents of the Maori War, New Zealand in 1860–1861* (London: Richard Bentley, 1863)

Alexander, R. O., 'The capture of Quebec: A manuscript journal relating to the operations before Quebec from 8th May 1759 to 17 May 1760 kept by Colonel Malcolm Fraser', *Journal of the Society for Army Historical Research*, 18/71 (Autumn 1939), 135–168

Anonymous, *An Authentic Account of the Reduction of Louisbourg, in June and July 1758, by a Spectator* (London: W. Owen, 1758)

Anonymous, *Observations on Mr Home's Account of the Battle of Culloden* (Exeter, 1802)

Anonymous, *The Personal Narrative of a Private Soldier who Served in the Forty-Second Highlanders for Twelve Years During the Late War* (London: John Murray, 1821)

Anonymous, *Remarks on the Military Operations of the English and French Armies, Commanded by his Royal Highness the Duke of Cumberland, and Marshal Saxe, During the Campaign of 1747* (London: T. Becket, 1760)

Aspinall, A. (ed.), *The Correspondence of George, Prince of Wales 1770–1812*, 8 vols (London: Cassell, 1964)

Aspinall, A. (ed.), *The Later Correspondence of George III*, 5 vols (Cambridge: Cambridge University Press, 1966)

Baker, Ezekiel, *Remarks on Rifles and Guns* (London: T. Egerton, 1803)

Baxter, James Phinney (ed.), *Collections of the Maine Historical Society, Second Series, Documentary History of the State of Maine, Vols. 4, 9–12, Containing the Baxter Manuscripts* (Portland: Maine Historical Society, 1889–1916)

Bayly, Ralph, *Diary of Colonel Bayly, 12th Regt, 1796–1830* (London: Army and Navy Cooperative Society, 1896)

Bell, R. F. (ed.), *Memorials of John Murray of Broughton Sometime Secretary to Prince Charles Edward* (Edinburgh: Scottish History Society, 1898)

Bernier, François, *Travels in the Mogul Empire, AD 1656–68*, A. Constable (ed.) & I. Brock (trans.) (London: Constable, 1891)

Bhargava, K. D. and S. N. Prasad (eds), *Fort William-India House Correspondence*, 20 vols (New Delhi: National Archives of India, 1949–1975)

Bingham, W. R., *The Field of Ferozeshah in Two Cantos, With Other Poems by a Young Soldier* (London: Charles Edward Bingham, 1848)

Blakiston, Ralph, *12 Years Military Adventure in Three-quarters of the Globe . . .* (London: Henry Coulburn, 1840)

Bradbury, J. M., 'Military Journal, April 1760 to August 1762', in *Bradbury Memorial* (Portland, MN, 1890), 261–295

Brown, Marvin L. (ed.), *Baroness von Riedesel and the American Revolution: Journal and Correspondence of a Tour of Duty, 1776–1783* (Chapel Hill: University of North Carolina Press, 1965)

Brown, Robert, *An Impartial Journal of a Detachment from the Brigade of Foot Guards Commencing 25th February 1793 and Ending 9 May 1795 by Robert Brown, Corporal in the Coldstream Guards* (London: John Stockdale, 1795)

Bruce, H. A., *Life of General William Napier*, 2 vols (London: John Murray, 1864)

Bunbury, Henry, *A Narrative of the Campaign in North Holland, 1799* (London: Boone, 1849)

Burgoyne, Bruce E. (ed.), *Enemy Views: The American Revolutionary War as Recorded by the Hessian Participants* (Westminster, MD: Heritage Books, 1996)

Burgoyne, John, *A State of the Expedition From Canada as Laid Before the House of Commons . . .* (London: J. Almon, 1780)

Campbell, Alexander, 'Letter from Lt Alexander Campbell, 74th Foot, to his brother Lt Frederick Campbell, RA, dated Seringapatam, 20 June 1799, describing the battle there', *Journal of the Royal Highland Fusiliers*, 6/1 (June 1969), 80

Campbell, James, *Memoirs of Sir James Campbell of Ardkinglas*, 2 vols (London: Colburn & Bentley, 1832)

Campbell, Neil, *Instructions for Light Infantry and Riflemen: Founded Upon the Regulations for the Exercise of Riflemen and Light Infantry in Close Order, and the Regulations for the Exercise of Riflemen and Light Infantry* (London: T. Egerton, 1807, reprinted 1813)

Carver, P. L. (ed.), 'Wolfe to the Duke of Richmond: unpublished letters', *University of Toronto Quarterly*, 8/1 (1938), 11–40

Cassels, S. A. C. (ed.), *Peninsular Portrait, 1811–1814. The Letters of Captain William Bragge Third (King's Own) Dragoons* (London: Oxford University Press, 1963)

Chadwick, French Ensor (ed.), *The Graves Papers and Other Documents Relating to the Naval Operations of the Yorktown Campaign, July to October 1781* (New York: De Vinne Press for the Navy History Society, 1916)

Church, Benjamin, *Diary of King Philip's War, 1675–1676* (Little Compton: Little Compton Historical Society, 1975)

Churchill, John, Duke of Marlborough, *The Case of his Grace the D— of M—. As Design'd To be Represented by him to the Honourable House of Commons, in Vindication of Himself from the Charge of the Commissioners of Accounts in Relation to the Two and Half per Cent Bread and Bread Waggons* (London: A. Baldwin, 1712)

Clarke, J., *An Impartial and Authentic Narrative of the Battle Fought on the 17th of June 1775, between His Britannic Majesty's Troops and the American Provincial Army, on Bunker's Hill* (London: J. Millan, 1775)

Colebrook, Thomas Edward, *The Life of the Honourable Mountstuart Elphinstone*, 2 vols (London: John Murray, 1884)

Collins, Dennis, *An Account of the English Colony of New South Wales, 1788–1801*, 2 vols (London: T. Cadell, 1802)

Commager, Henry Steele and Richard B. Morris (eds), *The Spirit of '76: The Story of the American Revolution as Told by Participants*, 2 vols (Indianapolis: Bobbs-Merrill, 1958)

Commonwealth of Australia, *Historical Records of Australia: Series I: Governors' Despatches to and from England*, 37 vols (Sydney: Library Committee of the Commonwealth Parliament, 1917)

Cooke, Captain J., *Memoirs of the Late War: The Personal Narrative of Captain Cooke of the 43rd Regiment, Light Infantry*, 2 vols (London: Colburn & Bentley, 1831)

Costello, Edward, *The Adventures of a Soldier; or Memoirs of Edward Costello* (London: Henry Colburn, 1841)

Crichton, Patrick, *The Woodhouselee MS. A Narrative of Events in Edinburgh and District During the Jacobite Occupation* (London: W. & R. Chambers, 1907)

Cumming, William P., *British Maps of Colonial America* (Chicago: University of Chicago Press, 1974)

Dacombe, M. R. and B. J. H. Rowe, 'The adventures of Serjeant Benjamin Miller during his service with the 4th Battalion, Royal Artillery, from 1796 to 1815', *Journal of the Society for Army Historical Research*, 7/27 (January 1928), 9–51.

Davies, K. G. (ed.), *Documents of the American Revolution, 1770–1783*, 21 vols (Shannon: Irish University Press, 1972–1981)

De Brahm, Romans, Cook, Jackson & Collet, *The American Military Pocket Atlas; Being an approved Collection of Correct Maps, Both General and Particular, of the British Colonies; Especially those which now are, or probably may be The Theatre of War: Taken principally from the actual Surveys and judicious Observations of Engineers, De Brahm and Romans; Cook, Jackson and Collet; Maj. Holland, and other Officers, Employed in His Majesty's Fleets and Armies* (London: Sayer & Bennet, 1776)

Dirom, Alexander, *A Narrative of the Campaign in India, Which Terminated the War with Tippoo Sultan, in 1792* (London: Bulmer & Co., 1793)

Dobbs, John, *Recollections of an Old 52nd Man* (Waterford: T. S. Harvey, 1859)

Donaldson, Joseph, *Recollections of an Eventful Life, Chiefly Passed in the Army* (Glasgow: W. R. McPhun, 1824)

Doughty, A. G., 'A new account of the death of Wolfe', *The Canadian Historical Review*, 4:1 (March 1923), 45–55

Doughty, A. G. and G. W. Parmelee (eds), *The Siege of Quebec and the Battle of the Plains of Abraham*, 6 vols (Quebec: Dussault & Proulx, 1901)

Duff, James Grant, *A History of the Mahrattas*, 3 vols (London: Longman, 1826)

Dunnigan, Brian Leigh (ed.), *Memoirs on the Late War in North America Between France and England* (New York: Old Fort Niagara Association, 1994)

Faden, William, *Atlas of the Battles of the American Revolution, Together with Maps Shewing the Routes of the British and American Armies, Plans of Cities, Surveys of Harbors, &c.* (New York: Bartlett & Welford, 1845)

Fitzpatrick, John C. (ed.), *The Writings of George Washington from the Original Manuscript Sources, 1745–1799*, 39 vols (Washington: Government Printing Office, 1931–1944)

Fonblanque, Edward Barrington de, *Political and Military Episodes in the Latter Half of the Eighteenth Century: Derived from the Life and Correspondence of the Right Hon. John Burgoyne, General, Statesman, Dramatist* (London: Macmillan, 1876)

Fortescue, John (ed.), *The Correspondence of King George the Third, From 1760 to December 1783*, 6 vols (London: Frank Cass, 1967)

French, Allen (ed.), *A British Fusilier in Revolutionary Boston: Being the Diary of Lieutenant Frederick Mackenzie, Adjutant of the Royal Welch Fusiliers, January 5–April 30, 1775, with a letter describing his voyage to America* (Cambridge, MA: Harvard University Press, 1924)

Gardyne, C. G., *The Life of a Regiment: The History of the Gordon Highlanders*, 2 vols (Edinburgh: Douglas, 1901–1903)

Gleig, George Robert, *A Memoir of the Late Major-General Robert Craufurd Reprinted from the Military Panorama of October 1812 with an Account of his Funeral* (London; Private Impression, 1842)

Gleig, George Robert, *The Life of Sir Thomas Munro*, 2 vols (London: Colburn & Bentley, 1830)

Gleig, George Robert, *The Subaltern: A Chronicle of the Peninsular War* (London: T. Cadell, 1825)

Glover, Michael (ed.), *A Gentleman Volunteer: The Letters of George Hennell from the Peninsular War, 1812–1813* (London: Heineman, 1979)

Gordon, Iain (ed.), *Soldier of the Raj: The Life of Richard Fortescue Purvis, 1789–1869, Soldier, Sailor and Parson* (Barnsley: Leo Cooper, 2001)

Gordon, W. A., 'Journal of the siege of Louisbourg from a MS in the Royal United Service Institution', *Journal of the Royal United Services Institute*, 60:439 (1915), 117–152

Grant, Ann, *Memoirs of an American Lady*, 2 vols (London: Longman, Hurst, Rees & Orme, 1809)

Grattan, William, 'Reminiscences of a subaltern: Battle of Salamanca', *United Services Journal* (June 1834), 175–187

Gruber, Ira D. (ed.), *John Peebles' American War: The Diary of a Scottish Grenadier, 1776–1782* (London: Stackpole Books, 1998)

Gurwood, John (ed.), *The Dispatches of Field Marshal the Duke of Wellington During His Various Campaigns in India, Denmark, Portugal, Spain, The Low Countries and France*, 13 vols (London: John Murray, 1852)

Hadden, James M., *A Journal Kept in Canada and Upon Burgoyne's Campaign in 1776 and 1777* (Albany: Munsell's, 1884)

Hamilton, Charles, *Braddock's Defeat: The Journal of Captain Robert Cholmley's Batman, the Journal of a British Officer, Halkett's Orderly Book* (Norman: University of Oklahoma Press, 1959)

Hibbert, Christopher (ed.), *Recollections of Rifleman Harris* (London: Archon Books, 1970)

Hitsman, J. Mackay, 'Order Before Landing at Louisbourg, 1758', *Military Affairs*, 15 (1958), 146–148

Holden, David, 'Journal kept by Sergeant David Holden of Groton, Massachusetts during the latter part of the French and Indian War, February 20–November 29, 1760', *Proceedings of the Massachusetts Historical Society* (June 1889), 384–407

Hook, Theodore, *The Life of General, the Right Honourable Sir David Baird*, 2 vols (London: Bentley, 1832)

Howe, W., *The Narrative of Lieut. Ge. Sir William Howe, in a Committee of the House of Commons, on the 29th of April, 1779, Relative to His Conduct, During His Late Command of the King's Troops in North America* (London: H. Baldwin, 1780)

Hutchinson, Thomas, *The History of the Province of Massachusetts Bay from 1749 to 1774* (London: John Murray, 1778)

James, Alfred Proctor, *Writings of General John Forbes Relating to his Service in North America* (Menasha, WI: The Collegiate Press, 1938)

Jefferys, Thomas, *A General Topography of North America and the West Indies. Being a Collection of all the Maps, Charts, Plans, and Particular Surveys, That Have Been Published of that Part of the World, Either in Europe or America* (London: R. Sayer, 1768)

Jenks, Samuel, 'Journal of Captain Jenks', *Proceedings of the Massachusetts Historical Society* (March 1890), 352–391

Jennings, Louis J. (ed.), *The Croker Papers: The Correspondence and Diaries of John Wilson Croker*, 3 vols (London: John Murray, 1884)

Johnson, Samuel, *The Works of Samuel Johnson*, 15 vols (London: Knapton, 1789)

Johnson, William, *Sketches in the Life and Correspondence of Nathanael Greene*, 2 vols (Charleston: Privately Published, 1822)

Johnstone, Chevalier de, *The Campaign of 1760: A Narrative Attributed to Chevalier Johnstone* (Quebec: Literary and Historical Society of Quebec, 1887)

Kennedy, James Shaw, *Notes on the Battle of Waterloo: With a Brief Memoir of His Life and Services and Plan for the Defence of Canada* (London: John Murray, 1865)

Kimball, Gertrude Selwyn (ed.), *Correspondence of William Pitt When Secretary of State with Colonial Governors and Military and Naval Commissioners in America*, 2 vols (New York: Macmillan, 1906)

Kincaid, John, *Adventures in the Rifle Brigade and Random Shots from a Rifleman* (York: Leonaur, 2010)

Kirk, Robert, *The Memoirs and Adventures of Robert Kirk, Late of the Royal Highland Regiment* (London: J. Ferrar, 1770)

Knox, John, *An Historical Journal of the Campaigns in North America for the Years 1757, 1758, 1759, and 1760*, 3 vols (Toronto: The Champlain Society, 1914)

Lamb, Roger, *A Memoir of His Own Life* (Dublin: J. Jones, 1811)

Larpent, F. S., *The Private Journal of F.S. Larpent, Esq. Judge Advocate General of the British Forces in the Peninsula Attached to the Headquarters of Lord Wellington During the Peninsular War from 1812 to its Close*, 3 vols (London: Richard Bentley, 1853)

Laughton, J. K. and J. Y. F. Sullivan (eds), *The Journal of Rear-Admiral Bartholomew James, 1752–1828* (London: Navy Records Society Publications, 1896)

Leach, Jonathan, *Rough Sketches of the Life of an Old Soldier* (London: Longman, 1831)

Le Couteur, John, *The Rifle: Its Effects on the War; Or National Military Organization; and Preparation for Defence* (London: Parker, Furnival & Parker, 1855)

Le Marchant, Denis, *Memoirs of the Late Major General Le Marchant* (London: Samuel Bentley, 1841)

Lee, Henry, *The Campaign of 1781 in the Carolinas* (Philadelphia: E. Littell, 1824)

Lee, Robert E. (ed.), *The Revolutionary War Memoirs of General Henry Lee* (New York: Da Capo Press, 1998)

Lindsay, Lord Alexander (ed.), *Lives of the Lindsays; Or, A Memoir of the Houses of Crawford and Balcarres*, 3 vols (London: John Murray, 1858)

Lloyd, C. C. (ed.), *The Keith Papers*, 3 vols (London: Navy Records Society, 1950–1955)

Lloyd, Hannibal, *Memoir of General Lloyd* (London: Printed for Private Circulation, 1842)

Lloyd, Henry, *The History of the Late War in Germany, Between the King of Prussia, and the Empress of Germany and her Allies* (London: Privately Published, 1766)

Lodge, Henry Cabot (ed.), *André's Journal: An Authentic Record of the Movements and Engagements of the British Army in America from June 1777 to November 1778 ...* (Boston: Bibliophile Society, 1903)

Lushington, S. R., *The Life and Services of General Lord Harris GCB, During His Campaigns in America, the West Indies and India* (London: John W. Parker, 1845)

Lydenberg, Harry Miller (ed.), *Archibald Robertson, Lieutenant-General Royal Engineers, His Diaries and Sketches in America, 1762–1780* (New York: New York Public Library, 1930)

Mackay, Hugh, *Memoirs of the War Carried on in Scotland and Ireland* (Edinburgh: Privately Published, 1833)

Mackenzie, Frederick, *Diary of Frederick Mackenzie*, 2 vols (Cambridge, MA: Harvard University Press, 1930)

Mackenzie, Roderick, *A Sketch of the War with Tippoo Sultan*, 2 vols (London: Sewell, 1793)

Manners, Walter Evelyn, *Some Account of the Military, Political, and Social Life of the Right Hon. John Manners, Marquis of Granby* (London: Macmillan, 1899)

Marchant, John, *The History of the Present Rebellion* (London: Hyndshaw & Thompson, 1746)

Markham, Clements R., *A Memoir of the Indian Surveys* (London: Allen & Co, 1871)

Marshall, Douglas W. and Howard H. Peckham, *Campaigns of the American Revolution: An Atlas of Manuscript Maps* (Ann Arbor: University of Michigan Press, 1976)

Martin, Montgomery (ed.), *The Dispatches, Minutes, and Correspondence of the Marquess Wellesley, K.G., During His Administration in India* (London: John Murray, 1836–1837)

Massie, Alistair and Jonathan Oates (eds), *The Duke of Cumberland's Campaigns in Britain and the Low Countries, 1745–1748: A Selection of His Letters* (Stroud: The History Press, 2018)

Maurice, J. F. (ed.), *The Diary of Sir John Moore*, 2 vols (London: Edward Arnold, 1904)

Middleton, Richard (ed.), *Amherst and the Conquest of Canada* (Stroud: Sutton Publishing, 2003)

Minis Hays, I., 'A journal kept during the siege of Fort William Henry, August 1757', *Proceedings of the American Philosophical Society*, 37/157 (January 1898), 143–150

Mitchell, John, *Biographies of Eminent Soldiers of the Last Four Centuries* (London: William Blackwood, 1865)

Money, John, *The History of the Campaign of 1792, Between the Armies of France Under General Dumourier, Valence etc, and the Allies Under the Duke of Brunswick* (London: E. Harlow, 1794)

Money, John, *To the Right Honourable William Windham on a Partial Reorganization of the British Army* (London: T. Egerton, 1799)

Moore, G. C. (ed.), *The Autobiography of Lieutenant-General Sir Harry Smith* (London: John Murray, 1901)

Moore, James Carrick, *The Life of Lieutenant-General Sir John Moore*, 2 vols (London: John Murray, 1834)

Moorsom, William Scarth, *Historical Record of the Fifty-second Regiment (Oxfordshire Light Infantry) from the Year 1755 to the Year 1858* (London: Bentley, 1860)

Muenchhausen, Friedrich Ernst von, *At General Howe's Side, 1776–1778: The Diary of General William Howe's Aide de Camp, Captain Friedrich von Muenchhausen* (Monmouth Beach, NJ: Philip Freneau Press, 1974)

Napier, W. C. E., *The Early Military Life of General Sir George T. Napier* (London: John Murray, 1886)

Napier, W. F. P., *History of the War in the Peninsula and in the South of France from the Year 1807 to the Year 1814*, 6 vols (London: Thomas and William Boone, 1847)

Napier, W. F. P., *The Life and Opinions of General Sir Charles James Napier*, 4 vols (London: John Murray, 1857)

Nolte, Vincent, *Fifty Years in Both Hemispheres: Or, Reminiscences of the Life of a Former Merchant* (New York: Redfield, 1854)

O'Callaghan, E. B. and B. Fernow (eds), *Documents Relative to the Colonial History of the State of New York*, 15 vols (Albany: Argus & Co., 1853–1887)

Page, Julia (ed.), *Intelligence Officer in the Peninsula: Letters & Diaries of Major the Hon. Edward Charles Cocks, 1786–1812* (London: Spellmount, 1986)

Pargellis, Stanley (ed.), *Military Affairs in North America, 1748–1765: Selected Documents From the Cumberland Papers in Windsor Castle* (New York: Appleton-Century, 1936)

Pearse, Hugh Wodehouse, *Memoir of the Life and Military Services of Viscount Lake, Baron Lake of Delhi and Laswarree, 1744–1808* (London: Blackwood, 1908)

Peckham, Howard H. (ed.), *Sources of American Independence: Selected Manuscripts from the Collections of the Williams L. Clements Library*, 2 vols (Chicago: University of Chicago Press, 1978)

Pester, John, *War and Sport in India, 1802–1806: An Officer's Diary* (London: Heath, Cranton & Ouseley, 1913)

Philippart, J. (ed.), *Royal Military Calendar*, 5 vols (London: T. Egerton, 1820)

Phillimore, R. H. (ed.), *Historical Records of the Survey of India*, 4 vols (Dehra Dun: Survey of India, 1945)

Pinkard, George, *Notes on the West Indies*, 3 vols (London: Longman, 1806)

Price, David, *Memoirs of the Early Life and Service of a Field Officer on the Retired List of the Indian Army* (London: Wm. H. Allen & Co., 1839)

Price, J. F. and K. Rangachari (eds), *The Private Diary of Ananda Ranga Pillai, Dubash to Joseph François Dupleix*, 12 vols (Madras: Government Press, 1904–1928)

Randolph, Herbert, *Life of General Sir Robert Wilson*, 2 vols (London: John Murray, 1862)

Récher, Jean-Felix, *Journal du siège de Québec en 1759* (Quebec: Société historique de Québec, 1959)

Rennell, James, *A Bengal Atlas: Containing Maps of the Theatre of War and Commerce on That Side of Hindostan* (London: Privately Published, 1781)

Rennell, James, *The Marches of the British Armies in the Peninsula of India During the Campaigns of 1790 and 1791* (London: Bulmer & co, 1792)

Rennell, James, *Memoir of a Map of Hindoostan: Or, The Mogul Empire: With an Introduction, Illustrative of the Geography and Present Division of that Country: and a Map of the Countries Situated Between the Heads of the Indian Rivers, and the Caspian Sea* (London: W. Bulmer & Co., 1793)

Rhodehamel, John H. (ed.), *Washington: Writings* (Washington: Library of America, 1997)

Rigaud, Gibbes, *Celer et Audax: A Sketch of the Services of the Fifth Battalion Sixtieth Regiment (Rifles) During the Twenty Years of Their Existence* (Oxford: Pickard Hall, 1879)

Rogers, Robert, *Journals of Major Robert Rogers* (Albany: Joel Munsell's Sons, 1883)

Romance, Germaine-Hyacinthe de, Marquis de Mesmon, *Mémoires militaires et politiques du Général Lloyd, servant d'introduction à l'histoire de la guerre . . .* (Paris: Magimel, 1801)

Ross, Charles (ed.), *Correspondence of Charles, First Marquis Cornwallis*, 3 vols (London: J. Murray, 1859)

Royal Military Academy, Woolwich, *Records of the Royal Military Academy, 1741–1892* (Woolwich: F. J. Cattermole, 1892)

Russell, Earl John, *Memoirs of the Affairs of Europe: From the Peace of Utrecht*, 2 vols (London: John Murray, 1829)

Ryder, John, *Four Years' Service in India by a Private Soldier* (Leicester: W. H. Burton, 1853)

Saint-Germain, Claude-Louis, *Mémoires de M. le comte de Saint-Germain* (Amsterdam: M. M. Rey, 1779)

Sarkar, Jadunath and G. S. Sardesai (eds), *English Records of Maratha History: The Poona Residency Correspondence* (Bombay: Modern India Press, 1936–1951)

Schenck, David, *North Carolina, 1780–'81: Being a History of the Invasion of the Carolinas by the British Army Under Lord Cornwallis in 1780–'81* (Raleigh: Edwards & Broughton, 1889)

Scull, G. D. (ed.), *The Montresor Journals* (New York: New York Historical Society, 1882)

Seaton, Thomas, *From Cadet to Colonel: The Record of a Life of Active Service*, 2 vols (London: Hurst and Blackett, 1866)

Shawe, John Robert, *John Robert Shawe: An Autobiography of Thirty Years, 1777–1807* (Athens: Ohio University Press, 1992)

Showman, Richard K. (ed.), *The Papers of Nathanael Greene*, 13 vols (Chapel Hill: University of North Carolina Press, 1976–2005)

Simcoe, John Graves, *A Journal of the Operations of the Queen's Rangers From the End of the Year 1777 to the Conclusion of the Late American War* (Exeter: Privately Published, 1787)

Smiles, Samuel, *A Publisher and his Friends: Memoir and Correspondence of John Murray, With an Account of the Origin and Progress of the House, 1768–1843*, 2 vols (New York: Dossier Press, 1904)

Smythies, R. H. Raymond, *Historical Records of the 40th (2nd Somersetshire) Regiment* (Devonport: A. H. Swiss, 1894)

Speelman, Patrick J. (ed.), *War, Society and Enlightenment: The Works of General Lloyd* (Leiden: Brill, 2005)

Stanhope, Philip Henry, *Notes of Conversations With the Duke of Wellington, 1831–1851* (London: John Murray, 1889)

Stanley, George F. (ed.), *For Want of a Horse: Being a Journal of the Campaigns Against the Americans in 1776 and 1777 Conducted from Canada by an Officer who Served with Lt. Gen. Burgoyne* (Sackville, NB: Tribune, 1961)

Stedman, Charles, *The History of the Origin, Progress, and Termination of the American War* (London: J. Debrett, 1794)

Steuart, A. Francis (ed.), *The Last Journals of Horace Walpole During the Reign of George III from 1771–1783*, 2 vols (London: The Bodley Head, 1910)

Stevens, Benjamin Franklin, *The Campaign in Virginia, 1781: An Exact Reprint of Six Rare Pamphlets on the Clinton-Cornwallis Controversy*, 2 vols (London: Privately Published, 1888)

Stevens, Benjamin Franklin (ed.), *General Sir William Howe's Orderly Book: at Charlestown, Boston and Halifax, June 17, 1775 to 1776, 26 May* (London: B. F. Stevens, 1890)

Stevens, S. K., Donald H. Kent and Autumn L. Leonard (eds), *The Papers of Henry Bouquet*, 6 vols (Harrisburg: Pennsylvania Historical and Museum Commission, 1951)

Stewart, Charles, *A Descriptive Catalogue of the Oriental Library of the Late Tippoo Sultan of Mysore* (Cambridge: The University Press, 1809)

Stewart, Irene (ed.), *Letters of General John Forbes Relating to the Expedition Against Fort Duquesne in 1758* (Pittsburgh: Allegheny County Committee, 1927)

Stewart, William, *The Cumloden Papers: The Correspondence of Lieutenant-General Sir William Stewart* (Edinburgh: Privately Published, 1871)

Sullivan, James (ed.), *The Papers of Sir William Johnson*, 14 vols (Albany: University of the State of New York, 1921–1965)

Surtees, William, *Twenty-five Years in the Rifle Brigade* (London: T. Cadell, 1833)

Syrett, David (ed.), *The Siege and Capture of Havana 1762* (London: Navy Records Society, 1970)

Tarleton, Banastre, *A History of the Campaigns of 1780 and 1781, in the Southern Provinces of North America* (London: Cadell, 1787)

Taylor, William, *Life in the Ranks* (London: T. C. Neby, 1847)

Thomson, William, *Memoirs of the Late War in Asia, With a Narrative of the Imprisonment and Sufferings of Our Officers and Soldiers, by an Officer of Colonel Baillie's Detachment*, 2 vols (London: John Murray, 1788)

Tomkinson, William, *The Diary of a Cavalry Officer in the Peninsular and Waterloo Campaigns, 1809–1815* (London: Swann Sonnenschein, 1894)

Townshend, George, *A Brief Narrative of the Late Campaigns in Germany and Flanders in a Letter to a Member of Parliament* (London: J. Lion, 1751)

Tucker, St George, 'St George Tucker to Francis Bland Tucker, 18 March 1781', *Magazine of American History*, 7 (September 1881)

Tupper, Ferdinand Brock (ed.), *The Life and Correspondence of Major-General Sir Isaac Brock* (London: Simpkin, Marshall & Co., 1845)

Tustin, Joseph P. (ed.), *Diary of the American War: A Hessian Journal of Captain Johan Ewald, Field Jäger Corps* (New Haven: Yale University Press, 1979)

Vane, Charles (ed.), *The Memoranda and Correspondence of Robert Stewart, Viscount Castlereagh*, 12 vols (London: Henry Coulburn, 1848–1854)

Varney, Harry (ed.), *The Journals and Correspondence of General Sir Harry Calvert ... Comprising the Campaigns in Flanders and Holland in 1793–4* (London: Hurst & Blackett, 1853)

Vattel, Emmerich de, *The Law of Nations: Or Principles of the Law of Nature Applied to the Conduct of Nations and Sovereigns*, 2 vols (London: Sweet & Maxwell, 1834)

Vibart, H. M., *The Military History of the Madras Engineers and Pioneers, From 1743 up to the Present Time*, 2 vols (London: W. H. Allen, 1888)

Watkins, John, *A Biographical Memoir of His Late Royal Highness Frederick, Duke of York and Albany* (London: Henry Fisher, 1827)

Webster, John C. (ed.), *Journal of William Amherst in America, 1758–1760* (London: Butler & Tanner, 1927)

Webster, John C. (ed.), *The Journal of Jeffrey Amherst* (Chicago: University of Chicago Press, 1931)

Wellington, 2nd Duke of (ed.), *Supplementary Dispatches and Memoranda of Field Marshall Arthur Duke of Wellington, 1797–1818*, 14 vols (London: John Murray, 1858)

Wells, F. P. (ed.), 'Part of the Journal of Capt. Jacob Bayley in the Old French War', in *History of Newbury, Vermont* (Newbury, VT: Caledonian Company, 1902), 376–380

Welsh, James, *Military Reminiscences: Extracted from a Journal of Nearly Forty Years Active Service in the East Indies*, 2 vols (London: Smith, Elder & Co., 1830)

Whitworth, Rex H., 'Some unpublished Wolfe letters, 1755–1758', *Journal of the Society for Army History Research*, 53/214 (Summer 1975), 65–86

Wilkin, W. H., *Some British Soldiers in America* (London: H. Rees, 1914)

Wilkinson, James, *Memoirs of My Own Times*, 3 vols (Philadelphia: Abraham Small, 1816)

Wilks, Mark, *Historical Sketches of the South of India in an Attempt to Trace the History of Mysoor*, 3 vols (London: Longman, 1817)

Willcox, William B. (ed.), *The American Rebellion: Sir Henry Clinton's Narrative of His Campaigns, 1775–1782, with an Appendix of Original Documents* (New Haven: Yale University Press, 1954)

Willson, Beckles, *The Life and Letters of James Wolfe* (London: William Heinemann, 1909)

Willyams, Cooper, *An Account of the Campaign in the West Indies in the Year 1794* (London: T. Bensley, 1796)

Wilson, Charles Robert (ed.), *Old Fort William in Bengal: A Selection of Official Documents Dealing with its History*, 2 vols (London: John Murray, 1906)

Wilson, R. T., *A Narrative of the Expedition to Egypt, Under Sir Ralph Abercrombie* (London: Dutton, 1803)

Winchester, Charles (ed.), *Memoirs of the Chevalier de Johnstone*, 3 vols (Aberdeen: Wyllie & Son, 1871)

Wittman, William, *Travels in Turkey, Asia-Minor, Syria, and Across the Desert Into Egypt During the Years 1799, 1800, and 1801, in Company with the Turkish Army, and the British Military Mission* (London: R. Phillips, 1803)

Wright, Robert, *The Life of Major-General Wolfe* (London: Chapman & Hall, 1864)

Wrottesley, George, *Life and Correspondence of Field Marshal Sir John Burgoyne*, 2 vols (London: Richard Bentley, 1873)

Wylly, Harold Carmichael, *A Life of Lieutenant-General Sir Eyre Coote* (Oxford: Clarendon Press, 1922)

Wylly, Harold Carmichael, *History of the King's Own Yorkshire Light Infantry From 1755 to 1914* (London: P. Lund, Humphries & co., 1924)

Young, Thomas, 'Memoir of Thomas Young', *Orion*, 3 (October 1843)

Yorke, Philip C. (ed.), *The Life and Correspondence of Philip Yorke, Earl of Hardwicke, Lord High Chancellor of Great Britain*, 3 vols (Cambridge: Cambridge University Press, 1913)

Official Reports and Publications

'Having been favoured with the Perusal of the following Instructions relative to the Military School at High Wycombe, we present the same to our Readers, as containing important Information', *British Military Library or Journal*, 2/17 (February 1800), 161–163

House of Commons, *Report from the Select Committee on Sandhurst Royal Military College* (London: HMSO, 1855)

Lefroy, J. H., *Report on the Regimental and Garrison Schools of the Army, and on Military Libraries and Reading Rooms* (London: HMSO, 1859)

The Report of the General Officers Appointed . . . to Inquire into the Causes of the Failure of the Late Expedition to the Coasts of France (London: A. Millar, 1758)

Stockdale, J. (ed.), *Parliamentary Register* (London: J. Almon, 1775–)

Doctrine Manuals, Drill Books and Military Treatises

Alexander, James E., *Bush Fighting Illustrated by Remarkable Actions and Incidents of the Maori War in New Zealand* (London: Low, Marston, Low & Searle, 1873)

Anonymous, *Essay of the Art of War: in which the General Principles of All the Operations of War in the Field are Fully Explained. The Whole Collected from the Opinions of the Best Authors* (London: A. Millar, 1761)

Anonymous, *The New Manual Exercise as Performed by His Majesty's Dragoons, Foot-Guards, Foot, Light Infantry, Artillery* (London: J. Millan, 1758)

Carnot, Lazare Nicholas Marguerite, *Règlement provisoire sur le service de l'infanterie en campagne du 5 avril 1792* (Paris: Magimel, 1792)

Cooper, T. H., *A Practical Guide for the Light Infantry Officer* (London: Robert Wilks, 1806)

Craufurd, C and R. Craufurd, *An Account of Some of the Most Remarkable Events of the War Between the Prussians, Austrians, and Russians, from 1756 to 1763, and a Treatise on Several Branches of the Military Art. With Plans and Maps, Translated from the Second Edition of the German Original of J.G. Tielke, by Captain C. Craufurd and Captain R. Craufurd*, 2 vols (London: J. Walter, 1788)

Cross, John, *A System of Drill and Manoeuvres as Practised in the 52nd Light Infantry Regiment* (London: T. Egerton, 1823)

Dalby, Isaac, *A Course of Mathematics, Designed for the Use of Officers and Cadets, of the Royal Military College* (London: W. Glendinning, 1807)

Dundas, David, *Principles of Military Movements* (London: T. Cadell, 1788)

Feuquières, Antoine de Pas, *Mémoires de M. le Marquis de Feuquière*, 4 vols (London: P. Dunoyer, 1740)

Fitzclarence, Frederick, *Suggestions for Brigade and Light Infantry Movements* (London: Parker, Furnival & Parker, 1851)

Fitzclarence, Frederick, *Memoranda by Lieut.-General Lord Frederick Fitzclarence, for the Use of Young Officers Assembled in Poona During the Period of Exercise in December 1853, Including Instructions Applicable to a Combination of the Three Arms* (London: Parker, Furnival & Parker, 1854)

Folard, Jean-Charles de, *Nouvelles découvertes sur la guerre* (Brussels: Foppens & Tilliard, 1726)

Folard, Jean-Charles de, *L'Esprit de Chevalier Folard, Tiré de ses Commentaires sur l'Histoire de Polybe* (Paris: Jean Marie Bruyzet by La Compagnie des Libraires, 1760)

Fossée, Charles-Louis-François de, *Idée d'un militaire pour la disposition des troupes [. . .] la défense et l'attaque des petits postes* (Paris: Jombert, 1783)

Hanger, George, *A Letter to . . . Lord Castlereagh . . . from G. H. . . . proving how one hundred and fifty thousand men . . . well disciplined . . . may be acquired in the short space of two months* (London: Privately Published, 1808)

Jarry, François, *Instruction Concerning the Duties of Light Infantry in the Field* (London: A Dulau & Co., 1803)

Jones, W. D., *Records of the Royal Military Academy* (Woolwich: Royal Military Academy, 1851)

Kane, Richard, *Campaigns of King William and Queen Anne; From 1689 to 1712. Also a New System of Military Discipline, for a Battalion of Foot on Action; With the Most Essential Exercise of the Cavalry* (London: J. Millan, 1745)

Lloyd, Henry, *Continuation of the History of the Late War in Germany Between the King of Prussia and the Empress of Germany and Her Allies* (London: Hooper, 1781)

Lloyd, Henry, *A Political and Military Rhapsody, on the Invasion and Defence of Great Britain and Ireland ... To Which is Annexed, a Short Account of the Author* [signed: John Drummond], *and a Supplement by the Editor*. The fourth edition. With additions, etc. (London: Edgerton, 1795)

Manningham, Coote, *Military Lectures Delivered to the Officers of the 95th (Rifle) Regiment at Shorn-Cliffe Barracks, Kent* (London: T. Egerton, 1803)

Mitchell, John, *Thoughts on Tactics and Military Organization: Together with an Enquiry into the Power and Position of Russia* (London: Longman, 1838)

Molesworth, Richard, *A Short Course of Standing Rules, for the Governments and Conduct of an Army, Designed for, or in The Field* (London: R. Dodsley, 1744)

Preuss, J. D. E. (ed.), *Œuvres de Frédéric le Grand*, 30 vols (Berlin: Impr. Royale, 1846–56)

Rottenburg, Baron Francis de, *Regulations for the Exercise of Riflemen and Light Infantry: Instructions for Their Conduct in the Field* (London: T. Egerton, 1803)

Saxe, Maurice, Comte de, *Reveries, or Memoirs Concerning the Art of War* (Edinburgh: Sands, Donaldson, Murray and Cochran, 1759)

Smith, George, *A Universal Military Dictionary* (London: J. Millan, 1779)

Smith, William, *An Historical Account of the Expedition Against the Ohio Indians ... Under the Command of Henry Bouquet* (Philadelphia: W. Bradford, 1766)

Stewart, William, *Outlines of a Plan for the General Reform of the British Land Forces* (London: T. Egerton, 1806)

Torrens, Henry, *Field Exercise and Evolutions of the Army* (London: William Clowes, 1824)

Townshend, George, *Rules and Orders for the Royal Military Academy at Woolwich* (London: Bullock & Spencer, 1776)

Turpin de Crissé, Lancelot, *An Essay on the Art of War. Translated from the French by Captain Joseph Otway*, 2 vols (London: Johnston, 1762)

Williamson, Adam, *Military Memoirs and Maxims of Marshal Turenne; Interspersed with Others, Taken from the Best Authors and Observation, with Remarks* (London: Knapton, 1740)

Wolfe, James, *General Wolfe's Instructions to Young Officers* (London: Millan, 1768)

Historical Manuscripts Commission

The Manuscripts of J. B. Fortescue, Preserved at Dropmore, 9 vols (London, 1892–1912)

The Manuscripts of the Marquess Townshend (London, 1887)

Report on the Laing Manuscripts Preserved at the University of Edinburgh, 3 vols (London, 1925)

Report on the Manuscripts of Earl Bathurst Preserved at Cirencester Park (London, 1923)

Report on the Manuscripts of Mrs. Frankland-Russell-Astley of Chequers Court, Bucks (London, 1900)

Report on the Manuscripts of Mrs. Stopford-Sackville of Drayton House, Northamptonshire, 2 vols (London, 1910)

Report on Manuscripts in Various Collections, 8 vols (London, 1909)

Newspapers, Periodicals and Magazines

Boston Gazette
Boston News-Letter
Calcutta Gazette
Colburn's United Service Magazine, and Naval and Military Journal
The Critical Review, Or, Annals of Literature
Edinburgh Review
The Gentleman's Magazine

Gentleman's Quarterly
London Evening Post
London and Westminster Review
Naval and Military Gazette
Quarterly Review
Royal Military Chronicle
Sydney Gazette
The Times
The United Service Journal and Naval and Military Magazine
United Service Magazine
Universal Magazine

Secondary Sources

Abel, Jonathan, *Guibert: Father of Napoleon's Grand Armée* (Norman: University of Oklahoma Press, 2016)

Adams, Randolph G., *British Headquarters Maps and Sketches Used by Sir Henry Clinton While in Command of the British Forces Operating in North America During the War for Independence, 1775–1782: A Descriptive List of the Original Manuscripts and Printed Documents Now Preserved in the William L. Clements Library at the University of Michigan* (Ann Arbor: William L. Clements Library, 1928)

Ahuja, Ravi and Martin Christof-Füchsle (eds), *A Great War in South India: German Accounts of the Anglo-Mysore Wars, 1766–1799* (Berlin: De Gruyter, 2020)

Anderson, Carolyn J., 'Military Intelligence: The Board of Ordnance Maps and Plans of Scotland, 1689–c.1760', in Gary A. Boyd and Denis Linehan (eds), *Ordnance: War + Architecture & Space* (London: Routledge, 2016), 157–178

Anderson, Fred, *Crucible of War: The Seven Years' War and the Fate of the British Empire in British North America, 1754–1766* (New York: Knopf, 2000)

Andrews, John Harwood, *Maps in Those Days: Cartographic Methods Before 1850* (Dublin: Four Court Press, 2009)

Atkinson, Christopher Thomas, *The South Wales Borderers, 24th Foot, 1689–1937* (Cambridge: Cambridge University Press, 1937)

Auerbach, Jeffrey A., *Imperial Boredom: Monotony and the British Empire* (Oxford: Oxford University Press, 2018)

Babits, Lawrence E., *A Devil of a Whipping: The Battle of Cowpens* (Chapel Hill: University of North Carolina Press, 1998)

Bainbridge, Simon, *British Poetry and the Revolutionary and Napoleonic Wars: Visions of Conflict* (Oxford: Oxford University Press, 2003)

Baker, Thomas, *Another Such Victory: The Story of the American Defeat at Guildford Courthouse That Helped Win the War for Independence* (New York: Eastern Acorn Press, 1981)

Ballantyne, Tony, 'Empire, Knowledge and Culture: From Proto-Globalization to Modern Globalization', in A. G. Hopkins (ed.), *Globalization in World History* (London: Pimlico, 2002), 115–140

Ballantyne, Tony, *Webs of Empire: Locating New Zealand's Colonial Past* (Wellington: Bridget Williams Books, 2014)

Baugh, Daniel, *The Global Seven Years War, 1754–1763* (Harlow: Longman, 2011)

Bayly, C. A., *Empire and Information: Intelligence Gathering and Social Communication in India, 1780–1870* (Cambridge: Cambridge University Press, 1996)

Beattie, Daniel J., 'The Adaptation of the British Army to Wilderness Warfare, 1755–1763', in Marten Ultee (ed.), *Adapting to Conditions: War and Society in the Eighteenth Century* (Huntsville: University of Alabama Press, 1986), 56–83.

Belich, James, *The New Zealand Wars and the Victorian Interpretation of Racial Conflict* (Auckland: Auckland University Press, 1998)

Berkovich, Ilya, *Motivation in War: The Experience of Command Soldiers in Old-Regime Europe* (Cambridge: Cambridge University Press, 2017)

Bew, John, 'Waterloo: beyond the battlefield', *History Today*, 63/9, 2013.

Black, Jeremy, 'A Military Revolution? A 1660–1792 Perspective', in Clifford J. Rogers (ed.), *The Military Revolution Debate: Readings on the Military Transformation of Early Modern Europe* (Boulder: Westview Press, 1995), 95–116

Black, Jeremy, *Britain as a Military Power, 1688–1815* (London: UCL Press, 1999)

Black, Jeremy, 'British Military Strategy', in Donald Stoker, Kenneth J. Hagan and Michael T. McMaster (eds), *Strategy in the American War of Independence: A Global Approach* (London: Routledge, 2010), 58–72

Black, Jeremy, *European Warfare, 1660–1815* (London: Yale University Press, 1994)

Black, Jeremy, *Fighting for America: The Struggle for Mastery in North America, 1519–1871* (Bloomington: Indiana University Press, 2011)

Black, Jeremy, *How the Army Made Britain a Global Power: 1688–1815* (Oxford: Casemate, 2021)

Black, Jeremy, *Military Strategy: A Global History* (London: Yale University Press, 2020)

Black, Jeremy, *The English Press in the Eighteenth Century* (London: Routledge, 1987)

Blackmore, David, *Destructive and Formidable: British Infantry Firepower, 1642–1745* (Barnsley: Frontline, 2014)

Blanning, T.C.W., *The Origins of the French Revolutionary Wars* (London: Routledge, 1986)

Blanning, Tim, *Frederick the Great: King of Prussia* (London: Allen Lane, 2015)

Boscawen, Hugh, *The Capture of Louisbourg, 1758* (Norman: Oklahoma University Press, 2011)

Brooks, Lisa, *Our Beloved Kin: A New History of King Philip's War* (New Haven: Yale University Press, 2018)

Brown, Steve, *The Duke of York's Flanders Campaign: Fighting the French Revolution, 1793–1795* (Barnsley: Frontline, 2018)

Browning, Reed, *The War of Austrian Succession* (New York: St Martin's Press, 1993)

Brumwell, Stephen, '"A Service Truly Critical": The British Army and warfare with the North American Indians, 1755–1764', *War in History*, 5/2 (April 1998), 146–175

Brumwell, Stephen, *Paths of Glory: The Life and Death of James Wolfe* (London: Hambledon Continuum, 2006)

Brumwell, Stephen, *Redcoats: The British Soldier and War in the Americas, 1755–1763* (Cambridge: Cambridge University Press, 2002)

Brumwell, Stephen, *White Devil: A True Story of War, Savagery, and Vengeance in Colonial America* (Cambridge, MA: Da Capo Press, 2004)

Bryant, G. J., *The Emergence of British Power in India, 1600–1784: A Grand Strategic Interpretation* (Woodbridge: Boydell Press, 2013)

Buchanan, John, *The Road to Guilford Courthouse: The American Revolution in the Carolinas* (New York: Wiley, 1997)

Buckley, Roger, *Slaves in Red Coats: The British West India Regiments, 1795–1815* (New Haven: Yale University Press, 1979)

Buckley, Roger, *The British Army in the West Indies: Society and the Military in the Revolutionary Age* (Tallahassee: University Press of Florida, 1998)

Callahan, Raymond, *The East India Company and Army Reform, 1783–1798* (Cambridge, MA: Harvard University Press, 1972)

Calloway, Colin G., *The Scratch of a Pen: 1763 and the Transformation of North America* (Oxford: Oxford University Press, 2006)

Campbell, Alexander V., *The Royal American Regiment: An Atlantic Microcosm, 1755–1772* (Norman: Oklahoma University Press, 2010)

Carpenter, Stanley D. M., *Southern Gambit: Cornwallis and the British March to Yorktown* (Norman: University of Oklahoma Press, 2018)

Chambers, Thomas A., *Memories of War: Visiting Battlegrounds and Bonefields in the Early American Republic* (Ithaca: Cornell University Press, 2012)

Chandler, David, *The Art of Warfare in the Age of Marlborough* (London: Batsford, 1976)

Chatterjee, Partha, *The Black Hold of Empire: History of a Global Practice of Power* (Princeton: Princeton University Press, 2012)

Chet, Guy, *Conquering the American Wilderness: The Triumph of European Warfare in the Colonial Northeast* (Amherst: University of Massachusetts, 2003)

Chickering, Roger and Stig Förster (eds), *War in an Age of Revolution, 1775–1815* (Cambridge: Cambridge University Press, 2010)

Childs, John, *The Nine Years' War and the British Army 1688 97: The Operations in the Low Countries* (Manchester: Manchester University Press, 2013)

Clarke, Joseph and John Horne (eds), *Militarized Cultural Encounters in the Long Nineteenth Century: Making War, Mapping Europe* (Basingstoke: Palgrave, 2018)

Cohn, Bernard S., *Colonialism and its Forms of Knowledge: The British in India* (Princeton: Princeton University Press, 1996)

Colley, Linda, 'Going native, telling tales: captivity, collaborations and empire', *Past & Present*, 168 (August 2000), 170–193

Collins, Bruce, *War and Empire: The Expansion of Britain, 1790–1830* (London: Routledge, 2010)

Connor, John, *The Australian Frontier Wars 1788–1838* (Sydney: University of New South Wales Press, 2002)

Conway, Stephen, *The British Army, 1714–1783: An Institutional History* (Barnsley: Pen & Sword, 2021)

Conway, Stephen, 'The British Army, "military Europe," and the American War of Independence', *The William and Mary Quarterly*, 67/1 (January 2010), 69–100

Cooper, Randolf G. S., *The Anglo-Maratha Campaigns and the Contest for India: The Struggle for Control of the South Asian Military Economy* (Cambridge: Cambridge University Press, 2004)

Cooper, Randolf G. S., 'Culture, combat and colonialism in eighteenth and nineteenth century India', *International History Review*, 27/3 (September 2005), 534–549

Coss, Edward J., *All for the King's Shilling: The British Soldier Under Wellington, 1808–1814* (Norman: University of Oklahoma Press, 2010)

Cubbison, Douglas R., *All Canada in the Hands of the British: General Jeffrey Amherst and the 1760 Campaign to Conquer New France* (Norman: University of Oklahoma Press, 2014)

Cumpston, J. H. L., *Thomas Mitchell: Surveyor General & Explorer* (Oxford: Oxford University Press, 1965)

Dalrymple, William, *The Anarchy: The East India Company, Corporate Violence and the Pillage of an Empire* (New York: Bloomsbury, 2019)

Dalrymple, William, *Return of a King: The Battle for Afghanistan, 1839–42* (London: Bloomsbury, 2013)

Daughan, George C., *Revolution on the Hudson: New York City and the Hudson River Valley in the American War of Independence* (New York: W. W. Norton, 2016)

David, Saul, *All the King's Men: The British Soldier from the Restoration to Waterloo* (London: Penguin, 2012)

David, Saul, *Victoria's Wars: The Rise of Empire* (London: Penguin, 2006)

Davies, Huw J., 'Military Print Culture, Knowledge and Terrain: Knowledge Mobility and Eighteenth-century Military Colonialism', in David Lambert and Peter Merriman (eds), *Empire and Mobility in the Long Nineteenth Century* (Manchester: Manchester University Press, 2020), 29–49

Davies, Huw J., *Spying for Wellington: British Military Intelligence in the Peninsular War* (Norman: University of Oklahoma Press, 2018)

Davies, Huw J., *Wellington's Wars: The Making of a Military Genius* (London: Yale University Press, 2012)

Deloche, Jean, *Transport and Communications in India Prior to Steam Locomotion; Volume 1: Land Transport* (Delhi: Oxford University Press, 1993)

Dennis, Peter, Jeffrey Grey, Ewan Morris and Robin Prior (eds), *Oxford Companion to Australian Military History* (Oxford: Oxford University Press, 2008)

Dias, Rosie, 'Memory and the Aesthetics of Military Experience: Viewing the Landscape of the Anglo-Mysore Wars', *Tate Papers*, no.19, Spring 2013.

Divall, Carole, *General Sir Ralph Abercromby and the French Revolutionary Wars, 1793–1801* (London: Pen & Sword, 2019)

Dixon, David, *Never Come to Peace Again: Pontiac's Uprising and the Fate of the British Empire in North America* (Norman: Oklahoma University Press, 2005)

Dobie, Madeleine, "The enlightenment at war", *PMLA*, 124/5 (October 2009), 1851–1854

Dodwell, H. H., 'Transport and the Second Mysore War', *Journal of the Society for Army Historical Research* 3 (1924), 266–272

Duffy, Christopher, *The Army of Frederick the Great* (London: David & Charles, 1974)

Duffy, Christopher, *The Army of Maria Theresa: The Armed Forces of Imperial Austria, 1740–1780* (London: Hippocrene Books, 1977)

Duffy, Christopher, *Fight for a Throne: The Jacobite '45 Reconsidered* (Solihull: Helion, 2015)

Duffy, Christopher, *Frederick the Great: A Military Life* (London: Routledge, 1985)

Duffy, Christopher, *The Military Experience in the Age of Reason* (New York: Atheneum, 1988)

Duffy, Michael, *Soldiers, Sugar and Seapower: The British Expeditions to the West Indies and the War Against Revolutionary France* (Oxford: Clarendon Press, 1987)

Dupree, Louis, *Afghanistan* (Princeton: Princeton University Press, 1973)

Edelson, S. Max, *The New Map of Empire: How Britain Imagined America Before Independence* (Cambridge, MA: Harvard University Press, 2017)

Edney, Matthew, *Mapping an Empire: The Geographical Construction of India, 1765–1843* (Chicago: University of Chicago Press, 1997)

Ehrlich, Joshua, 'Plunder and prestige: Tipu Sultan's library and the making of British India', *South Asia: Journal of South Asian Studies*, 43:3 (May 2020), 478–492

Engberg-Petersen, Anders, *Empires of Chance: The Napoleonic Wars and the Disorder of Things* (Cambridge, MA: Harvard University Press, 2015)

Esdaile, Charles J., *Napoleon's Wars* (London: Penguin, 2008)

Esdaile, Charles J., *Outpost of Empire: The Napoleonic Occupation of Andalucía, 1810–1812* (Norman: Oklahoma University Press, 2012)

Esdaile, Charles J., *The Peninsular War* (London: Penguin, 2002)

Esdaile, Charles J., *The Spanish Army in the Peninsular War* (Manchester: Manchester University Press, 1988)

Esdaile, Charles J., *The Wars of the French Revolution, 1792–1801* (Abingdon: Routledge, 2019)

Esdaile, Charles and Philip Freeman, *Burgos in the Peninsular War, 1808–1814: Occupation, Siege, Aftermath* (London: Palgrave, 2015)

Fenn, Elizabeth A., 'Biological warfare in eighteenth-century North America: Beyond Jeffrey Amherst', *Journal of American History*, 86 (1999–2000), 1552–80.

Ferlier, Louisiane and Bénédicte Miyamoto, *Forms, Formats and the Circulation of Knowledge: British Printscape's Innovations, 1688–1832* (Leiden: Brill, 2020)

Ferling, John, *Almost a Miracle: The American Victory in the War of Independence* (Oxford: Oxford University Press, 2007)

Figes, Orlando, *Crimea: The Last Crusade* (London: Allen Lane, 2010)

Fischer, David Hackett, *Washington's Crossing* (Oxford: Oxford University Press, 2004)

Fisher, Michael H., *Indirect Rule in India: Residents and the Residency System, 1764–1858* (Oxford: Oxford University Press, 1991)

Flavell, Julie, *The Howe Dynasty: The Untold Story of a Military Family and the Women Behind Britain's Wars for America* (New York: Liveright, 2021)

Fletcher, Ian, *Craufurd's Light Division: The Life of Robert Craufurd and his Command of the Light Division* (Tunbridge Wells: Spellmount, 1991)

Fletcher, Ian, *Robert Craufurd, The Man and the Myth: The Life and Times of Wellington's Wayward Martinet* (Oxford: Pen & Sword, 2021)

Forrest, Alan, *Waterloo* (Oxford: Oxford University Press, 2015)

Fortescue, J. W., *A History of the British Army*, 12 vols (London: Macmillan, 1899–1927)

Frégault, Guy, *Canada: The War of Conquest* (Oxford: Oxford University Press, 1969)

Gapps, Stephen, *The Sydney Wars: Conflict in the Early Colony, 1788–1817* (Sydney: University of New South Wales Press, 2018)

Gat, Azar, *The Origins of Military Thought: From the Enlightenment to Clausewitz* (Oxford: Oxford University Press, 1989)

Gates, David, *The British Light Infantry Arm, c.1790–1815* (London: Batsford, 1987)

Geggus, David P., *Slavery, War and Revolution: The British Occupation of Saint Domingue, 1793–1798* (Oxford: Oxford University Press, 1982)

Gilbert, Arthur N., 'Recruitment and reform in the East India Company Army, 1760–1800', *Journal of British Studies*, 15:1 (Autumn 1975), 89–111

Gipson, Lawrence, *The Great War for Empire: The Victorious Years, 1758–1760* (New York: Knopf, 1950)

Gipson, Lawrence, *The Great War for the Empire: The Years of Defeat, 1754–1757* (New York: Knopf, 1948)

Glover, Richard, *Peninsular Preparation: The Reform of the British Army, 1795–1809* (Cambridge: Cambridge University Press, 1963)

Goldsmith, Sarah, *Masculinity and Danger on the Eighteenth-Century Grand Tour* (London: University of London Press, 2020)

Golway, Terry, *Washington's General: Nathanael Greene and the Triumph of the American Revolution* (New York: Henry Holt, 2005)

Gordon, Stewart, *The Marathas: 1600–1818* (Cambridge: Cambridge University Press, 1993)

Grenier, John, *The First Way of War: American War Making on the Frontier* (Cambridge: Cambridge University Press, 2005)

Gruber, Ira D., *The Howe Brothers and the American Revolution* (Chapel Hill: University of North Carolina Press, 1972)

Gruber, Ira D., *Books and the British Army in the Age of the American Revolution* (Chapel Hill: University of North Carolina Press, 2010)

Gruber, Ira D., 'The education of Sir Henry Clinton', *Bulletin of the John Rylands University Library of Manchester*, 72 (1990), 131–53.

Guedella, Philip, *The Duke* (London: Hodder & Stoughton, 1931)

Hackman, W. K., 'The British raid on Rochefort, 1757', *Mariner's Mirror*, 64/3 (August 1978), 263–275

Hagist, Don, *British Soldiers of the American War: Voices of the American Revolution* (Yardley: Westholme Publishing, 2012)

Harari, Yuval Noah, *The Ultimate Experience: Battlefield Revelations and the Making of Modern War Culture, 1450–2000* (London: Palgrave, 2008)

Harding, D. F., *Small Arms of the East India Company*, 4 vols (London: Foresight, 1999)

Harding-Edgar, John, *Next to Wellington. General Sir George Murray: The Story of a Scottish Soldier and Statesman, Wellington's Quartermaster General* (London: Helion & Co., 2018)

Harlow, Vincent T., *The Founding of the Second British Empire, 1763–1793*, 2 vols (London: Longman, 1952)

Hartley, J. B., 'The bankruptcy of Thomas Jeffreys: An episode in the economic history of eighteenth century map-making', *Imago Mundi*, 20 (1966), 33–47

Hartley, J. B., *The New Nature of Maps: Essays in the History of Cartography* (Baltimore: Johns Hopkins University Press, 2001)

Hartley, J. B., Barbara Bartz Petchenick and Lawrence W. Towner, *Mapping the American Revolutionary War* (Chicago: University of Chicago Press, 1978)

Hasrat, Bikrama Jit, *Anglo-Sikh Relations, 1799–1849: A Reappraisal of the Rise and Fall of the Sikhs* (New Delhi: V.V. Research Institute Book Agency, 1968)

Haynes, Christine, *Our Friends the Enemies: The Occupation of France After Napoleon* (Cambridge, MA: Harvard University Press, 2018)

Hayworth, Jordan R., *Revolutionary France's War of Conquest in the Rhineland: Conquering the Natural Frontier, 1792–1797* (Cambridge: Cambridge University Press, 2019)

Headrick, Daniel R., *The Tools of Empire: Technology and European Imperialism in the Nineteenth Century* (Oxford: Oxford University Press, 1981)

Heathcote, T. A., *The Military in British India: The Development of British Land Forces in South Asia, 1600–1947* (Barnsley: The Praetorian Press, 2013)

Hilaire-Perez, Liliane and Catherine Verna, 'Dissemination of technical knowledge in the Middle Ages and the Early Modern era: new approaches and methodological issues', *Technology and Culture*, 47/3 (2006), 536–565.

Hill, Joanna, *Wellington's Right Hand: Rowland, Viscount Hill* (Stroud: Spellmount, 2011)

Hillemann, Ulrike, *Asian Empire and British Knowledge: China and the Networks of British Imperial Expansion* (Basingstoke: Palgrave, 2009)

Hochman, Leah, *The Ugliness of Moses Mendelssohn: Aesthetics, Religion and Morality in the Eighteenth Century* (New York: Routledge, 2014)

Hoffman, Ronald and Peter J. Albert (eds), *Arms and Independence: The Military Character of the American Revolution* (Charlottesville: University Press of Virginia, 1984)

Hopkins, Benjamin D., *The Making of Modern Afghanistan* (Basingstoke: Palgrave, 2008)

Hornsby, Stephen J., *Surveyors of Empire: Samuel Holland, J. W. F. des Barres and the Making of the Atlantic Neptune* (Montreal: McGill-Queen's University Press, 2016)

Houlding, J. A., *Fit for Service: The Training of the British Army 1715–1795* (Oxford: Oxford University Press, 1981)

Howard, Michael, 'Wellington and the British Army', in Michael Howard (ed.), *Wellingtonian Studies* (Aldershot: Gale & Polden, 1959)

Jennings, Francis, *Empire of Fortune: Crowns, Colonies & Tribes in the Seven Years War in America* (New York: W. W. Norton, 1988)

Johnson, Richard R., 'The search for a usable Indian: An aspect of the defense of Colonial New England', *Journal of American History*, 64/3 (1977), 623–651

Kamissek, Christoph and Jonas Kreienbaum, 'An imperial cloud? Conceptualising inter-imperial connections and transimperial knowledge', *Journal of Modern European History*, 14/2 (2016), 164–181

Kennedy, Catriona, 'Military Ways of Seeing: British Soldiers' Sketches from the Egyptian Campaign of 1801', in Joseph Clarke and John Horne (eds), *Militarized Cultural Encounters in the Long Nineteenth Century: Making War, Mapping Europe* (Basingstoke: Palgrave, 2018), 197–222

Kennedy, Catriona, *Narratives of the Revolutionary and Napoleonic Wars: Military and Civilian Experience in Britain and Ireland* (Basingstoke: Palgrave, 2013)

Kennedy, Catriona and Matthew McCormack (eds), *Soldiering in Britain and Ireland, 1750–1850: Men of Arms* (London: Palgrave, 2013)

Khule, Arthur, 'War without contact: Berenhorst, Bülow, and the avoidance of violence as the core paradigm of military science', *War in History* (May 2020), 1–26

Knight, Roger, *Britain Against Napoleon: The Organization of Victory, 1793–1815* (London: Allen Lane, 2013)

Laidlaw, Zoe, *Colonial Connections, 1815–45: Patronage, the Information Revolution and Colonial Government* (Manchester: Manchester University Press, 2012)

LaFont, Jean-Marie, *Fauj-i-Khas: Maharaja Ranjit Singh and His French Officers* (Amritsar: Guru Nanak Dev University, 2002)

Lambert, David and Alan Lester (eds), *Colonial Lives Across the British Empire: Imperial Careering in the Long Nineteenth Century* (Cambridge: Cambridge University Press, 2006)

Lambert, David and Peter Merriman (eds), *Empire and Mobility in the Long Nineteenth Century* (Manchester: Manchester University Press, 2020)

Landis, Charles I. et al, 'Jasper Yeates and his times', *Pennsylvania Magazine of History and Biography*, 46/3 (1922), 212–213

Lawson, Cecil C. P., *A History of the Uniforms of the British Army*, 5 vols (London: Norman, 1961)

Leach, Douglas Edward, *Arms for Empire: A Military History of the British Colonies in North America, 1607–1763* (New York: Macmillan, 1973)

Lee, Wayne E., *Barbarians and Brothers: Anglo-American Warfare, 1500–1865* (Oxford: Oxford University Press, 2011)

Lee, Wayne E., 'Fortify, fight, or flee: Tuscarora and Cherokee defensive warfare and military culture adaptation', *Journal of Military History*, 3/68 (July 2004), 713–770.

Lender, Mark Edward and Garry Wheeler Stone, *Fatal Sunday: George Washington, the Monmouth Campaign and the Politics of Battle* (Norman: University of Oklahoma Press, 2016)

Lester, Alan, *Imperial Networks: Creating Identities in Nineteenth-Century South Africa and Britain* (London: Routledge, 2001)

Long, John Cuthbert, *Lord Jeffrey Amherst: A Soldier of the King* (London: Macmillan, 1933)

Luvaas, Jay, *The Education of an Army: British Military Thought, 1815–1940* (London: Cassell, 1964)

Lynn, John, *Battle: A History of Combat and Culture from Ancient Greece to Modern America* (New York: Basic Books, 2003)

MacDonald, Janet, *Sir John Moore: The Making of a Controversial Hero* (Barnsley: Pen & Sword, 2016)

Mackesy, Piers, *British Victory in Egypt: The End of Napoleon's Conquest* (London: Routledge, 1995)

Mackesy, Piers, *Statesmen at War: Strategy of Overthrow, 1798–1799* (London: Longman, 1974)

Mackesy, Piers, *The War for America: 1775–1783* (Lincoln: University of Nebraska, 1964)

Mackesy, Piers, 'What the British Army Learned', in Ronald Hoffman and Peter J. Albert (eds), *Arms and Independence: The Military Character of the American Revolution* (Charlottesville: University Press of Virginia, 1984), 191–215

MacKillop, Andrew, *'More Fruitful Than the Soil': Army, Empire and the Scottish Highlands, 1715–1815* (East Lothian: Tuckwell Press, 2000)

Mahon, R. H., *Life of General the Hon. James Murray: A Builder of Canada* (London: John Murray, 1921)

Manning, Stephen, *Quebec: The Story of Three Sieges* (London: Continuum, 2009)

Markham, Clements R., *Major James Rennell and the Rise of Modern English Geography* (London: Cassell and Co, 1895)

Markovits, Claude, Jacques Pouchepadass and Sanjay Subrahmanyam (eds), *Society and Circulation: Mobile People and Itinerant Cultures in South Asia, 1750–1950* (London: Anthem Press, 2006)

Marshall, Douglas W., 'The British Engineers in America: 1755–1783', *Journal of the Society for Army Historical Research*, 51/207 (1973), 155–163

Marshall, Douglas W., 'Military maps of the eighteenth-century and the Tower of London Drawing Room', *Imago Mundi*, 32 (1980), 21–44.

Marshall, P. J., *The Making and Unmaking of Empires: Britain, India, and America, c. 1750–1783* (Oxford: Oxford University Press, 2005)

Matheson, Cyril, *The Life of Henry Dundas, First Viscount Melville, 1742–1811* (London: Constable, 1933)

McCavitt, John and Christopher T. George, *The Man Who Captured Washington: Major General Robert Ross and the War of 1812* (Norman: University of Oklahoma Press, 2016)

McConnell, Michael N., *Army & Empire: British Soldiers on the American Frontier, 1758–1775* (Lincoln: University of Nebraska, 2004)

McCormack, Matthew, 'Liberty and Discipline: Militia Training Literature in Mid-Georgian England', in Catriona Kennedy and Matthew McCormack (eds), *Soldiering in Britain and Ireland, 1750–1850: Men of Arms* (London: Palgrave, 2013), 159–178

McCulloch, I. M., *Sons of the Mountains: The Highland Regiments in the French and Indian War, 1756–67*, 2 vols (New York: Purple Mountain, 2006)

McCurdy, John Gilbert, *Quarters: The Accommodation of the British Army and the Coming of the American Revolution* (Ithaca: Cornell University Press, 2019)

Miakinkov, Eugene, *War and Enlightenment in Russia: Military Culture in the Age of Catherine II* (Toronto: University of Toronto Press, 2020)

Middleton, Richard, 'British coastal expeditions to France, 1757–1758', *Journal of the Society for Army History Research*, 71/286 (Summer 1993), 74–92

Middleton, Richard, *Cornwallis: Soldier and Statesman in a Revolutionary World* (London: Yale University Press, 2022)

Mikaberidze, Alexander, *The Napoleonic Wars: A Global History* (Oxford: Oxford University Press, 2020)

Moon, Penderel, *The British Conquest and Dominion of India* (London: Duckworth, 1989)

Muir, Rory, *Wellington: The Path to Victory, 1769–1814* (London: Yale University Press, 2013)

Muir, R. J. B. and C. J. Esdaile, 'Strategic Planning in a Time of Small Government: The Wars Against Revolutionary and Napoleonic France, 1793–1815', in C. M. Woolgar (ed.), *Wellington Studies I* (Southampton: University of Southampton Press, 1996), 1–90

Murphy, Sharon, *The British Soldier and His Libraries, c.1822–1901* (Basingstoke: Palgrave, 2016)

Nester, William R., *The French and Indian War and the Conquest of New France* (Norman: University of Oklahoma Press, 2014)

Nosworthy, Brent, *Battle Tactics of Napoleon and His Enemies* (London: Constable, 1995)

Oliphant, John, *John Forbes: Scotland, Flanders and the Seven Years' War, 1707–1759* (London: Bloomsbury, 2015)

Oman, Charles, *Wellington's Army, 1809–1814* (London: E. Arnold, 1913)

O'Neil, Lindsay, *The Opened Letter: Networking in the Early Modern British World* (Philadelphia: University of Pennsylvania Press, 2014)

O'Shaughnessy, Andrew, *The Men Who Lost America: British Command During the Revolutionary War and the Preservation of Empire* (New Haven: Yale University Press, 2013)

Page, Anthony, *Britain and the Seventy Years War, 1744–1815* (Basingstoke: Palgrave, 2015)

Pancake, John S., *This Destructive War: The British Campaign in the Carolinas, 1780–1782* (Tuscaloosa: University of Alabama Press, 2003)

Paret, Peter, 'Colonial experience and European military reform at the end of the eighteenth century', *Bulletin of the Institute of Historical Research*, 37/95 (1964), 47–59

Paret, Peter, 'The Relationship Between the Revolutionary War and European Military Thought and Practice in the Second Half of the Eighteenth Century', in Don Higginbotham (ed.), *Reconsiderations on the Revolutionary War* (Westport, GT, 1978), 144–157

Pargellis, Stanley, *Lord Loudoun in North America* (New Haven: Yale University Press, 1934)

Parker, Geoffrey, *The Military Revolution: Military Innovation and the Rise of the West, 1500–1800* (Cambridge: Cambridge University Press, 1988)

Peaty, John, 'Architect of victory: the reforms of the Duke of York', *Journal of the Society of Army Historical Research*, 84/340 (Winter 2006), 339–348

Peckham, Howard H., *The Colonial Wars, 1689–1762* (Chicago: University of Chicago Press, 1964)

Peckham, Howard H., *The War for Independence* (Chicago: University of Chicago Press, 1958)

Pichichero, Christy, *The Military Enlightenment: War and Culture in the French Empire from Louis XIV to Napoleon* (Ithaca: Cornell University Press, 2017)

Plank, Geoffrey, *Rebellion and Savagery: The Jacobite Rising of 1745 and the British Empire* (Philadelphia: University of Pennsylvania Press, 2006)

Preston, David, *Braddock's Defeat: The Battle of the Monongahela and the Road to Revolution* (Oxford: Oxford University Press, 2015)

Price, Richard, *Making Empire: Colonial Encounters and the Creation of Imperial Rule in Nineteenth-Century Africa* (Cambridge: Cambridge University Press, 2008)

Rae, Thomas I., 'The Loudoun Scottish Papers in the Huntington Library', *The Scottish Historical Review*, 49/148 (October 1970)

Reilly, Robin, *The Rest to Fortune: The Life of Major-General James Wolfe* (London: White Lion, 1960)

Richards, Thomas, *The Imperial Archive: Knowledge and the Fantasy of Empire* (London: Verso, 1993)

Robertson, Ian, *Wellington Invades France: The Final Phase of the Peninsular War, 1813–1814* (London: Greenhill, 2003)

Robertson, Richie, *The Enlightenment: The Pursuit of Happiness, 1680–1790* (London: Allen Lane, 2020)

Rogers, Clifford J. (ed.), *The Military Revolution Debate: Readings on the Military Transformation of Early Modern Europe* (Boulder: Westview Press, 1995)

Rogers, H. C. B., *The British Army in the Eighteenth Century* (London: Allen & Unwin, 1977)

Roider, Karl A., *Baron Thugut and Austria's Response to the French Revolution* (Princeton: Princeton University Press, 1987)

Rose, J. H. and A. M. Broadly, *Dumouriez and the Defence of England Against Napoleon* (London: J. Lane, 1909)

Rowe, Michael, 'Lessons from the American Revolutionary War: Sir Henry Clinton's Analysis of the Allied Invasion of France, 1792', Georgian Papers Programme Blog

Roy, Kaushik, 'Military synthesis in South Asia: armies, warfare, and Indian society, c. 1740–1849', *Journal of Military History*, 69 (July 2005), 651–90.

Rukhsana, Parveen, 'Military administration under Tipu Sultan – A study', *Quarterly Journal of the Mythic Society*, 93/1 (2002), 70–77

Russell, Peter E., 'Redcoats in the wilderness: British officers and irregular warfare in Europe and America, 1740–1760', *The William and Mary Quarterly*, 35/4 (October 1978), 629–652.

Saunders, Tim and Rob Yuill, *The Light Division in the Peninsular War, 1808–1811* (Barnsley: Pen & Sword, 2020)

Savory, Reginald, *His Britannic Majesty's Army in Germany During the Seven Years War* (Oxford: Clarendon Press, 1966)

Schneider, Elena A., *The Occupation of Havana: War, Trade and Slavery in the Atlantic World* (Chapel Hill: University of North Carolina Press, 2018)

Severn, John, *Architects of Empire: The Duke of Wellington and His Brothers* (Norman: University of Oklahoma Press, 2007)

Shaw, Matthew J., *An Inky Business: A History of Newspapers from the English Civil War to the American Civil War* (London: Reaktion, 2021)

Shy, John, *Toward Lexington: The Role of the British Army in the Coming of the American Revolution* (Princeton: Princeton University Press, 1965)

Smith, David, *William Howe and the American War of Independence* (London: Bloomsbury, 2015)

Snow, Dan, *Death or Victory: The Battle for Quebec and the Birth of Empire* (London: HarperCollins, 2010)

Sosin, Jack M., *Whitehall and the Wilderness: The Middle West in British Colonial Policy, 1760–1775* (Lincoln: University of Nebraska Press, 1961)

Speelman, Patrick J., *Henry Lloyd and the Military Enlightenment of Eighteenth-Century Europe* (Westport: Greenwood Press, 2002)

Spiers, Edward M., *The Late Victorian Army, 1868–1902* (Manchester: Manchester University Press, 1992)

Spring, Matthew H., *With Zeal and With Bayonets Only: The British Army on Campaign in North America, 1775–1783* (Norman: University of Oklahoma Press, 2008)

Stanley, Peter, *White Mutiny: British Military Culture in India, 1825–1875* (London: Hurst & Co, 1998)

Starkey, Armstrong, *European and Native American Warfare, 1675–1815* (London: UCL Press, 1998)

Starkey, Armstrong, *War in the Age of Enlightenment, 1700–1789* (London: Praeger, 2003)

Steele, Ian K., *Warpaths: Invasions of North America* (Oxford: Oxford University Press, 1994)

Stoker, Donald, Kenneth J. Hagan and Michael T. McMaster (eds), *Strategy in the American War of Independence: A Global Approach* (London: Routledge, 2010)

Stoker, Donald and Michael W. Jones, 'Colonial Military Strategy', in Stoker et al., *Strategy in the American War*, 5–34

Stokes, I. N. Phelps, *The Iconography of Manhattan Island, 1498–1909*, 6 vols (New York: Robert H. Dodd, 1915–1928)

Strachan, Hew, *From Waterloo to Balaclava: Tactics, Technology, and the British Army 1815–1854* (Cambridge: Cambridge University Press, 1985)

Strachan, Hew, *Wellington's Legacy: Reform of the British Army, 1830–54* (Manchester: Manchester University Press, 1986)

Taylor, Charles, *Sources of the Self: The Making of Modern Identity* (Cambridge, MA: Harvard University Press, 1989)

Thompson, Andrew C., *George II* (London: Yale University Press, 2011)

Thoumine, R. H., *Scientific Soldier: A Life of General Le Marchant, 1766–1812* (Oxford: Oxford University Press, 1968)

Till, Karen E., *The New Berlin: Memory, Politics, Place* (Minneapolis: University of Minnesota Press, 2005)

Towsey, Mark, *Reading History in Britain and America, c.1750–c.1840* (Cambridge: Cambridge University Press, 2021)

Tritton, Alan, *When the Tiger Fought the Thistle: The Tragedy of Colonel William Baillie of the Madras Army* (London: Radcliffe Press, 2013)

Urban, Mark, *The Man Who Broke Napoleon's Codes: The Story of George Scovell* (London: Faber, 2001)

Urban, Mark, *Fusiliers: How the British Army Lost America but Learned to Fight* (London: Faber & Faber, 2008)

Vandervort, Bruce, *Wars of Imperial Conquest in Africa, 1830–1914* (London: UCL Press, 1998)

Vartavarian, Mesrob, 'An open military economy: the British conquest of South India reconsidered, 1780–1799', *Journal of the Economic and Social History of the Orient*, 57/4 (2014), 486–510.

Venturi, Franco, 'Le avventure del generale Henry Lloyd', *Rivista Storia Italiana*, 151 (1979), 369–433

Wald, Erica, *Vice in the Barracks: Medicine, the Military and the Making of Colonial India, 1780–18688* (Basingstoke: Palgrave, 2014)

Walter, Dierk, *Colonial Violence: European Armies and the Use of Force* (London: Hurst, 2017)

Ward, Matthew, *Breaking the Backcountry: The Seven Years' War in Virginia and Pennsylvania, 1754–1765* (Pittsburgh: University of Pittsburgh Press, 2003)

Weigley, Russell F., *The Age of Battles: The Quest for Decisive Warfare from Breitenfeld to Waterloo* (Bloomington: Indiana University Press, 1991)

White, Charles Edward, *The Enlightened Soldier: Scharnhorst and the Militärische Gesellschaft in Berlin, 1801–1805* (New York: Praeger, 1989)

White, Jon Manchip, *Marshal of France: The Life and Times of Maurice de Saxe* (London: Hamish Hamilton, 1962)

Whitworth, Rex, *Field Marshal Lord Ligonier: A Story of the British Army, 1702–1770* (Oxford: Oxford University Press, 1958)

Whitworth, Rex, *William Augustus, Duke of Cumberland: A Life* (London: Leo Cooper, 1992)

Wickwire, Franklin and Mary, *Cornwallis and the War of Independence* (London: Faber & Faber, 1971)

Wickwire, Franklin and Mary, *Cornwallis: The Imperial Years* (Chapel Hill: University of North Carolina Press, 1980)

Widder, Keith, 'The cartography of Dietrich Brehm and Thomas Hutchins and the establishment of British authority in the Western Great Lakes region, 1760–1763', *Cartographica: The International Journal for Geographic Information and Geovisualisation*, 36/1 (April 1999), 1–23

Willcox, William B., *Portrait of a General: Sir Henry Clinton in the War of Independence* (New York: Knopf, 1962)

Wrong, George McKinnon, *The Fall of Canada: A Chapter in the History of the Seven Years' War* (Oxford: Clarendon Press, 1914)

Yagi, George, *The Struggle for North America, 1754–1758: Britannia's Tarnished Laurels* (London: Bloomsbury, 2017)

Yazdani, Kaveh, 'Mysore at War: The Military Structure During the Reigns of Haidar 'Ali and Tipu Sultan', in Ravi Ahuja and Martin Christof-Füchsle (eds), *A Great War in South India: German Accounts of the Anglo-Mysore Wars, 1766–1799* (Berlin: De Gruyter, 2020), 17–54

Unpublished Papers

Miyamoto, Bénédicte, 'Artistic Training in the Military Enlightenment: Drawing and Color-Coding to Circulate Knowledge in the British Army', at the Consortium on the Revolutionary Era, Tallahassee, Florida, February 2020

Ramsey, Neil, 'Military History and Eighteenth Century Print Culture', New Direction in War and History Conference, Canberra, 5 February 2016

Unpublished Theses

Anderson, Carolyn J., 'Constructing the Military Landscape: The Board of Ordnance Maps and Plans of Scotland, 1689–1815' (PhD Thesis, University of Edinburgh, 2009)

Bartlett, Keith John, 'The Development of the British Army During the Wars with France, 1793–1815' (PhD Thesis, University of Durham, 1998)

Beattie, Daniel J., 'General Jeffrey Amherst and the Conquest of Canada, 1758–1760' (PhD Thesis, Duke University, 1976)

Bowyer-Bower, T.A., 'The Development of Educational Ideas and Curricula in the Army During the Eighteenth and Nineteenth Centuries' (M.Ed. Thesis, Nottingham University, 1954)

Fletcher, William Rudolf, ' "Scientifics" and "Wycombites": A Study of the Quartermaster General's Department of the British Army, 1799–1814' (Phd Thesis, King's College London, 2019)

Hubner, Brian E., 'The Formation of the British Light Infantry Companies and Their Employment in the Saratoga Campaign of 1777' (MA Thesis, University of Saskatchewan, 1986)

Pimlott, John L., 'The Administration of the British Army, 1783–1793' (PhD Thesis, University of Leicester, 1975)

Springer, W. H., 'The Military Apprenticeship of Arthur Wellesley in India, 1791–1805' (PhD Dissertation, Yale University, 1965)

Storring, Adam Lindsay, 'Frederick the Great and the Meanings of War, 1730–1755' (PhD Thesis, Cambridge University, 2017)

Thompson, Mark S., 'The Rise of the Scientific Soldier as Seen Through the Performance of the Corps of Royal Engineers during the Early 19th Century' (PhD Dissertation, University of Sunderland, 2009)

Websites

Colonial America
    http://www.colonialamerica.amdigital.co.uk
George III's Collection of Military Maps
    https://militarymaps.rct.uk
Georgian Papers Programme
    https://georgianpapers.com
Library of Congress, Washington, DC
    https://www.loc.gov
Lachlan and Elizabeth Macquarie Archive, Macquarie University, New South Wales
    https://www.mq.edu.au/macquarie-archive/lema
Soldiers of Empire: Garrison & Empire in the 19th Century
    http://www.soldiersofempire.nz
Stephen S. Clark Map Library, University of Michigan, Maps and Map-making in India online exhibit
    https://apps.lib.umich.edu/online-exhibits/exhibits/show/india-maps
Tate Research Publications
    https://www.tate.org.uk/research/publications
Victoria & Albert Museum Articles
    https://www.vam.ac.uk/articles

Index

Army personnel are indexed under the highest rank they achieved.

Entries for maps are in *italics*.

Forts, lakes and rivers are indexed under their names and not under F, L or R.

Surnames including a preposition or nobiliary particle ('von' or 'de') are indexed respectively under V and D.